Artificial Intelligence Python

Second Edition

Your complete guide to building intelligent apps using Python 3.x

Alberto Artasanchez

Prateek Joshi

BIRMINGHAM - MUMBAI

Artificial Intelligence with Python

Second Edition

Producer: Tushar Gupta
Acquisition Editor – Peer Reviews: Suresh Jain
Content Development Editor: Ian Hough
Technical Editor: Aniket Shetty
Project Editor: Carol Lewis
Proofreader: Safis Editing
Indexer: Tejal Daruwale Soni
Presentation Designer: Sandip Tadge

First published: January 2017

Second edition: January 2020

Production reference: 3020620

Published by Packt Publishing Ltd.
Livery Place
35 Livery Street
Birmingham B3 2PB, UK.

ISBN 978-1-83921-953-5

www.packt.com

packt.com

Subscribe to our online digital library for full access to over 7,000 books and videos, as well as industry leading tools to help you plan your personal development and advance your career. For more information, please visit our website.

Why subscribe?

- Spend less time learning and more time coding with practical eBooks and Videos from over 4,000 industry professionals
- Learn better with Skill Plans built especially for you
- Get a free eBook or video every month
- Fully searchable for easy access to vital information
- Copy and paste, print, and bookmark content

Did you know that Packt offers eBook versions of every book published, with PDF and ePub files available? You can upgrade to the eBook version at www.Packt.com and as a print book customer, you are entitled to a discount on the eBook copy. Get in touch with us at customercare@packtpub.com for more details.

At www.Packt.com, you can also read a collection of free technical articles, sign up for a range of free newsletters, and receive exclusive discounts and offers on Packt books and eBooks.

Contributors

About the authors

Alberto Artasanchez is a data scientist with over 25 years of consulting experience with Fortune 500 companies as well as startups. He has an extensive background in artificial intelligence and advanced algorithms. Mr. Artasanchez holds 9 AWS certifications including the Big Data Specialty and the Machine Learning Specialty certifications. He is an AWS Ambassador and publishes frequently in a variety of data science blogs. He is often tapped as a speaker on topics ranging from Data Science, Big Data, and Analytics to underwriting optimization and fraud detection. He has a strong and extensive track record designing and building end-to-end machine learning platforms at scale.

He graduated with a Master of Science degree from Wayne State University and a Bachelor of Arts degree from Kalamazoo College. He is particularly interested in using Artificial Intelligence to build Data Lakes at scale. He is married to his lovely wife Karen and is addicted to CrossFit.

I would like to thank the wonderful editors at Packt for all the help. This book would have never been completed without their invaluable assistance. They are Ian Hough, Carol Lewis, Ajinkya Kolhe, Aniket Shetty, and Tushar Gupta. I would also like to thank my amazing wife Karen Artasanchez for her support and patience, not just with this book but for her continued support in all my crazy endeavors. I would like to dedicate this book to my father Alberto Artasanchez Madrigal and my mother Laura Loy Loy.

Prateek Joshi is the founder of Plutoshift and a published author of 9 books on artificial intelligence. He has been featured on Forbes 30 Under 30, NBC, Bloomberg, CNBC, TechCrunch, and The Business Journals. He has been an invited speaker at conferences such as TEDx, Global Big Data Conference, Machine Learning Developers Conference, and Silicon Valley Deep Learning. His tech blog (`www.prateekjoshi.com`) has received more than 2M page views from 200+ countries and has 7,500+ followers. You can learn more about him on `www.prateekj.com`. Apart from artificial intelligence, some of the topics that excite him are number theory, cryptography, and quantum computing. His greater goal is to make artificial intelligence accessible to everyone so that it can impact billions of people around the world.

About the reviewer

Ajinkya Kolhe is a Data Analytics and Machine Learning Instructor. He started his journey as a software developer at Morgan Stanley and transitioned into the machine learning field. He is now working as an instructor to help companies and individuals to get started with Artificial Intelligence.

Table of Contents

Preface

Recent advances in **artificial intelligence** (**AI**) have placed great power into the hands of humans. With great power comes a proportional level of responsibility. Self-driving cars, chatbots, and increasingly accurate predictions of the future are but a few examples of AI's ability to supercharge humankind's capacity for growth and advancement.

AI is becoming a core, transformative path that is changing the way we think about every aspect of our lives. It is impacting industry. It is becoming pervasive and embedded in our everyday lives. Most excitingly, this is a field that is still in its infancy: the AI revolution has only just begun.

As we collect more and more data and tackle that data with better and faster algorithms, we can use AI to build increasingly accurate models and to answer increasingly complex, previously intractable questions.

From this, it will come as no surprise that the ability to work with and fully utilize AI will be a skill that is set only to increase in value. In this book, we explore various real-world scenarios and learn how to apply relevant AI algorithms to a wide swath of problems.

The book starts with the most basic AI concepts and progressively builds on these concepts to solve increasingly difficult problems. It will use the initial knowledge gleaned during the beginning chapters as a foundation to allow the reader to explore and tackle some of the more complicated problems in AI. By the end of the book, the reader will have gained a solid understanding of many AI techniques and will have gained confidence about when to use these techniques.

We will start by talking about various realms of AI. We'll then move on to discuss more complex algorithms, such as extremely random forests, Hidden Markov Models, genetic algorithms, artificial neural networks, convolutional neural networks, and so on.

This book is for Python programmers looking to use AI algorithms to create real-world applications. This book is friendly to Python beginners, but familiarity with Python programming would certainly be helpful so you can play around with the code. It is also useful to experienced Python programmers who are looking to implement artificial intelligence techniques.

You will learn how to make informed decisions about the type of algorithms you need to use and how to implement those algorithms to get the best possible results. If you want to build versatile applications that can make sense of images, text, speech, or some other form of data, this book on artificial intelligence will definitely come to your rescue!

Who this book is for

This book is for Python developers who want to build real-world artificial intelligence applications. This book is friendly to Python beginners, but being familiar with Python would be useful to play around with the code. It will also be useful for experienced Python programmers who are looking to use artificial intelligence techniques in their existing technology stacks.

What this book covers

Chapter 1, Introduction to Artificial Intelligence

This chapter provides some basic definitions and groupings that will be used throughout the book. It will also provide an overall classification of the artificial intelligence and machine learning fields as they exist today.

Chapter 2, Fundamental Use Cases for Artificial Intelligence

Artificial Intelligence is a fascinating topic and a vast field of knowledge. In its current state it generates more questions than it answers, but there are certainly many places where artificial intelligence is being applied, in many instances without us even realizing. Before we delve into the fundamental algorithms that drive AI, we will analyze some of the most popular use cases for the technology as of today.

Chapter 3, Machine Learning Pipelines

Model training is only a small piece of the machine learning process. Data scientists often spend a significant amount of time cleansing, transforming, and preparing data to get it ready to be consumed by an AI model. Since data preparation is such a time-consuming activity, we will present state-of-the-art techniques to facilitate this activity as well as other components that a well-designed production data pipeline should possess.

Chapter 4, Feature Selection and Feature Engineering

Model performance can be improved by selecting the right dimensions to pass to the model as well as discovering new dimensions that can enrich the input datasets. This chapter will demonstrate how new features can be created from existing ones as well as from external sources. It will also cover how to eliminate redundant or low-value features.

Chapter 5, Classification and Regression Using Supervised Learning

This chapter defines in detail supervised learning. It provides a taxonomy of the various methods and algorithms for problems that fall under this classification.

Chapter 6, Predictive Analytics with Ensemble Learning

Ensemble learning is a powerful technique that allows you to aggregate the power of individual models. This chapter goes over the different ensemble methods as well as guidance on when to use each of them. Finally, the chapter will cover how to apply these techniques to real-world event prediction.

Chapter 7, Detecting Patterns with Unsupervised Learning

This chapter will explore the concepts of clustering and data segmentation and how they are related to unsupervised learning. It will also cover how to perform clustering and how to apply various clustering algorithms. It will show several examples that allow the reader to visualize how these algorithms work. Lastly, it will cover the application of these algorithms to perform clustering and segmentation in real-world situations.

Chapter 8, Building Recommender Systems

This chapter will demonstrate how to build recommender systems. It will also show how to persist user preferences. It will cover the concepts of nearest neighbor search and collaborative filtering. Finally, there will be an example showing how to build a movie recommendation system.

Chapter 9, Logic Programming

This chapter will cover how to write programs using logic programming. It will discuss various programming paradigms and see how programs are constructed with logic programming. It will highlight the building blocks of logic programming and see how to solve problems in this domain. Finally, various Python program implementations will be built for various solvers that tackle a variety of problems.

Chapter 10, Heuristic Search Techniques

This chapter covers heuristic search techniques. Heuristic search techniques are used to search through the solution space to come up with answers. The search is conducted using heuristics that guide the search algorithm. Heuristics allow the algorithm to speed up the process, which would otherwise take a long time to arrive at the solution.

Chapter 11, Genetic Algorithms and Genetic Programming

We will discuss the basics of genetic programming and its importance in the field of AI. We will learn how to solve simple problems using genetic algorithms. We will understand some underlying concepts that are used to do genetic programming. We will then see how to apply this to a real-world problem.

Chapter 12, Artificial Intelligence on the Cloud

The cloud enables us to accelerate AI development, workloads, and deployment. In this chapter, we will explore the different offerings from the most popular vendors that enable and accelerate AI projects.

Chapter 13, Building Games with Artificial Intelligence

This chapter will cover how to build games using artificial intelligence techniques. Search algorithms will be used to develop winning game strategies and tactics. Finally, intelligent bots will be built for a variety of games.

Chapter 14, Building a Speech Recognizer

This chapter will cover how to perform speech recognition. It will show how to process speech data and extract features from it. Finally, it will demonstrate how to use the extracted features to build a speech recognition system.

Chapter 15, Natural Language Processing

This chapter will focus on the important area of AI known as **Natural Language Processing** (**NLP**). It will discuss various concepts such as tokenization, stemming, and lemmatization to process text. It will also cover how to build a Bag of Words model and use it to classify text. It will demonstrate how machine learning can be used to analyze the sentiment of a given sentence. Lastly, it will show topic modeling and go over the implementation of a system to identify topics in a document.

Chapter 16, Chatbots

Chatbots can help to save money and better serve customers by increasing productivity and deflecting calls. In this chapter, we will cover the basics of chatbots and the tools available to build them.

Finally, we will build a full-blown chatbot from scratch that will implement a real-world use case including error handling, connecting it to an external API, and deploying the chatbot.

Chapter 17, Sequential Data and Time Series Analysis

We will discuss the concept of probabilistic reasoning. We will learn how to apply that concept to build models for sequential data. We will learn about the various characteristics of time-series data. We will discuss Hidden Markov Models and how to use them to analyze sequential data. We will then use this technique to analyze stock market data.

Chapter 18, Image Recognition

We will discuss how to work with images in this chapter. We will learn how to detect and track objects in a live video. We will then learn how to apply those techniques to track parts of the human face.

Chapter 19, Neural Networks

We will discuss artificial neural networks. We will learn about perceptrons and see how they are used to build neural networks. We will learn how to build single-layered and multi-layered neural networks. We will discuss how a neural network learns about the training data and builds a model. We will learn about the cost function and backpropagation. We will then use these techniques to perform optical character recognition.

Chapter 20, Deep Learning with Convolutional Neural Networks

We will discuss the basics of deep learning in this chapter. The reader will be introduced to various concepts in convolutional neural networks and how they can be used for image recognition. We will discuss various layers in a convolutional neural network. We will then use these techniques to build a real-world application.

Chapter 21, Recurrent Neural Networks and Other Deep Learning Models

This chapter will continue to cover other types of deep learning algorithms. It will start with coverage of recurrent neural networks and it will then cover newer algorithms such as the Attention, Self-Attention, and Transformer models. This chapter will cover the use cases where these networks are used and the advantages of using these kinds of model architecture, as well as their limitations. Finally, the techniques discussed will be used to build a real-world application.

Chapter 22, Creating Intelligent Agents with Reinforcement Learning

This chapter will define **reinforcement learning** (**RL**) as well as cover the components within an RL model. It will detail the techniques used to build RL systems. Finally, it will demonstrate how to build learning agents that can learn by interacting with the environment.

Chapter 23, Artificial Intelligence and Big Data

This chapter will analyze how big data techniques can be applied to accelerate machine learning pipelines as well as covering different techniques that can be used to streamline dataset ingestion, transformation, and validation. Finally, it will walk the reader through an actual example using Apache Spark to demonstrate the concepts covered in the chapter.

What you need for this book

This book is focused on AI in Python as opposed to Python itself. We have used Python 3 to build various applications. We focus on how to utilize various Python libraries in the best possible way to build real world applications. In that spirit, we have tried to keep all of the code as friendly and readable as possible. We feel that this will enable our readers to easily understand the code and readily use it in different scenarios.

Download the example code files

You can download the example code files for this book from your account at `http://www.packtpub.com`. If you purchased this book elsewhere, you can visit `http://www.packtpub.com/support` and register to have the files emailed directly to you.

You can download the code files by following these steps:

1. Log in or register at `http://www.packtpub.com`.
2. Select the **SUPPORT** tab.
3. Click on **Code Downloads & Errata**.
4. Enter the name of the book in the **Search** box and follow the on-screen instructions.

Once the file is downloaded, please make sure that you unzip or extract the folder using the latest version of:

- WinRAR / 7-Zip for Windows

- Zipeg / iZip / UnRarX for Mac
- 7-Zip / PeaZip for Linux

The code bundle for the book is also hosted on GitHub at `https://github.com/PacktPublishing/Artificial-Intelligence-with-Python-Second-Edition`. We also have other code bundles from our rich catalog of books and videos available at `https://github.com/PacktPublishing/`. Check them out!

Download the color images

We also provide a PDF file that has color images of the screenshots/diagrams used in this book. You can download it here: `https://static.packt-cdn.com/downloads/9781839219535_ColorImages.pdf`.

Conventions used

In this book, you will find a number of text styles that distinguish between different kinds of information. Here are some examples of these styles and an explanation of their meaning.

`CodeInText`: Indicates code words in text, database table names, folder names, filenames, file extensions, pathnames, dummy URLs, user input, and Twitter handles. For example: "The `n_estimators` parameter refers to the number of trees that will be constructed."

A block of code is set as follows:

```
# Create label encoder and fit the labels
encoder = preprocessing.LabelEncoder()
encoder.fit(input_labels)
```

When we wish to draw your attention to a particular part of a code block, the relevant lines or items are set in bold:

```
# Create label encoder and fit the labels
encoder = preprocessing.LabelEncoder()
encoder.fit(input_labels)
```

Any command-line input or output is written as follows:

```
$ python3 random_forests.py --classifier-type rf
```

Bold: Indicates a new term, an important word, or words that you see on the screen, for example, in menus or dialog boxes, also appear in the text like this. For example: "**Supervised learning** refers to the process of building a machine learning model that is based on labeled training data."

Warnings or important notes appear in a box like this.

Tips and tricks appear like this.

Get in touch

Feedback from our readers is always welcome.

General feedback: If you have questions about any aspect of this book, mention the book title in the subject of your message and email us at `customercare@packtpub.com`.

Errata: Although we have taken every care to ensure the accuracy of our content, mistakes do happen. If you have found a mistake in this book we would be grateful if you would report this to us. Please visit, `www.packtpub.com/support/errata`, selecting your book, clicking on the Errata Submission Form link, and entering the details.

Piracy: If you come across any illegal copies of our works in any form on the Internet, we would be grateful if you would provide us with the location address or website name. Please contact us at `copyright@packt.com` with a link to the material.

If you are interested in becoming an author: If there is a topic that you have expertise in and you are interested in either writing or contributing to a book, please visit `authors.packtpub.com`.

Reviews

Please leave a review. Once you have read and used this book, why not leave a review on the site that you purchased it from? Potential readers can then see and use your unbiased opinion to make purchase decisions, we at Packt can understand what you think about our products, and our authors can see your feedback on their book. Thank you!

For more information about Packt, please visit `packt.com`.

1
Introduction to Artificial Intelligence

In this chapter, we are going to discuss the concept of **artificial intelligence** (**AI**) and how it's applied in the real world. We spend a significant portion of our everyday life interacting with smart systems. This can be in the form of searching for something on the internet, biometric facial recognition, or converting spoken words to text. AI is at the heart of all this and it's becoming an important part of our modern lifestyle. All these systems are complex real-world applications and AI solves these problems with mathematics and algorithms. Throughout the book, we will learn the fundamental principles that can be used to build such applications. Our overarching goal is to enable you to take up new and challenging AI problems that you might encounter in your everyday life.

By the end of this chapter, you will know:

- What is AI and why do we need to study it?
- What are some applications of AI?
- A classification of AI branches
- The five tribes of machine learning
- What is the Turing test?
- What are rational agents?
- What are General Problem Solvers?
- How to build an intelligent agent
- How to install Python 3 and related packages

What is AI?

How one defines AI can vary greatly. Philosophically, what is "intelligence?" How one perceives intelligence in turn defines its artificial counterpart. A broad and optimistic definition of the field of AI could be: "the area of computer science that studies how machines can perform tasks that would normally require a sentient agent." It could be argued from such a definition that something as simple as a computer multiplying two numbers is "artificial intelligence." This is because we have designed a machine capable of taking an input and independently producing a logical output that usually would require a living entity to process.

A more skeptical definition might be more narrow, for example: "the area of computer science that studies how machines can closely imitate human intelligence." From such definition skeptics may argue that what we have today is not artificial intelligence. Up until now, they have been able to point to examples of tasks that computers cannot perform, and therefore claim that computers cannot yet "think" or exhibit artificial intelligence if they cannot satisfactorily perform such functions.

This book leans towards the more optimistic view of AI and we prefer to marvel at the number of tasks that a computer can currently perform.

In our aforementioned multiplication task, a computer will certainly be faster and more accurate than a human if the two numbers are large enough. There are other areas where humans can currently perform much better than computers. For example, a human can recognize, label, and classify objects with a few examples, whereas currently a computer might require thousands of examples to perform at the same level of accuracy. Research and improvement continue relentlessly, and we will continue to see computers solving more and more problems that just a few years ago we could only dream of them solving. As we progress in the book, we will explore many of these use cases and provide plenty of examples.

An interesting way to consider the field of AI is that AI is in some ways one more branch of science that is studying the most fascinating computer we know: the brain. With AI, we are attempting to reflect some of the systems and mechanics of the brain within computing, and thus find ourselves borrowing from, and interacting with, fields such as neuroscience.

Why do we need to study AI?

AI can impact every aspect of our lives. The field of AI tries to understand patterns and behaviors of entities. With AI, we want to build smart systems and understand the concept of intelligence as well. The intelligent systems that we construct are very useful in understanding how an intelligent system like our brain goes about constructing another intelligent system.

Let's look at how our brain processes information:

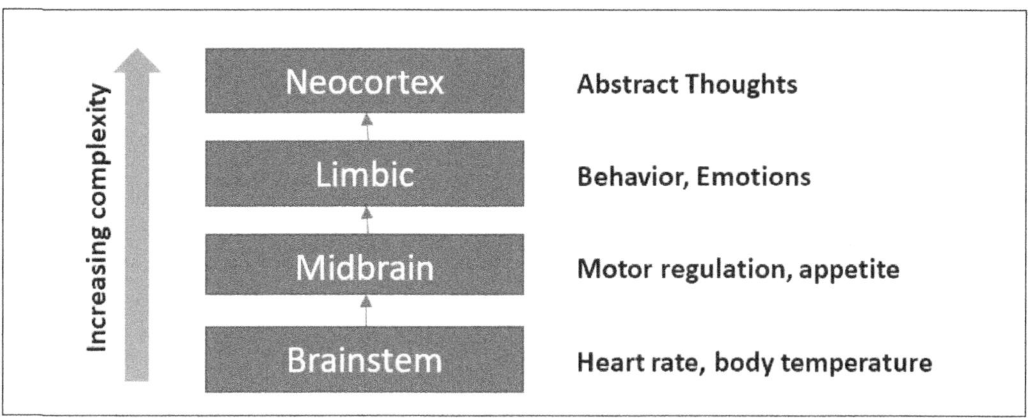

Figure 1: Basic brain components

Compared to some other fields such as mathematics or physics that have been around for centuries, AI is relatively in its infancy. Over the last couple of decades, AI has produced some spectacular products such as self-driving cars and intelligent robots that can walk. Based on the direction in which we are heading, it's obvious that achieving intelligence will have a great impact on our lives in the coming years.

We can't help but wonder how the human brain manages to do so much with such effortless ease. We can recognize objects, understand languages, learn new things, and perform many more sophisticated tasks with our brain. How does the human brain do this? We don't yet have many answers to that question. When you try to replicate tasks that the brain performs, using a machine, you will see that it falls way behind! Our own brains are far more complex and capable than machines, in many respects.

When we try to look for things such as extraterrestrial life or time travel, we don't know if those things exist; we're not sure if these pursuits are worthwhile. The good thing about AI is that an idealized model for it already exists: our brain is the holy grail of an intelligent system! All we have to do is to mimic its functionality to create an intelligent system that can do something similarly to, or better than, our brain.

Let's see how raw data gets converted into intelligence through various levels of processing:

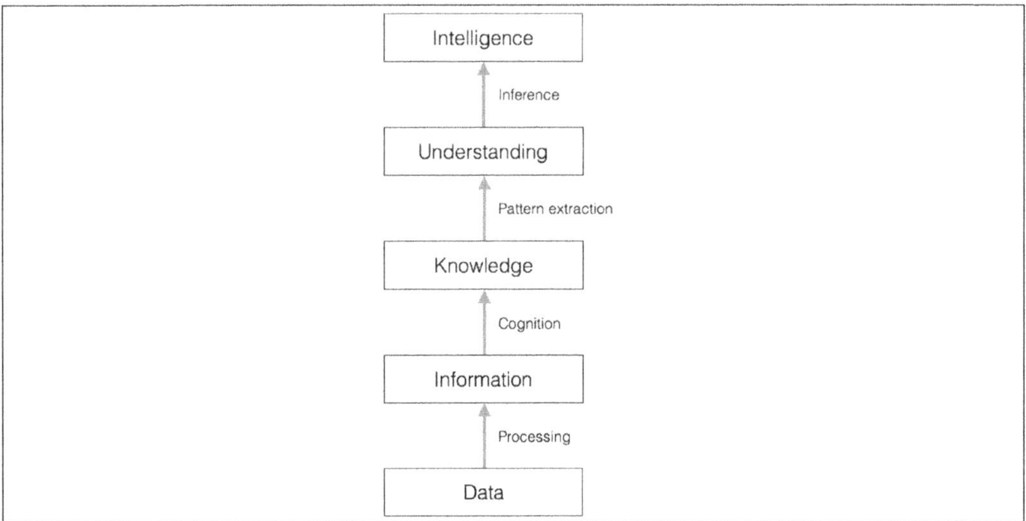

Figure 2: Conversion of data into intelligence

One of the main reasons we want to study AI is to automate many things. We live in a world where:

- We deal with huge and insurmountable amounts of data. The human brain can't keep track of so much data.
- Data originates from multiple sources simultaneously. The data is unorganized and chaotic.
- Knowledge derived from this data must be updated constantly because the data itself keeps changing.
- The sensing and actuation must happen in real-time with high precision.

Even though the human brain is great at analyzing things around us, it cannot keep up with the preceding conditions. Hence, we need to design and develop intelligent machines that can do this. We need AI systems that can:

- Handle large amounts of data in an efficient way. With the advent of Cloud Computing, we are now able to store huge amounts of data.
- Ingest data simultaneously from multiple sources without any lag. Index and organize data in a way that allows us to derive insights.
- Learn from new data and update constantly using the right learning algorithms. Think and respond to situations based on the conditions in real time.
- Continue with tasks without getting tired or needing breaks.

AI techniques are actively being used to make existing machines smarter so that they can execute faster and more efficiently.

Branches of AI

It is important to understand the various fields of study within AI so that we can choose the right framework to solve a given real-world problem. There are several ways to classify the different branches of AI:

- Supervised learning vs. unsupervised learning vs. reinforcement learning
- Artificial general intelligence vs. narrow intelligence
- By human function:
    - Machine vision
    - Machine learning
    - Natural language processing
    - Natural language generation

Following, we present a common classification:

- **Machine learning and pattern recognition**: This is perhaps the most popular form of AI out there. We design and develop software that can learn from data. Based on these learning models, we perform predictions on unknown data. One of the main constraints here is that these programs are limited to the power of the data.

If the dataset is small, then the learning models would be limited as well. Let's see what a typical machine learning system looks like:

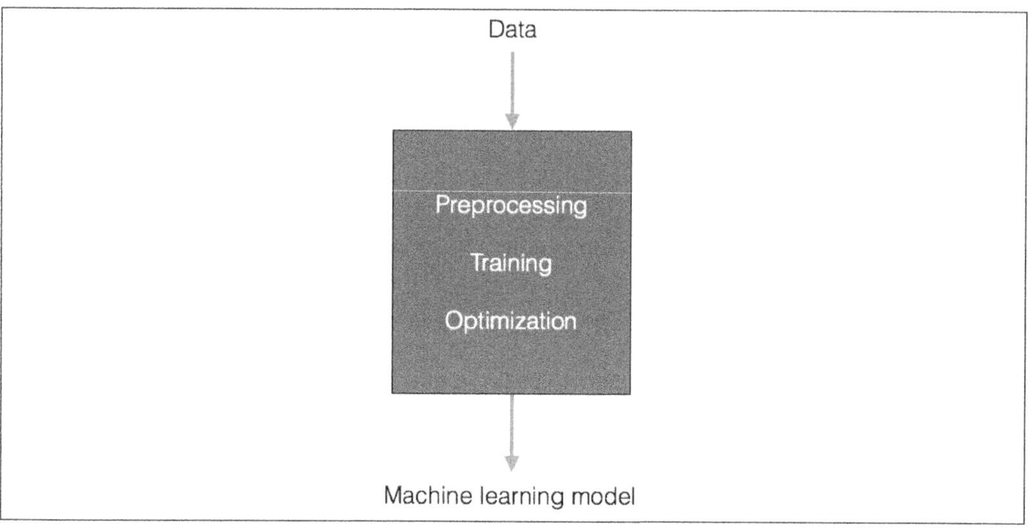

Figure 3: A typical computer system

When a system receives a previously unseen data point, it uses the patterns from previously seen data (the training data) to make inferences on this new data point. For example, in a facial recognition system, the software will try to match the pattern of eyes, nose, lips, eyebrows, and so on in order to find a face in the existing database of users.

- **Logic-based AI**: Mathematical logic is used to execute computer programs in logic-based AI. A program written in logic-based AI is basically a set of statements in logical form that expresses facts and rules about a problem domain. This is used extensively in pattern matching, language parsing, semantic analysis, and so on.
- **Search**: Search techniques are used extensively in AI programs. These programs examine many possibilities and then pick the most optimal path. For example, this is used a lot in strategy games such as chess, networking, resource allocation, scheduling, and so on.
- **Knowledge representation**: The facts about the world around us need to be represented in some way for a system to make sense of them. The languages of mathematical logic are frequently used here. If knowledge is represented efficiently, systems can be smarter and more intelligent. Ontology is a closely related field of study that deals with the kinds of objects that exist.

It is a formal definition of the properties and relationships of the entities that exist in a domain. This is usually done with a taxonomy or a hierarchical structure of some kind. The following diagram shows the difference between information and knowledge:

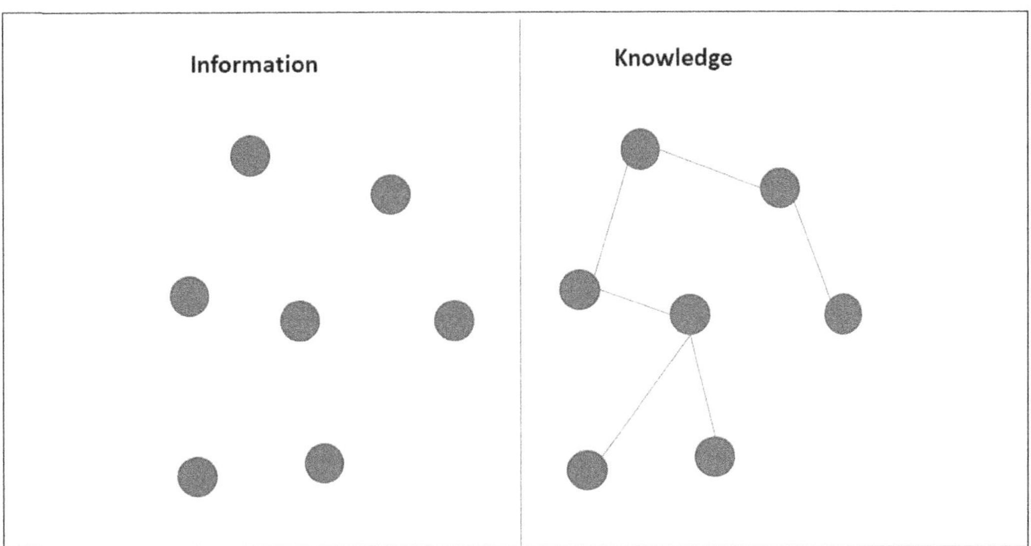

Figure 4: Information vs. Knowledge

- **Planning**: This field deals with optimal planning that gives us maximum returns with minimal costs. These software programs start with facts about the situation and a statement of a goal. These programs are also aware of the facts of the world, so that they know what the rules are. From this information, they generate the most optimal plan to achieve the goal.
- **Heuristics**: A heuristic is a technique used to solve a given problem that's practical and useful in solving the problem in the short term, but not guaranteed to be optimal. This is more like an educated guess on what approach we should take to solve a problem. In AI, we frequently encounter situations where we cannot check every single possibility to pick the best option. Thus, we need to use heuristics to achieve the goal. They are used extensively in AI in fields such as robotics, search engines, and so on.
- **Genetic programming**: Genetic programming is a way to get programs to solve a task by mating programs and selecting the fittest. The programs are encoded as a set of genes, using an algorithm to get a program that can perform the given task well.

The five tribes of machine learning

Machine learning can be further classified in a variety of ways. One of our favorite classifications is the one provided by Pedro Domingos in his book *The Master Algorithm*. In his book, he classifies machine learning by the field of science that sprouted the ideas. For example, genetic algorithms sprouted from Biology concepts. Here are the full classifications, the name Domingos uses for the tribes, and the dominant algorithms used by each tribe, along with noteworthy proponents:

Tribe	**Origins**	**Dominant algorithm**	**Proponents**
Symbolists	Logic and Philosophy	Inverse deduction	Tom Mitchell Steve Muggleton Ross Quinlan
Connectionists	Neuroscience	Backpropagation	Yan LeCun Geoffrey Hinton Yoshua Bengio
Evolutionaries	Biology	Genetic programming	John Koza John Holland Hod Lipson
Bayesians	Statistics	Probabilistic inference	David Heckerman Judea Pearl Michael Jordan
Analogizers	Psychology	Kernel machines	Peter Hart Vladimir Vapnik Douglas Hofstadter

Symbolists – Symbolists use the concept of induction or inverse deduction as their main tool. When using induction, instead of starting with a premise and looking for conclusions, inverse deduction starts with a set of premises and conclusions and works backwards to fill in the missing pieces.

An example of deduction:

Socrates is human + All humans are mortal = What can be deduced? (Socrates is mortal)

An example of induction:

Socrates is human + ?? = Socrates is mortal (Humans are mortal?)

Connectionists - Connectionists use the brain, or at least our very crude understanding of the brain, as their primary tool - mainly neural networks. Neural networks are a type of algorithm, modeled loosely after the brain, which are designed to recognize patterns. They can recognize numerical patterns contained in vectors. In order to use them, all inputs, be they images, sound, text, or time series need to be translated into these numerical vectors. It is hard to open a magazine or a news site and not read about examples of "deep learning." Deep learning is a specialized type of a neural network.

Evolutionaries - Evolutionaries focus on using the concepts of evolution, natural selection, genomes, and DNA mutation and applying them to data processing. Evolutionary algorithms will constantly mutate, evolve, and adapt to unknown conditions and processes.

Bayesians - Bayesians focus on handling uncertainty using probabilistic inference. Vision learning and spam filtering are some of the problems tackled by the Bayesian approach. Typically, Bayesian models will take a hypothesis and apply a type of "a priori" reasoning, assuming that some outcomes will be more likely. They then update a hypothesis as they see more data.

Analogizers - Analogizers focus on techniques that find similarities between examples. The most famous analogizer model is the *k-nearest neighbor* algorithm.

Defining intelligence using the Turing test

The legendary computer scientist and mathematician, *Alan Turing*, proposed the Turing test to provide a definition of intelligence. It is a test to see if a computer can learn to mimic human behavior. He defined intelligent behavior as the ability to achieve human-level intelligence during a conversation. This performance should be enough to trick an interrogator into thinking that the answers are coming from a human.

To see if a machine can do this, he proposed a test setup: he proposed that a human should interrogate the machine through a text interface. Another constraint is that the human cannot know who's on the other side of the interrogation, which means it can either be a machine or a human. To enable this setup, a human will be interacting with two entities through a text interface. These two entities are called respondents. One of them will be a human and the other one will be the machine.

The respondent machine passes the test if the interrogator is unable to tell whether the answers are coming from a machine or a human. The following diagram shows the setup of a Turing test:

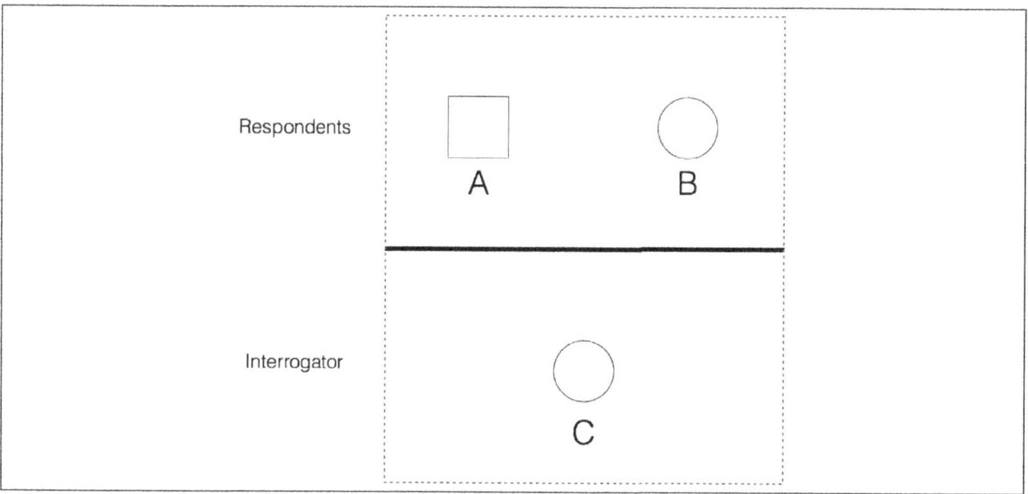

Figure 5: The Turing Test

As you can imagine, this is quite a difficult task for the respondent machine. There are a lot of things going on during a conversation. At the very minimum, the machine needs to be well versed with the following things:

- **Natural language processing**: The machine needs this to communicate with the interrogator. The machine needs to parse the sentence, extract the context, and give an appropriate answer.
- **Knowledge representation**: The machine needs to store the information provided before the interrogation. It also needs to keep track of the information being provided during the conversation so that it can respond appropriately if it comes up again.
- **Reasoning**: It's important for the machine to understand how to interpret the information that gets stored. Humans tend to do this automatically in order to draw conclusions in real time.
- **Machine learning**: This is needed so that the machine can adapt to new conditions in real time. The machine needs to analyze and detect patterns so that it can draw inferences.

You must be wondering why the human is communicating with a text interface. According to Turing, physical simulation of a person is unnecessary for intelligence. That's the reason the Turing test avoids direct physical interaction between the human and the machine.

There is another thing called the Total Turing Test that deals with vision and movement. To pass this test, the machine needs to see objects using computer vision and move around using robotics.

Making machines think like humans

For decades, we have been trying to get the machine to think more like humans. In order to make this happen, we need to understand how humans think in the first place. How do we understand the nature of human thinking? One way to do this would be to note down how we respond to things. But this quickly becomes intractable, because there are too many things to note down. Another way to do this is to conduct an experiment based on a predefined format. We develop a certain number of questions to encompass a wide variety of human topics, and then see how people respond to it.

Once we gather enough data, we can create a model to simulate the human process. This model can be used to create software that can think like humans. Of course, this is easier said than done! All we care about is the output of the program given an input. If the program behaves in a way that matches human behavior, then we can say that humans have a similar thinking mechanism.

The following diagram shows different levels of thinking and how our brain prioritizes things:

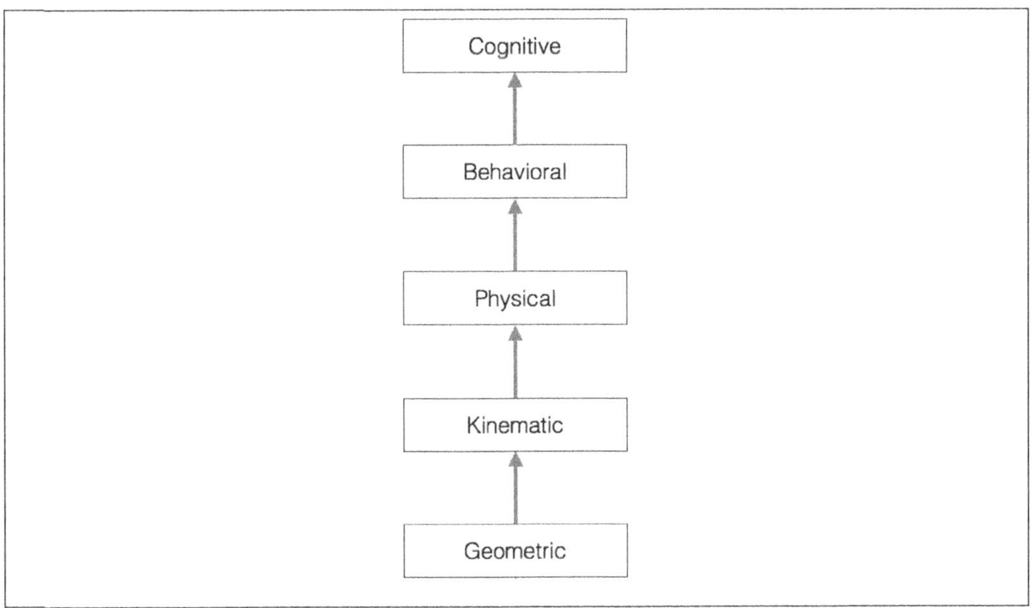

Figure 6: The levels of thought

Within computer science, there is a field of study called **Cognitive Modeling** that deals with simulating the human thinking process. It tries to understand how humans solve problems. It takes the mental processes that go into this problem-solving process and turns it into a software model. This model can then be used to simulate human behavior.

Cognitive modeling is used in a variety of AI applications such as deep learning, expert systems, natural language processing, robotics, and so on.

Building rational agents

A lot of research in AI is focused on building rational agents. What exactly is a rational agent? Before that, let us define the word *rationality* within the context of AI. Rationality refers to observing a set of rules and following their logical implications in order to achieve a desirable outcome. This needs to be performed in such a way that there is maximum benefit to the entity performing the action. An agent, therefore, is said to act rationally if, given a set of rules, it takes actions to achieve its goals. It just perceives and acts according to the information that's available. This system is used a lot in AI to design robots when they are sent to navigate unknown terrains.

How do we define what is *desirable*? The answer is that it depends on the objectives of the agent. The agent is supposed to be intelligent and independent. We want to impart the ability to adapt to new situations. It should understand its environment and then act accordingly to achieve an outcome that is in its best interests. The best interests are dictated by the overall goal it wants to achieve. Let's see how an input gets converted to action:

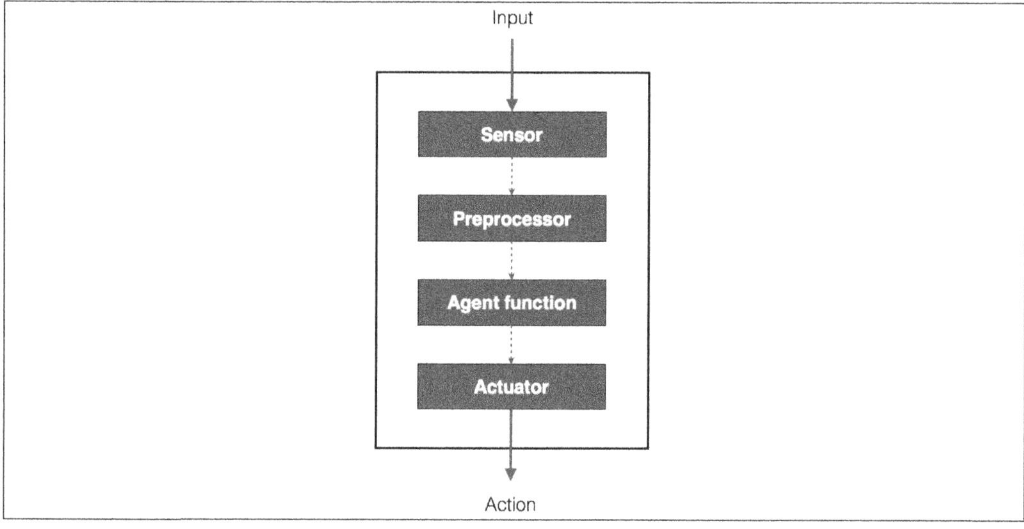

Figure 7: Converting input into action

How do we define the performance measure for a rational agent? One might say that it is directly proportional to the degree of success. The agent is set up to achieve a task, so the performance measure depends on what percentage of that task is complete. But we must think as to what constitutes rationality in its entirety. If it's just about results, we don't consider the actions leading up to the result.

Making the right inferences is a part of being rational, because the agent must act rationally to achieve its goals. This will help it draw conclusions that can be used successively.

But, what about situations where there are no provably right things to do? There are situations where the agent doesn't know what to do, but it still must do something.

Let's set up a scenario to make this last point clearer. Imagine a self-driving car that's going at 60 miles an hour and suddenly someone crosses its path. For the sake of the example, assume that given the speed the car is going, it only has two choices. Either the car crashes against a guard rail knowing that it will kill the car occupant, or it runs over the pedestrian and kills them. What's the right decision? How does the algorithm know what to do? If you were driving, would you know what to do?

We now are going to learn about one of the earliest examples of a rational agent – the General Problem Solver. As we'll see, despite the lofty name, it really wasn't capable of solving any problem, but it was a big leap in the field of computer science nonetheless.

General Problem Solver

The **General Problem Solver** (**GPS**) was an AI program proposed by Herbert Simon, J.C. Shaw, and Allen Newell. It was the first useful computer program that came into existence in the AI world. The goal was to make it work as a universal problem-solving machine. Of course, there were many software programs that existed before, but these programs performed specific tasks. GPS was the first program that was intended to solve any general problem. GPS was supposed to solve all the problems using the same base algorithm for every problem.

As you must have realized, this is quite an uphill battle! To program the GPS, the authors created a new language called **Information Processing Language** (**IPL**). The basic premise is to express any problem with a set of well-formed formulas. These formulas would be a part of a directed graph with multiple sources and sinks. In a graph, the source refers to the starting node and the sink refers to the ending node. In the case of GPS, the source refers to axioms and the sink refers to the conclusions.

Even though GPS was intended to be a general purpose, it could only solve well-defined problems, such as proving mathematical theorems in geometry and logic. It could also solve word puzzles and play chess. The reason was that these problems could be formalized to a reasonable extent. But in the real world, this quickly becomes intractable because of the number of possible paths you can take. If it tries to brute force a problem by counting the number of walks in a graph, it becomes computationally infeasible.

Solving a problem with GPS

Let's see how to structure a given problem to solve it using GPS:

1. The first step is to define the goals. Let's say our goal is to get some milk from the grocery store.
2. The next step is to define the preconditions. These preconditions are in reference to the goals. To get milk from the grocery store, we need to have a mode of transportation and the grocery store should have milk available.
3. After this, we need to define the operators. If my mode of transportation is a car and if the car is low on fuel, then we need to ensure that we can pay the fueling station. We need to ensure that you can pay for the milk at the store.

An operator takes care of the conditions and everything that affects them. It consists of actions, preconditions, and the changes resulting from taking actions. In this case, the action is giving money to the grocery store. Of course, this is contingent upon you having the money in the first place, which is the precondition. By giving them the money, you are changing your money condition, which will result in you getting the milk.

GPS will work if you can frame the problem like we did just now. The constraint is that it uses the search process to perform its job, which is way too computationally complex and time consuming for any meaningful real-world application.

In this section we learned what a rational agent is. Now let's learn how to make these rational agents more intelligent and useful.

Building an intelligent agent

There are many ways to impart intelligence to an agent. The most commonly used techniques include machine learning, stored knowledge, rules, and so on. In this section, we will focus on machine learning. In this method, the way we impart intelligence to an agent is through data and training.

Let's see how an intelligent agent interacts with the environment:

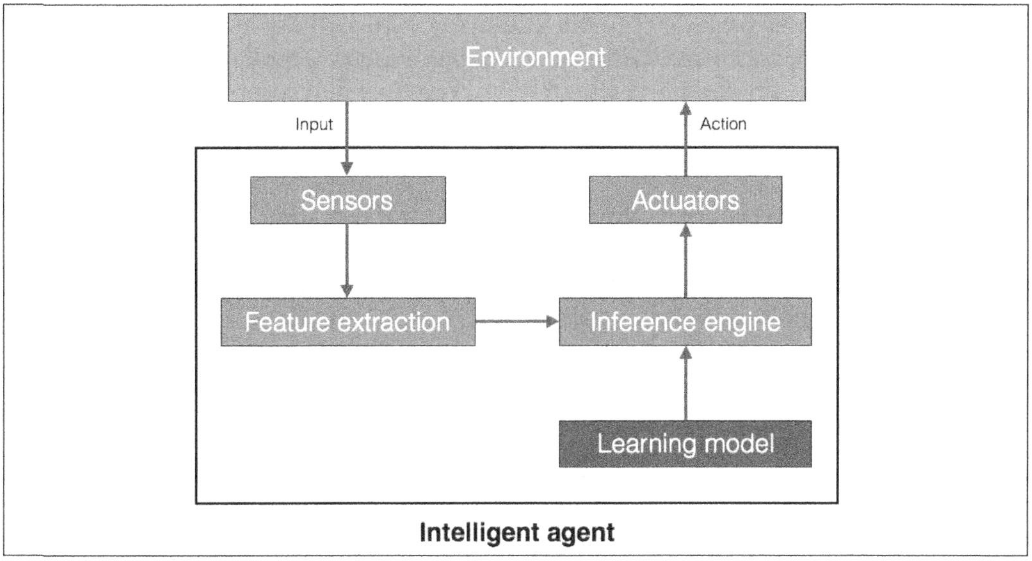

Figure 8: An intelligent agent interaction with its environment

With machine learning, sometimes we want to program our machines to use labeled data to solve a given problem. By going through the data and the associated labels, the machine learns how to extract patterns and relationships.

In the preceding example, the intelligent agent depends on the learning model to run the inference engine. Once the sensor perceives the input, it sends it to the feature extraction block. Once the relevant features are extracted, the trained inference engine performs a prediction based on the learning model. This learning model is built using machine learning. The inference engine then takes a decision and sends it to the actuator, which then takes the required action in the real world.

There are many applications of machine learning that exist today. It is used in image recognition, robotics, speech recognition, predicting stock market behavior, and so on. In order to understand machine learning and build a complete solution, you will have to be familiar with many techniques from different fields such as pattern recognition, artificial neural networks, data mining, statistics, and so on.

Types of models

There are two types of models in the AI world: Analytical models and learned models. Before we had machines that could compute, people used to rely on analytical models.

Analytical models were derived using a mathematical formulation, which is basically a sequence of steps followed to arrive at a final equation. The problem with this approach is that it was based on human judgment. Hence, these models were simplistic and often inaccurate, with just a few parameters. Think of how Newton and other scientists of old made calculations before they had computers. Such models often involved prolonged derivations and long periods of trial and error before a working formula was arrived at.

We then entered the world of computers. These computers were good at analyzing data. So, people increasingly started using learned models. These models are obtained through the process of training. During training, the machines look at many examples of inputs and outputs to arrive at the equation. These learned models are usually complex and accurate, with thousands of parameters. This gives rise to a very complex mathematical equation that governs the data that can assist in making predictions.

Machine learning allows us to obtain these learned models that can be used in an inference engine. One of the best things about this is the fact that we don't need to derive the underlying mathematical formula. You don't need to know complex mathematics, because the machine derives the formula based on data. All we need to do is create the list of inputs and the corresponding outputs. The learned model that we get is just the relationship between labeled inputs and the desired outputs.

Installing Python 3

We will be using Python 3 throughout this book. Make sure you have installed the latest version of Python 3 on your machine. Type the following command to check:

```
$ python3 --version
```

If you see something like Python 3.x.x (where x.x are version numbers) printed out, you are good to go. If not, installing it is straightforward.

Installing on Ubuntu

Python 3 is already installed by default on Ubuntu 14.xx and above. If not, you can install it using the following command:

```
$ sudo apt-get install python3
```

Run the check command like we did earlier:

```
$ python3 --version
```

You should see the version number as output.

Installing on Mac OS X

If you are on Mac OS X, it is recommended that you use Homebrew to install Python 3. It is a great package installer for Mac OS X and it is really easy to use. If you don't have Homebrew, you can install it using the following command:

```
$ ruby -e "$(curl -fsSL https://raw.githubusercontent.com/Homebrew/
install/master/install)"
```

Let's update the package manager:

```
$ brew update
```

Let's install Python 3:

```
$ brew install python3
```

Run the check command like we did earlier:

```
$ python3 --version
```

You should see the version number printed as output.

Installing on Windows

If you use Windows, it is recommended that you use a `SciPy-stack` compatible distribution of Python 3. Anaconda is pretty popular and easy to use. You can find the installation instructions at: `https://www.continuum.io/downloads`.

If you want to check out other `SciPy-stack` compatible distributions of Python 3, you can find them at `http://www.scipy.org/install.html`. The good part about these distributions is that they come with all the necessary packages preinstalled. If you use one of these versions, you don't need to install the packages separately.

Once you install it, run the check command like we did earlier:

```
$ python3 --version
```

You should see the version number printed as output.

Installing packages

Throughout this book, we will use various packages such as NumPy, SciPy, scikit-learn, and matplotlib. Make sure you install these packages before you proceed.

If you use Ubuntu or Mac OS X, installing these packages is straightforward. All these packages can be installed using a one-line command. Here are the relevant links for installation:

- NumPy: `http://docs.scipy.org/doc/numpy-1.10.1/user/install.html`
- SciPy: `http://www.scipy.org/install.html`
- scikit-learn: `http://scikit-learn.org/stable/install.html`
- matplotlib: `http://matplotlib.org/1.4.2/users/installing.html`

If you are on Windows, you should have installed a `SciPy-stack` compatible version of Python 3.

Loading data

In order to build a learning model, we need data that's representative of the world. Now that we have installed the necessary Python packages, let's see how to use the packages to interact with data. Enter the Python command prompt by typing the following command:

```
$ python3
```

Let's import the package containing all the datasets:

```
>>> from sklearn import datasets
```

Let's load the house prices dataset:

```
>>> house_prices = datasets.load_boston()
```

Print the data:

```
>>> print(house_prices.data)
```

You will see an output similar to this:

```
>>> print(house_prices.data)
[[ 6.32000000e-03   1.80000000e+01   2.31000000e+00 ...,   1.53000000e+01
   3.96900000e+02   4.98000000e+00]
 [ 2.73100000e-02   0.00000000e+00   7.07000000e+00 ...,   1.78000000e+01
   3.96900000e+02   9.14000000e+00]
 [ 2.72900000e-02   0.00000000e+00   7.07000000e+00 ...,   1.78000000e+01
   3.92830000e+02   4.03000000e+00]
 ...,
 [ 6.07600000e-02   0.00000000e+00   1.19300000e+01 ...,   2.10000000e+01
   3.96900000e+02   5.64000000e+00]
 [ 1.09590000e-01   0.00000000e+00   1.19300000e+01 ...,   2.10000000e+01
   3.93450000e+02   6.48000000e+00]
 [ 4.74100000e-02   0.00000000e+00   1.19300000e+01 ...,   2.10000000e+01
   3.96900000e+02   7.88000000e+00]]
```

Figure 9: Output of input home prices

Let's check out the labels.

You will see this output:

```
>>> print(house_prices.target)
[ 24.   21.6  34.7  33.4  36.2  28.7  22.9  27.1  16.5  18.9  15.   18.9
  21.7  20.4  18.2  19.9  23.1  17.5  20.2  18.2  13.6  19.6  15.2  14.5
  15.6  13.9  16.6  14.8  18.4  21.   12.7  14.5  13.2  13.1  13.5  18.9
  20.   21.   24.7  30.8  34.9  26.6  25.3  24.7  21.2  19.3  20.   16.6
  14.4  19.4  19.7  20.5  25.   23.4  18.9  35.4  24.7  31.6  23.3  19.6
  18.7  16.   22.2  25.   33.   23.5  19.4  22.   17.4  20.9  24.2  21.7
  22.8  23.4  24.1  21.4  20.   20.8  21.2  20.3  28.   23.9  24.8  22.9
  23.9  26.6  22.5  22.2  23.6  28.7  22.6  22.   22.9  25.   20.6  28.4
  21.4  38.7  43.8  33.2  27.5  26.5  18.6  19.3  20.1  19.5  19.5  20.4
  19.8  19.4  21.7  22.8  18.8  18.7  18.5  18.3  21.2  19.2  20.4  19.3
  22.   20.3  20.5  17.3  18.8  21.4  15.7  16.2  18.   14.3  19.2  19.6
  23.   18.4  15.6  18.1  17.4  17.1  13.3  17.8  14.   14.4  13.4  15.6
  11.8  13.8  15.6  14.6  17.8  15.4  21.5  19.6  15.3  19.4  17.   15.6
  13.1  41.3  24.3  23.3  27.   50.   50.   50.   22.7  25.   50.   23.8
  23.8  22.3  17.4  19.1  23.1  23.6  22.6  29.4  23.2  24.6  29.9  37.2
  39.8  36.2  37.9  32.5  26.4  29.6  50.   32.   29.8  34.9  37.   30.5
  36.4  31.1  29.1  50.   33.3  30.3  34.6  34.9  32.9  24.1  42.3  48.5
  50.   22.6  24.4  22.5  24.4  20.   21.7  19.3  22.4  28.1  23.7  25.
  23.3  28.7  21.5  23.   26.7  21.7  27.5  30.1  44.8  50.   37.6  31.6
  46.7  31.5  24.3  31.7  41.7  48.3  29.   24.   25.1  31.5  23.7  23.3
```

Figure 10: Output of predicted home prices

The actual array is larger, so the image represents the first few values in that array.

There are also image datasets available in the scikit-learn package. Each image is of shape 8×8. Let's load it:

```
>>> digits = datasets.load_digits()
```

Print the fifth image:

```
>>> print(digits.images[4])
```

You will see this output:

```
>>> print(digits.images[4])
[[ 0.   0.   0.   1.  11.   0.   0.   0.]
 [ 0.   0.   0.   7.   8.   0.   0.   0.]
 [ 0.   0.   1.  13.   6.   2.   2.   0.]
 [ 0.   0.   7.  15.   0.   9.   8.   0.]
 [ 0.   5.  16.  10.   0.  16.   6.   0.]
 [ 0.   4.  15.  16.  13.  16.   1.   0.]
 [ 0.   0.   0.   3.  15.  10.   0.   0.]
 [ 0.   0.   0.   2.  16.   4.   0.   0.]]
...
```

Figure 11: Output of scikit-learn array of images

As you can see, it has eight rows and eight columns.

Summary

In this chapter, we discussed:

- What AI is all about and why we need to study it
- Various applications and branches of AI
- What the Turing test is and how it's conducted
- How to make machines think like humans
- The concept of rational agents and how they should be designed
- General Problem Solver (GPS) and how to solve a problem using GPS
- How to develop an intelligent agent using machine learning
- Different types of machine learning models

We also went through how to install Python 3 on various operating systems, and how to install the necessary packages required to build AI applications. We discussed how to use these packages to load data that's available in scikit-learn.

In the next chapter, we will learn about supervised learning and how to build models for classification and regression.

2
Fundamental Use Cases for Artificial Intelligence

In this chapter, we are going to discuss some of the use cases for **Artificial Intelligence (AI)**. This by no means is an exhaustive list. Many industries have been impacted by AI, and the list of those industries not yet impacted gets shorter every day. Ironically, some of the jobs that robots, automation, and AI will not be able to take over are jobs with a low pay rate that require less "brain" power. For example, it will be a while until we are able to replace hair stylists and plumbers. Both of these jobs require a lot of finesse and detail that robots have yet to master. I know it will be a long time before my wife trusts her hair to anyone else other than her current hair stylist, let alone a robot.

This chapter will discuss:

- Some representative AI use cases
- The jobs that will take the longest to replace by automation
- The industries that will be most impacted by AI

Representative AI use cases

From finance to medicine, it is difficult to find an industry that is not being disrupted by Artificial Intelligence. We will focus on real-world examples of the most popular applications of AI in our everyday life. We will explore the current state of the art as well as what is coming soon. Most importantly, maybe this book will spark your imagination and you will come up with some new and innovative ideas that will positively impact society and we can add it to the next edition of our book.

Artificial Intelligence, cognitive computing, machine learning, and deep learning are only some of the disruptive technologies that are enabling rapid change today. These technologies can be adopted quicker because of advances in cloud computing, **Internet of Things** (**IoT**), and edge computing. Organizations are reinventing the way they do business by cobbling together all these technologies. This is only the beginning; we are not even in the first inning, we haven't even recorded the first strike!

With that, let's begin to look at some contemporary applications of AI.

Digital personal assistants and chatbots

Unfortunately, it is still all too common for some call centers to use legacy **Interactive Voice Response** (**IVR**) **systems** that make calling them an exercise in patience. However, we have made great advances in the area of natural language processing: chatbots. Some of the most popular examples are:

- **Google Assistant**: Google Assistant was launched in 2016 and is one of the most advanced chatbots available. It can be found in a variety of appliances such as telephones, headphones, speakers, washers, TVs, and refrigerators. Nowadays, most Android phones include Google Assistant. Google Home and Nest Home Hub also support Google Assistant.
- **Amazon Alexa**: Alexa is a virtual assistant developed and marketed by Amazon. It can interact with users by voice and by executing commands such as playing music, creating to-do lists, setting up alarms, playing audiobooks, and answering basic questions. It can even tell you a joke or a story on demand. Alexa can also be used to control compatible smart devices. Developers can extend Alexa's capabilities by installing skills. An Alexa skill is additional functionality developed by third-party vendors.
- **Apple Siri**: Siri can accept user voice commands and a natural language user interface to answer questions, make suggestions, and perform actions by parsing these voice commands and delegating these requests to a set of internet services. The software can adapt to users' individual language usage, their searches, and preferences. The more it is used the more it learns and the better it gets.
- **Microsoft Cortana**: Cortana is another digital virtual assistant, designed and created by Microsoft. Cortana can set reminders and alarms, recognize natural voice commands, and it answers questions using information.

All these assistants will allow you to perform all or at least most of these tasks:

- Control devices in your home
- Play music and display videos on command
- Set timers and reminders
- Make appointments
- Send text and email messages
- Make phone calls
- Open applications
- Read notifications
- Perform translations
- Order from e-commerce sites

Some of the tasks that might not be supported but will start to become more pervasive are:

- Checking into your flight
- Booking a hotel
- Making a restaurant reservation

All these platforms also support 3rd party developers to develop their own applications or "skills" as Amazon calls them. So, the possibilities are endless.

Some examples of existing Alexa skills:

- **MySomm**: Recommends what wine goes with a certain meat
- **The bartender**: Provides instructions on how to make alcoholic drinks
- **7-minute workout**: Will guide you through a tough 7-minute workout
- **Uber**: Allows you to order an Uber ride through Alexa

All the preceding services listed continue to get better. They continuously learn from interactions with customers. They are improved both by the developers of the services as well as by the systems taking advantage of new data points created daily by users of the services.

Most cloud providers make it extremely easy to create chatbots and for some basic examples it is not necessary to use a programming language. In addition, it is not difficult to deploy these chatbots to services such as Slack, Facebook Messenger, Skype, and WhatsApp.

Personal chauffeur

Self-driving or driverless cars are vehicles that can travel along a pre-established route with no human assistance. Most self-driving cars in existence today do not rely on a single sensor and navigation method and use a variety of technologies such as radar, sonar, lidar, computer vision, and GPS.

As technologies emerge, industries start creating standards to implement and measure their progress. Driverless technologies are no different. SAE International has created standard J3016, which defines six levels of automation for cars so that automakers, suppliers, and policymakers can use the same language to classify the vehicle's level of sophistication:

Level 0 (No automation)

The car has no self-driving capabilities. The driver is fully involved and responsible. The human driver steers, brakes, accelerates, and negotiates traffic. This describes most current cars on the road today.

Level 1 (Driver assistance)

System capability: Under certain conditions, the car controls either the steering or the vehicle speed, but not both simultaneously.

Driver involvement: The driver performs all other aspects of driving and has full responsibility for monitoring the road and taking over if the assistance system fails to act appropriately. For example, Adaptive cruise control.

Level 2 (Partial automation)

The car can steer, accelerate, and brake in certain circumstances. The human driver still performs many maneuvers like interpreting and responding to traffic signals or changing lanes. The responsibility for controlling the vehicle largely falls on the driver. The manufacturer still requires the driver to be fully engaged. Examples of this level are:

- Audi Traffic Jam Assist
- Cadillac Super Cruise
- Mercedes-Benz Driver Assistance Systems
- Tesla Autopilot
- Volvo Pilot Assist

Level 3 (Conditional automation)

The pivot point between levels 2 and 3 is critical. The responsibility for controlling and monitoring the car starts to change from driver to computer at this level. Under the right conditions, the computer can control the car, including monitoring the environment. If the car encounters a scenario that it cannot handle, it requests that the driver intervene and take control. The driver normally does not control the car but must be available to take over at any time. An example of this is Audi Traffic Jam Pilot.

Level 4 (High automation)

The car does not need human involvement under most conditions but still needs human assistance under some road, weather, or geographic conditions. Under a shared car model restricted to a defined area, there may not be any human involvement. But for a privately-owned car, the driver might manage all driving duties on surface streets and the system takes over on the highway. Google's now defunct Firefly pod-car is an example of this level. It didn't have pedals or a steering wheel. It was restricted to a top speed of 25 mph and it was not used in public streets.

Level 5 (Full automation)

The driverless system can control and operate the car on any road and under any conditions that a human driver could handle. The "operator" of the car only needs to enter a destination. Nothing at this level is in production yet but a few companies are close and might be there by the time the book is published.

We'll now review some of the leading companies working in the space:

Google's Waymo

As of 2018, Waymo's autonomous cars have driven eight million miles on public roads as well as five billion miles in simulated environments. In the next few years, it is all but a certainty that we will be able to purchase a car capable of full driving autonomy. Tesla, among others, already offers driver assistance with their Autopilot feature and possibly will be the first company to offer full self-driving capabilities. Imagine a world where a child born today will never have to get a driver's license! The disruption caused in our society by this advance in AI alone will be massive. The need for delivery drivers, taxi drivers, and truckers will be obviated. Even if there are still car accidents in a driverless future, millions of lives will be saved because we will eliminate distracted driving and drunk driving.

Waymo launched the first commercial driverless service in 2018 in Arizona, USA with plans to expand nationally and worldwide.

Uber ATG

Uber's **Advanced Technology Group** (**ATG**) is an Uber subsidiary working on developing self-driving technology. In 2016, Uber launched an experimental car service on the streets of Pittsburgh. Uber has plans to buy up to 24,000 Volvo XC90 and equip them with their self-driving technology and start commercializing them in some capacity by 2021.

Tragically, in March 2018, Elaine Herzberg was involved in an incident with an Uber driverless car and died. According to police reports, she was struck by the Uber vehicle while trying to cross the street, while she was watching a video on her phone. Ms. Herzberg became one of the first individuals to die in an incident involving a driverless car. Ideally, we would like to see no accidents ever happen with this technology, yet the level of safety that we demand needs to be tempered with the current crisis we have with traffic accidents. For context, there were 40,100 motor vehicle deaths in the US in 2017; even if we continue to see accidents with automated cars, if this death toll was slashed by say, half, thousands of lives would be saved each year.

It is certainly possible to envision a driverless vehicle that looks more like a living room than the interior of our current cars. There would be no need for steering wheels, pedals or any kind of manual control. The only input the car would need is your destination, which could be given at the beginning of your journey by "speaking" to your car. There would be no need to keep track of a maintenance schedule as the car would be able to sense when a service is due or there is an issue with the car's function.

Liability for car accidents will shift from the driver of the vehicle to the manufacturer of the vehicle doing away with the need to have car insurance. This last point is probably one of the reasons why car manufacturers have been slow to deploy this technology. Even car ownership might be flipped on its head since we could summon a car whenever we need one instead of needing one all the time.

Shipping and warehouse management

An Amazon sorting facility is one of the best examples of the symbiotic relationship that is forming between humans, computers, and robots. Computers take customer orders and decide where to route merchandise, the robots act as mules carrying the pallets and inventory around the warehouse. Humans plug the "last mile" problem by hand picking the items that are going into each order. Robots are proficient in mindlessly repeating a task many times as long as there is a pattern involved and some level of pretraining is involved to achieve this. However, having a robot pick a 20-pound package and immediately being able to grab an egg without breaking it is one of the harder robotics problems.

Robots struggle dealing with objects of different sizes, weights, shapes, and fragility; a task that many humans can perform effortlessly. People, therefore, handle the tasks that the robots encounter difficulty with. The interaction of these three types of different actors translates into a finely tuned orchestra that can deliver millions of packages everyday with very little mistakes.

Even Scott Anderson, Amazon's director of robotics fulfillment acknowledged in May 2019 that a fully automated warehouse is at least 10 years away. So, we will continue to see this configuration in warehouses across the world for a little longer.

Human health

The ways that AI can be applied in health science is almost limitless. We will discuss a few of them here, but it will by no means be an exhaustive list.

Drug discovery

AI can assist in generating drug candidates (that is, molecules to be tested for medical application) and then quickly eliminating some of them using constraint satisfaction or experiment simulation. We will learn more about constraint satisfaction programming in later chapters. In a nutshell, this approach allows us to speed up drug discovery by quickly generating millions of possible drug candidates and just as quickly rejecting them if the candidates do not satisfy certain predetermined constraints.

In addition, in some cases we can simulate experiments in the computer that otherwise would be much more expensive to perform in real life.

Furthermore, in some instances researchers still conduct real-world experiments but rely on robots to perform the experiments and speed up the process with them. These emerging fields are dubbed **high throughput screening** (HTS) and **virtual high throughput screening** (VHTS).

Machine learning is starting to be used more and more to enhance clinical trials. The consulting company of Accenture has developed a tool called **intelligent clinical trials** (ITP). It is used to predict the length of clinical trials.

Another approach that can surprisingly be used is to apply to drug discovery is **Natural Language Processing** (NLP). Genomic data can be represented using a string of letters and the NLP techniques can be used to process or "understand" what the genomic sequences mean.

Insurance pricing

Machine learning algorithms can be used to better price insurance by more accurately predicting how much will be spent on a patient, how good a driver an individual is, or how long a person will live.

As an example, the *young.ai* project from Insilico Medicine can predict with some accuracy how long someone will live from a blood sample and a photograph. The blood sample provides 21 biomarkers such as cholesterol level, inflammation markers, hemoglobin counts and albumin level that are used as input to a machine learning model. Other inputs into the model are ethnicity and age, as well as a photograph of the person.

Interestingly, as of now, anyone can use this service for free by visiting young.ai (`https://young.ai`) and providing the required information.

Patient diagnosis

Doctors can make better diagnosis on their patients and be more productive in their practice by using sophisticated rules engines and machine learning. As an example, in a recent study at the University of California in San Diego conducted by Kang Zhang [1], one system could diagnose children's illnesses with a higher degree of accuracy than junior pediatricians. The system was able to diagnose the following diseases with a degree of accuracy of between 90% and 97%:

- Glandular fever
- Roseola
- Influenza
- Chicken pox
- Hand, foot, and mouth disease

The input dataset consisted of medical records from 1.3 million children visits to the doctor from the Guangzhou region in China between 2016 and 2017.

Medical imaging interpretation

Medical imaging data is a complex and rich source of information about patients. CAT scans, MRIs, and X-rays contain information that is otherwise unavailable. There is a shortage of radiologists and clinicians that can interpret them. Getting results from these images can sometimes take days and can sometimes be misinterpreted. Recent studies have found that machine learning models can perform just as well, if not better, than their human counterparts.

Data scientists have developed AI enabled platforms that can interpret MRI scans and radiological images in a matter of minutes instead of days and with a higher degree of accuracy when compared with traditional methods.

Perhaps surprisingly, far from being concerned, leaders from the American College for Radiology see the advent of AI as a valuable tool for physicians. In order to foster further development in the field, the **American College for Radiology Data Science Institute** (**ACR DSI**) released several AI use cases in medical imaging and plans to continue releasing more.

Psychiatric analysis

An hour-long session with a psychiatrist can costs hundreds of dollars. We are on the cusp of being able to simulate the behavior with AI chatbots. At the very least, these bots will be able to offer follow-up care from the sessions with the psychiatrist and help with a patient's care between doctor's visits.

One early example of an automated counselor is Eliza. It was developed in 1966 by Joseph Weizenbaum. It allows users to have a "conversation" with the computer mimicking a Rogerian psychotherapist. Remarkably, Eliza feels natural, but its code is only a few hundred lines and it doesn't really use much AI at its core.

A more recent and advanced example is Ellie. Ellie was created by the Institute for Creative Technologies at the University of Southern California. It helps with the treatment of people with depression or post-traumatic stress disorder. Ellie is a virtual therapist (she appears on screen), responds to emotional cues, nods affirmatively when appropriate and shifts in her seat. She can sense 66 points on a person's face and use these inputs to read a person's emotional state. One of Ellie's secrets is that she is obviously not human and that makes people feel less judged and more comfortable opening up to her.

Smart health records

Medicine is notorious for being a laggard in moving to electronic records. Data science provides a variety of methods to streamline the capture of patient data including OCR, handwriting recognition, voice to text capture, and real-time reading and analysis of patient's vital signs. It is not hard to imagine a future coming soon where this information can be analyzed in real-time by AI engines to take decisions such as adjusting body glucose levels, administering a medicine, or summoning medical help because a health problem is imminent.

Disease detection and prediction

The human genome is the ultimate dataset. At some point soon, we will be able to use the human genome as input to machine learning models and be able to detect and predict a wide variety of diseases and conditions using this vast dataset.

Using genomic datasets as an input in machine learning is an exciting area that is evolving rapidly and will revolutionize medicine and health care.

The human genome contains over 3 billion base pairs. We are making progress on two fronts that will accelerate progress:

- Continuous advancements in the understanding of genome biology
- Advances in big data computing to process vast amounts of data faster

There is much research applying deep learning to the field of genomics. Although it is still in early stages, deep learning in genomics has the potential to inform fields including:

- Functional genomics
- Oncology
- Population genetics
- Clinical genetics
- Crop yield improvement
- Epidemiology and public health
- Evolutionary and phylogenetic analysis

Knowledge search

We have gotten to a point where, in some cases, we don't even realize we are using artificial intelligence. A sign that a technology or product is good is when we don't necessarily stop to think how it's doing what it is doing. A perfect example of this is Google Search. The product has become ubiquitous in our lives and we don't realize how much it relies on artificial intelligence to produce its amazing results. From its Google Suggest technology to its constant improvement of the relevancy of its results, AI is deeply embedded in its search process.

Early in 2015, as was reported by Bloomberg, Google began using a deep learning system called RankBrain to assist in generating search query responses. The Bloomberg article describes RankBrain as follows:

> *"RankBrain uses artificial intelligence to embed vast amounts of written language into mathematical entities – called vectors – that the computer can understand. If RankBrain sees a word or phrase it isn't familiar with, the machine can make a guess as to what words or phrases might have a similar meaning and filter the result accordingly, making it more effective at handling never-before-seen search queries."*
>
> – *Clark, Jack [2]*

As of the last report, RankBrain plays a role in a large percentage of the billions of Google Search queries. As one can imagine, the company is tight lipped about how exactly RankBrain works, and furthermore even Google might have a hard time explaining how it works. You see, this is one of the dilemmas of deep learning. In many cases, it can provide highly accurate results, but deep learning algorithms are usually hard to understand in terms of why an individual answer was given. Rule-based systems and even other machine learning models (such as Random Forest) are much easier to interpret.

The lack of explainability of deep learning algorithms has major implications, including legal implications. Lately, Google and Facebook among others, have found themselves under the microscope to determine if their results are biased. In the future, legislators and regulators might require that these tech giants provide a justification for a certain result. If deep learning algorithms do not provide explainability, they might be forced to use other less accurate algorithms that do.

Initially, RankBrain only assisted in about 15 percent of Google queries, but now it is involved in almost all user queries.

However, if a query is a common query, or something that the algorithm understands, the RankBrain rank score is given little weight. If the query is one that the algorithm has not seen before or it does not know its meaning, RankBrain score is much more relevant.

Recommendation systems

Recommendation systems are another example of AI technology that has been weaved into our everyday lives. Amazon, YouTube, Netflix, LinkedIn, and Facebook all rely on recommendation technology and we don't even realize we are using it. Recommendation systems rely heavily on data and the more data that is at their disposable, the more powerful they become. It is not coincidence that these companies have some of the biggest market caps in the world and their power comes from them being able to harness the hidden power in their customer's data. Expect this trend to continue in the future.

What is a recommendation? Let's answer the question by first exploring what it is not. It is not a definitive answer. Certain questions like "what is two plus two?" or "how many moons does Saturn have?" have a definite answer and there is no room for subjectivity. Other questions like "what is your favorite movie?" or "do you like radishes?" are completely subjective and the answer is going to depend on the person answering the question. Some machine learning algorithms thrive with this kind of "fuzziness." Again, these recommendations can have tremendous implications.

Think of the consequences of Amazon constantly recommending a product versus another. The company that makes the recommended product will thrive and the company that makes the product that was not recommended could go out of business if it doesn't find alternative ways to distribute and sell its product.

One of the ways that a recommender system can improve is by having previous selections from users of the system. If you visit an e-commerce site for the first time and you don't have an order history, the site will have a hard time making a recommendation tailored to you. If you purchase sneakers, the website now has one data point that it can start using as a starting point. Depending on the sophistication of the system, it might recommend a different pair of sneakers, a pair of athletic socks, or maybe even a basketball (if the shoes were high-tops).

An important component of good recommendation systems is a randomization factor that occasionally "goes out on a limb" and makes oddball recommendations that might not be that related to the initial user's choices. Recommender systems don't just learn from history to find similar recommendations, but they also attempt to make new recommendations that might not be related at first blush. For example, a Netflix user might watch "The Godfather" and Netflix might start recommending Al Pacino movies or mobster movies. But it might recommend "Bourne Identity," which is a stretch. If the user does not take the recommendation or does not watch the movie, the algorithm will learn from this and avoid other movies like the "Bourne Identity" (for example any movies that have Jason Bourne as the main character).

As recommender systems get better, the possibilities are exciting. They will be able to power personal digital assistants and become your personal butler that has intimate knowledge of your likes and dislikes and can make great suggestions that you might have not thought about. Some of the areas where recommendations can benefit from these systems are:

- Restaurants
- Movies
- Music
- Potential partners (online dating)
- Books and articles
- Search results
- Financial services (robo-advisors)

Some notable specific examples of recommender systems follow:

Netflix Prize

A contest that created a lot of buzz in the recommender system community was the Netflix Prize. From 2006 to 2009, Netflix sponsored a competition with a grand prize of one million US dollars. Netflix made available a dataset of 100 million plus ratings.

Netflix offered to pay the prize to the team that offered the highest accuracy in their recommendations and was 10% more accurate than the recommendations from Netflix's existing recommender system. The competition energized research for new and more accurate algorithms. In September 2009, the grand prize was awarded to the BellKor's Pragmatic Chaos team.

Pandora

Pandora is one of the leading music services. Unlike other companies like Apple and Amazon, Pandora's exclusive focus is as a music service. One of Pandora's salient service features is the concept of customized radio stations. These "stations" allow users to play music by genre. As you can imagine, recommender systems are at the core of this functionality.

Pandora's recommender is built on multiple tiers:

- First, their team of music experts annotates songs based on genre, rhythm, and progression.
- These annotations are transformed into a vector for comparing song similarity. This approach promotes the presentation of "long tail" or obscure music from unknown artists that nonetheless could be a good fit for individual listeners.
- The service also heavily relies on user feedback and uses it to continuously enhance the service. Pandora has collected over 75 billion feedback data points on listener preferences.
- The Pandora recommendation engine can then perform personalized filtering based on a listener's preferences using their previous selections, geography, and other demographic data.

In total, Pandora's recommender uses around 70 different algorithms, including 10 to analyze content, 40 to process collective intelligence, and about another 30 to do personalized filtering.

Betterment

Robo-advisors are recommendation engines that provide investment or financial advice and management with minimal human involvement. These services use machine learning to automatically allocate, manage, and optimize a customer's asset mix. They can offer these services at a lower cost than traditional advisors because their overhead is lower, and their approach is more scalable.

There is now fierce competition in this space with well over 100 companies offering these kinds of services. Robo-advisors are considered a tremendous breakthrough. Formerly, wealth management services were an exclusive and expensive service reserved for high net worth individuals. Robo-advisors promise to bring a similar service to a broader audience with lower costs compared to the traditional human-enabled services. Robo-advisors could potentially allocate investments in a wide variety of investment products like stocks, bonds, futures, commodities, real estate, and other exotic investments. However, to keep things simple investments are often constrained to **exchange traded funds** (**ETFs**).

As we mentioned there are many companies offering robo-advice. As an example, you might want to investigate Betterment to learn more about this topic. After filling out a risk questionnaire, Betterment will provide users with a customized, diversified portfolio. Betterment will normally recommend a mix of low-fee stock and bond index funds. Betterment charges an administration fee (as a percentage of the portfolio) but it is lower than most human-powered services. Please note that we are not endorsing this service and we only mention it as an example of a recommendation engine in the financial sector.

The smart home

Whenever you bring up the topic of AI to the common folk on the street, they are usually skeptical about how soon it is going to replace human workers. They can rightly point to the fact that we still need to do a lot of housework around the house. AI needs to become not only technologically possible, but it also needs to be economically feasible for adoption to become widespread. House help is normally a low-wage profession and, for that reason, automation to replace it needs to be the same price or cheaper. In addition, house work requires a lot of finesse and it comprises tasks that are not necessarily repetitive. Let's list out some of the tasks that this automaton will need to perform in order to be proficient:

- Wash and dry clothes
- Fold clothes
- Cook dinner

- Make beds
- Pick up items off the floor
- Mop, dust and vacuum
- Wash dishes
- Monitor the home

As we already know, some of these tasks are easy to perform for machines (even without AI) and some of them are extremely hard. For this reason and because of the economic considerations, the home will probably be one of the last places to become fully automated. Nonetheless, let's look at some of the amazing advances that have been made in this area.

Home Monitoring

Home monitoring is one area where great solutions are generally available already. The Ring video doorbell from Amazon and the Google Nest thermostat are two inexpensive options that are widely available and popular. These are two simple examples of smart home devices that are available for purchase today.

The Ring video doorbell is a smart home device connected to the internet that can notify the homeowner of activity at their home, such as a visitor, via their smartphone. The system does not continuously record but rather it activates when the doorbell is pressed, or when the motion detector is activated. The Ring doorbell can then let the home owner watch the activity or communicate with the visitor using the built-in microphone and speakers. Some models also allow the homeowner to open the door remotely via a smart lock and let the visitor into the house.

The Nest Learning Thermostat is a smart home device initially developed by Nest Labs, a company that was later bought by Google. It was designed by Tony Fadell, Ben Filson, and Fred Bould. It is programmable, Wi-Fi-enabled, and self-learning. It uses artificial intelligence to optimize the temperature of the home while saving energy.

In the first weeks of use you set the thermostat to your preferred settings and this will serve as a baseline. The thermostat will learn your schedule and your preferred temperatures. Using built-in sensors and your phones' locations, the thermostat will shift into energy saving mode when no one is home.

Since 2011, the Nest Thermostat has saved billions of kWh of energy in millions of homes worldwide. Independent studies have shown that it saves people an average of 10% to 12% on their heating bills and 15% on their cooling bills so in about 2 years it may pay for itself.

Vacuuming and mopping

Two tasks that have been popular to hand off to robots are vacuuming and mopping. A robotic vacuum cleaner is an autonomous robotic vacuum cleaner that uses AI to vacuum a surface. Depending on the design, some of these machines use spinning brushes to reach tight corners and some models include several other features in addition to being able to vacuum, such as mopping and UV sterilization. Much of the credit for popularizing this technology goes to the company (not the film), *iRobot*.

iRobot was started in 1990 by Rodney Brooks, Colin Angle, and Helen Greiner after meeting each other while working in MIT's Artificial Intelligence Lab. iRobot is best known for its vacuuming robot (Roomba), but for a long time they also had a division devoted to the development of military robots. The Roomba started selling in 2002. As of 2012 iRobot had sold more than eight million home robots as well as creating more than 5,000 defense and security robots. The company's PackBot is a bomb-disposal robot used by the US military that has been used extensively in Iraq and Afghanistan. PackBots were also used to gather information under dangerous conditions at the Fukushima Daiichi nuclear disaster site. iRobot's Seaglider was used to detect underwater pools of oil after the Deepwater Horizon oil spill in the Gulf of Mexico.

Another iRobot product is the Braava series of cleaners. The Braava is a small robot that can mop and sweep floors. It is meant for small spaces like bathrooms and kitchens. It sprays water and uses an assortment of different pads to clean effectively and quietly. Some of the Braava models have a built-in navigation system. The Braava doesn't have enough power to remove deep-set stains, so it's not a complete human replacement, but it does have wide acceptance and high ratings. We expect them to continue to gain popularity.

The potential market for intelligent devices in the home is huge and it is all but certain that we will continue to see attempts from well established companies and startups alike to exploit this largely untapped market.

Picking up your mess

As we learned in the shipping use case, picking objects of different weights, dimensions, and shapes is one of the most difficult tasks to automate. Robots can perform efficiently under homogeneous conditions like a factory floor where certain robots specialize in certain tasks. Picking up a pair of shoes after picking up a chair, however, can be immensely challenging and expensive. For this reason, do not expect this home chore to be pervasively performed by machines in a cost-effective fashion any time soon.

Personal chef

Like picking up items off the floor, cooking involves picking up disparate items. Yet there are two reasons why we can expect "automated cooking" to happen sooner:

- Certain restaurants may charge hundreds of dollars for their food and be paying high prices for skilled chefs. Therefore, they might be open to using technology to replace their high-priced staff if this should work out to be more profitable. An example for this is a five-star sushi restaurant.
- Some tasks in the kitchen are repetitive and therefore lend themselves to automation. Think of a fast food joint where hamburgers and fries might have to be made by the hundreds. Thus, rather than having one machine handle the entire disparate cooking process, a series of machines could deal with individual repetitive stages of the process.

Smart prosthetics are great examples of artificial intelligence augmenting humans rather than replacing them. There are more than a few chefs that lost their arm in an accident or were born without a limb.

One example is chef Michael Caines who runs a two Michelin star restaurant and lost his arm in a horrific car accident. Chef Caines was head chef of Gidleigh Park in Devon in England until January 2016.[3] He is currently the executive chef of the Lympstone Manor hotel between Exeter and Exmouth. He now cooks with a prosthetic arm, but you'd never know it given the quality of his food.

Another example is Eduardo Garcia who is a sportsman and a chef - both of which are made possible by the most advanced bionic hand in the world.

On October 2011, while bow-hunting elk he was electrocuted in the Montana backcountry. Eduardo was hunting by himself in October 2011. He was in back country when he saw a dead baby black bear. He stopped to check it out, knelt, and used his knife to prod it.

While doing so, 2,400 volts coursed through his body - the baby bear had been killed by a buried, live electrical wire. He survived but lost his arm during the incident.

In September 2013, Garcia was fitted by Advanced Arm Dynamics with a bionic hand designed by Touch Bionics. The bionic hand is controlled by Garcia's forearm muscles and can grip in 25 different ways. With his new hand, Garcia can perform tasks that normally require great dexterity. His new hand still has some limitations. For example, Garcia cannot lift heavy weights. However, there are things that he can perform now that he couldn't before. For example, he can grab things out of a hot oven and not get burnt and it is impossible to cut his fingers.

Conversely, rather than augmenting humans, robots may replace humans in the kitchen entirely. An example of this is Moley, the robotic kitchen. Moley is not currently in production but the most advanced prototype of the Moley Robotic Kitchen consists of two robotic arms with hands equipped with tactile sensors, a stove top, an oven, a dishwasher, and a touchscreen unit. These artificial hands can lift, grab, and interact with most kitchen equipment including knives, whisks, spoons, and blenders.

Using a 3D camera and a glove it can record a human chef preparing a meal and then upload detailed steps and instructions into a repository. The chef's actions are then translated into robotic movements using gesture recognition models. These models were created in collaboration with Stanford University and Carnegie Mellon University. After that Moley can reproduce the same steps and cooks the exact same meal from scratch.

In the current prototype, the user can operate it using a touchscreen or smartphone application with ingredients prepared in advance and placed in preset locations. The company's long-term goal is to allow users to simply select an option from a list of more 2,000 recipes and Moley will have the meal prepared in minutes.

Gaming

There is perhaps no better example to demonstrate the awe-inspiring advances in Artificial Intelligence than the progress that has been made in the area of gaming. Humans are competitive by nature and having machines beat us at our own games is an interesting yardstick to measure the breakthroughs in the field. Computers have long been able to beat us in some of the more basic, more deterministic, less compute-intensive games like say checkers. It's only in the last few years that machines have been able to consistently beat the masters of some of the harder games. In this section we go over three of these examples.

StarCraft 2

Video games have been used for decades as a benchmark to test the performance of AI systems. As capabilities increase, researchers work with more complex games that require different types of intelligence. The strategies and techniques developed from this game playing can transfer to solving real-world problems. The game of StarCraft II is considered one of the hardest, though it is an ancient game by video game standards.

The team at DeepMind introduced a program dubbed AlphaStar that can play StarCraft II and was for the first time able to defeat a top professional player. In matches held in December 2018, AlphaStar whooped a team put together by Grzegorz "MaNa" Komincz, one of the world's strongest professional StarCraft players with a score of 5-0. The games took place under professional match conditions and without any game restrictions.

In contrast to previous attempts to master the game using AI that required restrictions, AlphaStar can play the full game with no restrictions. It uses a deep neural network that is trained directly from raw game data using supervised learning and reinforcement learning.

One of the things that makes StarCraft II so difficult is the need to balance short- and long-term goals and adapt to unexpected scenarios. This has normally posed a tremendous challenge for previous systems.

While StarCraft is just a game, albeit a difficult one, the concepts and techniques coming out of AlphaStar can be useful in solving other real-world challenges. As an example, AlphaStar's architecture is capable of modeling very long sequences of likely actions - with games often lasting up to an hour with tens of thousands of moves - based on imperfect information. The primary concept of making complicated predictions over long sequences of data can be found in many real-world problems, such as:

- Weather prediction
- Climate modelling
- Natural Language Understanding

The success that AlphaStar has demonstrated playing StarCraft represents a major scientific breakthrough in one of the hardest video games in existence. These breakthroughs represent a big leap in the creation of artificial intelligence systems that can be transferred and that can help solve fundamental real-world practical problems.

Jeopardy

IBM and the Watson team made history in 2011 when they devised a system that was able to beat two of the most successful Jeopardy champions.

Ken Jennings has the longest unbeaten run in the show's history with 74 consecutive appearances. Brad Rutter had the distinction of winning the biggest prize pot with a total of $3.25 million.

Both players agreed to an exhibition match against Watson.

Watson is a question-answering system that can answer questions posed in natural language. It was initially created by IBM's DeepQA research team, led by principal investigator David Ferrucci.

The main difference between the question-answering technology used by Watson and general search (think Google searches) is that general search takes a keyword as input and responds with a list of documents with a ranking based on the relevance to the query. Question-answering technology like what is used by Watson takes a question expressed in natural language, tries to understand the question at a deeper level, and tries to provide the precise answer to the question.

The software architecture of Watson uses:

- IBM's DeepQA software
- Apache UIMA (Unstructured Information Management Architecture)
- A variety of languages, including Java, C++, and Prolog
- SUSE Linux Enterprise Server
- Apache Hadoop for distributed computing

Chess

Many of us remember the news when Deep Blue famously beat chess grand master Gary Kasparov in 1996. Deep Blue was a chess-playing application created by IBM.

In the first round of play Deep Blue won the first game against Gary Kasparov. However, they were scheduled to play six games. Kasparov won three and drew two of the following five games thus defeating Deep Blue by a score of 4–2.

The Deep Blue team went back to the drawing board, made a lot of enhancements to the software, and played Kasparov again in 1997. Deep Blue won the second round against Kasparov winning the six-game rematch by a score of 3½–2½. It then became the first computer system to beat a current world champion in a match under standard chess tournament rules and time controls.

A lesser known example, and a sign that machines beating humans is becoming common place, is the achievement in the area of chess by the AlphaZero team.

Google scientists from their AlphaZero research team created a system in 2017 that took just four hours to learn the rules of chess before crushing the most advanced world champion chess program at the time called *Stockfish*. By now the question as to whether computers or humans are better at chess has been resolved.

Let's pause for a second and think about this. All of humanity's knowledge about the ancient game of chess was surpassed by a system that, if it started learning in the morning, would be done by lunch time.

The system was given the rules of chess, but it was not given any strategies or further knowledge. Then, in a few hours, AlphaZero mastered the game to the extent it was able to beat Stockfish.

In a series of 100 games against Stockfish, AlphaZero won 25 games while playing as white (white has an advantage because it goes first). It also won three games playing as black. The rest of the games were ties. Stockfish did not obtain a single win.

AlphaGo

As hard as chess is, its difficulty does not compare to the ancient game of Go.

Not only are there more possible (19 x 19) Go-board positions than there are atoms in the visible universe and the number of possible chess positions is negligible to the number of Go positions. But Go is at least several orders of magnitude more complex than a game of chess because of the large number of possible ways to let the game flow with each move towards another line of development. With Go, the number of moves in which a single stone can affect and impact the whole-board situation is also many orders of magnitude larger than that of a single piece movement with chess.

There is great example of a powerful program that can play the game of Go also developed by DeepMind called AlphaGo. AlphaGo also has three far more powerful successors, called AlphaGo Master, AlphaGo Zero, and AlphaZero.

In October 2015, the original AlphaGo became the first computer Go program to beat a human professional Go player without handicaps on a full-sized 19 x 19 board. In March 2016, it beat Lee Sedol in a five-game match. This became the first time a Go program beat a 9-dan professional without handicaps. Although AlphaGo lost to Lee Sedol in the fourth game, Lee resigned in the final game, giving a final score of 4 games to 1.

At the 2017 Future of Go Summit, the successor to AlphaGo called AlphaGo Master beat the master Ke Jie in a three-game match. Ke Jie was ranked the world No.1 ranked player at the time. After this, AlphaGo was awarded professional 9-dan by the Chinese Weiqi Association.

AlphaGo and its successors use a Monte Carlo tree search algorithm to find their moves based on knowledge previously "learned" by machine learning, specifically using deep learning and training, both playing with humans and by itself. The model is trained to predict AlphaGo's own moves and the winner's games. This neural net improves the strength of tree search, resulting in better moves and stronger play in following games.

Movie making

It is all but a certainty that within the next few decades it will be possible to create movies that are 100% computer generated. It is not unfathomable to envision a system where the input is a written script and the output is a full-length feature film. In addition, some strides have been made in natural generators. So, eventually not even the script will be needed. Let's explore this further.

Deepfakes

A deepfake is a *portmanteau*, or blend, of "deep learning" and "fake." It is an AI technique to merge video images. A common application is to overlap someone's face onto another. A nefarious version of this was used to merge pornographic scenes with famous people or to create revenge porn. Deepfakes can also be used to create fake news or hoaxes. As you can imagine, there are severe societal implications if this technology is misused.

One recent version of similar software was developed by a Chinese company called Momo who developed an app called *Zao*. It allows you to overlap someone's face over short movie clips like Titanic and the results are impressive. This and other similar applications do not come without controversy. Privacy groups are complaining that the photos submitted to the site per the terms of the user agreement become property of Momo and then can later be used for other applications.

It will be interesting to see how technology continues to advance in this area.

Movie Script Generation

They are not going to win any Academy Awards any time soon, but there are a couple projects dedicated to producing movie scripts. One of the most famous examples is Sunspring.

Sunspring is an experimental science fiction short film released in 2016. It was entirely written by using deep learning techniques. The film's script was created using a **long short-term memory** (**LSTM**) model dubbed Benjamin. Its creators are BAFTA-nominated filmmaker Oscar Sharp and NYU AI researcher Ross Goodwin. The actors in the film are Thomas Middleditch, Elisabeth Grey, and Humphrey Ker. Their character names are H, H2, and C, living in the future. They eventually connect with each other and a love triangle forms.

Originally shown at the Sci-Fi-London film festival's 48hr Challenge, it was also released online by technology news website Ars Technica in June 2016.

Underwriting and deal analysis

What is underwriting? In short, underwriting is the process by which an institution determines if they want to take a financial risk in exchange for a premium. Examples of transactions that require underwriting are:

- Issuing an insurance policy
    - Health
    - Life
    - Home
    - Driving
- Loans
    - Installment loans
    - Credit cards
    - Mortgages
    - Commercial lines of credit
- Securities underwriting and Initial Public Offerings (IPOs)

As can be expected, determining whether an insurance policy or a loan should be issued and at what price can be very costly if the wrong decision is made. For example, if a bank issues a loan and the loan defaults, it would require dozens of other performing loans to make up for that loss. Inversely, if the bank passes up on a loan where the borrower was going to make all their payments is also detrimental to the bank finances. For this reason, the bank spends considerable time analyzing or "underwriting" the loan to determine the credit worthiness of the borrower as well as the value of the collateral securing the loan.

Even with all these checks, underwriters still get it wrong and issue loans that default or bypass deserving borrowers. The current underwriting process follows a set of criteria that must be met but specially for smaller banks there is still a degree of human subjectivity in the process. This is not necessarily a bad thing. Let's visit a scenario to explore this further:

A high net worth individual recently came back from a tour around the world. Three months ago, they got a job at a prestigious medical institution and their credit score is above 800.

Would you lend money to this individual? With the characteristics given, they seem to be a good credit risk. However, normal underwriting rules might disqualify them because they haven't been employed for the last two years. Manual underwriting would look at the whole picture and probably approve them.

Similarly, a machine learning model would probably be able to flag this as a worthy account and issue the loan. Machine learning models don't have hard and fast rules but rather "learn by example."

Many lenders are already using machine learning in their underwriting. An interesting example of a company that specializes in this space is Zest Finance. Zest Finance uses AI techniques to assist lenders with their underwriting. AI can help to increase revenue and reduce risk. Most importantly well applied AI in general and Zest Finance in particular can help companies to ensure that the AI models used are compliant with a country's regulations. Some AI models can be a "black box" where it is difficult to explain why one borrower was rejected and another one was accepted. Zest Finance can fully explain data modeling results, measure business impact, and comply with regulatory requirements. One of Zest Finance's secret weapons is the use of non-traditional data, including data that a lender might have in-house, such as:

- Customer support data
- Payment histories
- Purchase transactions

They might also consider nontraditional credit variables such as:

- The way a customer fills out a form
- The method a customer uses to arrive at the site or how they navigate the site
- The amount of time taken to fill out an application

Data cleansing and transformation

Just as gas powers a car, data is the lifeblood of AI. The age-old adage of "garbage in, garbage out" remains painfully true. For this reason, having clean and accurate data is paramount to producing consistent, reproducible, and accurate AI models. Some of this data cleansing has required painstaking human involvement. By some measures, it is said that a data scientist spends about 80% of their time cleaning, preparing, and transforming their input data and 20% of the time running and optimizing their models. Examples of this are the ImageNet and MS-COCO image datasets. Both contain over a million labeled images of various objects and categories. These datasets are used to train models that can distinguish between different categories and object types. Initially, these datasets were painstakingly and patiently labeled by humans. As these systems become more prevalent, we can use AI to perform the labeling. Furthermore, there is a plethora of AI-enabled tools that help with the cleansing and deduplication process.

One good example is Amazon Lake Formation. In August 2019, Amazon made its service Lake Formation generally available. Amazon Lake Formation automates some of the steps typically involved in the creation of a data lake including the collection, cleansing, deduplication, cataloging, and publication of data. The data then can be made available for analytics and to build machine models. To use Lake Formation, a user can bring data into the lake from a range of sources using predefined templates. They can then define policies that govern data access depending on the level of access that groups across the organization require.

Some automatic preparation, cleansing, and classification that the data undergoes uses machine learning to automatically perform these tasks.

Lake Formation also provides a centralized dashboard where administrators can manage and monitor data access policies, governance, and auditing across multiple analytics engines. Users can also search for datasets in the resulting catalog. As the tool evolves in the next few months and years, it will facilitate the analysis of data using their favorite analytics and machine learning services, including:

- Databricks
- Tableau
- Amazon Redshift
- Amazon Athena
- AWS Glue
- Amazon EMR
- Amazon QuickSight
- Amazon SageMaker

Summary

This chapter provided a few examples of the applications of AI. That said, the content here doesn't begin to scratch the surface! We tried to keep the use cases to either technology that is widely available, or at least that has the potential to become available soon. It is not difficult to extrapolate how this technology is going to continue to improve, become cheaper, and be more widely available. For example, it will be quite exciting when self-driving cars start becoming popular.

However, we can all be certain that the bigger applications of AI have not yet even been conceived. Also, advances in AI will have wide implications for our society and at some point, we will have to deal with these questions:

- What happens if an AI became so evolved that it became conscious? Should it be given rights?
- If a robot replaces a human, should companies be required to continue paying payroll tax for that displaced worker?
- Will we get to a point where computers are doing everything, and if so, how will we adapt to this; how will we spend our time?
- Worse yet, does the technology enable a few individuals to control all resources? Will a universal income society emerge in which individuals can pursue their own interests? Or will the displaced masses live in poverty?

Bill Gates and Elon Musk have warned about AIs either destroying the planet in a frenzied pursuit of their own goals or doing away with humans by accident (or not so much by accident). We will take a more optimistic "half-full" view of the impact of AI, but one thing that is certain is that it will be an interesting journey.

References

1. Willingham, Emily, *A Machine Gets High Marks for Diagnosing Sick Children*, Scientific American, October 7th, 2019, `https://www.scientificamerican.com/article/a-machine-gets-high-marks-for-diagnosing-sick-children/`
2. Clark, Jack, *Google Turning Its Lucrative Web Search Over to AI Machines*, Bloomberg, October 26th, 2015, `https://www.bloomberg.com/news/articles/2015-10-26/google-turning-its-lucrative-web-search-over-to-ai-machines`
3. `https://www.michaelcaines.com/michael-caines/about-michael/`

3
Machine Learning Pipelines

Model training is only a small piece of the machine learning process. Data scientists often spend a significant amount of time cleansing, transforming, and preparing data to get it ready to be consumed by a machine learning model. Since data preparation is such a time-consuming activity, we will present state of the art techniques to facilitate this activity as well as other components that together form a well-designed production machine learning pipeline.

In this chapter, we will cover the following key topics:

- What exactly is a machine learning pipeline?
- What are the components of a production-quality machine learning pipeline?
- What are the best practices when deploying machine learning models?
- Once a machine learning pipeline is in place, how can we shorten the deployment cycle?

What is a machine learning pipeline?

Many young data scientists starting their machine learning training immediately want to jump into model building and model tuning. They fail to realize that creating successful machine learning systems involves a lot more than choosing between a random forest model and a support vector machine model.

From choosing the proper ingestion mechanism to data cleansing to feature engineering, the initial steps in a machine learning pipeline are just as important as model selection. Also being able to properly measure and monitor the performance of your model in production and deciding when and how to retrain your models can be the difference between great results and mediocre outcomes. As the world changes, your input variables change, and your model must change with them.

As data science progresses, expectations get higher. Data sources become more varied, voluminous (in terms of size) and plentiful (in terms of number), and the pipelines and workflows get more complex. It doesn't help that more and more of the data we are expected to process is real-time in nature. Think of web logs, click data, e-commerce transactions, and self-driving car inputs. The data from these systems comes in fast and furious and we must have methods that can process the information faster than it is received.

Many machine learning solutions exist to implement these pipelines. It is certainly possible to set up basic machine learning pipelines using just the Python or R languages. We'll begin to build up our understanding by laying out an example of a pipeline using Python. In this chapter we will explore in detail a few architectures that utilize some of the most popular tools out there today. Some of the tools that data pipelines commonly leverage are:

- Hadoop
- Spark
- Spark Streaming
- Kafka
- Azure
- AWS
- Google Cloud Platform
- R
- SAS
- Databricks
- Python

As we'll see, some of these are more appropriate for certain stages of the pipeline. Let's perform a quick overview of the minimum steps required to set up a machine learning pipeline.

One important item to consider is that each step in the pipeline produces an output that becomes the input for the next step in the pipeline. The term *pipeline* is somewhat misleading as it implies a one-way flow of data. In reality, machine learning pipelines can be cyclical and iterative. Every step in the pipeline might be repeated to achieve better results or cleaner data. Finally, the output variable might be used as input the next time the pipeline cycle is performed.

The main steps in a machine learning pipeline are:

1. **Problem Definition**: Define the business problem.
2. **Data Ingestion**: Identify and collect the dataset.
3. **Data Preparation**: Process and prepare the data using techniques such as:
    - Impute missing values
    - Remove duplicate records
    - Normalize values (change numeric values in a dataset to use a common scale)
    - Perform another type of cleanup or mappings
    - Complete feature extraction
    - Eliminate correlated features
    - Perform feature engineering
4. **Data Segregation**: Split the data into a training set, validation set, and testing set.
5. **Model Training**: Train the machine models against the training dataset. This is the core of data science. In this chapter, we will only scratch the surface of this step and the steps that follow. There are other chapters in the book that will cover model training in more detail. It is listed here mostly to give the reader a full picture of the complete pipeline.
6. **Candidate Model Evaluation**: Measure the performance of the models using test and validation subsets of data to determine model accuracy.
7. **Model Deployment**: Once a model is chosen, deploy it into production for inference.

8. **Performance Monitoring**: Continuously monitor model performance, retrain, and calibrate accordingly. Collect new data to continue to improve the model and prevent it from becoming stale:

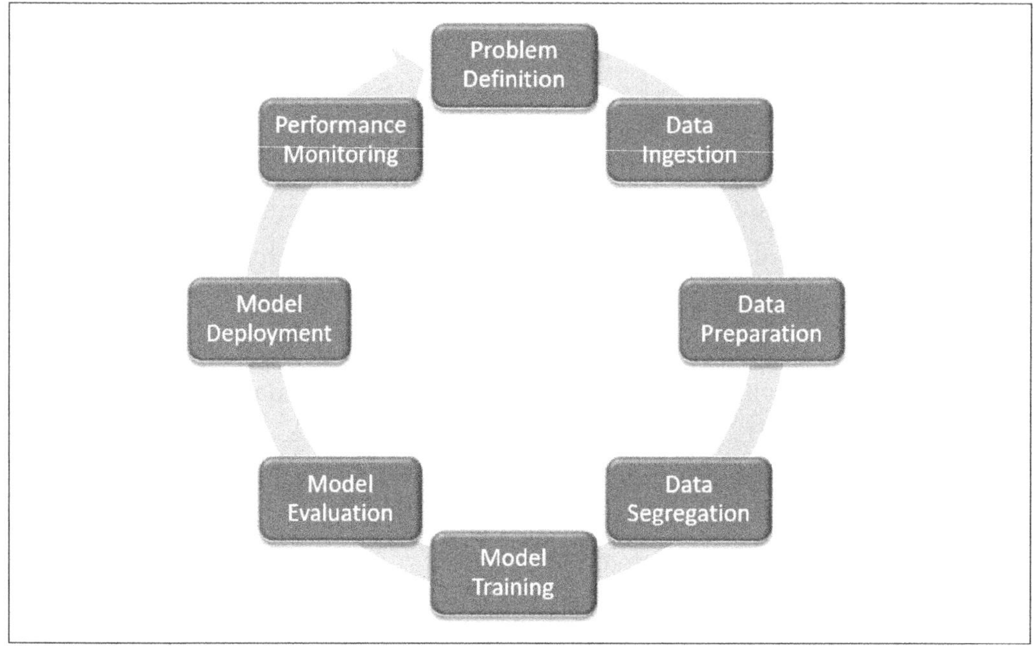

Figure 1: The machine learning pipeline

Let's explore further and dive into the components of the pipeline.

Problem definition

This might be the most critical step when setting up your pipeline. Time spent here can save you orders of magnitude of time on the later stages of the pipeline. It might mean the difference between making a technological breakthrough or failing, or it could be the difference between a startup company succeeding or the company going bankrupt. Asking and framing the right question is paramount. Consider the following cautionary tale:

> *"Bob spent years planning, executing, and optimizing how to conquer a hill. Unfortunately, it turned out to be the wrong hill."*

For example, let's say you want to create a pipeline to determine loan default prediction. Your initial question might be:

For a given loan, will it default or not?

Now, this question does not distinguish between a loan defaulting in the first month or 20 years into the loan. Obviously, a loan that defaults upon issuance is a lot less profitable than a loan that stopped performing 20 years in. So, a better question might be:

When will the loan default?

This is a more valuable question to answer. Can we make it better? It is sometimes possible that a borrower will not send in the full due payment every month. Sometimes, a borrower might send sporadic payments. To account for this, we might refine the question further:

How much money will be received for a given loan?

Let's improve it even more. A dollar today is worth more than a dollar in the future. For this reason, financial analysts use a formula to calculate the present value of money. Just as important as to how much a borrower pays on their loan is the question of when do they pay it. Also, you have the issue of prepayment. If a borrower prepays a loan, that might make the loan less profitable since less interest will be collected. Let's change the question again:

What will be the profit made on a given loan?

Are we done crafting the question? Maybe. Let's consider one more thing. There are certain input variables that by law are not allowed to be used to determine default rates. For example, race and sex are two factors that cannot be used to determine loan eligibility. One more attempt:

What will be the profit made on a given loan without using disallowed input features?

We will leave it to the reader to further refine the question. As you can see, a lot of thought needs to be given to the first and critical step in the machine learning pipeline.

Data ingestion

Once you have crafted and polished your question to a degree to which you are satisfied with, it is now time to gather the raw data that will help you answer the question. This doesn't mean that your question cannot be changed once you go on to the next steps of the pipeline. You should continuously refine your problem statement and adjust it as necessary.

Collecting the right data for your pipeline might be a tremendous undertaking. Depending on the problem you are trying to solve, obtaining relevant datasets might be quite difficult.

Another important consideration is to decide how will the data be sourced, ingested, and stored:

- What data provider or vendor should we use? Can they be trusted?
- How will it be ingested? Hadoop, Impala, Spark, just Python, and so on?
- Should it be stored as a file or in a database?
- What type of database? Traditional RDBMS, NoSQL, graph.
- Should it even be stored? If we have a real-time feed into the pipeline, it might not even be necessary or efficient to store the input.
- What format should the input be? Parquet, JSON, CSV.

Many times, we might not even have control of the input sources to decide what form it should take, and we should take it as is and then decide how it needs to be transformed. Additionally, we might not have a sole data source. There might be multiple sources that need to be consolidated, merged, and joined before we can feed them into the model (more on that later).

As much as we would like it, and even though artificial intelligence makes the long-term promise to replace human intelligence, deciding what variables should be contained in the input datasets still requires human intelligence and maybe even some good old human intuition.

If you are trying to predict stock prices, the price of the stock the previous day seems like an obvious input. Maybe not so obvious might be other inputs like interest rates, company earnings, news headlines, and so forth.

For restaurant daily sales, the previous day's sales are probably also important. Others might include: Day of the week, holiday or not holiday, rain or no rain, daily foot traffic, and so on.

For game-playing systems like chess and Go, we might provide previous games or successful strategies. As an example, one of the best ways for humans to learn chess is to learn opening and gambits that master players have used successfully in the past as well as watching completed games from past tournaments. Computers can learn in the same way by using this previous knowledge and history to decide how to play in the future.

As of now, picking relevant input variables and setting up successful models still requires the data scientist to have domain knowledge. And in some cases intimate and deep domain knowledge. Let's explore an example further.

Staying on the loan default example, let's think of some of the most important features that are relevant in order to make accurate predictions. This is a first stab at that list. Due to space limitations, we're not going to list all the features that would normally be used. We'll add and remove items as we learn from our data:

Feature Name	Feature Description	Why is it useful?
Delinquent Accounts	# of accounts on which the borrower is now delinquent.	If a borrower is having trouble paying their bills, they will probably have trouble paying new loans.
Trade Accounts	# of trades opened in past 24 months.	This is only a problem if there are too few.
Borrower Address	The address provided by the borrower in the loan application.	Drop this. Addresses are unique. Unique variables do not provide predictive ability.
Zip Code	The zip code provided by the borrower in the loan application.	This is not unique and can have predictive power.
Annual Income	The self-reported annual income provided by the borrower during registration.	More income allows the borrower to handle bigger payments more easily.
Current Balance	Average current balance of all accounts.	Not valuable in isolation. Needs to be relative.
Charge-offs	Number of charge-offs within 12 months.	Indicative of borrower's previous default behavior.
Past Due Amount	The past-due amount owed for the accounts on which the borrower is now delinquent.	Indicative of borrower's previous default behavior.
Oldest Account	Months since the oldest revolving account opened.	Indicative of a borrower's experience borrowing money.
Employment Length	Employment length in years.	Indicative of borrower's stability.
Loan Amount	The total amount committed to that loan at that point in time.	Not valuable in isolation. Needs to be relative.
Number of Inquiries	Number of personal finance inquiries.	Borrower looking for credit.
Interest Rate	Interest rate on the loan.	If a loan has a high interest rate, the payments will be more and might be harder to pay back.
Maximum Balance	Maximum current balance owed on all revolving accounts.	If it's close to 100%, this might indicate the borrower is having financial difficulties.

Months Since Last Public Record	The number of months since the last public record.	Indicative of previous financial difficulties
Number of accounts past due	Number of accounts 120 or more days past due	Indicative of current financial difficulties
Public Records	Number of derogatory public records	Indicative of previous financial difficulties
Term	The number of monthly payments on the loan.	The longer the loan, potentially the more possibility for default.
Total Current Balance	Total current balance of all accounts	Not valuable in isolation. Needs to be relative.

As we saw, some of these variables do not provide meaning on their own and they need to be combined to become predictive. This would be an example of feature engineering. Two examples of new variables are:

Credit Utilization	Balance to credit limit on all trades. Current balance compared to the credit limit.	A high percentage indicates that the borrower is "maxed out" and is having trouble obtaining new credit.
Debt to Income	Calculated using the total monthly debt payments on the total debt obligations, excluding mortgage and the requested loan, divided by the borrower's self-reported monthly income.	A low debt-to-income ratio indicates that the borrower has ample resources to pay back their obligations and should not have issues meeting them.

Data preparation

The next step is a data transformation tier that processes the raw data; some of the transformations that need to be done are:

- Data Cleansing
- Filtration
- Aggregation
- Augmentation
- Consolidation
- Storage

The cloud providers have become the major data science platforms. Some of the most popular stacks are built around:

- Azure ML service
- AWS SageMaker
- GCP Cloud ML Engine
- SAS
- RapidMiner
- Knime

One of the most popular tools to perform these transformations is Apache Spark, but it still needs a data store. For persistence, the most common solutions are:

- Hadoop Distributed File System (HDFS)
- HBase
- Apache Cassandra
- Amazon S3
- Azure Blob Storage

It's also possible to process data for machine learning in-place, inside the database; databases like SQL Server and SQL Azure are adding specific machine learning functionality to support machine learning pipelines. Spark has that built in with Spark Streaming. It can read data from HDFS, Kafka, and other sources.

There are also other alternatives like Apache Storm and Apache Heron. Whatever else is in the pipeline, initial exploration of the data is often done in interactive Jupyter notebooks or R Studio.

Some of the real-time data processing solutions out there provide fault-tolerant, scalable, low-latency data ingestion. Some of the favorite ones are:

- Apache Kafka
- Azure Event Hubs
- AWS Kinesis

Let's now explore one of the critical operations of data preparation – data cleansing. We need to ensure that the data is clean. More likely than not, the data will not be perfect, and the data quality will be less than optimal. The data can be unfit for several reasons:

Missing values

Quite often our data contains missing values or missing values are replaced by zeros or N/A. How do we deal with this problem? Following are six different ways to deal with missing values:

- **Do Nothing**: Sometimes the best action is no action. Depending on the algorithm being used, it is not always the case that we need to do anything with missing values. XGBoost is an example of an algorithm that can gracefully handle missing values.
- **Imputation using median values**: When values are missing, a reasonable value to assign to the missing data is the median of all the rest of the non-missing values for that variable. This alternative is easy and fast to calculate, and it works well for small datasets. However, it does not provide much accuracy and it doesn't consider correlations with other variables.
- **Imputation using the most frequent value or a constant**: Another option is to assign the most frequent value or a constant like zero. One advantage of this method is that it works for non-numerical variables. Like the previous method, it doesn't factor correlations with other variables and, depending on the frequency of the nulls, it can introduce a bias into the dataset.

Duplicate records or values

If two values are truly identical, it is easy to create a query or a program that can find duplicate values. The trouble starts if two records or values are supposed to identify the same entity but there is a slight difference between the two values. A traditional database query for duplicates might not find spelling errors, missing values, address changes, or people who left out their middle name. Some people use aliases.

Until recently, finding and fixing duplicate records has been a manual process that is time-intensive and resource-consuming. However, some techniques and research are starting to emerge that use AI to find duplicates. Unless all the details match exactly, it is difficult to determine whether different records refer to the same entity. Additionally, often most duplicates are false positives. Two individuals might share the same name, address, and date of birth but still be different people.

The solution to identifying duplicates is to use fuzzy matching instead of exact matching. Fuzzy matching is a computer-assisted technique to score data similarity. It is used extensively to perform fuzzy matching. Discussing fuzzy matching is beyond the scope of this book, but it may be useful for the reader to investigate this topic further.

Feature scaling

Datasets often contain features with varying magnitudes. This kind of variation in the magnitudes in the features often has a detrimental effect on the accuracy of predictions (but not always; for example, Random Forest does not need feature scaling). Many machine learning algorithms use Euclidean distance between the data points for their calculations. If we don't make this adjustment, features with a high order of magnitude will have an over-weighted impact on the results.

The most common methods for feature scaling are:

- Rescaling (min-max normalization)
- Mean normalization
- Standardization (Z-score normalization)
- Scaling to unit length

Inconsistent values

Data can contain often contain inconsistent values. Furthermore, data can be inconsistent in a variety of ways. An example of inconsistent data is a street address modifier. Consider these data points:

- Fifth Avenue
- Fifth Ave
- Fifth Av
- Fifth Av.

As humans, we can quickly determine that all these examples are truly the same value. Computers have a harder time in drawing this conclusion.

Two approaches to handle this are rule-based and example-based. A rule-based system will work better when there is less variability in the data, and it doesn't change quickly. The rule-based approach breaks when we have fast moving data.

Consider a spam filter. We could create a rule that marks as spam anything that has the word "Viagra," but spammers might get smart and start changing the data to bypass the rule ("Vi@gra"). A machine learning example-based cleanser would work better in this case.

Sometimes, we might want to consider a hybrid approach and use both methods. For instance, a person's height should always be a positive value. So, we could write a rule for that. For other values with more variability, we can use a machine learning approach.

Inconsistent date formatting

- 11/1/2016
- 11/01/2016
- 11/1/16
- Nov 1 16
- November 1st, 2016

These are all the same value. So, we need to standardize dates.

This is not a comprehensive list of data preparation but instead is designed to give a taste of the different transformations that need to be done to cleanse and prepare data in order to be useful.

Data segregation

In order to train a model using the processed data, it is recommended to split the data into two subsets:

- Training data
- Testing data

and sometimes into three:

- Training data
- Validation data
- Testing data

You can then train the model on the training data in order to later make predictions on the test data. The training set is visible to the model and it is trained on this data. The training creates an inference engine that can be later applied to new data points that the model has not previously seen. The test dataset (or subset) represents this unseen data and it now can be used to make predictions on this previously unseen data.

Model training

Once we split the data it is now time to run the training and test data through a series of models and assess the performance of a variety of models and determine how accurate each candidate model is. This is an iterative process and various algorithms might be tested until you have a model that sufficiently answers your question.

We will delve deeper into this step within later chapters. Plenty of material is provided on model selection in the rest of the book.

Candidate model evaluation and selection

After we train our model with various algorithms comes another critical step. It is time to select which model is optimal for the problem at hand. We don't always pick the best performing model. An algorithm that performs well with the training data might not perform well in production because it might have overfitted the training data. At this point in time, model selection is more of an art than a science but there are some techniques that are explored further to decide which model is best.

Model deployment

Once a model is chosen and finalized, it is now ready to be used to make predictions. It is typically exposed via an API and embedded in decision-making frameworks as part of an analytics solution.

How it gets exposed and deployed should be determined by the business requirements. Some questions to consider in the deployment selection:

- Does the system need to be able to make predictions in real-time (if yes, how fast: in milliseconds, seconds, minutes, hours?)
- How often do the models need to be updated?
- What amount of volume or traffic is expected?
- What is the size of the datasets?
- Are there regulations, policies and other constraints that need to be followed and abided by?

Once you've solidified the requirements, we can now consider a high-level architecture for the deployment of the model. Following are a variety of options. This is not an exhaustive list by any means, but it does encompass some of the more popular architectures:

	RESTful API Architecture	**Shared DB Architecture**	**Streaming Architecture**	**Mobile App Architecture**
Training Method	Batch	Batch	Streaming	Streaming
Prediction Method	Real-time	Batch	Streaming	Real-time

Result Delivery	Via RESTful API	Via Shared Database	Streaming via Message Queue	Via in-process API on mobile device
Prediction Latency	Low	High	Very Low	Low
System Maintainability	Medium	Easy	Difficult	Medium

As summarized in the table, each of these four options has its pros and cons. Many more considerations need to be accounted for as we drill down into the specifics of the architecture. As an example, each of these architectures can be implemented using a modularized microservice architecture or in a monolithic manner. Again, the choice should be driven by the business requirements. For example, the monolithic approach might be picked because we have a very limited use case that required an extremely low latency.

Regardless of the architecture chosen for the model deployment it is a good idea to use the following principles:

- **Reproducibility**: Store all the model inputs and outputs, as well as all relevant metadata such as configuration, dependencies, geography, and time zones. required to explain a past prediction. Ensure the latest versioning for each of these deployment bundles is available, which should also include the training data. This is especially important for domains that are highly regulated, banking, for example.
- **Automation**: As early as possible, automate as much as possible of the training and model publishing.
- **Extensibility**: If models need to be updated on a regular basis, a plan needs to be put in place from the beginning.
- **Modularity**: As much as possible, modularize your code and make sure that controls are put in place to faithfully reproduce the pipelines across environments (DEV, QA, TEST).
- **Testing**: Allocate a significant part of your schedule for testing the machine learning pipeline. Automate the testing as much as possible and integrate into your process from the beginning. Explore **Test Driven Development** (**TDD**) and **Behavior Driven Development** (**BDD**).

Performance monitoring

Once a model makes it into production, our work is not finished. Moving a model into production may not be easy, but once the model is deployed it must be closely monitored to make sure that the model is performing satisfactorily. There are various steps involved in getting the model into production. The model is continuously monitored to observe how it behaved in the real world and calibrated accordingly. New data is collected to incrementally improve it. Similarly, monitoring a deployed machine learning model requires attention from various perspectives to make sure that the model is performing. Let's analyze these different metrics that need to be considered when monitoring machine learning models, and why each one of them is important:

Model performance

Performance in the data science context does not mean how fast the model is running, but rather how accurate are the predictions. Data scientists monitoring machine learning models are primarily looking at a single metric: drift. Drift happens when the data is no longer a relevant or useful input to the model. Data can change and lose its predictive value. Data scientists and engineers must monitor the models constantly to make sure that the model features continue to be like the data points used during the model training. If the data drifts, the prediction results will become less accurate because the input features are out of date or no longer relevant. As an example, think of stock market data. Thirty years ago, the market was dramatically different. Some ways in which it was different include the following:

- Volume in the stock exchanges was significantly lower than it is today
- High-frequency trading was not even an idea
- Passive index funds were much less popular

As you can imagine, these characteristics make stock performance significantly different. If we train our models with 30-year-old data, they are more than likely not going to be able to perform with today's data.

Operational performance

Machine learning pipelines at the end of the day are still software systems. For this reason, it's still important to monitor resource consumption, including:

- **CPU utilization**: Identifies spikes and whether or not they can be explained.
- **Memory usage**: How much memory is being consumed.
- **Disk usage**: How much disc space is our application consuming.

- **Network I/O traffic**: If our application spans across instances, it is important to measure the network traffic.
- **Latency**: The amount of time it takes for a data transfer to occur.
- **Throughput**: The amount of data successfully transferred.

If these metrics change, they need to be analyzed to understand why these changes are happening.

Total cost of ownership (TCO)

Data scientists need to monitor their model performance in terms of records per second. Although this gives some insight into the efficiency of the model, companies should also be focused on the benefit they gain from the model versus the cost. It is recommended to monitor the cost of all the steps of the machine learning pipeline. If this information is closely tracked, the business can make smart decisions on how to keep costs down and how to take advantage of new opportunities or whether certain pipelines are not providing enough value and they need to be changed or shut down.

Service performance

Technology not in the context of a business problem is useless. Businesses often have, or at least should have, **service level agreements** (**SLAs**) in place with the technology department. Examples of SLAs:

- Fix all critical bugs within one day
- Ensure that an API responds within 100 ms
- Process at least a million predictions per hour
- Complex models must be designed, developed, and deployed within 3 months

For the business to perform optimally it's important to establish, monitor, and meet previously agreed upon SLAs.

Machine learning models can be mission critical to a business. A key to ensure that they do not become a bottleneck is to properly monitor the deployed models. As part of your machine learning pipelines, make sure that deployed machine learning models are monitored and compared against SLAs to ensure satisfactory business results.

Summary

This chapter laid out in detail what are the different steps involved in creating a machine learning pipeline. This tour should be considered an initial overview of the steps involved. As the book progresses you will learn how to improve your own pipelines, but we did learn some of the best practices and most popular tools that are used to set up pipelines today. In review the steps to a successful pipeline are:

- Problem definition
- Data ingestion
- Data preparation
- Data segregation
- Candidate model selection
- Model deployment
- Performance monitoring

In the next chapter we'll delve deeper into one of the steps of the machine learning pipeline. We'll learn how to perform feature selection and we'll learn what is feature engineering. These two techniques are critically important to improve model performance.

4

Feature Selection and Feature Engineering

Feature selection - also known as variable selection, attribute selection, or variable subset selection - is a method used to select a subset of features (variables, dimensions) from an initial dataset. Feature selection is a key step in the process of building machine learning models and can have a huge impact on the performance of a model. Using correct and relevant features as the input to your model can also reduce the chance of overfitting, because having more relevant features reduces the opportunity of a model to use noisy features that don't add signal as input. Lastly, having less input features decreases the amount of time that it will take to train a model. Learning which features to select is a skill developed by data scientists that usually only comes from months and years of experience and can be more of an art than a science. Feature selection is important because it can:

- Shorten training times
- Simplify models and make them easier to interpret
- Enhances testing set performance by reducing overfitting

One important reason to drop features is the high correlation and redundancy between input variables or the irrelevancy of certain features. These input variables can thus be removed without incurring much loss of information. Redundant and irrelevant are two distinct notions, since one relevant feature may be redundant in the presence of another relevant feature with which it is strongly correlated.

Feature engineering in some ways is the opposite of feature selection. With feature selection, you remove variables. In feature engineering, you create new variables to enhance the model. In many cases, you are using domain knowledge for the enhancement.

Feature selection and feature engineering is an important component of your machine learning pipeline, and that's why a whole chapter is devoted to this topic.

By the end of this chapter, you will know:

- How to decide if a feature should be dropped from a dataset
- Learn about the concepts of collinearity, correlation, and causation
- Understand the concept of feature engineering and how it differs from feature selection
- Learn about the difference between manual feature engineering and automated feature engineering. When is it appropriate to use each one?

Feature selection

In the previous chapter, we explored the components of a machine learning pipeline. A critical component of the pipeline is deciding which features will be used as inputs to the model. For many models, a small subset of the input variables provide the lion's share of the predictive ability. In most datasets, it is common for a few features to be responsible for the majority of the information signal and the rest of the features are just mostly noise.

It is important to lower the amount of input features for a variety of reasons including:

- Reducing the multi collinearity of the input features will make the machine learning model parameters easier to interpret. *Multicollinearity* (also *collinearity*) is a phenomenon observed with features in a dataset where one predictor feature in a regression model can be linearly predicted from the other's features with a substantial degree of accuracy.
- Reducing the time required to run the model and the amount of storage space the model needs will allow us to run more variations of the models leading to quicker and better results.
- The smaller number of input features a model requires, the easier it is to explain it. When the number of features goes up, the explainability of the model goes down. Reducing the amount of input features also makes it easier to visualize the data when reduced to low dimensions (for example, 2D or 3D).
- As the number of dimensions increases, the possible configurations increase exponentially, and the number of configurations covered by an observation decreases. As you have more features to describe your target, you might be able to describe the data more precisely, but your model will not generalize with new data points - your model will overfit the data. This is known as the *curse of dimensionality*.

Let's think about this intuitively by going through an example. There is a real estate site in the US that allows real estate agents and homeowners to list homes for rent or for sale. Zillow is famous, among other things, for its Zestimate. The Zestimate is an estimated price using machine learning. It is the price that Zillow estimates a home will sell for if it was put on the market today. The Zestimates are constantly updated and recalculated. How does Zillow come up with this number? If you want to learn more about it, there was a competition on Kaggle that has great resources on the Zestimate. You can find out more here:

`https://www.kaggle.com/c/zillow-prize-1`

The exact details of the Zestimate algorithm are proprietary, but we can make some assumptions. We will now start to explore how we can come up with our own Zestimate. Let's come up with a list of potential input variables for our machine learning model and the reasons why they might be valuable:

- **Square footage**: Intuitively, the bigger the home, the more expensive it will be.
- **Number of bedrooms**: More rooms, more cost.
- **Number of bathrooms**: Bedrooms need bathrooms.
- **Mortgage interest rates**: If rates are low, that makes mortgage payments lower, which means potential homeowners can afford a more expensive home.
- **Year built**: In general, newer homes are typically more expensive than older homes. Older homes normally need more repairs.
- **Property taxes**: If property taxes are high, that will increase the monthly payments and homeowners will only be able to afford a less expensive home.
- **House color**: At first glance, this might not seem like a relevant variable, but what if the home is painted lime green?
- **Zip code**: Location, location, location. In real estate, where the home is located is an important determinant of price. In some cases, a house in one block can be hundreds of thousands of dollars more than a house on the next block. Location can be that important.
- **Comparable sales**: One of the metrics that is commonly used by appraisers and real estate agents to value a home is to look for similar properties to the "subject" property that have been recently sold or at least are listed for sale, to see what the sale price was or what the listing price currently is.
- **Tax assessment**: Property taxes are calculated based on what the county currently thinks the property is worth. This is publicly accessible information.

These could all potentially be variables that have high predictive power, but intuitively we can probably assume that square footage, the number of bedrooms, and number of bathrooms are highly correlated. Also, intuitively, square footage provides more precision than the number of bedrooms or the number of bathrooms. So, we can probably drop the number of bedrooms and the number bathrooms and keep the square footage and don't lose much accuracy. Indeed, we could potentially increase the accuracy, by reducing the noise.

Furthermore, we can most likely drop the house color without losing precision.

Features that can be dropped without impacting the model's precision significantly fall into two categories:

- **Redundant**: This is a feature that is highly correlated to other input features and therefore does not add much new information to the signal.
- **Irrelevant**: This is a feature that has a low correlation with the target feature and for that reason provides more noise than signal.

One way to find out if our assumptions are correct is to train our model with and without our assumptions and see what produces the better results. We could use this method with every single feature, but in cases where we have a high number of features the possible number of combinations can escalate quickly.

As we mentioned previously, exploratory data analysis can be a good way to get an intuitive understanding and to obtain insights into the dataset we are working with. Let's analyze three approaches that are commonly used to obtain these insights. They are:

- Feature importance
- Univariate selection
- Correlation matrix with heatmap

Feature importance

The importance of each feature of a dataset can be established by using this method.

Feature importance provides a score for each feature in a dataset. A higher score means the feature has more importance or relevancy in relation to the output feature.

Feature importance is normally an inbuilt class that comes with *Tree-Based Classifiers*. In the following example, we use the *Extra Tree Classifier* to determine the top five features in a dataset:

```
import pandas as pd
```

```
from sklearn.ensemble import ExtraTreesClassifier
import numpy as np
import matplotlib.pyplot as plt

data = pd.read_csv("train.csv")
X = data.iloc[:,0:20]  #independent columns
y = data.iloc[:,-1]    # pick last column for the target feature

model = ExtraTreesClassifier()
model.fit(X,y)
print(model.feature_importances_) #use inbuilt class
#feature_importances of tree based classifiers
#plot graph of feature importances for better visualization
feat_importances = pd.Series(model.feature_importances_, index=X.
columns)
feat_importances.nlargest(5).plot(kind='barh')
plt.show()
```

You should see this as output:

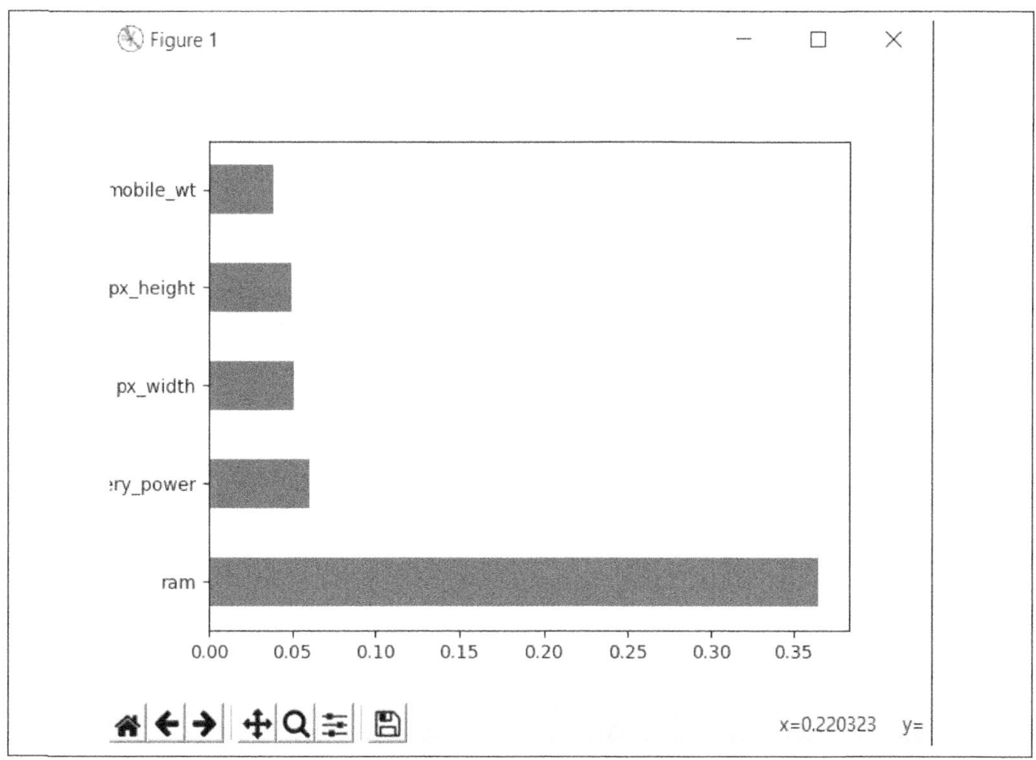

Figure 1: Feature importance graph

Univariate selection

Statistical tests can be used to determine which features have the strongest correlation to the output variable. The scikit-learn library has a class called `SelectKBest` that provides a set of statistical tests to select the K "best" features in a dataset.

The following is an example that uses the *chi-squared (*chi^2*) statistical test for non-negative features* to select the five best features in an input dataset:

```
import pandas as pd
import numpy as np
from sklearn.feature_selection import SelectKBest
from sklearn.feature_selection import chi2
data = pd.read_csv("train.csv")
X = data.iloc[:,0:20]  #independent columns
y = data.iloc[:,-1]    #pick last column for the target feature
#apply SelectKBest class to extract top 5 best features
bestfeatures = SelectKBest(score_func=chi2, k=5)
fit = bestfeatures.fit(X,y)
dfscores = pd.DataFrame(fit.scores_)

dfcolumns = pd.DataFrame(X.columns)
scores = pd.concat([dfcolumns,dfscores],axis=1)
scores.columns = ['specs','score']
print(scores.nlargest(5,'score'))  #print the 5 best features
```

And you should see something like this as your output:

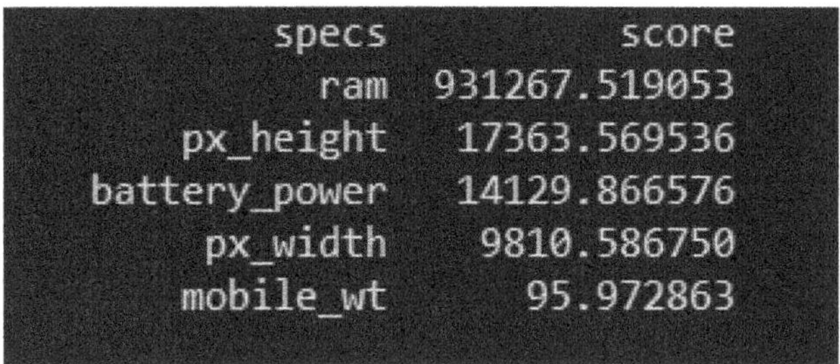

specs	score
ram	931267.519053
px_height	17363.569536
battery_power	14129.866576
px_width	9810.586750
mobile_wt	95.972863

Figure 2: Best features graph

Correlation heatmaps

A correlation exists between two features when there is a relationship between the different values of the features. For example, if home prices go up as the square footage goes up, these two features are said to be positively correlated. There can be different degrees of correlation. If a feature changes consistently in relation to another feature, these features are said to be highly correlated.

Correlation can be positive (an increase in one value of a feature increases the value of the target variable) or negative (an increase in one value of a feature decreases the value of the target variable).

Correlation is a continuous value between -1 and 1:

- If the correlation between two variables is 1, there is a perfect direct correlation.
- If the correlation between two features is -1, a perfect inverse correlation exists.
- If the correlation is 0 between two features, there is no correlation between the two features.

A heatmap makes it easy to identify which features are most correlated to the target variable. We will plot a heatmap of correlated features using the `seaborn` library, using the following code:

```
import pandas as pd
import numpy as np
import seaborn as sns
import matplotlib.pyplot as plt

data = pd.read_csv("train.csv")
X = data.iloc[:,0:20]  #independent columns
y = data.iloc[:,-1]    # pick last column for the target feature
#get the correlations of each feature in the dataset
correlation_matrix = data.corr()
top_corr_features = correlation_matrix.index
plt.figure(figsize=(20,20))
#plot heat map
g=sns.heatmap(data[top_corr_features].corr(),annot=True,cmap="RdYlGn")
```

You should get a similar output to:

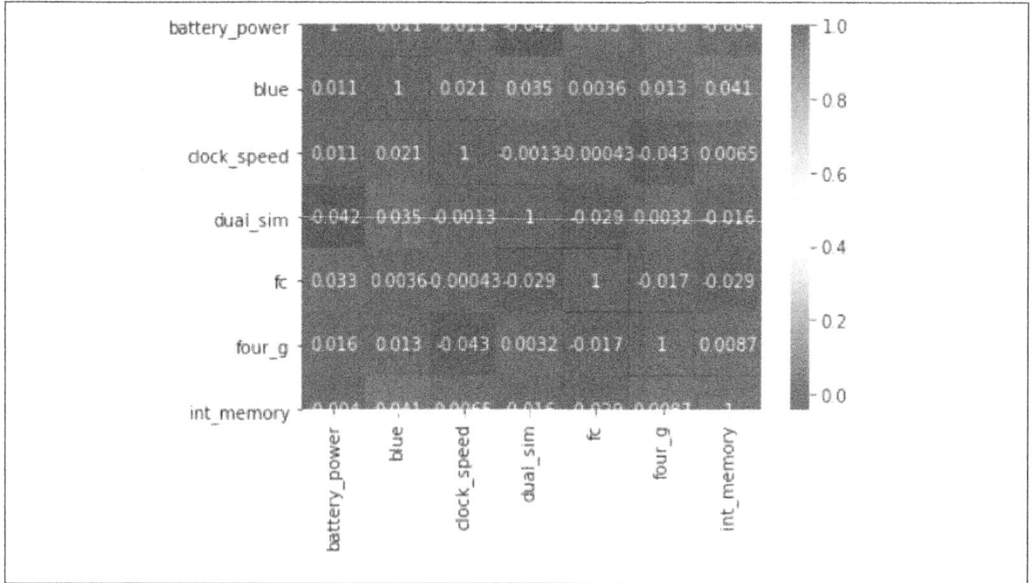

Figure 3: Correlation heat map

More formal and less intuitive methods exist to automatically select features. Many of these methods exist and quite a few are implemented in the scikit-learn package. One way to classify these approaches is mentioned next.

Wrapper-based methods

When using wrapper methods, the problem of feature selection is essentially reduced to a search problem using these steps:

1. A subset of features is used to train a model
2. Based on the results of each iteration, features are added to or removed from the subset

Wrapper methods are usually computationally expensive. The following are a few examples:

- **Forward Selection**: The forward selection method is an iterative process that starts by having no features in the dataset. During each iteration, features are added with the intent of improving the performance of the model. If performance is improved, the features are kept. Features that do not improve the results are discarded. The process continues until improvement of the model stalls.

- **Backward Elimination**: When using the backward elimination method, all features are initially present in the dataset. Features with the least significance are removed during each iteration, and the process then checks if the performance of the model improves. The process is repeated until no significant improvement is observed.
- **Recursive Feature Elimination**: The recursive feature elimination method is a greedy optimization algorithm with a stated goal of finding the best performing feature subset. It iteratively creates models and stores the best or the worst performing feature during each iteration. It constructs the next model with the remaining features until all the features are exhausted. The features are then ranked based on the order of their elimination.

Filter-based methods

A metric is specified and based on that metric features are filtered. Examples of filter-based methods are:

- **Pearson's Correlation**: This algorithm is used as a measure of quantifying the linear dependence between two continuous variables X and Y. Its value can lie anywhere between -1 to +1.
- **Linear discriminant analysis (LDA)**: LDA can be used to find a linear combination of features that characterizes or separates two or more levels (or classes) of a categorical variable.
- **Analysis of Variance (ANOVA)**: ANOVA is like LDA except that it is calculated using one or more categorical independent variables and one continuous dependent variable. It provides a statistical test to know whether the mean of several groups is equal or not.
- **Chi-Square**: Chi-Square is a statistical test applied to groups of categorical variables to determine the likelihood of correlation or association between them using their frequency distribution.

One issue to keep in mind is that *filter-based methods* do not remove multicollinearity. So, additional processing must be performed to deal with feature multicollinearity before creating models from your input data.

Embedded methods

Embedded methods use algorithms with built-in feature selection methods. Embedded methods combine the advantages of filter and wrapper methods. They are normally implemented using algorithms with built-in feature selection methods.

Two popular embedded method implementations follow:

- **Lasso regression**: It performs L1 regularization, which adds a penalty equivalent to the absolute value of the magnitude of coefficients
- **Ridge regression**: It performs L2 regularization, which adds a penalty equivalent to the square of the magnitude of coefficients

These algorithms are also commonly used:

- Memetic algorithm
- Random multinomial logit
- Regularized trees

This concludes the first section of this chapter. You should feel more prepared to tackle your own feature selection projects. Now get ready to take a plunge into the world of feature engineering. Feature selection is all about how we can reduce the number of variables to increase accuracy. Feature engineering is the opposite. It asks: how can we create new variables that will make our models be more performant?

Feature engineering

According to a recent survey performed by the folks at Forbes, data scientists spend around 80% of their time on data preparation:

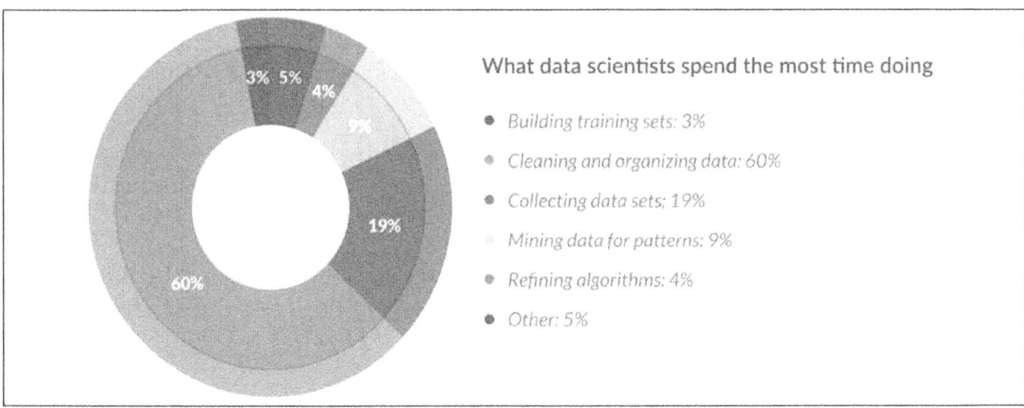

Figure 4: Breakdown of time spent by data scientists (source: Forbes)

This statistic highlights the importance of data preparation and feature engineering in data science.

Just like judicious and systematic feature selection can make models faster and more performant by removing features, feature engineering can accomplish the same by adding new features. This seems contradictory at first blush, but the features that are being added are not features that were removed by the feature selection process. The features being added are features that might have not been in the initial dataset. You might have the most powerful and well-designed machine learning algorithm in the world, but if your input features are not relevant, you will never be able to produce useful results. Let's analyze a couple of simple examples to get some intuition.

In a previous chapter, we visited the problem of loan defaults. Intuitively, it might be surmised that a borrower will have lower default ratios if they have a high salary. Similarly, we might assume that borrowers that have a large balance on their credit cards might have a difficult time paying back those balances compared to someone who has low balances.

Now that we have that fresh knowledge, let's try to intuitively determine who is going to pay back a loan and who is not. If borrower *A* has a balance in his credit cards of $10,000 and borrower *B* has a balance of $20,000, who do you think has a better chance of paying back their debt? If no other information is given, we would say borrower *A* is a safer choice. Now, what if I told you that borrower *A* has an annual income of $20,000 per year and borrower *B* has an income of $100,000? That changes everything, doesn't it? How can we quantitively capture the relationship between the two features? Banks often use what they call the **debt to income** (**DTI**) ratio and it is calculated as you would imagine:

$$DTI = \frac{Debt}{Income}$$

So, borrower A would have a DTI of 0.50 and borrower *B* has a debt to income ratio of 0.20. In other words, borrower *A* makes twice what their debt is, and borrower *B* makes 5 times their debt. Borrower *B* has more room to pay their debt. We can certainly add other features to the profiles of these borrowers that would change the makeup of their profile, but hopefully this helped illustrate the concept of feature engineering.

More formally, feature engineering is the process a data scientist or a computer goes through to generate features that will enhance the predictive ability of a machine learning model. Feature engineering is a fundamental concept in machine learning and can be both difficult and expensive. Many data scientists want to directly jump to model selection, but the ability to discern which new features will enhance a model is a critical skill that may take years to master.

The evolution of better feature engineering algorithms is in full swing right now, and one day these may prove to be better than senior data scientists when it comes to feature engineering decision making, but, for the next few years, we predict that good data scientists will still be in demand.

The feature engineering process can be described as follows:

1. Brainstorm about which features are relevant
2. Decide what features might improve the model performance
3. Create new features
4. Determine if the new features add to the model performance; if not, drop them
5. Go back to *Step 1* until the performance of the model meets expectations

As we saw in the example, having domain knowledge and getting familiar with the dataset can be useful for feature engineering. However, there are also some generic data science techniques that can be applied in data preparation and feature engineering steps regardless of the domain. Let's spend some time analyzing these techniques.

The techniques we will explore are:

- Imputation
- Outlier management
- One-hot encoding
- Log transform
- Scaling
- Date manipulation

Imputation

It is not uncommon for datasets to be "dirty" and imperfect. Rows with missing values is a common problem. There might be many reasons why values are missing:

- Inconsistent datasets
- Clerical error
- Privacy issues

Regardless of the reason, having missing values can affect the performance of a model, and in some cases, it can bring things to a screeching halt since some algorithms do not take kindly to missing values. There are multiple techniques to handle missing values. They include:

Removing the row with missing values - This technique can reduce the performance of the model because it reduces the number of data points that the model will have to train.

Let's look at an example that drops columns where more than 60% of the data is missing:

```
threshold = 0.6
#Drop columns with a missing value rate higher than threshold
data = data[data.columns[data.isnull().mean() < threshold]]

#Drop rows with missing value rate higher than threshold
data = data.loc[data.isnull().mean(axis=1) < threshold]
threshold = 0.6
#Drop columns with a missing value rate higher than threshold
data = data[data.columns[data.isnull().mean() < threshold]]

#Drop rows with missing value rate higher than threshold
data = data.loc[data.isnull().mean(axis=1) < threshold]
print(data)
```

The output should look like this:

```
    battery_power  blue  clock_speed  dual_sim  fc  four_g  int_memory  \
0             842     0          2.2         0   1       0           7
1            1021     1          0.5         1   0       1          53
2             563     1          0.5         1   2       1          41
3             615     1          2.5         0   0       0          10
4            1821     1          1.2         0  13       1          44
5            1859     0          0.5         1   3       0          22
6            1821     0          1.7         0   4       1          10
7            1954     0          0.5         1   0       0          24
8            1445     1          0.5         0   0       0          53
9             509     1          0.6         1   2       1           9
10            769     1          2.9         1   0       0           9
11           1520     1          2.2         0   5       1          33
12           1815     0          2.8         0   2       0          33
13            803     1          2.1         0   7       0          17
14           1866     0          0.5         0  13       1          52
15            775     0          1.0         0   3       0          46
16            838     0          0.5         0   1       1          13
17            595     0          0.9         1   7       1          23
```

Figure 5: Drop missing values output

Numerical Imputation - Imputation is another method to deal with missing values. Imputation simply means replacing the missing value with another value that "makes sense".

In the case of numerical variables, these are common replacements:

- Using zero as the replacement value is one option
- Calculate the mean for the full dataset and replace the missing value with the mean
- Calculate the average for the full dataset and replace the missing value with the average

Using the mean rather than average is normally preferable because the average is more susceptible to be affected by outliers. Let's look at a couple examples to make this replacement:

```
#Filling all missing values with 0
data = data.fillna(0)

#Filling missing values with medians of the columns
data = data.fillna(data.median())
print(data)
```

You will be able to scroll through the output and see the changed values:

	battery_power	blue	clock_speed	dual_sim	fc	four_g	int_memory
0	842	0	2.2	0	1	0	7
1	1021	1	0.5	1	0	1	53
2	563	1	0.5	1	2	1	41
3	615	1	2.5	0	0	0	10
4	1821	1	1.2	0	13	1	44
5	1859	0	0.5	1	3	0	22
6	1821	0	1.7	0	4	1	10
7	1954	0	0.5	1	0	0	24
8	1445	1	0.5	0	0	0	53
9	509	1	0.6	1	2	1	9
10	769	1	2.9	1	0	0	9
11	1520	1	2.2	0	5	1	33
12	1815	0	2.8	0	2	0	33
13	803	1	2.1	0	7	0	17
14	1866	0	0.5	0	13	1	52
15	775	0	1.0	0	3	0	46
16	838	0	0.5	0	1	1	13
17	595	0	0.9	1	7	1	23

Figure 5: Drop missing values output

Categorical Imputation - Categorical variables do not contain numbers, rather they contain categories. For example, red, green, and yellow. Or banana, apple, and orange. Therefore, averages and means cannot be used with categorical variables. A common technique used is to replace any missing value with the value that appears the most.

In cases where many categories exist, or the categories are distributed uniformly, using something like "Other" might make sense. Let's look at an example in Python that replaces all of the missing values with the value that occurs most often (`idxmax` in Python returns the most common value across a feature):

```
#Max fill function for categorical columns
import pandas as pd

data = pd.read_csv("dataset.csv")

data['color'].fillna(data['color'].value_counts().idxmax(),
inplace=True)
print(data)
```

The output should be similar to this:

```
    index   color
0       0   green
1       1  yellow
2       2     red
3       3     red
4       4  purple
5       5     red
6       6     red
7       7  purple
8       8     red
9       9     red
10     10  yellow
11     11     red
12     12   black
13     13   white
```

Figure 7: Fill missing values output

Outlier management

Home prices are a good domain to analyze to understand why we need to pay special attention to outliers. Regardless of what region of the world you live in, most houses in your neighborhood are going to fall in a certain range and they are going to have certain characteristics. Maybe something like this:

- 1 to 4 bedrooms
- 1 kitchen
- 500 to 3000 square feet
- 1 to 3 bathrooms

The average home price in the US in 2019 is $226,800. And you can guess that kind of house will probably share some of the characteristics above. But there might also be a couple houses that are *outliers*. Maybe a house that has 10 or 20 bedrooms. Some of these houses might be a 1 million or 10 million dollars, depending on the number of crazy customizations that these houses might have. As you might imagine, these outliers are going to affect the mean in a data set, and it will affect the average even more. For this reason, and given that there are not too many of these houses, it might be best to remove these outliers as to not affect predictions with the other more common data points. Let's look at a graph of some house values and then try to draw two best fit lines: one with all the data and one done with the high-price home outliers removed:

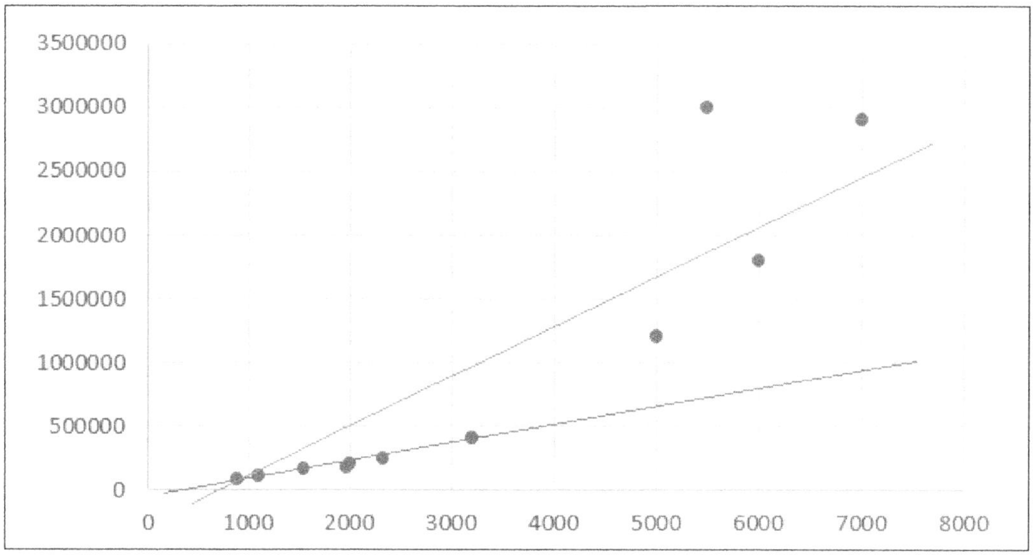

Figure 8: Best fit graph

As you can see, if you remove the outliers from the calculation of the best fit line, the line predicts the lower priced home much more accurately. For this reason, simply removing outliers is a simple yet powerful way to deal with the influence of outliers.

So how can we determine if a value is an outlier and should be removed? One common method is to remove outliers that fall a certain multiple of the standard deviation of the values for a feature in a dataset. What constant to use for the multiplication factor is more of an art than a science, but a value between 2 and 4 is common:

```
#Dropping the outlier rows with standard deviation
import pandas as pd
```

```
data = pd.read_csv("train.csv")

#Dropping the outlier rows with standard deviation
factor = 2
upper_lim = data['battery_power'].mean () + data['battery_power'].std
() * factor
lower_lim = data['battery_power'].mean () - data['battery_power'].std
() * factor

data = data[(data['battery_power'] < upper_lim) & (data['battery_
power'] > lower_lim)]
print(data)
```

The output should be similar to:

	battery_power	blue	clock_speed	dual_sim	fc	four_g	int_memory
0	842	0	2.2	0	1	0	7
1	1021	1	0.5	1	0	1	53
2	563	1	0.5	1	2	1	41
3	615	1	2.5	0	0	0	10
4	1821	1	1.2	0	13	1	44
5	1859	0	0.5	1	3	0	22
6	1821	0	1.7	0	4	1	10
7	1954	0	0.5	1	0	0	24
8	1445	1	0.5	0	0	0	53
9	509	1	0.6	1	2	1	9
10	769	1	2.9	1	0	0	9
11	1520	1	2.2	0	5	1	33
12	1815	0	2.8	0	2	0	33
13	803	1	2.1	0	7	0	17
14	1866	0	0.5	0	13	1	52
15	775	0	1.0	0	3	0	46
16	838	0	0.5	0	1	1	13
17	595	0	0.9	1	7	1	23

Figure 9: Drop outlier rows output

Another method to detect and remove outliers is to use percentiles. With this method, we simply assume that a certain percentage of the values for a feature are outliers. What percentage of values to drop is again subjective and it is going to be domain-dependent.

Let's look at a Python example where we drop the top and bottom 1%:

```
#Dropping the outlier rows with Percentiles
upper_lim = data['battery_power'].quantile(.99)
lower_lim = data['battery_power'].quantile(.01)
```

```
data = data[(data['battery_power'] < upper_lim) & (data['battery_
power'] > lower_lim)]
print(data)
```

The expected output follows:

	battery_power	blue	clock_speed	dual_sim	fc	four_g	int_memory
1	1021	1	0.5	1	0	1	53
8	1445	1	0.5	0	0	0	53
11	1520	1	2.2	0	5	1	33
18	1131	1	0.5	1	11	0	49
25	961	1	1.4	1	0	1	57
27	956	0	0.5	0	1	1	41
28	1453	0	1.6	1	12	1	52
30	1579	1	0.5	1	0	0	5
31	1568	1	0.5	0	16	0	33
32	1319	1	0.9	0	3	1	41
33	1310	1	2.2	1	0	1	51
40	1347	0	2.9	0	5	0	44
42	1253	1	0.5	1	5	1	5
44	1195	1	2.8	0	1	1	20
45	1514	0	2.9	0	0	0	27
47	1054	1	1.8	1	3	1	40
50	1547	1	3.0	1	2	1	14
53	1457	0	1.9	1	1	1	16

Figure 10: Drop outlier rows output

An alternative way to handle outliers is to cap values instead of dropping values. Capping values instead of dropping rows allows you to keep the data point and can potentially increase the performance of your models. However, keeping the data point but capping the value makes that data point an estimation rather than a real observation, which might also affect the results. Deciding which method to use will depend on analysis of the specific dataset at hand. Here is an example that uses capping values instead of dropping rows:

```
#Capping the outlier rows with percentiles
upper_lim = data['battery_power'].quantile(.99)
lower_lim = data['battery_power'].quantile(.01)

data.loc[(data['battery_power'] > upper_lim), 'battery_power'] =
upper_lim
data.loc[(data['battery_power'] < lower_lim), 'battery_power'] =
lower_lim
print(data)
```

The following is the output that should be observed. If you should scroll through the output, you might be able to notice some of the changed values:

	battery_power	blue	clock_speed	dual_sim	fc	four_g	int_memory
1	1021.00	1	0.5	1	0	1	53
8	1445.00	1	0.5	0	0	0	53
11	1520.00	1	2.2	0	5	1	33
18	1131.00	1	0.5	1	11	0	49
25	961.00	1	1.4	1	0	1	57
27	956.00	0	0.5	0	1	1	41
28	1453.00	0	1.6	1	12	1	52
30	1579.00	1	0.5	1	0	0	5
31	1568.00	1	0.5	0	16	0	33
32	1319.00	1	0.9	0	3	1	41
33	1310.00	1	2.2	1	0	1	51
40	1347.00	0	2.9	0	5	0	44
42	1253.00	1	0.5	1	5	1	5
44	1195.00	1	2.8	0	1	1	20
45	1514.00	0	2.9	0	0	0	27
47	1054.00	1	1.8	1	3	1	40
50	1547.00	1	3.0	1	2	1	14
53	1457.00	0	1.9	1	1	1	16

Figure 11: Cap outlier rows output

One-hot encoding

One-hot encoding is an often-used technique in machine learning for feature engineering. Some machine learning algorithms cannot handle categorical features, so one-hot encoding is a way to convert these categorical features into numerical features. Let's say that you have a feature labeled "status" that can take one of three values (red, green, or yellow). Because these values are categorical, there is no concept of which value is *higher* or *lower*. We could convert these values to numerical values and that would give them this characteristic. For example:

Yellow = 1

Red = 2

Green = 3

But this seems somewhat arbitrary. If we knew that red is bad and green is good, and yellow is somewhere in the middle, we might change the mapping to something like:

Red = -1

Yellow = 0

Green = 1

And that might produce better performance. But now let's see how this example can be one-hot encoded. To achieve the one-hot encoding of this one variable, we create a new feature for each one of the values. In this case, some of our data (something you might encounter in the wild) might look like this:

red	**yellow**	**green**	**status**
1	0	0	red
0	1	0	yellow
0	0	1	green
0	0	1	green

Since we have one-hot encoded the data, the status feature now becomes redundant, so we can eliminate it from our dataset:

red	**yellow**	**green**
1	0	0
0	1	0
0	0	1
0	0	1

Additionally, we can calculate the value of any of the color features from the other two. If red and yellow are both 0, that means that green needs to be 1 and so forth. So, in one-hot encoding, we can always drop one of the features without losing information. Something like this:

red	**yellow**
1	0
0	1
0	0
0	0

Let's now look at an example on how we can use the Pandas library to one-hot encode a feature using the `get_dummies` function:

```
import pandas as pd

data = pd.read_csv("dataset.csv")

encoded_columns = pd.get_dummies(data['color'])
data = data.join(encoded_columns).drop('color', axis=1)
print(data)
```

The output should look like this:

	index	black	green	purple	red	white	yellow
0	0	0	1	0	0	0	0
1	1	0	0	0	0	0	1
2	2	0	0	0	0	0	0
3	3	0	0	0	1	0	0
4	4	0	0	1	0	0	0
5	5	0	0	0	1	0	0
6	6	0	0	0	1	0	0
7	7	0	0	1	0	0	0
8	8	0	0	0	0	0	0
9	9	0	0	0	1	0	0
10	10	0	0	0	0	0	1
11	11	0	0	0	0	0	0
12	12	1	0	0	0	0	0
13	13	0	0	0	0	1	0

Figure 12: One hot encoding output

Log transform

Logarithm transformation (or log transform) is a common feature engineering transformation. Log transform helps to flatten highly skewed values. After the log transformation is applied, the data distribution is normalized.

Let's go over another example to again gain some intuition. Remember when you were 10-year-old and looking at 15-year-old boys and girls and thinking "They are so much older than me!" Now think of a 50-year-old person and another that is 55-year-old. In this case, you might think that the age difference is not that much. In both cases, the age difference is 5 years. However, in the first case a 15-year-old is 50 percent older than the 10-year-old, and in the second case the 55-year-old is only 10 percent older than the 50-year-old.

If we apply a log transform to all these data points it normalizes magnitude differences like this.

Applying a log transform also decreases the effect of the outliers, due to the normalization of magnitude differences and models that use log transforms become more robust.

One key restriction to consider when using this technique is that you should only apply log transforms when all data points are positive values. Also, you can add 1 to your data before applying the transformation. Thus, you ensure the output of the transformation to be positive:

Log (x+1)

Here is how you can perform log transform in Python:

```
#Log Transform Example
data = pd.DataFrame({'value':[3,67, -17, 44, 37, 3, 31, -38]})
data['log+1'] = (data['value']+1).transform(np.log)

#Negative Values Handling
#Note that the values are different
data['log'] = (data['value']-data['value'].min()+1) .transform(np.log)
print(data)
```

This is the output that should be produced:

```
   value     log+1       log
0      3  1.386294  3.737670
1     67  4.219508  4.663439
2    -17       NaN  3.091042
3     44  3.806662  4.418841
4     37  3.637586  4.330733
5      3  1.386294  3.737670
6     31  3.465736  4.248495
7    -38       NaN  0.000000
```

Figure 13: Log transform output

Scaling

In many instances, numerical features in a dataset can vary greatly in scale with other features. For example, the typical square footage of a house might be a number between 1000 and 3000 square feet, whereas 2, 3, or 4 might be a more typical number for the number of bedrooms in a house. If we leave these values alone, the features with a higher scale might be given a higher weighting if left alone. How can this issue be fixed?

Scaling can be a way to solve this problem. Continuous features become comparable in terms of the range after scaling is applied. Not all algorithms require scaled values (Random Forest comes to mind), but other algorithms will produce meaningless results if the dataset is not scaled beforehand (examples are k-nearest neighbors or k-means). We will now explore the two most common scaling methods.

Normalization (or minmax normalization) scales all values for a feature within a fixed range between 0 and 1. More formally, each value for a feature can be normalized using the formula:

$$X_{norm} = \frac{X - X_{min}}{X_{max} - X_{min}}$$

Where:

- X - any given value for a feature
- X_{min} - the smallest value of all the data points in the dataset
- X_{max} - the largest value of all the data points in the dataset
- X_{norm} - the normalized value after applying the formula

Normalization does not change the distribution of the feature, and because of decreased standard deviations the effect of outliers increases. For this reason, it is recommended to handle outliers before normalizing. And now, let's look at a Python example:

```
data = pd.DataFrame({'value':[7,25, -47, 73, 8, 22, 53, -25]})

data['normalized'] = (data['value'] - data['value'].min()) /
(data['value'].max() - data['value'].min())
print(data)
```

Expect to see the following output:

```
   value  normalized
0      7    0.450000
1     25    0.600000
2    -47    0.000000
3     73    1.000000
4      8    0.458333
5     22    0.575000
6     53    0.833333
7    -25    0.183333
```

Figure 14: Normalization output

Standardization (or z-score normalization) is a scaling method that includes standard deviation as part of its calculation. Standardization minimizes and smoothens the effect of outliers in the scaling. Let's see how it can be calculated:

$$z = \frac{x - \mu}{\sigma}$$

Where:

- μ = mean
- σ = standard deviation
- x = the data point

And calculating in Python:

```
data = pd.DataFrame({'value':[7,25, -47, 73, 8, 22, 53, -25]})

data['standardized'] = (data['value'] - data['value'].mean()) /
data['value'].std()
print(data)
```

And you should see this in your console:

```
   value  standardized
0      7     -0.193539
1     25      0.270954
2    -47     -1.587017
3     73      1.509601
4      8     -0.167733
5     22      0.193539
6     53      0.993498
7    -25     -1.019303
```

Figure 15: Standardization output

Date manipulation

Time features can be of critical importance for some data science problems. In time series analysis, dates are obviously critical. Predicting that the S&P 500 is going to 3,000 means nothing if you don't attach a date to the prediction.

Dates without any processing might not provide much significance to most models and the values are going to be too unique to provide any predictive power. Why is 10/21/2019 different from 10/19/2019? If we use some of the domain knowledge, we might be able to greatly increase the information value of the feature. For example, converting the date to a categorical variable might help. If the target feature is that you are trying to determine when rent is going to get paid, convert the date to a binary value where the possible values are:

- Before the 5th of the month = 1
- After the 5th of the month = 0

If you are asked to predict foot traffic and sales at a restaurant, there might not be any pattern in traffic looking at the 21st of every month, but as you can imagine there might be a pattern in traffic if the date is a Sunday versus a Tuesday, or if the month is October versus December (think Christmas). If this is an international chain of restaurants, the restaurant location together with the month might be highly significant (Christmas in the USA versus Diwali in India).

Other possible ways that dates can be manipulated include:

- Divide the date into different components: Year, month, day, and so on
- Calculate the time period between the current date and the value in question in terms of years, months, days, and so on
- Extract specific features from the date:
    - Day of the week (Monday, Tuesday, and so on)
    - Weekend or not
    - Holiday or not

There are plenty of other possibilities. We leave it to the reader to brainstorm or research other approaches.

Summary

In this chapter we analyzed two important steps in the machine learning pipeline:

- Feature selection
- Feature engineering

As we saw, these two processes currently are as much an art as they are a science. Picking a model to use in the pipeline potentially is an easier task than deciding which features to drop and which features to generate to add to the model. This chapter is not meant to be a comprehensive analysis of feature selection and feature engineering, but rather it's a small taste and hopefully it whets your appetite to explore this topic further.

In the next chapter, we'll start getting into the meat of machine learning. We will be building machine learning models starting with supervised learning models.

5

Classification and Regression Using Supervised Learning

In this chapter, we are going to learn about classification and regression of data using supervised learning techniques. By the end of this chapter, you will have a better understanding of these topics:

- Differences between supervised and unsupervised learning
- Classification methods
- Data preprocessing methods
- Label encoding
- Logistic regression classifiers
- The Naïve Bayes classifier
- Confusion matrixes
- Support Vector Machines and SVM classifiers
- Linear and polynomial regression
- Single-variable and multivariable linear regressors
- Estimating housing prices using Support Vector Regressors

Supervised versus unsupervised learning

It's not hard to see from looking at the popular press that one of the hottest areas in artificial intelligence today is machine learning. Machine learning is commonly classified into supervised and unsupervised learning. Other classifications exist, but we'll discuss those later.

Let's get some intuitive understanding about supervised learning versus unsupervised learning before we give a more formal definition. Assume you have a set of portraits of people. The people in this set are a very diverse group of men and women and you have all kinds of nationalities, ages, body weights, and so on. Initially, you put the dataset through an unsupervised learning algorithm. In this case, without any a priori knowledge, the unsupervised algorithm will start classifying these photographs depending on some feature that it recognizes as similar. For example, on its own, it might start recognizing that men and women are different, and it might start clustering the men in one group and the women in another. But there is no guarantee that it will find that pattern. It might cluster the images because some portraits have a dark background and others have a light background, which would likely be a useless inference.

Now picture the same set of photographs, but this time we also have a label that goes with each photograph. Let's say the label is gender. Because we now have a label for the data, we can put this data through a supervised algorithm and use input variables (in this case the input variables are the photograph pixels) to calculate the target variable (in this case, gender). More formally:

Supervised learning refers to the process of building a machine learning model that is based on labeled training data. In supervised learning, each example or row is a tuple consisting of input variables and a desired target variable. For example, a common dataset used in machine learning is the "Titanic" dataset. This dataset contains features to describe the passengers of the famous ship RMS Titanic. Some of the input features are:

- Passenger name
- Sex
- Cabin class
- Age
- Place of embarkment

And the target variable in this case would be whether the passenger survived or not.

Unsupervised learning refers to the process of building a machine learning model without relying on labeled training data. In some sense, it is the opposite of supervised learning. Since there are no labels available, you need to extract insights based on just the data given to you. With unsupervised learning, we are training a system where separate datapoints will potentially be separated into multiple clusters or groups. A key point to highlight is that we don't know exactly what the criteria of separation should be. Hence, an unsupervised learning algorithm needs to separate the given dataset into several groups in the best way possible.

Now that we've described one of the main ways in which machine learning approaches are classified, let's get into how we classify data.

What is classification?

In this section, we will discuss supervised classification techniques. The classification process is a technique used to arrange data into a fixed number of categories so that it can be used effectively and efficiently.

In machine learning, classification is used to identify the category to which a new datapoint belongs. A classification model is built based on the training dataset containing datapoints and the corresponding labels. For example, let's say that we want to determine whether a given image contains a person's face or not. We would build a training dataset containing classes corresponding to two classes: face and no-face. A model would then be trained based on the available training samples. The trained model can then be used for inference.

A good classification system makes it easy to find and retrieve data. Classification is used extensively in face recognition, spam identification, recommendation engines, and so on. A good data classification algorithm will automatically generate the right criteria to separate the given data into the given number of classes.

For classification to generate decent results, a sufficiently large number of samples will be required so that it can generalize those criteria. If there is an insufficient number of samples, the algorithm will overfit to the training data. This means that it won't perform well on unknown data because it fine-tuned the model too much to fit into the patterns observed in training data. This is actually a common problem that occurs in the world of machine learning. It's a good idea to consider this factor when building various machine learning models.

Preprocessing data

Raw data is the fuel of machine learning algorithms. But just like we cannot put crude oil into a car and instead we must use gasoline, machine learning algorithms expect data to be formatted in a certain way before the training process can begin. In order to prepare the data for ingestion by machine learning algorithms, the data must be preprocessed and converted into the right format. Let's look at some of the ways this can be accomplished.

For the examples we will analyze to work, we will need to import a few Python packages:

```
import numpy as np
from sklearn import preprocessing
```

Also, let's define some sample data:

```
input_data = np.array([[5.1, -2.9, 3.3],
                       [-1.2, 7.8, -6.1],
                       [3.9, 0.4, 2.1],
                       [7.3, -9.9, -4.5]])
```

These are the preprocessing techniques we will be analyzing:

- Binarization
- Mean removal
- Scaling
- Normalization

Binarization

Binarization is used to convert numerical values into Boolean values. Let's use an inbuilt method to binarize input data using `2.1` as the threshold value.

Add the following lines to the same Python file:

```
# Binarize data
data_binarized = preprocessing.Binarizer(threshold=2.1).
transform(input_data)
print("\nBinarized data:\n", data_binarized)
```

If you run the code, you will see the following output:

```
Binarized data:
[[ 1.  0.  1.]
[ 0.  1.  0.]
[ 1.  0.  0.]
[ 1.  0.  0.]]
```

As we can see here, all the values above `2.1` become `1`. The remaining values become `0`.

Mean removal

Removing the mean is a common preprocessing technique used in machine learning. It's usually useful to remove the mean from a feature vector, so that each feature is centered on zero. We do this in order to remove bias from the features in our feature vector.

Add the following lines to the same Python file as in the previous section:

```
# Print mean and standard deviation
print("\nBEFORE:")
print("Mean =", input_data.mean(axis=0))
print("Std deviation =", input_data.std(axis=0))
```

The preceding line displays the mean and standard deviation of the input data. Let's remove the mean:

```
# Remove mean
data_scaled = preprocessing.scale(input_data)
print("\nAFTER:")
print("Mean =", data_scaled.mean(axis=0))
print("Std deviation =", data_scaled.std(axis=0))
```

If you run the code, you will see the following output:

```
BEFORE:
Mean = [ 3.775 -1.15  -1.3  ]
Std deviation = [ 3.12039661  6.36651396  4.0620192 ] AFTER:
Mean = [  1.11022302e-16  0.00000000e+00  2.77555756e-17]
Std deviation = [ 1.  1.  1.]
```

As seen from the values obtained, the mean value is very close to `0` and the standard deviation is `1`.

Scaling

As we have done in previous sections, let's build some intuition on what scaling is by visiting an example. Let's assume that you have a dataset that contains features related to homes and you are trying to predict the prices of those homes. The ranges of the numeric values of those features can vary greatly. For example, the square footage of the home is normally in the thousands, whereas the number of rooms is usually less than 10. Additionally, some of those features might contain some outliers. For example, there might be some mansions in our dataset that skew the rest of the dataset.

We need to find a way to scale those features so that the weighting given to each feature is about the same and outliers do not have an outsized importance. One way to do this is to readjust all features so that they fall within a small range such as `0` and `1`. The MinMaxScaler algorithm is probably the most efficient way to achieve this. The formula for this algorithm is:

$$\frac{x_i - \min(x)}{\max(x) - \min(x)}$$

Where *max(x)* is the largest value for a variable, *min(x)* is the smallest value and x_i is each individual value.

In our feature vector, the value of each feature can vary between many random values. So, it becomes important to scale those features to have a level playing field for the training of the machine learning algorithm. No feature should be artificially large or small just because of the nature of the measurements.

To implement this in Python, add the following lines in the file:

```
# Min max scaling
data_scaler_minmax = preprocessing.MinMaxScaler(feature_range=(0, 1))
data_scaled_minmax = data_scaler_minmax.fit_transform(input_data)
print("\nMin max scaled data:\n", data_scaled_minmax)
```

If you run the code, you will see the following output:

```
Min max scaled data:
 [[ 0.74117647  0.39548023  1.        ]
 [ 0.          1.          0.        ]
 [ 0.6         0.5819209   0.87234043]
 [ 1.          0.          0.17021277]]
```

Each row is scaled so that the maximum value is `1` and all the other values are relative to this value.

Normalization

Folks often confuse scaling and normalization. One of the reasons why the terms are often confused is because they are in fact quite similar. In both cases, you are transforming the data to make the data more useful. But whereas in scaling you are changing the *range* of values for a variable, with normalization you are changing the *shape of the distribution* of the data. For machine learning models to work better, it is desirable for the values of a feature to be normally distributed.

But reality is messy, and sometimes this is not the case. For example, the distribution of values might be skewed. Normalization normally distributes the data. The following is a graph of the data before being normalized and after:

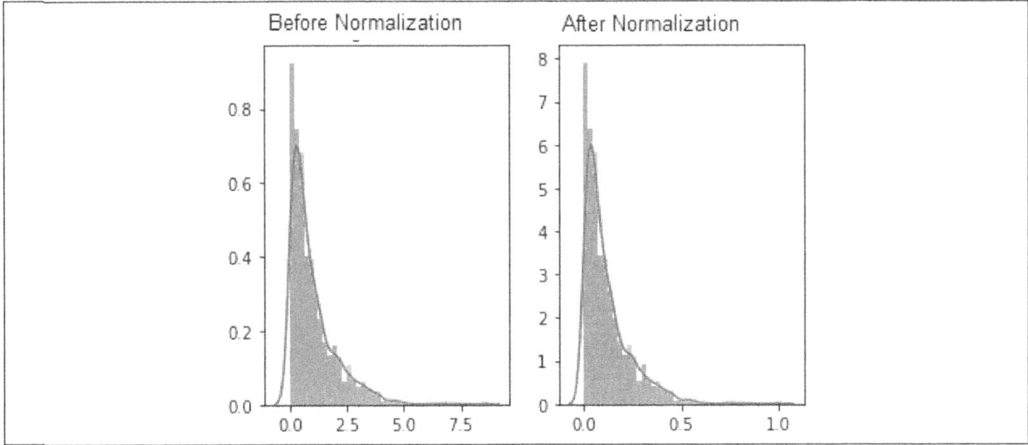

Figure 1: Before and After Normalization

We use the process of normalization to modify the values in the feature vector so that we can measure them on a common scale. In machine learning, we use many different forms of normalization. Some of the most common forms of normalization aim to modify the values so that they sum up to 1. **L1 normalization**, which refers to **Least Absolute Deviations**, works by making sure that the sum of absolute values is *1* in each row. **L2 normalization**, which refers to least squares, works by making sure that the sum of squares is *1*.

In general, the L1 normalization technique is considered more robust than the L2 normalization technique. The L1 normalization technique is robust because it is resistant to outliers in the data. A lot of times, data tends to contain outliers and we cannot do anything about it. We want to use techniques that can safely and effectively ignore them during the calculations. If we are solving a problem where outliers are important, then maybe L2 normalization becomes a better choice.

Add the following lines to the same Python file:

```
# Normalize data
data_normalized_l1 = preprocessing.normalize(input_data, norm='l1')
data_normalized_l2 = preprocessing.normalize(input_data, norm='l2')
print("\nL1 normalized data:\n", data_normalized_l1)
print("\nL2 normalized data:\n", data_normalized_l2)
```

If you run the code, you will see the following output:

```
L1 normalized data:
 [[ 0.45132743  -0.25663717    0.2920354 ]
 [-0.0794702    0.51655629   -0.40397351]
 [ 0.609375     0.0625  0.328125 ]
 [ 0.33640553 -0.4562212    -0.20737327]]
L2 normalized data:
 [[ 0.75765788      -0.43082507   0.49024922]
 [-0.12030718 0.78199664  -0.61156148]
 [ 0.87690281 0.08993875    0.47217844]
 [ 0.55734935 -0.75585734  -0.34357152]]
```

The code for this entire section is given in the `data_preprocessor.py` file.

Label encoding

When performing classification, we usually deal with lots of labels. These labels can be in the form of words, numbers, or something else. Many machine learning algorithms require numbers as input. So, if they are already numbers, they can be directly used for training. But this is not always the case.

Labels are normally words, because words can be understood by humans. Training data is labeled with words so that the mapping can be tracked. To convert word labels into numbers, a label encoder can be used. Label encoding refers to the process of transforming word labels into numbers. This enables the algorithms to be able to process the data. Let's look at an example:

Create a new Python file and import the following packages:

```
import numpy as np
from sklearn import preprocessing
```

Define some sample labels:

```
# Sample input labels
input_labels = ['red', 'black', 'red', 'green', 'black', 'yellow',
'white']
```

Create the label encoder object and train it:

```
# Create label encoder and fit the labels
encoder = preprocessing.LabelEncoder()
encoder.fit(input_labels)
```

Print the mapping between words and numbers:

```
# Print the mapping
print("\nLabel mapping:")
for i, item in enumerate(encoder.classes_):
    print(item, '-->', i)
```

Let's encode a set of randomly ordered labels to see how it performs:

```
# Encode a set of labels using the encoder
test_labels = ['green', 'red', 'black']
encoded_values = encoder.transform(test_labels)
print("\nLabels =", test_labels)
print("Encoded values =", list(encoded_values))
```

Let's decode a random set of numbers:

```
# Decode a set of values using the encoder
encoded_values = [3, 0, 4, 1]
decoded_list = encoder.inverse_transform(encoded_values)
print("\nEncoded values =", encoded_values)
print("Decoded labels =", list(decoded_list))
```

If you run the code, you will see the following output:

```
Label mapping:
black --> 0
green --> 1
red --> 2
white --> 3
yellow --> 4

Labels = ['green', 'red', 'black']
Encoded values = [1, 2, 0]

Encoded values = [3, 0, 4, 1]
Decoded labels = ['white', 'black', 'yellow', 'green']
```

Figure 2: Encoding and decoding outputs

You can check the mapping to see that the encoding and decoding steps are correct. The code for this section is given in the `label_encoder.py` file.

Logistic regression classifiers

Logistic regression is a technique that is used to explain the relationship between input variables and output variables. Regression can be used to make predictions on continuous values, but it can also be useful to make discrete predictions where the result is *True* or *False*, for example, or *Red*, *Green*, or *Yellow* as another example.

The input variables are assumed to be independent and the output variable is referred to as the dependent variable. The dependent variable can take only a fixed set of values. These values correspond to the classes of the classification problem.

Our goal is to identify the relationship between the independent variables and the dependent variables by estimating the probabilities using a logistic function. This logistic function in this case will be a **sigmoid curve** that's used to build the function with various parameters. Some of the reasons a sigmoid function is used in logistic regression models are:

- It is bounded between 0 and 1
- Its derivate is easier to compute
- It is a simple method to introduce non-linearity to the model

It is closely related to generalized linear model analysis, where we try to fit a line to a bunch of points to minimize the error. Instead of using linear regression, we use logistic regression. Logistic regression by itself is not a classification technique, but it is used in this way to facilitate classification. It is used commonly in machine learning because of its simplicity. Let's see how to build a classifier using logistic regression. Make sure the `Tkinter` package is installed before you proceed. If it is not, it can be found here: `https://docs.python.org/2/library/tkinter.html`.

Create a new Python file and import the following packages:

```
import numpy as np
from sklearn import linear_model
import matplotlib.pyplot as plt

from utilities import visualize_classifier
```

Define sample input data with two-dimensional vectors and corresponding labels:

```
# Define sample input data
X = np.array([[3.1, 7.2], [4, 6.7], [2.9, 8], [5.1, 4.5], [6, 5],
[5.6, 5], [3.3, 0.4], [3.9, 0.9], [2.8, 1], [0.5, 3.4], [1, 4], [0.6,
4.9]])
y = np.array([0, 0, 0, 1, 1, 1, 2, 2, 2, 3, 3, 3])
```

We will train the classifier using this labeled data. Now create the logistic regression classifier object:

```
# Create the logistic regression classifier
classifier = linear_model.LogisticRegression(solver='liblinear', C=1)
```

Train the classifier using the data defined earlier:

```
# Train the classifier
classifier.fit(X, y)
```

Visualize the performance of the classifier by looking at the boundaries of the classes:

```
# Visualize the performance of the classifier
visualize_classifier(classifier, X, y)
```

The function needs to be defined before it can be used. We will be using this function multiple times in this chapter, so it's better to define it in a separate file and import the function. This function is given in the `utilities.py` file provided.

Create a new Python file and import the following packages:

```
import numpy as np
import matplotlib.pyplot as plt
```

Create the function definition by taking the `classifier` object, input data, and labels as input parameters:

```
def visualize_classifier(classifier, X, y):
    # Define the minimum and maximum values for X and Y
    # that will be used in the mesh grid
    min_x, max_x = X[:, 0].min() - 1.0, X[:, 0].max() + 1.0
    min_y, max_y = X[:, 1].min() - 1.0, X[:, 1].max() + 1.0
```

We also defined the minimum and maximum values of `X` and `Y` directions that will be used in our mesh grid. This grid is basically a set of values that is used to evaluate the function, so that we can visualize the boundaries of the classes. Define the step size for the grid and create it using the minimum and maximum values:

```
    # Define the step size to use in plotting the mesh grid
    mesh_step_size = 0.01

    # Define the mesh grid of X and Y values
    x_vals, y_vals = np.meshgrid(np.arange(min_x, max_x, mesh_step_
size), np.arange(min_y, max_y, mesh_step_size))
```

Run the classifier on all the points on the grid:

```
    # Run the classifier on the mesh grid
    output = classifier.predict(np.c_[x_vals.ravel(), y_vals.ravel()])

    # Reshape the output array
    output = output.reshape(x_vals.shape)
```

Create the figure, pick a color scheme, and overlay all the points:

```
    # Create a plot
    plt.figure()

    # Choose a color scheme for the plot
    plt.pcolormesh(x_vals, y_vals, output, cmap=plt.cm.gray)

    # Overlay the training points on the plot
    plt.scatter(X[:, 0], X[:, 1], c=y, s=75, edgecolors='black',
linewidth=1, cmap=plt.cm.Paired)
```

Specify the boundaries of the plots using the minimum and maximum values, add the check marks, and display the figure:

```
    # Specify the boundaries of the plot
    plt.xlim(x_vals.min(), x_vals.max())
    plt.ylim(y_vals.min(), y_vals.max())

    # Specify the ticks on the X and Y axes
    plt.xticks((np.arange(int(X[:, 0].min() - 1), int(X[:, 0].max() +
1), 1.0)))
    plt.yticks((np.arange(int(X[:, 1].min() - 1), int(X[:, 1].max() +
1), 1.0)))

    plt.show()
```

If the code is run, you will see the following screenshot:

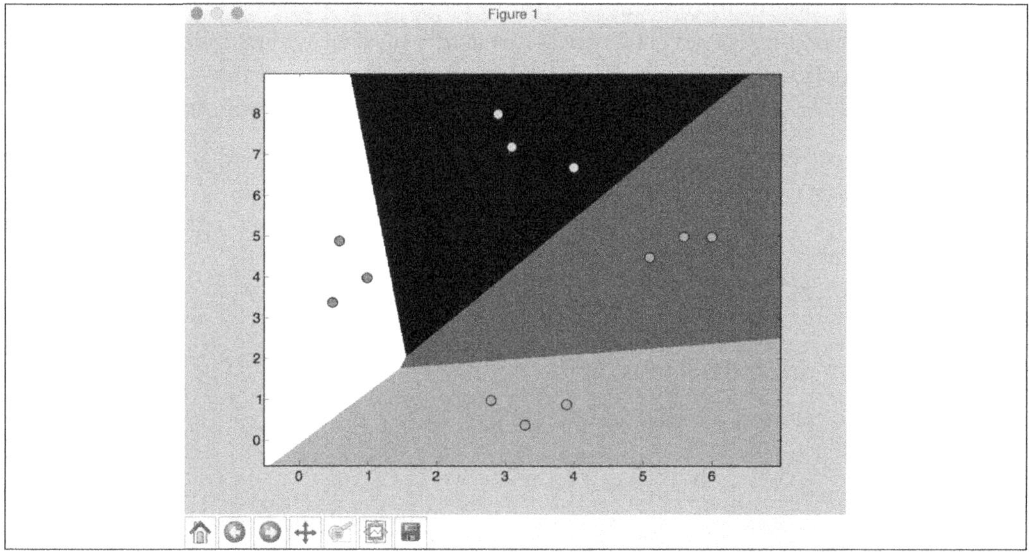

Figure 3: The displayed figure once the boundaries of the plots have been set

If you change the value of `C` to `100` in the following line, you will see that the boundaries become more accurate:

```
classifier = linear_model.LogisticRegression(solver='liblinear',
C=100)
```

The reason is that `C` imposes a certain penalty on misclassification, so the algorithm customizes more to the training data. You should be careful with this parameter, because if you increase it by a lot, it will overfit to the training data and it won't generalize well.

If you run the code with `C` set to `100`, you will see the following screenshot:

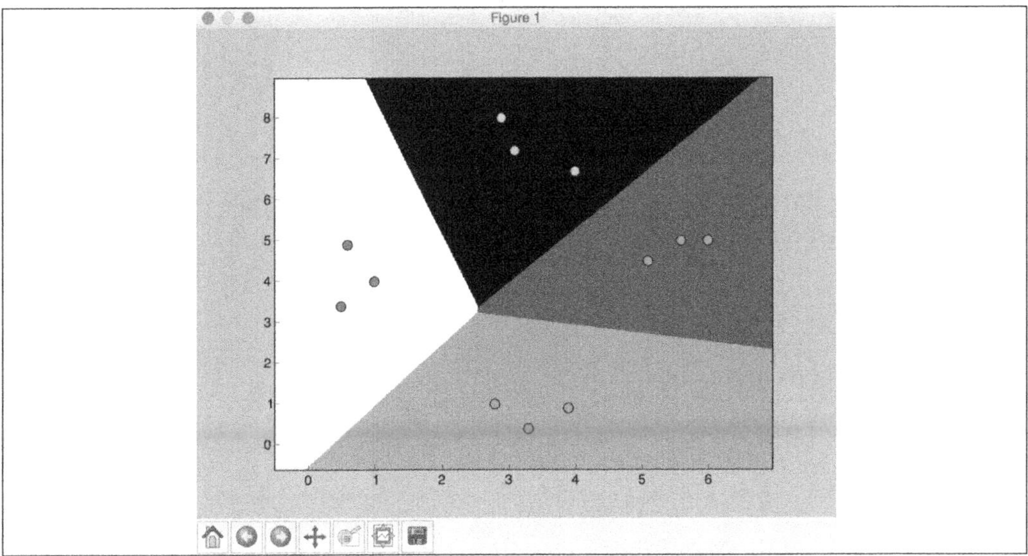

Figure 4: Results when running the code with C set to 100

If you compare with the earlier figure, you will see that the boundaries are now better. The code for this section is given in the `logistic_regression.py` file.

The Naïve Bayes classifier

Naïve Bayes is a technique used to build classifiers using Bayes, theorem. Bayes, theorem describes the probability of an event occurring based on different conditions that are related to that event. We build a Naïve Bayes classifier by assigning class labels to problem instances. These problem instances are represented as vectors of feature values. The assumption here is that the value of any given feature is independent of the value of any other feature. This is called the independence assumption, which is the naïve part of a Naïve Bayes classifier.

Given the class variable, we can just see how a given feature affects it regardless of its effect on other features. For example, an animal may be considered a cheetah if it is spotted, has four legs, has a tail, and runs at about 70 MPH. A Naïve Bayes classifier considers that each of these features contributes independently to the outcome. The outcome refers to the probability that this animal is a cheetah. We don't concern ourselves with the correlations that may exist between skin patterns, number of legs, presence of a tail, and movement speed. Let's see how to build a Naïve Bayes classifier.

Create a new Python file and import the following packages:

```
import numpy as np
import matplotlib.pyplot as plt
from sklearn.naive_bayes import GaussianNB
from sklearn.model_selection import train_test_split
from sklearn.model_selection import cross_val_score

from utilities import visualize_classifier
```

We will be using the file `data_multivar_nb.txt` as the source data. This file contains comma-separated values in each line:

```
# Input file containing data
input_file = 'data_multivar_nb.txt'
```

Let's load the data from this file:

```
# Load data from input file
data = np.loadtxt(input_file, delimiter=',')
X, y = data[:, :-1], data[:, -1]
```

Create an instance of the Naïve Bayes classifier. We will be using the Gaussian Naïve Bayes classifier here. In this type of classifier, we assume that the values associated with each class follow a Gaussian distribution:

```
# Create Naïve Bayes classifier
classifier = GaussianNB()
```

Train the classifier using the training data:

```
# Train the classifier
classifier.fit(X, y)
```

Run the classifier on the training data and predict the output:

```
# Predict the values for training data
y_pred = classifier.predict(X)
```

Let's compute the accuracy of the classifier by comparing the predicted values with the true labels, and then visualize the performance:

```
# Compute accuracy
accuracy = 100.0 * (y == y_pred).sum() / X.shape[0]
print("Accuracy of Naïve Bayes classifier =", round(accuracy, 2), "%")

# Visualize the performance of the classifier
visualize_classifier(classifier, X, y)
```

The preceding method to compute the accuracy of the classifier is not robust. We need to perform cross-validation, so that we don't use the same training data when we are testing it.

Split the data into training and testing subsets. As specified by the `test_size` parameter in the following line, we will allocate 80% for training and the remaining 20% for testing. We'll then train a Naïve Bayes classifier on this data:

```
# Split data into training and test data
X_train, X_test, y_train, y_test = train_test_split(X, y, test_
size=0.2, random_state=3)
classifier_new = GaussianNB()
classifier_new.fit(X_train, y_train)
y_test_pred = classifier_new.predict(X_test)
```

Compute the accuracy of the classifier and visualize the performance:

```
# compute accuracy of the classifier
accuracy = 100.0 * (y_test == y_test_pred).sum() / X_test.shape[0]
print("Accuracy of the new classifier =", round(accuracy, 2), "%")

# Visualize the performance of the classifier
visualize_classifier(classifier_new, X_test, y_test)
```

Let's use the inbuilt functions to calculate the accuracy, precision, and recall values based on three-fold cross-validation:

```
num_folds = 3
accuracy_values = cross_val_score(classifier,
        X, y, scoring='accuracy', cv=num_folds)
print("Accuracy: " + str(round(100*accuracy_values.mean(), 2)) + "%")

precision_values = cross_val_score(classifier,
         X, y, scoring='precision_weighted', cv=num_folds)
print("Precision: " + str(round(100*precision_values.mean(), 2)) +
"%")
```

```
recall_values = cross_val_score(classifier,
        X, y, scoring='recall_weighted', cv=num_folds)
print("Recall: " + str(round(100*recall_values.mean(), 2)) + "%")

f1_values = cross_val_score(classifier,
        X, y, scoring='f1_weighted', cv=num_folds)
print("F1: " + str(round(100*f1_values.mean(), 2)) + "%")
```

If you run the code, you will see this for the first training run:

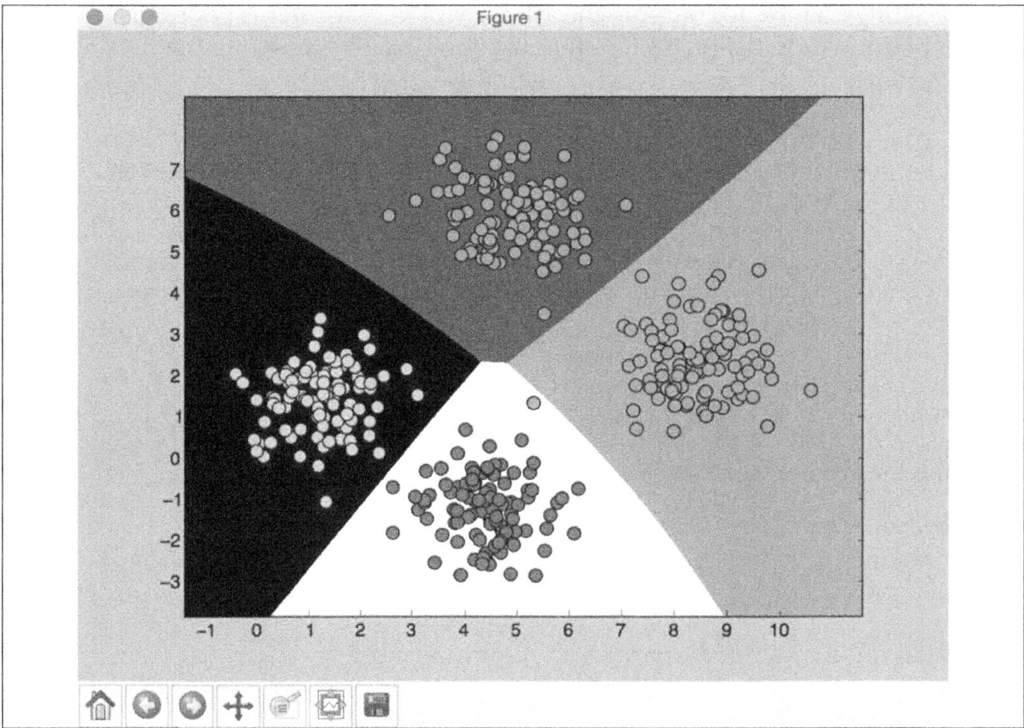

Figure 5: Clustering and boundaries following the first training run

The preceding screenshot shows the boundaries obtained from the classifier. We can see that they separate the four clusters well and create regions with boundaries based on the distribution of the input datapoints. You will see in the following screenshot the second training run with cross-validation:

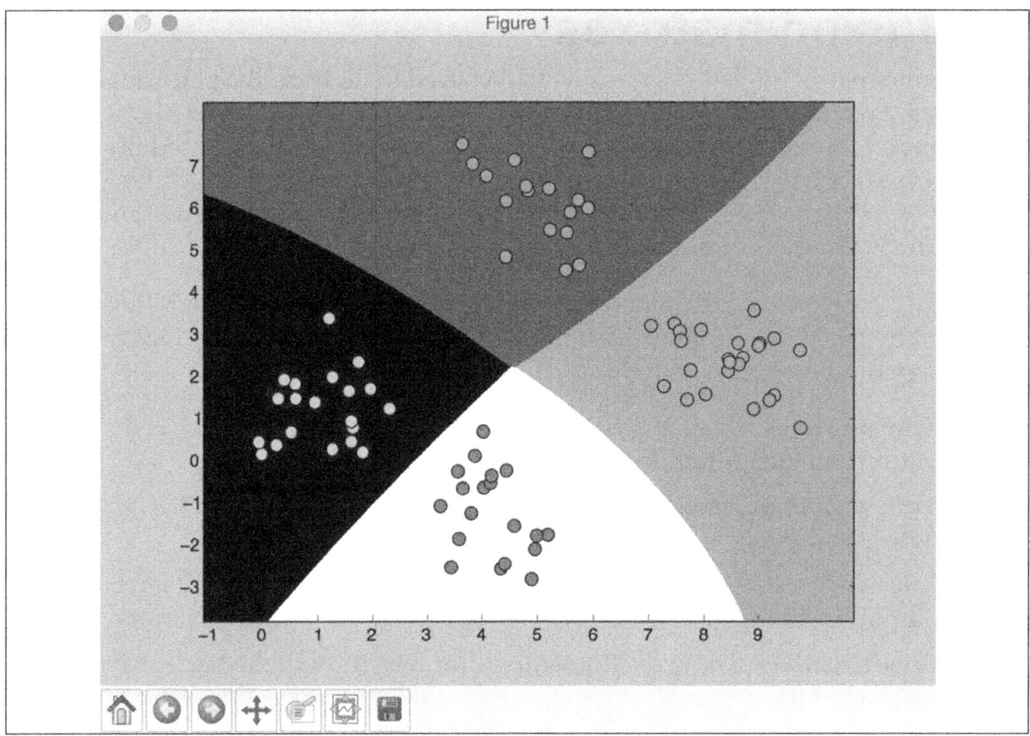

Figure 6: Results of the second training, using cross-validation

You will see the following printed output:

```
Accuracy of Naïve Bayes classifier = 99.75 %
Accuracy of the new classifier = 100.0 %
Accuracy: 99.75%
Precision: 99.76%
Recall: 99.75%
F1: 99.75%
```

The code for this section is given in the file `naive_bayes.py`.

Confusion matrixes

A **confusion matrix** is a figure or a table that is used to describe the performance of a classifier. Each row in the matrix represents the instances in a predicted class and each column represents the instances in an actual class. This name is used because the matrix makes it easy to visualize if the model confused or mislabeled two classes. We compare each class with every other class and see how many samples are classified correctly or misclassified.

During the construction of this table, we come across several key metrics that are important in the field of machine learning. Let's consider a binary classification case where the output is either *0* or *1*:

- **True positives**: These are the samples for which we predicted *1* as the output and the ground truth is *1* too.
- **True negatives**: These are the samples for which we predicted *0* as the output and the ground truth is *0* too.
- **False positives**: These are the samples for which we predicted *1* as the output but the ground truth is *0*. This is also known as a *Type I error*.
- **False negatives**: These are the samples for which we predicted *0* as the output but the ground truth is *1*. This is also known as a *Type II error*.

Depending on the problem at hand, we may have to optimize our algorithm to reduce the false positive or the false negative rate. For example, in a biometric identification system, it is very important to avoid false positives, because the wrong people might get access to sensitive information. Let's see how to create a confusion matrix.

Create a new Python file and import the following packages:

```
import numpy as np
import matplotlib.pyplot as plt
from sklearn.metrics import confusion_matrix
from sklearn.metrics import classification_report
```

Define some sample labels for the ground truth and the predicted output:

```
# Define sample labels
true_labels = [2, 0, 0, 2, 4, 4, 1, 0, 3, 3, 3]
pred_labels = [2, 1, 0, 2, 4, 3, 1, 0, 1, 3, 3]
```

Create the confusion matrix using the labels we just defined:

```
# Create confusion matrix
confusion_mat = confusion_matrix(true_labels, pred_labels)
```

Visualize the confusion matrix:

```
# Visualize confusion matrix
plt.imshow(confusion_mat, interpolation='nearest', cmap=plt.cm.gray)
plt.title('Confusion matrix')
plt.colorbar()
ticks = np.arange(5)
plt.xticks(ticks, ticks)
plt.yticks(ticks, ticks)
plt.ylabel('True labels')
plt.xlabel('Predicted labels')
plt.show()
```

In the preceding visualization code, the `ticks` variable refers to the number of distinct classes. In our case, we have five distinct labels.

Let's print the classification report:

```
# Classification report
targets = ['Class-0', 'Class-1', 'Class-2', 'Class-3', 'Class-4']
print('\n', classification_report(true_labels, pred_labels, target_
names=targets))
```

The classification report prints the performance for each class. If you run the code, you will see the following screenshot:

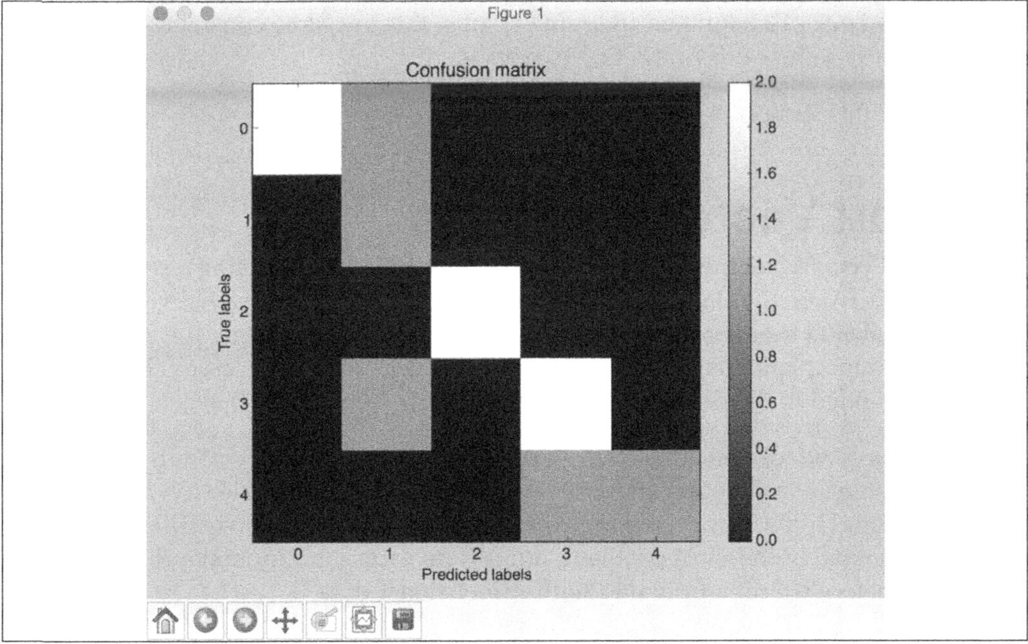

Figure 7: Performance of each class from the classification report

White indicates higher values, whereas black indicates lower values, as seen on the color map key on the right of the image. In an ideal scenario, the diagonal squares will be all white and everything else will be black. This indicates 100% accuracy.

The output should be as follows:

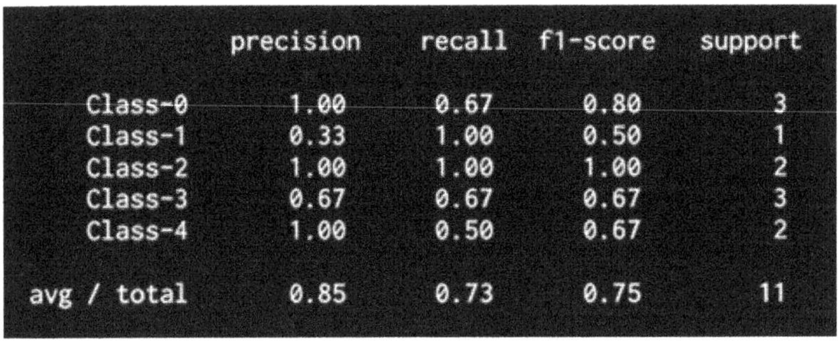

	precision	recall	f1-score	support
Class-0	1.00	0.67	0.80	3
Class-1	0.33	1.00	0.50	1
Class-2	1.00	1.00	1.00	2
Class-3	0.67	0.67	0.67	3
Class-4	1.00	0.50	0.67	2
avg / total	0.85	0.73	0.75	11

Figure 8: Values from the classification report

As we can see the average `precision` was 85% and the average `recall` was 73%. Whereas the `f1-score` was 75%. Depending on the domain we are working with, these might be great results or poor results. If the domain in question was to try to determine whether a patient has cancer and we were only able to have precision of 85%, 15% of the population would have been misclassified and would be quite unhappy. If the domain we were analyzing was whether someone was going to buy a product and our precision had the same results, this might be considered a home run and greatly reduce our marketing expenses.

The code for this section is given in the file `confusion_matrix.py`.

Support Vector Machines

A **Support Vector Machine** (**SVM**) is a classifier that is defined using a separating hyperplane between the classes. This **hyperplane** is the N-dimensional version of a line. Given labeled training data and a binary classification problem, the SVM finds the optimal hyperplane that separates the training data into two classes. This can easily be extended to the problem with `N` classes.

Let's consider a two-dimensional case with two classes of points. Given that it's 2D, we only must deal with points and lines on a 2D plane. This is easier to visualize than vectors and hyperplanes in a high-dimensional space. Of course, this is a simplified version of the SVM problem, but it is important to understand it and visualize it before we can apply it to high-dimensional data.

Consider the following figure:

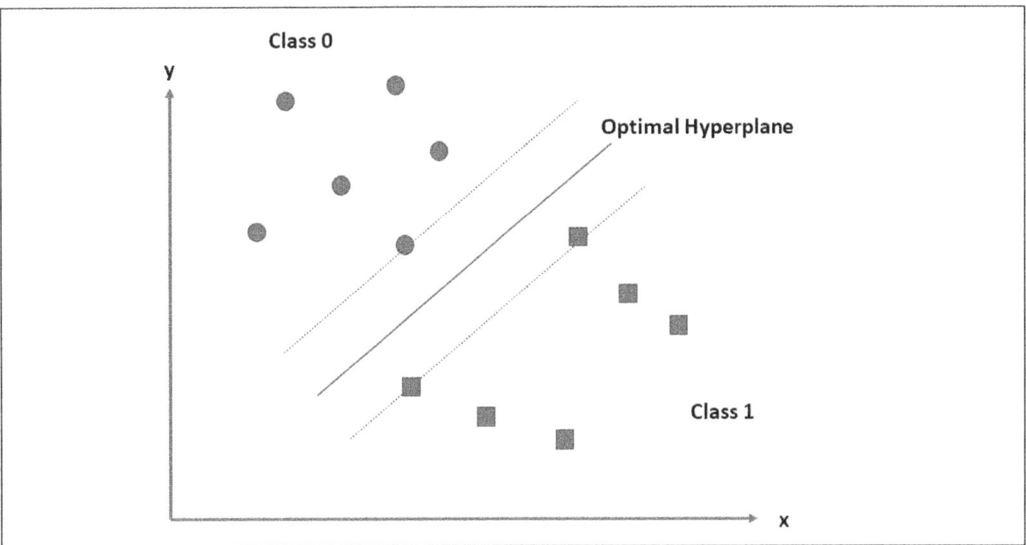

Figure 9: Separating two classes with a hyperplane

There are two classes of points and we want to find the optimal hyperplane to separate the two classes. But how do we define optimal? In this picture, the solid line represents the best hyperplane. You can draw many different lines to separate the two classes of points, but this line is the best separator, because it maximizes the distance of each point from the separating line. The points on the dotted lines are called Support Vectors. The perpendicular distance between the two dotted lines is called the maximum margin. You can think of the maximum margin as the thickest border that can be drawn for a given dataset.

Classifying income data using Support Vector Machines

We will build a Support Vector Machine classifier to predict the income bracket of a given person based on 14 attributes. Our goal is to see whether the income is higher or lower than $50,000 per year. Hence this is a binary classification problem. We will be using the census income dataset available at `https://archive.ics.uci.edu/ml/datasets/Census+Income`. One item to note in this dataset is that each datapoint is a mixture of words and numbers. We cannot use the data in its raw format, because the algorithms don't know how to deal with words. We cannot convert everything using a label encoder because numerical data is valuable. Hence, we need to use a combination of label encoders and raw numerical data to build an effective classifier.

Create a new Python file and import the following packages:

```
import numpy as np
import matplotlib.pyplot as plt
from sklearn import preprocessing
from sklearn.svm import LinearSVC
from sklearn.multiclass import OneVsOneClassifier
from sklearn.model_selection import train_test_split
```

We will be using the file `income_data.txt` to load the data. This file contains the income details:

```
# Input file containing
data input_file = 'income_data.txt'
```

In order to load the data from the file, we need to preprocess it to prepare it for classification. We will use at most 25,000 datapoints for each class:

```
# Read the data
X = []
y = []
count_class1 = 0
count_class2 = 0
max_datapoints = 25000
```

Open the file and start reading the lines:

```
with open(input_file, 'r') as f:
    for line in f.readlines():
        if count_class1 >= max_datapoints and count_class2 >= max_
datapoints:
            break

        if '?' in line:
            continue
```

Each line is comma-separated, so we need to split it accordingly. The last element in each line represents the label. Depending on that label, we will assign it to a class:

```
        data = line[:-1].split(', ')

        if data[-1] == '<=50K' and count_class1 < max_datapoints:
            X.append(data)
            count_class1 += 1

        if data[-1] == '>50K' and count_class2 < max_datapoints:
            X.append(data)
            count_class2 += 1
```

Convert the list into a `numpy` array so that it can be used as an input to the `sklearn` function:

```
# Convert to numpy array
X = np.array(X)
```

If any attribute is a string, it needs to be encoded. If it is a number, it can be kept as is. Note that we will end up with multiple label encoders and we need to keep track of all of them:

```
# Convert string data to numerical data
label_encoder = []
X_encoded = np.empty(X.shape)
for i,item in enumerate(X[0]):
    if item.isdigit():
        X_encoded[:, i] = X[:, i]
    else:
        label_encoder.append(preprocessing.LabelEncoder())
        X_encoded[:, i] = label_encoder[-1].fit_transform(X[:, i])

X = X_encoded[:, :-1].astype(int)
y = X_encoded[:, -1].astype(int)
```

Create the `SVM` classifier with a linear kernel:

```
# Create SVM classifier
classifier = OneVsOneClassifier(LinearSVC(random_state=0))
```

Train the classifier:

```
# Train the classifier
classifier.fit(X, y)
```

Perform cross-validation using an 80/20 split for training and testing, and then predict the output for the training data:

```
# Cross validation
X_train, X_test, y_train, y_test = train_test_split.train_test_
split(X, y, test_size=0.2, random_state=5)
classifier = OneVsOneClassifier(LinearSVC(random_state=0))
classifier.fit(X_train, y_train)
y_test_pred = classifier.predict(X_test)
```

Compute the F1 score for the classifier:

```
# Compute the F1 score of the SVM classifier
f1 = train_test_split.cross_val_score(classifier, X, y, scoring='f1_
weighted', cv=3)
```

```
print("F1 score: " + str(round(100*f1.mean(), 2)) + "%")
```

Now that the classifier is ready, let's see how to take a random input datapoint and predict the output. Let's define one such datapoint:

```
# Predict output for a test datapoint
input_data = ['37', 'Private', '215646', 'HS-grad', '9', 'Never-
married', 'Handlers-cleaners', 'Not-in-family', 'White', 'Male', '0',
'0', '40', 'United-States']
```

Before predictions can be performed, the datapoint needs to be encoded using the label encoders created earlier:

```
# Encode test datapoint
input_data_encoded = [-1] * len(input_data)
count = 0
for i, item in enumerate(input_data):
    if item.isdigit():
        input_data_encoded[i] = int(input_data[i])
    else:
        input_data_encoded[i] = int(label_encoder[count].
transform(input_data[i]))
        count += 1

input_data_encoded = np.array(input_data_encoded)
```

We are now ready to predict the output using the classifier:

```
# Run classifier on encoded datapoint and print output
predicted_class = classifier.predict(input_data_encoded)
print(label_encoder[-1].inverse_transform(predicted_class)[0])
```

If you run the code, it will take a few seconds to train the classifier. Once it's done, you will see the following output:

```
F1 score: 66.82%
```

You will also see the output for the test datapoint:

```
<=50K
```

If you check the values in that datapoint, you will see that it closely corresponds to the datapoints in the less-than-50K class. You can change the performance of the classifier (F1 score, precision, or recall) by using different kernels and trying out multiple combinations of the parameters.

The code for this section is given in the file `income_classifier.py`.

What is regression?

Regression is the process of estimating the relationship between input and output variables. One item to note is that output variables are continuous-valued real numbers. Hence, there are an infinite number of possibilities. This is in contrast with classification, where the number of output classes is fixed. The classes belong to a finite set of possibilities.

In regression, it is assumed that the output variables depend on the input variables, so we want to see how they are related. Consequently, the input variables are called *independent variables*, also known as *predictors*, and output variables are called *dependent variables*, also known as *criterion variables*. It is not necessary that the input variables are independent of one another; indeed, there are a lot of situations where there are correlations between input variables.

Regression analysis helps us in understanding how the value of the output variable changes when we vary some input variables while keeping other input variables fixed. In linear regression, we assume that the relationship between input and output is linear. This puts a constraint on our modeling procedure, but it's fast and efficient.

Sometimes, linear regression is not enough to explain the relationship between input and output. Hence, we use polynomial regression, where we use a polynomial to explain the relationship between input and output. This is computationally more complex but gives higher accuracy. Depending on the problem at hand, we use different forms of regression to extract the relationship. Regression is frequently used for the prediction of prices, economics, variations, and so on.

Building a single-variable regressor

Let's see how to build a single-variable regression model. Create a new Python file and import the following packages:

```
import pickle

import numpy as np
from sklearn import linear_model
import sklearn.metrics as sm
import matplotlib.pyplot as plt
```

We will use the file `data_singlevar_regr.txt` provided to you. This is our source of data:

```
# Input file containing data
input_file = 'data_singlevar_regr.txt'
```

It's a comma-separated file, so we can easily load it using a one-line function call:

```
# Read data
data = np.loadtxt(input_file, delimiter=',')
X, y = data[:, :-1], data[:, -1]
```

Split it into training and testing:

```
# Train and test split
num_training = int(0.8 * len(X))
num_test = len(X) - num_training

# Training data
X_train, y_train = X[:num_training], y[:num_training]

# Test data
X_test, y_test = X[num_training:], y[num_training:]
```

Create a linear regressor object and train it using the training data:

```
# Create linear regressor object
regressor = linear_model.LinearRegression()

# Train the model using the training sets
regressor.fit(X_train, y_train)
```

Predict the output for the testing dataset using the training model:

```
# Predict the output
y_test_pred = regressor.predict(X_test)
```

Plot the output:

```
# Plot outputs
plt.scatter(X_test, y_test, color='green')
plt.plot(X_test, y_test_pred, color='black', linewidth=4)
plt.xticks(())
plt.yticks(())
plt.show()
```

Compute the performance metrics for the regressor by comparing the ground truth, which refers to the actual outputs, with the predicted outputs:

```
# Compute performance metrics
print("Linear regressor performance:")
print("Mean absolute error =", round(sm.mean_absolute_error(y_test,
y_test_pred), 2))
print("Mean squared error =", round(sm.mean_squared_error(y_test, y_
```

```
test_pred), 2))
print("Median absolute error =", round(sm.median_absolute_error(y_
test, y_test_pred), 2))
print("Explain variance score =", round(sm.explained_variance_score(y_
test, y_test_pred), 2))
print("R2 score =", round(sm.r2_score(y_test, y_test_pred), 2))
```

Once the model has been created, we can save it into a file so that we can use it later. Python provides a nice module called `pickle` that enables us to do this:

```
# Model persistence
output_model_file = 'model.pkl'

# Save the model
with open(output_model_file, 'wb') as f:
    pickle.dump(regressor, f)
```

Let's load the model from the file on the disk and perform prediction:

```
# Load the model
with open(output_model_file, 'rb') as f:
    regressor_model = pickle.load(f)

# Perform prediction on test data
y_test_pred_new = regressor_model.predict(X_test)
print("\nNew mean absolute error =", round(sm.mean_absolute_error(y_
test, y_test_pred_new), 2))
```

If you run the code, you will see the following screen:

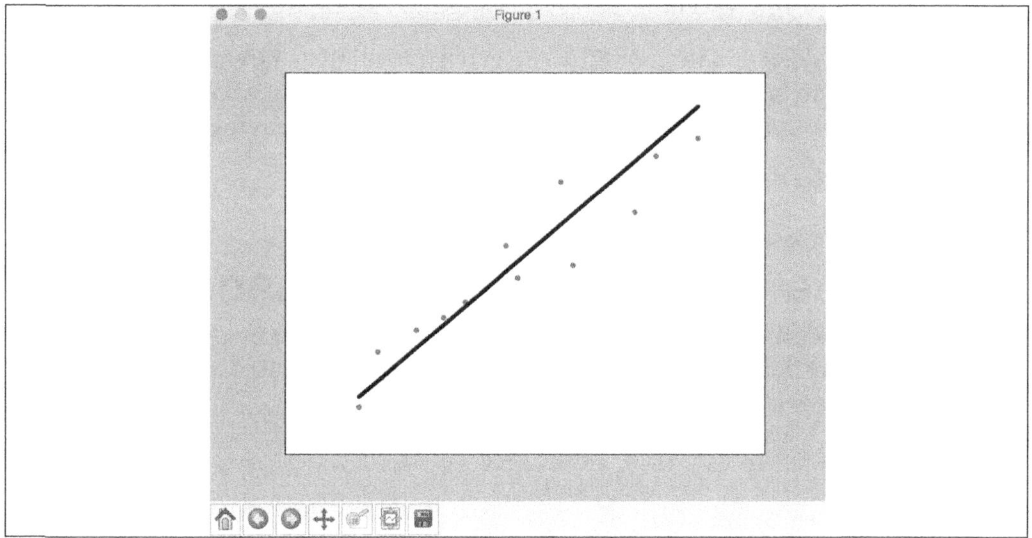

Figure 10: Output after performing prediction

You should see the following output:

```
Linear regressor performance:
Mean absolute error = 0.59
Mean squared error = 0.49
Median absolute error = 0.51
Explain variance score = 0.86
R2 score = 0.86
New mean absolute error = 0.59
```

The **mean absolute error** (**MAE**) is the average of the absolute errors:

$$|e_i| = |y_i - x_i|$$

Where y_i is the prediction and x_i is the actual value.

The **mean squared error** (**MSE**) is the average of the squares of the errors—that is, the average squared difference between the predicted value and the actual value. MSE is almost always strictly positive (and not zero) because of randomness. The MSE is a measure of the quality of an estimator. It is always non-negative, and the closer the value is to zero the better.

Explained variation measures the proportion to which a model accounts for the variation in a dataset. Often, the variation is quantified as variance; the more specific term explained variance can also be used. The rest of the total variation is the unexplained or residual variation.

The coefficient of determination or R2 score is used to analyze how the differences for one variable can be explained by a difference in a second variable. For example, if a woman gets pregnant, it has a high correlation with them having a child.

The code for this section is given in the file `regressor_singlevar.py`.

Building a multivariable regressor

In the previous section, we discussed how to build a regression model for a single variable. In this section, we will deal with multidimensional data. Create a new Python file and import the following packages:

```
import numpy as np
from sklearn import linear_model
import sklearn.metrics as sm
from sklearn.preprocessing import PolynomialFeatures
```

We will use the file `data_multivar_regr.txt` provided to you.

```
# Input file containing data
input_file = 'data_multivar_regr.txt'
```

This is a comma-separated file, so we can load it easily with a one-line function call:

```
# Load the data from the input file
data = np.loadtxt(input_file, delimiter=',')
X, y = data[:, :-1], data[:, -1]
```

Split the data into training and testing:

```
# Split data into training and testing
num_training = int(0.8 * len(X))
num_test = len(X) - num_training

# Training data
X_train, y_train = X[:num_training], y[:num_training]

# Test data
X_test, y_test = X[num_training:], y[num_training:]
```

Create and train the linear regressor model:

```
# Create the linear regressor model
linear_regressor = linear_model.LinearRegression()

# Train the model using the training sets
linear_regressor.fit(X_train, y_train)#
```

Predict the output for the test dataset:

```
# Predict the output
y_test_pred = linear_regressor.predict(X_test)
```

Print the performance metrics:

```
# Measure performance
print("Linear Regressor performance:")
print("Mean absolute error =", round(sm.mean_absolute_error(y_test,
y_test_pred), 2))
print("Mean squared error =", round(sm.mean_squared_error(y_test, y_
test_pred), 2))
print("Median absolute error =", round(sm.median_absolute_error(y_
test, y_test_pred), 2))
print("Explained variance score =", round(sm.explained_variance_
score(y_test, y_test_pred), 2))
print("R2 score =", round(sm.r2_score(y_test, y_test_pred), 2))
```

Create a polynomial regressor of degree 10. Train the regressor on the training dataset. Let's take a sample datapoint and see how to perform prediction. The first step is to transform it into a polynomial:

```
# Polynomial regression
polynomial = PolynomialFeatures(degree=10)
X_train_transformed = polynomial.fit_transform(X_train)
datapoint = [[7.75, 6.35, 5.56]]
poly_datapoint = polynomial.fit_transform(datapoint)
```

If you look closely, this datapoint is very close to the datapoint on line 11 in our data file, which is *[7.66, 6.29, 5.66]*. So, a good regressor should predict an output that's close to *41.35*. Create a linear regressor object and perform the polynomial fit. Perform the prediction using both linear and polynomial regressors to see the difference:

```
poly_linear_model = linear_model.LinearRegression()
poly_linear_model.fit(X_train_transformed, y_train)
print("\nLinear regression:\n", linear_regressor.predict(datapoint))
print("\nPolynomial regression:\n", poly_linear_model.predict(poly_
datapoint))
```

If you run the code, the output should be as follows:

```
Linear Regressor performance:
Mean absolute error = 3.58
Mean squared error = 20.31
Median absolute error = 2.99
Explained variance score = 0.86
R2 score = 0.86
```

You will see the following as well:

```
Linear regression:
 [ 36.05286276]
Polynomial regression:
 [ 41.46961676]
```

As you can see, the linear regression is `36.05`; the polynomial regressor is closer to 41.35 so the polynomial regression model was able to make a better prediction.

The code for this section is given in the file `regressor_multivar.py`.

Estimating housing prices using a Support Vector Regressor

Let's see how to use the SVM concept to build a regressor to estimate housing prices. We will use the dataset available in `sklearn` where each datapoint is defined by 13 attributes.

Our goal is to estimate housing prices based on these attributes. Create a new Python file and import the following packages:

```
import numpy as np
from sklearn import datasets
from sklearn.svm import SVR
from sklearn.metrics import mean_squared_error, explained_variance_
score
from sklearn.utils import shuffle
```

Load the housing dataset:

```
# Load housing data
data = datasets.load_boston()
```

Let's shuffle the data so that we don't bias our analysis:

```
# Shuffle the data
X, y = shuffle(data.data, data.target, random_state=7)
```

Split the dataset into training and testing in an 80/20 format:

```
# Split the data into training and testing datasets
num_training = int(0.8 * len(X))
X_train, y_train = X[:num_training], y[:num_training]
X_test, y_test = X[num_training:], y[num_training:]
```

Create and train the Support Vector Regressor using a linear kernel. The `C` parameter represents the penalty for training error. If you increase the value of `C`, the model will fine-tune it more to fit the training data. But this might lead to overfitting and cause it to lose its generality. The epsilon parameter specifies a threshold; there is no penalty for training error if the predicted value is within this distance from the actual value:

```
# Create Support Vector Regression model
sv_regressor = SVR(kernel='linear', C=1.0, epsilon=0.1)

# Train Support Vector Regressor
sv_regressor.fit(X_train, y_train)
```

Evaluate the performance of the regressor and print the metrics:

```
# Evaluate performance of Support Vector Regressor
y_test_pred = sv_regressor.predict(X_test)
mse = mean_squared_error(y_test, y_test_pred)
evs = explained_variance_score(y_test, y_test_pred)
print("\n#### Performance ####")
print("Mean squared error =", round(mse, 2))
print("Explained variance score =", round(evs, 2))
```

Let's take a test datapoint and perform prediction:

```
# Test the regressor on test datapoint
test_data = [3.7, 0, 18.4, 1, 0.87, 5.95, 91, 2.5052, 26, 666, 20.2,
351.34, 15.27]
print("\nPredicted price:", sv_regressor.predict([test_data])[0])
```

If you run the code, you should see the following output:

```
#### Performance ####
Mean squared error = 15.41
Explained variance score = 0.82
Predicted price: 18.5217801073
```

The code for this section is given in the file `house_prices.py`. Look at the first row in the file and see how close the prediction of `18.52` is to the actual target variable.

Summary

In this chapter, we learned the difference between supervised and unsupervised learning. We discussed the data classification problem and how to solve it. We understood how to preprocess data using various methods. We also learned about label encoding and how to build a label encoder. We discussed logistic regression and built a logistic regression classifier. We understood what a Naïve Bayes classifier is and learned how to build one. We also learned how to build a confusion matrix.

We discussed Support Vector Machines and understood how to build a classifier based on that. We learned about regression and understood how to use linear and polynomial regression for single-and multivariable data. We then used a Support Vector Regressor to estimate housing prices using input attributes.

In the next chapter, we will learn about predictive analytics and how to build a predictive engine using ensemble learning.

6

Predictive Analytics with Ensemble Learning

In this chapter, we will learn about ensemble learning and how to use it for predictive analytics. By the end of this chapter, you will have a better understanding of these topics:

- Decision trees and decision trees classifiers
- Learning models with ensemble learning
- Random forests and extremely random forests
- Confidence measure estimation of predictions
- Dealing with class imbalance
- Finding optimal training parameters using grid search
- Computing relative feature importance
- Traffic prediction using the extremely random forests regressor

Let's begin with decision trees. Firstly, what are they?

What are decision trees?

A **decision tree** is a way to partition a dataset into distinct branches. The branches or partitions are then traversed to make simple decisions. Decision trees are produced by training algorithms, which identify how to split the data in an optimal way.

The decision process starts at the root node at the top of the tree. Each node in the tree is a decision rule. Algorithms construct these rules based on the relationship between the input data and the target labels in the training data. The values in the input data are utilized to estimate the value of the output.

Now that we understand the basic concept behind decision trees, the next concept to understand is how the trees are automatically constructed. We need algorithms that can construct the optimal tree based on the data. In order to understand it, we need to understand the concept of entropy. In this context, entropy refers to information entropy and not thermodynamic entropy. Information entropy is basically a measure of uncertainty. One of the main goals of a decision tree is to reduce uncertainty as we move from the root node towards the leaf nodes. When we see an unknown data point, we are completely uncertain about the output. By the time we reach the leaf node, we are certain about the output. This means that the decision tree needs to be constructed in a way that will reduce the uncertainty at each level. This implies that we need to reduce the entropy as we progress down the tree.

You can learn more about this at `https://prateekvjoshi.com/2016/03/22/how-are-decision-trees-constructed-in-machine-learning`

Building a decision tree classifier

Let's see how to build a classifier using decision trees in Python. Create a new Python file and import the following packages:

```
import numpy as np
import matplotlib.pyplot as plt
from sklearn.metrics import classification_report
from sklearn.model_selection import train_test_split
from sklearn.tree import DecisionTreeClassifier

from utilities import visualize_classifier
```

We will be using the data in the `data_decision_trees.txt` file that's provided to you. In this file, each line contains comma-separated values. The first two values correspond to the input data and the last value corresponds to the target label. Let's load the data from that file:

```
# Load input data
input_file = 'data_decision_trees.txt'
data = np.loadtxt(input_file, delimiter=',')
X, y = data[:, :-1], data[:, -1]
```

Separate the input data into two separate classes based on the labels:

```
# Separate input data into two classes based on labels
class_0 = np.array(X[y==0])
class_1 = np.array(X[y==1])
```

Let's visualize the input data using a scatter plot:

```
# Visualize input data
plt.figure()
plt.scatter(class_0[:, 0], class_0[:, 1], s=75, facecolors='black',
        edgecolors='black', linewidth=1, marker='x')
plt.scatter(class_1[:, 0], class_1[:, 1], s=75, facecolors='white',
        edgecolors='black', linewidth=1, marker='o')
plt.title('Input data')
```

We need to split the data into training and testing datasets:

```
# Split data into training and testing datasets
X_train, X_test, y_train, y_test = train_test_split.train_test_split (
        X, y, test_size=0.25, random_state=5)
```

Create, build, and visualize a decision tree classifier based on the training dataset. The `random_state` parameter refers to the seed used by the random number generator required for the initialization of the decision tree classification algorithm. The `max_depth` parameter refers to the maximum depth of the tree that we want to construct:

```
# Decision Trees classifier
params = {'random_state': 0, 'max_depth': 4}
classifier = DecisionTreeClassifier(**params)
classifier.fit(X_train, y_train)
visualize_classifier(classifier, X_train, y_train, 'Training dataset')
```

Compute the output of the classifier on the test dataset and visualize it:

```
y_test_pred = classifier.predict(X_test)
visualize_classifier(classifier, X_test, y_test, 'Test dataset')
```

Evaluate the performance of the classifier by printing the classification report:

```
# Evaluate classifier performance
class_names = ['Class-0', 'Class-1']
print("\n" + "#"*40)
print("\nClassifier performance on training dataset\n")
print(classification_report(y_train, classifier.predict(X_train),
target_names=class_names))
print("#"*40 + "\n")

print("#"*40)
print("\nClassifier performance on test dataset\n")
print(classification_report(y_test, y_test_pred, target_names=class_
names))
print("#"*40 + "\n")

plt.show()
```

The full code is given in the `decision_trees.py` file. If you run the code, you will see a few figures. The first screenshot is the visualization of input data:

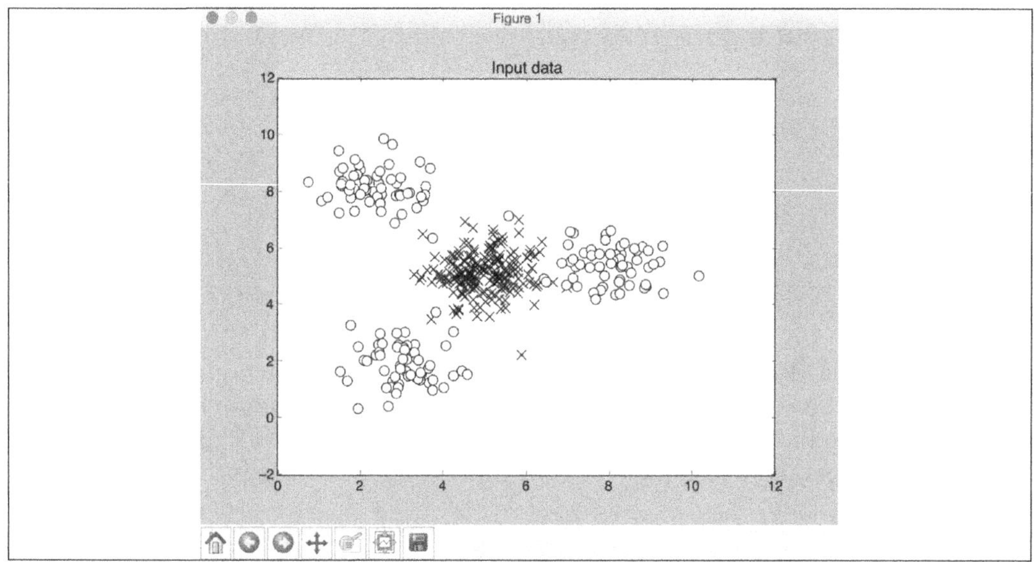

Figure 1: Visualization of input data

The second screenshot shows the classifier boundaries on the test dataset:

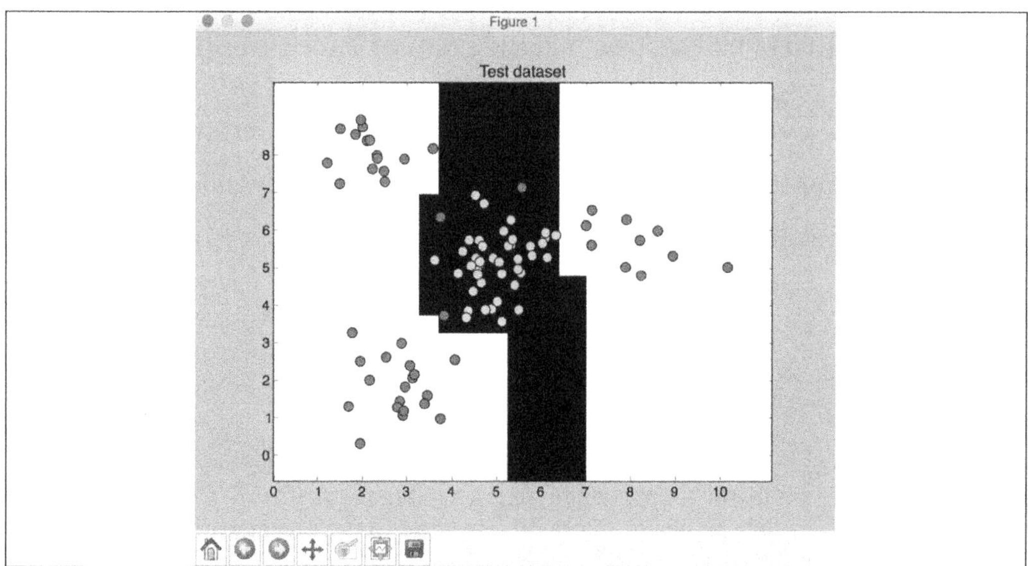

Figure 2: Classifier boundaries of the test dataset

You should also see the following output:

```
########################################

Classifier performance on training dataset

             precision    recall  f1-score   support

    Class-0       0.99      1.00      1.00       137
    Class-1       1.00      0.99      1.00       133

avg / total       1.00      1.00      1.00       270

########################################

########################################

Classifier performance on test dataset

             precision    recall  f1-score   support

    Class-0       0.93      1.00      0.97        43
    Class-1       1.00      0.94      0.97        47

avg / total       0.97      0.97      0.97        90

########################################
```

Figure 3: Classifier performance on training dataset

The performance of a classifier is characterized by `precision`, `recall`, and `f1-scores`. Precision refers to the accuracy of the classification, and recall refers to the number of items that were retrieved as a percentage of the overall number of items that were supposed to be retrieved. A good classifier will have high precision and high recall, but there is usually a trade-off between the two. Hence, we have `f1-score` to characterize that. F1 score is the harmonic mean of precision and recall, which gives it a good balance between precision and recall values.

Decision trees are an example of using a single model to make a prediction. It is possible to sometimes create stronger models and better predictions by combining and aggregating the results of multiple models. One way to do is to use ensemble learning, which will be discussed in the next section.

What is ensemble learning?

Ensemble learning involves building multiple models and then combining them in such a way that it produces better results than what the models could produce individually. These individual models can be classifiers, regressors, or other models.

Ensemble learning is used extensively across multiple fields, including data classification, predictive modeling, and anomaly detection.

So why use ensemble learning? In order to gain understanding, let's use a real-life example. You want to buy a new TV, but you don't know what the latest models are. Your goal is to get the best value for your money, but you don't have enough knowledge on this topic to make an informed decision. When you must decide about something like this, you might get the opinions of multiple experts in the domain. This will help you make the best decision. Often, instead of relying on one opinion, you can decide by combining the individual decisions of those experts. Doing this minimizes the possibility of making a wrong or suboptimal decision.

Building learning models with ensemble learning

While selecting a model, a commonly used procedure is to choose the one with the smallest error on the training dataset. The problem with this approach is that it will not always work. The model might become biased or overfit the training data. Even when training the model using cross-validation, it can perform poorly on unknown data.

A reason why ensemble learning models are effective is because they reduce the overall risk of making a poor model selection. This enables it to train in a diverse manner and then perform well on unknown data. When a model is built using ensemble learning, the individual models need to exhibit some diversity. This allows them to capture various nuances in the data; hence the overall model becomes more accurate.

The diversity is achieved by using different training parameters for each individual model. This allows individual models to generate different decision boundaries for training data. This means that each model will use different rules to make an inference, which is a powerful way of validating the result. If there is agreement among the models, this increases the confidence in the prediction.

A special type of an ensemble learning is when you combine decision trees into an ensemble. These models are usually known as random forests and extremely random forests, which we'll describe in the coming sections.

What are random forests and extremely random forests?

A **random forest** is an instance of ensemble learning where individual models are constructed using decision trees. This ensemble of decision trees is then used to predict the output value. We use a random subset of training data to construct each decision tree.

This will ensure diversity among various decision trees. In the first section, we discussed that one of the most important attributes when building good ensemble learning models is that we ensure that there is diversity among individual models.

One of the advantages of random forests is that they do not overfit. Overfitting is a frequent problem in machine learning. Overfitting is more likely with nonparametric and nonlinear models that have more flexibility when learning a target function. By constructing a diverse set of decision trees using various random subsets, we ensure that the model does not overfit the training data. During the construction of the tree, the nodes are split successively, and the best thresholds are chosen to reduce the entropy at each level. This split doesn't consider all the features in the input dataset. Instead, it chooses the best split among the random subset of the features that is under consideration. Adding this randomness tends to increase the bias of the random forest, but the variance decreases because of averaging. Hence, we end up with a robust model.

Extremely random forests take randomness to the next level. Along with taking a random subset of features, the thresholds are chosen randomly as well. These randomly generated thresholds are chosen as the splitting rules, which reduce the variance of the model even further. Hence, the decision boundaries obtained using extremely random forests tend to be smoother than the ones obtained using random forests. Some implementations of extremely random forest algorithms also enable better parallelization and can scale better.

Building random forest and extremely random forest classifiers

Let's see how we can build a classifier based on random forests and extremely random forests. The way to construct both classifiers is very similar, so an input flag is used to specify which classifier needs to be built.

Create a new Python file and import the following packages:

```
import argparse

import numpy as np
import matplotlib.pyplot as plt
from sklearn.metrics import classification_report
from sklearn.model_selection import train_test_split
from sklearn.ensemble import RandomForestClassifier,
ExtraTreesClassifier
from sklearn.metrics import classification_report

from utilities import visualize_classifier
```

Define an argument parser for Python so that we can take the classifier type as an input parameter. Depending on this parameter, we can construct a random forest classifier or an extremely random forest classifier:

```
# Argument parser
def build_arg_parser():
    parser = argparse.ArgumentParser(description='Classify data using
\
            Ensemble Learning techniques')
    parser.add_argument('--classifier-type', dest='classifier_type',
            required=True, choices=['rf', 'erf'], help="Type of
classifier \
                    to use; can be either 'rf' or 'erf'")
    return parser
```

Define the `main` function and parse the input arguments:

```
if __name__=='__main__':
    # Parse the input arguments
    args = build_arg_parser().parse_args()
    classifier_type = args.classifier_type
```

We will be using the data from the `data_random_forests.txt` file that is provided to you. Each line in this file contains comma-separated values. The first two values correspond to the input data and the last value corresponds to the target label. We have three distinct classes in this dataset. Let's load the data from that file:

```
    # Load input data
    input_file = 'data_random_forests.txt'
    data = np.loadtxt(input_file, delimiter=',')
    X, y = data[:, :-1], data[:, -1]
```

Separate the input data into three classes:

```
    # Separate input data into three classes based on labels
    class_0 = np.array(X[y==0])
    class_1 = np.array(X[y==1])
    class_2 = np.array(X[y==2])
```

Let's visualize the input data:

```
    # Visualize input data
    plt.figure()
    plt.scatter(class_0[:, 0], class_0[:, 1], s=75,
facecolors='white',
                    edgecolors='black', linewidth=1, marker='s')
    plt.scatter(class_1[:, 0], class_1[:, 1], s=75,
```

```
facecolors='white',
                    edgecolors='black', linewidth=1, marker='o')
    plt.scatter(class_2[:, 0], class_2[:, 1], s=75,
facecolors='white',
                    edgecolors='black', linewidth=1, marker='^')
    plt.title('Input data')
```

Split the data into training and testing datasets:

```
    # Split data into training and testing datasets
    X_train, X_test, y_train, y_test = train_test_split.train_test_
split (
            X, y, test_size=0.25, random_state=5)
```

Define the parameters to be used when we construct the classifier. The `n_estimators` parameter refers to the number of trees that will be constructed. The `max_depth` parameter refers to the maximum number of levels in each tree. The `random_state` parameter refers to the seed value of the random number generator needed to initialize the random forest classifier algorithm:

```
    # Ensemble Learning classifier
    params = {'n_estimators': 100, 'max_depth': 4, 'random_state': 0}
```

Depending on the input parameter, we either construct a random forest classifier or an extremely random forest classifier:

```
    if classifier_type == 'rf':
        classifier = RandomForestClassifier(**params)
    else:
        classifier = ExtraTreesClassifier(**params)
```

Train and visualize the classifier:

```
    classifier.fit(X_train, y_train)
    visualize_classifier(classifier, X_train, y_train, 'Training
dataset')
```

Compute the output based on the test dataset and visualize it:

```
    y_test_pred = classifier.predict(X_test)
    visualize_classifier(classifier, X_test, y_test, 'Test dataset')
```

Evaluate the performance of the classifier by printing the classification report:

```
    # Evaluate classifier performance
    class_names = ['Class-0', 'Class-1', 'Class-2']
    print("\n" + "#"*40)
    print("\nClassifier performance on training dataset\n")
```

```
    print(classification_report(y_train, classifier.predict(X_train),
target_names=class_names))
    print("#"*40 + "\n")

    print("#"*40)
    print("\nClassifier performance on test dataset\n")
    print(classification_report(y_test, y_test_pred, target_
names=class_names))
    print("#"*40 + "\n")
```

The full code is given in the `random_forests.py` file. Let's run the code with the random forest classifier using the `rf` flag in the input argument. Run the following command:

```
$ python3 random_forests.py --classifier-type rf
```

You will see a few figures pop up. The first screenshot is the input data:

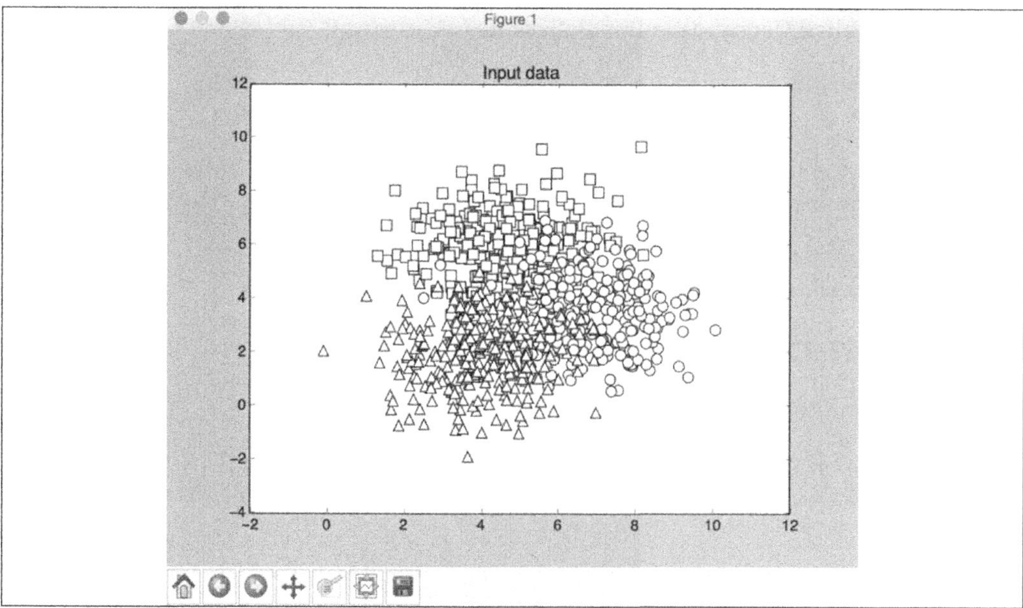

Figure 4: Visualization of input data

In the preceding screenshot, the three classes are being represented by squares, circles, and triangles. We see that there is a lot of overlap between classes, but that should be fine for now. The second screenshot shows the classifier boundaries:

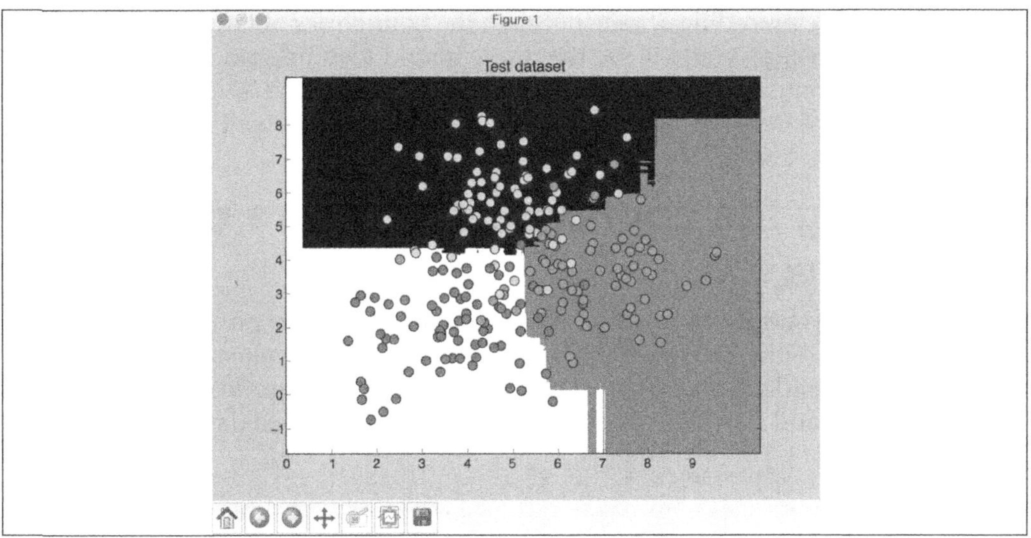

Figure 5: Classifier boundaries on the test dataset

Now let's run the code with the extremely random forest classifier by using the `erf` flag in the input argument. Run the following command:

```
$ python3 random_forests.py --classifier-type erf
```

You will see a few figures pop up. We already know what the input data looks like. The second screenshot shows the classifier boundaries:

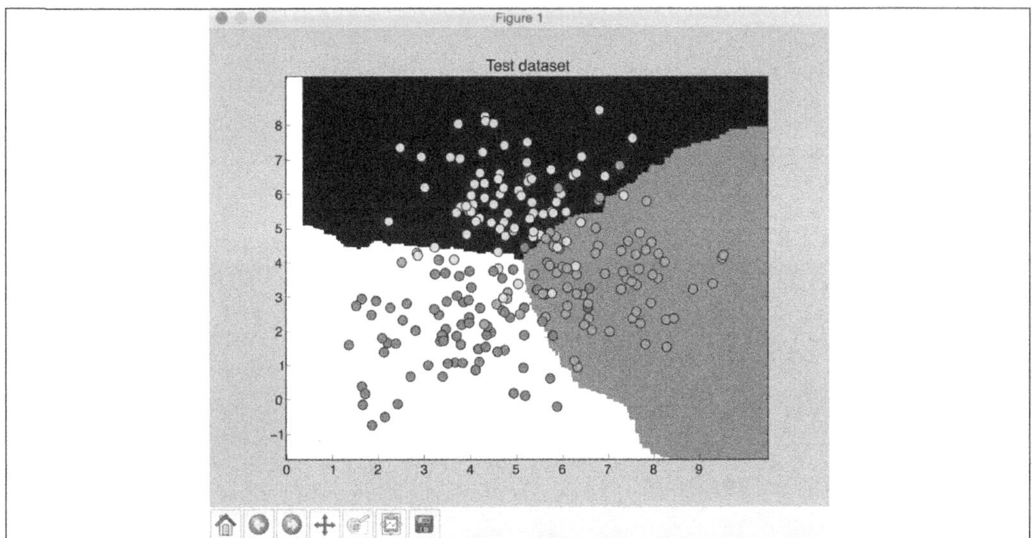

Figure 6: Classifier boundaries on the test dataset

If you compare the preceding screenshot with the boundaries obtained from the random forest classifier, you will see that these boundaries are smoother. The reason is that extremely random forests have more freedom during the training process to come up with good decision trees, hence they usually produce better boundaries.

Estimating the confidence measure of the predictions

If you analyze the output, you will see that the probabilities are printed for each data point. These probabilities are used to measure the confidence values for each class. Estimating the confidence values is an important task in machine learning. In the same Python file, add the following line to define an array of test data points:

```
    # Compute confidence
    test_datapoints = np.array([[5, 5], [3, 6], [6, 4], [7, 2], [4,
4], [5, 2]])
```

The classifier object has an inbuilt method to compute the confidence measure. Let's classify each point and compute the confidence values:

```
    print("\nConfidence measure:")
    for datapoint in test_datapoints:
        probabilities = classifier.predict_proba([datapoint])[0]
        predicted_class = 'Class-' + str(np.argmax(probabilities))
        print('\nDatapoint:', datapoint)
        print('Predicted class:', predicted_class)
```

Visualize the test data points based on classifier boundaries:

```
    # Visualize the datapoints
    visualize_classifier(classifier, test_datapoints, [0]*len(test_
datapoints),
            'Test datapoints')

    plt.show()
```

If you run the code with the `erf` flag, you will get the following output:

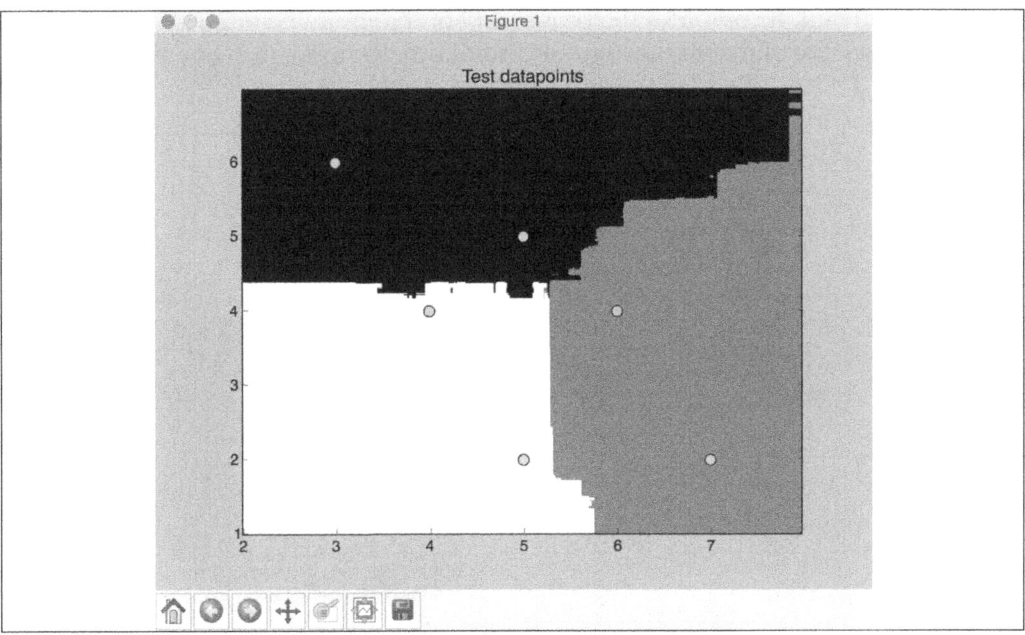

Figure 7: Classifier boundaries on the test dataset

Without the `erf` flag, it will produce the following output:

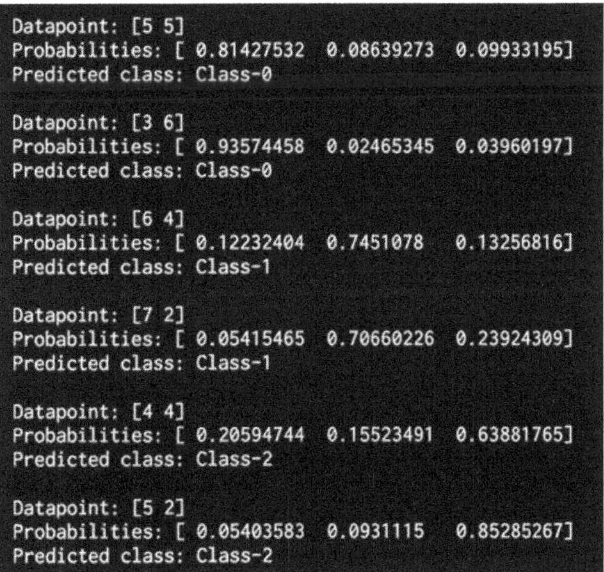

Figure 8: Dataset probabilities output

For each data point, it computes the probability of that point belonging to our three classes. We pick the one with the highest confidence. Running the code with the `erf` flag, you will get the following output:

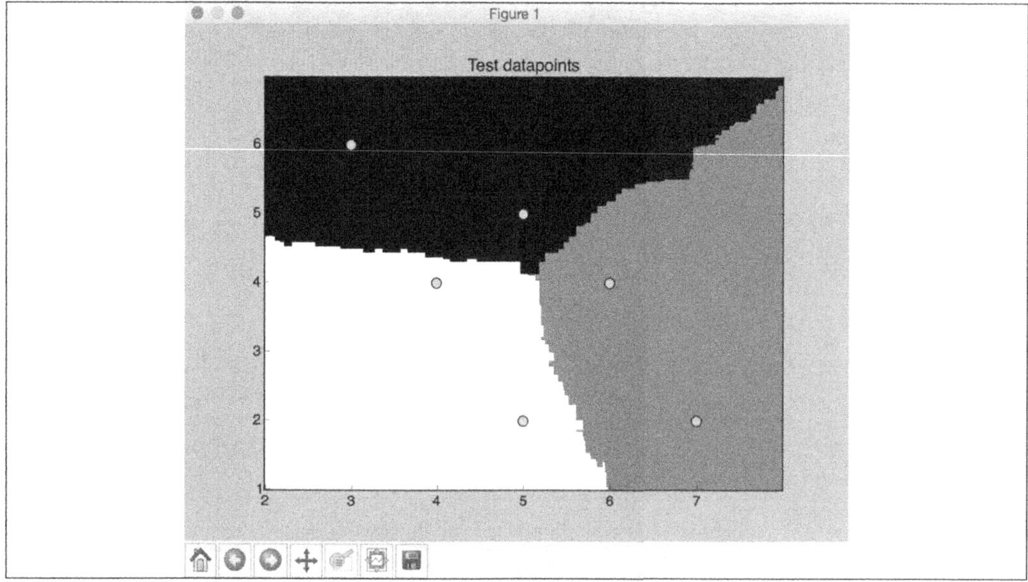

Figure 9: Classifier boundaries on the test dataset

Without the `erf` flag, the following output should be produced:

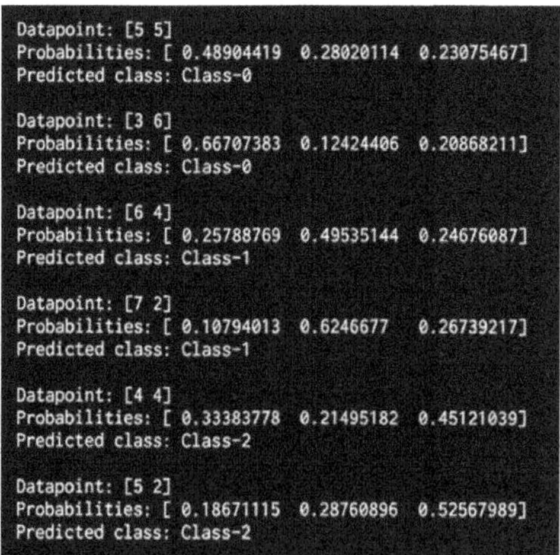

```
Datapoint: [5 5]
Probabilities: [ 0.48904419  0.28020114  0.23075467]
Predicted class: Class-0

Datapoint: [3 6]
Probabilities: [ 0.66707383  0.12424406  0.20868211]
Predicted class: Class-0

Datapoint: [6 4]
Probabilities: [ 0.25788769  0.49535144  0.24676087]
Predicted class: Class-1

Datapoint: [7 2]
Probabilities: [ 0.10794013  0.6246677   0.26739217]
Predicted class: Class-1

Datapoint: [4 4]
Probabilities: [ 0.33383778  0.21495182  0.45121039]
Predicted class: Class-2

Datapoint: [5 2]
Probabilities: [ 0.18671115  0.28760896  0.52567989]
Predicted class: Class-2
```

Figure 10: Dataset probabilities output

As can be observed, the outputs are consistent with the previous results.

Dealing with class imbalance

A classifier is only as good as the data that is used for training. A common problem faced in the real world is issues with data quality. For a classifier to perform well, it needs to see an equal number of points for each class. But when data is collected in the real world, it's not always possible to ensure that each class has the exact same number of data points. If one class has 10 times the number of data points than another class, then the classifier tends to get biased towards the more numerous class. Hence, we need to make sure that we account for this imbalance algorithmically. Let's see how to do that.

Create a new Python file and import the following packages:

```
import sys

import numpy as np
import matplotlib.pyplot as plt
from sklearn.ensemble import ExtraTreesClassifier
from sklearn.model_selection import train_test_split
from sklearn.metrics import classification_report

from utilities import visualize_classifier
```

We will use the data in the file `data_imbalance.txt` for our analysis. Let's load the data.

Each line in this file contains comma-separated values. The first two values correspond to the input data, and the last value corresponds to the target label. We have two classes in this dataset. Let's load the data from that file:

```
# Load input data
input_file = 'data_imbalance.txt'
data = np.loadtxt(input_file, delimiter=',')
X, y = data[:, :-1], data[:, -1]
```

Separate the input data into two classes:

```
# Separate input data into two classes based on labels
class_0 = np.array(X[y==0])
class_1 = np.array(X[y==1])
```

Visualize the input data using a scatter plot:

```
# Visualize input data
plt.figure()
plt.scatter(class_0[:, 0], class_0[:, 1], s=75, facecolors='black',
                edgecolors='black', linewidth=1, marker='x')
```

```
plt.scatter(class_1[:, 0], class_1[:, 1], s=75, facecolors='white',
                edgecolors='black', linewidth=1, marker='o')
plt.title('Input data')
```

Split the data into training and testing datasets:

```
# Split data into training and testing datasets
X_train, X_test, y_train, y_test = train_test_split.train_test_split(
        X, y, test_size=0.25, random_state=5)
```

Next, we define the parameters for the extremely random forest classifier. Note that there is an input parameter called `balance` that controls whether to algorithmically account for class imbalance. If so, another parameter needs to be added called `class_weight` that tells the classifier that it should balance the weight so that it's proportional to the number of data points in each class:

```
# Extremely Random Forests classifier
params = {'n_estimators': 100, 'max_depth': 4, 'random_state': 0}
if len(sys.argv) > 1:
    if sys.argv[1] == 'balance':
        params = {'n_estimators': 100, 'max_depth': 4, 'random_state':
0, 'class_weight': 'balanced'}
    else:
        raise TypeError("Invalid input argument; should be 'balance'")
```

Build, train, and visualize the classifier using training data:

```
classifier = ExtraTreesClassifier(**params)
classifier.fit(X_train, y_train)
visualize_classifier(classifier, X_train, y_train, 'Training dataset')
```

Predict the output for the test dataset and visualize the output:

```
y_test_pred = classifier.predict(X_test)
visualize_classifier(classifier, X_test, y_test, 'Test dataset')
```

Compute the performance of the classifier and print the classification report:

```
# Evaluate classifier performance
class_names = ['Class-0', 'Class-1']
print("\n" + "#"*40)
print("\nClassifier performance on training dataset\n")
print(classification_report(y_train, classifier.predict(X_train),
```

```
target_names=class_names))
print("#"*40 + "\n")

print("#"*40)
print("\nClassifier performance on test dataset\n")
print(classification_report(y_test, y_test_pred, target_names=class_
names))
print("#"*40 + "\n")

plt.show()
```

The full code is given in the file `class_imbalance.py`. If you run the code, you will see the following graphics. The first graphic shows the input data:

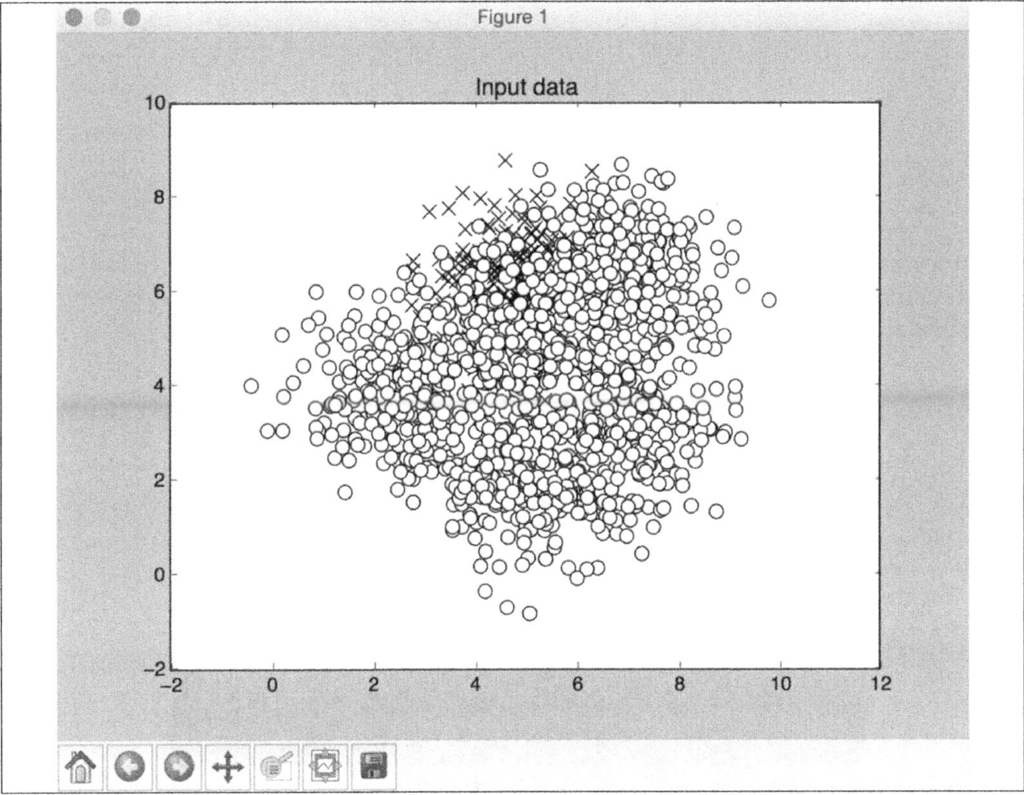

Figure 11: Visualization of input data

The second graphic shows the classifier boundary for the test dataset:

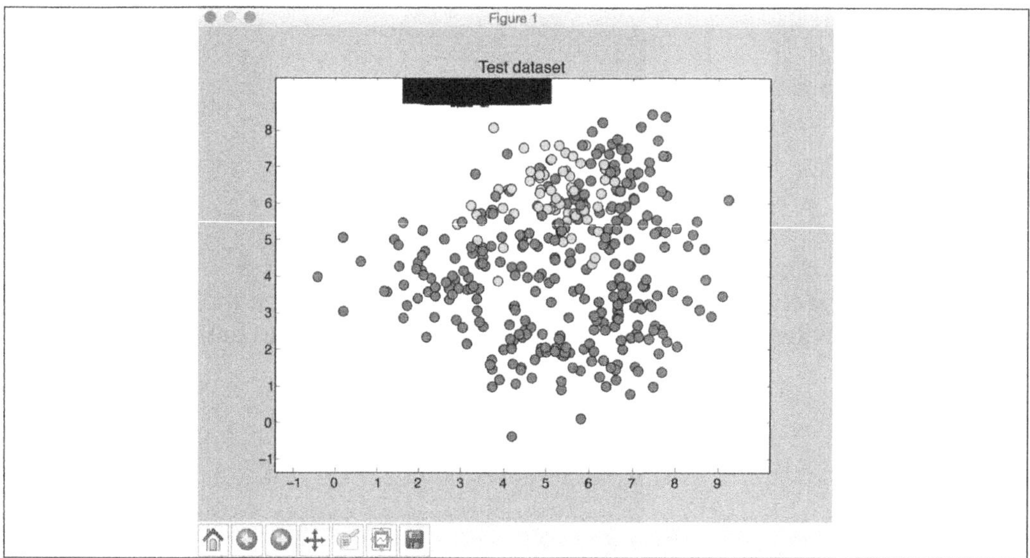

Figure 12: Classifier boundaries on the test dataset

The preceding graphic indicates that the boundary was not able to capture the actual boundary between the two classes. The black patch near the top represents the boundary. Finally, you should see the following output:

```
########################################

Classifier performance on test dataset

             precision    recall  f1-score   support

    Class-0       0.00      0.00      0.00        69
    Class-1       0.82      1.00      0.90       306

avg / total       0.67      0.82      0.73       375

########################################
```

Figure 13: Classifier performance on the test dataset

You see a warning because the values are `0` in the first row, which leads to a divide-by-zero error (`ZeroDivisionError` exception) when we compute the `f1-score`. Run the code using the `ignore` flag so that you do not see the divide-by-zero warning:

```
$ python3 --W ignore class_imbalance.py
```

Now, if you want to account for class imbalance, run it with the `balance` flag:

```
$ python3 class_imbalance.py balance
```

The classifier output looks like this:

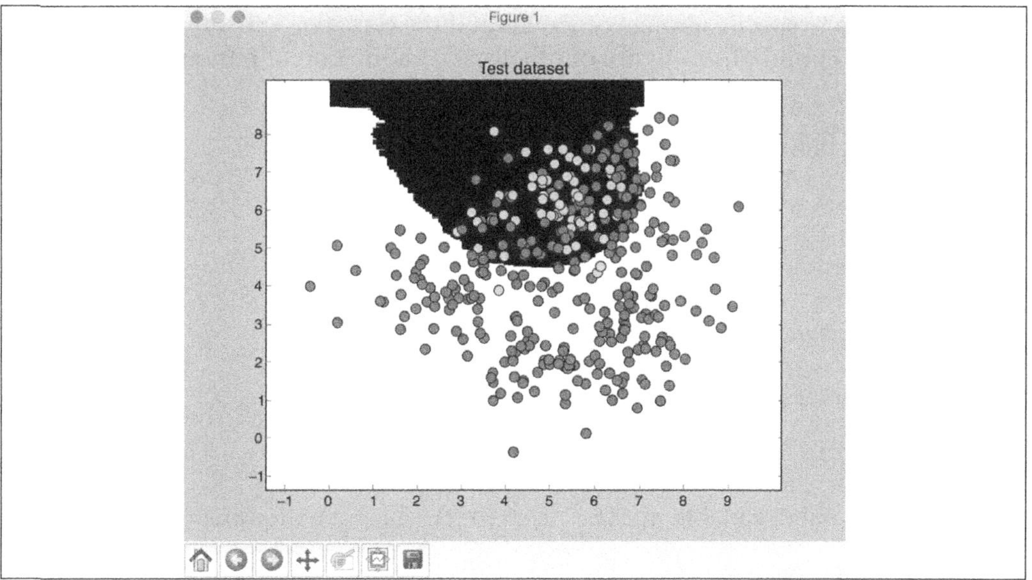

Figure 14: Visualization of test dataset with balance

You should see the following output:

```
########################################

Classifier performance on test dataset

             precision    recall  f1-score   support

    Class-0       0.45      0.94      0.61        69
    Class-1       0.98      0.74      0.84       306

avg / total       0.88      0.78      0.80       375

########################################
```

Figure 15: Classifier performance on the test dataset

By accounting for the class imbalance, we were able to classify the data points in `Class-0` with nonzero throughout accuracy.

Finding optimal training parameters using grid search

When working with classifiers, it is not always possible to know what the best parameters are to use. It is not efficient to use brute force by checking for all possible combinations manually. This is where grid search becomes useful. Grid search allows us to specify a range of values and the classifier will automatically run various configurations to figure out the best combination of parameters. Let's see how to do it.

Create a new Python file and import the following packages:

```
import numpy as np
import matplotlib.pyplot as plt
from sklearn.metrics import classification_report
from sklearn import grid_search
from sklearn.ensemble import ExtraTreesClassifier
from sklearn.model_selection import train_test_split
from sklearn.metrics import classification_report

from utilities import visualize_classifier
```

We will use the data available in `data_random_forests.txt` for analysis:

```
# Load input data
input_file = 'data_random_forests.txt'
data = np.loadtxt(input_file, delimiter=',')
X, y = data[:, :-1], data[:, -1]
```

Separate the data into three classes:

```
# Separate input data into three classes based on labels
class_0 = np.array(X[y==0])
class_1 = np.array(X[y==1])
class_2 = np.array(X[y==2])
```

Split the data into training and testing datasets:

```
# Split the data into training and testing datasets
X_train, X_test, y_train, y_test = train_test_split.train_test_split(
        X, y, test_size=0.25, random_state=5)
```

Specify the grid of parameters for the classifier to test. Usually one parameter is kept constant and the other parameter is varied. Then the inverse is done to figure out the best combination. In this case, we want to find the best values for `n_estimators` and `max_depth`. Let's specify the parameter grid:

```
# Define the parameter grid
parameter_grid = [{'n_estimators': [100], 'max_depth':[2, 4, 7, 12,
16]},
                  {'max_depth': [4], 'n_estimators': [25, 50, 100,
250]}
                 ]
```

Let's define the metrics that the classifier should use to find the best combination of parameters:

```
metrics = ['precision_weighted', 'recall_weighted']
```

For each metric, we need to run the grid search, where we train the classifier for a combination of parameters:

```
for metric in metrics:
    print("\n##### Searching optimal parameters for", metric)

    classifier = grid_search.GridSearchCV(
            ExtraTreesClassifier(random_state=0),
            parameter_grid, cv=5, scoring=metric)
    classifier.fit(X_train, y_train)
```

Print the score for each parameter combination:

```
    print("\nGrid scores for the parameter grid:")
    for params, avg_score, _ in classifier.grid_scores_:
        print(params, '-->', round(avg_score, 3))

    print("\nBest parameters:", classifier.best_params_)
```

Print the performance report:

```
    y_pred = classifier.predict(X_test)
    print("\nPerformance report:\n")
    print(classification_report(y_test, y_pred))
```

The full code is given in the file `run_grid_search.py`. If the code is run, the following output will be produced with the precision metric:

```
##### Searching optimal parameters for precision_weighted

Grid scores for the parameter grid:
{'n_estimators': 100, 'max_depth': 2} --> 0.847
{'n_estimators': 100, 'max_depth': 4} --> 0.841
{'n_estimators': 100, 'max_depth': 7} --> 0.844
{'n_estimators': 100, 'max_depth': 12} --> 0.836
{'n_estimators': 100, 'max_depth': 16} --> 0.818
{'n_estimators': 25, 'max_depth': 4} --> 0.846
{'n_estimators': 50, 'max_depth': 4} --> 0.84
{'n_estimators': 100, 'max_depth': 4} --> 0.841
{'n_estimators': 250, 'max_depth': 4} --> 0.845

Best parameters: {'n_estimators': 100, 'max_depth': 2}

Performance report:

             precision    recall  f1-score   support

        0.0       0.94      0.81      0.87        79
        1.0       0.81      0.86      0.83        70
        2.0       0.83      0.91      0.87        76

avg / total       0.86      0.86      0.86       225
```

Figure 16: Optimal parameter search output

Based on the combinations in the grid search, it will print out the best combination for the precision metric. To find the best combination for recall, the following output can be checked:

```
##### Searching optimal parameters for recall_weighted

Grid scores for the parameter grid:
{'n_estimators': 100, 'max_depth': 2} --> 0.84
{'n_estimators': 100, 'max_depth': 4} --> 0.837
{'n_estimators': 100, 'max_depth': 7} --> 0.841
{'n_estimators': 100, 'max_depth': 12} --> 0.834
{'n_estimators': 100, 'max_depth': 16} --> 0.816
{'n_estimators': 25, 'max_depth': 4} --> 0.843
{'n_estimators': 50, 'max_depth': 4} --> 0.836
{'n_estimators': 100, 'max_depth': 4} --> 0.837
{'n_estimators': 250, 'max_depth': 4} --> 0.841

Best parameters: {'n_estimators': 25, 'max_depth': 4}

Performance report:

             precision    recall  f1-score   support

        0.0       0.93      0.84      0.88        79
        1.0       0.85      0.86      0.85        70
        2.0       0.84      0.92      0.88        76

avg / total       0.87      0.87      0.87       225
```

Figure 17: Optimal parameter search output

It is a different combination for recall, which makes sense because precision and recall are different metrics that demand different parameter combinations.

Computing relative feature importance

When working with a dataset that contains N-dimensional data points, it must be understood that not all features are equally important. Some are more discriminative than others. If we have this information, we can use it to reduce the dimensionality. This is useful in reducing the complexity and increasing the speed of the algorithm. Sometimes, a few features are completely redundant. Hence, they can be easily removed from the dataset.

We will be using the `AdaBoost` regressor to compute feature importance. AdaBoost, short for Adaptive Boosting, is an algorithm that's frequently used in conjunction with other machine learning algorithms to improve their performance. In AdaBoost, the training data points are drawn from a distribution to train the current classifier. This distribution is updated iteratively so that the subsequent classifiers get to focus on the more difficult data points. The difficult data points are the ones that are misclassified. This is done by updating the distribution at each step. This will make the data points that were previously misclassified more likely to come up in the next sample dataset that's used for training.

These classifiers are then cascaded, and the decision is taken through weighted majority voting.

Create a new Python file and import the following packages:

```
import numpy as np
import matplotlib.pyplot as plt
from sklearn.tree import DecisionTreeRegressor
from sklearn.ensemble import AdaBoostRegressor
from sklearn import datasets
from sklearn.metrics import mean_squared_error, explained_variance_
score
from sklearn.model_selection import train_test_split
from sklearn.utils import shuffle

from utilities import visualize_feature_importances
```

We will use the inbuilt housing dataset available in scikit-learn:

```
# Load housing data
housing_data = datasets.load_boston()
```

Shuffle the data so that we don't bias our analysis:

```
# Shuffle the data
X, y = shuffle(housing_data.data, housing_data.target, random_state=7)
```

Split the dataset into training and testing:

```
# Split data into training and testing datasets
X_train, X_test, y_train, y_test = train_test_split(
        X, y, test_size=0.2, random_state=7)
```

Define and train an `AdaBoostregressor` using the decision tree regressor as the individual model:

```
# AdaBoost Regressor model
regressor = AdaBoostRegressor(DecisionTreeRegressor(max_depth=4),
        n_estimators=400, random_state=7)
regressor.fit(X_train, y_train)
```

Estimate the performance of the regressor:

```
# Evaluate performance of AdaBoost regressor
y_pred = regressor.predict(X_test)
mse = mean_squared_error(y_test, y_pred)
evs = explained_variance_score(y_test, y_pred )
print("\nADABOOST REGRESSOR")
print("Mean squared error =", round(mse, 2))
print("Explained variance score =", round(evs, 2))
```

This regressor has an inbuilt method that can be called to compute the relative feature importance:

```
# Extract feature importances
feature_importances = regressor.feature_importances_
feature_names = housing_data.feature_names
```

Normalize the values of the relative feature importance:

```
# Normalize the importance values
feature_importances = 100.0 * (feature_importances / max(feature_
importances))
```

Sort them so that they can be plotted:

```
# Sort the values and flip them
index_sorted = np.flipud(np.argsort(feature_importances))
```

Arrange the ticks on the x axis for the bar graph:

```
# Arrange the X ticks
pos = np.arange(index_sorted.shape[0]) + 0.5
```

Plot the bar graph:

```
# Plot the bar graph
plt.figure()
```

```
plt.bar(pos, feature_importances[index_sorted], align='center')
plt.xticks(pos, feature_names[index_sorted])
plt.ylabel('Relative Importance')
plt.title('Feature importance using AdaBoost regressor')
plt.show()
```

The full code is given in the file `feature_importance.py`. If you run the code, you should see the following output:

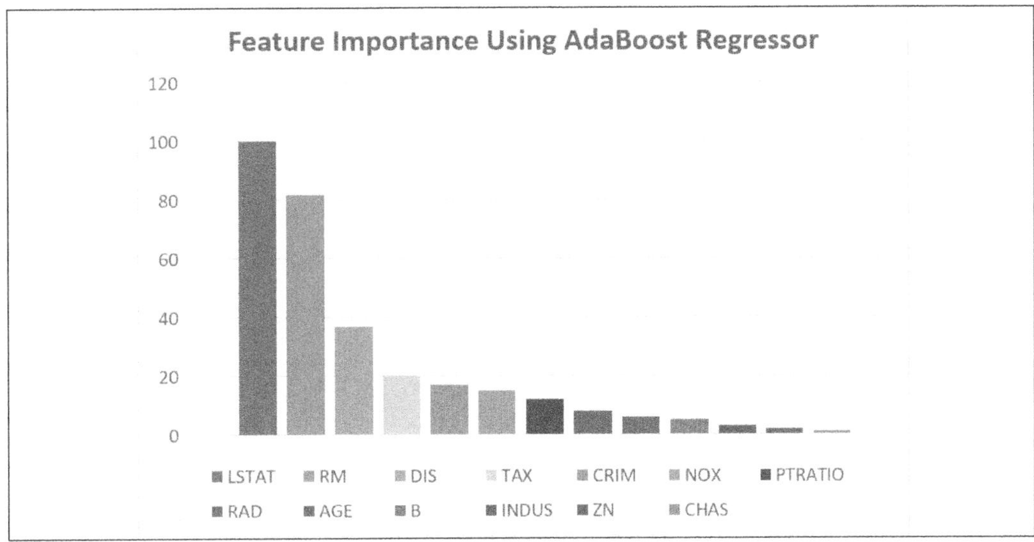

Figure 18: Feature importance using Adaboost Regressor

According to this analysis, the feature LSTAT is the most important feature in that dataset.

Predicting traffic using an extremely random forest regressor

Let's apply the concepts learned in the previous sections to a real-world problem. A dataset available at will be used: `https://archive.ics.uci.edu/ml/datasets/Dodgers+Loop+Sensor`. This dataset consists of data that counts the number of vehicles passing by on the road during baseball games played at Los Angeles Dodgers stadium. In order to make the data readily available for analysis, we need to pre-process it. The pre-processed data is in the file `traffic_data.txt`. In this file, each line contains comma-separated strings. Let's take the first line as an example:

```
Tuesday,00:00,San Francisco,no,3
```

With reference to the preceding line, it is formatted as follows:

Day of the week, time of the day, opponent team, binary value indicating whether a baseball game is currently going on (yes/no), number of vehicles passing by.

Our goal is to predict the number of vehicles going by using the given information. Since the output variable is continuous valued, we need to build a regressor that can predict the output. We will be using extremely random forests to build this regressor. Let's go ahead and see how to do that.

Create a new Python file and import the following packages:

```
import numpy as np
import matplotlib.pyplot as plt
from sklearn.metrics import classification_report, mean_absolute_error
from sklearn.model_selection import train_test_split
from sklearn import preprocessing
from sklearn.ensemble import ExtraTreesRegressor
from sklearn.metrics import classification_report
```

Load the data in the file `traffic_data.txt`:

```
# Load input data
input_file = 'traffic_data.txt'
data = []
with open(input_file, 'r') as f:
    for line in f.readlines():
        items = line[:-1].split(',')
        data.append(items)

data = np.array(data)
```

The non-numerical features in the data need to be encoded. It is also important not to encode numerical features. Each feature that needs to be encoded needs to have a separate label encoder. We need to keep track of these encoders because we will need them when we want to compute the output for an unknown data point. Let's create those label encoders:

```
# Convert string data to numerical data
label_encoder = []
X_encoded = np.empty(data.shape)
for i, item in enumerate(data[0]):
    if item.isdigit():
        X_encoded[:, i] = data[:, i]
```

```
        else:
            label_encoder.append(preprocessing.LabelEncoder())
            X_encoded[:, i] = label_encoder[-1].fit_transform(data[:, i])

X = X_encoded[:, :-1].astype(int)
y = X_encoded[:, -1].astype(int)
```

Split the data into training and testing datasets:

```
# Split data into training and testing datasets
X_train, X_test, y_train, y_test = train_test_split(
        X, y, test_size=0.25, random_state=5)
```

Train an extremely random forests regressor:

```
# Extremely Random Forests regressor
params = {'n_estimators': 100, 'max_depth': 4, 'random_state': 0}
regressor = ExtraTreesRegressor(**params)
regressor.fit(X_train, y_train)
```

Compute the performance of the regressor on testing data:

```
# Compute the regressor performance on test data
y_pred = regressor.predict(X_test)
print("Mean absolute error:", round(mean_absolute_error(y_test,
y_pred), 2))
```

Let's see how to compute the output for an unknown data point. Label encoders will be used to convert non-numerical features into numerical values:

```
# Testing encoding on single data instance
test_datapoint = ['Saturday', '10:20', 'Atlanta', 'no']
test_datapoint_encoded = [-1] * len(test_datapoint)
```

Predict the output:

```
# Predict the output for the test datapoint
print("Predicted traffic:", int(regressor.predict([test_datapoint_
encoded])[0]))
```

The full code is given in the file `traffic_prediction.py`. If you run the code, you will get `6` as the output, which is close to the actual value, and it confirms that our model is making decent predictions. You can confirm this from the data file.

Summary

In this chapter, we learned about ensemble learning and how it can be used in the real world. We discussed decision trees and how to build a classifier based on it.

We learned about random forests and extremely random forests, which are created from ensembling multiple decision trees. We discussed how to build classifiers based on them. We understood how to estimate the confidence measure of the predictions. We also learned how to deal with the class imbalance problem.

We discussed how to find the most optimal training parameters to build the models using grid search. We learned how to compute relative feature importance. We then applied ensemble learning techniques to a real-world problem, where we predicted traffic using an extremely random forest regressor.

In the next chapter, we will discuss unsupervised learning and how to detect patterns in stock market data.

7

Detecting Patterns with Unsupervised Learning

In this chapter, we are going to learn about unsupervised learning and how to use it in real-world situations. By the end of this chapter, you will have a better understanding of the following topics:

- Unsupervised learning definition
- Clustering data with the K-Means algorithm
- Estimating the number of clusters with the Mean Shift algorithm
- Estimating the quality of clustering with silhouette scores
- Gaussian Mixture Models
- Building a classifier based on Gaussian Mixture Models
- Finding subgroups in stock markets the using Affinity Propagation model
- Segmenting the market based on shopping patterns

What is unsupervised learning?

Unsupervised learning refers to the process of building machine learning models without using labeled training data. Unsupervised learning finds applications in diverse fields of study, including market segmentation, stock markets, natural language processing, and computer vision, to name a few.

In the previous chapters, we were dealing with data that had labels associated with it. When we have labeled training data, algorithms learn to classify data based on those labels. In the real world, labeled data might not always be available.

Sometimes, a large quantity of data exists without labeling and it needs to be categorized in some way. This is the perfect use case for unsupervised learning. Unsupervised learning algorithms attempt to classify data into subgroups within a given dataset using some similarity metric.

When we have a dataset without any labels, we assume that the data is generated because of latent variables that govern the distribution in some way. The process of learning can then proceed in a hierarchical manner, starting from the individual data points. We can build deeper levels of representation for the data by finding natural clusters of similarities and trying to obtain signal and insights by classifying and segmenting the data. Let's see some of the ways in which data can be classified using unsupervised learning.

Clustering data with the K-Means algorithm

Clustering is one of the most popular unsupervised learning techniques. This technique is used to analyze data and find clusters within that data. In order to find these clusters, we use a similarity measurement such as the Euclidean distance to find subgroups. This similarity measure can estimate the tightness of a cluster. Clustering is the process of organizing data into subgroups whose elements are like each other.

The goal of the algorithm is to identify the intrinsic properties of data points that make them belong to the same subgroup. There is no universal similarity metric that works in all cases. For example, we might be interested in finding the representative data point for each subgroup, or we might be interested in finding the outliers in the data. Depending on the situation, different metrics might be more appropriate than others.

The K-Means algorithm is a well-known algorithm for clustering data. In order to use it, the number of clusters is assumed beforehand. The data is segmented into *K* subgroups using various data attributes. The number of clusters is fixed, and the data is classified based on that number. The main idea here is that we need to update the locations of the centroids with each iteration. A centroid is the location representing the center of the cluster. We continue iterating until we have placed the centroids at their optimal locations.

We can see that the initial placement of centroids plays an important role in the algorithm. These centroids should be placed in a clever manner, because this directly impacts the results. A good strategy is to place them as far away from each other as possible.

The basic K-Means algorithm places these centroids randomly where `K-Means++` chooses these points algorithmically from the input list of data points. It tries to place the initial centroids far from each other so that they converge quickly. We then go through the training dataset and assign each data point to the closest centroid.

Once we go through the entire dataset, the first iteration is over. The points have been grouped based on the initialized centroids. The location of the centroids is recalculated based on the new clusters that were obtained at the end of the first iteration. Once a new set of *K* centroids is obtained, the process is repeated. We iterate through the dataset and assign each point to the closest centroid.

As the steps keep on getting repeated, the centroids keep moving to their equilibrium position. After a certain number of iterations, the centroids do not change their locations anymore. The centroids converge to a final location. These *K* centroids are the values that will be used for inference.

Let's apply K-Means clustering on two-dimensional data to see how it works. We will be using the data in the `data_clustering.txt` file provided to you. Each line contains two comma-separated numbers.

Create a new Python file and import the following packages:

```
import numpy as np
import matplotlib.pyplot as plt
from sklearn.cluster import KMeans
from sklearn import metrics
```

Load the input data from the file:

```
# Load input data
X = np.loadtxt('data_clustering.txt', delimiter=',')
```

Define the number of clusters before applying the K-Means algorithm:

```
num_clusters = 5
```

Visualize the input data to see what the spread looks like:

```
# Plot input data
plt.figure()
plt.scatter(X[:,0], X[:,1], marker='o', facecolors='none',
        edgecolors='black', s=80)
x_min, x_max = X[:, 0].min() - 1, X[:, 0].max() + 1
y_min, y_max = X[:, 1].min() - 1, X[:, 1].max() + 1
plt.title('Input data')
plt.xlim(x_min, x_max)
plt.ylim(y_min, y_max)
plt.xticks(())
plt.yticks(())
```

It can be seen that there are five groups within this data. Create the `KMeans` object using the initialization parameters. The `init` parameter represents the method of initialization to select the initial centers of clusters. Instead of selecting them randomly, we use `k-means++` to select these centers in a smarter way. This ensures that the algorithm converges quickly. The `n_clusters` parameter refers to the number of clusters. The `n_init` parameter refers to the number of times the algorithm should run before deciding upon the best outcome:

```
# Create KMeans object
kmeans = KMeans(init='k-means++', n_clusters=num_clusters, n_init=10)
```

Train the K-Means model with the input data:

```
# Train the KMeans clustering model
kmeans.fit(X)
```

To visualize the boundaries, we need to create a grid of points and evaluate the model on all those points. Let's define the step size of this grid:

```
# Step size of the mesh
step_size = 0.01
```

We define the grid of points and ensure that we are covering all the values in the input data:

```
# Define the grid of points to plot the boundaries
x_min, x_max = X[:, 0].min() - 1, X[:, 0].max() + 1
y_min, y_max = X[:, 1].min() - 1, X[:, 1].max() + 1
x_vals, y_vals = np.meshgrid(np.arange(x_min, x_max, step_size),
        np.arange(y_min, y_max, step_size))
```

Predict the outputs for all the points on the grid using the trained K-Means model:

```
# Predict output labels for all the points on the grid
output = kmeans.predict(np.c_[x_vals.ravel(), y_vals.ravel()])
```

Plot all output values and color each region:

```
# Plot different regions and color them
output = output.reshape(x_vals.shape)
plt.figure()
plt.clf()
plt.imshow(output, interpolation='nearest',
           extent=(x_vals.min(), x_vals.max(),
               y_vals.min(), y_vals.max()),
           cmap=plt.cm.Paired,
           aspect='auto',
           origin='lower')
```

Overlay input data points on top of these colored regions:

```
# Overlay input points
plt.scatter(X[:,0], X[:,1], marker='o', facecolors='none',

        edgecolors='black', s=80)
```

Plot the centers of the clusters obtained using the K-Means algorithm:

```
# Plot the centers of clusters
cluster_centers = kmeans.cluster_centers_
plt.scatter(cluster_centers[:,0], cluster_centers[:,1],
        marker='o', s=210, linewidths=4, color='black',
        zorder=12, facecolors='black')

x_min, x_max = X[:, 0].min() - 1, X[:, 0].max() + 1
y_min, y_max = X[:, 1].min() - 1, X[:, 1].max() + 1
plt.title('Boundaries of clusters')
plt.xlim(x_min, x_max)
plt.ylim(y_min, y_max)
plt.xticks(())
plt.yticks(())
plt.show()
```

The full code is given in the `kmeans.py` file. If you run the code, you will see two screenshots. The first screenshot is the input data:

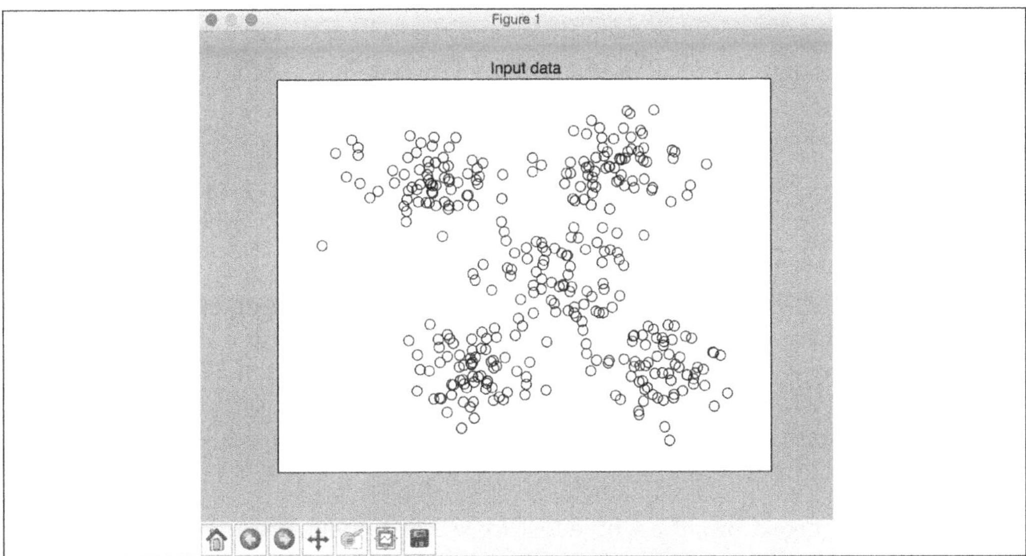

Figure 1: Visualization of input data

The second screenshot represents the boundaries obtained using K-Means:

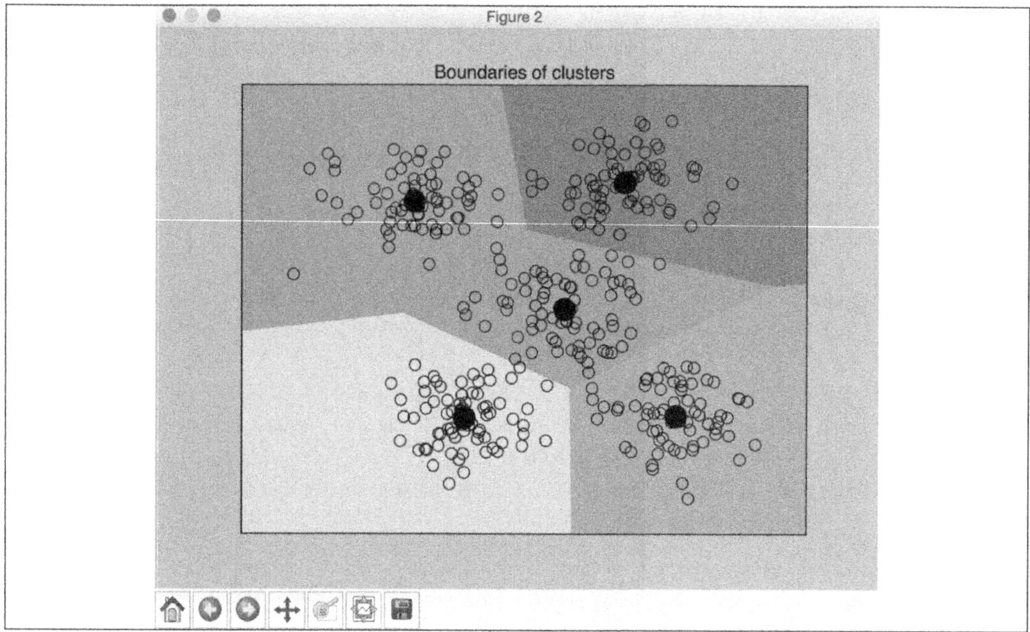

Figure 2: Kmeans boundaries

The black-filled circle at the center of each cluster represents the centroid of that cluster.

With the K-Means algorithm covered, we'll now move on to another approach – the Mean Shift algorithm.

Estimating the number of clusters with the Mean Shift algorithm

Mean Shift is a powerful algorithm used in unsupervised learning. It is a non-parametric algorithm used frequently for clustering. It is non-parametric because it does not make any assumptions about the underlying distributions. This contrasts with parametric techniques, where it is assumed that the underlying data follows a standard probability distribution. Mean Shift finds a lot of applications in fields such as object tracking and real-time data analysis.

In the Mean Shift algorithm, the whole feature space is considered as a probability density function. We start with the training dataset and assume that it has been sampled from a probability density function.

In this framework, the clusters correspond to the local maxima of the underlying distribution. If there are *K* clusters, then there are *K* peaks in the underlying data distribution and Mean Shift will identify those peaks.

The goal of Mean Shift is to identify the location of centroids. For each data point in the training dataset, it defines a window around it. It then computes the centroid for this window and updates the location to this new centroid. It then repeats the process for this new location by defining a window around it. As we keep doing this, we move closer to the peak of the cluster. Each data point will move towards the cluster it belongs to. The movement is towards a region of higher density.

The centroids (also called means) keep on getting shifted towards the peaks of each cluster. The algorithm gets its name from the fact that the means keep getting shifted. The shift continues to happen until the algorithm converges, at which stage the centroids don't move anymore.

Let's see how to use `MeanShift` to estimate the optimal number of clusters in the given dataset. The data in the `data_clustering.txt` file will be used for analysis. It is the same file that was used in the *Clustering data with the K-Means algorithm* section.

Create a new Python file and import the following packages:

```
import numpy as np
import matplotlib.pyplot as plt
from sklearn.cluster import MeanShift, estimate_bandwidth
from itertools import cycle
```

Load the input data:

```
# Load data from input file
X = np.loadtxt('data_clustering.txt', delimiter=',')
```

Estimate the bandwidth of the input data. Bandwidth is a parameter of the underlying kernel density estimation process used in the Mean Shift algorithm. The bandwidth affects the overall convergence rate of the algorithm and the number of clusters that we will end up with in the end. Hence, this is a crucial parameter - if the bandwidth is too small, it might result in too many clusters, whereas if the value is too large, then it will merge distinct clusters.

The `quantile` parameter impacts how the bandwidth is estimated. A higher value for a quantile will increase the estimated bandwidth, resulting in fewer clusters:

```
# Estimate the bandwidth of X
bandwidth_X = estimate_bandwidth(X, quantile=0.1, n_samples=len(X))
```

Then train the Mean Shift clustering model using the estimated bandwidth:

```
# Cluster data with MeanShift
meanshift_model = MeanShift(bandwidth=bandwidth_X, bin_seeding=True)
meanshift_model.fit(X)
```

Extract the centers of all the clusters:

```
# Extract the centers of clusters
cluster_centers = meanshift_model.cluster_centers_
print('\nCenters of clusters:\n', cluster_centers)
```

Extract the number of clusters:

```
# Estimate the number of clusters
labels = meanshift_model.labels_
num_clusters = len(np.unique(labels))
print("\nNumber of clusters in input data =", num_clusters)
```

Visualize the data points:

```
# Plot the points and cluster centers
plt.figure()
markers = 'o*xvs'
for i, marker in zip(range(num_clusters), markers):
    # Plot points that belong to the current cluster
    plt.scatter(X[labels==i, 0], X[labels==i, 1], marker=marker,
color='black')
```

Plot the center of the current cluster:

```
    # Plot the cluster center
    cluster_center = cluster_centers[i]
    plt.plot(cluster_center[0], cluster_center[1], marker='o',
            markerfacecolor='black', markeredgecolor='black',
            markersize=15)

plt.title('Clusters')
plt.show()
```

The full code is given in the `mean_shift.py` file. If you run the code, you will see the following screenshot, representing the clusters and their centers:

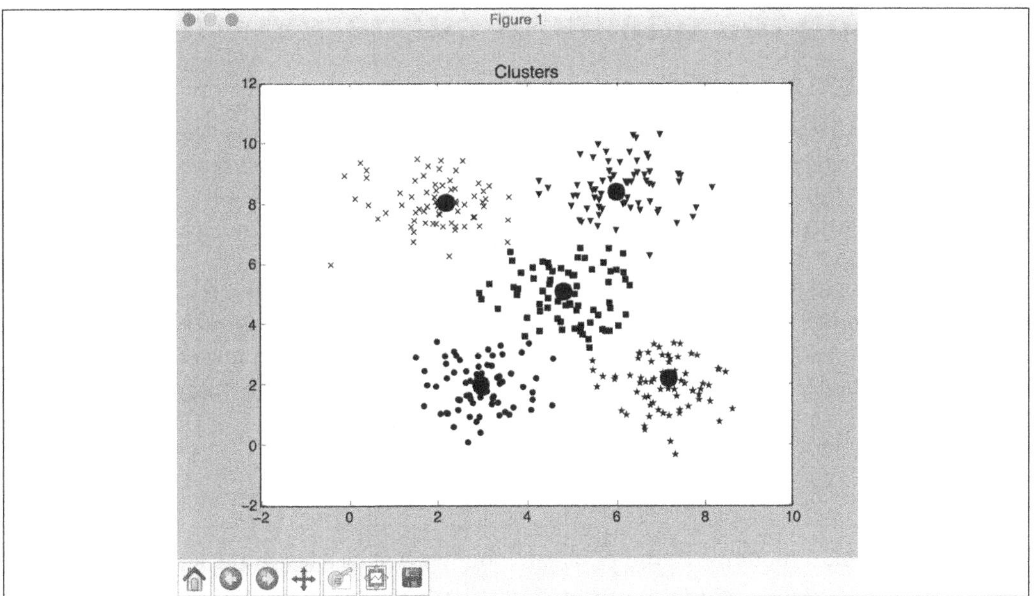

Figure 3: Centers of the cluster plot

You will see the following output:

```
Centers of clusters:
 [[ 2.95568966  1.95775862]
 [ 7.17563636  2.18145455]
 [ 2.17603774  8.03283019]
 [ 5.97960784  8.39078431]
 [ 4.81044444  5.07111111]]

Number of clusters in input data = 5
```

Figure 4: Centers of the cluster output

This completes our overview of Mean Shift. So far, we've dealt with how to cluster out data. Next, we'll move on to how we can estimate the quality of clustering, using the silhouette method.

Estimating the quality of clustering with silhouette scores

If data is naturally organized into several distinct clusters, then it is easy to visually examine it and draw some inferences. This is rarely the case in the real world, unfortunately. Data in the real world is huge and messy. So, we need a way to quantify the quality of the clustering.

Silhouette refers to a method used to check the consistency of clusters in data. It gives an estimate of how well each data point fits with its cluster. The silhouette score is a metric that measures the similarity of a data point to its own cluster, as compared to other clusters. The silhouette score works with any similarity metric.

For each data point, the silhouette score is computed using the following formula:

$$silhouette\ score = (p - q) / max(p, q)$$

Here, p is the mean distance to the points in the nearest cluster that the data point is not a part of, and q is the mean intra-cluster distance to all the points in its own cluster.

The value of the silhouette score range lies between *-1* and *1*. A score closer to *1* indicates that the data point is very similar to other data points in the cluster, whereas a score closer to *-1* indicates that the data point is not like other data points in the cluster. One way to think about it is if there are too many points with negative silhouette scores, then there may be too few or too many clusters in the data. We need to run the clustering algorithm again to find the optimal number of clusters. Ideally, we want to have a high positive value. Depending on the business problem, we do not need to optimize and have the highest possible value, but in general, if we have a silhouette score that is close to *1*, it indicates that the data clustered nicely. If the scores are close to *-1*, it indicates that the variable that we are using to classify is noisy and does not contain much of a signal.

Let's see how to estimate the clustering performance using silhouette scores. Create a new Python file and import the following packages:

```
import numpy as np
import matplotlib.pyplot as plt
from sklearn import metrics
from sklearn.cluster import KMeans
```

We will be using the data in the `data_quality.txt` file provided to you. Each line contains two comma-separated numbers:

```
# Load data from input file
X = np.loadtxt('data_quality.txt', delimiter=',')
```

Initialize the variables. The `values` array will contain a list of values to iterate over and to find the optimal number of clusters:

```
# Initialize variables
scores = []
values = np.arange(2, 10)
```

Iterate through all the values and build a K-Means model during each iteration:

```
# Iterate through the defined range
for num_clusters in values:
    # Train the KMeans clustering model
    kmeans = KMeans(init='k-means++', n_clusters=num_clusters, n_
init=10)
    kmeans.fit(X)
```

Estimate the silhouette score for the current clustering model using the Euclidean distance metric:

```
    score = metrics.silhouette_score(X, kmeans.labels_,
                metric='euclidean', sample_size=len(X))
```

Print the silhouette score for the current value:

```
    print("\nNumber of clusters =", num_clusters)
    print("Silhouette score =", score)

    scores.append(score)
```

Visualize the silhouette scores for various values:

```
# Plot silhouette scores
plt.figure()
plt.bar(values, scores, width=0.7, color='black', align='center')
plt.title('Silhouette score vs number of clusters')
```

Extract the best score and the corresponding value for the number of clusters:

```
# Extract best score and optimal number of clusters
num_clusters = np.argmax(scores) + values[0]
print('\nOptimal number of clusters =', num_clusters)
```

Visualize the input data:

```
# Plot data
plt.figure()
plt.scatter(X[:,0], X[:,1], color='black', s=80, marker='o',
facecolors='none')
x_min, x_max = X[:, 0].min() - 1, X[:, 0].max() + 1
y_min, y_max = X[:, 1].min() - 1, X[:, 1].max() + 1
```

```
plt.title('Input data')
plt.xlim(x_min, x_max)
plt.ylim(y_min, y_max)
plt.xticks(())
plt.yticks(())

plt.show()
```

The full code is given in the file `clustering_quality.py`. If you run the code, you will see two screenshots. The first screenshot is the input data:

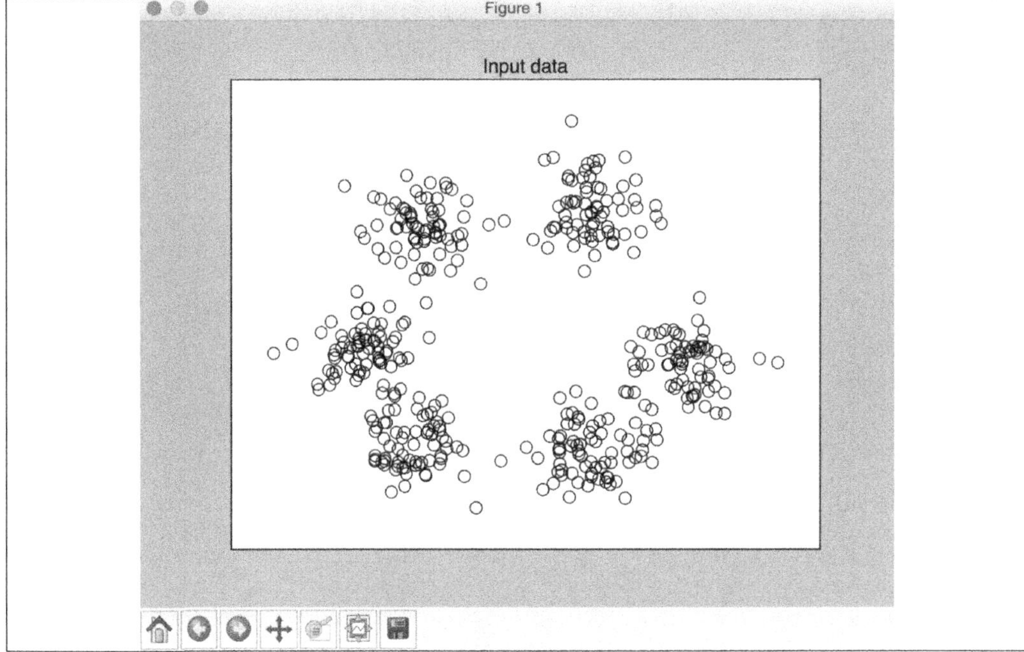

Figure 5: Visualization of the input data

We can see that there are six clusters in the data. The second screenshot represents the scores for various values of the number of clusters:

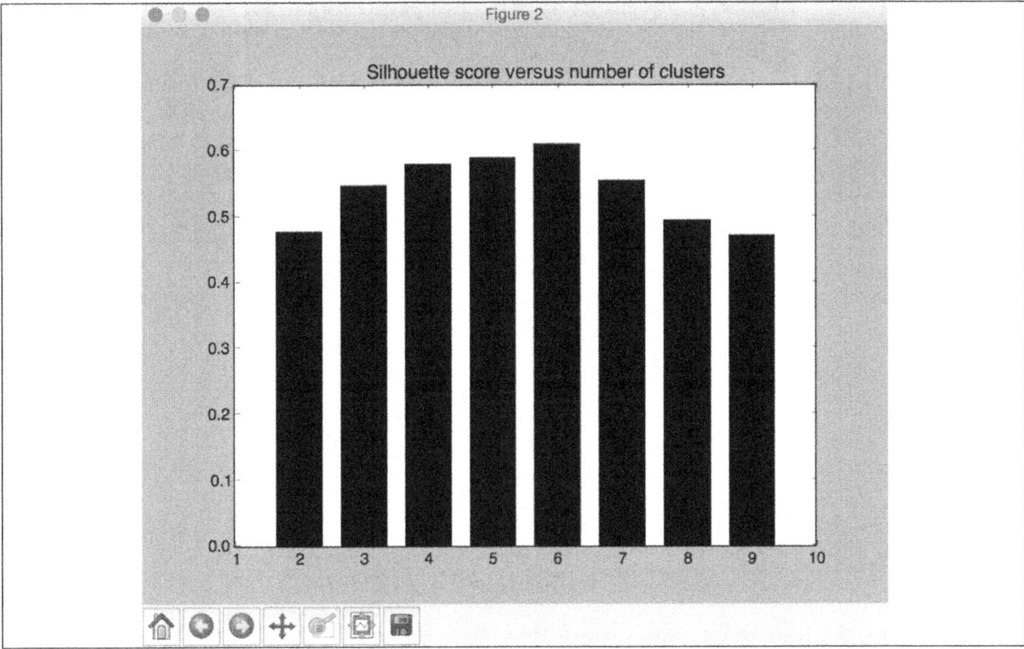

Figure 6: Silhoutte score vs number of clusters

We can verify that the silhouette score is peaking at the value of `0.6`, which is consistent with the data. You will see the following output:

```
Number of clusters = 2
Silhouette score = 0.477626248705

Number of clusters = 3
Silhouette score = 0.547174241173

Number of clusters = 4
Silhouette score = 0.579480188969

Number of clusters = 5
Silhouette score = 0.589003263565

Number of clusters = 6
Silhouette score = 0.609690411895

Number of clusters = 7
Silhouette score = 0.554310234032

Number of clusters = 8
Silhouette score = 0.494433661954

Number of clusters = 9
Silhouette score = 0.471414689437

Optimal number of clusters = 6
```

Figure 7: Optimal number of clusters output

In this section, we learned about silhouette scores and how they help us understand clusters. We will now learn about Gaussian Mixture models, which are yet another unsupervised learning technique to classify and cluster data.

What are Gaussian Mixture Models?

Before we discuss **Gaussian Mixture Models (GMMs)**, let's first understand what a Mixture Model is. A Mixture Model is a type of probability density model where it is assumed that the data is governed by several component distributions. If these distributions are Gaussian, then the model becomes a Gaussian Mixture Model. These component distributions are combined in order to provide a multi-modal density function, which becomes a mixture model.

Let's look at an example to understand how Mixture Models work. We want to model the shopping habits of all the people in South America. One way to do it would be to model the whole continent and fit everything into a single model, but people in different countries shop differently. We therefore need to understand how people in individual countries shop and how they behave.

To get a good representative model, we need to account for all the variations within the continent. In this case, we can use mixture models to model the shopping habits of individual countries and then combine all of them into a Mixture Model.

This way, nuances in the data of the underlying behavior of individual countries are not missed. By not enforcing a single model on all of the countries, a more accurate model is created.

An interesting point to note is that mixture models are semi-parametric, which means that they are partially dependent on a set of predefined functions. They can provide greater precision and flexibility in modeling the underlying distributions of the data. They can smooth the gaps that result from having sparse data.

Once the function is defined, the mixture model goes from being semi-parametric to parametric. Hence a GMM is a parametric model represented as a weighted summation of component Gaussian functions. We assume that the data is being generated by a set of Gaussian models that are combined in some way. GMMs are very powerful and are used in many fields. The parameters of the GMM are estimated from training data using algorithms like **Expectation–Maximization** (**EM**) or **Maximum A-Posteriori** (**MAP**) estimation. Some of the popular applications of GMM include image database retrieval, modeling stock market fluctuations, biometric verification, and so on.

Now that we've described what GMMs are, let's see how they can be applied.

Building a classifier based on Gaussian Mixture Models

Let's build a classifier based on a Gaussian Mixture Model. Create a new Python file and import the following packages:

```
import numpy as np
import matplotlib.pyplot as plt
from matplotlib import patches

from sklearn import datasets
from sklearn.mixture import GaussianMixture
from sklearn.model_selection import StratifiedKFold
from sklearn.model_selection import train_test_split
```

Let's use the Iris dataset available in scikit-learn for analysis:

```
# Load the iris dataset
iris = datasets.load_iris()

X, y = datasets.load_iris(return_X_y=True)
```

Split the dataset into training and testing using an 80/20 split. The `n_splits` parameter specifies the number of subsets you'll obtain. We are using a value of `5`, which means the dataset will be split into five parts.

We will use four parts for training and one part for testing, which gives a split of 80/20:

```
# Split dataset into training and testing (80/20 split)
skf = StratifiedKFold(n_splits=5) #
skf.get_n_splits(X, y)

X_train, X_test, y_train, y_test = train_test_split(X, y, test_
size=0.4, random_state=0)
```

Extract the number of classes in the training data:

```
# Extract the number of classes
num_classes = len(np.unique(y_train))
```

Build a GMM-based classifier using the relevant parameters. The `n_components` parameter specifies the number of components in the underlying distribution. In this case, it will be the number of distinct classes in the data. We need to specify the type of covariance to use. In this case, full covariance will be used. The `init_params` parameter controls the parameters that need to be updated during the training process. The value `kmeans` was used, which means weights and covariance parameters will be updated during training. The `max_iter` parameter refers to the number of Expectation-Maximization iterations that will be performed during training:

```
# Build GMM
classifier = GaussianMixture(n_components=num_classes, covariance_
type='full', init_params='kmeans', max_iter=20)
```

Initialize the means of the classifier:

```
# Initialize the GMM means
classifier.means_ = np.array([X_train[y_train == i].mean(axis=0) for i
in range(num_classes)])
```

Train the Gaussian mixture model classifier using the training data:

```
# Train the GMM classifier
classifier.fit(X_train)
```

Visualize the boundaries of the classifier. Then extract the eigenvalues and eigenvectors to estimate how to draw the elliptical boundaries around the clusters. For a quick refresher on eigenvalues and eigenvectors, refer to: `https://math.mit.edu/~gs/linearalgebra/ila0601.pdf`. Let's go ahead and plot the following:

```
# Draw boundaries
plt.figure()
colors = 'bgr'
for i, color in enumerate(colors):
    # Extract eigenvalues and eigenvectors
    eigenvalues, eigenvectors = np.linalg.eigh(
            classifier.covariances_[i][:2, :2])
```

Normalize the first eigenvector:

```
    # Normalize the first eigenvector
    norm_vec = eigenvectors[0] / np.linalg.norm(eigenvectors[0])
```

The ellipses need to be rotated to accurately show the distribution. Estimate the angle:

```
    # Extract the angle of tilt
    angle = np.arctan2(norm_vec[1], norm_vec[0])
    angle = 180 * angle / np.pi
```

Magnify the ellipses for visualization. The eigenvalues control the size of the ellipses:

```
    # Scaling factor to magnify the ellipses
    # (random value chosen to suit our needs)
    scaling_factor = 8
    eigenvalues *= scaling_factor
```

Draw the ellipses:

```
    # Draw the ellipse
    ellipse = patches.Ellipse(classifier.means_[i, :2],
            eigenvalues[0], eigenvalues[1], 180 + angle,
            color=color)
    axis_handle = plt.subplot(1, 1, 1)
    ellipse.set_clip_box(axis_handle.bbox)
    ellipse.set_alpha(0.6)
    axis_handle.add_artist(ellipse)
```

Overlay input data on the figure:

```
# Plot the data
colors = 'bgr'
for i, color in enumerate(colors):
    cur_data = iris.data[iris.target == i]
    plt.scatter(cur_data[:,0], cur_data[:,1], marker='o',
            facecolors='none', edgecolors='black', s=40,
            label=iris.target_names[i])
```

Overlay test data on this figure:

```
        test_data = X_test[y_test == i]
        plt.scatter(test_data[:,0], test_data[:,1], marker='s',
                facecolors='black', edgecolors='black', s=40 ,
                label=iris.target_names[i])
```

Compute the predicted output for the training and testing data:

```
    # Compute predictions for training and testing data
    y_train_pred = classifier.predict(X_train)
    accuracy_training = np.mean(y_train_pred.ravel() == y_train.ravel()) *
    100
    print('Accuracy on training data =', accuracy_training)

    y_test_pred = classifier.predict(X_test)
    accuracy_testing = np.mean(y_test_pred.ravel() == y_test.ravel()) *
    100
    print('Accuracy on testing data =', accuracy_testing)

    plt.title('GMM classifier')
    plt.xticks(())
    plt.yticks(())

    plt.show()
```

The full code is given in the file `gmm_classifier.py`. After running the code, you will see the following output:

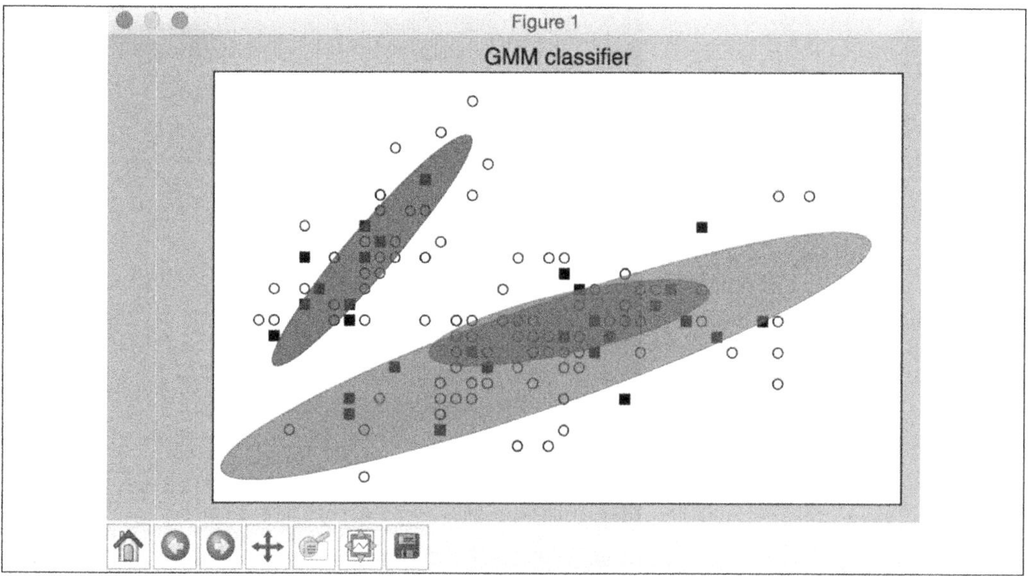

Figure 8: Gaussian Mixture Model classifier plot

The input data consists of three distributions. The three ellipses of various sizes and angles represent the underlying distributions in the input data. You will see the following output:

```
Accuracy on training data = 87.5
Accuracy on testing data = 86.6666666667
```

In this section, we learned about Gaussian Mixture Models and we developed an example using Python. In the next section, we will learn about another unsupervised learning technique to classify data, called the Affinity Propagation model and use it to find subgroups in stock market data.

Finding subgroups in stock market using the Affinity Propagation model

Affinity Propagation is a clustering algorithm that doesn't require a number of clusters to be specified beforehand. Because of its generic nature and simplicity of implementation, it has found a lot of applications in many fields. It finds out representative clusters, called exemplars, using a technique called message passing. It starts by specifying the measures of similarity that need to be considered. It simultaneously considers all training data points as potential exemplars. It then passes messages between the data points until it finds a set of exemplars.

The message passing happens in two alternate steps, called **responsibility** and **availability**. Responsibility refers to the message sent from members of the cluster to candidate exemplars, indicating how well suited the data point would be as a member of this exemplar's cluster. Availability refers to the message sent from candidate exemplars to potential members of the cluster, indicating how well suited it would be as an exemplar. It keeps doing this until the algorithm converges on an optimal set of exemplars.

There is also a parameter called preference, which controls the number of exemplars that will be found. If a high value is chosen, it will cause the algorithm to find too many clusters. If a low value is chosen, it will lead to a small number of clusters. An optimal value would be the median similarity between the points.

Let's use the Affinity Propagation model to find subgroups in the stock market. We will be using the stock quote variation between opening and closing as the governing feature. Create a new Python file and import the following packages:

```
import datetime
import json
```

```
import numpy as np
import matplotlib.pyplot as plt
from sklearn import covariance, cluster
import yfinance as yf
```

The stock market data available in matplotlib will be used as input. The company symbols are mapped to their full names in the file `company_symbol_mapping.json`:

```
# Input file containing company symbols
input_file = 'company_symbol_mapping.json'
```

Load the company symbol map from the file:

```
# Load the company symbol map
with open(input_file, 'r') as f:
    company_symbols_map = json.loads(f.read())

symbols, names = np.array(list(company_symbols_map.items())).T
```

Load the stock quotes from matplotlib:

```
# Load the historical stock quotes
start_date = datetime.datetime(2019, 1, 1)
end_date = datetime.datetime(2019, 1, 31)
quotes = [yf.Ticker(symbol).history(start=start_date, end=end_date)
                for symbol in symbols]
```

Compute the difference between opening and closing quotes:

```
# Extract opening and closing quotes
opening_quotes = np.array([quote.Open for quote in quotes]).astype(np.
float)
closing_quotes = np.array([quote.Close for quote in quotes]).
astype(np.float)

# Compute differences between opening and closing quotes
quotes_diff = closing_quotes - opening_quotes
```

Normalize the data:

```
# Normalize the data
X = quotes_diff.copy().T
X /= X.std(axis=0)
```

Create a graph model:

```
# Create a graph model
edge_model = covariance.GraphLassoCV()
```

Train the model:

```
# Train the model
with np.errstate(invalid='ignore'):
    edge_model.fit(X)
```

Build the Affinity Propagation clustering model using the edge model we just trained:

```
# Build clustering model using Affinity Propagation model
_, labels = cluster.affinity_propagation(edge_model.covariance_)
num_labels = labels.max()
```

Print the output:

```
# Print the results of clustering
print('\nClustering of stocks based on difference in opening and
closing quotes:\n')
for i in range(num_labels + 1):
    print("Cluster", i+1, "==>", ', '.join(names[labels == i]))
```

The full code is given in the file `stocks.py`. When running the code, you will see the following output:

```
Clustering of stocks based on difference in opening and closing quotes:

Cluster 1 ==> Kraft Foods
Cluster 2 ==> CVS, Walgreen
Cluster 3 ==> Amazon, Yahoo
Cluster 4 ==> Cablevision
Cluster 5 ==> Pfizer, Sanofi-Aventis, GlaxoSmithKline, Novartis
Cluster 6 ==> HP, General Electrics, 3M, Microsoft, Cisco, IBM, Texas instruments, Dell
Cluster 7 ==> Coca Cola, Kimberly-Clark, Pepsi, Procter Gamble, Kellogg, Colgate-Palmolive
Cluster 8 ==> Comcast, Wells Fargo, Xerox, Home Depot, Wal-Mart, Marriott, Navistar, DuPont de Nemours, A
merican express, Ryder, JPMorgan Chase, AIG, Time Warner, Bank of America, Goldman Sachs
Cluster 9 ==> Canon, Unilever, Mitsubishi, Apple, Mc Donalds, Boeing, Toyota, Caterpillar, Ford, Honda, S
AP, Sony
Cluster 10 ==> Valero Energy, Exxon, ConocoPhillips, Chevron, Total
Cluster 11 ==> Raytheon, General Dynamics, Lookheed Martin, Northrop Grumman
```

Figure 9: Clustering of stocks based on difference in opening and closing quotes

This output represents the various subgroups in the stock market during that time period. Please note that the clusters might appear in a different order when you run the code.

Now that we've covered the Affinity Propagation model and learned some new concepts, we'll move on to the final section of the chapter, in which we will use unsupervised learning techniques to segment market data using customer shopping habits.

Segmenting the market based on shopping patterns

Let's see how to apply unsupervised learning techniques to segment the market based on customer shopping habits. You have been provided with a file named `sales.csv`. This file contains the sales details of a variety of tops from several retail clothing stores. The goal is to identify the patterns and segment the market based on the number of units sold in those stores.

Create a new Python file and import the following packages:

```
import csv

import numpy as np
import matplotlib.pyplot as plt
from sklearn.cluster import MeanShift, estimate_bandwidth
```

Load the data from the input file. Since it's a CSV file, we can use the csv reader in Python to read the data from this file and convert it into a `NumPy` array:

```
# Load data from input file
input_file = 'sales.csv'
file_reader = csv.reader(open(input_file, 'r'), delimiter=',')
X = []
for count, row in enumerate(file_reader):
    if not count:
        names = row[1:]
        continue

    X.append([float(x) for x in row[1:]])

# Convert to numpy array
X = np.array(X)
```

Let's estimate the bandwidth of the input data:

```
# Estimating the bandwidth of input data
bandwidth = estimate_bandwidth(X, quantile=0.8, n_samples=len(X))
```

Train a mean shift model based on the estimated bandwidth:

```
# Compute clustering with MeanShift
meanshift_model = MeanShift(bandwidth=bandwidth, bin_seeding=True)
meanshift_model.fit(X)
```

Extract the labels and the centers of each cluster:

```
labels = meanshift_model.labels_
cluster_centers = meanshift_model.cluster_centers_
num_clusters = len(np.unique(labels))
```

Print the number of clusters and the cluster centers:

```
print("\nNumber of clusters in input data =", num_clusters)

print("\nCenters of clusters:")
print('\t'.join([name[:3] for name in names]))
for cluster_center in cluster_centers:
    print('\t'.join([str(int(x)) for x in cluster_center]))
```

We are dealing with six-dimensional data. In order to visualize the data, let's take two-dimensional data formed using second and third dimensions:

```
# Extract two features for visualization
cluster_centers_2d = cluster_centers[:, 1:3]
```

Plot the centers of the clusters:

```
# Plot the cluster centers
plt.figure()
plt.scatter(cluster_centers_2d[:,0], cluster_centers_2d[:,1],
        s=120, edgecolors='black', facecolors='none')

offset = 0.25
plt.xlim(cluster_centers_2d[:,0].min() - offset * cluster_
centers_2d[:,0].ptp(),
        cluster_centers_2d[:,0].max() + offset * cluster_
centers_2d[:,0].ptp(),)
plt.ylim(cluster_centers_2d[:,1].min() - offset * cluster_
centers_2d[:,1].ptp(),
        cluster_centers_2d[:,1].max() + offset * cluster_
centers_2d[:,1].ptp())

plt.title('Centers of 2D clusters')
plt.show()
```

The full code is given in the file `market_segmentation.py`. When running the code, you will see the following output:

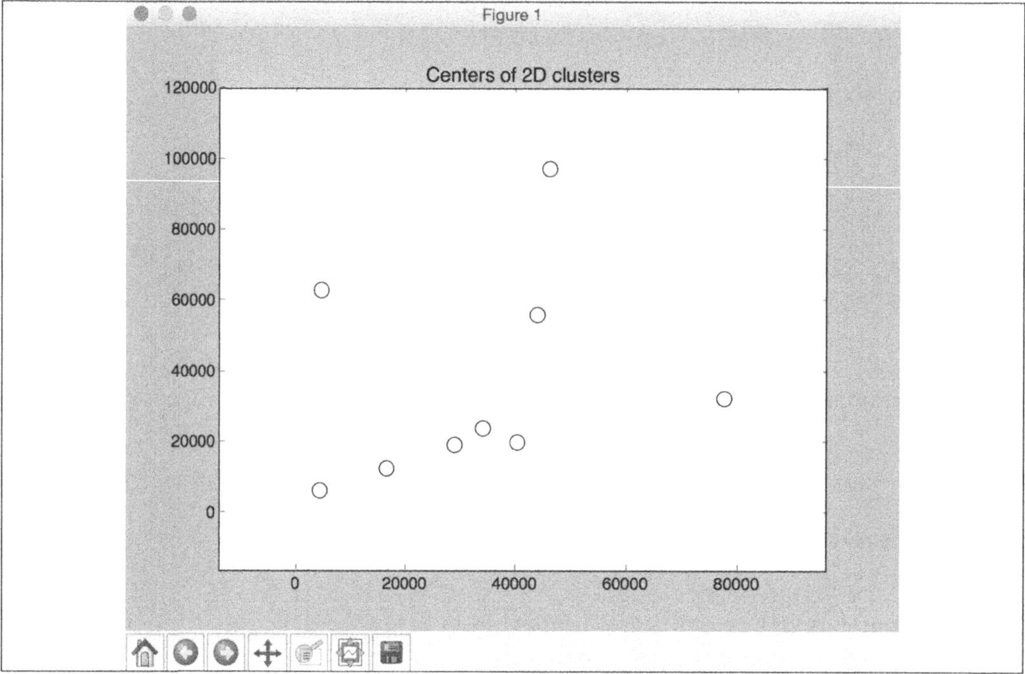

Figure 10: Centers of 2D clusters plot

In this last section of the chapter, we applied the Mean Shift algorithm, which we learned about earlier in the chapter, and used it to analyze and segment customer shopping habits.

And you will also see the following output:

```
Number of clusters in input data = 9

Centers of clusters:
Tsh     Tan     Hal     Tur     Tub     Swe
9823    4637    6539    2607    2228    1239
38589   44199   56158   5030    24674   4125
7852    4939    63081   134     40066   1332
35314   16745   12775   66900   1298    5613
22617   77873   32543   1005    21035   837
104972  29186   19415   16016   5060    9372
38741   40539   20120   35059   255     50710
28333   34263   24065   5575    4229    18076
14987   46397   97393   1127    37315   3235
```

Figure 11: Center of clusters output

Summary

In this chapter, we started by discussing unsupervised learning and its applications. We then learned about clustering and how to cluster data using the K-Means algorithm. We discussed how to estimate the number of clusters with the Mean Shift algorithm. We talked about silhouette scores and how to estimate the quality of clustering. We learned about Gaussian Mixture Models and how to build a classifier based on them. We also discussed the Affinity Propagation model and used it to find subgroups within the stock market. We then applied the Mean Shift algorithm to segment the market based on shopping patterns.

In the next chapter, we will learn how to build a recommendation engine.

8
Building Recommender Systems

In this chapter, we will learn how to build a recommendation system that will recommend movies that people might like to watch. We will learn about the K-nearest neighbors classifier and see how to implement it. We use these concepts to discuss collaborative filtering and then use it to build a recommender system.

By the end of this chapter, you will have learned about the following:

- Extracting the nearest neighbors
- Building a *K-Nearest Neighbors* classifier
- Computing similarity scores
- Finding similar users using collaborative filtering
- Building a movie recommendation system

Extracting the nearest neighbors

Recommender systems employ the concept of nearest neighbors to find good recommendations. The name *nearest neighbors* refers to the process of finding the closest data points to the input point from the given dataset. This is frequently used to build classification systems that classify a data point based on the proximity of the input data point to various classes. Let's see how to find the nearest neighbors for a given data point.

First, create a new Python file and import the following packages:

```
import numpy as np
import matplotlib.pyplot as plt
from sklearn.neighbors import NearestNeighbors
```

Define sample 2D data points:

```
# Input data
X = np.array([[2.1, 1.3], [1.3, 3.2], [2.9, 2.5], [2.7, 5.4], [3.8,
0.9],
        [7.3, 2.1], [4.2, 6.5], [3.8, 3.7], [2.5, 4.1], [3.4, 1.9],
        [5.7, 3.5], [6.1, 4.3], [5.1, 2.2], [6.2, 1.1]])
```

Define the number of nearest neighbors you want to extract:

```
# Number of nearest neighbors
k = 5
```

Define a test data point that will be used to extract the K-nearest neighbors:

```
# Test data point
test_data_point = [4.3, 2.7]
```

Plot the input data using circular black markers:

```
# Plot input data
plt.figure()
plt.title('Input data')
plt.scatter(X[:,0], X[:,1], marker='o', s=75, color='black')
```

Create and train a K-nearest neighbors model using the input data. Use this model to extract the nearest neighbors to the test data point:

```
# Build K Nearest Neighbors model
knn_model = NearestNeighbors(n_neighbors=k, algorithm='ball_tree').
fit(X)
distances, indices = knn_model.kneighbors(test_data_point)
```

Print the nearest neighbors extracted from the model:

```
# Print the 'k' nearest neighbors
print("\nK Nearest Neighbors:")
for rank, index in enumerate(indices[0][:k], start=1):
    print(str(rank) + " ==>", X[index])
```

Visualize the nearest neighbors:

```
# Visualize the nearest neighbors along with the test datapoint
plt.figure()
plt.title('Nearest neighbors')
plt.scatter(X[:, 0], X[:, 1], marker='o', s=75, color='k')
plt.scatter(X[indices][0][:][:, 0], X[indices][0][:][:, 1],
        marker='o', s=250, color='k', facecolors='none')
plt.scatter(test_data_point[0], test_data_point[1],
        marker='x', s=75, color='k')

plt.show()
```

The full code is given in the file `k_nearest_neighbors.py`. If you run the code, you will see two screenshots. The first screenshot represents the input data:

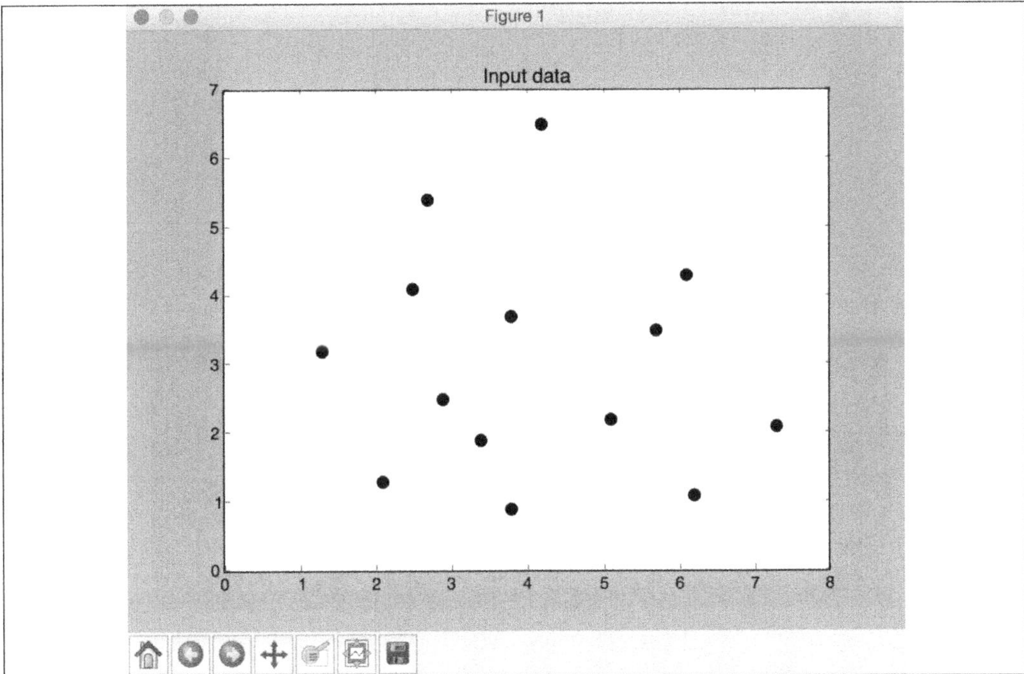

Figure 1: Visualization of the input dataset

The second screenshot represents the five nearest neighbors. The test data point is shown using a cross and the nearest neighbor points have been circled:

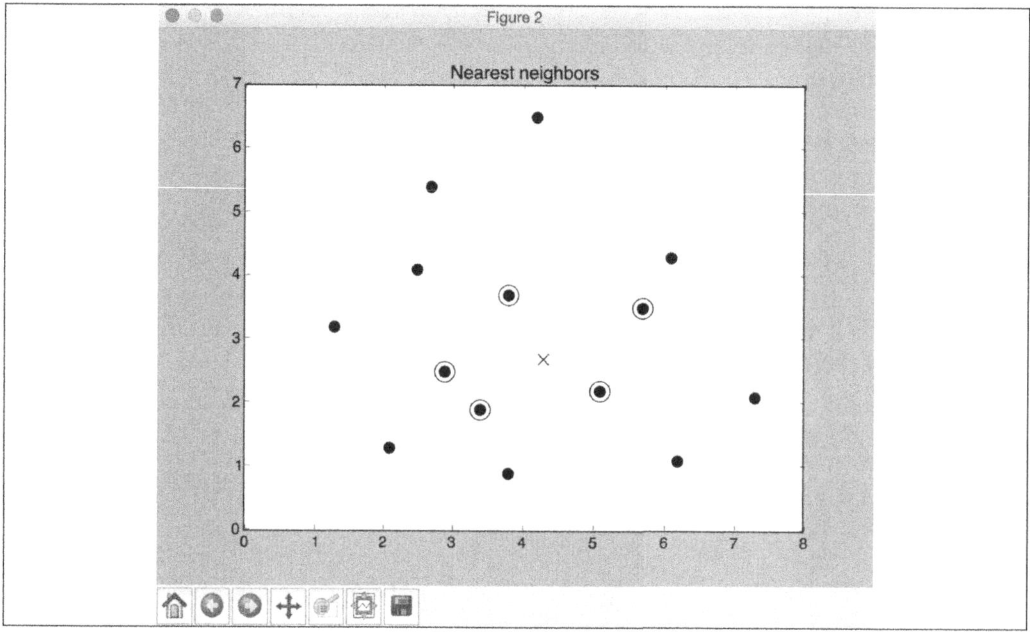

Figure 2: Five nearest neighbors plot

You will see the following output:

```
K Nearest Neighbors:
1 ==> [ 5.1  2.2]
2 ==> [ 3.8  3.7]
3 ==> [ 3.4  1.9]
4 ==> [ 2.9  2.5]
5 ==> [ 5.7  3.5]
```

Figure 3: K Nearest Neighbor ouput

The preceding figure shows the five points that are closest to the test data point. Now that we have learned how to construct and run a K-nearest neighbors model, in the next section, we will build on that knowledge and use it to build a K-nearest neighbors classifier.

Building a K-nearest neighbors classifier

A K-nearest neighbors classifier is a classification model that uses the K-nearest neighbors algorithm to classify a given data point. The algorithm finds the *K* closest data points in the training dataset to identify the category of the input data point. It will then assign a class to this data point based on a majority vote. From the list of those *K* data points, we look at the corresponding classes and pick the one with the highest number of votes. The value of *K* will depend on the problem at hand. Let's see how to build a classifier using this model.

Create a new Python file and import the following packages:

```
import numpy as np
import matplotlib.pyplot as plt
import matplotlib.cm as cm
from sklearn import neighbors, datasets
```

Load the input data from `data.txt`. Each line contains comma-separated values and the data contains four classes:

```
# Load input data
input_file = 'data.txt'
data = np.loadtxt(input_file, delimiter=',')
X, y = data[:, :-1], data[:, -1].astype(np.int)
```

Visualize the input data using four different marker shapes. We need to map the labels to corresponding markers, which is where the `mapper` variable comes into the picture:

```
# Plot input data
plt.figure()
plt.title('Input data')
marker_shapes = 'v^os'
mapper = [marker_shapes[i] for i in y]
for i in range(X.shape[0]):
    plt.scatter(X[i, 0], X[i, 1], marker=mapper[i],
            s=75, edgecolors='black', facecolors='none')
```

Define the number of nearest neighbors to be used:

```
# Number of nearest neighbors
num_neighbors = 12
```

Define the step size of the grid that will be used to visualize the boundaries of the classifier model:

```
# Step size of the visualization grid
step_size = 0.01
```

Create the K-nearest neighbors classifier model:

```
# Create a K Nearest Neighbors classifier model
classifier = neighbors.KNeighborsClassifier(num_neighbors,
weights='distance')
```

Train the model using the training data:

```
# Train the K Nearest Neighbors model
classifier.fit(X, y)
```

Create the mesh grid of values that will be used to visualize the grid:

```
# Create the mesh to plot the boundaries
x_min, x_max = X[:, 0].min() - 1, X[:, 0].max() + 1
y_min, y_max = X[:, 1].min() - 1, X[:, 1].max() + 1
x_values, y_values = np.meshgrid(np.arange(x_min, x_max, step_size),
        np.arange(y_min, y_max, step_size))
```

Evaluate the classifier on all the points on the grid to create a visualization of the boundaries:

```
# Evaluate the classifier on all the points on the grid
output = classifier.predict(np.c_[x_values.ravel(), y_values.ravel()])
```

Create a color mesh to visualize the output:

```
# Visualize the predicted output
output = output.reshape(x_values.shape)
plt.figure()
plt.pcolormesh(x_values, y_values, output, cmap=cm.Paired)
```

Overlay the training data on top of this color mesh to visualize the data relative to the boundaries:

```
# Overlay the training points on the map
for i in range(X.shape[0]):
    plt.scatter(X[i, 0], X[i, 1], marker=mapper[i],
            s=50, edgecolors='black', facecolors='none')
```

Set the X and Y limits along with the title:

```
plt.xlim(x_values.min(), x_values.max())
plt.ylim(y_values.min(), y_values.max())
plt.title('K Nearest Neighbors classifier model boundaries')
```

Define a test data point to see how the classifier performs. Create a figure with training data points and a test data point to see where it lies:

```
# Test input data point
test_data_point = [5.1, 3.6]
plt.figure()
plt.title('Test data_point')
for i in range(X.shape[0]):
    plt.scatter(X[i, 0], X[i, 1], marker=mapper[i],
            s=75, edgecolors='black', facecolors='none')

plt.scatter(test_data_point[0], test_data_point[1], marker='x',
        linewidth=6, s=200, facecolors='black')
```

Extract the K-nearest neighbors to the test data point, based on the classifier model:

```
# Extract the K nearest neighbors
_, indices = classifier.kneighbors([test_data_point])
indices = indices.astype(np.int)[0]
```

Plot the K-nearest neighbors obtained in the previous step:

```
# Plot k nearest neighbors
plt.figure()
plt.title('K Nearest Neighbors')

for i in indices:
    plt.scatter(X[i, 0], X[i, 1], marker=mapper[y[i]],
            linewidth=3, s=100, facecolors='black')
```

Overlay the test data point:

```
plt.scatter(test_data_point[0], test_data_point[1], marker='x',
        linewidth=6, s=200, facecolors='black')
```

Overlay the input data:

```
for i in range(X.shape[0]):
    plt.scatter(X[i, 0], X[i, 1], marker=mapper[i],
            s=75, edgecolors='black', facecolors='none')
```

Print the predicted output:

```
print("Predicted output:", classifier.predict([test_data_point])[0])

plt.show()
```

The full code is given in the file `nearest_neighbors_classifier.py`. If you run the code, you will see four screenshots. The first screenshot represents the input data:

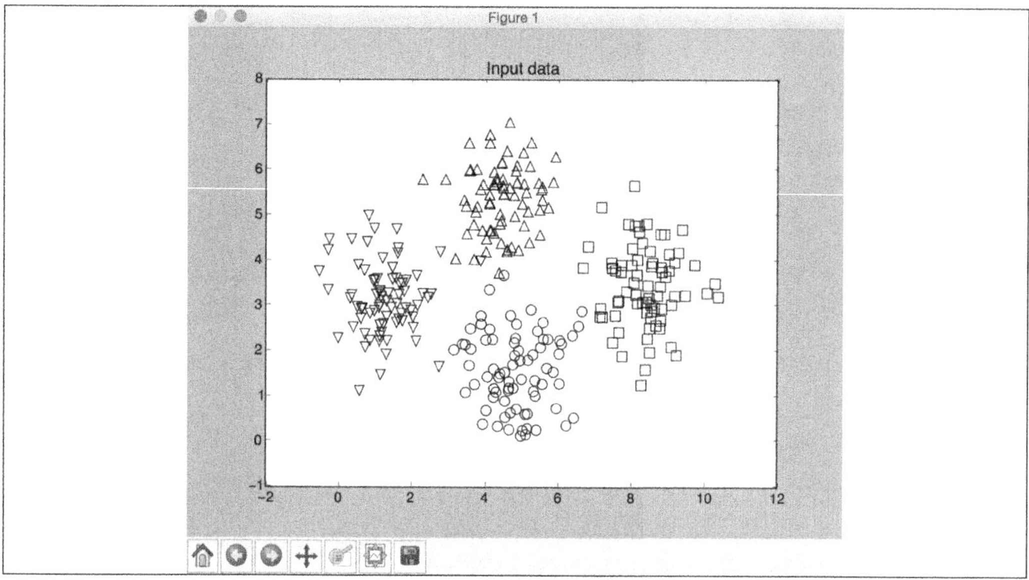

Figure 4: Visualization of input data

The second screenshot represents the classifier boundaries:

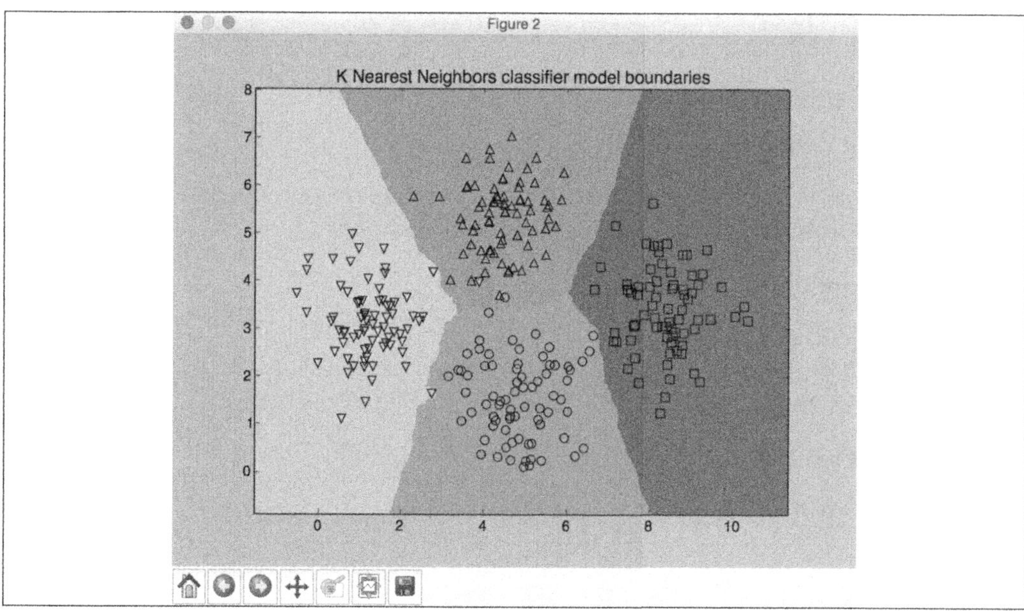

Figure 5: Classifier model boundaries

The third screenshot shows the test data point relative to the input dataset. The test data point is shown using a cross:

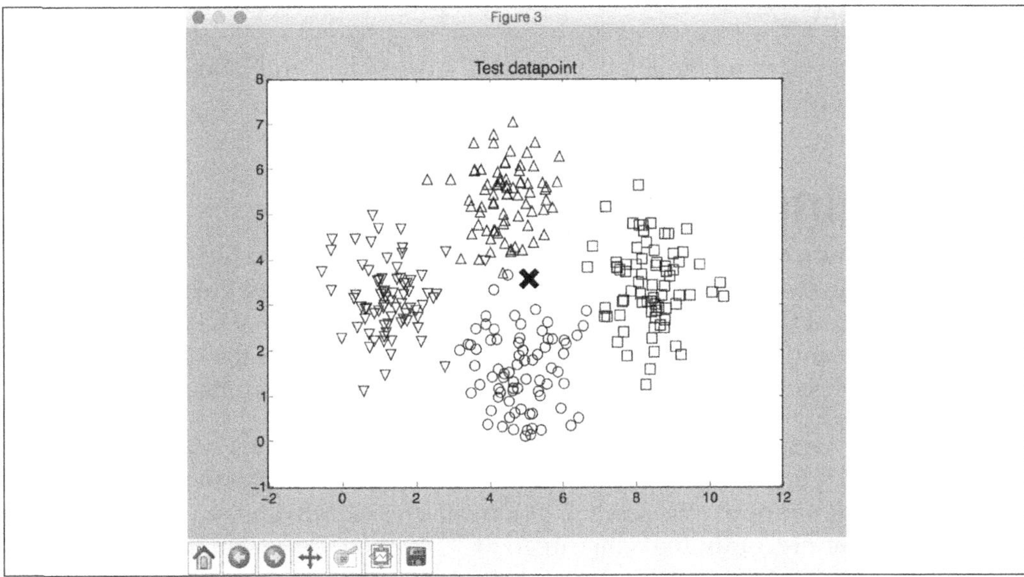

Figure 6: Test data point relative to the input dataset

The fourth screenshot shows the 12 nearest neighbors to the test data point:

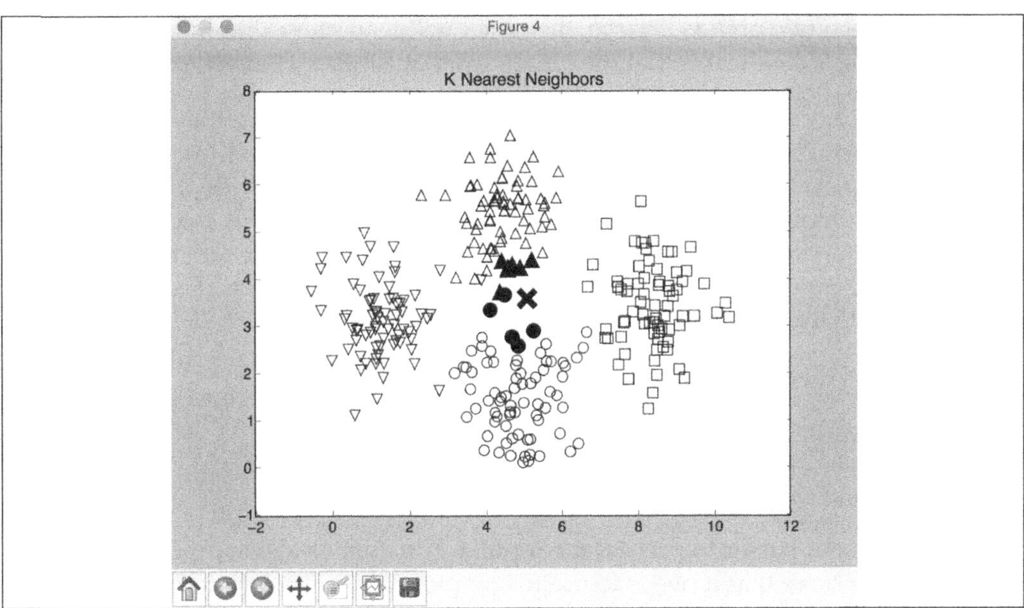

Figure 7: 12 nearest neighbor plot

You will see the following output, indicating that the model is predicting that the test data point belongs to class `1`:

```
Predicted output: 1
```

Like any machine learning model, the output is a prediction and might or might not match the actual result.

Computing similarity scores

To build a recommendation system, it is important to understand how to compare various objects in the dataset. If the dataset consists of people and their various movie preferences, then in order to make a recommendation we need to understand how to compare any two people with one another. This is where the similarity score is important. The similarity score gives an idea of how similar two data points are.

There are two scores that are used frequently in this domain - the Euclidean score and the Pearson score. The **Euclidean score** uses the Euclidean distance between two data points to compute the score. If you need a quick refresher on how Euclidean distance is computed, you can go to:

`https://en.wikipedia.org/wiki/Euclidean_distance`

The value of the Euclidean distance can be unbounded. Hence, we take this value and convert it in a way that the Euclidean score ranges from *0* to *1*. If the Euclidean distance between two objects is large, then the Euclidean score should be low because a low score indicates that the objects are not similar. Hence Euclidean distance is inversely proportional to Euclidean score.

The **Pearson score** is a measure of correlation between two data points. It uses the covariance between the two data points along with their individual standard deviations to compute the score. The score can range from *-1* to *+1*. A score of *+1* indicates that the data points are similar, and a score of *-1* indicates that they are dissimilar. A score of *0* indicates that there is no correlation between them. Let's see how to compute these scores.

Create a new Python file and import the following packages:

```
import argparse
import json
import numpy as np
```

Build an argument parser to process the input arguments. It will accept two users and the type of score that it needs to use to compute the similarity score:

```
def build_arg_parser():
```

```
    parser = argparse.ArgumentParser(description='Compute similarity
score')
    parser.add_argument('--user1', dest='user1', required=True,
            help='First user')
    parser.add_argument('--user2', dest='user2', required=True,
            help='Second user')
    parser.add_argument("--score-type", dest="score_type",
required=True,
            choices=['Euclidean', 'Pearson'], help='Similarity metric
to be used')
    return parser
```

Define a function to compute the Euclidean score between the input users. If the users are not in the dataset, the code will raise an error:

```
# Compute the Euclidean distance score between user1 and user2
def euclidean_score(dataset, user1, user2):
    if user1 not in dataset:
        raise TypeError('Cannot find ' + user1 + ' in the dataset')

    if user2 not in dataset:
        raise TypeError('Cannot find ' + user2 + ' in the dataset')
```

Define a variable to track the movies that have been rated by both users:

```
    # Movies rated by both user1 and user2
    common_movies = {}
```

Extract the movies rated by both users:

```
    for item in dataset[user1]:
        if item in dataset[user2]:
            common_movies[item] = 1
```

If there are no common movies, then the similarity score cannot be computed:

```
    # If there are no common movies between the users,
    # then the score is 0
    if len(common_movies) == 0:
        return 0
```

Compute the squared differences between the ratings and use it to compute the Euclidean score:

```
    squared_diff = []

    for item in dataset[user1]:
        if item in dataset[user2]:
```

```
            squared_diff.append(np.square(dataset[user1][item] -
dataset[user2][item]))

    return 1 / (1 + np.sqrt(np.sum(squared_diff)))
```

Define a function to compute the Pearson score between the users in the given dataset. If the users are not found in the dataset, it raises an error:

```
# Compute the Pearson correlation score between user1 and user2
def pearson_score(dataset, user1, user2):
    if user1 not in dataset:
        raise TypeError('Cannot find ' + user1 + ' in the dataset')

    if user2 not in dataset:
        raise TypeError('Cannot find ' + user2 + ' in the dataset')
```

Define a variable to track the movies that have been rated by both users:

```
    # Movies rated by both user1 and user2
    common_movies = {}
```

Extract the movies rated by both users:

```
    for item in dataset[user1]:
        if item in dataset[user2]:
            common_movies[item] = 1
```

If there are no common movies, then we cannot compute the similarity score:

```
    num_ratings = len(common_movies)

    # If there are no common movies between
    #user1 and user2, then the score is 0

    if num_ratings == 0:
        return 0
```

Calculate the sum of ratings of all the movies that have been rated by both users:

```
    # Calculate the sum of ratings of all the common movies
    user1_sum = np.sum([dataset[user1][item] for item in common_
movies])
    user2_sum = np.sum([dataset[user2][item] for item in common_
movies])
```

Calculate the sum of squares of the ratings all the movies that have been rated by both the users:

```
    # Calculate the sum of squares of ratings
    # of all the common movies
    user1_squared_sum = np.sum([np.square(dataset[user1][item]) for
item in common_movies])
    user2_squared_sum = np.sum([np.square(dataset[user2][item]) for
item in common_movies])
```

Calculate the sum of products of the ratings of all the movies rated by both the input users:

```
    # Calculate the sum of products of the
    # ratings of the common movies
    sum_of_products = np.sum([dataset[user1][item] * dataset[user2]
[item] for item in common_movies])
```

Calculate the various parameters required to compute the Pearson score using the preceding computations:

```
    # Calculate the Pearson correlation score
    Sxy = sum_of_products - (user1_sum * user2_sum / num_ratings)
    Sxx = user1_squared_sum - np.square(user1_sum) / num_ratings
    Syy = user2_squared_sum - np.square(user2_sum) / num_ratings
```

If there is no deviation, then the score is `0`:

```
    if Sxx * Syy == 0:

        return 0
```

Return the Pearson score:

```
    return Sxy / np.sqrt(Sxx * Syy)
```

Define the `main` function and parse the input arguments:

```
if __name__=='__main__':
    args = build_arg_parser().parse_args()
    user1 = args.user1
    user2 = args.user2
    score_type = args.score_type
```

Load the ratings from the file `ratings.json` into a dictionary:

```
ratings_file = 'ratings.json'

with open(ratings_file, 'r') as f:
    data = json.loads(f.read())
```

Compute the similarity score based on the input arguments:

```
if score_type == 'Euclidean':
    print("\nEuclidean score:")
    print(euclidean_score(data, user1, user2))
else:
    print("\nPearson score:")
    print(pearson_score(data, user1, user2))
```

The full code is given in the file `compute_scores.py`. Let's run the code with a few combinations. To compute the Euclidean score between `David Smith` and `Bill Duffy`:

```
$ python3 compute_scores.py --user1 "David Smith" --user2 "Bill Duffy"
--score-type Euclidean
```

If you run the preceding command, you will get the following output:

```
Euclidean score:
0.585786437627
```

If you want to compute the Pearson score between the same pair, run the following command:

```
$ python3 compute_scores.py --user1 "David Smith" --user2 "Bill Duffy"
--score-type Pearson
```

You will see the following output:

```
Pearson score:
0.99099243041
```

It can be run using other combinations of parameters as well.

In this section, we learned how to compute similarity scores and learned why that an important component in the construction of a recommender system. In the next section, we will learn how to identify users with similar preferences by using collaborative filtering.

Finding similar users using collaborative filtering

Collaborative filtering refers to the process of identifying patterns among the objects in a dataset in order to decide about a new object. In the context of recommendation engines, collaborative filtering is used to provide recommendations by looking at similar users in the dataset.

By collecting the preferences of different users in the dataset, we collaborate that information to filter the users. Hence the name collaborative filtering.

The assumption here is that if two people have similar ratings for a set of movies, then their choices for a set of new unknown movies would be similar too. By identifying patterns in those common movies, predictions can be made about new movies. In the previous section, we learned how to compare different users in the dataset. The scoring techniques discussed will now be used to find similar users in the dataset. Collaborative filtering algorithms can be parallelized and be implemented in big data systems such as AWS EMR and Apache Spark, enabling the processing of hundreds of terabytes worth of data. These methods can be used for various verticals like finance, online shopping, marketing, customer studies, among others.

Let's get started and build our collaborative filtering system.

Create a new Python file and import the following packages:

```
import argparse
import json
import numpy as np

from compute_scores import pearson_score
```

Define a function to parse the input arguments. The input argument is the name of the user:

```
def build_arg_parser():
    parser = argparse.ArgumentParser(description='Find users who are
similar to the input user')
    parser.add_argument('--user', dest='user', required=True,
            help='Input user')
    return parser
```

Define a function to find the users in the dataset that are similar to the given user. If the user is not in the dataset, raise an error:

```
# Finds users in the dataset that are similar to the input user
def find_similar_users(dataset, user, num_users):
    if user not in dataset:
        raise TypeError('Cannot find ' + user + ' in the dataset')
```

The function to compute the Pearson score has been imported. Let's use that function to compute the Pearson score between the input user and all the other users in the dataset:

```
    # Compute Pearson score between input user
    # and all the users in the dataset
    scores = np.array([[x, pearson_score(dataset, user,
            x)] for x in dataset if x != user])
```

Sort the scores in descending order:

```
    # Sort the scores in decreasing order
    scores_sorted = np.argsort(scores[:, 1])[::-1]
```

Extract the top `num_users` number of users as specified by the input argument and return the array:

```
    # Extract the top 'num_users' scores
    top_users = scores_sorted[:num_users]

    return scores[top_users]
```

Define the `main` function and parse the input arguments to extract the name of the user:

```
if __name__=='__main__':
    args = build_arg_parser().parse_args()
    user = args.user
```

Load the data from the movie ratings file `ratings.json`. This file contains the names of the people and their ratings for various movies:

```
    ratings_file = 'ratings.json'

    with open(ratings_file, 'r') as f:
        data = json.loads(f.read())
```

Find the top three users who are like the user specified by the input argument. You can change it to any number of users depending on your choice. Print the output along with the scores:

```
print('\nUsers similar to ' + user + ':\n')
similar_users = find_similar_users(data, user, 3)
print('User\t\t\tSimilarity score')
print('-'*41)
for item in similar_users:
    print(item[0], '\t\t', round(float(item[1]), 2))
```

The full code is given in the file `collaborative_filtering.py`. Let's run the code and find the users who are like Bill Duffy:

```
$ python3 collaborative_filtering.py --user "Bill Duffy"
```

You will get the following output:

```
Users similar to Bill Duffy:

User                    Similarity score
-----------------------------------------
David Smith              0.99
Samuel Miller            0.88
Adam Cohen               0.86
```

Figure 8: User similarity output

Let's run the code and find the users who are like Clarissa Jackson:

```
$ python3 collaborative_filtering.py --user "Clarissa Jackson"
```

You will get the following output:

```
Users similar to Clarissa Jackson:

User                    Similarity score
-----------------------------------------
Chris Duncan             1.0
Bill Duffy               0.83
Samuel Miller            0.73
```

Figure 9: User similarity output

In this section, we learned how we can find users in a dataset that are like each other as well as being able to assign a score to determine how similar a user is to another. In the next section, we will put it all together and build our recommendation system.

Building a movie recommendation system

So far, we have laid the foundation to build our recommendation system by learning about:

- Extracting the nearest neighbors
- Building a K-nearest neighbors classifier
- Computing similarity scores
- Finding similar users using collaborative filtering

Now that all the building blocks in place, it's time to build a movie recommendation system. We learned all the underlying concepts that are needed to build a recommendation system. In this section, we will build a movie recommendation system based on the data provided in the file `ratings.json`. This file contains a set of people and their ratings for various movies. To find movie recommendations for a given user, we need to find similar users in the dataset and then come up with recommendations for this person. Let's get started.

Create a new Python file and import the following packages:

```
import argparse
import json
import numpy as np

from compute_scores import pearson_score
from collaborative_filtering import find_similar_users
```

Define a function to parse the input arguments. The input argument is the name of the user:

```
def build_arg_parser():
    parser = argparse.ArgumentParser(description='Find recommendations
for the given user')
    parser.add_argument('--user', dest='user', required=True,
            help='Input user')
    return parser
```

Define a function to get the movie recommendations for a given user. If the user doesn't exist in the dataset, the code will raise an error:

```
# Get movie recommendations for the input user
def get_recommendations(dataset, input_user):
    if input_user not in dataset:
        raise TypeError('Cannot find ' + input_user + ' in the
dataset')
```

Define the variables to track the scores:

```
    overall_scores = {}
    similarity_scores = {}
```

Compute a similarity score between the input user and all the other users in the dataset:

```
    for user in [x for x in dataset if x != input_user]:
        similarity_score = pearson_score(dataset, input_user, user)
```

If the similarity score is less than `0`, you can continue with the next user in the dataset:

```
        if similarity_score <= 0:
            continue
```

Extract a list of movies that have been rated by the current user but haven't been rated by the input user:

```
        filtered_list = [x for x in dataset[user] if x not in \
                dataset[input_user] or dataset[input_user][x] == 0]
```

For each item in the filtered list, keep a track of the weighted rating based on the similarity score. Also keep a track of the similarity scores:

```
        for item in filtered_list:
            overall_scores.update({item: dataset[user][item] *
similarity_score})
            similarity_scores.update({item: similarity_score})
```

If there are no such movies, then we cannot recommend anything:

```
    if len(overall_scores) == 0:
        return ['No recommendations possible']
```

Normalize the scores based on the weighted scores:

```
    # Generate movie ranks by normalization
    movie_scores = np.array([[score/similarity_scores[item], item]
            for item, score in overall_scores.items()])
```

Sort the scores and extract the movie recommendations:

```
    # Sort in decreasing order
    movie_scores = movie_scores[np.argsort(movie_scores[:, 0])[::-1]]

    # Extract the movie recommendations
    movie_recommendations = [movie for _, movie in movie_scores]

    return movie_recommendations
```

Define the `main` function and parse the input arguments to extract the name of the input user:

```
if __name__=='__main__':
    args = build_arg_parser().parse_args()
    user = args.user
```

Load the movie ratings data from the file `ratings.json`:

```
    ratings_file = 'ratings.json'

    with open(ratings_file, 'r') as f:
        data = json.loads(f.read())
```

Extract the movie recommendations and print the output:

```
    print("\nMovie recommendations for " + user + ":")
    movies = get_recommendations(data, user)
    for i, movie in enumerate(movies):
        print(str(i+1) + '. ' + movie)
```

The full code is given in the file `movie_recommender.py`. Let's find the movie recommendations for `Chris Duncan`:

```
$ python3 movie_recommender.py --user "Chris Duncan"
```

You will see the following output:

```
Movie recommendations for Chris Duncan:
1. Vertigo
2. Goodfellas
3. Scarface
4. Roman Holiday
```

Figure 10: Movie recommendations

Let's find the movie recommendations for `Julie Hammel`:

```
$ python3 movie_recommender.py --user "Julie Hammel"
```

You will see the following output:

```
Movie recommendations for Julie Hammel:
1. The Apartment
2. Vertigo
3. Raging Bull
```

Figure 11: Movie recommendations

The movies in the output are the actual recommendations by the system, based on previous preferences observed for Julie Hammel. Potentially, the system could continue to get better simply by observing more and more data points.

Summary

In this chapter, we learned how to extract K-nearest neighbors for a given data point from a given dataset. We then used this concept to build the K-nearest neighbors classifier. We discussed how to compute similarity scores such as the Euclidean and Pearson scores. We learned how to use collaborative filtering to find similar users from a given dataset and used it to build a movie recommendation system. Finally, we were able to test our model and run it against data points that the system had not previously seen.

In the next chapter, we will learn about logic programming and see how to build an inference engine that can solve real-world problems.

9
Logic Programming

In this chapter, we are going to learn how to write programs using logic programming. We will discuss various programming paradigms and see how programs are constructed with logic programming. We will learn about the building blocks of logic programming and see how to solve problems in this domain. We will implement Python programs to build various solvers that solve a variety of problems.

By the end of this chapter, you will know about the following:

- What is logic programming?
- Understanding the building blocks of logic programming
- Solving problems using logic programming
- Installing Python packages
- Matching mathematical expressions
- Validating primes
- Parsing a family tree
- Analyzing geography
- Building a puzzle solver

What is logic programming?

Logic programming is a programming paradigm, which basically means it is a way to approach programming. Before we talk about what it constitutes and how it is relevant in **Artificial Intelligence** (**AI**), let's talk a bit about programming paradigms.

The concept of programming paradigms originates from the need to classify programming languages. It refers to the way computer programs solve problems through code.

Some programming paradigms are primarily concerned with implications or the sequence of operations used to achieve a particular result. Other programming paradigms are concerned about how we organize the code.

Here are some of the more popular programming paradigms:

- **Imperative**: Uses statements to change a program's state, thus allowing for side effects.
- **Functional**: Treats computation as an evaluation of mathematical functions and does not allow changing states or mutable data.
- **Declarative**: A way of programming where programs are written by describing what needs to be done and not how to do it. The logic of the underlying computation is expressed without explicitly describing the control flow.
- **Object oriented**: Groups the code within a program in such a way that each object is responsible for itself. Objects contain data and methods that specify how changes happen.
- **Procedural**: Groups the code into functions and each function is responsible for a series of steps.
- **Symbolic**: Uses a style of syntax and grammar through which the program can modify its own components by treating them as plain data.
- **Logic**: Views computation as automatic reasoning over a database of knowledge consisting of facts and rules.

Logic programming has been around for a while. A language that was quite popular during one of the last heydays of AI was Prolog. It is a language that uses only three constructs:

- Facts
- Rules
- Questions

But with these three constructs you were able to build some powerful systems. One popular usage was in the construction of "expert systems." The idea behind was to interview human experts that had been working in a given field for a long time and codify the interview into AI systems. Some examples of fields for which expert systems where built were:

- **Medicine** - Famous examples include MYCIN, INTERNIST-I, and CADUCEUS
- **Chemical analysis** - DENDRAL is an analysis system used to predict molecular structure

- **Finance** - Advisory programs to assist bankers in making loans
- **Debugging programs** - SAINT, MATLAB, and MACSYMA

In order to understand logic programming, it's necessary to understand the concepts of computation and deduction. To compute something, we start with an expression and a set of rules. This set of rules is basically the program.

Expressions and rules are used to generate the output. For example, let's say we want to compute the sum of 23, 12, and 49:

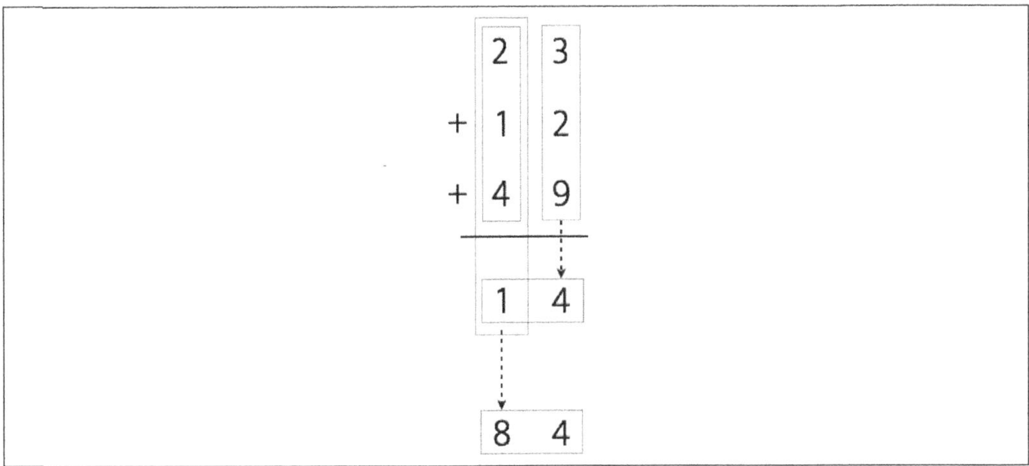

Figure 1: Addition operation mechanics

The procedure to complete the operation would be as follows:

1. Add 3 + 2 + 9 = 14
2. We need to keep a single digit, which is the 4, and then we carry the 1
3. Add 2 + 1 + 4 (plus the 1 we carried) = 8
4. Combine 8 and 4. The final result is: 84

On the other hand, to deduce something, we need to start from a conjecture. A proof is constructed according to a set of rules. The process of computation is mechanical, whereas the process of deduction is more creative.

When writing a program using the logic programming paradigm, a set of statements is specified based on facts and rules about the problem domain, and the solver solves it using this information.

Understanding the building blocks of logic programming

In programming object-oriented or imperative paradigms, a variable always needs to be defined. In logic programming, things work a bit differently. An uninstantiated argument can be passed to a function and the interpreter will instantiate these variables by looking at the facts defined by the user. This is a powerful way of approaching the variable matching problem. The process of matching variables with different items is called unification. This is one of the ways logic programming is different. Relations can also be specified in logic programming. Relations are defined by means of clauses called facts and rules.

Facts are just statements that are truths about the program and the data. The syntax is straightforward. For example, *Donald is Allan's son* is a fact, whereas *Who is Allan's son?* is not be a fact. Every logic program needs facts so that it can achieve the given goal based on them.

Rules are the things we have learned in terms of how to express various facts and how to query them. They are the constraints that must be met, and they enable you to make conclusions about the problem domain. For example, let's say you are working on building a chess engine. You need to specify all the rules about how each piece can move on the chessboard.

Solving problems using logic programming

Logic programming looks for solutions by using facts and rules. A goal must be specified for each program. When a logic program and a goal don't contain any variables, the solver comes up with a tree that constitutes the search space for solving the problem and getting to the goal.

One of the most important things about logic programming is how we treat the rules. Rules can be viewed as logical statements. Let's consider the following:

Kathy orders dessert => Kathy is happy

This can be read as an implication that says, *If Kathy is happy, then Kathy orders dessert*. It can also be construed as Kathy orders dessert whenever she is happy.

Similarly, let's consider the following rules and facts:

canfly(X) :- bird(X), not abnormal(X).

abnormal(X) :- wounded(X).

bird(john).

bird(mary).

wounded(john).

Here is how to interpret the rules and facts:

- John is wounded
- Mary is a bird
- John is a bird
- Wounded birds are abnormal
- Birds that are not abnormal can fly

From this, we can conclude that Mary can fly, and John cannot fly.

This construction is used in various forms throughout logic programming to solve various types of problems. Let's go ahead and see how to solve these problems in Python.

Installing Python packages

Before we start logic programming in Python, we need to install a couple of packages. The package `logpy` is a Python package that enables logic programming in Python. We will also be using SymPy for some of the problems. So, let's go ahead and install `logpy` and `sympy` using `pip`:

```
$ pip3 install logpy
$ pip3 install sympy
```

If you get an error during the installation process for `logpy`, you can install it from source at `https://github.com/logpy/logpy`. Once you have successfully installed these packages, you can proceed to the next section.

Matching mathematical expressions

We encounter mathematical operations all the time. Logic programming is an efficient way of comparing expressions and finding out unknown values. Let's see how to do that.

Create a new Python file and import the following packages:

```
from logpy import run, var, fact
import logpy.assoccomm as la
```

Define a couple of mathematical operations:

```
# Define mathematical operations
add = 'addition'
mul = 'multiplication'
```

Both addition and multiplication are commutative operations (meaning the operands can be flipped without changing the result). Let's specify that:

```
# Declare that these operations are commutative
# using the facts system
fact(la.commutative, mul)
fact(la.commutative, add)
fact(la.associative, mul)
fact(la.associative, add)
```

Let's define some variables:

```
# Define some variables
a, b, c = var('a'), var('b'), var('c')
```

Consider the following expression:

```
expression_orig = 3 x (-2) + (1 + 2 x 3) x (-1)
```

Let's generate this expression with masked variables. The first expression would be:

expression1 = (1 + 2 x a) x b + 3 x c

The second expression would be:

expression2 = c x 3 + b x (2 x a + 1)

The third expression would be:

expression3 = (((2 x a) x b) + b) + 3 x c

If you observe carefully, all three expressions represent the same basic expression. The goal is to match these expressions with the original expression to extract the unknown values:

```
# Generate expressions
expression_orig = (add, (mul, 3, -2), (mul, (add, 1, (mul, 2, 3)),
-1))
```

```
expression1 = (add, (mul, (add, 1, (mul, 2, a)), b), (mul, 3, c))
expression2 = (add, (mul, c, 3), (mul, b, (add, (mul, 2, a), 1)))
expression3 = (add, (add, (mul, (mul, 2, a), b), b), (mul, 3, c))
```

Compare the expressions with the original expression. The method run is commonly used in `logpy`. This method takes the input arguments and runs the expression. The first argument is the number of values, the second argument is a variable, and the third argument is a function:

```
# Compare expressions
print(run(0, (a, b, c), la.eq_assoccomm(expression1, expression_
orig)))
print(run(0, (a, b, c), la.eq_assoccomm(expression2, expression_
orig)))
print(run(0, (a, b, c), la.eq_assoccomm(expression3, expression_
orig)))
```

The full code is given in `expression_matcher.py`. If you run the code, you will see the following output:

```
((3, -1, -2),)
((3, -1, -2),)
()
```

The three values in the first two lines represent the values for `a`, `b`, and `c`. The first two expressions matched with the original expression, whereas the third one returned nothing. This is because, even though the third expression is mathematically the same, it is structurally different. Pattern comparison works by comparing the structure of the expressions.

Validating primes

Let's see how to use logic programming to check for prime numbers. We will use the constructs available in `logpy` to determine which numbers in the given list are prime, as well as finding out if a given number is a prime or not.

Create a new Python file and import the following packages:

```
import itertools as it
import logpy.core as lc
from sympy.ntheory.generate import prime, isprime
```

Next, define a function that checks if the given number is prime depending on the type of data. If it's a number, then it's straightforward. If it's a variable, then we must run the sequential operation. To give a bit of background, the method `conde` is a goal constructor that provides logical AND and OR operations.

The method `condeseq` is like `conde`, but it supports the generic iteration of goals:

```
# Check if the elements of x are prime
def check_prime(x):
    if lc.isvar(x):
        return lc.condeseq([(lc.eq, x, p)] for p in map(prime,
it.count(1)))
    else:
        return lc.success if isprime(x) else lc.fail
```

Declare the variable x that will be used:

```
# Declate the variable
x = lc.var()
```

Define a set of numbers and check which numbers are prime. The method `membero` checks if a given number is a member of the list of numbers specified in the input argument:

```
# Check if an element in the list is a prime number
list_nums = (23, 4, 27, 17, 13, 10, 21, 29, 3, 32, 11, 19)
print('\nList of primes in the list:')
print(set(lc.run(0, x, (lc.membero, x, list_nums), (check_prime, x))))
```

Let's use the function in a slightly different way now by printing the first 7 prime numbers:

```
# Print first 7 prime numbers
print('\nList of first 7 prime numbers:')
print(lc.run(7, x, check_prime(x)))
```

The full code is given in `prime.py`. If you run the code, you will see the following output:

```
List of primes in the list:
{3, 11, 13, 17, 19, 23, 29}
List of first 7 prime numbers: (2, 3, 5, 7, 11, 13, 17)
```

You can confirm that the output values are correct.

Parsing a family tree

Now that we are more familiar with logic programming, let's use it to solve an interesting problem. Consider the following family tree:

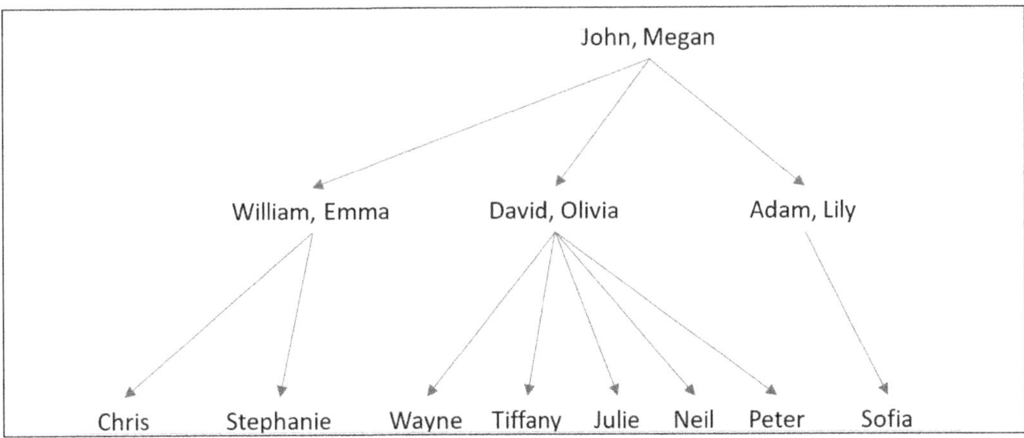

Figure 2: Sample family tree

John and Megan have three sons - William, David, and Adam. The wives of William, David, and Adam are Emma, Olivia, and Lily respectively. William and Emma have two children - Chris and Stephanie. David and Olivia have five children - Wayne, Tiffany, Julie, Neil, and Peter. Adam and Lily have one child - Sophia. Based on these facts, we can create a program that can tell us the name of Wayne's grandfather or Sophia's uncles. Even though we have not explicitly specified anything about the grandparent or uncle relationships, logic programming can infer them.

These relationships are specified in a file called `relationships.json` provided for you. The file looks like the following:

```
{
        "father":
        [
                {"John": "William"},
                {"John": "David"},
                {"John": "Adam"},
                {"William": "Chris"},
                {"William": "Stephanie"},
                {"David": "Wayne"},
                {"David": "Tiffany"},
                {"David": "Julie"},
                {"David": "Neil"},
                {"David": "Peter"},
                {"Adam": "Sophia"}
        ],
        "mother":
        [
                {"Megan": "William"},
```

```
                {"Megan": "David"},
                {"Megan": "Adam"},
                {"Emma": "Stephanie"},
                {"Emma": "Chris"},
                {"Olivia": "Tiffany"},
                {"Olivia": "Julie"},
                {"Olivia": "Neil"},
                {"Olivia": "Peter"},
                {"Lily": "Sophia"}
        ]
}
```

It is a simple JSON file that specifies the father and mother relationships. Note that we haven't specified anything about the husbands and wives, grandparents, or uncles.

Create a new Python file and import the following packages:

```
import json
from logpy import Relation, facts, run, conde, var, eq
```

Define a function to check if `x` is the parent of `y`. We will use the logic that if `x` is the parent of `y`, then `x` is either the father or the mother. We have already defined "father" and "mother" in the fact base:

```
# Check if 'x' is the parent of 'y'
def parent(x, y):
    return conde([father(x, y)], [mother(x, y)])
```

Define a function to check if `x` is the grandparent of `y`. We will use the logic that if `x` is the grandparent of `y`, then the offspring of `x` will be the parent of `y`:

```
# Check if 'x' is the grandparent of 'y'
def grandparent(x, y):
    temp = var()
    return conde((parent(x, temp), parent(temp, y)))
```

Define a function to check if `x` is the sibling of `y`. We will use the logic that if `x` is the sibling of `y`, then `x` and `y` will have the same parents. Notice that there is a slight modification needed here because when we list out all the siblings of `x`, `x` will be listed as well because `x` satisfies these conditions. So, when we print the output, we will have to remove `x` from the list. We will discuss this in the `main` function:

```
# Check for sibling relationship between 'a' and 'b'
def sibling(x, y):
    temp = var()
    return conde((parent(temp, x), parent(temp, y)))
```

Define a function to check if x is y's uncle. We will use the logic that if x is y's uncle, then x grandparents will be the same as y's parents. Notice that there is a slight modification needed here because when we list out all the uncles of x, x's father will be listed as well because x's father satisfies these conditions. So, when we print the output, we will have to remove x's father from the list. We will discuss this in the main function:

```
# Check if x is y's uncle
def uncle(x, y):
    temp = var()
    return conde((father(temp, x), grandparent(temp, y)))
```

Define the main function and initialize the relations father and mother:

```
if __name__=='__main__':
    father = Relation()
    mother = Relation()
```

Load the data from the relationships.json file:

```
    with open('relationships.json') as f:
        d = json.loads(f.read())
```

Read the data and add it to the fact base:

```
    for item in d['father']:
        facts(father, (list(item.keys())[0], list(item.values())[0]))

    for item in d['mother']:
        facts(mother, (list(item.keys())[0], list(item.values())[0]))
```

Define the variable x:

```
    x = var()
```

We are now ready to ask some questions and see if the solver can come up with the right answers. Let's ask who John's children are:

```
    # John's children
    name = 'John'
    output = run(0, x, father(name, x))
    print("\nList of " + name + "'s children:")
    for item in output:
        print(item)
```

Who is William's mother?

```
    # William's mother
```

```
name = 'William'
output = run(0, x, mother(x, name))[0]
print("\n" + name + "'s mother:\n" + output)
```

Who are Adam's parents?

```
# Adam's parents name = 'Adam'
output = run(0, x, parent(x, name))
print("\nList of " + name + "'s parents:")
for item in output:
    print(item)
```

Who are Wayne's grandparents?

```
# Wayne's grandparents name = 'Wayne'
output = run(0, x, grandparent(x, name))
print("\nList of " + name + "'s grandparents:")
for item in output:
    print(item)
```

Who are Megan's grandchildren?

```
# Megan's grandchildren
name = 'Megan'
output = run(0, x, grandparent(name, x))
print("\nList of " + name + "'s grandchildren:")
for item in output:
    print(item)
```

Who are David's siblings?

```
# David's siblings
name = 'David'
output = run(0, x, sibling(x, name))
siblings = [x for x in output if x != name]
print("\nList of " + name + "'s siblings:")
for item in siblings:
    print(item)
```

Who are Tiffany's uncles?

```
# Tiffany's uncles
name = 'Tiffany'
name_father = run(0, x, father(x, name))[0]
output = run(0, x, uncle(x, name))
output = [x for x in output if x != name_father]
print("\nList of " + name + "'s uncles:")
for item in output:
    print(item)
```

List all of the spouses in the family:

```
# All spouses
a, b, c = var(), var(), var()
output = run(0, (a, b), (father, a, c), (mother, b, c))
print("\nList of all spouses:")
for item in output:
    print('Husband:', item[0], '<==> Wife:', item[1])
```

The full code is given in `family.py`. If you run the code, you will see some outputs. The first half looks like the following:

```
List of John's children:
David
William
Adam

William's mother:
Megan

List of Adam's parents:
John
Megan

List of Wayne's grandparents:
John
Megan
```

Figure 3: Family tree example output

The second half looks like the following:

```
List of Megan's grandchildren:
Chris
Sophia
Peter
Stephanie
Julie
Tiffany
Neil
Wayne

List of David's siblings:
William
Adam

List of Tiffany's uncles:
William
Adam

List of all spouses:
Husband: Adam <==> Wife: Lily
Husband: David <==> Wife: Olivia
Husband: John <==> Wife: Megan
Husband: William <==> Wife: Emma
```

Figure 4: Family tree example output

You can compare the output with the family tree to ensure that the answers are indeed correct.

Analyzing geography

Let's use logic programming to build a solver to analyze geography. In this problem, we will specify information about the location of various states in the US and then query the program to answer various questions based on those facts and rules. The following is a map of the US:

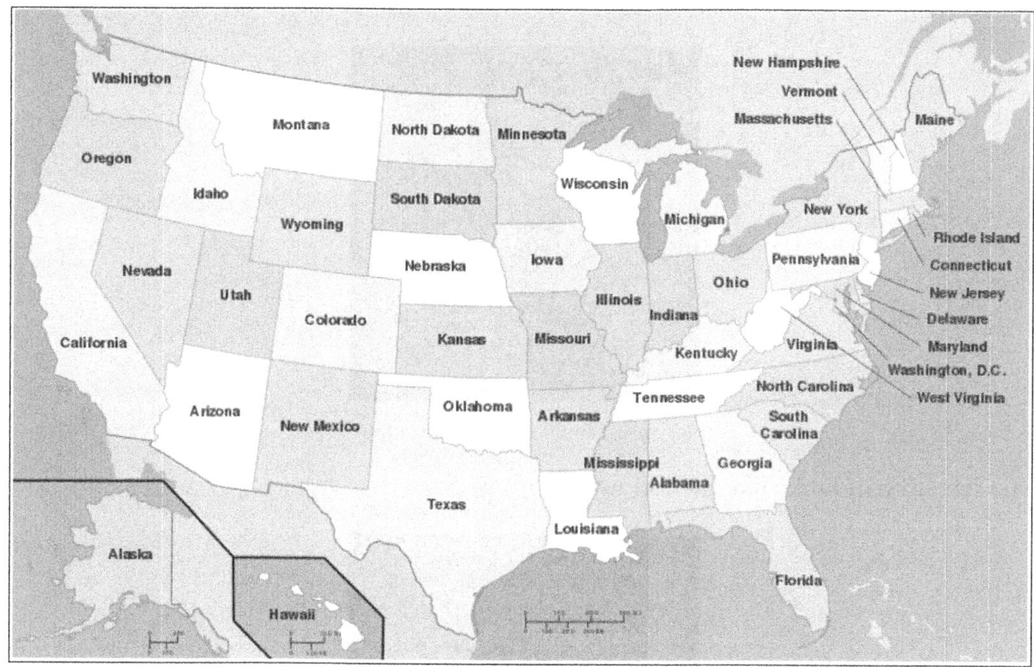

Figure 5: Adjacent and coastal states example map

You have been provided with two text files named `adjacent_states.txt` and `coastal_states.txt`. These files contain the details about which states are adjacent to each other and which states are coastal. Based on this, we can get interesting information like "What states are adjacent to both Oklahoma and Texas?" or "Which coastal state is adjacent to both New Mexico and Louisiana?"

Create a new Python file and import the following:

```
from logpy import run, fact, eq, Relation, var
```

Initialize the relations:

```
adjacent = Relation()
coastal = Relation()
```

Define the input files to load the data from:

```
file_coastal = 'coastal_states.txt'
file_adjacent = 'adjacent_states.txt'
```

Load the data:

```
# Read the file containing the coastal states
with open(file_coastal, 'r') as f:
    line = f.read()
    coastal_states = line.split(',')
```

Add the information to the fact base:

```
# Add the info to the fact base
for state in coastal_states:
    fact(coastal, state)
```

Read the adjacent data:

```
# Read the file containing the coastal states
with open(file_adjacent, 'r') as f:
    adjlist = [line.strip().split(',') for line in f if line and
line[0].isalpha()]
```

Add the adjacency information to the fact base:

```
# Add the info to the fact base
for L in adjlist:
    head, tail = L[0], L[1:]
    for state in tail:
        fact(adjacent, head, state)
```

Initialize the variables `x` and `y`:

```
# Initialize the variables
x = var()
y = var()
```

We are now ready to ask some questions. Check if Nevada is adjacent to Louisiana:

```
# Is Nevada adjacent to Louisiana?
output = run(0, x, adjacent('Nevada', 'Louisiana'))
print('\nIs Nevada adjacent to Louisiana?:')
print('Yes' if len(output) else 'No')
```

Print out all the states that are adjacent to Oregon:

```
# States adjacent to Oregon
```

```
output = run(0, x, adjacent('Oregon', x))
print('\nList of states adjacent to Oregon:')
for item in output:
    print(item)
```

List all the coastal states that are adjacent to Mississippi:

```
# States adjacent to Mississippi that are coastal
output = run(0, x, adjacent('Mississippi', x), coastal(x))
print('\nList of coastal states adjacent to Mississippi:')
for item in output:
    print(item)
```

List seven states that border a coastal state:

```
# List of 'n' states that border a coastal state
n = 7
output = run(n, x, coastal(y), adjacent(x, y))
print('\nList of ' + str(n) + ' states that border a coastal state:')
for item in output:
    print(item)
```

List states that are adjacent to both Arkansas and Kentucky:

```
# List of states that adjacent to the two given states
output = run(0, x, adjacent('Arkansas', x), adjacent('Kentucky', x))
print('\nList of states that are adjacent to Arkansas and Kentucky:')
for item in output:
    print(item)
```

The full code is given in `states.py`. If you run the code, you will see the following output:

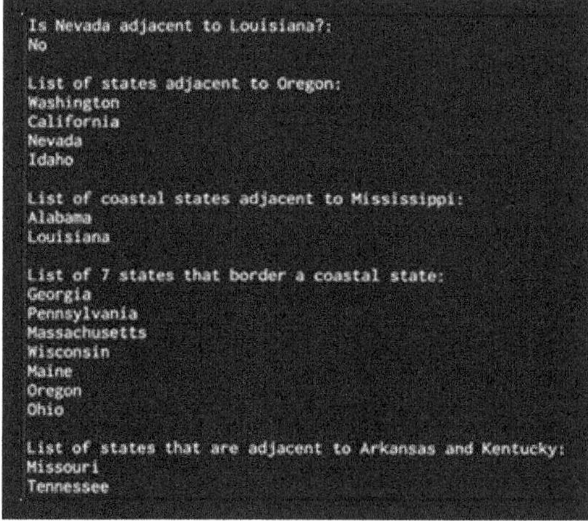

Figure 6: Adjacent and coastal state example output

You can cross-check the output with the US map to verify whether the answers are right. You can also add more questions to the program to see if it can answer them.

Building a puzzle solver

Another interesting application of logic programming is solving puzzles. We can specify the conditions of a puzzle and the program will come up with a solution. In this section, we will specify various bits and pieces of information about four people and ask for the missing piece of information.

In the logic program, we specify the puzzle as follows:

- Steve has a blue car.
- The person who owns a cat lives in Canada. Matthew lives in the USA.
- The person with a black car lives in Australia.
- Jack has a cat.
- Alfred lives in Australia.
- The person who has a dog lives in France.
- Who has a rabbit?

The goal is the find the person who has a rabbit. Here are the full details about the four people:

	Pet	Car Color	Country
Steve	dog	blue	France
Jack	cat	green	Canada
Matthew	rabbit	yellow	USA
Alfred	parrot	black	Australia

Figure 7: Puzzle solver input data

Create a new Python file and import the following packages:

```
from logpy import *
from logpy.core import lall
```

Declare the variable `people`:

```
# Declare the variable people
people = var()
```

Define all the rules using `lall`. The first rule is that there are four people:

```
# Define the rules
rules = lall(
    # There are 4 people
    (eq, (var(), var(), var(), var()), people),
```

The person named Steve has a blue car:

```
    # Steve's car is blue
    (membero, ('Steve', var(), 'blue', var()), people),
```

The person who has a cat lives in Canada:

```
    # Person who has a cat lives in Canada
    (membero, (var(), 'cat', var(), 'Canada'), people),
```

The person named Matthew lives in the USA:

```
    # Matthew lives in USA
    (membero, ('Matthew', var(), var(), 'USA'), people),
```

The person who has a black car lives in Australia:

```
    # The person who has a black car lives in Australia
    (membero, (var(), var(), 'black', 'Australia'), people),
```

The person named Jack has a cat:

```
    # Jack has a cat
    (membero, ('Jack', 'cat', var(), var()), people),
```

The person named Alfred lives in Australia:

```
    # Alfred lives in Australia
    (membero, ('Alfred', var(), var(), 'Australia'), people),
```

The person who has a dog lives in France:

```
    # Person who owns the dog lives in France
    (membero, (var(), 'dog', var(), 'France'), people),
```

One of the people in this group has a rabbit. Who is that person?

```
    # Who has a rabbit?
    (membero, (var(), 'rabbit', var(), var()), people)
)
```

Run the solver with the preceding constraints:

```
# Run the solver
solutions = run(0, people, rules)
```

Extract the output from the solution:

```
# Extract the output
output = [house for house in solutions[0] if 'rabbit' in house][0][0]
```

Print the full matrix obtained from the solver:

```
# Print the output
print('\n' + output + ' is the owner of the rabbit')
print('\nHere are all the details:')
attribs = ['Name', 'Pet', 'Color', 'Country']
print('\n' + '\t\t'.join(attribs))
print('=' * 57)
for item in solutions[0]:
    print('')
    print('\t\t'.join([str(x) for x in item]))
```

The full code is given in `puzzle.py`. If you run the code, you will see the following output:

```
Matthew is the owner of the rabbit

Here are all the details:

Name            Pet             Color           Country
=========================================================

Steve           dog             blue            France

Jack            cat             ~_9             Canada

Matthew         rabbit          ~_11            USA

Alfred          ~_13            black           Australia
```

Figure 8: Puzzle solver output

The preceding figure shows all the values obtained using the solver. Some of them are still unknown as indicated by the numbered names. Even though the information was incomplete, the solver was able to answer the question. But in order to answer every single question, you may need to add more rules. This program was to demonstrate how to solve a puzzle with incomplete information. You can play around with it and see how you can build puzzle solvers for various scenarios.

Summary

In this chapter, we learned how to write Python programs using logic programming. We discussed how various programming paradigms deal with building programs. We understood how programs are built in logic programming. We learned about various building blocks of logic programming and discussed how to solve problems in this domain. We implemented various Python programs to solve interesting problems and puzzles.

In the next chapter, we will learn about heuristic search techniques and use those algorithms to solve real-world problems.

10
Heuristic Search Techniques

In this chapter, we are going to learn about heuristic search techniques. Heuristic search techniques are used to search through the solution space to come up with answers. The search is conducted using heuristics that guide the search algorithm. This heuristic allows the algorithm to speed up the process, which would otherwise take a long time to arrive at the solution.

By the end of this chapter, you will know about the following:

- What is heuristic search?
- Uninformed vs. informed search
- Constraint satisfaction problems
- Local search techniques
- Simulated annealing
- Constructing a string using greedy search
- Solving a problem with constraints
- Solving the region coloring problem
- Building an 8-puzzle solver
- Building a maze solver

Is heuristic search artificial intelligence?

In *Chapter 2, Fundamental Use Cases for Artificial Intelligence*, we learned about the five tribes as defined by Pedro Domingos. One of the most "ancient" tribes is the *symbolist* tribe. At least to me, this fact is not surprising. As humans, we try to find rules and patterns in everything. Unfortunately, the world is sometimes messy and not everything follows simple rules.

This is the reason why other tribes emerged to help us when we don't have an orderly world. However, when our search spaces are small and the domain is limited, using heuristics, constraint satisfaction, and other techniques laid out in this chapter, is useful for this set of problems. These techniques are useful when the number of combinations is relatively small and combinatorial explosion is limited. For example, solving the traveling salesman problem is simple with these techniques when the number of cities is around 20. If we try to solve the same problem for n=2000, other techniques will have to be used that don't explore the complete space and only give an approximation of the result.

What is heuristic search?

Searching and organizing data is an important topic within artificial intelligence. There are many problems that require searching for an answer within the solution domain. There are many possible solutions to a given problem and we do not know which ones are correct. By efficiently organizing the data, we can search for solutions quickly and effectively.

More often, there are so many possible options to solve a given problem that no single algorithm can be developed to find a definite best solution. Also, going through every solution is not possible because it is prohibitively expensive. In such cases, we rely on a rule of thumb that helps us narrow down the search by eliminating the options that are obviously wrong. This rule of thumb is called a **heuristic**. The method of using heuristics to guide the search is called **heuristic search**.

Heuristic techniques are powerful because they speed up the process. Even if the heuristic is not able to eliminate some options, it will help ordering those options so that better solutions are likely to come up first. As mentioned previously, heuristic searches can be computationally expensive. We will now learn how we can take *shortcuts* and *prune* the search tree.

Uninformed versus informed search

If you are familiar with computer science, you might have heard about search techniques such as **Depth First Search** (**DFS**), **Breadth First Search** (**BFS**), and **Uniform Cost Search** (**UCS**). These are search techniques that are commonly used on graphs to get to the solution. These are examples of uninformed searches. They do not use any prior information or rules to eliminate some paths. They check all the plausible paths and pick the optimal one.

A heuristic search, on the other hand, is called an **informed search** because it uses prior information or rules to eliminate unnecessary paths. Uninformed search techniques do not take the goal into account. Uninformed search techniques search blindly and have no a priori knowledge about the final solution.

In the graph problem, heuristics can be used to guide the search. For example, at each node we can define a heuristic function that returns a score that represents the estimate of the cost of the path from the current node to the goal. By defining this heuristic function, we are informing the search technique about the right direction to reach the goal. This will allow the algorithm to identify which neighbor will lead to the goal.

We need to note that heuristic searches might not always find the most optimal solution. This is because we are not exploring every single possibility and we are relying on a heuristic. The search is guaranteed to find a good solution in a reasonable time, however, which is what we expect from a practical solution. In real-world scenarios, we need solutions that are fast and effective. Heuristic searches provide an efficient solution by arriving at a reasonable solution quickly. They are used in cases where the problems cannot be solved in any other way or would take a long time to solve. Another way to *prune* the tree is by taking advantage of constraints inherent in the data. In the next section, we will learn more pruning techniques leveraging these constraints.

Constraint satisfaction problems

There are many problems that must be solved under constraints. These constraints are basically conditions that cannot be violated during the process of solving the problem.

These problems are referred to as **Constraint Satisfaction Problems** (**CSPs**).

To gain some intuitive understanding, let's quickly look at an example section of a Sudoku puzzle. Sudoku is a game where we cannot have the same number twice across a horizontal line, vertical line, or in the same square. Here is an example Sudoku board:

<table>
<tr><td></td><td></td><td></td><td>2</td><td>6</td><td></td><td>7</td><td></td><td>1</td></tr>
<tr><td>6</td><td>8</td><td></td><td></td><td>7</td><td></td><td></td><td>9</td><td></td></tr>
<tr><td>1</td><td>9</td><td></td><td></td><td></td><td>4</td><td>5</td><td></td><td></td></tr>
<tr><td>8</td><td>2</td><td></td><td>1</td><td></td><td></td><td></td><td>4</td><td></td></tr>
<tr><td></td><td></td><td>4</td><td>6</td><td></td><td>2</td><td>9</td><td></td><td></td></tr>
<tr><td></td><td>5</td><td></td><td></td><td></td><td>3</td><td></td><td>2</td><td>8</td></tr>
<tr><td></td><td></td><td>9</td><td>3</td><td></td><td></td><td></td><td>7</td><td>4</td></tr>
<tr><td></td><td>4</td><td></td><td></td><td>5</td><td></td><td></td><td>3</td><td>6</td></tr>
<tr><td>7</td><td></td><td>3</td><td></td><td>1</td><td>8</td><td></td><td></td><td></td></tr>
</table>

Figure 1: Example of a Sudoku board

Using constraint satisfaction and the rules of Sudoku we can quickly determine which numbers to try and which numbers not to try to solve the puzzle. For example, in this square:

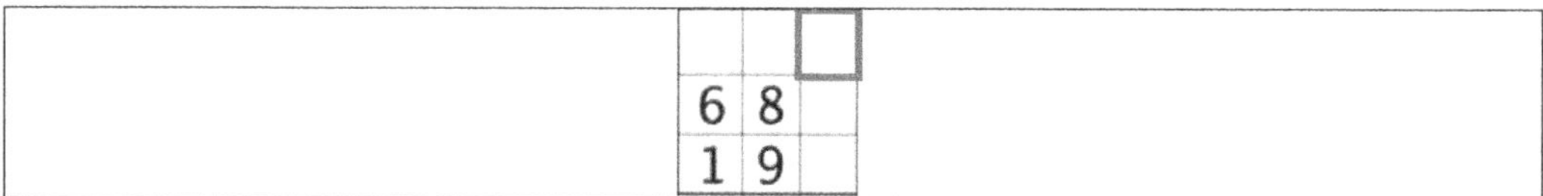

Figure 2: Considering a problem in Sudoku

If we were not using CSP, one brute force approach would be to try all of the combinations of numbers in the slots and then check if the rules applied. For example, our first attempt might be to fill out all the squares with the number 1, and then check the result.

Using CSP, we can prune the attempts before we try them.

Let's walk through what we think the number should be for the square highlighted in red. We know that the number cannot be a 1, 6, 8 or a 9 because those numbers already exist in the square. We also know that it cannot be a 2 or 7 because those number exist in the horizontal line. We also know that it cannot be a 3 or a 4 because those number are already in the vertical line. That leaves us with the only possibility of what the number should be – 5.

CSPs are mathematical problems that are defined as a set of variables that must satisfy some constraints. When we arrive at the final solution, the states of the variables must obey all the constraints. This technique represents the entities involved in a given problem as a collection of a fixed number of constraints over the variables. These variables need to be solved by constraint satisfaction methods.

These problems require a combination of heuristics and other search techniques to be solved in a reasonable amount of time. In this case, we will use constraint satisfaction techniques to solve problems on finite domains. A finite domain consists of a finite number of elements. Since we are dealing with finite domains, we can use search techniques to arrive at the solution. To get further clarity on CSP we will now learn how to use local search techniques to solve CSP problems.

Local search techniques

Local search is a way of solving a CSP. It keeps optimizing the solution until all the constraints are satisfied. It iteratively keeps updating the variables until we arrive at the destination. These algorithms modify the value during each step of the process that gets us closer to the goal. In the solution space, the updated value is closer to the goal than the previous value. Hence, it is known as a local search.

A local search algorithm is a type of heuristic search algorithm. These algorithms use a function that calculates the quality of each update. For example, it can count the number of constraints that are being violated by the current update or it can see how the update affects the distance to the goal. This is referred to as the cost of the assignment. The overall goal of local search is to find the minimum cost update at each step.

Hill climbing is a popular local search technique. It uses a heuristic function that measures the difference between the current state and the goal. When we start, it checks if the state is the final goal. If it is, then it stops. If not, then it selects an update and generates a new state. If it's closer to the goal than the current state, then it makes that the current state. If not, it ignores it and continues the process until it checks all possible updates. It basically climbs the hill until it reaches the summit.

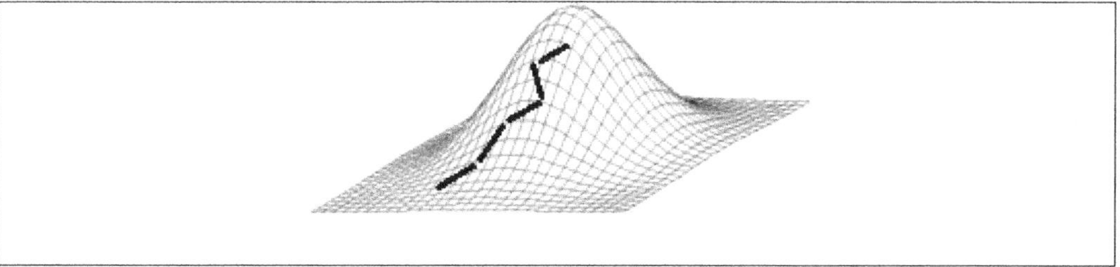

Figure 3: Hill climbing

Simulated annealing

Simulated annealing is a type of local search, as well as a stochastic search technique. Stochastic search techniques are used extensively in various fields, such as robotics, chemistry, manufacturing, medicine, and economics. Stochastic algorithms are used to solve many real-world problems: we can perform things like optimizing the design of a robot, determining the timing strategies for automated control in factories, and planning traffic.

Simulated annealing is a variation of the hill climbing technique. One of the main problems of hill climbing is that it ends up climbing false foothills; this means that it gets stuck in local maxima. So, it is better to check out the whole space before we make any climbing decisions. In order to achieve this, the whole space is initially explored to see what it is like. This helps us avoid getting stuck in a plateau or local maxima.

In simulated annealing, we reformulate the problem and solve it for minimization, as opposed to maximization. So, we are now descending into valleys as opposed to climbing hills. We are pretty much doing the same thing, but in a different way.

We use an objective function to guide the search. This objective function serves as the heuristic.

The reason it is called *simulated annealing* is because it is derived from the metallurgical process. In that process, we first heat metals up, allowing atoms to diffuse within the metal, and then let them cool until they reach their optimal desired state in terms of atomic structural arrangement. This is typically to change a metal's physical properties to become softer and easier to work.

The rate at which we cool the system is called the **annealing schedule**. The rate of cooling is important because it directly impacts the result. In the real-world case of metals, if the rate of cooling is too fast, it ends up settling too quickly into a non-ideal state (atomic structure). For example, if the heated metal is put into cold water, it ends up quickly settling into a structure that was not desired, making the metal brittle, for instance.

If the rate of cooling is slow and controlled, the metal has a chance to arrive at the optimal atomic structure, leading to the desired physical properties. The chances of taking big steps quickly towards any hill are lower in this case. Since the rate of cooling is slow, it will take its time to move into the optimal state. Something similar can be done with data.

We first evaluate the current state and see if it has reached the goal. If it has, then we stop. If not, then we set the best state variable to the current state. We then define an annealing schedule that controls how quickly it descends into a valley. The difference is computed between the current state and the new state. If the new state is not better, then we make it the current state with a certain predefined probability. This is done using a random number generator and deciding based on a threshold. If it is above the threshold, then we set the best state to this state. Based on this, the annealing schedule is updated depending on the number of nodes. We keep doing this until we arrive at the goal. Another local search technique is the greedy search algorithm. We will learn more about that in the next section.

Constructing a string using greedy search

Greedy search is an algorithmic paradigm that makes the locally optimal choice at each stage in order to find the global optimum. But in many problems, greedy algorithms do not produce globally optimum solutions. An advantage of using greedy algorithms is that they produce an approximate solution in a reasonable time. The hope is that this approximate solution is reasonably close to the global optimal solution.

Greedy algorithms do not refine their solutions based on new information during the search. For example, let's say you are planning on a road trip and you want to take the best route possible. If you use a greedy algorithm to plan the route, it might ask you to take routes that are have a shorter distance but might end up taking more time. It may also lead you to paths that may seem faster in the short term but might lead to traffic jams later. This happens because greedy algorithms only see the next step and not the globally-optimal final solution.

Let's see how to solve a problem using a greedy search. In this problem, we will try to recreate the input string based on the alphabets. We will ask the algorithm to search the solution space and construct a path to the solution.

We will be using a package called `simpleai` throughout this chapter. It contains various routines that are useful in building solutions using heuristic search techniques. It's available at `https://github.com/simpleai-team/simpleai`. We need to make a few changes to the source code in order to make it work in Python 3. A file called `simpleai.zip` has been provided along with the code for the book. Unzip this file into a folder called `simpleai`. This folder contains all the necessary changes to the original library necessary to make it work in Python 3. Place the `simpleai` folder in the same folder as your code and you'll be able to run your code smoothly.

Create a new Python file and import the following packages:

```
import argparse
import simpleai.search as ss
```

Define a function to parse the input arguments:

```
def build_arg_parser():
    parser = argparse.ArgumentParser(description='Creates the input 
string \
            using the greedy algorithm')
    parser.add_argument("--input-string", dest="input_string", 
required=True,
            help="Input string")
    parser.add_argument("--initial-state", dest="initial_state", 
required=False,
            default='', help="Starting point for the search")
    return parser
```

Create a class that contains the methods needed to solve the problem. This class inherits the `SearchProblem` class available in the library. A few methods need to be overridden to solve the problem at hand. The first method `set_target` is a custom method that defines the target string:

```
class CustomProblem(ss.SearchProblem):
    def set_target(self, target_string):
        self.target_string = target_string
```

The actions is a method that comes with a `SearchProblem` and that needs to be overridden. It's responsible for taking the right steps towards the goal. If the length of the current string is less than the length of the target string, it will return the list of possible alphabets to choose from. If not, it will return an empty string:

```
    # Check the current state and take the right action
    def actions(self, cur_state):
        if len(cur_state) < len(self.target_string):
            alphabets = 'abcdefghijklmnopqrstuvwxyz'
            return list(alphabets + ' ' + alphabets.upper())
        else:
            return []
```

Now create a method to compute the result by concatenating the current string and the action that needs to be taken. This method comes with a `SearchProblem` and we are overriding it:

```
    # Concatenate state and action to get the result
    def result(self, cur_state, action):
        return cur_state + action
```

The method `is_goal` is a part of the `SearchProblem` and it's used to check if the goal has been reached:

```
    # Check if goal has been achieved
    def is_goal(self, cur_state):
        return cur_state == self.target_string
```

The method `heuristic` is also a part of the `SearchProblem` and we need to override it. A heuristic is defined that will be used to solve the problem. A calculation is performed to see how far the goal is and use that as the heuristic to guide it towards the goal:

```
    # Define the heuristic that will be used
    def heuristic(self, cur_state):
        # Compare current string with target string
        dist = sum([1 if cur_state[i] != self.target_string[i] else 0
                    for i in range(len(cur_state))])

        # Difference between the lengths
        diff = len(self.target_string) - len(cur_state)


        return dist + diff
```

Initialize the input arguments:

```
if __name__=='__main__':
    args = build_arg_parser().parse_args()
```

Initialize the CustomProblem object:

```
    # Initialize the object
    problem = CustomProblem()
```

Set the starting point as well as the goal we want to achieve:

```
    # Set target string and initial state
    problem.set_target(args.input_string)
    problem.initial_state = args.initial_state
```

Run the solver:

```
    # Solve the problem
    output = ss.greedy(problem)
```

Print the path to the solution:

```
    print('\nTarget string:', args.input_string)
    print('\nPath to the solution:')
    for item in output.path():
        print(item)
```

The full code is given in the file `greedy_search.py`. If you run the code with an empty initial state:

```
$ python3 greedy_search.py --input-string 'Artificial Intelligence'
--initial-state ''
```

You will get the following output:

```
Path to the solution:
(None, '')
('A', 'A')
('r', 'Ar')
('t', 'Art')
('i', 'Arti')
('f', 'Artif')
('i', 'Artifi')
('c', 'Artific')
('i', 'Artifici')
('a', 'Artificia')
('l', 'Artificial')
(' ', 'Artificial ')
('I', 'Artificial I')
('n', 'Artificial In')
('t', 'Artificial Int')
('e', 'Artificial Inte')
('l', 'Artificial Intel')
('l', 'Artificial Intell')
('i', 'Artificial Intelli')
('g', 'Artificial Intellig')
('e', 'Artificial Intellige')
('n', 'Artificial Intelligen')
('c', 'Artificial Intelligenc')
('e', 'Artificial Intelligence')
```

Figure 4: Code output when ran with an empty initial state

If you run the code with a non-empty starting point:

```
$ python3 greedy_search.py --input-string 'Artificial Intelligence with
Python' --initial-state 'Artificial Inte'
```

You will get the following output:

```
Path to the solution:
(None, 'Artificial Inte')
('l', 'Artificial Intel')
('l', 'Artificial Intell')
('i', 'Artificial Intelli')
('g', 'Artificial Intellig')
('e', 'Artificial Intellige')
('n', 'Artificial Intelligen')
('c', 'Artificial Intelligenc')
('e', 'Artificial Intelligence')
(' ', 'Artificial Intelligence ')
('w', 'Artificial Intelligence w')
('i', 'Artificial Intelligence wi')
('t', 'Artificial Intelligence wit')
('h', 'Artificial Intelligence with')
(' ', 'Artificial Intelligence with ')
('P', 'Artificial Intelligence with P')
('y', 'Artificial Intelligence with Py')
('t', 'Artificial Intelligence with Pyt')
('h', 'Artificial Intelligence with Pyth')
('o', 'Artificial Intelligence with Pytho')
('n', 'Artificial Intelligence with Python')
```

Figure 5: Code output when ran with a non-empty initial state

Now that we have covered some popular search techniques, we will move on to solving some real-world problems using these search algorithms.

Solving a problem with constraints

We have already discussed how CSPs are formulated. Let's apply them to a real-world problem. In this problem, we have a list of names and each name can take a fixed set of values. We also have a set of constraints between these people that needs to be satisfied. Let's see how to do it.

Create a new Python file and import the following packages:

```
from simpleai.search import CspProblem, backtrack, \
        min_conflicts, MOST_CONSTRAINED_VARIABLE, \
        HIGHEST_DEGREE_VARIABLE, LEAST_CONSTRAINING_VALUE
```

Define the constraint that specifies that all the variables in the input list should have unique values:

```
# Constraint that expects all the different variables
# to have different values
def constraint_unique(variables, values):
    # Check if all the values are unique
    return len(values) == len(set(values))
```

Define the constraint that specifies that the first variable should be bigger than the second variable:

```
# Constraint that specifies that one variable
# should be bigger than other
def constraint_bigger(variables, values):
    return values[0] > values[1]
```

Define the constraint that specifies that if the first variable is odd, then the second variable should be even and vice versa:

```
# Constraint that specifies that there should be
# one odd and one even variables in the two variables
def constraint_odd_even(variables, values):
    # If first variable is even, then second should
    # be odd and vice versa
    if values[0] % 2 == 0:
        return values[1] % 2 == 1
    else:
        return values[1] % 2 == 0
```

Define the `main` function and define the variables:

```
if __name__=='__main__':
    variables = ('John', 'Anna', 'Tom', 'Patricia')
```

Define the list of values that each variable can take:

```
    domains = {
        'John': [1, 2, 3],
        'Anna': [1, 3],
        'Tom': [2, 4],
        'Patricia': [2, 3, 4],
    }
```

Define the constraints for various scenarios. In this case, we specify three constraints as follows:

- John, Anna, and Tom should have different values
- Tom's value should be bigger than Anna's value
- If John's value is odd, then Patricia's value should be even and vice versa

Use the following code:

```
constraints = [
    (('John', 'Anna', 'Tom'), constraint_unique),
    (('Tom', 'Anna'), constraint_bigger),
    (('John', 'Patricia'), constraint_odd_even),
]
```

Use the preceding variables and the constraints to initialize the `CspProblem` object:

```
problem = CspProblem(variables, domains, constraints)
```

Compute the solution and print it:

```
print('\nSolutions:\n\nNormal:', backtrack(problem))
```

Compute the solution using the `MOST_CONSTRAINED_VARIABLE` heuristic:

```
print('\nMost constrained variable:', backtrack(problem,
        variable_heuristic=MOST_CONSTRAINED_VARIABLE))
```

Compute the solution using the `HIGHEST_DEGREE_VARIABLE` heuristic:

```
print('\nHighest degree variable:', backtrack(problem,
        variable_heuristic=HIGHEST_DEGREE_VARIABLE))
```

Compute the solution using the `LEAST_CONSTRAINING_VALUE` heuristic:

```
print('\nLeast constraining value:', backtrack(problem,
        value_heuristic=LEAST_CONSTRAINING_VALUE))
```

Compute the solution using the `MOST_CONSTRAINED_VARIABLE` variable heuristic and the `LEAST_CONSTRAINING_VALUE` value heuristic:

```
print('\nMost constrained variable and least constraining value:',
        backtrack(problem, variable_heuristic=MOST_CONSTRAINED_
VARIABLE,
        value_heuristic=LEAST_CONSTRAINING_VALUE))
```

Compute the solution using the `HIGHEST_DEGREE_VARIABLE` variable heuristic and the `LEAST_CONSTRAINING_VALUE` value heuristic:

```
print('\nHighest degree and least constraining value:',
        backtrack(problem, variable_heuristic=HIGHEST_DEGREE_
VARIABLE,
        value_heuristic=LEAST_CONSTRAINING_VALUE))
```

Compute the solution using the minimum conflicts heuristic:

```
print('\nMinimum conflicts:', min_conflicts(problem))
```

The full code is given in the file `constrained_problem.py`. If you run the code, you will get the following output:

```
Solutions:

Normal: {'Patricia': 2, 'John': 1, 'Anna': 3, 'Tom': 4}

Most constrained variable: {'Patricia': 2, 'John': 3, 'Anna': 1, 'Tom': 2}

Highest degree variable: {'Patricia': 2, 'John': 1, 'Anna': 3, 'Tom': 4}

Least constraining value: {'Patricia': 2, 'John': 1, 'Anna': 3, 'Tom': 4}

Most constrained variable and least constraining value: {'Patricia': 2, 'John': 3, 'Anna': 1, 'Tom': 2}

Highest degree and least constraining value: {'Patricia': 2, 'John': 1, 'Anna': 3, 'Tom': 4}

Minimum conflicts: {'Patricia': 4, 'John': 1, 'Anna': 3, 'Tom': 4}
```

Figure 6: Computing the solution with the minimum conflicts heuristic

You can check the constraints to see if the solutions satisfy all those constraints.

Solving the region-coloring problem

Let's use the constraint satisfaction framework to solve the region-coloring problem. Consider the following screenshot:

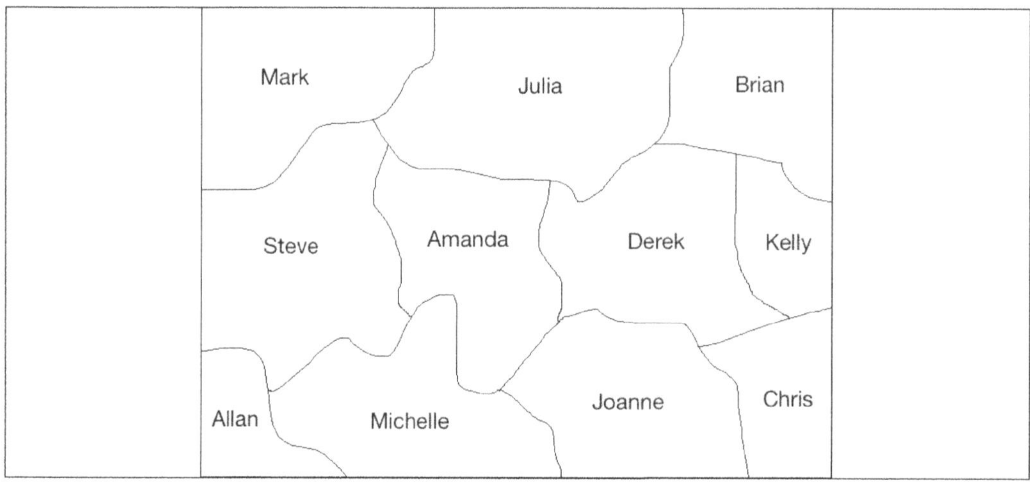

Figure 7: Framework for the region-coloring problem

We have a few regions in the preceding figure that are labeled with names. The goal is to color with four colors so that no adjacent regions have the same color.

Create a new Python file and import the following packages:

```
from simpleai.search import CspProblem, backtrack
```

Define the constraint that specifies that the values should be different:

```
# Define the function that imposes the constraint
# that neighbors should be different
def constraint_func(names, values):
    return values[0] != values[1]
```

Define the `main` function and specify the list of names:

```
if __name__=='__main__':
    # Specify the variables
    names = ('Mark', 'Julia', 'Steve', 'Amanda', 'Brian',
            'Joanne', 'Derek', 'Allan', 'Michelle', 'Kelly')
```

Define the list of possible colors:

```
    # Define the possible colors
    colors = dict((name, ['red', 'green', 'blue', 'gray']) for name in
names)
```

We need to convert the map information into something that the algorithm can understand. Let's define the constraints by specifying the list of people who are adjacent to each other:

```
    # Define the constraints
    constraints = [
        (('Mark', 'Julia'), constraint_func),
        (('Mark', 'Steve'), constraint_func),
        (('Julia', 'Steve'), constraint_func),
        (('Julia', 'Amanda'), constraint_func),
        (('Julia', 'Derek'), constraint_func),
        (('Julia', 'Brian'), constraint_func),
        (('Steve', 'Amanda'), constraint_func),
        (('Steve', 'Allan'), constraint_func),
        (('Steve', 'Michelle'), constraint_func),
        (('Amanda', 'Michelle'), constraint_func),
        (('Amanda', 'Joanne'), constraint_func),
        (('Amanda', 'Derek'), constraint_func),
        (('Brian', 'Derek'), constraint_func),
        (('Brian', 'Kelly'), constraint_func),
```

```
            (('Joanne', 'Michelle'), constraint_func),
            (('Joanne', 'Amanda'), constraint_func),
            (('Joanne', 'Derek'), constraint_func),
            (('Joanne', 'Kelly'), constraint_func),
            (('Derek', 'Kelly'), constraint_func),
        ]
```

Use the variables and constraints to initialize the object:

```
        # Solve the problem
        problem = CspProblem(names, colors, constraints)
```

Solve the problem and print the solution:

```
        # Print the solution
        output = backtrack(problem)
        print('\nColor mapping:\n')
        for k, v in output.items():
            print(k, '==>', v)
```

The full code is given in the file `coloring.py`. If you run the code, you will get the following output:

Figure 8: Color mapping output

If you color the regions based on this output, you will get the following:

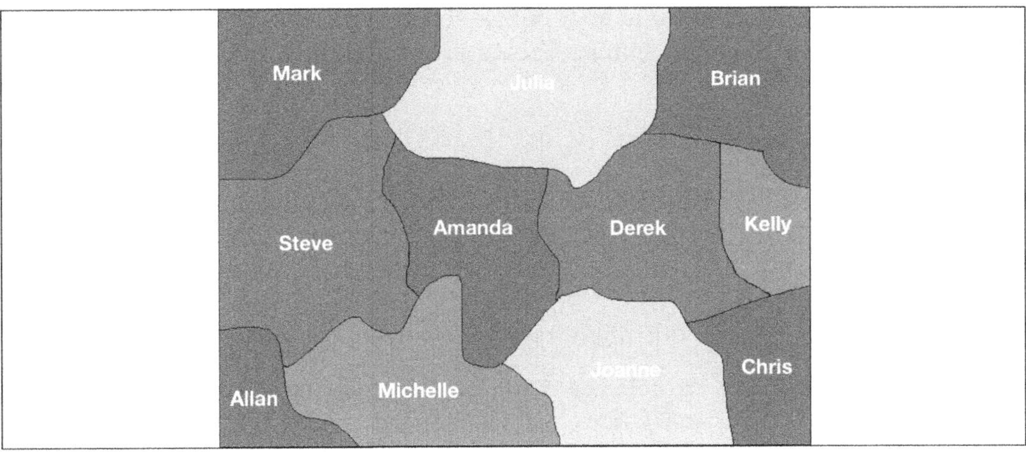

Figure 9: Solution to the region-coloring problem

You can check that no two adjacent regions have the same color.

Building an 8-puzzle solver

The 8-puzzle is a variant of the 15-puzzle. You can check it out at `https://en.wikipedia.org/wiki/15_puzzle`. You will be presented with a randomized grid and your goal is to get it back to the original ordered configuration. You can play the game to get familiar with it at `http://mypuzzle.org/sliding`.

We will use an **A* algorithm** to solve this problem. It is an algorithm that's used to find paths to the solution in a graph. This algorithm is a combination of **Dijkstra's algorithm** and a greedy best-first search. Instead of blindly guessing where to go next, the A* algorithm picks the one that looks the most promising. At each node, the list of all possibilities is generated and then the one with the minimal cost required to reach the goal is picked.

Let's see how to define the cost function. At each node, the cost needs to be computed. This cost is basically the sum of two costs – the first cost is the cost of getting to the current node and the second cost is the cost of reaching the goal from the current node.

We use this summation as a heuristic. As we can see, the second cost is basically an estimate that's not perfect. If it was perfect, then the A* algorithm would arrive at the solution quickly. But it's not usually the case. It takes some time to find the best path to the solution. A* is effective in finding the optimal paths, however, and is one of the most popular techniques out there.

Let's use the A* algorithm to build an 8-puzzle solver. This is a variant of the solution given in the `simpleai` library. Create a new Python file and import the following packages:

```
from simpleai.search import astar, SearchProblem
```

Define a class that contains the methods to solve the 8-puzzle:

```
# Class containing methods to solve the puzzle
class PuzzleSolver(SearchProblem):
```

Override the `actions` method to align it with the current problem:

```
    # Action method to get the list of the possible
    # numbers that can be moved into the empty space
    def actions(self, cur_state):
        rows = string_to_list(cur_state)
        row_empty, col_empty = get_location(rows, 'e')
```

Check the location of the empty space and create the new action:

```
        actions = []
        if row_empty > 0:
            actions.append(rows[row_empty - 1][col_empty])
        if row_empty < 2:
            actions.append(rows[row_empty + 1][col_empty])
        if col_empty > 0:
            actions.append(rows[row_empty][col_empty - 1])
        if col_empty < 2:
            actions.append(rows[row_empty][col_empty + 1])

        return actions
```

Override the `result` method. Convert the string to a list and extract the location of the empty space. Generate the result by updating the locations:

```
    # Return the resulting state after moving
    # a piece to the empty space
    def result(self, state, action):
        rows = string_to_list(state)
        row_empty, col_empty = get_location(rows, 'e')
        row_new, col_new = get_location(rows, action)

        rows[row_empty][col_empty], rows[row_new][col_new] = \
                rows[row_new][col_new], rows[row_empty][col_empty]

        return list_to_string(rows)
```

Check if the goal has been reached:

```
    # Returns true if a state is the goal state
    def is_goal(self, state):
        return state == GOAL
```

Define the heuristic method. We will use the heuristic that computes the distance between the current state and goal state using Manhattan distance:

```
    # Returns an estimate of the distance from a state to
    # the goal using the manhattan distance
    def heuristic(self, state):
        rows = string_to_list(state)

        distance = 0
```

Compute the distance:

```
        for number in '12345678e':
            row_new, col_new = get_location(rows, number)
            row_new_goal, col_new_goal = goal_positions[number]

            distance += abs(row_new - row_new_goal) + abs(col_new -
col_new_goal)

        return distance
```

Define a function to convert a list to string:

```
# Convert list to string
def list_to_string(input_list):
    return '\n'.join(['-'.join(x) for x in input_list])
```

Define a function to convert a string to a list:

```
# Convert string to list
def string_to_list(input_string):
    return [x.split('-') for x in input_string.split('\n')]
```

Define a function to get the location of a given element in the grid:

```
# Find the 2D location of the input element
def get_location(rows, input_element):
    for i, row in enumerate(rows):
        for j, item in enumerate(row):
            if item == input_element:
                return i, j
```

Define the initial state and the final goal we want to achieve:

```
# Final result that we want to achieve
GOAL = '''1-2-3
4-5-6
7-8-e'''

# Starting point
INITIAL = '''1-e-2
6-3-4
7-5-8'''
```

Track the goal positions for each piece by creating a variable:

```
# Create a cache for the goal position of each piece
goal_positions = {}
rows_goal = string_to_list(GOAL)
for number in '12345678e':
    goal_positions[number] = get_location(rows_goal, number)
```

Create the A* solver object using the initial state we defined earlier and extract the result:

```
# Create the solver object
result = astar(PuzzleSolver(INITIAL))
```

Print the solution:

```
# Print the results
for i, (action, state) in enumerate(result.path()):
    print()
    if action == None:
        print('Initial configuration')
    elif i == len(result.path()) - 1:
        print('After moving', action, 'into the empty space. Goal
achieved!')
    else:
        print('After moving', action, 'into the empty space')

    print(state)
```

The full code is given in the file `puzzle.py`. If you run the code, you will get a long output.

It will start as follows:

```
Initial configuration
1-e-2
6-3-4
7-5-8

After moving 2 into the empty space
1-2-e
6-3-4
7-5-8

After moving 4 into the empty space
1-2-4
6-3-e
7-5-8

After moving 3 into the empty space
1-2-4
6-e-3
7-5-8

After moving 6 into the empty space
1-2-4
e-6-3
7-5-8
```

Figure 10: PuzzleSolver output

If you scroll down, you will see the steps taken to arrive at the solution. At the end, you will see the following:

```
After moving 2 into the empty space
e-2-3
1-4-6
7-5-8

After moving 1 into the empty space
1-2-3
e-4-6
7-5-8

After moving 4 into the empty space
1-2-3
4-e-6
7-5-8

After moving 5 into the empty space
1-2-3
4-5-6
7-e-8

After moving 8 into the empty space. Goal achieved!
1-2-3
4-5-6
7-8-e
```

Figure 11: End of the PuzzleSolver output - Goal achieved!

As you can see, the goal is achieved and the puzzle is solved.

Building a maze solver

Let's use the A* algorithm to solve a maze. Consider the following figure:

```
##############################
#         #              #   #
# ####    ########       #   #
#  o #    #              #   #
#    ###     #####  ######   #
#      #   ###   #           #
#      #     #   #  #  #   ###
#     #####    #    #  # x   #
#              #       #     #
##############################
```

Figure 12: Example of a maze problem

The **#** symbols indicate obstacles. The symbol **o** represents the starting point, and **x** represents the goal. The goal is to find the shortest path from the start to the end point. Let's see how to do it in Python. The following solution is a variant of the solution provided in the `simpleai` library. Create a new Python file and import the following packages:

```
import math
from simpleai.search import SearchProblem, astar
```

Create a class that contains the methods needed to solve the problem:

```
# Class containing the methods to solve the maze
class MazeSolver(SearchProblem):
```

Define the initializer method:

```
    # Initialize the class
    def __init__(self, board):
        self.board = board
        self.goal = (0, 0)
```

Extract the initial and final positions:

```
        for y in range(len(self.board)):
            for x in range(len(self.board[y])):
                if self.board[y][x].lower() == "o":
```

```
                self.initial = (x, y)
            elif self.board[y][x].lower() == "x":
                self.goal = (x, y)

    super(MazeSolver, self).__init__(initial_state=self.initial)
```

Override the `actions` method. At each position, we need to check the cost of going to the neighboring cells and then append all the possible actions. If the neighboring cell is blocked, then that action is not considered:

```
# Define the method that takes actions
# to arrive at the solution
def actions(self, state):
    actions = []
    for action in COSTS.keys():
        newx, newy = self.result(state, action)
        if self.board[newy][newx] != "#":
        actions.append(action)

        return actions
```

Override the `result` method. Depending on the current state and the input action, update the `x` and `y` coordinates:

```
# Update the state based on the action
def result(self, state, action):
    x, y = state

    if action.count("up"):
        y -= 1
    if action.count("down"):
        y += 1
    if action.count("left"):
        x -= 1
    if action.count("right"):
        x += 1

    new_state = (x, y)

    return new_state
```

Check if we have arrived at the goal:

```
# Check if we have reached the goal
def is_goal(self, state):
    return state == self.goal
```

We need to define the cost function. This is the cost of moving to a neighboring cell, and it's different for vertical/horizontal and diagonal moves. We will define these later:

```
    # Compute the cost of taking an action
    def cost(self, state, action, state2):
        return COSTS[action]
```

Define the heuristic that will be used. In this case, we will use the Euclidean distance:

```
    # Heuristic that we use to arrive at the solution
    def heuristic(self, state):
        x, y = state
        gx, gy = self.goal

        return math.sqrt((x - gx) ** 2 + (y - gy) ** 2)
```

Define the main function and define the map we discussed earlier:

```
if __name__ == "__main__":
    # Define the map
    MAP = """
    ##############################
    #         #              #   #
    # ####    ########       #   #
    #  o #    #              #   #
    #    ###     #####  ######   #
    #      #   ###   #           #
    #      #     #   #  #  #   ###
    #     #####    #    #  # x   #
    #              #       #     #
    ##############################
    """
```

Convert the map information into a list:

```
    # Convert map to a list
    print(MAP)
    MAP = [list(x) for x in MAP.split("\n") if x]
```

Define the cost of moving around the map. A diagonal move is more expensive than horizontal or vertical moves:

```
    # Define cost of moving around the map
    cost_regular = 1.0
    cost_diagonal = 1.7
```

Assign the costs to the corresponding moves:

```
# Create the cost dictionary
COSTS = {
    "up": cost_regular,
    "down": cost_regular,
    "left": cost_regular,
    "right": cost_regular,
    "up left": cost_diagonal,
    "up right": cost_diagonal,
    "down left": cost_diagonal,
    "down right": cost_diagonal,
}
```

Create a solver object using the custom class that was defined earlier:

```
# Create maze solver object
problem = MazeSolver(MAP)
```

Run the solver on the map and extract the result:

```
# Run the solver
result = astar(problem, graph_search=True)
```

Extract the path from the result:

```
# Extract the path
path = [x[1] for x in result.path()]
```

Print the output:

```
# Print the result
print()
for y in range(len(MAP)):
    for x in range(len(MAP[y])):
        if (x, y) == problem.initial:
            print('o', end='')
        elif (x, y) == problem.goal:
            print('x', end='')
        elif (x, y) in path:
            print('·', end='')
        else:
            print(MAP[y][x], end='')


    print()
```

The full code is given in the file `maze.py`. If you run the code, you will get the following output:

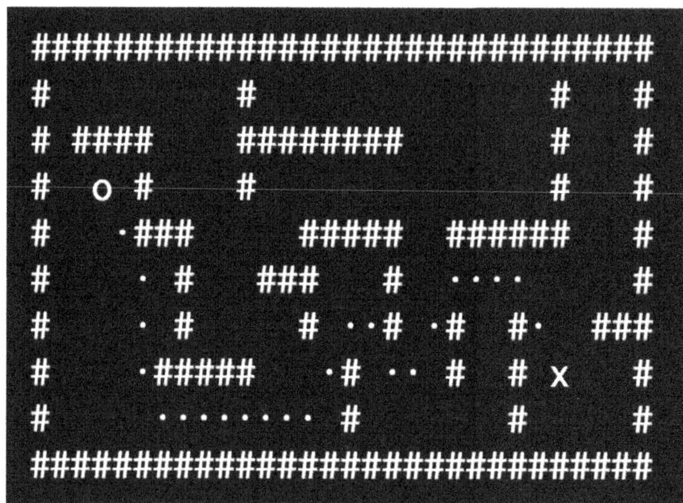

Figure 13: A solution to the maze problem

As you can see, the algorithm left a trail of dots and found the solution from the starting point **o** to the end point **x**. This concludes our demonstration of the A* algorithm in this final section of the chapter.

Summary

In this chapter, we learned how heuristic search techniques work. We discussed the difference between uninformed and informed searches. We learned about constraint satisfaction problems and how we can solve problems using this paradigm. We discussed how local search techniques work and why simulated annealing is used in practice. We implemented a greedy search for a string problem. We solved a problem using the CSP formulation.

We used this approach to solve the region-coloring problem. We then discussed the A* algorithm and how it can used to find the optimal paths to the solution. We used it to build an 8-puzzle solver as well as a maze solver. In the next chapter, we will discuss genetic algorithms and how they can used to solve real-world problems.

11
Genetic Algorithms and Genetic Programming

In this chapter, we are going to learn about genetic algorithms. First, we'll describe what a genetic algorithm is, then we will discuss the concepts of evolutionary algorithms and genetic programming and see how these relate to genetic algorithms. We will learn about the fundamental building blocks of genetic algorithms including crossover, mutation, and fitness functions. We will then use these concepts to build various systems.

By the end of this chapter, you will have a better understanding of the following:

- Evolutionary and genetic algorithms
- Fundamental concepts in genetic algorithms
- Generating bit patterns with predefined parameters
- Visualizing the progress of an evolution
- Solving the symbol regression problem
- Building an intelligent robot controller

The evolutionists tribe

As we mentioned at the beginning of the book, the computer science and data science researchers studying genetic algorithms and genetic programming are part of the evolutionist tribe as defined by Pedro Domingos. In some ways, this tribe is not front and center. The connectionists are having their day in the sun and seem to be enjoying their time in the spotlight. As highlighted by Dr. Domingos, as CPUs get faster and more research is performed in this area, do not be surprised if new and exciting cutting-edge research emerges in this area in the next couple years. They already have made many strong and innovative contributions to the field and will continue to do so.

Understanding evolutionary and genetic algorithms

A genetic algorithm is a type of evolutionary algorithm. So, in order to understand genetic algorithms, we need to discuss evolutionary algorithms. An evolutionary algorithm is a meta-heuristic optimization algorithm that applies the principles of evolution to solve problems. The concept of evolution is like the one we find in nature; much like the environment actively drives the "solution" arrived at through evolution, we directly use the problem's functions and variables to arrive at a solution. But in a genetic algorithm, any given problem is encoded in bit patterns that are manipulated by the algorithm.

Computer solving of problems autonomously is the central goal of Artificial Intelligence and machine learning. **Genetic Algorithms (GAs)** are an evolutionary computation technique that automatically solves problems without requiring the user to know or specify the form or structure of the solution in advance. At the most abstract level, GAs are a systematic, domain-independent method for computers to solve problems automatically, beginning from a high-level statement of what needs to be done.

The underlying steps in evolutionary algorithms are as follows:

Step 1

Generate the initial population of data points or *individuals* randomly. An individual as defined by GAs is member of population that has certain *characteristics* or *traits*. In later steps of the algorithm, we'll determine if these traits allow the individual to adapt to the environment and survive long enough to have offspring.

Step 2

Perform these steps in a loop until termination:

1. Evaluate the fitness of everyone in that population.
2. Select the best-fit individuals for reproduction.
3. Breed new individuals through crossover and mutation operations to give birth to offspring.
4. Evaluate the individual fitness of new individuals.
5. Replace the least-fit population with new individuals.

The *fitness* of individuals is determined using a **fitness function** that's predefined. This where the phrase *survival of the fittest* comes into play.

We then take these selected individuals and create the next generation of individuals by recombination and mutation. We will discuss the concepts of recombination and mutation in the next section. For now, let's think of these techniques as mechanisms to create the next generation by treating the selected individuals as parents.

Once we execute recombination and mutation, we create a new set of individuals who will compete with the old ones for a place in the next generation. By discarding the weakest individuals and replacing them with offspring, we are increasing the overall fitness level of the population. We continue to iterate until the desired overall fitness is achieved.

A GA is an evolutionary algorithm where we use a heuristic to find a string of bits that solves a problem. We continuously iterate on a population to arrive at a solution.

We do this by generating new populations containing fitter individuals. We apply probabilistic operators such as **selection**, **crossover**, and **mutation** in order to generate the next generation of individuals. The individuals are represented as strings, where every string is the encoded version of a potential solution.

A fitness function is used that evaluates the fitness measure of each string telling us how well-suited it is to solve the problem in question. This fitness function is also referred to as an **evaluation function**. GAs apply operators that are inspired by nature, which is why the nomenclature is closely related to the terms found in biology.

Fundamental concepts in genetic algorithms

In order to build a GA, we need to understand several key concepts and terms. These concepts are used extensively throughout the field of GAs to build solutions to various problems. One of the most important aspects of GAs is *randomness*. In order to iterate, it relies on the random sampling of individuals. This means that the process is non-deterministic. So, if you run the same algorithm multiple times, you might end up with different solutions.

Let's now define the term *population*. A population is a set of individuals that are possible candidate solutions. In a GA, the single best solution is not maintained at any given stage but rather a set of potential solutions, one of which could be the best. But the other solutions play an important role during the search. Since the population of solutions is tracked, it is less likely to get stuck in a local optimum. Getting stuck in a local optimum is a classic problem faced by other optimization techniques.

Now that we know about populations and the stochastic nature of GAs, let's talk about the operators. When creating the next generation of individuals, the algorithm tries to make sure that they come from the fittest individuals in the current generation.

Mutation is one of the ways to achieve this. A GA makes random changes to one or more individuals of the current generation to yield a new candidate solution. This change is called mutation. Now this change might make that individual better or worse than existing individuals.

The next concept that needs to be defined is *recombination*, which is also called *crossover*. This is directly related to the role of reproduction in the evolution process. A GA tries to combine individuals from the current generation to create a new solution. It combines some of the features of each parent individual to create this offspring. This process is called crossover. The goal is to replace the "less fit" individuals in the current generation with offspring generated from "fitter" individuals in the population.

In order to apply crossover and mutation, we need to have selection criteria. The concept of *selection* is inspired by the theory of natural selection. During each iteration, the GA performs a selection process. The fittest individuals are chosen using this selection process and the weaker individuals are terminated. This is where the survival of the fittest concept comes into play. The selection process is carried out using a function that computes the fitness of individuals.

Generating a bit pattern with predefined parameters

Now that we know the basic concepts behind a GA, let's see how to use it to solve some problems. We will be using a Python package called `DEAP`. You can find all the details about it at `http://deap.readthedocs.io/en/master`. Let's go ahead and install it by running the following command:

```
$ pip3 install deap
```

Now that the package is installed, let's quickly test it. Go into the Python shell by typing the following command:

```
$ python3
```

Once you are inside, type the following:

```
>>> import deap
```

If you do not see an error message, you are good to go.

In this section, we will use a variant of the **One Max algorithm**. The One Max algorithm tries to generate a bit string that contains the maximum number of ones. It is a simple algorithm, but it's helpful to get familiar with the library in order to better understand how to implement solutions using GAs. In this case, a bit string may be generated that contains a predefined number of ones. You will see that the underlying structure and part of the code is like the example used in the `DEAP` library.

Create a new Python file and import the following:

```
import random

from deap import base, creator, tools
```

Let's say we want to generate a bit pattern of length 75, and we want it to contain `45` ones. We need to define an evaluation function that can be used to target this objective:

```
# Evaluation function
def eval_func(individual):
    target_sum = 45
    return len(individual) - abs(sum(individual) - target_sum),
```

The formula used in the preceding function reaches its maximum value when the number of ones is equal to `45`. The length of all individuals is 75. When the number of ones is equal to `45`, the return value would be `75`.

Now let's define a function to create the `toolbox`. First, define a `creator` object for the fitness function and to keep track of the individuals. The `Fitness` class used here is an abstract class and it needs the `weights` attribute to be defined. We are building a maximizing fitness using positive weights:

```
# Create the toolbox with the right parameters def
def create_toolbox(num_bits):
    creator.create("FitnessMax", base.Fitness, weights=(1.0,))
    creator.create("Individual", list, fitness=creator.FitnessMax)
```

The first line creates a single objective maximizing fitness named `FitnessMax`. The second line deals with producing the individual. The first individual that is created is a list of floats. In order to produce this individual, we must create an `Individual` class using the `creator`. The fitness attribute will use `FitnessMax` defined earlier.

A toolbox is an object that is commonly used in DEAP. It is used to store various functions along with their arguments. Let's create this object:

```
# Initialize the toolbox
toolbox = base.Toolbox()
```

We will now start registering various functions to this toolbox. Let's start with the random number generator that generates a random integer between 0 and 1. This is basically to generate the bit strings:

```
    # Generate attributes
    toolbox.register("attr_bool", random.randint, 0, 1)
```

Let's register the individual function. The method initRepeat takes three arguments – a container class for the individual, a function used to fill the container, and the number of times we want the function to repeat itself:

```
    # Initialize structures
    toolbox.register("individual", tools.initRepeat, creator.
Individual,
        toolbox.attr_bool, num_bits)
```

We need to register the population function. We want the population to be a list of individuals:

```
    # Define the population to be a list of individuals
    toolbox.register("population", tools.initRepeat, list, toolbox.
individual)
```

We now need to register the genetic operators. Register the evaluation function that we defined earlier, which will act as the fitness function. We want the individual, which is a bit pattern, to have 45 ones:

```
    # Register the evaluation operator
    toolbox.register("evaluate", eval_func)
```

Register the crossover operator named mate using the cxTwoPoint method:

```
    # Register the crossover operator
    toolbox.register("mate", tools.cxTwoPoint)
```

Register the mutation operator named mutate using mutFlipBit. We need to specify the probability of each attribute to be mutated using indpb:

```
    # Register a mutation operator
    toolbox.register("mutate", tools.mutFlipBit, indpb=0.05)
```

Register the selection operator using `selTournament`. It specifies which individuals will be selected for breeding:

```
    # Operator for selecting individuals for breeding
    toolbox.register("select", tools.selTournament, tournsize=3)

    return toolbox
```

This is the implementation of all the concepts discussed in the preceding section. A `toolbox` generator function is common in `DEAP` and we will use it throughout this chapter. So, it's important to spend some time to understand how the `toolbox` was generated.

Define the `main` function by starting with the length of the bit pattern:

```
if __name__ == "__main__":
    # Define the number of bits
    num_bits = 75
```

Create a `toolbox` using the function we defined earlier:

```
    # Create a toolbox using the above parameter
    toolbox = create_toolbox(num_bits)
```

Seed the random number generator to get repeatable results:

```
    # Seed the random number generator
    random.seed(7)
```

Create an initial population of, say, `500` individuals using the method available in the `toolbox` object. Feel free to change this number and experiment with it:

```
    # Create an initial population of 500 individuals
    population = toolbox.population(n=500)
```

Define the probabilities of crossing and mutating. Again, these are parameters that are defined by the user. So, you can change these parameters and see how they affect the result:

```
    # Define probabilities of crossing and mutating
    probab_crossing, probab_mutating = 0.5, 0.2
```

Define the number of generations needed to iterate until the process is terminated. If you increase the number of generations, you are giving it more cycles to improve the fitness of the population:

```
    # Define the number of generations
    num_generations = 60
```

Evaluate all the individuals in the population using the fitness functions:

```
    print('\nStarting the evolution process')

    # Evaluate the entire population
    fitnesses = list(map(toolbox.evaluate, population))
    for ind, fit in zip(population, fitnesses):
        ind.fitness.values = fit
```

Start iterating through the generations:

```
    print('\nEvaluated', len(population), 'individuals')

    # Iterate through generations
    for g in range(num_generations):
        print("\n===== Generation", g)
```

In each generation, select the next generation individuals using the selection operator that we registered to the `toolbox` earlier:

```
        # Select the next generation individuals
        offspring = toolbox.select(population, len(population))
```

Clone the selected individuals:

```
        # Clone the selected individuals
        offspring = list(map(toolbox.clone, offspring))
```

Apply crossover and mutation on the next generation individuals using the probability values defined earlier. Once it's done, reset the fitness values:

```
        # Apply crossover and mutation on the offspring
        for child1, child2 in zip(offspring[::2], offspring[1::2]):
            # Cross two individuals
            if random.random() < probab_crossing:
                toolbox.mate(child1, child2)

                # "Forget" the fitness values of the children
                del child1.fitness.values
                del child2.fitness.values
```

Apply mutation to the next generation individuals using the corresponding probability value that was defined earlier. Once it's done, reset the fitness value:

```
        # Apply mutation
        for mutant in offspring:
            # Mutate an individual
            if random.random() < probab_mutating:
                toolbox.mutate(mutant)
                del mutant.fitness.values
```

Evaluate the individuals with invalid fitness values:

```
        # Evaluate the individuals with an invalid fitness
        invalid_ind = [ind for ind in offspring if not ind.fitness.
valid]
        fitnesses = map(toolbox.evaluate, invalid_ind)
        for ind, fit in zip(invalid_ind, fitnesses):
            ind.fitness.values = fit

        print('Evaluated', len(invalid_ind), 'individuals')
```

Replace the population with the next generation of individuals:

```
        # The population is entirely replaced by the offspring
        population[:] = offspring
```

Print the stats for the current generation to see how it's progressing:

```
        # Gather all the fitnesses in one list and print the stats
        fits = [ind.fitness.values[0] for ind in population]

        length = len(population)
        mean = sum(fits) / length
        sum2 = sum(x*x for x in fits)
        std = abs(sum2 / length - mean**2)**0.5

        print('Min =', min(fits), ', Max =', max(fits))
        print('Average =', round(mean, 2), ', Standard deviation =',
                round(std, 2))

    print("\n==== End of evolution")
```

Print the final output:

```
    best_ind = tools.selBest(population, 1)[0]
    print('\nBest individual:\n', best_ind)
    print('\nNumber of ones:', sum(best_ind))
```

The full code is given in the file `bit_counter.py`. If you run the code, you will see iterations printed out. At the start, you will see something like the following:

```
Starting the evolution process

Evaluated 500 individuals

===== Generation 0
Evaluated 297 individuals
Min = 58.0 , Max = 75.0
Average = 70.43 , Standard deviation = 2.91

===== Generation 1
Evaluated 303 individuals
Min = 63.0 , Max = 75.0
Average = 72.44 , Standard deviation = 2.16

===== Generation 2
Evaluated 310 individuals
Min = 65.0 , Max = 75.0
Average = 73.31 , Standard deviation = 1.6

===== Generation 3
Evaluated 273 individuals
Min = 67.0 , Max = 75.0
Average = 73.76 , Standard deviation = 1.41
```

Figure 1: Initial evolution output (Generations 0 to 3)

At the end, you will see something like the following that indicates the end of the evolution:

```
===== Generation 57
Evaluated 306 individuals
Min = 68.0 , Max = 75.0
Average = 74.02 , Standard deviation = 1.27

===== Generation 58
Evaluated 276 individuals
Min = 69.0 , Max = 75.0
Average = 74.15 , Standard deviation = 1.18

===== Generation 59
Evaluated 288 individuals
Min = 69.0 , Max = 75.0
Average = 74.12 , Standard deviation = 1.24

==== End of evolution

Best individual:
 [1, 1, 0, 1, 1, 0, 1, 0, 1, 0, 0, 1, 0, 1, 0, 1, 1, 1, 1, 0, 1, 0, 0, 1, 1, 1, 0, 1, 1, 1, 1, 1, 1, 1, 1
, 1, 1, 1, 0, 0, 1, 0, 0, 1, 1, 0, 0, 1, 1, 0, 1, 1, 0, 0, 0, 1, 0, 0, 1, 1, 1, 0, 1, 1, 1, 0, 1, 1, 0, 0
, 1, 0, 0, 0, 1]

Number of ones: 45
```

Figure 2: Evolution final output

As seen in the preceding figure, the evolution process ends after 60 generations (zero-indexed). Once it's done, the best individual is picked and printed on the output. It has 45 ones in the best individual, which is a confirmation of the result because the target sum is `45` in the evaluation function.

Visualizing the evolution

Let's see how to visualize the evolution process. In DEAP, there is a method called **Covariance Matrix Adaptation Evolution Strategy** (**CMA-ES**) to visualize evolutions. It is an evolutionary algorithm that's used to solve non-linear problems in the continuous domain. The CMA-ES technique is robust, well studied, and is considered "state-of-the-art" in evolutionary algorithms. Let's see how it works by delving into the source code. The following code is a slight variation of the example shown in the DEAP library.

Create a new Python file and import the following:

```
import numpy as np
import matplotlib.pyplot as plt
from deap import algorithms, base, benchmarks, \
        cma, creator, tools
```

Define a function to create the toolbox. We will define a FitnessMin function using negative weights:

```
# Function to create a toolbox
def create_toolbox(strategy):
    creator.create("FitnessMin", base.Fitness, weights=(-1.0,))
    creator.create("Individual", list, fitness=creator.FitnessMin)
```

Create the toolbox and register the evaluation function, as follows:

```
    toolbox = base.Toolbox()
    toolbox.register("evaluate", benchmarks.rastrigin)

    # Seed the random number generator
    np.random.seed(7)
```

Register the generate and update methods. This will use the generate-update paradigm and generate a population from a strategy, and then the strategy is updated based on the population:

```
    toolbox.register("generate", strategy.generate, creator.
Individual)
    toolbox.register("update", strategy.update)

    return toolbox
```

Define the main function. Start by defining the number of individuals and the number of generations:

```
if __name__ == "__main__":
```

```
# Problem size
num_individuals = 10
num_generations = 125
```

Define a `strategy` before starting the process:

```
# Create a strategy using CMA-ES algorithm
strategy = cma.Strategy(centroid=[5.0]*num_individuals, sigma=5.0,
        lambda_=20*num_individuals)
```

Create the `toolbox` based on the strategy:

```
# Create toolbox based on the above strategy
toolbox = create_toolbox(strategy)
```

Create a `HallOfFame` object. The `HallOfFame` object contains the best individual that ever existed in the population. This object is always kept in a sorted format. This way, the first element in this object is the individual that has the best fitness value seen during the evolution process:

```
# Create hall of fame object
hall_of_fame = tools.HallOfFame(1)
```

Register the stats using the `Statistics` method:

```
# Register the relevant stats
stats = tools.Statistics(lambda x: x.fitness.values)
stats.register("avg", np.mean)
stats.register("std", np.std)
stats.register("min", np.min)
stats.register("max", np.max)
```

Define the `logbook` to keep track of the evolution records. It is basically a chronological list of dictionaries:

```
logbook = tools.Logbook()
logbook.header = "gen", "evals", "std", "min", "avg", "max"
```

Define objects to compile all the data:

```
# Objects that will compile the data
sigma = np.ndarray((num_generations, 1))
axis_ratio = np.ndarray((num_generations, 1))
diagD = np.ndarray((num_generations, num_individuals))
fbest = np.ndarray((num_generations,1))
best = np.ndarray((num_generations, num_individuals))
std = np.ndarray((num_generations, num_individuals))
```

Iterate through the generations:

```
    for gen in range(num_generations):
        # Generate a new population
        population = toolbox.generate()
```

Evaluate individuals using the fitness function:

```
        # Evaluate the individuals
        fitnesses = toolbox.map(toolbox.evaluate, population)
        for ind, fit in zip(population, fitnesses):
            ind.fitness.values = fit
```

Update the strategy based on the population:

```
        # Update the strategy with the evaluated individuals
        toolbox.update(population)
```

Update the hall of fame and statistics with the current generation of individuals:

```
        # Update the hall of fame and the statistics with the
        # currently evaluated population
        hall_of_fame.update(population)
        record = stats.compile(population)
        logbook.record(evals=len(population), gen=gen, **record)

        print(logbook.stream)
```

Save the data for plotting:

```
        # Save more data along the evolution for plotting
        sigma[gen] = strategy.sigma
        axis_ratio[gen] = max(strategy.diagD)**2/min(strategy.
diagD)**2
        diagD[gen, :num_individuals] = strategy.diagD**2
        fbest[gen] = hall_of_fame[0].fitness.values
        best[gen, :num_individuals] = hall_of_fame[0]
        std[gen, :num_individuals] = np.std(population, axis=0)
```

Define the x axis and plot the stats:

```
    # The x-axis will be the number of evaluations
    x = list(range(0, strategy.lambda_ * num_generations, strategy.
lambda_))
    avg, max_, min_ = logbook.select("avg", "max", "min")
    plt.figure()
    plt.semilogy(x, avg, "--b")
    plt.semilogy(x, max_, "--b")
    plt.semilogy(x, min_, "-b")
    plt.semilogy(x, fbest, "-c")
    plt.semilogy(x, sigma, "-g")
```

```
    plt.semilogy(x, axis_ratio, "-r")
    plt.grid(True)
    plt.title("blue: f-values, green: sigma, red: axis ratio")
```

Plot the progress:

```
    plt.figure()
    plt.plot(x, best)
    plt.grid(True)
    plt.title("Object Variables")

    plt.figure()
    plt.semilogy(x, diagD)
    plt.grid(True)
    plt.title("Scaling (All Main Axes)")

    plt.figure()
    plt.semilogy(x, std)
    plt.grid(True)
    plt.title("Standard Deviations in All Coordinates")

    plt.show()
```

The full code is given in the file `visualization.py`. If you run the code, you will see four screenshots. The first screenshot shows various parameters:

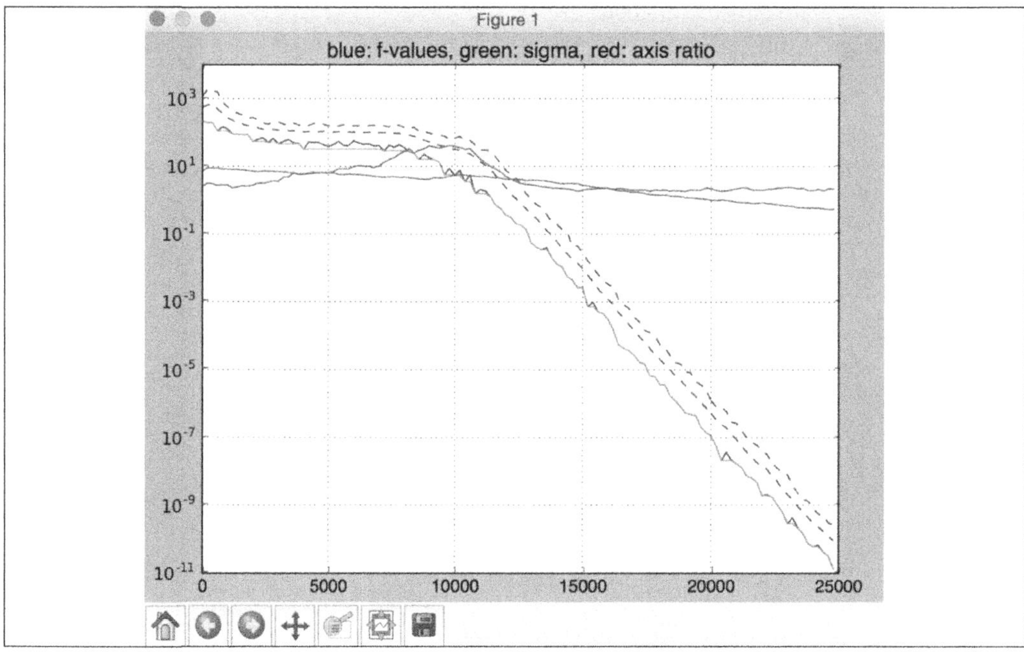

Figure 3: Plotted parameters from the evolution process

The second screenshot shows object variables:

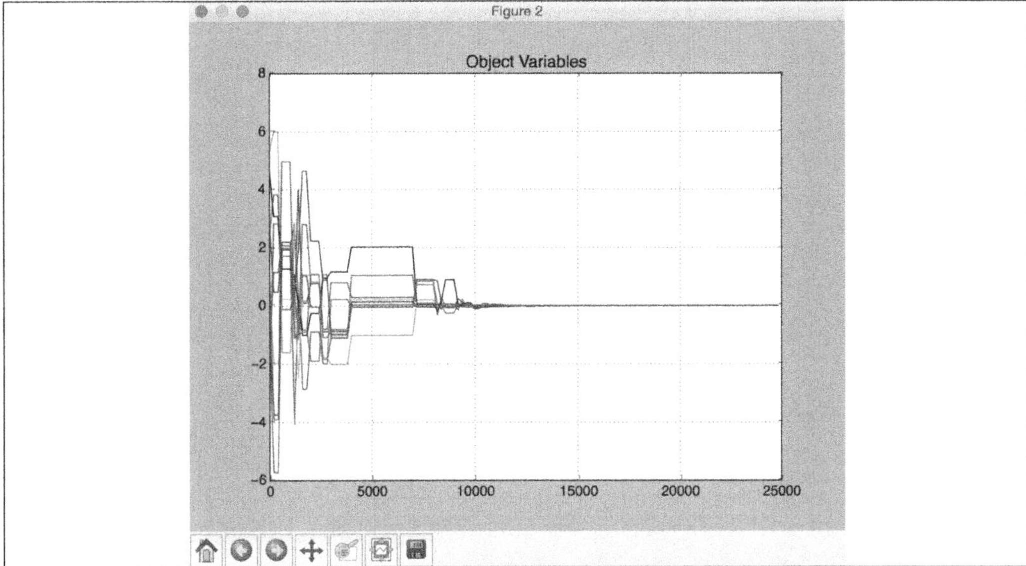

Figure 4: Plotted object variables from the evolution process

The third screenshot shows scaling:

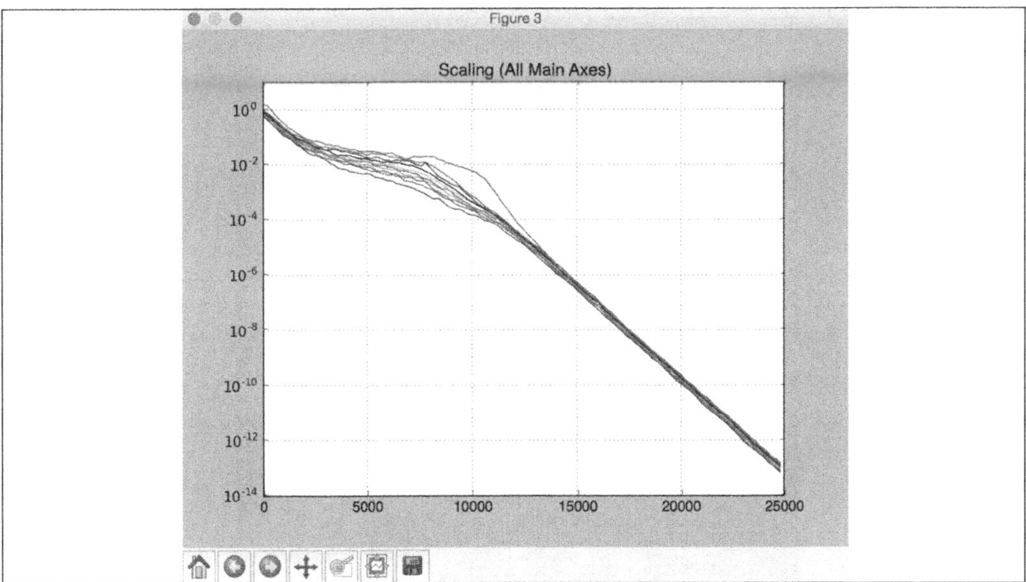

Figure 5: Plotted scaling from the evolution process

The fourth screenshot shows standard deviations:

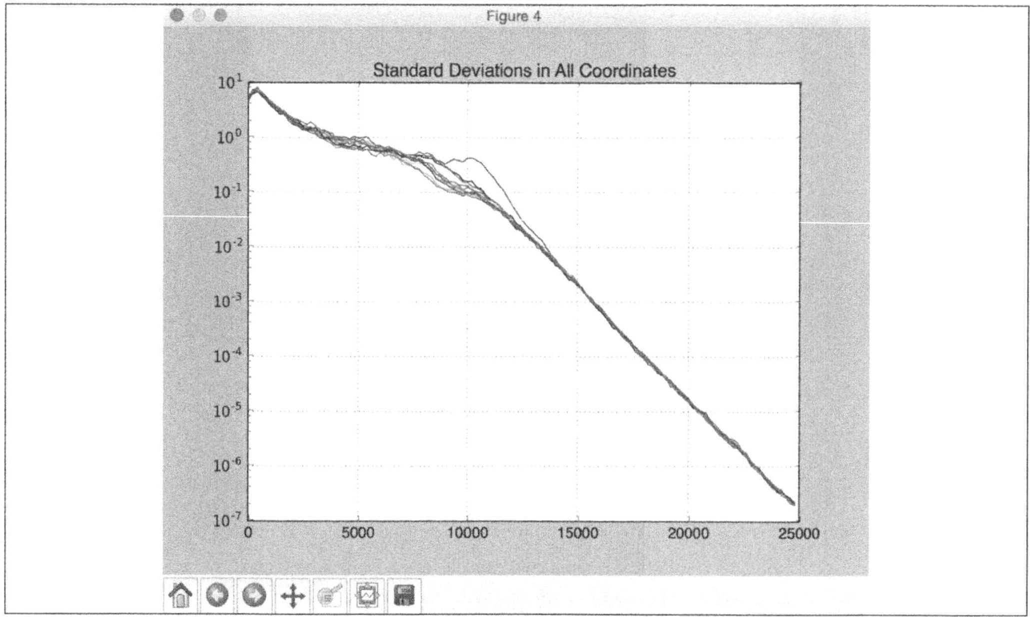

Figure 6: Plotted standard deviations from the evolution process

You will see the progress printed out. At the start, you will see something like the following:

```
gen     evals   std     min     avg     max
0       200     188.36  217.082 576.281 1199.71
1       200     250.543 196.583 659.389 1869.02
2       200     273.081 199.455 683.641 1770.65
3       200     215.326 111.298 503.933 1579.3
4       200     133.046 149.47  373.124 790.899
5       200     75.4405 131.117 274.092 585.433
6       200     61.2622 91.7121 232.624 426.666
7       200     49.8303 88.8185 201.117 373.543
8       200     39.9533 85.0531 178.645 326.209
9       200     31.3781 87.4824 159.211 261.132
10      200     31.3488 54.0743 144.561 274.877
11      200     30.8796 63.6032 136.791 240.739
12      200     24.1975 70.4913 125.691 190.684
13      200     21.2274 50.6409 122.293 177.483
14      200     25.4931 67.9873 124.132 199.296
15      200     26.9804 46.3411 119.295 205.331
16      200     24.8993 56.0033 115.614 176.702
17      200     21.9789 61.4999 113.417 170.156
18      200     21.2823 50.2455 112.419 190.677
19      200     22.5016 48.153  111.543 166.2
20      200     21.1602 32.1864 106.044 171.899
21      200     23.3864 52.8601 107.301 163.617
22      200     23.1008 51.1226 109.628 185.777
23      200     22.0836 51.3058 106.402 179.673
```

Figure 7: Evolution process initial output

At the end, you will see the following:

```
100   200   2.38865e-07   1.12678e-07   5.18814e-07   1.23527e-06
101   200   1.49444e-07   5.56979e-08   3.3199e-07    7.98774e-07
102   200   1.11635e-07   2.07109e-08   2.41361e-07   7.96738e-07
103   200   9.50257e-08   3.69117e-08   1.94641e-07   5.75896e-07
104   200   5.63849e-08   2.09827e-08   1.26148e-07   2.887e-07
105   200   4.42488e-08   1.64212e-08   8.6972e-08    2.58639e-07
106   200   2.34933e-08   1.28302e-08   5.47789e-08   1.54658e-07
107   200   1.74434e-08   7.13185e-09   3.64705e-08   9.88235e-08
108   200   1.17157e-08   6.32208e-09   2.54673e-08   7.13075e-08
109   200   8.73027e-09   4.60369e-09   1.79681e-08   5.88066e-08
110   200   6.39874e-09   1.92573e-09   1.43229e-08   4.00087e-08
111   200   5.31196e-09   2.05551e-09   1.13736e-08   3.16793e-08
112   200   3.15607e-09   1.72427e-09   7.28548e-09   1.67727e-08
113   200   2.3789e-09    1.01164e-09   5.01177e-09   1.24541e-08
114   200   1.38424e-09   6.43112e-10   2.94696e-09   9.25819e-09
115   200   1.04172e-09   2.87571e-10   2.06068e-09   7.90436e-09
116   200   6.08685e-10   4.32905e-10   1.4704e-09    3.80221e-09
117   200   4.51515e-10   2.1538e-10    9.23627e-10   2.2759e-09
118   200   2.77204e-10   1.46869e-10   6.3507e-10    1.44637e-09
119   200   2.06475e-10   7.54881e-11   4.41427e-10   1.33167e-09
120   200   1.3138e-10    5.97282e-11   2.98116e-10   8.60453e-10
121   200   9.52385e-11   6.753e-11     2.32358e-10   5.45441e-10
122   200   7.55001e-11   4.1851e-11    1.72688e-10   5.05054e-10
123   200   5.52125e-11   3.2216e-11    1.23505e-10   3.10081e-10
124   200   4.38068e-11   1.32871e-11   8.94929e-11   2.57202e-10
```

Figure 8: Evolution progress final output

As seen from the preceding figure, all the values keep decreasing as we progress. This indicates that it's converging.

Solving the symbol regression problem

We will see at the end of this chapter the many applications of GAs to a vast amount of industries and domains. From finance to traffic optimization, the applications of GAs are almost endless. For now, though, we continue with another simple example. Let's see how to use genetic programming to solve the symbol regression problem. It is important to understand that genetic programming is not the same as GAs. Genetic programming is a type of evolutionary algorithm in which the solutions occur in the form of computer programs. The individuals in each generation would be computer programs and their fitness level correspond to their ability to solve problems. These programs are modified, at each iteration, using a GA. Genetic programming is the application of a GA.

Coming to the symbol regression problem, we have a polynomial expression that needs to be approximated here. It's a classic regression problem where we try to estimate the underlying function. In this example, we will use the expression: *f(x) = 2x^3 - 3x^2 + 4x - 1*

The code discussed here is a variant of the symbol regression problem given in the `DEAP` library. Create a new Python file and import the following:

```
import operator
import math
import random

import numpy as np
from deap import algorithms, base, creator, tools, gp
```

Create a division operator that can handle the divide-by-zero error gracefully:

```
# Define new functions
def division_operator(numerator, denominator):
    if denominator == 0:
        return 1

    return numerator / denominator
```

Define the evaluation function that will be used for fitness calculation. We need to define a callable function to run computations on the input individual:

```
# Define the evaluation function
def eval_func(individual, points):
    # Transform the tree expression in a callable function
    func = toolbox.compile(expr=individual)
```

Compute the **mean squared error** (**MSE**) between the function defined earlier and the original expression:

```
    # Evaluate the mean squared error
    mse = ((func(x) - (2 * x**3 - 3 * x**2 + 4 * x - 1))**2 for x in
points)

    return math.fsum(mse) / len(points),
```

Define a function to create the `toolbox`. In order to create the `toolbox` here, a set of primitives needs to be created. These primitives are operators that will be used during the evolution. They serve as building blocks for the individuals. The primitives will be basic arithmetic functions:

```
# Function to create the toolbox
def create_toolbox():
    pset = gp.PrimitiveSet("MAIN", 1)
    pset.addPrimitive(operator.add, 2)
    pset.addPrimitive(operator.sub, 2)
    pset.addPrimitive(operator.mul, 2)
```

```
pset.addPrimitive(division_operator, 2)
pset.addPrimitive(operator.neg, 1)
pset.addPrimitive(math.cos, 1)
pset.addPrimitive(math.sin, 1)
```

Next, declare an ephemeral constant. An ephemeral constant is a special terminal type that does not have a fixed value. When a given program appends such an ephemeral constant to the tree, the function gets executed. The result is then inserted into the tree as a constant terminal.

These constant terminals can take the values `-1`, `0`, or `1`:

```
pset.addEphemeralConstant("rand101", lambda: random.randint(-1,1))
```

The default name for the arguments is `ARGx`. Let's rename it to `x`:

```
pset.renameArguments(ARG0='x')
```

We need to define two object types – fitness and an individual. Let's do it using the `creator`:

```
    creator.create("FitnessMin", base.Fitness, weights=(-1.0,))
    creator.create("Individual", gp.PrimitiveTree, fitness=creator.
FitnessMin)
```

Create the `toolbox` and `register` the functions. The registration process is done like in previous sections:

```
    toolbox = base.Toolbox()

    toolbox.register("expr", gp.genHalfAndHalf, pset=pset, min_=1,
max_=2)
    toolbox.register("individual", tools.initIterate, creator.
Individual, toolbox.expr)
    toolbox.register("population", tools.initRepeat, list, toolbox.
individual)
    toolbox.register("compile", gp.compile, pset=pset)
    toolbox.register("evaluate", eval_func, points=[x/10. for x in
range(-10,10)])
    toolbox.register("select", tools.selTournament, tournsize=3)
    toolbox.register("mate", gp.cxOnePoint)
    toolbox.register("expr_mut", gp.genFull, min_=0, max_=2)
    toolbox.register("mutate", gp.mutUniform, expr=toolbox.expr_mut,
pset=pset)

    toolbox.decorate("mate", gp.staticLimit(key=operator.
attrgetter("height"), max_value=17))
    toolbox.decorate("mutate", gp.staticLimit(key=operator.
```

```
attrgetter("height"), max_value=17))

    return toolbox
```

Define the main function and start by seeding the random number generator:

```
if __name__ == "__main__":
    random.seed(7)
```

Create the toolbox object:

```
    toolbox = create_toolbox()
```

Define the initial population using the method available in the toolbox object using 450 individuals. The number of individuals is can be changed. Feel free to experiment with it. Also define the hall_of_fame object:

```
    population = toolbox.population(n=450)
    hall_of_fame = tools.HallOfFame(1)
```

Statistics are useful when building GAs. Define the stats objects:

```
    stats_fit = tools.Statistics(lambda x: x.fitness.values)
    stats_size = tools.Statistics(len)
```

Register the stats using the objects defined previously:

```
    mstats = tools.MultiStatistics(fitness=stats_fit, size=stats_size)
    mstats.register("avg", np.mean)
    mstats.register("std", np.std)
    mstats.register("min", np.min)
    mstats.register("max", np.max)
```

Define the crossover probability, mutation probability, and the number of generations:

```
    probab_crossover = 0.4
    probab_mutate = 0.2
    num_generations = 60
```

Run the evolutionary algorithm using the above parameters:

```
    population, log = algorithms.eaSimple(population, toolbox,
            probab_crossover, probab_mutate, num_generations,
            stats=mstats, halloffame=hall_of_fame, verbose=True)
```

The full code is given in the file symbol_regression.py. If you run the code, you will see the following at the start of the evolution:

		fitness				size			
gen	nevals	avg	max	min	std	avg	max	min	std
0	450	18.6918	47.1923	7.39087	6.27543	3.73556	7	2	1.62449
1	251	15.4572	41.3823	4.46965	4.54993	3.80222	12	1	1.81316
2	236	13.2545	37.7223	4.46965	4.06145	3.96889	12	1	1.98861
3	251	12.2299	60.828	4.46965	4.70055	4.19556	12	1	1.9971
4	235	11.001	47.1923	4.46965	4.48841	4.84222	13	1	2.17245
5	229	9.44483	31.478	4.46965	3.8796	5.56	19	1	2.43168
6	225	8.35975	22.0546	3.02133	3.40547	6.38889	15	1	2.40875
7	237	7.99309	31.1356	1.81133	4.08463	7.14667	16	1	2.57782
8	224	7.42611	359.418	1.17558	17.0167	8.33333	19	1	3.11127
9	237	5.70308	24.1921	1.17558	3.71991	9.64444	23	1	3.31365
10	254	5.27991	30.4315	1.13301	4.13556	10.5089	25	1	3.51898

Figure 9: Evolution process initial output

At the end, you will see the following:

36	209	1.10464	22.0546	0.0474957	2.71898	26.4867	46	1	5.23289
37	258	1.61958	86.0936	0.0382386	6.1839	27.2111	45	3	4.75557
38	257	2.03651	70.4768	0.0342642	5.15243	26.5311	49	1	6.22327
39	235	1.95531	185.328	0.0472693	9.32516	26.9711	48	1	6.00345
40	234	1.51403	28.5529	0.0472693	3.24513	26.6867	52	1	5.39811
41	230	1.4753	70.4768	0.0472693	5.4607	27.1	46	3	4.7433
42	233	12.3648	4880.09	0.0396503	229.754	26.88	53	1	5.18192
43	251	1.807	86.0936	0.0396503	5.85281	26.4889	50	1	5.43741
44	236	9.30096	3481.25	0.0277886	163.888	26.9622	55	1	6.27169
45	231	1.73196	86.7372	0.0342642	6.8119	27.4711	51	2	5.27807
46	227	1.86086	185.328	0.0342642	10.1143	28.0644	56	1	6.10812
47	216	12.5214	4923.66	0.0342642	231.837	29.1022	54	1	6.45898
48	232	14.3469	5830.89	0.0322462	274.536	29.8244	58	3	6.24093
49	242	2.56984	272.833	0.0322462	18.2752	29.9267	51	1	6.31446
50	227	2.80136	356.613	0.0322462	21.0416	29.7978	56	4	6.50275
51	243	1.75099	86.0936	0.0322462	5.70833	29.8089	56	1	6.62379
52	253	10.9184	3435.84	0.0227048	163.602	29.9911	55	1	6.66833
53	243	1.80265	48.0418	0.0227048	4.73856	29.88	55	1	7.33084
54	234	1.74487	86.0936	0.0227048	6.0249	30.6067	55	1	6.85782
55	220	1.58888	31.094	0.0132398	3.82809	30.5644	54	1	6.96669
56	234	1.46711	103.287	0.00766444	6.81157	30.6689	55	3	6.6806
57	250	17.0896	6544.17	0.00424267	308.689	31.1267	60	4	7.25837
58	231	1.66757	141.584	0.00144401	7.35306	32	52	1	7.23295
59	229	2.22325	265.224	0.00144401	13.388	33.5489	64	1	8.38351
60	248	2.60303	521.804	0.00144401	24.7018	35.2533	58	1	7.61506

Figure 10: Evolution progress final output

We can see the value in the min column getting smaller and smaller, indicating that the error for the approximation of the solution of the equation is getting smaller.

Building an intelligent robot controller

Let's see how to build a robot controller using a GA. We are given a map with targets sprinkled all over it.

The map looks like this. The hashes represent the targets that the robot needs to hit:

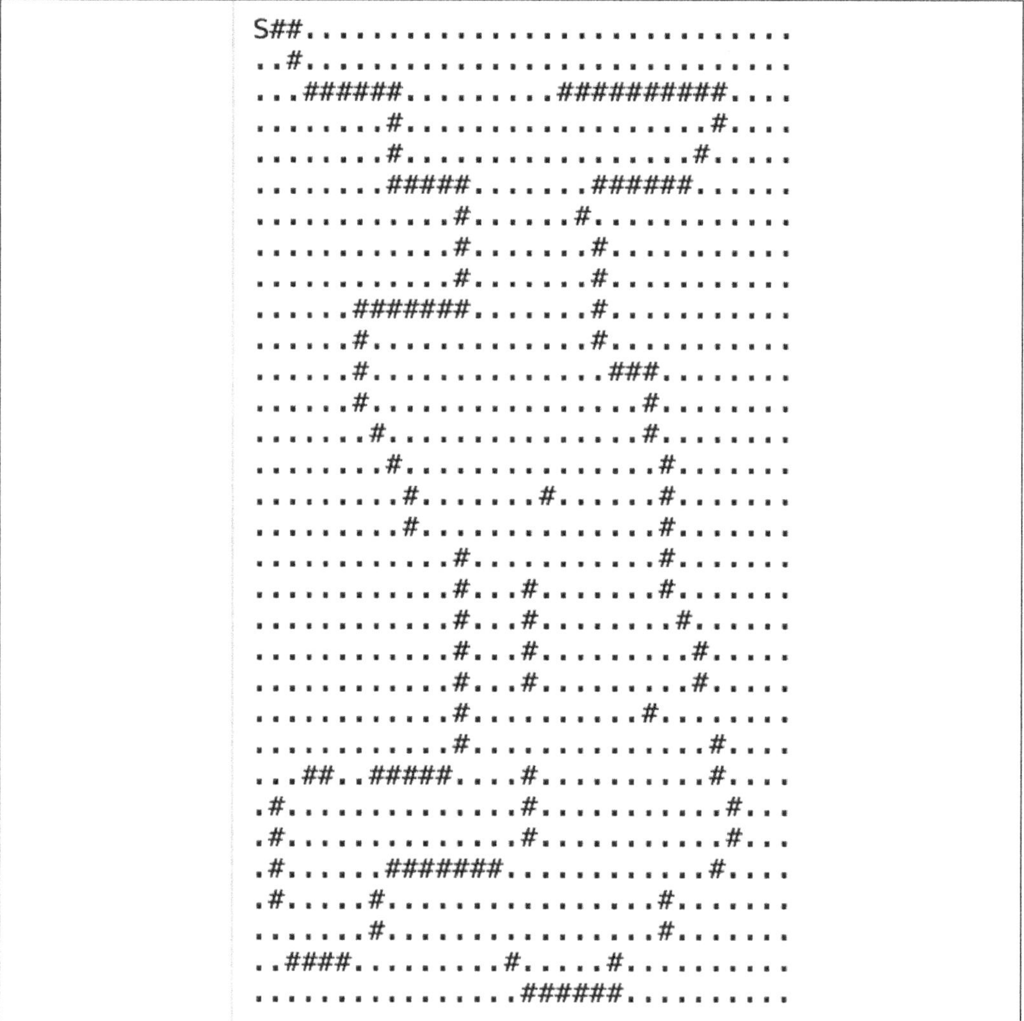

```
S##.............................
..#.............................
...######.........##########....
........#..................#....
........#.................#.....
........#####.......######......
............#......#............
............#.......#...........
............#.......#...........
......#######.......#...........
......#.............#...........
......#..............###........
......#................#........
.......#...............#........
........#...............#.......
.........#.......#......#.......
.........#..............#.......
............#...........#.......
............#...#.......#.......
............#...#........#......
............#...#.........#.....
............#...#.........#.....
............#..........#........
............#..............#....
...##..#####....#..........#....
.#..............#...........#...
.#..............#...........#...
.#......#######............#....
.#.....#................#.......
.......#................#.......
..####.........#.....#..........
................######..........
```

Figure 11: A map with targets that an AI robot needs to hit, with targets represented by hashes

There are 124 targets in the preceding map. The goal of the robot controller is to automatically traverse the map and consume all those targets. This program is a variant of the artificial ant program given in the `DEAP` library.

Create a new Python file and import the following:

```
import copy
import random
from functools import partial
```

```
import numpy as np
from deap import algorithms, base, creator, tools, gp
```

Create the class to control the robot:

```
class RobotController(object):
    def __init__(self, max_moves):
        self.max_moves = max_moves
        self.moves = 0
        self.consumed = 0
        self.routine = None
```

Define the directions and movements:

```
    self.direction = ["north", "east", "south", "west"]
    self.direction_row = [1, 0, -1, 0]
    self.direction_col = [0, 1, 0, -1]
```

Define the reset functionality:

```
    def _reset(self):
        self.row = self.row_start
        self.col = self.col_start
        self.direction = 1
        self.moves = 0
        self.consumed = 0
        self.matrix_exc = copy.deepcopy(self.matrix)
```

Define the conditional operator:

```
    def _conditional(self, condition, out1, out2):
        out1() if condition() else out2()
```

Define the left turning operator:

```
    def turn_left(self):
        if self.moves < self.max_moves:
            self.moves += 1
            self.direction = (self.direction - 1) % 4
```

Define the right turning operator:

```
    def turn_right(self):
        if self.moves < self.max_moves:
            self.moves += 1
            self.direction = (self.direction + 1) % 4
```

Define the method to control how the robot moves forward:

```
        def move_forward(self):
            if self.moves < self.max_moves:
                self.moves += 1
                self.row = (self.row + self.direction_row[self.direction])
    % self.matrix_row
               self.col = (self.col + self.direction_col[self.direction])
    % self.matrix_col

                if self.matrix_exc[self.row][self.col] == "target":
                    self.consumed += 1

                self.matrix_exc[self.row][self.col] = "passed"
```

Define a method to sense the target. If you see the target ahead, then update the matrix accordingly:

```
        def sense_target(self):
            ahead_row = (self.row + self.direction_row[self.direction]) %
    self.matrix_row
            ahead_col = (self.col + self.direction_col[self.direction]) %
    self.matrix_col
            return self.matrix_exc[ahead_row][ahead_col] == "target"
```

If you see the target ahead, then create the relevant function and return it:

```
        def if_target_ahead(self, out1, out2):
            return partial(self._conditional, self.sense_target, out1,
    out2)
```

Define the method to run it:

```
        def run(self,routine):
            self._reset()
            while self.moves < self.max_moves:
                routine()
```

Define a function to traverse the input map. The symbol # indicates all the targets on the map and the symbol `S` indicates the starting point. The symbol `.` denotes empty cells:

```
        def traverse_map(self, matrix):
            self.matrix = list()
            for i, line in enumerate(matrix):
                self.matrix.append(list())

                for j, col in enumerate(line):
```

```
                if col == "#":
                    self.matrix[-1].append("target")

                elif col == ".":
                    self.matrix[-1].append("empty")

                elif col == "S":
                    self.matrix[-1].append("empty")
                    self.row_start = self.row = i
                    self.col_start = self.col = j
                    self.direction = 1

        self.matrix_row = len(self.matrix)
        self.matrix_col = len(self.matrix[0])
        self.matrix_exc = copy.deepcopy(self.matrix)
```

Define a class to generate functions depending on the number of input arguments:

```
class Prog(object):
    def _progn(self, *args):
        for arg in args:
            arg()

    def prog2(self, out1, out2):
        return partial(self._progn, out1, out2)

    def prog3(self, out1, out2, out3):
        return partial(self._progn, out1, out2, out3)
```

Define an evaluation function for individuals:

```
def eval_func(individual):
    global robot, pset

    # Transform the tree expression to functional Python code
    routine = gp.compile(individual, pset)
```

Run the program:

```
    # Run the generated routine
    robot.run(routine)
    return robot.consumed,
```

Define a function to create the `toolbox` and add primitives:

```
def create_toolbox():
    global robot, pset
```

```
    pset = gp.PrimitiveSet("MAIN", 0)
    pset.addPrimitive(robot.if_target_ahead, 2)
    pset.addPrimitive(Prog().prog2, 2)
    pset.addPrimitive(Prog().prog3, 3)
    pset.addTerminal(robot.move_forward)
    pset.addTerminal(robot.turn_left)
    pset.addTerminal(robot.turn_right)
```

Create the object types using the fitness function:

```
    creator.create("FitnessMax", base.Fitness, weights=(1.0,))
    creator.create("Individual", gp.PrimitiveTree, fitness=creator.
FitnessMax)
```

Create the `toolbox` and register all the operators:

```
    toolbox = base.Toolbox()

    # Attribute generator
    toolbox.register("expr_init", gp.genFull, pset=pset, min_=1,
max_=2)

    # Structure initializers
    toolbox.register("individual", tools.initIterate, creator.
Individual, toolbox.expr_init)
    toolbox.register("population", tools.initRepeat, list, toolbox.
individual)

    toolbox.register("evaluate", eval_func)
    toolbox.register("select", tools.selTournament, tournsize=7)
    toolbox.register("mate", gp.cxOnePoint)

    toolbox.register("expr_mut", gp.genFull, min_=0, max_=2)
    toolbox.register("mutate", gp.mutUniform, expr=toolbox.expr_mut,
pset=pset)

    return toolbox
```

Define the `main` function and start by seeding the random number generator:

```
if __name__ == "__main__":
    global robot

    # Seed the random number generator
    random.seed(7)
```

Create the robot controller object using the initialization parameter:

```
# Define the maximum number of moves
max_moves = 750

# Create the robot object
robot = RobotController(max_moves)
```

Create the `toolbox` using the function we defined earlier:

```
# Create the toolbox
toolbox = create_toolbox()
```

Read the map data from the input file:

```
# Read the map data
with open('target_map.txt', 'r') as f:
  robot.traverse_map(f)
```

Define the population with `400` individuals and define the `hall_of_fame` object:

```
# Define population and hall of fame variables
population = toolbox.population(n=400)
hall_of_fame = tools.HallOfFame(1)
```

Register the `stats`:

```
# Register the stats
stats = tools.Statistics(lambda x: x.fitness.values)
stats.register("avg", np.mean)
stats.register("std", np.std)
stats.register("min", np.min)
stats.register("max", np.max)
```

Define the crossover probability, mutation probability, and the number of generations:

```
# Define parameters
probab_crossover = 0.4
probab_mutate = 0.3
num_generations = 50
```

Run the evolutionary algorithm using the parameters defined earlier:

```
# Run the algorithm to solve the problem
algorithms.eaSimple(population, toolbox, probab_crossover,
        probab_mutate, num_generations, stats,
        halloffame=hall_of_fame)
```

The full code is given in the file `robot.py`. If you run the code, you will get the following:

gen	nevals	avg	std	min	max
0	400	1.4875	4.37491	0	62
1	231	4.285	7.56993	0	73
2	235	10.8925	14.8493	0	73
3	231	21.72	22.1239	0	73
4	238	29.9775	27.7861	0	76
5	224	37.6275	31.8698	0	76
6	231	42.845	33.0541	0	80
7	223	43.55	33.9369	0	83
8	234	44.0675	34.5201	0	83
9	231	49.2975	34.3065	0	83
10	249	47.075	36.4106	0	93
11	222	52.7925	36.2826	0	97
12	248	51.0725	37.2598	0	97
13	234	54.01	37.4614	0	97
14	229	59.615	37.7894	0	97
15	228	63.3	39.8205	0	97
16	220	64.605	40.3962	0	97
17	236	62.545	40.5607	0	97
18	233	67.99	38.9033	0	97
19	236	66.4025	39.6574	0	97
20	221	69.785	38.7117	0	97
21	244	65.705	39.0957	0	97
22	230	70.32	37.1206	0	97
23	241	67.3825	39.4028	0	97

Figure 12: Evolution process initial output

Towards the end, you will see the following:

26	214	71.505	36.964	0	97
27	246	72.72	37.1637	0	97
28	238	73.5975	36.5385	0	97
29	239	76.405	35.5696	0	97
30	246	78.6025	33.4281	0	97
31	240	74.83	36.5157	0	97
32	216	80.2625	32.6659	0	97
33	220	80.6425	33.0933	0	97
34	247	78.245	34.6022	0	97
35	241	81.22	32.1885	0	97
36	234	83.6375	29.0002	0	97
37	228	82.485	31.7354	0	97
38	219	83.4625	30.0592	0	97
39	212	88.64	24.2702	0	97
40	231	86.7275	27.0879	0	97
41	229	89.1825	23.8773	0	97
42	216	87.96	25.1649	0	97
43	218	86.85	27.1116	0	97
44	236	88.78	23.7278	0	97
45	225	89.115	23.4212	0	97
46	232	88.5425	24.187	0	97
47	245	87.7775	25.3909	0	97
48	231	87.78	26.3786	0	97
49	238	88.8525	24.5115	0	97
50	233	87.82	25.4164	1	97

Figure 13: Evolution process final output

As seen from the preceding figure, the standard deviation keeps decreasing as we progress. This indicates that it's converging. In this output, we only show 50 generations. You can expect the values to converge even further if we run further generations.

Genetic programming use cases

As discussed in one of the early chapters, Genetic Algorithms (GA) and Genetic Programming (GP) are one of the "five tribes" of machine learning.

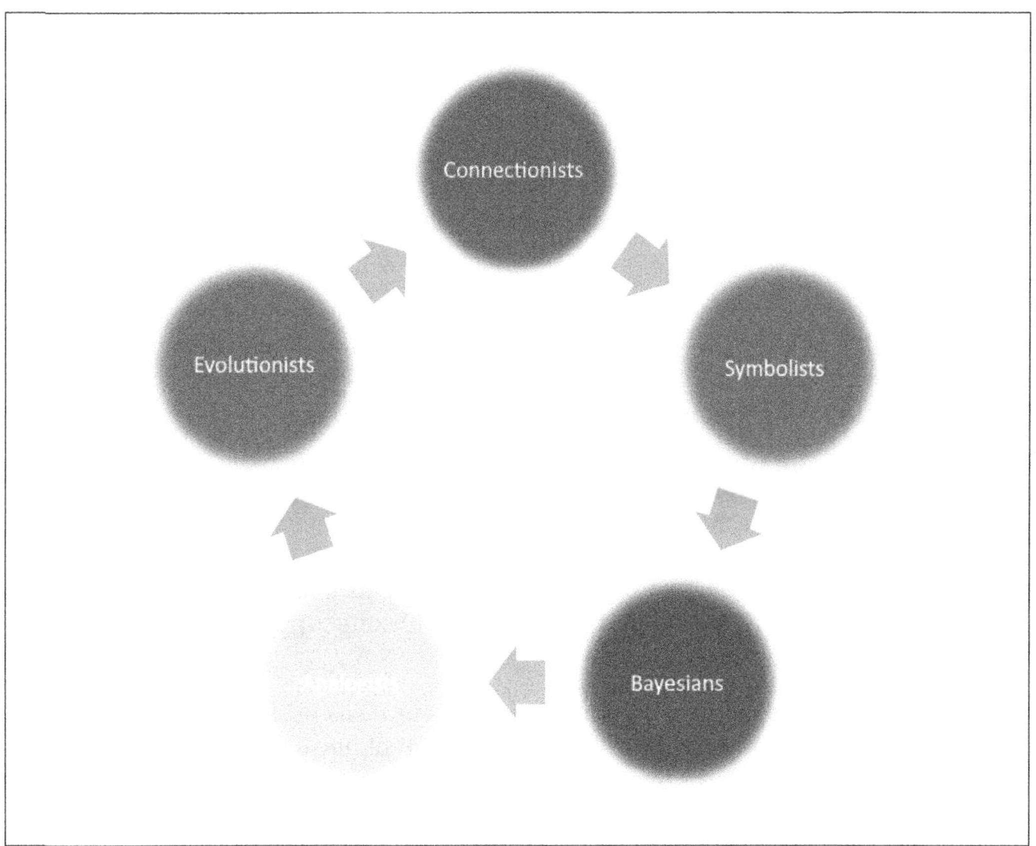

Figure 14: The five tribes (Pedro Domingos)

Since its early beginnings, GP has produced a wide variety of advances. The literature, which covers thousands of applications of GP contains many use cases where GP has been applied successfully. Exhaustively covering that list would be beyond the scope of the book, but we list a few of the more important ones here.

Here, we begin a discussion of the general kinds of problems where GP has been applied successfully, and then review a representative subset of each of the main application areas of GP. Areas where GP has done well, based on the experience of a diverse and wide group of researchers over the years, include:

Poorly understood domains

This is where the interrelationships among the relevant variables is unknown or poorly understood (or where it is suspected that the current understanding may possibly be wrong). One of the benefits of GP (and other evolutionary algorithms) is in exploring poorly understood domains. If the problem domain is well understood, there are other analytical tools and methods that can provide quality solutions without the uncertainty inherent in a stochastic search process of GP.

GP, on the other hand, has produced results when the domain is not well understood. GP can assist in the determination of which attributes and dimensions are relevant, provide novel and creative solutions, reveal unexpected relationships among attributes, and discover new concepts that can then be applied in other domains.

Finding the size and shape of the eventual solution is a major part of the problem. If the form of the solution is known, then alternative search mechanisms that work on fixed size representations (for example, GAs) may be more efficient because they won't have to discover the size and shape of the solution.

Data is available and plentiful

GP in particular, and machine learning and search techniques in general, normally require vast amounts of test data to perform. Finding relevant datasets for a problem can be a big hurdle. But in cases when big datasets are readily available, it can be a data scientist's dream, and it might be a good idea to come up with questions that can be posed simply because the data is available.

It is also helpful if the test data are as clean and accurate as possible. However, GP algorithms can deal gracefully with a certain amount of noise in the data, especially if steps are taken to minimize over-fitting.

Approximate solutions are acceptable

GP works well in situations where an approximate solution is acceptable, or an approximate solution is the best possible. Evolution in general, and GP in particular, is typically about being "good enough" rather than "the best." If a bear is chasing you through the woods, you don't have to be the fastest person in the world. You just need to be faster than the bear or than the person running next to you. As a result, evolutionary algorithms tend to work best in domains where close approximations are both possible and acceptable.

Small but highly valued improvements

GP has been found to work well in domains where technological efforts tend to concentrate in areas of high economic importance. In these domains, previous researchers have probably spent considerable amounts of time and effort, and the "state of the art" tends to be advanced. In this case, it is difficult to improve current solutions. However, in these same domains small improvements can be extremely valuable. In cases like this, GP can sometimes make small but valuable and profitable contributions. Examples might be oil exploration, materials management, and financial applications.

Now let's look at some industry-specific applications of GA and GP:

Movies

As with other professions, the days of the movie stuntman are numbered. A start-up called *NaturalMotion* uses GP with incredibly realistic results to generate people in motion. These virtual actors fall, jump, and perform other stunts with real-world precision. These virtual actors can react like real humans to forces applied to them and display a wide variety of lifelike movements. All this, and it only requires the power of a desktop PC. Movies are just the start. In the next few years, NaturalMotion has plans to unleash these lifelike figures in the next generation of video games.

NaturalMotion is a new company started by former Oxford researchers Torsten Reil and Colm Massey. The company has only one product as of now, called Endorphin, which employs neural networks and artificial evolution to produce software automatons that can walk, run, fall, and fly with human-like precision.

Endorphin made its feature film debut in the movie *The Return of the King*, where it was used to make a particularly tricky stunt come to life. But that was just the beginning. A few months later, the company's robots fought to the death on the plains of Ilium, taking falls and daggers in Wolfgang Petersen's film *Troy*.

Source: `https://www.naturalmotion.com/`

Computer games

Today everyone is enamored with deep learning algorithms. They have certainly produced some impressive results in many domains and against many benchmarks. But GP is no slouch. Thanks to the work of Dennis Wilson and a few colleagues at the University of Toulouse in France some impressive results have been observed. Their work on GP has been able to outperform humans in quite a few classic games. Wilson and his team of researchers have shown how GP can match the performance of deep learning algorithms at the emblematic task that powered deep learning to fame in 2013 - the ability to outperform humans at arcade video games such as Pong, Breakout, and Space Invaders.

Wilson has demonstrated convincingly that GP can produce impressive results comparable and maybe better to deep learning.

Source: `https://github.com/d9w`

File compression

One of the first lossless compression techniques used GP evolving non-linear predictors for images. The algorithm predicted the gray level a pixel can take based on the gray values of a subset of the neighboring pixels. The prediction errors in conjunction with the model's description can represent a compressed version of the image. The images were compressed using Huffman encoding. Results on a wide variety of images have shown promising results using GP compression. In some cases, the GP algorithms have outperformed some of the best human-designed lossless compression algorithms.

Source: Fukunaga and Stechert, 1998 [1]

Financial trading

The efficient markets hypothesis is a fundamental tenet of economics. It is founded on the idea that every market participant has *perfect information* and they act *rationally*. If the efficient markets hypothesis is true, everyone should assign the same price to all assets in a market and agree on a price. If price differences didn't exist, there would be no way to beat the market. Whether it's a commodity, currency, or stock market, no market participant is equal and there exists considerable doubt that *efficient markets* truly exist. The more illiquid the market is, the less efficient the market will be. And so, people continue to research the stock market and try to find ways to beat it. There are a few folks and companies that based on their track record make a compelling case that the market is beatable. Some examples include:

- Warren Buffet and Berkshire Hathaway
- Peter Lynch and the Fidelity Magellan Fund
- Ray Dalio and Bridgewater Associates
- Jim Simons and Renaissance Technologies

The latter two examples rely heavily on computer algorithms to achieve market beating results.

Game theory has been a standard tool used by economists to try to understand markets but is increasingly supplemented by simulations with both human and computerized agents. GP is increasingly being used as part of these simulations of social systems.

GP algorithms are widely used in the areas of financial trading, time series prediction, and economic modeling; it would take a whole book to list all its applications.

It this section we will scratch the surface and visit a few examples. A particularly prodigious researcher that stands out in this field is Sheng-Hung Chen. Chen has written more than 60 papers on using GP in finance and economics. Some of his recent papers have looked at the modeling of agents in stock markets (Chen and Liao, 2005), game theory (Chen, Duffy, and Yeh, 2002), evolving trading rules for the S&P 500 (Yu and Chen, 2004) and forecasting the Heng-Sheng index (Chen, Wang, and Zhang, 1999).

Other applications

Optimization – GAs and GP are commonly used in optimization problems wherein values must be maximized or minimized given an objective function under a set of constraints.

Parallelization – GAs also possess parallel processing capabilities and prove to be an effective method to solve problems that require parallel processing. Parallelization is an active area of research in GA and GP.

Neural networks – GAs are used to train neural networks, particularly recurrent neural networks (RNNs).

Economics – GAs are commonly used to model economic systems such as:

- The cobweb model
- Game theory equilibrium resolution
- Asset pricing

Image processing – GAs are used for various digital image processing (DIP) tasks as well, such as dense pixel matching.

Scheduling applications – GAs can be used to solve many scheduling problems, particularly the timetabling problem. Simply explained, the timetabling problem occurs when we have a set of resources, a set of activities, and a set of dependencies between the activities and the resources. An example is class schedules at a university where we have classrooms, professors, and students and at the end of the exercise, hopefully a big percentage of the students are able to take all the classes that they want to take.

Parametric design – GAs have been used to design vehicles, machinery, and airplanes by varying the parameters and evolving better solutions.

DNA analysis – GAs can and have been used to determine DNA structures using sample spectrometric data.

Multimodal optimization – GAs are a great approach to solve multimodal optimization problems where multiple optimum solutions are being sought.

Traveling salesman problem (TSP) – GAs have been used to solve the TSP and all its related applications such as vehicle routing and robot trajectory problems, which is a well-known combinatorial problem using novel crossover and packing strategies.

Hopefully the vast and diverse applications of GP and GAs are clear to you. Maybe you will be able to come up with your own unique applications and use the gained knowledge to move the field forward.

Summary

In this chapter, we learned about GAs and their underlying concepts. We discussed evolutionary algorithms and genetic programming. We understood how they are related to GAs. We discussed the fundamental building blocks of GAs including the concepts of population, crossover, mutation, selection, and fitness function. We learned how to generate a bit pattern with predefined parameters. We discussed how to visualize the evolution process using CMA-ES. We learned how to solve the symbol regression problem in this paradigm. We then used these concepts to build a robot controller to traverse a map and consume all the targets. In the next chapter, we will learn about reinforcement learning and see how to build a smart agent.

References

1. A. Fukunaga and A. Stechert. Evolving nonlinear predictive models for lossless image compression with genetic programming. In J. R. Koza, et al., editors, *Genetic Programming 1998: Proceedings of the Third Annual Conference*, pages 95-102, University of Wisconsin, Madison, Wisconsin, USA, 22-25 July 1998. Morgan Kaufmann. ISBN 1-55860-548-7.

12
Artificial Intelligence on the Cloud

In this chapter, we are going to learn about the cloud and artificial intelligence workloads on the cloud. We will discuss the benefits and the risks of migrating AI projects to the cloud. We will also learn about the offerings provided by the major cloud providers. We will learn about the services and features that they offer and hopefully get an understanding of why those providers are the market leaders.

By the end of this chapter, you will have a better understanding of the following:

- The benefits, risks, and costs of migrating to the cloud
- Fundamental cloud concepts such as elasticity
- The top cloud providers
- Amazon Web Services:
    - Amazon SageMaker
    - Alexa, Lex, and Polly - conversational agents
    - Amazon Comprehend - natural language processing
    - Amazon Rekognition - image and video
    - Amazon Translate
    - Amazon machine learning
    - Amazon Transcribe - transcription
    - Amazon Textract - document analysis
- Microsoft Azure:
    - Machine Learning Studio

    - Azure Machine Learning interactive workspace
    - Azure Cognitive Services

- Google AI and its machine learning products:
    - AI Hub
    - AI building blocks

Why are companies migrating to the cloud?

It is hard turning anywhere these days without being hit with the term "the cloud." Our present-day society has hit a tipping point where businesses big and small are seeing that the benefits of moving their workloads to the cloud outweigh the costs and risks. As an example, the US Department of Defense, as of 2019, is in the process of selecting a cloud provider and awarding a 10-year $10 billion-dollar contract. Moving your systems to the cloud has many advantages, but one of the main reasons companies move to the cloud is its elastic capabilities.

When deploying a new project in an on-premises environment, we always start with capacity planning. Capacity planning is the exercise that enterprises go through to determine how much hardware they will need for a new system to run efficiently. Depending on the size of the project, the cost of this hardware can run into the millions. For that reason, it could take months to complete the process. One of the reasons it can take so long is because many approvals might be required to complete the purchase. We can't blame business for being so slow and judicious with these kinds of decisions.

Even though great planning and thought might go into these purchases, it is not uncommon to either buy less equipment than required or to buy underpowered equipment. Maybe just as often, too much equipment is bought or equipment that is overkill for the project at hand. The reason this happens is because in many cases, it is difficult to determine demand a priori.

Additionally, even if we get the capacity required properly at the beginning, the demand might continue to grow and force us to go through the provisioning process all over again. Or the demand might be variable. For example, we might have a website that gets a lot of traffic during the day, but demand drops way down at night. In this case, when using on-premises environments, we have no choice but to account for the worst-case scenario and buy enough resources so that we can handle peak periods of demand, but resources will be wasted when demand decreases in slow periods.

All these issues are non-existent in a cloud environment. All the major cloud providers, in different ways, provide elastic environments. Not only can we easily scale up, but we can just as easily scale down.

If we have a website that has variable traffic, we could put the servers that handle the traffic behind a load balancer and set up alerts that automatically add more servers to handle traffic spikes and other alerts to terminate the servers once the storm passes.

The top cloud providers

Given the tsunami that is the cloud, many vendors are vying to quench the demand for cloud services. However, as is often the case in technology markets, only a few have bubbled to the top and dominate the space. In this section, we'll analyze the top players.

Amazon Web Services (AWS)

Amazon Web Services is one of the cloud pioneers. Since it launched in 2006, AWS has ranked highly in the greatly respected Gartner's Magic Quadrant in both vision and execution. Since its inception, AWS has held a big chunk of the cloud market. AWS is an appealing option both for legacy players as well as start-ups. According to Gartner:

> *"AWS is the provider most commonly chosen for strategic, organization-wide adoption"*

AWS also has an army of consultants and advisors dedicated to helping its customers deploy AWS services as well as to teach them how to best leverage the services available. In summary, it is safe to say that AWS is the most mature, most advanced cloud provider, with a strong track record of customer success, as well as a strong stable of partners in AWS Marketplace.

On the flip side, since AWS is the leader and they know it, they are not always the least expensive option. Another knock for AWS is that since they highly value being first to market with new services and features, it seems like they are willing to launch services quickly that might not be fully mature and feature-complete, and work out the kinks once they are released. In fairness, this is not a tactic exclusive to AWS and other cloud providers also release beta versions of their services. In addition, since Amazon competes in markets other than the cloud, it is not uncommon for some potential customers to go with other providers in order to not "feed the beast." For example, Walmart is well known for avoiding using AWS at all costs because of their fierce competition in the e-commerce space.

Microsoft Azure

For the past few years, Microsoft Azure has held the second position in the Gartner Magic Quadrant, trailing AWS, lagging significantly on their ability to execute better than AWS. But the good news is that they only trail AWS and they are a strong number two.

Microsoft's solution is appealing to customers hosting legacy workloads as well as brand new cloud deployments, but for different reasons.

Legacy workloads are normally run on Azure by clients that have traditionally been Microsoft customers and are trying to leverage their previous investments in that technology stack.

For new cloud deployments, Azure cloud services hold appeal because of Microsoft's strong offerings for application development, specialized **Platform as a Service** (**PaaS**) capabilities, data storage, machine learning, and **Internet of Things** (**IoT**) services.

Enterprises that are strategically committed to the Microsoft technology stack have been able to deploy many large-scale applications in production. Azure specifically shines when developers fully commit to the suite of Microsoft products, such as .NET applications, and then deploy them on Azure. Another reason Microsoft has deep market penetration is its experienced sales staff and its extensive partner network.

In addition, Microsoft realizes that the next battle in technology will not revolve around operating systems but rather in the cloud and they have become increasingly open to adopting non-Microsoft operating systems. As proof of this, as of now, about half of Azure workloads run on Linux or other open source operating systems and technology stacks.

A Gartner report notes "*Microsoft has a unique vision for the future that involves bringing in technology partners through native, first-party offerings such as those from VMware, NetApp, Red Hat, Cray, and Databricks.*"

On the downside, there have been some reports of reliability, downtime, and service disruptions as well as some customers taking issue with the quality of Microsoft's technical support.

Google Cloud Platform (GCP)

In 2018, Google broke into the prestigious Gartner's leaders' quadrant with its GCP offering, joining only AWS and Azure in the exclusive club. In 2019, GCP remained in the same quadrant with its two fierce competitors. However, in terms of market share, GCP is a distant third.

They recently beefed up their sales staff, they have deep pockets, and they have a strong incentive to not be left behind so don't discount them yet.

Google's reputation as a leader in machine learning is undisputed so it is no surprise that GCP has strong big data and machine learning offerings. But GCP is also making some headway, attracting bigger enterprises looking to host legacy workloads such as SAP and other traditional **customer relationship management** (**CRMs**) systems.

Google's internal innovations around machine learning, automation, containers, and networking, with offerings such as TensorFlow and Kubernetes, have advanced cloud development. GPS's technology offerings revolve around their contributions to open source.

Be careful about centering your cloud strategy exclusively around GCP, however. In a recent report, Gartner declared:

> *"Google demonstrates an immaturity of process and procedures when dealing with enterprise accounts, which can make the company difficult to transact with at times."*

And:

> *"Google has a much smaller pool of experienced Managed Service Providers (MSP) and infrastructure-centric professional services partners than other vendors in this Magic Quadrant."*

However, Gartner also states:

> *"Google is aggressively targeting these shortcomings."*

Gartner also notes that Google's channel needs development.

Alibaba Cloud

Alibaba Cloud made its first appearance in Gartner's Magic Quadrant in 2017, and as of 2019, Alibaba's cloud offering called Aliyun remains in the Niche Player category.

Gartner only evaluated the company's international service, headquartered in Singapore.

Alibaba Cloud is the market leader in China, and many Chinese businesses, as well as the Chinese government, have been served well by using Alibaba as their cloud provider. However, a big part of this market share leadership might be given up if China ever decides to remove some of the restrictions on other international cloud vendors.

The company provides support in China for building hybrid clouds. But, outside of China, it's mostly used by cloud-centric workloads. In 2018, it forged partnerships with VMware and SAP.

Alibaba has a suite of services that is comparable in scope to the service portfolios of other global providers.

The company's close relationships with the Alibaba Group helps the cloud service to be a bridge for international companies looking to do business in China, and out of China for Chinese companies.

Alibaba does not yet seem to have the service and feature depth of competitors such as AWS, Azure, and GCP. And in many regions, services are only available for specific compute instances. They also need to strengthen their MSP ecosystem, third-party enterprise software integration, and operational tools.

Oracle Cloud Infrastructure (OCI)

In 2017, Oracle's cloud offering made a debut on Gartner's Magic Quadrant as a Visionary. But in 2018, due to a change to Gartner's evaluation criteria, Oracle was moved to Niche Player status. It remained there as of 2019.

Oracle Cloud Infrastructure, or OCI, was a second-generation service launched in 2016 to phase out the legacy offering, now referred to as Oracle Cloud Infrastructure Classic.

OCI offers both virtualized and bare-metal servers, with one-click installation and configuration of Oracle databases and container services.

OCI appeals to customers with Oracle workloads that don't need more than basic **Infrastructure as a Service** (**IaaS**) capabilities.

Oracle's cloud strategy relies on its applications, database, and middleware.

Oracle has made some headway in attracting talent from other cloud providers to beef up its offerings. It's also made some progress in winning new business and getting existing Oracle customers to move to the OCI cloud. However, Oracle still has a long road ahead of it before it can catch up with the big three.

IBM Cloud

In the mainframe era, IBM was the undisputed computing king of the hill. It lost that title when we started moving away from mainframes and personal computers became ubiquitous. IBM is again trying to reclaim a leadership position in this new paradigm shift. IBM Cloud is IBM's answer to this challenge.

The company's diversified cloud services include container platforms, serverless services, and PaaS offerings. They are complemented by IBM Cloud Private for hybrid architectures.

Like some of the other lower-tier cloud providers, IBM appeals to its existing customers who have a strong preference to purchase most of their technology from Big Blue (IBM's nickname).

These existing customers usually have traditional workloads. IBM is also leveraging these long relationships to transition these customers into emerging IBM solutions, such as Watson's artificial intelligence.

IBM benefits from a large base of existing customers running critical production services and that are just starting to get comfortable with cloud adoption. This existing customer base positions IBM well to assist these customers as they embrace the cloud and begin their transformation journeys.

Like Oracle, IBM is fighting an uphill battle to gain market share from AWS, Azure, and Google.

Amazon Web Services (AWS)

We'll now focus on the top three cloud providers. As you are probably already aware, cloud providers offer much more than artificial services, starting with barebones compute and storage services, all the way to very sophisticated high-level services. As with everything else in this book, we will specifically drill into the artificial intelligence and machine learning services that cloud providers offer, starting with AWS.

Amazon SageMaker

Amazon SageMaker was launched at Amazon's annual re:Invent conference in Las Vegas, Nevada in 2017. SageMaker is a machine learning platform that enables developers and data scientists to create, train, and deploy machine learning (ML) models in the cloud.

A common tool used by data scientists in their day-to-day work is a Jupyter Notebook. These notebooks are documents that contain a combination of computer code such as Python, rich text elements such as paragraphs, equations, graphs, and URLs. Jupyter notebooks can easily be understood by humans because they contain analysis, descriptions, and results (figures, graphs, tables, and so on), and they are also executable programs that can be processed online or on a laptop.

You can think of Amazon SageMaker as a Jupyter Notebook on *steroids*. These are some of the advantages of SageMaker over traditional Jupyter notebooks. In other words, these are the different steroid flavors:

- Like many of the machine learning services offered by Amazon, SageMaker is a fully managed machine learning service so you do not have to worry about upgrading operating systems or installing drivers.
- Amazon SageMaker provides implementations of some of the most common machine learning models, but these implementations are highly optimized and, in some cases, run up to 10 times faster than other implementations of the same algorithm. In addition, you can bring in your own algorithms if the machine learning model is not provided *out of the box* by SageMaker.
- Amazon SageMaker provides the right amount of muscle for a variety of workloads. The type of machine that can be used to either train or deploy your algorithm can be selected from the wide variety of machine types that Amazon provides. If you are just experimenting with SageMaker, you might decide to use an *ml.t2.medium* machine, which is one of the smallest machines you can use with SageMaker. If you require some real power, you can their accelerated computer instances, such as an *ml.p3dn.24xlarge* machine. The power delivered by such an instance is equivalent to what just a few years ago was considered a supercomputer and would cost millions of dollars to purchase.

Amazon SageMaker allows developers to increase their productivity across the entire machine learning pipeline, including:

Data preparation – Amazon SageMaker can seamlessly integrate with many other AWS services, including S3, RDS, DynamoDB, and Lambda, making it simple to ingest and prepare data for consumption by machine learning algorithms.

Algorithm selection and training – Out of the box, Amazon SageMaker has a variety of high-performance, scalable machine learning algorithms optimized for speed and accuracy. These algorithms can perform training on petabyte-size datasets and can increase performance by up to 10 times the performance of similar implementations. These are some of the algorithms that are included with SageMaker:

- BlazingText
- DeepAR forecasting
- Factorization machines
- K-Means
- Random Cut Forest (RCF)

- Object detection
- Image classification
- Neural Topic Model (NTM)
- IP Insights
- K-Nearest Neighbors (k-NN)
- Latent Dirichlet Allocation (LDA)
- Linear Learner
- Object2Vec
- Principal Component Analysis (PCA)
- Semantic segmentation
- Sequence-to-sequence
- XGBoost

Algorithm tuning and optimizing - Amazon SageMaker offers automatic model tuning, also known as hyperparameter tuning. The tuning finds the best parameter set for a model by running multiple iterations using the same input dataset running the same algorithm over a range of specified hyperparameters. As the training jobs run, a scorecard is kept of the best performing version of the model. The definition of "best" is based on a pre-defined metric.

As an example, let's assume we are trying to solve a binary classification problem. The goal is to maximize the **area under the curve** (**AUC**) metric of the algorithm by training an XGBoost algorithm model. We can tune the following hyperparameters for the algorithm:

- `alpha`
- `eta`
- `min_child_weight`
- `max_depth`

In order to find the best values for these hyperparameters, we can specify a range of values for the hyperparameter tuning. A series of training jobs will be kicked off and the best set of hyperparameters will be stored depending on which version provides the highest AUC.

Amazon SageMaker's automatic model tuning can be used both with SageMaker's built-in algorithms as well as with custom algorithms.

Algorithm deployment - Deploying a model in Amazon SageMaker is a two-step process:

1. Create an endpoint configuration specifying the ML compute instances that are used to deploy the model.
2. Launching one or more ML compute instances to deploy the model and exposing the URI to invoke that will allow users to make predictions.

The endpoint configuration API accepts the ML instance type and the initial count of instances. In the case of neural networks, the configuration may include the type of GPU-backed instance. The endpoint API provisions the infrastructure as defined in the previous step.

SageMaker deployment supports both one-off and batch predictions. Batch predictions make predictions on datasets that can be stored in Amazon S3 or other AWS storage solutions.

Integration and invocation - Amazon SageMaker provides a variety of ways and interfaces to interact with the service:

- **Web API** - Sagemaker has a web API that can be used to control and invoke a SageMaker server instance.
- **SageMaker API** - As with other services, Amazon has an API for SageMaker that supports the following list of programming languages:
    - Go
    - C++
    - Java
    - JavaScript
    - Python
    - PHP
    - Ruby
    - Java
- **Web interface** - If you are familiar with Jupyter Notebooks, you will feel right at home with Amazon SageMaker since the web interface to interact with SageMaker is Jupyter Notebooks.
- **AWS CLI** - The AWS command-line interface (CLI).

Alexa, Lex, and Polly – conversational gents

In previous chapters, we discussed Alexa and its increasingly pervasive presence in homes. We'll now delve into the technologies that power Alexa and allow you to create your own conversational bots.

Amazon Lex is a service for building conversational agents. Amazon Lex, along with other chatbots, is our generation's attempt at passing the Turing Test, which we discussed in previous chapters. It will be a while before anyone confuses a conversation with Alexa with a human conversation. However, Amazon and other companies keep on making strides in making these conversations more and more natural. Amazon Lex, which uses the same technologies that power Amazon Alexa allows developers to quickly build sophisticated, natural language, conversational agents or *chatbots*. For simple cases, it's possible to build some of these chatbots without any programming. However, it is possible to integrate Lex with other services in the AWS stack with AWS Lambda as the integration technology.

We will devote a whole chapter to creating chatbots later, so we will keep this section short for now.

Amazon Comprehend – natural language processing

Amazon Comprehend is a **natural language processing** (**NLP**) service provided by AWS. It uses machine learning to analyze content, perform entity recognition, and find implicit and explicit relationships. Companies are starting to realize that they have valuable information in the mounds of data that they generate every day. Valuable insights can be ascertained from customer emails, support tickets, product reviews, call center conversations, and social media interactions. Up until recently, it was cost-prohibitive to try to obtain these insights, but tools like Amazon Comprehend make it cost-effective to perform analysis on vast amounts of data.

Another advantage of this service is that is it yet another AWS service that is fully managed, so there is no need to provision servers, install drivers, and upgrade software. It is simple to use and deep experience in NLP is not required to quickly become productive with it.

Like other AWS AI/ML services, Amazon Comprehend integrates with other AWS services such as AWS Lambda and AWS Glue.

Use cases – Amazon Comprehend can be used to scan documents and identify patterns in those documents. This capability can be applied to a range of use cases, such as sentiment analysis, entity extraction, and document organization by topic.

As an example, Amazon Comprehend could analyze text from a social media interaction with a customer, identify key phrases, and determine whether the customer's experience was positive or negative.

Console Access - Amazon Comprehend can be accessed from the AWS Management Console. One of the easiest ways to ingest data into the service is by using Amazon S3. We can then make a call to the Comprehend service to analyze text for key phrases and relationships. Comprehend can return a confidence score for each user request to determine the confidence level of accuracy; the higher the percentage, the more confident the service is. Comprehend can easily process a single request or multiple requests in a batch.

Available **Application Programming Interface (APIs)** - As of this writing, Comprehend provides six different APIs to enable insights. They are:

- **Key phrase Extraction API** - Identifies key phrases and terms.
- **Sentiment Analysis API** - Returns the overall meaning and feeling of the text, either positive, negative, neutral, or mixed.
- **Syntax API** - Allows a user to tokenize text to define word boundaries and label words in their different parts of speech, such as nouns and verbs.
- **Entity Recognition API** - Identifies and labels different entities in the text, such as people, places, and companies.
- **Language Detection API** - Identifies the primary language in which a text is written. The service can identify over a hundred languages.
- **Custom Classification API** - Enables a user to build a custom text classification model.

Industry-specific services - Amazon Comprehend Medical was released at AWS re:Invent in 2018. It is built specifically for the medical industry and can identify industry-specific terminology. Comprehend also offers a specific Medical Named Entity and Relationship Extraction API. AWS does not store or use any text inputs from Amazon Comprehend Medical for future machine learning training.

Amazon Rekognition – image and video

No, it's not a typo. Amazon named its recognition service with a k and not a c. Amazon Rekognition can perform image and video analysis and enables users to add this functionality to their applications. Amazon Rekognition has been pretrained with millions of labeled images. Because of this, the service can quickly recognize:

- **Object types** - Chairs, tables, cars, and so on
- **Celebrities** - Actors, politicians, athletes, and so on

- **People** - Facial analysis, facial expressions, facial quality, user verification, and so on
- **Text** - Recognize an image as text and convert it to text
- **Scenes** - Dancing, celebrating, eating, and so on
- **Inappropriate content** - Adult, violent, or visually disturbing content

Amazon Rekognition has already recognized billions of images and videos and it uses them to continuously get better and better. The application of deep learning in the domain of image recognition might arguably be the most successful machine learning application in the last few years and Amazon Rekognition leverages deep learning to deliver impressive results. To use it, it is not required to have a high level of machine learning expertise. Amazon Rekognition provides a simple API. To use it, an image is passed along to the services along with a few parameters and that is it. Amazon Rekognition will only continue to get better. The more it gets used, the more inputs it receives, and the more it learns from those inputs. In addition, Amazon continues to enhance and to add new features and functionality to the service.

Some of the most popular use cases and applications for Amazon Rekognition are:

Object, scene, and activity detection - With Amazon Rekognition, you can identify thousands of different types of objects (for example, cars, houses, chairs, and so on) and scenes (for example, cities, malls, beaches, and so on). When analyzing video, specific activities that are happening in the frame can be identified, such as "emptying a car trunk" or "children playing."

Gender recognition - Amazon Rekognition can be used to make an educated guess to determine whether a person in an image is a male or a female. The functionality should not be used as the sole determinant of a person's gender. It is not meant to be used in such a way. For example, if a male actor is wearing a long-haired wig and earrings for a role, they might be identified as a female.

Facial recognition and analysis - One of the uses of facial recognition systems is to identify and authenticate a person from an image or video. This technology has been around for decades, but it's not until recently that its application has become more popular, cheaper, and more available, due in no small part to deep learning techniques and the ubiquity of services such as Rekognition. Facial recognition technologies power many of today's applications, such as photo sharing and storage services and as a second factor in authentication workflows for smartphones.

Once we recognize that an object is a face, we might want to perform further facial analysis. Some of the attributes that Amazon Rekognition can assist in determining are:

- Eyes open or closed

- Mood:
    - Happy
    - Sad
    - Angry
    - Surprised
    - Disgusted
    - Calm
    - Confused
    - Fear
- Hair color
- Eye color
- Beards or mustaches
- Glasses
- Age range
- Gender
- Visual geometry of a face

These detected attributes are useful when there is a need to search through and organize millions of images in seconds, generating metadata tags such as a person's mood or to identify a person.

Pathing - The path of a person can be tracked in the scene using Amazon Rekognition using video files. For example, if we see an image that contains a person with bags around a trunk, we might not know whether the person is taking the bags out of the trunk and arriving or if they are putting the bags into the trunk and leaving. By analyzing the video using pathing, we will be able to make this determination.

Unsafe content detection - Amazon Rekognition can assist in identifying potentially unsafe or inappropriate content in images and video content and it can provide detailed labels that accurately control access to those assets based on previously determined criteria.

Celebrity recognition - Celebrities and famous people can be quickly identified in image and video libraries to catalog photos and footage. This functionality can be used in marketing, advertising, and media industry use cases.

Text in images - Once we identify that an image contains text, it is only natural to want to convert the letters and words in that image into text. As an example, if Rekognition is able to not only recognize that an object is a license plate but additionally convert the image into text, it will then be easy to index that against Department of Motor Vehicle records and track individuals and their whereabouts.

Amazon Translate

Amazon Translate is another Amazon service that can be used to translate large amounts of text written in one language to another language. Amazon Translate is pay-per-use, so you will only be charged when you submit something that needs translation. As of October 2019, Amazon Translate supports 32 languages:

Language	Language Code
Arabic	ar
Chinese (Simplified)	zh
Chinese (Traditional)	zh-TW
Czech	cs
Danish	da
Dutch	nl
English	en
Finnish	fi
French	fr
German	de
Greek	el
Hebrew	he
Hindi	hi
Hungarian	hu
Indonesian	id
Italian	it
Japanese	ja
Korean	ko
Malay	ms
Norwegian	no
Persian	fa
Polish	pl
Portuguese	pt

Romanian	ro
Russian	ru
Spanish	es
Swedish	sv
Thai	th
Turkish	tr
Ukrainian	uk
Urdu	ur
Vietnamese	vi

With a few exceptions, most of these languages can be translated from one to the other. Users can also add items to the dictionary to customize the terminology and include terms that are specific to their organization or use case, such as brand and product names.

Amazon Translate uses machine learning and a continuous learning model to improve the performance of its translation over time.

The service can be accessed in three different ways, in the same way that many of the AWS services can be accessed:

- From the AWS console, to translate small snippets of text and to sample the service.
- Using the AWS API (supported languages are C++, Go, Java, JavaScript, .NET, Node.js, PHP, Python, and Ruby).
- Amazon Translate can be accessed via the AWS CLI.

Uses for Amazon Translate

Many companies use Amazon Translate together with other external services. Additionally, Amazon Translate can be integrated with other AWS services. For example, Translate can be used in conjunction with Amazon Comprehend to pull out predetermined entities, sentiments, or keywords from a social media feed and then translate the extracted terms. In another example, the service can be paired with Amazon S3 to translate document repositories and speak a translated language with Amazon Polly.

However, using Amazon Translate does not mean that human translators don't have a role anymore. Some companies are pairing Amazon Translate with human translators to increase the speed of the translation process.

Amazon Machine Learning

Before there was Amazon SageMaker, there was Amazon Machine Learning or Amazon ML. Amazon ML is a simpler service that can still be a powerful tool for some use cases. Amazon ML was initially released in April 2015 at the AWS Summit in San Francisco. Amazon ML makes it easy for developers of all skill levels to use machine learning technology. Amazon ML provides visualization tools and wizards that guide users through the process of creating machine learning models without having to learn complex ML algorithms and technology. Once your models are ready, Amazon ML makes it a snap to obtain predictions. Applications can use a straightforward API without having to implement custom prediction code, all within a fully managed service.

Amazon Transcribe – transcription

Another service that was released at the re:Invent conference in 2017 was Amazon Transcribe. You can think of Amazon Transcribe as your personal secretary, taking notes as you speak.

Amazon Transcribe is an **automatic speech recognition** (**ASR**) service that allows developers to add speech-to-text capabilities to various applications. The Amazon Transcribe API can be used to analyze stored audio files. The service returns a text file containing transcribed speech. Amazon Transcribe can also be used in real time. It can receive a live audio stream and it will generate a real-time stream containing the transcribed text.

Amazon Transcribe can be used to transcribe customer service calls and to generate subtitles for audio and video content. The service supports common audio formats such as WAV and MP3. It can generate a timestamp for every word. This facilitates locating the original audio source quickly using the generated text. Like other Amazon machine learning services, Amazon Transcribe continuously learns from the text that it is processing to constantly improve the service.

Amazon Textract – document analysis

One of the hardest problems in machine learning is recognizing handwriting. Everybody's handwriting is different and some of us have horrible handwriting that sometimes even we can't understand a few minutes after writing it. No, Amazon has not mastered a way to decipher your chicken scratch, but Amazon Textract is a service that can convert images that contain text into its text equivalent. There are many scanned and faxed documents that are sitting in drawers that could provide much value to their owners if we were able to scan those documents, convert them to text, index them, and enable users to search the content of those documents.

Amazon Textract enables users to extract text from documents, forms, and tables. Amazon Textract can automatically detect the layout of a document and key page elements. It can identify data in embedded forms or tables and extract that data within the context of the page. This information can then be integrated with other AWS services and used as input for an AWS Lambda call or as a stream into Amazon Kinesis.

Microsoft Azure

Having covered AWS, let's take a look at the features of Microsoft's offering within the area of cloud services: Microsoft Azure.

Microsoft Azure Machine Learning Studio

Microsoft Azure Machine Learning Studio is Microsoft's answer to Amazon SageMaker. Machine Learning Studio is a collaborative tool with a simple drag-and-drop interface that allows the user to build, test, and deploy machine learning models. Machine Learning Studio enables model publishing that can be consumed by other applications and can easily integrate with BI tools such as Excel.

Machine Learning Studio interactive workspace – In *Chapter 3, Machine Learning Pipelines*, we learned about the machine learning pipeline. The Machine Learning Studio interactive workspace simplifies pipeline development by allowing users to easily ingest data into the workspace, transform the data, then analyze that data through various data manipulation and statistical functions, and finally generate predictions. Developing a machine learning pipeline is normally an iterative process and the workspace makes it simple to perform this iterative development. While modifying the various functions and their parameters, you will be able to visualize and analyze the performance of your model until you are satisfied with the results.

Azure Machine Learning Studio provides an interactive, visual workspace to easily build, test, and iterate on a predictive analysis model. To bring datasets into the workspace, you can drag-and-drop them. You can also drag analysis modules onto an interactive canvas and connect them together to form an initial *experiment*, which can then be run in Machine Learning Studio. If the results are not satisfactory, the parameters of the experiment can be modified and run again and again until the results are satisfactory. Once the performance is satisfactory, the *training experiment* can be converted to a *predictive experiment*, and it can be published as a web service so that the model can be accessed by users and other services.

Learning Studio does not require any programming. Experiments are constructed by visually connecting datasets and modules to build a predictive analysis model.

Getting started with Machine Learning Studio - To get started, you can create a free tier account with Azure. As of this writing, the benefits of a free account were:

- 12 months of free products such as virtual machines, storage, and databases
- $200 in credits for services that don't qualify for the free tier
- No automatic charges unless you specifically upgrade to a paid account
- Additionally, Azure has more than 25 products that are always free, including serverless products and AI services

Once you create your account, you can visit the Azure Machine Learning Studio.

After you sign in, you'll see the following tabs on the left:

- **Projects** - Projects are collections of experiments, datasets, notebooks, and other resources
- **Experiments** - Experiments can be created, edited, run, and saved
- **Web Services** - Experiments can be deployed and exposed as web services
- **Notebooks** - The Studio also supports Jupyter Notebooks
- **Datasets** - Datasets that have been uploaded into Studio
- **Trained Models** - Models that have been trained and saved in experiments
- **Settings** - Settings can be used to configure accounts and resources.

Azure Machine Learning Gallery - The Gallery is a place where data science communities can share solutions that they have previously created using components from the Cortana Intelligence Suite.

Components of an experiment - An experiment consists of datasets and analytical modules, which can be connected to construct a predictive analysis model. A valid experiment has these characteristics:

- The experiment has at least one dataset and one module
- Datasets may be connected only to modules
- Modules may be connected to either datasets or other modules
- All input ports for modules must have some connection to the data flow
- All required parameters for each module must be set

Experiments can be created from scratch or using an existing experiment as a template.

Datasets - A dataset is data that has been uploaded to Machine Learning Studio so that it can be used in an experiment. Several sample datasets are included with Machine Learning Studio, and more datasets can be uploaded as needed.

Modules - A module is an algorithm that you can perform on your data. Machine Learning Studio has a variety of modules, including:

- Data ingestion processes
- Training functions
- Scoring functions
- Validation processes

More specific examples:

- **ARFF Conversion Module** - Converts a .NET serialized dataset to Attribute-Relation File Format (ARFF)
- **Compute Elementary Statistics Module** - Calculates elementary statistics such as mean, standard deviation, and so on
- **Linear Regression Model** - Creates an online gradient descent-based linear regression model
- **Scoring Model** - Scores a trained classification or regression model

A module may have a set of parameters that can be used to configure the module's internal algorithms.

Model Deployment - Once your predictive analytics model is ready, you can deploy it as a web service right from Machine Learning Studio.

Azure Machine Learning Service

Azure Machine Learning (**AML**) Service is a platform that allows data scientists and data engineers to train, deploy, automate, and manage machine learning models at scale and in the cloud. Users of the service can create powerful applications and workflows using Python-based libraries. The AML Service is a framework that allows developers to train models using predefined datasets and then wrap their model as a web service in a Docker container and deploy them using a variety of container orchestrators.

Azure Machine Learning Services can be accessed and used in one of two ways:

- Via the Software Developer Kit (SDK)
- Using the service visual interface

If you are thinking that this sounds a lot like Azure Machine Learning Studio, you would be right to think that. These are similar services and at some point, Microsoft might decide to merge them together or deprecate one of them. If they deprecate one of them, you can assume with a high degree of certainty that Microsoft will offer a way to migrate workflows and applications developed in one of the services into the other.

How is Machine Learning Studio different from the Azure Machine Learning Services? These are the main differences, which will allow you to decide which one to use:

Azure Machine Learning Services	Azure Machine Learning Studio
• Hybrid deployment of training and scoring models. Models can be trained on-prem and deployed on the cloud or vice versa • Freedom to use different frameworks and machine instance types • Support for Auto ML and auto hyperparameter tuning	• Ideal for beginners • Standard experiments can be quickly created but are harder to customize • Fully managed service • Not available on-premise

Here, we present a chart that highlights the differences and the various features that are supported by each service:

Feature	Azure Machine Learning Studio	Azure Machine Learning Service SDK	Azure Machine Learning Service Visual Interface
Year released	2015	2018	2019 (in preview)
User interface	Web-based	API-based	Web-based
Cloud support	Yes	Yes	Yes
On-prem	No	Yes	No
Tool support	Web-based	• Visual Studio • Azure Notebooks • Python interfaces	Web-based
GPU supported	No	Yes	Yes

Built-in algorithms	• Classification • Regression • Clustering • Time Series • Text Analytics • Anomaly Detection	External packages can be imported	• Classification • Regression • Clustering
Auto hyperparameter tuning	No	Yes	No
Auto ML	No	Yes	No
Ease of extensibility	Not straightforward	Python packages can be easily installed via pip	Not straightforward
Python support	Yes	Yes	Yes
R support	Yes	No	Not yet
Built-in containers	No	Yes	No

Azure Cognitive Services

Decision service - Allows users to build applications that provide recommendations and support efficient decision-making.

Vision service - Enables applications that can recognize, identify, caption, index, and moderate images and videos.

Speech service - This service converts speech into text and text into natural-sounding speech. It can also perform translation from one language to another. Additionally, it supports speaker verification and recognition.

Search service - Bing Search support can be added to applications and enable users to search through billions of web pages, images, videos, and news articles with a single API call.

Language service - Enables applications to process natural language with pre-built scripts to evaluate text sentiment and determine the text's intent.

Google Cloud Platform (GCP)

Having looked at the services provided by Microsoft Azure, let's move on to discussing another alternative cloud platform: GCP. First, we'll talk about GCP's AI Hub service.

AI Hub

One of the available services in the Google Cloud Platform is AI Hub. AI Hub is a fully managed repository of plug-and-play AI components that enable the creation of end-to-end machine learning pipelines. AI Hub provides a wide variety of out-of-the-box machine learning algorithms. AI Hub provides enterprise-grade collaboration capabilities that let companies privately host their machine learning workflows and foster reuse and sharing. You can also easily deploy your models into production on the Google Cloud as well as other environments and cloud providers. AI Hub was released in 2018 so it is in its early stages. Given the importance that Google has assigned to AI research, we expect AI Hub to quickly mature and continue to provide more features and functionality at a fast pace.

Component and code discovery - AI Hub is a content repository that allows users to quickly discover quality content. Some of the publishers that are accessible via AI Hub are:

- Google AI
- Google Cloud AI
- Google Cloud Partners

If the Hub is used within an enterprise, users can also find other components built by other teams within the company.

Collaboration - AI Hub improves user productivity and allows them to avoid effort duplication. AI Hub provides highly granular controls to share components only with users within the organization that are supposed to have access to the components. It also provides users with access to predefined machine learning algorithms created by Google engineers and researchers and other code shared by Azure partners and other publishers.

Deployment - AI Hub enables the modification and customization of algorithms and pipelines for specific business needs. It also provides intuitive mechanisms for the deployment of trained models. These models can be deployed on Google Cloud or in other environments and cloud providers.

Google Cloud AI Building Blocks

In addition to AI Hub, which can be compared to Amazon SageMaker and Azure Machine Learning Studio, Google Cloud also has similar offerings to what AWS and Azure provide in terms of fully managed services that simplify the application of machine learning to text, language, images, and video. Google organizes many of these managed services under the *Google Cloud AI Building Blocks* umbrella. For many of these managed services, there are two ways to interact with them - AutoML and APIs. AutoML is used for custom models and APIs are used for pre-trained models. AutoML and APIs can be used individually or together.

Google Cloud AutoML custom models - The AutoML services use Google's state-of-the-art transfer learning and neural architecture search technology to allow users to create domain-specific custom models for a variety of use cases.

Google Cloud pre-trained APIs - When dealing with common use cases, users of a Google service can immediately become productive using pre-trained APIs without having to previously train the model. The pre-trained APIs are continuously and transparently upgraded to increase the speed and accuracy of these models.

Vision AI and AutoML Vision - This service allows users to derive insights from images with AutoML Vision or using pre-trained Vision API models. This service can detect emotion, understand text, and more.

To use the service, images can be uploaded and analyzed using custom image models. The service has an easy-to-use visual interface. The service allows you to optimize models for accuracy, latency, and size. Results can be exported to other applications in the cloud or to an array of devices at the edge.

Google Cloud's Vision API offers powerful pre-trained machine learning models that can be accessed using RESTful and RPC API calls. The service can quickly label images and classify them. The service is pretrained and it already contains millions of categories. It can also be used for facial recognition and analysis, as well as to recognize captions within images and convert them into text.

AutoML Video Intelligence and Video Intelligence API - The AutoML Video Intelligence service has a simple interface that can identify, track, and classify objects in videos using custom models. The service does not require an extensive background in programming or artificial intelligence. This service is used for applications that require custom labels that cannot be generated by the pre-trained Video Intelligence API.

The Video Intelligence API has pre-trained models that can recognize a wide variety of common objects, scenes, and activities. In addition to stored video, it also supports streaming video. As more images are processed, it automatically and transparently improves over time.

AutoML Translation and Translation API - Both developers and translators with little or no programming experience can create production-quality models. The Translation API uses pre-trained neural net algorithms to provide world-class machine translation that in some instances is starting to rival human-level performance.

AutoML Natural Language and Natural Language API - This service can be used to classify text, perform entity extraction, and sentiment detection, all with a simple-to-use API. Users can leverage the AutoML natural language interface to provide datasets and determine which custom models will be used.

The Natural Language API has pre-trained models that let users of the API access **natural language understanding** (**NLU**) features including:

- Entity analysis
- Sentiment analysis
- Content classification
- Entity sentiment analysis
- Syntax analysis

Dialogflow - Dialogflow is a development service that allows users to create conversational agents. It can be used to build chatbots that enable natural and rich interactions. It allows users of the service to develop agents once and then they can be deployed to a variety of platforms, including:

- Google Assistant
- Facebook Messenger
- Slack
- Alexa Voice Services

Text-to-Speech - Google Cloud Text-to-Speech can convert text into human-like speech in more than 180 voices across over 30 languages and accents. For example, it can imitate an American accent or a British accent. It uses speech synthesis (WaveNet) and neural networks developed by Google to deliver high-fidelity audio. Users can call the API and create lifelike interactions. It is not difficult to imagine that we will soon be seeing this technology embedded in a variety of customer service applications.

Speech-to-Text - You can think of this service as the opposite of the previous service. If *Text-to-Speech* is the voice, *Speech-to-Text* provides the ears. Google Cloud Speech-to-Text enables users of the service to convert audio files into text utilizing neural network models. The complexity of these models is completely hidden from the users of the service and they can just invoke it calling an easy-to-use API. As of this writing, the API supports over 120 languages and variants. It can be used to:

- Enable voice commands in an application
- Transcribe call center conversations
- Integrate with other Google and non-Google services in a workflow
- Process audio in real time as well as prerecorded versions

AutoML Tables - This service enables analysts, developers, and data scientists to build and deploy machine learning models on structured data. For many use cases, it requires little to no coding, so it can greatly enhance the speed of deployment. In these cases, configuration is done through a wizard-like interface. When coding is required, AutoML Tables supports *Colab Notebooks*. These notebooks are powerful notebooks that are like Jupyter notebooks and have many added features that make them easy to use and to collaborate with other users. The service is domain-agnostic so it can be used to tackle a wide variety of problems. As of October 2019, the service was still not generally available, but it is accessible in its beta version.

Recommendations AI - This Google service can deliver highly personalized product recommendations at scale. For over two decades, Google has been providing recommendations across its flagship properties, such as Google Ads, Google Search, and YouTube. Recommendations AI draws on that experience to enable users of the service to deliver personalized recommendations that cater to individual customer's needs and preferences across a wide swath of applications and use cases. As of this writing, this product is also in beta and is not generally available.

Summary

In this chapter, we saw that all major technology companies are involved in a high-stakes arms race to be the cloud lead dog. Through the history of computing, and as different technologies emerge, the most common outcome is to have one player that dominates the space and all the other competitors are relegated to feed on the scraps. The cloud might be the most important technology to emerge in the history of computing. As customers decide who their preferred cloud provider is, even though they might not realize it now, they are making a decision that will lock them into that cloud provider's ecosystem, and it will be quite difficult to extricate themselves from it and jump to another cloud provider down the road.

Cloud vendors realize the importance of this and are rushing to match competitors' capabilities. We clearly saw this in this chapter, when we analyzed the machine learning offerings from the top three cloud vendors. They are fighting hard to differentiate from each other and at the same time try to match each other tit for tat on every service and feature offering. It will be exciting to see in the next few years how these cloud offerings evolve and what great new services these vendors will offer, especially in the areas of artificial intelligence and machine learning.

One drawback for us as technologists is that it will be hard to keep up with all the fun toys and technologies, but if nothing else, it should a thrilling ride to explore them.

Speaking of toys, in the next chapter, we will explore how to build games using artificial intelligence and put some of the concepts that we have learned to good use.

13 Building Games with Artificial Intelligence

In this chapter, we are going to learn how to build games using an artificial intelligence technique called combinatorial search. In its most basic form, it can be thought of as a *brute-force approach*. We explore every single possible solution. Later in the chapter, we will get smarter and find a way to short circuit the search and not have to try every single possibility. We will learn how to use search algorithms to effectively come up with strategies to win a set of games. We will then use these algorithms to build intelligent bots for different games.

By the end of this chapter, you will have a better understanding of the following concepts:

- Search algorithms in games
- Combinatorial search
- The Minimax algorithm
- Alpha-Beta pruning
- The Negamax algorithm
- Building a bot to play Last Coin Standing
- Building a bot to play Tic-Tac-Toe
- Building two bots to play Connect Four against each other
- Building two bots to play Hexapawn against each other

Using search algorithms in games

Search algorithms are commonly used in games to figure out a strategy. The algorithms search through possible game moves and pick the best one. There are various parameters to consider when implementing these searches - speed, accuracy, complexity, and so on. These algorithms consider all possible game moves given a current game state and then evaluate each possible move to determine the best one. The goal of these algorithms is to find the optimal move that will eventually lead to winning the game. Also, every game has a different set of rules and constraints. These algorithms consider these rules and constraints when exploring the best moves.

Games without opponents are easier to optimize than games with opponents. Gameplay becomes more complicated with games that have multiple players. Let's consider a two-player game. For every move made by a player to try to win the game, the opposing player will make a move to prevent the player from winning. So, when a search algorithm finds the optimal set of moves from the current state, it cannot just make moves without considering the opposing player's countermoves. This means that search algorithms need to constantly be re-evaluated after each move.

Let's discuss how a computer perceives any given game. We can think of a game as a search tree. Each node in this tree represents a future state. For example, if you are playing **Tic-Tac-Toe** (Noughts and Crosses), you can construct a tree to represent all possible moves. We start from the root of the tree, which is the starting point of the game. This node will have several children that represent various possible moves. Those children, in turn, will have more children that represent game states after more moves by the opponent. The terminal nodes of the tree represent the final moves of the game. The game will either end in a draw or one of the players will win it. The search algorithms search through this tree to make decisions at each step of the game. We will now learn a variety of search techniques of how to include an exhaustive combinatorial search to help us to never lose at Tic-Tac-Toe and solve a variety of many other problems.

Combinatorial search

Search algorithms appear to solve the problem of adding intelligence to games, but there's a drawback. These algorithms employ a type of search called exhaustive search, which is also known as a *brute-force* search. It basically explores the entire search space and tests every possible solution. It means that the algorithm will have to explore all the possible solutions before obtaining the optimal solution.

As the games get more complex, brute-force search may not be the best approach, because the number of possibilities becomes enormous. The search quickly becomes computationally intractable. In order to solve this problem, combinatorial search can be used to solve problems. Combinatorial search refers to a field of study where search algorithms efficiently explore the solution space using heuristics to reduce the size of the search space. This is useful in games such as Chess or Go.

Combinatorial search works efficiently by using pruning strategies. These strategies avoid testing all possible solutions by eliminating the ones that are obviously wrong. This helps to save time and effort. Now that we have learned about exhaustive combinatorial search and its limitations, we'll start exploring ways to take short cuts, "prune" the search tree, and avoid having to test every single combination. In the following sections, we'll explore some specific algorithms that enable us to perform a combinatorial search.

The Minimax algorithm

Now that we have briefly discussed combinatorial search in general, let's talk about the heuristics that are employed by combinatorial search algorithms. These heuristics are used to speed up the search strategy and the Minimax algorithm is one such strategy used by combinatorial search. When two players are playing against each other, their goals are diametrically opposed. Each player is trying to win. So, each side needs to predict what the opposing player is going to do in order to win the game. Keeping this in mind, Minimax tries to achieve this through strategy. It will try to minimize the function that the opponent is trying to maximize.

As discussed earlier, brute force only works in simple games with a small number of possible moves. In more complicated cases, the computer cannot go through all the possible states to find the optimal gameplay. In this case, the computer can try to calculate the optimal move based on the current state using a heuristic. The computer constructs a tree and it starts from the bottom. It evaluates which moves would benefit its opponent. The algorithm knows which moves the opponent is going to make based on the premise that the opponent will make the moves that would benefit them the most, and thereby be of the least benefit to the computer. This outcome is one of the terminal nodes of the tree and the computer uses this position to work backwards. Each option that's available to the computer can be assigned a value and it can then pick the highest value to take an action.

Alpha-Beta pruning

Minimax search is an efficient strategy, but it still ends up exploring parts of the tree that are irrelevant. When an indicator on a node is found showing that a solution does not exist in that sub-tree, there is no need to evaluate that sub-tree. But Minimax search is too conservative, so it ends up exploring some of these sub-trees.

The Alpha-Beta algorithm is smarter and avoids searching parts of the tree that it discovers will not have the solution. This process is called **pruning** and Alpha-Beta pruning is a type of strategy that is used to avoid searching parts of the tree that do not contain the solution.

The Alpha and Beta parameters in Alpha-Beta pruning refer to the two bounds that are used during the calculation. These parameters refer to the values that restrict the set of possible solutions. This is based on the section of the tree that has already been explored. Alpha is the maximum lower bound on the number of possible solutions and Beta is the minimum upper bound on the number of possible solutions.

As discussed earlier, each node can be assigned a value based on the current state. When the algorithm considers any new node as a potential path to the solution, it can work out if the current estimate of the value of the node lies between Alpha and Beta. This is how it prunes the search.

The Negamax algorithm

The **Negamax** algorithm is a variant of Minimax that's frequently used in real-world implementations. A two-player game is usually a zero-sum game, which means that one player's loss is equal to another player's gain and vice versa. Negamax uses this property extensively to come up with a strategy to increases its chances of winning the game.

In terms of a game, the value of a given position to the first player is the negation of the value to the second player. Each player looks for a move that will maximize the damage to the opponent. The value resulting from the move should be such that the opponent gets the least value. This works both ways seamlessly, which means that a single method can be used to value the positions. This is where it has an advantage over Minimax in terms of simplicity. Minimax requires that the first player select the move with the maximum value, whereas the second player must select a move with the minimum value. Alpha-Beta pruning is used here as well. Now that we've looked at a few of the most popular combinatorial search algorithms, let's install a library so that we can build some AI and see these algorithms in action.

Installing the easyAI library

We will be using a library called `easyAI` in this chapter. It is an artificial intelligence framework and it provides all the functionality necessary to build two-player games. You can learn more about it here:

`http://zulko.github.io/easyAI`

Install it by running the following command:

```
$ pip3 install easyAI
```

Some of the files need to be accessible in order to use some of the pre-built routines. For ease of use, the code provided with this book contains a folder called `easyAI`. Make sure you place this folder in the same folder as your code files. This folder is basically a subset of the `easyAI` GitHub repository available here:

`https://github.com/Zulko/easyAI`

You can go through the source code to make yourself more familiar with it.

Building a bot to play Last Coin Standing

In this game, there is a pile of coins and each player takes turns to take a number of coins from the pile. There is a lower and an upper bound on the number of coins that can be taken from the pile. The goal of the game is to avoid taking the last coin in the pile. This recipe is a variant of the Game of Bones recipe given in the `easyAI` library. Let's see how to build a game where the computer can play against the user.

Create a new Python file and import the following packages:

```
from easyAI import TwoPlayersGame, id_solve, Human_Player, AI_Player
from easyAI.AI import TT
```

Create a class to handle all the operations of the game. The code inherits from the base class `TwoPlayersGame` available in the `easyAI` library. There are a couple of parameters that must be defined for the code to function properly. The first one is the `players` variable. The `player` object will be discussed later. Create the class using the following code:

```
class LastCoinStanding(TwoPlayersGame):
    def __init__(self, players):
        # Define the players. Necessary parameter.
        self.players = players
```

Define the player that is going to start the game. The players are numbered starting with one. So, in this case, player one starts the game:

```
        # Define who starts the game. Necessary parameter.
        self.nplayer = 1
```

Define the number of coins in the pile. You are free to choose any number here. In this case, let's choose `25`:

```
        # Overall number of coins in the pile
        self.num_coins = 25
```

Define the maximum number of coins that can be taken out in any move. You are free to choose any number for this parameter as well. Let's choose `4` in our case:

```
        # Define max number of coins per move
        self.max_coins = 4
```

Define all the possible moves. In this case, players can take either 1, 2, 3, or 4 coins in each move:

```
    # Define possible moves
    def possible_moves(self):
        return [str(x) for x in range(1, self.max_coins + 1)]
```

Define a method to remove the coins and keep track of the number of coins remaining in the pile:

```
    # Remove coins
    def make_move(self, move):
        self.num_coins -= int(move)
```

Check if somebody won the game by checking the number of coins remaining:

```
    # Did the opponent take the last coin?
    def win(self):
        return self.num_coins <= 0
```

Stop the game after somebody wins it:

```
    # Stop the game when somebody wins
    def is_over(self):
        return self.win()
```

Compute the score based on the `win` method. It's necessary to define this method:

```
    # Compute score
    def scoring(self):
        return 100 if self.win() else 0
```

Define a method to show the current status of the pile:

```
    # Show number of coins remaining in the pile
    def show(self):
        print(self.num_coins, 'coins left in the pile')
```

Define the `main` function and start by defining the transposition table. Transposition tables are used in games to store the positions and movements to speed up the algorithm.

Type in the following code:

```
if __name__ == "__main__":
    # Define the transposition table
    tt = TT()
```

Define the method `ttentry` to get the number of coins. It's an optional method that's used to create a string to describe the game:

```
    # Define the method
    LastCoinStanding.ttentry = lambda self: self.num_coins
```

Let's solve the game using AI. The function `id_solve` is used to solve a given game using iterative deepening. It basically determines who can win a game using all the paths. It looks to answer questions such as:

- Can the first player force a win by playing perfectly?
- Will the computer always lose against a perfect opponent?

The method `id_solve` explores various options in the game's Negamax algorithm several times. It always starts at the initial state of the game and takes increasing depth to keep going. It will do so until the score indicates that somebody will win or lose. The second argument in the method takes a list of depths that it will try out. In this case, it will try all the values from `2` to `20`:

```
    # Solve the game
    result, depth, move = id_solve(LastCoinStanding,
            range(2, 20), win_score=100, tt=tt)
    print(result, depth, move)
```

Start the game against the computer:

```
    # Start the game
    game = LastCoinStanding([AI_Player(tt), Human_Player()])
    game.play()
```

The full code is given in the file `coins.py`. It's an interactive program, so it will expect input from the user. If you run the code, you will be basically playing against the computer. Your goal is to force the computer to take the last coin so that you win the game. If you run the code, you will initially get the following output:

```
d:2, a:0, m:1
d:3, a:0, m:1
d:4, a:0, m:1
d:5, a:0, m:1
d:6, a:0, m:1
d:7, a:0, m:1
d:8, a:0, m:1
d:9, a:0, m:1
d:10, a:100, m:4
1 10 4
25 coins left in the pile

Move #1: player 1 plays 4 :
21 coins left in the pile

Player 2 what do you play ? 1

Move #2: player 2 plays 1 :
20 coins left in the pile

Move #3: player 1 plays 4 :
16 coins left in the pile
```

Figure 1: Last coin standing game initial output

If you scroll down, you will see the following towards the end:

```
Move #5: player 1 plays 2 :
11 coins left in the pile

Player 2 what do you play ? 4

Move #6: player 2 plays 4 :
7 coins left in the pile

Move #7: player 1 plays 1 :
6 coins left in the pile

Player 2 what do you play ? 2

Move #8: player 2 plays 2 :
4 coins left in the pile

Move #9: player 1 plays 3 :
1 coins left in the pile

Player 2 what do you play ? 1

Move #10: player 2 plays 1 :
0 coins left in the pile
```

Figure 2: Last coin standing game final output

As we can see, the computer wins the game because the user picked up the last coin.

Let's look at building a bot for another game: Tic-Tac-Toe.

Building a bot to play Tic-Tac-Toe

Tic-Tac-Toe (Noughts and Crosses) is perhaps one of the most famous games in the world. Let's see how to build a game where the computer can play against the user. This is a minor variant of the Tic-Tac-Toe recipe given in the `easyAI` library.

Create a new Python file and import the following packages:

```
from easyAI import TwoPlayersGame, AI_Player, Negamax
from easyAI.Player import Human_Player
```

Define a class that contains all the methods to play the game. Start by defining the players and who starts the game:

```
class GameController(TwoPlayersGame):
    def __init__(self, players):
        # Define the players
        self.players = players

        # Define who starts the game
        self.nplayer = 1
```

We will be using a 3×3 board numbered from one to nine row-wise:

```
        # Define the board
        self.board = [0] * 9
```

Define a method to compute all the possible moves:

```
    # Define possible moves
    def possible_moves(self):
        return [a + 1 for a, b in enumerate(self.board) if b == 0]
```

Define a method to update the board after making a move:

```
    # Make a move
    def make_move(self, move):
        self.board[int(move) - 1] = self.nplayer
```

Define a method to see if somebody has lost the game. We will be checking if somebody has three in a row:

```
    # Does the opponent have three in a line?
```

```
    def loss_condition(self):
        possible_combinations = [[1,2,3], [4,5,6], [7,8,9],
            [1,4,7], [2,5,8], [3,6,9], [1,5,9], [3,5,7]]

        return any([all([(self.board[i-1] == self.nopponent)
                for i in combination]) for combination in possible_
combinations])
```

Check if the game is done using the `loss_condition` method:

```
    # Check if the game is over
    def is_over(self):
        return (self.possible_moves() == []) or self.loss_condition()
```

Define a method to show the current progress:

```
    # Show current position
    def show(self):
        print('\n'+'\n'.join([' '.join([['.', 'O', 'X'][self.board[3*j
+ i]]
                for i in range(3)]) for j in range(3)]))
```

Compute the score using the `loss_condition` method:

```
    # Compute the score
    def scoring(self):
        return -100 if self.loss_condition() else 0
```

Define the `main` function and start by defining the algorithm. Negamax will be used as the AI algorithm for this game. The number of steps that the algorithm should think ahead can be specified in advance. In this case, let's choose `7`:

```
if __name__ == "__main__":
    # Define the algorithm
    algorithm = Negamax(7)
```

Start the game:

```
   # Start the game
   GameController([Human_Player(), AI_Player(algorithm)]).play()
```

The full code is given in the file `tic_tac_toe.py`. It's an interactive game where you play against the computer. If you run the code, you will initially get the following output:

```
. . .
. . .
. . .

Player 1 what do you play ? 5

Move #1: player 1 plays 5 :

. . .
. O .
. . .

Move #2: player 2 plays 1 :

X . .
. O .
. . .

Player 1 what do you play ? 9

Move #3: player 1 plays 9 :

X . .
. O .
. . O
```

Figure 3: Tic-tac-toe game initial output

If you scroll down, you will see the following output printed:

```
X O X
. O .
. X O

Player 1 what do you play ? 4

Move #7: player 1 plays 4 :

X O X
O O .
. X O

Move #8: player 2 plays 6 :

X O X
O O X
. X O

Player 1 what do you play ? 7

Move #9: player 1 plays 7 :

X O X
O O X
O X O
```

Figure 4: Tic-tac-toe game final output

As we can see, the game ends in a draw. We've looked at bots that can play against a user. Now let's build two bots to play against one another; this time, in Connect Four™.

Building two bots to play Connect Four™ against each other

Connect Four™ is a popular two-player game sold under the Milton Bradley trademark. It is also known by other names such as Four in a Row or Four Up. In this game, the players take turns dropping discs into a vertical grid consisting of six rows and seven columns. The goal is to get four discs in a line. This is a variant of the Connect Four recipe given in the `easyAI` library. Let's see how to build it. In this recipe, instead of playing against the computer, we will create two bots that will play against each other. A different algorithm will be used for each to see which one wins.

Create a new Python file and import the following packages:

```
import numpy as np
from easyAI import TwoPlayersGame, Human_Player, AI_Player, \
        Negamax, SSS
```

Define a class that contains all the methods needed to play the game:

```
class GameController(TwoPlayersGame):
    def __init__(self, players, board = None):
        # Define the players
        self.players = players
```

Define the board with six rows and seven columns:

```
        # Define the configuration of the board
        self.board = board if (board != None) else (
            np.array([[0 for i in range(7)] for j in range(6)]))
```

Define who's going to start the game. In this case, let's have player one start the game:

```
        # Define who starts the game
        self.nplayer = 1
```

Define the positions:

```
        # Define the positions
        self.pos_dir = np.array([[[i, 0], [0, 1]] for i in range(6)] +
                [[[0, i], [1, 0]] for i in range(7)] +
```

```
            [[[i, 0], [1, 1]] for i in range(1, 3)] +
            [[[0, i], [1, 1]] for i in range(4)] +
            [[[i, 6], [1, -1]] for i in range(1, 3)] +
            [[[0, i], [1, -1]] for i in range(3, 7)])
```

Define a method to get all the possible moves:

```
    # Define possible moves
    def possible_moves(self):
        return [i for i in range(7) if (self.board[:, i].min() == 0)]
```

Define a method to control how to make a move:

```
    # Define how to make the move
    def make_move(self, column):
        line = np.argmin(self.board[:, column] != 0)
        self.board[line, column] = self.nplayer
```

Define a method to show the current status:

```
    # Show the current status
    def show(self):
        print('\n' + '\n'.join(
                ['0 1 2 3 4 5 6', 13 * '-'] +
                [' '.join([['.', 'O', 'X'][self.board[5 - j][i]]
                for i in range(7)]) for j in range(6)]))
```

Define a method to compute what a loss looks like. Whenever somebody gets four in a line, that player wins the game:

```
    # Define what a loss_condition looks like
    def loss_condition(self):
        for pos, direction in self.pos_dir:
            streak = 0
            while (0 <= pos[0] <= 5) and (0 <= pos[1] <= 6):
                if self.board[pos[0], pos[1]] == self.nopponent:
                    streak += 1
                    if streak == 4:
                        return True
                else:
                    streak = 0

                pos = pos + direction


        return False
```

Check if the game is over by using the `loss_condition` method:

```
# Check if the game is over
def is_over(self):
    return (self.board.min() > 0) or self.loss_condition()
```

Compute the score:

```
# Compute the score
def scoring(self):
    return -100 if self.loss_condition() else 0
```

Define the `main` function and start by defining the algorithms. Then, the two algorithms will play against each other. Negamax will be used for the first computer player and the **SSS*** algorithm for the second computer player. SSS* is a search algorithm that conducts a state space search by traversing the tree in a best-first style. Both methods take, as an input argument, the number of turns in advance to think about. In this case, let's use `5` for both:

```
if __name__ == '__main__':
    # Define the algorithms that will be used
    algo_neg = Negamax(5)
    algo_sss = SSS(5)
```

Start playing the game:

```
    # Start the game
    game = GameController([AI_Player(algo_neg), AI_Player(algo_sss)])
    game.play()
```

Print the result:

```
    # Print the result
    if game.loss_condition():
        print('\nPlayer', game.nopponent, 'wins.')
    else:
        print("\nIt's a draw.")
```

The full code is given in the file `connect_four.py`. This is not an interactive game. The code pits one algorithm against another. The Negamax algorithm is player one and the SSS* algorithm is player two.

If you run the code, you will initially get the following output:

```
0 1 2 3 4 5 6
-------------
. . . . . . .
. . . . . . .
. . . . . . .
. . . . . . .
. . . . . . .
. . . . . . .

Move #1: player 1 plays 0 :

0 1 2 3 4 5 6
-------------
. . . . . . .
. . . . . . .
. . . . . . .
. . . . . . .
. . . . . . .
O . . . . . .

Move #2: player 2 plays 0 :

0 1 2 3 4 5 6
-------------
. . . . . . .
```

Figure 5: Connect Four game initial output

If you scroll down, you will see the following toward the end:

```
O O O X O O .

Move #35: player 1 plays 6 :

0 1 2 3 4 5 6
-------------
X X O O X . .
O O X X O . .
X X O O X X .
O O X X O O .
X X O X X X .
O O O X O O O

Move #36: player 2 plays 6 :

0 1 2 3 4 5 6
-------------
X X O O X . .
O O X X O . .
X X O O X X .
O O X X O O .
X X O X X X X
O O O X O O O

Player 2 wins.
```

Figure 6: Connect Four game final output

As we can see, player two wins the game. Let's try one more game: Hexapawn.

Building two bots to play Hexapawn against each other

Hexapawn is a two-player game starting with a chessboard of size $N \times M$. Pawns exist on each side of the board and the goal is to advance a pawn all the way to the other end of the board. The standard pawn rules of chess apply. This is a variant of the Hexapawn recipe given in the `easyAI` library. Two bots will be created and pitted against each other. Let's create the code.

Create a new Python file and import the following packages:

```
from easyAI import TwoPlayersGame, AI_Player, \
        Human_Player, Negamax
```

Define a class that contains all the methods necessary to control the game. Start by defining the number of pawns on each side and the length of the board. Create a list of tuples containing the positions:

```
class GameController(TwoPlayersGame):
    def __init__(self, players, size = (4, 4)):
        self.size = size
        num_pawns, len_board = size
        p = [[(i, j) for j in range(len_board)] \
                for i in [0, num_pawns - 1]]
```

Assign the direction, goals, and pawns to each player:

```
        for i, d, goal, pawns in [(0, 1, num_pawns - 1,
                p[0]), (1, -1, 0, p[1])]:
            players[i].direction = d
            players[i].goal_line = goal
            players[i].pawns = pawns
```

Define the players and specify who starts first:

```
        # Define the players
        self.players = players

        # Define who starts first
        self.nplayer = 1
```

Define the alphabets that will be used to identify positions such as B6 or C7 on a chessboard:

```
        # Define the alphabets
        self.alphabets = 'ABCDEFGHIJ'
```

Define a `lambda` function to convert the strings to tuples:

```
        # Convert B4 to (1, 3)
        self.to_tuple = lambda s: (self.alphabets.index(s[0]),
                int(s[1:]) - 1)
```

Define a `lambda` function to convert the tuples to strings:

```
        # Convert (1, 3) to B4
        self.to_string = lambda move: ' '.join([self.alphabets[
                move[i][0]] + str(move[i][1] + 1)
                for i in (0, 1)])
```

Define a method to compute the possible moves:

```
    # Define the possible moves
    def possible_moves(self):
        moves = []
        opponent_pawns = self.opponent.pawns
        d = self.player.direction
```

If you don't find an opponent pawn in a position, then that's a valid move:

```
        for i, j in self.player.pawns:
            if (i + d, j) not in opponent_pawns:
                moves.append(((i, j), (i + d, j)))

            if (i + d, j + 1) in opponent_pawns:
                moves.append(((i, j), (i + d, j + 1)))

            if (i + d, j - 1) in opponent_pawns:
                moves.append(((i, j), (i + d, j - 1)))

        return list(map(self.to_string, [(i, j) for i, j in moves]))
```

Define how to make a move and update the pawns based on that:

```
    # Define how to make a move
    def make_move(self, move):
        move = list(map(self.to_tuple, move.split(' ')))
        ind = self.player.pawns.index(move[0])
        self.player.pawns[ind] = move[1]

        if move[1] in self.opponent.pawns:
            self.opponent.pawns.remove(move[1])
```

Define the conditions for a loss. If a player gets 4 in a line, then the opponent loses:

```
    # Define what a loss looks like
    def loss_condition(self):
        return (any([i == self.opponent.goal_line
                for i, j in self.opponent.pawns])
                or (self.possible_moves() == []) )
```

Check if the game is done using the `loss_condition` method:

```
    # Check if the game is over
    def is_over(self):
        return self.loss_condition()
```

Print the current status:

```
    # Show the current status
    def show(self):
        f = lambda x: '1' if x in self.players[0].pawns else (
                '2' if x in self.players[1].pawns else '.')

        print("\n".join([" ".join([f((i, j)) for j in
          range(self.size[1])]) for i in range(self.size[0])]))
```

Define the `main` function and start by defining the `scoring` lambda function:

```
if __name__=='__main__':
    # Compute the score
    scoring = lambda game: -100 if game.loss_condition() else 0
```

Define the algorithm to be used. In this case, we will use Negamax, which can calculate `12` moves in advance and uses a `scoring` lambda function for strategy:

```
    # Define the algorithm
    algorithm = Negamax(12, scoring)
```

Start playing the game:

```
    # Start the game
    game = GameController([AI_Player(algorithm),
            AI_Player(algorithm)])
    game.play()
    print('\nPlayer', game.nopponent, 'wins after', game.nmove,
'turns')
```

The full code is given in the file `hexapawn.py`. It's not an interactive game. Two bots are created and pitted against each other. If you run the code, you will initially get the following output:

```
1 1 1 1
. . . .
. . . .
2 2 2 2

Move #1: player 1 plays A1 B1 :
. 1 1 1
1 . . .
. . . .
2 2 2 2

Move #2: player 2 plays D1 C1 :
. 1 1 1
1 . . .
2 . . .
. 2 2 2

Move #3: player 1 plays A2 B2 :
. . 1 1
1 1 . .
2 . . .
. 2 2 2

Move #4: player 2 plays D2 C2 :
. . 1 1
```

Figure 7: Hexapawn game initial output

If you scroll down, you will see the following toward the end:

```
Move #4: player 2 plays D2 C2 :
. . 1 1
1 1 . .
2 2 . .
. . 2 2

Move #5: player 1 plays B1 C2 :
. . 1 1
. 1 . .
2 1 . .
. . 2 2

Move #6: player 2 plays C1 B1 :
. . 1 1
2 1 . .
. 1 . .
. . 2 2

Move #7: player 1 plays C2 D2 :
. . 1 1
2 1 . .
. . . .
. 1 2 2

Player 1 wins after 8 turns
```

Figure 8: Hexapawn game final output

As we can see, player one wins the game.

Summary

In this chapter, we discussed how to build games using a special type of artificial intelligence technique called combinatorial search. We learned how to use these types of search algorithms to effectively come up with strategies to win games. These algorithms can be used to build game playing machines for more complicated games as well as solve a wide variety of problems. We talked about combinatorial search and how it can be used to speed up the search process. We learned about Minimax and Alpha-Beta pruning. We learned how the Negamax algorithm is used in practice. We then used these algorithms to build bots to play Last Coin Standing and Tic-Tac-Toe.

We learned how to build two bots to play against each other in Connect Four and Hexapawn. In the next chapter, we will learn about speech recognition and build a system to automatically recognize spoken words.

14
Building a Speech Recognizer

In this chapter, we are going to learn about speech recognition. We will discuss how to work with speech signals and learn how to visualize various audio signals. By utilizing various techniques to process speech signals, we will learn how to build a speech recognition system.

By the end of this chapter, you will know more about:

- Working with speech signals
- Visualizing audio signals
- Transforming audio signals to the frequency domain
- Generating audio signals
- Synthesizing tones
- Extracting speech features
- Recognizing spoken words

We'll begin by discussing how we can work with speech signals.

Working with speech signals

Speech recognition is the process of understanding the words that are spoken by humans. The speech signals are captured using a microphone and the system tries to understand the words that are being captured. Speech recognition is used extensively in human-computer interaction, smartphones, speech transcription, biometric systems, security, and more.

It is important to understand the nature of speech signals before they are analyzed. These signals happen to be complex mixtures of various signals. There are many different aspects of speech that contribute to its complexity. They include emotion, accent, language, and noise.

Because of this complexity, it is difficult to define a robust set of rules to analyze speech signals. In contrast, humans are outstanding at understanding speech even though it can have so many variations. Humans seem to do it with relative ease. For machines to do the same, we need to help them understand speech the same way humans do.

Researchers work on various aspects and applications of speech, such as understanding spoken words, identifying who the speaker is, recognizing emotions, and identifying accents. In this chapter, we will focus on understanding spoken words. Speech recognition represents an important step in the field of human-computer interaction. If we want to build cognitive robots that can interact with humans, they need to talk to us in natural language. This is the reason that automatic speech recognition has been the center of attention for many researchers in recent years. Let's go ahead and see how to deal with speech signals and build a speech recognizer.

Visualizing audio signals

Let's see how to visualize an audio signal. We will learn how to read an audio signal from a file and work with it. This will help us understand how an audio signal is structured. When audio files are recorded using a microphone, they are sampling the actual audio signals and storing the digitized versions. The real audio signals are continuous valued waves, which means we cannot store them as they are. We need to sample the signal at a certain frequency and convert it into discrete numerical form.

Most commonly, speech signals are sampled at 44,100 Hz. This means that each second of the speech signal is broken down into 44,100 parts and the values at each of these timestamps is stored in an output file. We save the value of the audio signal every 1/44,100 seconds. In this case, we say that the sampling frequency of the audio signal is 44,100 Hz. By choosing a high sampling frequency, it will appear that the audio signal is continuous when humans listen to it. Let's go ahead and visualize an audio signal.

Create a new Python file and import the following packages:

```
import numpy as np
import matplotlib.pyplot as plt
from scipy.io import wavfile
```

Read the input audio file using the `wavefile.read` method. It returns two values - sampling frequency and the audio signal:

```
# Read the audio file
sampling_freq, signal = wavfile.read('random_sound.wav')
```

Print the shape of the signal, the datatype, and the duration of the audio signal:

```
# Display the params
print('\nSignal shape:', signal.shape)
print('Datatype:', signal.dtype)
print('Signal duration:', round(signal.shape[0] / float(sampling_
freq), 2), 'seconds')
```

Normalize the signal:

```
# Normalize the signal
signal = signal / np.power(2, 15)
```

Extract the first `50` values from the `numpy` array for plotting:

```
# Extract the first 50 values
signal = signal[:50]
```

Construct the time axis in seconds:

```
# Construct the time axis in milliseconds
time_axis = 1000 * np.arange(0, len(signal), 1) / float(sampling_freq)
```

Plot the audio signal:

```
# Plot the audio signal
plt.plot(time_axis, signal, color='black')
plt.xlabel('Time (milliseconds)')
plt.ylabel('Amplitude')
plt.title('Input audio signal')
plt.show()
```

The full code is given in the file `audio_plotter.py`. If you run the code, you will see the following screenshot:

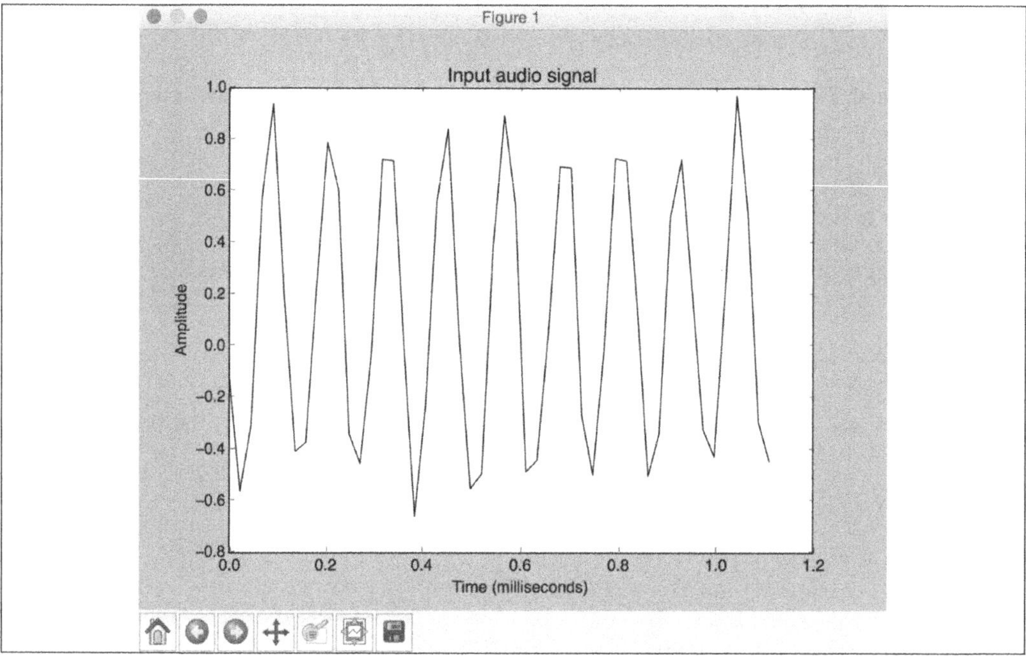

Figure 1: Visualization of input audio signal

The preceding screenshot shows the first 50 samples of the input audio signal. You will see the following output:

```
Signal shape: (132300,)
Datatype: int16
Signal duration: 3.0 seconds
```

Figure 2: Input audio signal output

The output printed in the preceding figure shows the information that we extracted from the signal.

Transforming audio signals to the frequency domain

In order to analyze audio signals, we need to understand the underlying frequency components. This gives us insights into how to extract meaningful information from this signal. Audio signals are composed of a mixture of sine waves of varying frequencies, phases, and amplitudes.

If we dissect the frequency components, we can identify a lot of characteristics. Any given audio signal is characterized by its distribution in the frequency spectrum. In order to convert a time domain signal into the frequency domain, we need to use a mathematical tool such as the **Fourier Transform**. If you need a quick refresher on the Fourier Transform, check out this link: `http://www.thefouriertransform.com`. Let's see how to transform an audio signal from the time domain to the frequency domain.

Create a new Python file and import the following packages:

```
import numpy as np
import matplotlib.pyplot as plt
from scipy.io import wavfile
```

Read the input audio file using the `wavefile.read` method. It returns two values - sampling frequency and the audio signal:

```
# Read the audio file
sampling_freq, signal = wavfile.read('spoken_word.wav')
```

Normalize the audio signal:

```
# Normalize the values
signal = signal / np.power(2, 15)
```

Extract the length and half-length of the signal:

```
# Extract the length of the audio signal
len_signal = len(signal)

# Extract the half length
len_half = np.ceil((len_signal + 1) / 2.0).astype(np.int)
```

Apply the Fourier transform to the signal:

```
# Apply Fourier transform
freq_signal = np.fft.fft(signal)
```

Normalize the frequency domain signal and take the square:

```
# Normalization
freq_signal = abs(freq_signal[0:len_half]) / len_signal

# Take the square
freq_signal **= 2
```

Adjust the Fourier-transformed signal for even and odd cases:

```
# Extract the length of the frequency transformed signal
len_fts = len(freq_signal)

# Adjust the signal for even and odd cases
if len_signal % 2:
    freq_signal[1:len_fts] *= 2
else:
    freq_signal[1:len_fts-1] *= 2
```

Extract the power signal in `dB`:

```
# Extract the power value in dB
signal_power = 10 * np.log10(freq_signal)
```

Build the *X* axis, which is frequency measured in `kHz` in this case:

```
# Build the X axis
x_axis = np.arange(0, len_half, 1) * (sampling_freq / len_signal) /
1000.0
```

Plot the figure:

```
# Plot the figure
plt.figure()
plt.plot(x_axis, signal_power, color='black')
plt.xlabel('Frequency (kHz)')
plt.ylabel('Signal power (dB)')
plt.show()
```

The full code is given in the file `frequency_transformer.py`. If you run the code, you will see the following screenshot:

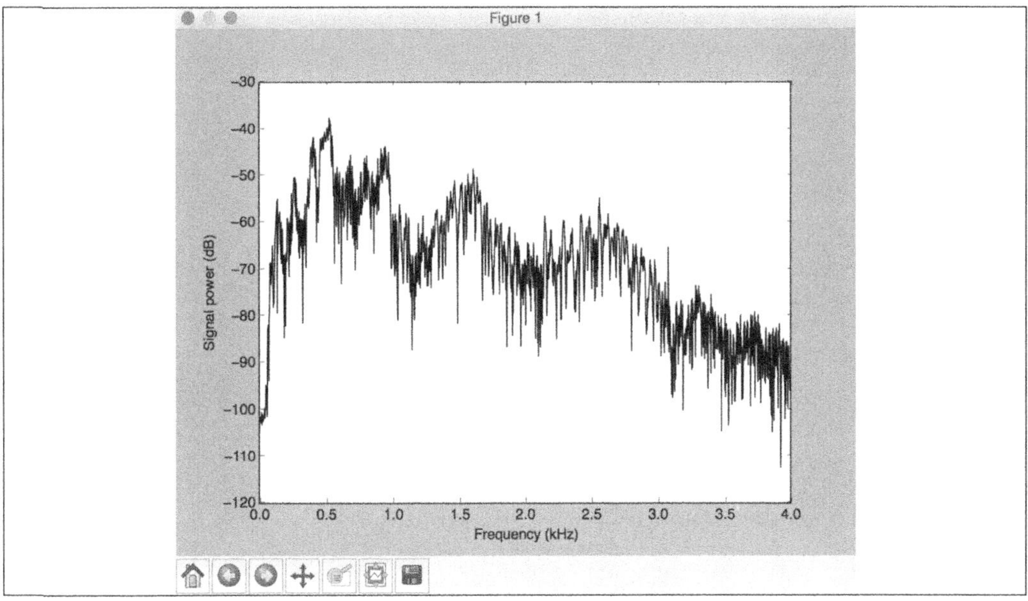

Figure 3: Visualization of audio signal transformation

The preceding screenshot shows how powerful the signal is across the frequency spectrum. In this case, the power of the signal goes down in the higher frequencies.

Generating audio signals

Now that we know how audio signals work, let's see how we can generate one such signal. We can use the NumPy package to generate various audio signals. Since audio signals are mixtures of **sinusoids**, we can use this to generate an audio signal with some predefined parameters.

Create a new Python file and import the following packages:

```
import numpy as np
import matplotlib.pyplot as plt
from scipy.io.wavfile import write
```

Define the output audio file's name:

```
# Output file where the audio will be saved
output_file = 'generated_audio.wav'
```

Specify the audio parameters, such as duration, sampling frequency, tone frequency, minimum value, and maximum value:

```
# Specify audio parameters
```

```
duration = 4  # in seconds
sampling_freq = 44100  # in Hz
tone_freq = 784
min_val = -4 * np.pi
max_val = 4 * np.pi
```

Generate the audio signal using the defined parameters:

```
# Generate the audio signal
t = np.linspace(min_val, max_val, duration * sampling_freq)
signal = np.sin(2 * np.pi * tone_freq * t)
```

Add some noise to the signal:

```
# Add some noise to the signal
noise = 0.5 * np.random.rand(duration * sampling_freq)
signal += noise
```

Normalize and scale the signal:

```
# Scale it to 16-bit integer values
scaling_factor = np.power(2, 15) - 1
signal_normalized = signal / np.max(np.abs(signal))
signal_scaled = np.int16(signal_normalized * scaling_factor)
```

Save the generated audio signal in the output file:

```
# Save the audio signal in the output file
write(output_file, sampling_freq, signal_scaled)
```

Extract the first `200` values for plotting:

```
# Extract the first 200 values from the audio signal
signal = signal[:200]
```

Construct the time axis in milliseconds:

```
# Construct the time axis in milliseconds
time_axis = 1000 * np.arange(0, len(signal), 1) / float(sampling_freq)
```

Plot the audio signal:

```
# Plot the audio signal
plt.plot(time_axis, signal, color='black')
plt.xlabel('Time (milliseconds)')
plt.ylabel('Amplitude')
plt.title('Generated audio signal')
plt.show()
```

The full code is given in the file `audio_generator.py`. If you run the code, you will see the following screenshot:

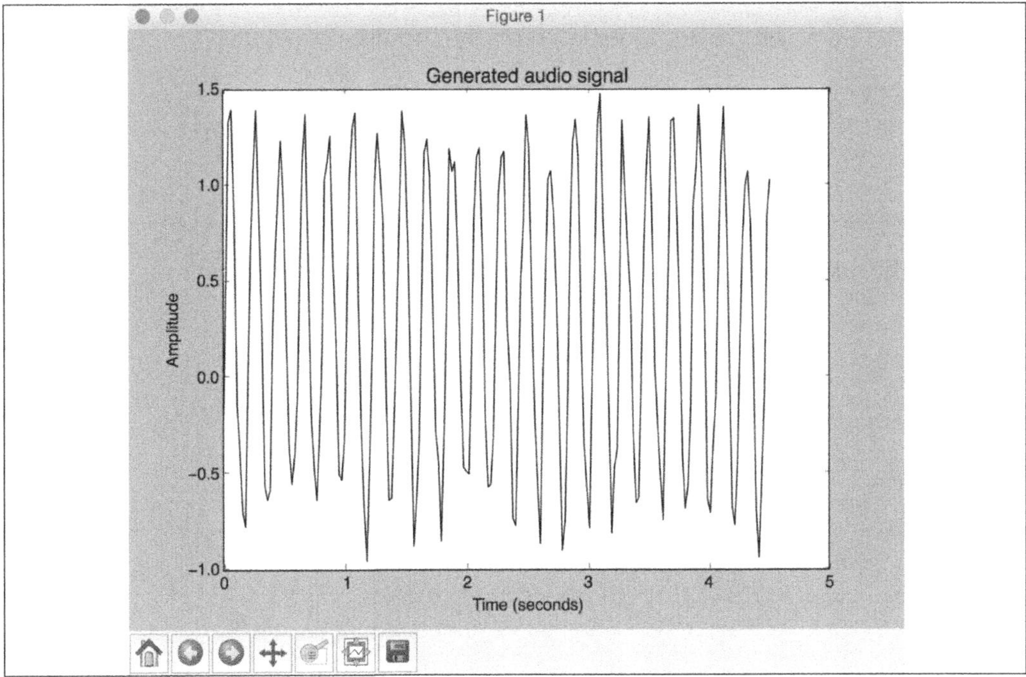

Figure 4: Visualization of audio signal generation

Play the file `generated_audio.wav` using your media player to see what it sounds like. It will be a signal that's a mixture of a *784 Hz* signal and the noise signal.

Synthesizing tones to generate music

The previous section described how to generate a simple monotone, but it's not very meaningful. It was just a single frequency through the signal. Let's use that principle to synthesize music by stitching different tones together. We will be using standard tones such as *A*, *C*, *G*, and *F* to generate music. In order to see the frequency mapping for these standard tones, check out this link: `http://www.phy.mtu.edu/~suits/notefreqs.html`.

Let's use this information to generate a musical signal.

Create a new Python file and import the following packages:

```
import json
```

```
import numpy as np
import matplotlib.pyplot as plt
from scipy.io.wavfile import write
```

Define a function to generate a tone based on the input parameters:

```
# Synthesize the tone based on the input parameters
def tone_synthesizer(freq, duration, amplitude=1.0, sampling_
freq=44100):
    # Construct the time axis
    time_axis = np.linspace(0, duration, duration * sampling_freq)
```

Construct the audio signal using the parameters specified and return it:

```
    # Construct the audio signal
    signal = amplitude * np.sin(2 * np.pi * freq * time_axis)

    return signal.astype(np.int16)
```

Define the `main` function. Let's define the output audio filenames:

```
if __name__=='__main__':
    # Names of output files
    file_tone_single = 'generated_tone_single.wav'
    file_tone_sequence = 'generated_tone_sequence.wav'
```

We will be using a tone mapping file that contains the mapping from tone names (such as *A*, *C*, and *G*) to the corresponding frequencies:

```
    # Source: http://www.phy.mtu.edu/~suits/notefreqs.html
    mapping_file = 'tone_mapping.json'

    # Load the tone to frequency map from the mapping file
    with open(mapping_file, 'r') as f:
        tone_map = json.loads(f.read())
```

Let's generate the `F` tone with a duration of `3` seconds:

```
    # Set input parameters to generate 'F' tone
    tone_name = 'F'
    # seconds
    duration = 3
    # amplitude
    amplitude = 12000
    # Hz
    sampling_freq = 44100
```

Extract the corresponding tone frequency:

```
    # Extract the tone frequency
    tone_freq = tone_map[tone_name]
```

Generate the tone using the tone synthesizer function that was defined earlier:

```
    # Generate the tone using the above parameters
    synthesized_tone = tone_synthesizer(tone_freq, duration,
amplitude, sampling_freq)
```

Write the generated audio signal to the output file:

```
    # Write the audio signal to the output file
    write(file_tone_single, sampling_freq, synthesized_tone)
```

Let's generate a tone sequence to make it sound like music. Let's define a tone sequence with corresponding durations in seconds:

```
    # Define the tone sequence along with corresponding
    # durations in seconds
    tone_sequence = [('G', 0.4), ('D', 0.5), ('F', 0.3), ('C', 0.6),
('A', 0.4)]
```

Construct the audio signal based on the tone sequence:

```
    # Construct the audio signal based on the above sequence
    signal = np.array([])
    for item in tone_sequence:
        # Get the name of the tone
        tone_name = item[0]
```

For each tone, extract the corresponding frequency:

```
        # Extract the corresponding frequency of the tone
        freq = tone_map[tone_name]
```

Extract the corresponding duration:

```
        # Extract the duration
        duration = item[1]
```

Synthesize the tone using the `tone_synthesizer` function:

```
        # Synthesize the tone
        synthesized_tone = tone_synthesizer(freq, duration, amplitude,
sampling_freq)
```

Append it to the main output signal:

```
        # Append the output signal
        signal = np.append(signal, synthesized_tone, axis=0)
```

Save the main output signal to the output file:

```
    # Save the audio in the output file
    write(file_tone_sequence, sampling_freq, signal)
```

The full code is given in the file `synthesizer.py`. If you run the code, it will generate two output files – `generated_tone_single.wav` and `generated_tone_sequence.wav`.

You can play the audio files using a media player to hear what they sound like.

Extracting speech features

We learned how to convert a time domain signal into the frequency domain. Frequency domain features are used extensively in all speech recognition systems. The concept we discussed earlier is an introduction to the idea, but real-world frequency domain features are a bit more complex. Once we convert a signal into the frequency domain, we need to ensure that it's usable in the form of a feature vector. This is where the concept of **Mel Frequency Cepstral Coefficients** (**MFCCs**) becomes relevant. MFCC is a tool that's used to extract frequency domain features from a given audio signal.

In order to extract the frequency features from an audio signal, MFCC first extracts the power spectrum. It then uses filter banks and a **Discrete Cosine Transform** (**DCT**) to extract the features. If you are interested in exploring MFCCs further, check out this link:

`http://practicalcryptography.com/miscellaneous/machine-learning/guide-mel-frequency-cepstral-coefficients-mfccs`

We will be using a package called `python_speech_features` to extract the MFCC features. The package is available here:

`http://python-speech-features.readthedocs.org/en/latest`

For ease of use, the relevant folder has been included with the code bundle. You will see a folder called `features` in the code bundle that contains the files needed to use this package. Let's see how to extract MFCC features.

Create a new Python file and import the following packages:

```
import numpy as np
import matplotlib.pyplot as plt
from scipy.io import wavfile
from python_speech_features import mfcc, logfbank
```

Read the input audio file and extract the first `10,000` samples for analysis:

```
# Read the input audio file
sampling_freq, signal = wavfile.read('random_sound.wav')

# Take the first 10,000 samples for analysis
signal = signal[:10000]
```

Extract the MFCC:

```
# Extract the MFCC features
features_mfcc = mfcc(signal, sampling_freq)
```

Print the MFCC parameters:

```
# Print the parameters for MFCC
print('\nMFCC:\nNumber of windows =', features_mfcc.shape[0])
print('Length of each feature =', features_mfcc.shape[1])
```

Plot the MFCC features:

```
# Plot the features
features_mfcc = features_mfcc.T
plt.matshow(features_mfcc)
plt.title('MFCC')
```

Extract the filter bank features:

```
# Extract the Filter Bank features
features_fb = logfbank(signal, sampling_freq)
```

Print the parameters for the filter bank:

```
# Print the parameters for Filter Bank
print('\nFilter bank:\nNumber of windows =', features_fb.shape[0])
print('Length of each feature =', features_fb.shape[1])
```

Plot the features:

```
# Plot the features
features_fb = features_fb.T
plt.matshow(features_fb)
plt.title('Filter bank')

plt.show()
```

The full code is given in the file `feature_extractor.py`. If you run the code, you will see two screenshots. The first screenshot shows the MFCC features:

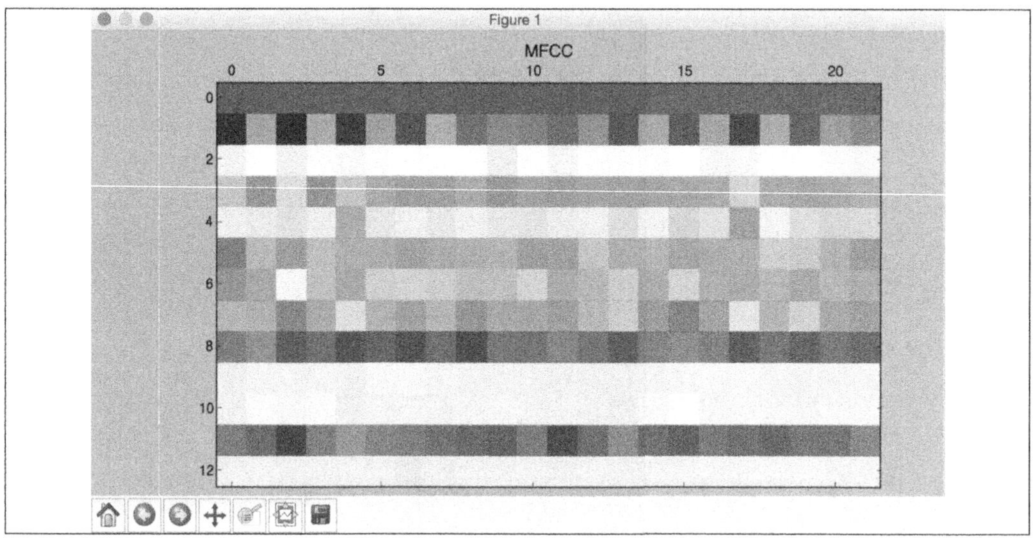

Figure 5: Plot of MFCC features

The second screenshot shows the filter bank features:

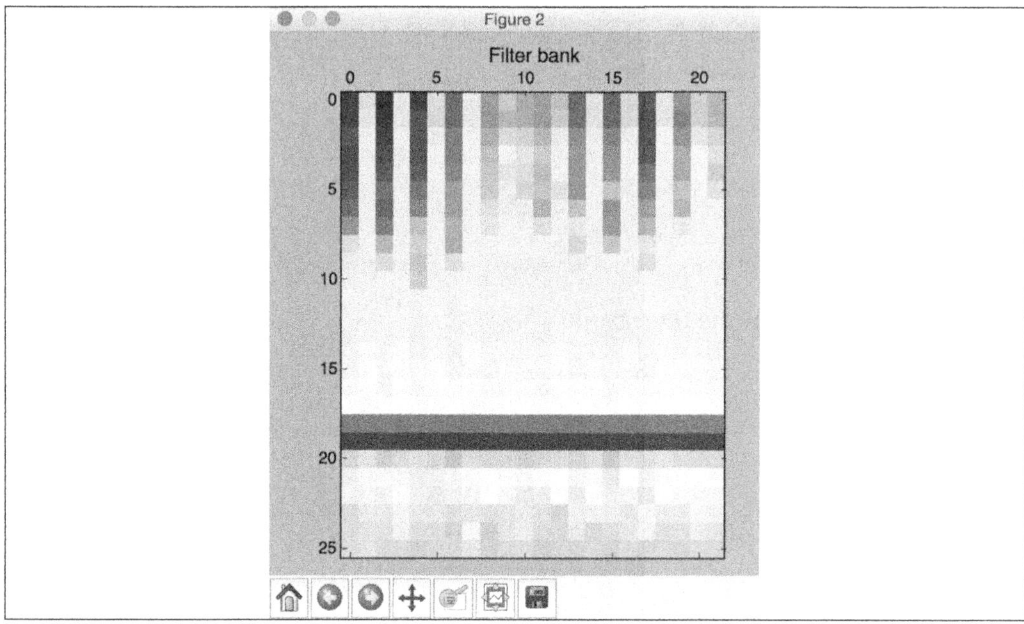

Figure 6: Plot of filter bank features

You will see the following printed out:

```
MFCC:
Number of windows = 22
Length of each feature = 13

Filter bank:
Number of windows = 22
Length of each feature = 26
```

Figure 7: MFCC and filter bank features output

As we see in the previous charts, and as we learned in this chapter, it can be very useful to convert sounds into pictures, and it can allow us to analyze the sounds in a different way and derive insights that we would have otherwise missed.

Recognizing spoken words

Now that we have learned all the techniques to analyze speech signals, let's go ahead and see how to recognize spoken words. Speech recognition systems take audio signals as input and recognize the words being spoken. **Hidden Markov Models (HMMs)** will be used for this task.

As we discussed in the previous chapter, HMMs are great at analyzing sequential data. An audio signal is a time series signal, which is a manifestation of sequential data. The assumption is that the outputs are being generated by the system going through a series of hidden states. Our goal is to find out what these hidden states are so that we can identify the words in our signal. If you are interested in digging deeper, check out this link: `https://web.stanford.edu/~jurafsky/slp3/A.pdf`.

We will be using a package called `hmmlearn` to build our speech recognition system. You can learn more about it here: `http://hmmlearn.readthedocs.org/en/latest`.

You can install the package by running the following command:

```
$ pip3 install hmmlearn
```

In order to train our speech recognition system, we need a dataset of audio files for each word. We will use the database available at `https://code.google.com/archive/p/hmm-speech-recognition/downloads`.

For ease of use, you have been provided with a folder called `data` in your code bundle that contains all these files. This dataset contains seven different words. Each word has a folder associated with it and each folder has 15 audio files.

We will use 14 for training and one for testing in each folder. Note that this is actually a very small dataset. In the real world, you will be using much larger datasets to build speech recognition systems. We are using this dataset to get familiar with speech recognition and see how we can build a system to recognize spoken words.

We will build an HMM model for each word and store all the models for reference. When we want to recognize the word in an unknown audio file, we will run it through all these models and pick the one with the highest score. Let's see how to build this system.

Create a new Python file and import the following packages:

```
import os
import argparse
import warnings

import numpy as np
from scipy.io import wavfile

from hmmlearn import hmm
from python_speech_features import mfcc
```

Define a function to parse the input arguments. We need to specify the input folder containing the audio files required to train our speech recognition system:

```
# Define a function to parse the input arguments
def build_arg_parser():
    parser = argparse.ArgumentParser(description='Trains the HMM-based
speech recognition system')
    parser.add_argument("--input-folder", dest="input_folder",
required=True, help="Input folder containing the audio files for
training")
    return parser
```

Define a class to train the HMMs:

```
# Define a class to train the HMM
class ModelHMM(object):
    def __init__(self, num_components=4, num_iter=1000):
        self.n_components = num_components
        self.n_iter = num_iter
```

Define the covariance type and the type of HMM:

```
        self.cov_type = 'diag'
        self.model_name = 'GaussianHMM'
```

Initialize the variable in which we will store the models for each word:

```
        self.models = []
```

Define the model using the specified parameters:

```
        self.model = hmm.GaussianHMM(n_components=self.n_components,
                covariance_type=self.cov_type, n_iter=self.n_iter)
```

Define a method to train the model:

```
    # 'training_data' is a 2D numpy array where each row is
13-dimensional
    def train(self, training_data):
        np.seterr(all='ignore')
        cur_model = self.model.fit(training_data)
        self.models.append(cur_model)
```

Define a method to compute the score for input data:

```
    # Run the HMM model for inference on input data
    def compute_score(self, input_data):
        return self.model.score(input_data)
```

Define a function to build a model for each word in the training dataset:

```
# Define a function to build a model for each word
def build_models(input_folder):
    # Initialize the variable to store all the models
    speech_models = []
```

Parse the input directory:

```
    # Parse the input directory
    for dirname in os.listdir(input_folder):
        # Get the name of the subfolder
        subfolder = os.path.join(input_folder, dirname)

        if not os.path.isdir(subfolder):
            continue
```

Extract the label:

```
        # Extract the label
        label = subfolder[subfolder.rfind('/') + 1:]
```

Initialize the variable to store the training data:

```
        # Initialize the variables
        X = np.array([])
```

Create a list of files to be used for training:

```
            # Create a list of files to be used for training
            # We will leave one file per folder for testing
            training_files = [x for x in os.listdir(subfolder) if
    x.endswith('.wav')][:-1]

            # Iterate through the training files and build the models
            for filename in training_files:
                # Extract the current filepath
                filepath = os.path.join(subfolder, filename)
```

Read the audio signal from the current file:

```
                # Read the audio signal from the input file
                sampling_freq, signal = wavfile.read(filepath)
```

Extract the MFCC features:

```
                # Extract the MFCC features
                with warnings.catch_warnings():
                    warnings.simplefilter('ignore')
                    features_mfcc = mfcc(signal, sampling_freq)
```

Append the data point to the variable `X`:

```
                # Append to the variable X
                if len(X) == 0:
                    X = features_mfcc
                else:
                    X = np.append(X, features_mfcc, axis=0)
```

Initialize the HMM model:

```
            # Create the HMM model
            model = ModelHMM()
```

Train the model using the training data:

```
            # Train the HMM
            model.train(X)
```

Save the model for the current word:

```
            # Save the model for the current word
            speech_models.append((model, label))

            # Reset the variable
            model = None

        return speech_models
```

Define a function to run the tests on the test dataset:

```
# Define a function to run tests on input files
def run_tests(test_files):
    # Classify input data
    for test_file in test_files:
        # Read input file
        sampling_freq, signal = wavfile.read(test_file)
```

Extract the MFCC features:

```
        # Extract MFCC features
        with warnings.catch_warnings():
            warnings.simplefilter('ignore')
            features_mfcc = mfcc(signal, sampling_freq)
```

Define the variables to store the maximum score and the output label:

```
        # Define variables
        max_score = -float('inf')
        output_label = None
```

Iterate through each model to pick the best one:

```
        # Run the current feature vector through all the HMM
        # models and pick the one with the highest score
        for item in speech_models:
            model, label = item
```

Evaluate the score and compare against the maximum score:

```
            score = model.compute_score(features_mfcc)
            if score > max_score:
                max_score = score
                predicted_label = label
```

Print the output:

```
        # Print the predicted output
        start_index = test_file.find('/') + 1
        end_index = test_file.rfind('/')
        original_label = test_file[start_index:end_index]
        print('\nOriginal: ', original_label)
        print('Predicted:', predicted_label)
```

Define the `main` function and get the input folder from the input parameter:

```
if __name__=='__main__':
    args = build_arg_parser().parse_args()
    input_folder = args.input_folder
```

Build an HMM model for each word in the input folder:

```
# Build an HMM model for each word
speech_models = build_models(input_folder)
```

We left one file for testing in each folder. Use that file to see how accurate the model is:

```
# Test files -- the 15th file in each subfolder
test_files = []
for root, dirs, files in os.walk(input_folder):
    for filename in (x for x in files if '15' in x):
        filepath = os.path.join(root, filename)
        test_files.append(filepath)

run_tests(test_files)
```

The full code is given in the file `speech_recognizer.py`. Make sure that the `data` folder is placed in the same folder as the code file. Run the code as follows:

```
$ python3 speech_recognizer.py --input-folder data
```

If you run the code, you will see the following output:

```
Original:  apple
Predicted: apple

Original:  banana
Predicted: banana

Original:  kiwi
Predicted: kiwi

Original:  lime
Predicted: lime

Original:  orange
Predicted: orange

Original:  peach
Predicted: peach

Original:  pineapple
Predicted: pineapple
```

Figure 8: Recognized word output

As we can see in the preceding screenshot, our speech recognition system identifies all the words correctly.

Summary

In this chapter, we learned about speech recognition. We discussed how to work with speech signals and the associated concepts. We learned how to visualize audio signals. We talked about how to transform time domain audio signals into the frequency domain using Fourier Transforms. We discussed how to generate audio signals using predefined parameters.

We then used this concept to synthesize music by stitching tones together. We talked about MFCCs and how they are used in the real world. We understood how to extract frequency features from speech. We learned how to use all these techniques to build a speech recognition system. In the next chapter, we will discuss natural language processing and how to use it to analyze text data by modeling and classifying it.

15

Natural Language Processing

In this chapter, we will learn about the exciting topic of natural language processing (NLP). As we have discussed in previous chapters, having computers that are able to understand human language is one of the breakthroughs that will truly make computers even more useful. NLP provides the foundation to begin to understand how this might be possible.

We will discuss and use various concepts, such as tokenization, stemming, and lemmatization, to process text. We will then discuss the *Bag of Words* model and how to use it to classify text. We will see how to use machine learning to analyze the sentiment of a sentence. We will then discuss topic modeling and implement a system to identify topics in a given document.

By the end of this chapter, you will be familiar with the following topics:

- Installing relevant NLP packages
- Tokenizing text data
- Converting words to their base forms using stemming
- Converting words to their base forms using lemmatization
- Dividing text data into chunks
- Extracting a document-term matrix using the Bag of Words model
- Building a category predictor
- Constructing a gender identifier
- Building a sentiment analyzer
- Topic modeling using Latent Dirichlet Allocation

Introduction and installation of packages

Natural Language Processing (**NLP**) has become an important part of modern systems. It is used extensively in search engines, conversational interfaces, document processors, and so on. Machines can handle structured data well, but when it comes to working with free-form text, they have a hard time. The goal of NLP is to develop algorithms that enable computers to understand free - form text and help them understand language.

One of the most challenging things about processing free - form natural language is the sheer amount of variation. Context plays a very important role in how a sentence is understood. Humans are innately great at understanding language. It is not clear yet how humans understand language so easily and intuitively. We use our past knowledge and experiences to understand conversations and we can quickly get the gist of what other people are talking about even with little explicit context.

To address this issue, NLP researchers started developing various applications using machine learning approaches. To build such applications, a large corpus of text is obtained and then algorithms are trained on this data to perform various tasks such as categorizing text, analyzing sentiments, and modeling topics. The algorithms are trained to detect patterns in the input text data and to derive insights from it.

In this chapter, we will discuss various underlying concepts that are used to analyze text and build NLP applications. This will enable us to understand how to extract meaningful information from the given text data. We will use a Python package called **Natural Language Toolkit** (**NLTK**) to build these applications. You can install it by running the following command:

```
$ pip3 install nltk
```

You can find more information about NLTK at `http://www.nltk.org`.

In order to access all the datasets provided by NLTK, we need to download it. Open a Python shell by typing the following:

```
$ python3
```

We are now inside the Python shell. Type the following to download the data:

```
>>> import nltk
>>> nltk.download()
```

We will also use a package called `gensim` in this chapter. `gensim` is a robust semantic modeling library that's useful for many applications. It can be installed by running the following command:

```
$ pip3 install gensim
```

You might need another package, called `pattern`, for `gensim` to function properly. You can install it by running the following command:

```
$ pip3 install pattern
```

You can find more information about gensim at `https://radimrehurek.com/gensim`. Now that you have installed the NLTK and `gensim`, let's proceed with the discussion.

Tokenizing text data

When we deal with text, we need to break it down into smaller pieces for analysis. To do this, tokenization can be applied. Tokenization is the process of dividing text into a set of pieces, such as words or sentences. These pieces are called tokens. Depending on what we want to do, we can define our own methods to divide the text into many tokens. Let's look at how to tokenize the input text using NLTK.

Create a new Python file and import the following packages:

```
from nltk.tokenize import sent_tokenize, \
        word_tokenize, WordPunctTokenizer
```

Define the input text that will be used for tokenization:

```
# Define input text
input_text = "Do you know how tokenization works? It's actually \
   quite interesting! Let's analyze a couple of sentences and \
   figure it out."
```

Divide the input text into sentence tokens:

```
# Sentence tokenizer
print("\nSentence tokenizer:")
print(sent_tokenize(input_text))
```

Divide the input text into word tokens:

```
# Word tokenizer
print("\nWord tokenizer:")
print(word_tokenize(input_text))
```

Divide the input text into word tokens using the `WordPunct` tokenizer:

```
# WordPunct tokenizer
print("\nWord punct tokenizer:")
print(WordPunctTokenizer().tokenize(input_text))
```

The full code is given in the file `tokenizer.py`. If you run the code, you will get the following output:

```
Sentence tokenizer:
['Do you know how tokenization works?', "It's actually quite interesting!", "Let's analyze a couple of se
ntences and figure it out."]

Word tokenizer:
['Do', 'you', 'know', 'how', 'tokenization', 'works', '?', 'It', "'s", 'actually', 'quite', 'interesting'
, '!', 'Let', "'s", 'analyze', 'a', 'couple', 'of', 'sentences', 'and', 'figure', 'it', 'out', '.']

Word punct tokenizer:
['Do', 'you', 'know', 'how', 'tokenization', 'works', '?', 'It', "'", 's', 'actually', 'quite', 'interest
ing', '!', 'Let', "'", 's', 'analyze', 'a', 'couple', 'of', 'sentences', 'and', 'figure', 'it', 'out', '.
']
```

Figure 1: Tokenizers output

The sentence tokenizer divides the input text into sentences. Two-word tokenizers behave differently when it comes to punctuation. For example, the word "It's" is divided differently by the punct tokenizer than by the regular tokenizer.

Converting words to their base forms using stemming

Working with text means working with a lot of variation. We must deal with different forms of the same word and enable the computer to understand that these different words have the same base form. For example, the word `sing` can appear in many forms, such as *singer, singing, song, sung,* and so on. This set of words share similar meanings. This process is known as stemming. Stemming is a way of producing morphological variants of a root/base word. Humans can easily identify these base forms and derive context.

When analyzing text, it's useful to extract these base forms. Doing so enables the extraction of useful statistics derived from the input text. Stemming is one way to achieve this. The goal of a stemmer is to reduce words from their different forms into a common base form. It is basically a heuristic process that cuts off the ends of words to extract their base forms. Let's see how to do it using NLTK.

Create a new Python file and import the following packages:

```
from nltk.stem.porter import PorterStemmer
from nltk.stem.lancaster import LancasterStemmer
from nltk.stem.snowball import SnowballStemmer
```

Define some input words:

```
input_words = ['writing', 'calves', 'be', 'branded', 'horse',
'randomize',
        'possibly', 'provision', 'hospital', 'kept', 'scratchy',
'code']
```

Create objects for the **Porter**, **Lancaster**, and **Snowball** stemmers:

```
# Create various stemmer objects
porter = PorterStemmer()
lancaster = LancasterStemmer()
snowball = SnowballStemmer('english')
```

Create a list of names for table display and format the output text accordingly:

```
# Create a list of stemmer names for display
stemmer_names = ['PORTER', 'LANCASTER', 'SNOWBALL']
formatted_text = '{:>16}' * (len(stemmer_names) + 1)
print('\n', formatted_text.format('INPUT WORD', *stemmer_names),
        '\n', '='*68)
```

Iterate through the words and stem them using the three stemmers:

```
# Stem each word and display the output
for word in input_words:
    output = [word, porter.stem(word),
            lancaster.stem(word), snowball.stem(word)]
    print(formatted_text.format(*output))
```

The full code is given in the file `stemmer.py`. If you run the code, you will get the following output:

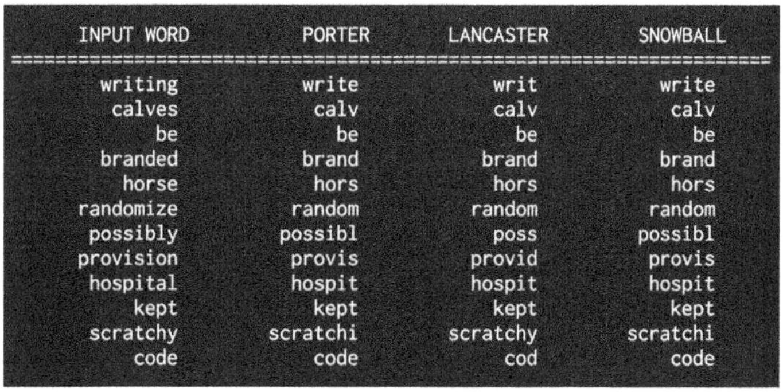

```
      INPUT WORD          PORTER       LANCASTER        SNOWBALL
 ====================================================================
         writing           write            writ           write
          calves            calv            calv            calv
              be              be              be              be
         branded           brand           brand           brand
           horse            hors            hors            hors
       randomize          random          random          random
        possibly         possibl            poss         possibl
       provision          provis          provid          provis
        hospital          hospit          hospit          hospit
            kept            kept            kept            kept
        scratchy        scratchi        scratchy        scratchi
            code            code             cod            code
```

Figure 2: Stemmer output

Let's talk about the three stemming algorithms that are being used here. All of them basically try to achieve the same goal. The difference between them is the level of strictness that's used to arrive at the base form.

The Porter stemmer is the least strict, and Lancaster is the strictest. If you closely observe the outputs, you will notice the differences. Stemmers behave differently when it comes to words such as `possibly` or `provision`. The stemmed outputs obtained from the Lancaster stemmer are a bit obfuscated because it reduces the words a lot. At the same time, the algorithm is fast. A good rule of thumb is to use the Snowball stemmer because it's a good trade-off between speed and strictness.

Converting words to their base forms using lemmatization

Lemmatization is another method of reducing words to their base forms. In the previous section, we saw that some of the base forms that were obtained from those stemmers didn't make sense. Lemmatization is the process of grouping together the different inflected forms of a word so they can be analyzed as a single item. Lemmatization is like stemming, but it brings context to the words. So, it links words with similar meanings to one word. For example, all three stemmers said that the base form of *calves* is *calv*, which is not a real word. Lemmatization takes a more structured approach to solve this problem. Here are some more examples of lemmatization:

- rocks : rock
- corpora : corpus
- worse : bad

The lemmatization process uses the lexical and morphological analysis of words. It obtains the base forms by removing the inflectional word endings such as *ing* or *ed*. This base form of any word is known as the lemma. If you lemmatize the word *calves*, you should get *calf* as the output. One thing to note is that the output depends on whether the word is a verb or a noun. Let's look at how to do this with NLTK.

Create a new Python file and import the following packages:

```
from nltk.stem import WordNetLemmatizer
```

Define some input words. We will be using the same set of words that we used in the previous section so that we can compare the outputs:

```
input_words = ['writing', 'calves', 'be', 'branded', 'horse',
'randomize',
```

```
        'possibly', 'provision', 'hospital', 'kept', 'scratchy',
'code']
```

Create a `lemmatizer` object:

```
# Create lemmatizer object
lemmatizer = WordNetLemmatizer()
```

Create a list of `lemmatizer` names for the table display and format the text accordingly:

```
# Create a list of lemmatizer names for display
lemmatizer_names = ['NOUN LEMMATIZER', 'VERB LEMMATIZER']
formatted_text = '{:>24}' * (len(lemmatizer_names) + 1)
print('\n', formatted_text.format('INPUT WORD', *lemmatizer_names),
        '\n', '='*75)
```

Iterate through the words and lemmatize the words using noun and verb lemmatizers:

```
# Lemmatize each word and display the output
for word in input_words:
    output = [word, lemmatizer.lemmatize(word, pos='n'),
           lemmatizer.lemmatize(word, pos='v')]
    print(formatted_text.format(*output))
```

The full code is given in the file `lemmatizer.py`. If you run the code, you will get the following output:

```
              INPUT WORD         NOUN LEMMATIZER         VERB LEMMATIZER
===========================================================================
                 writing                 writing                   write
                  calves                    calf                   calve
                      be                      be                      be
                 branded                 branded                   brand
                   horse                   horse                   horse
               randomize               randomize               randomize
                possibly                possibly                possibly
               provision               provision               provision
                hospital                hospital                hospital
                    kept                    kept                    keep
                scratchy                scratchy                scratchy
                    code                    code                    code
```

Figure 3: Lemmatizer output

We can see that the noun lemmatizer works differently than the verb lemmatizer when it comes to words such as `writing` or `calves`. If you compare these outputs to stemmer outputs, you will see that there are differences too. The lemmatizer outputs are all meaningful, whereas stemmer outputs may or may not be meaningful.

Dividing text data into chunks

Text data usually needs to be divided into pieces for further analysis. This process is known as **chunking**. This is used frequently in text analysis. The conditions that are used to divide the text into chunks can vary based on the problem at hand. This is not the same as tokenization, where text is also divided into pieces. During chunking, we do not adhere to any constraints, except for the fact that the output chunks need to be meaningful.

When we deal with large text documents, it becomes important to divide the text into chunks to extract meaningful information. In this section, we will see how to divide input text into several pieces.

Create a new Python file and import the following packages:

```
import numpy as np
from nltk.corpus import brown
```

Define a function to divide the input text into chunks. The first parameter is the text, and the second parameter is the number of words in each chunk:

```
# Split the input text into chunks, where
# each chunk contains N words
def chunker(input_data, N):
    input_words = input_data.split(' ')
    output = []
```

Iterate through the words and divide them into chunks using the input parameter. The function returns a list:

```
    cur_chunk = []
    count = 0
    for word in input_words:
        cur_chunk.append(word)
        count += 1
        if count == N:
            output.append(' '.join(cur_chunk))
            count, cur_chunk = 0, []

    output.append(' '.join(cur_chunk))

    return output
```

Define the main function and read the input data using the Brown corpus. We will read `12000` words in this case. You are free to read as many words as you want:

```
if __name__=='__main__':
    # Read the first 12000 words from the Brown corpus
    input_data = ' '.join(brown.words()[:12000])
```

Define the number of words in each chunk:

```
    # Define the number of words in each chunk
    chunk_size = 700
```

Divide the input text into chunks and display the output:

```
    chunks = chunker(input_data, chunk_size)
    print('\nNumber of text chunks =', len(chunks), '\n')
    for i, chunk in enumerate(chunks):
        print('Chunk', i+1, '==>', chunk[:50])
```

The full code is given in the file `text_chunker.py`. If you run the code, you will get the following output:

```
Number of text chunks = 18

Chunk 1 ==> The Fulton County Grand Jury said Friday an invest
Chunk 2 ==> '' . ( 2 ) Fulton legislators `` work with city of
Chunk 3 ==> . Construction bonds Meanwhile , it was learned th
Chunk 4 ==> , anonymous midnight phone calls and veiled threat
Chunk 5 ==> Harris , Bexar , Tarrant and El Paso would be $451
Chunk 6 ==> set it for public hearing on Feb. 22 . The proposa
Chunk 7 ==> College . He has served as a border patrolman and
Chunk 8 ==> of his staff were doing on the address involved co
Chunk 9 ==> plan alone would boost the base to $5,000 a year a
Chunk 10 ==> nursing homes In the area of `` community health s
Chunk 11 ==> of its Angola policy prove harsh , there has been
Chunk 12 ==> system which will prevent Laos from being used as
Chunk 13 ==> reform in recipient nations . In Laos , the admini
Chunk 14 ==> . He is not interested in being named a full-time
Chunk 15 ==> said , `` to obtain the views of the general publi
Chunk 16 ==> '' . Mr. Reama , far from really being retired , i
Chunk 17 ==> making enforcement of minor offenses more effectiv
Chunk 18 ==> to tell the people where he stands on the tax issu
```

Figure 4: Text chunker output

The preceding screenshot shows the first 50 characters of each chunk.

Now that we have explored techniques to divide and chunk the text, let's start looking at methods to start performing text analysis.

Extracting the frequency of terms using the Bag of Words model

One of the main goals of text analysis with the Bag of Words model is to convert text into a numerical form so that we can use machine learning on it. Let's consider text documents that contain many millions of words. In order to analyze these documents, we need to extract the text and convert it into a form of numerical representation.

Machine learning algorithms need numerical data to work with so that they can analyze the data and extract meaningful information. This is where the Bag of Words model comes in. This model extracts vocabulary from all the words in the documents and builds a model using a document-term matrix. This allows us to represent every document as a *bag of words*. We just keep track of word counts and disregard the grammatical details and the word order.

Let's see what a document-term matrix is all about. A document-term matrix is basically a table that gives us counts of various words that occur in a document. So, a text document can be represented as a weighted combination of various words. We can set thresholds and choose words that are more meaningful. In a way, we are building a histogram of all the words in the document that will be used as a feature vector. This feature vector is used for text classification.

Consider the following sentences:

- Sentence 1: The children are playing in the hall
- Sentence 2: The hall has a lot of space
- Sentence 3: Lots of children like playing in an open space

If you consider all three sentences, we have the following 14 unique words:

- the
- children
- are
- playing
- in
- hall
- has
- a
- lot

- of
- space
- like
- an
- open

Let's construct a histogram for each sentence by using the word count in each sentence. Each feature vector will be 14-dimensional because we have 14 unique words:

- Sentence 1: [2, 1, 1, 1, 1, 1, 0, 0, 0, 0, 0, 0, 0, 0]
- Sentence 2: [1, 0, 0, 0, 0, 1, 1, 1, 1, 1, 1, 0, 0, 0]
- Sentence 3: [0, 1, 0, 1, 1, 0, 0, 0, 1, 1, 1, 1, 1, 1]

Now that we have extracted these features with the Bag of Words model, we can use machine learning algorithms to analyze this data.

Let's see how to build a Bag of Words model in NLTK. Create a new Python file and import the following packages:

```
import numpy as np
from sklearn.feature_extraction.text import CountVectorizer
from nltk.corpus import brown
from text_chunker import chunker
```

Read the input data from the Brown corpus. We will use `5,400` words. Feel free to try it with as many words as you want:

```
# Read the data from the Brown corpus
input_data = ' '.join(brown.words()[:5400])
```

Define the number of words in each chunk:

```
# Number of words in each chunk
chunk_size = 800
```

Divide the input text into chunks:

```
text_chunks = chunker(input_data, chunk_size)
```

Convert the chunks into dictionary items:

```
# Convert to dict items
chunks = []
for count, chunk in enumerate(text_chunks):
    d = {'index': count, 'text': chunk}
    chunks.append(d)
```

Extract the document term matrix where we get the count of each word. We will achieve this using the `CountVectorizer` method, which takes two input parameters. The first parameter is the minimum document frequency, and the second parameter is the maximum document frequency. The frequency refers to the number of occurrences of a word in the text:

```
# Extract the document term matrix
count_vectorizer = CountVectorizer(min_df=7, max_df=20)
document_term_matrix = count_vectorizer.fit_transform([chunk['text']
for chunk in chunks])
```

Extract the vocabulary with the Bag of Words model and display it. The vocabulary refers to the list of distinct words that were extracted in the previous step:

```
# Extract the vocabulary and display it
vocabulary = np.array(count_vectorizer.get_feature_names())
print("\nVocabulary:\n", vocabulary)
```

Generate the names for display:

```
# Generate names for chunks
chunk_names = []
for i in range(len(text_chunks)):
    chunk_names.append('Chunk-' + str(i+1))
```

Print the document-term matrix:

```
# Print the document term matrix
print("\nDocument term matrix:")
formatted_text = '{:>12}' * (len(chunk_names) + 1)
print('\n', formatted_text.format('Word', *chunk_names), '\n')
for word, item in zip(vocabulary, document_term_matrix.T):
    # 'item' is a 'csr_matrix' data structure
    output = [word] + [str(freq) for freq in item.data]
    print(formatted_text.format(*output))
```

The full code is given in the file `bag_of_words.py`. If you run the code, you will get the following output:

Document term matrix:

Word	Chunk-1	Chunk-2	Chunk-3	Chunk-4	Chunk-5	Chunk-6	Chunk-7
and	23	9	9	11	9	17	10
are	2	2	1	1	2	2	1
be	6	8	7	7	6	2	1
by	3	4	4	5	14	3	6
county	6	2	7	3	1	2	2
for	7	13	4	10	7	6	4
in	15	11	15	11	13	14	17
is	2	7	3	4	5	5	2
it	8	6	8	9	3	1	2
of	31	20	20	30	29	35	26
on	4	3	5	10	6	5	2
one	1	3	1	2	2	1	1
said	12	5	7	7	4	3	7
state	3	7	2	6	3	4	1
that	13	8	9	2	7	1	7
the	71	51	43	51	43	52	49
to	11	26	20	26	21	15	11
two	2	1	1	1	1	2	2
was	5	6	7	7	4	7	3
which	7	4	5	4	3	1	1
with	2	2	3	1	2	2	3

Figure 5: Document term matrix output

All the words can be seen in the Bag of Words model document-term matrix along with the corresponding counts in each chunk.

Now that we have done a count of the words, we can build on this and start making some predictions based on the frequency of words.

Building a category predictor

A category predictor is used to predict the category to which a given piece of text belongs. This is frequently used in text classification to categorize text documents. Search engines frequently use this tool to order search results by relevance. For example, let's say that we want to predict whether a given sentence belongs to sports, politics, or science. To do this, we build a corpus of data and train an algorithm. This algorithm can then be used for inference on unknown data.

In order to build this predictor, we will use a metric called **Term Frequency – Inverse Document Frequency** (**tf-idf**). In a set of documents, we need to understand the importance of each word. The tf-idf metric helps us to understand how important a given word is to a document in a set of documents.

Let's consider the first part of this metric. The **Term Frequency** (**tf**) is basically a measure of how frequently each word appears in a given document. Since different documents have a different number of words, the exact numbers in the histogram will vary. In order to have a level playing field, we need to normalize the histograms. So, we divide the count of each word by the total number of words in a given document to obtain the term frequency.

The second part of the metric is the **Inverse Document Frequency** (**idf**), which is a measure of how unique a word is to a document in a given set of documents. When we compute the term frequency, the assumption is that all the words are equally important. But we cannot just rely on the frequency of each word because words such as *and*, *or*, and *the* appear a lot. To balance the frequencies of these commonly occurring words, we need to reduce their weights and increase the weights of the rare words. This helps us identify words that are unique to each document as well, which in turn helps us formulate a distinctive feature vector.

To compute this statistic, we need to compute the ratio of the number of documents with the given word and divide it by the total number of documents. This ratio is essentially the fraction of the documents that contain the given word. Inverse document frequency is then calculated by taking the negative algorithm of this ratio.

We then combine term frequency and inverse document frequency to formulate a feature vector to categorize documents. This work is the foundation for deeper analysis of the text to get deeper meaning, such as sentiment analysis, context of the text, or topic analysis. Let's see how to build a category predictor.

Create a new Python file and import the following packages:

```
from sklearn.datasets import fetch_20newsgroups
from sklearn.naive_bayes import MultinomialNB
from sklearn.feature_extraction.text import TfidfTransformer
from sklearn.feature_extraction.text import CountVectorizer
```

Define the map of categories that will be used for training. We will be using five categories in this case. The keys in this dictionary object refer to the names in the scikit-learn dataset:

```
# Define the category map
category_map = {'talk.politics.misc': 'Politics', 'rec.autos':
'Autos',
        'rec.sport.hockey': 'Hockey', 'sci.electronics':
'Electronics',
        'sci.med': 'Medicine'}
```

Get the training dataset using `fetch_20newsgroups`:

```
# Get the training dataset
training_data = fetch_20newsgroups(subset='train',
        categories=category_map.keys(), shuffle=True, random_state=5)
```

Extract the term counts using the `CountVectorizer` object:

```
# Build a count vectorizer and extract term counts
count_vectorizer = CountVectorizer()
```

```
train_tc = count_vectorizer.fit_transform(training_data.data)
print("\nDimensions of training data:", train_tc.shape)
```

Create the **tf-idf** transformer and train it using the data:

```
# Create the tf-idf transformer
tfidf = TfidfTransformer()
train_tfidf = tfidf.fit_transform(train_tc)
```

Define some sample input sentences that will be used for testing:

```
# Define test data
input_data = [
    'You need to be careful with cars when you are driving on slippery
roads',
    'A lot of devices can be operated wirelessly',
    'Players need to be careful when they are close to goal posts',
    'Political debates help us understand the perspectives of both
sides'
]
```

Train a multinomial Bayes classifier using the training data:

```
# Train a Multinomial Naive Bayes classifier
classifier = MultinomialNB().fit(train_tfidf, training_data.target)
```

Transform the input data using the count vectorizer:

```
# Transform input data using count vectorizer
input_tc = count_vectorizer.transform(input_data)
```

Transform the vectorized data using the `tf-idf` transformer so that it can be run through the inference model:

```
# Transform vectorized data using tfidf transformer
input_tfidf = tfidf.transform(input_tc)
```

Predict the output using the `tf-idf` transformed vector:

```
# Predict the output categories
predictions = classifier.predict(input_tfidf)
```

Print the output category for each sample in the input test data:

```
# Print the outputs
for sent, category in zip(input_data, predictions):
    print('\nInput:', sent, '\nPredicted category:', \
            category_map[training_data.target_names[category]])
```

The full code is given in the file `category_predictor.py`. If you run the code, you will get the following output:

```
Dimensions of training data: (2844, 40321)

Input: You need to be careful with cars when you are driving on slippery roads
Predicted category: Autos

Input: A lot of devices can be operated wirelessly
Predicted category: Electronics

Input: Players need to be careful when they are close to goal posts
Predicted category: Hockey

Input: Political debates help us understand the perspectives of both sides
Predicted category: Politics
```

Figure 6: Category predictor output

We can see intuitively that the predicted categories are correct. Next, we'll look at another form of text analysis - gender identification.

Constructing a gender identifier

Gender identification is an interesting problem and far from being an exact science. We can quickly think of names that can be used for both males and females:

- Dana
- Angel
- Lindsey
- Morgan
- Jessie
- Chris
- Payton
- Tracy
- Stacy
- Jordan
- Robin
- Sydney

In addition, in a heterogeneous society such as the United States, there are going to be many ethnic names that will not follow English rules. In general, we can take an educated guess for a wide range of names. In this simple example, we will use a heuristic to construct a feature vector and use it to train a classifier. The heuristic that will be used here is the last *N* letters of a given name. For example, if the name ends with *ia*, it's most likely a female name, such as *Amelia* or *Genelia*. On the other hand, if the name ends with *rk*, it's likely a male name, such as *Mark* or *Clark*. Since we are not sure of the exact number of letters to use, we will play around with this parameter and find out what the best answer is. Let's see how to do it.

Create a new Python file and import the following packages:

```
import random

from nltk import NaiveBayesClassifier
from nltk.classify import accuracy as nltk_accuracy
from nltk.corpus import names
```

Define a function to extract the last *N* letters from the input word:

```
# Extract last N letters from the input word
# and that will act as our "feature"
def extract_features(word, N=2):
    last_n_letters = word[-N:]
    return {'feature': last_n_letters.lower()}
```

Define the `main` function and extract training data from the `scikit-learn` package. This data contains labeled male and female names:

```
if __name__=='__main__':
    # Create training data using labeled names available in NLTK
    male_list = [(name, 'male') for name in names.words('male.txt')]
    female_list = [(name, 'female') for name in names.words('female.
txt')]
    data = (male_list + female_list)
```

Seed the random number generator and shuffle the data:

```
    # Seed the random number generator
    random.seed(5)

    # Shuffle the data
    random.shuffle(data)
```

Create some sample names that will be used for testing:

```
# Create test data
input_names = ['Alexander', 'Danielle', 'David', 'Cheryl']
```

Define the percentage of data that will be used for training and testing:

```
    # Define the number of samples used for train and test
    num_train = int(0.8 * len(data))
```

The last *N* characters will be used as the feature vector to predict the gender. This parameter will be changed to see how the performance varies. In this case, we will go from `1` to `6`:

```
    # Iterate through different lengths to compare the accuracy
    for i in range(1, 6):
        print('\nNumber of end letters:', i)
        features = [(extract_features(n, i), gender) for (n, gender)
in data]
```

Separate the data into training and testing:

```
        train_data, test_data = features[:num_train], features[num_
train:]
```

Build a `NaiveBayesClassifier` using the training data:

```
        classifier = NaiveBayesClassifier.train(train_data)
```

Compute the accuracy of the classifier using the inbuilt accuracy method that's available in NLTK:

```
        # Compute the accuracy of the classifier
        accuracy = round(100 * nltk_accuracy(classifier, test_data),
2)
        print('Accuracy = ' + str(accuracy) + '%')
```

Predict the output for each name in the input test list:

```
        # Predict outputs for input names using
        # the trained classifier model
        for name in input_names:
            print(name, '==>', classifier.classify(extract_
features(name, i)))
```

The full code is given in the file `gender_identifier.py`. If you run the code, you will get the following output:

```
Number of end letters: 1
Accuracy = 74.7%
Alexander ==> male
Danielle ==> female
David ==> male
Cheryl ==> male

Number of end letters: 2
Accuracy = 78.79%
Alexander ==> male
Danielle ==> female
David ==> male
Cheryl ==> female

Number of end letters: 3
Accuracy = 77.22%
Alexander ==> male
Danielle ==> female
David ==> male
Cheryl ==> female
```

Figure 7: Gender identification output

The preceding screenshot shows the accuracy as well as the predicted outputs for the test data. Let's go further and see what happens:

```
Number of end letters: 4
Accuracy = 69.98%
Alexander ==> male
Danielle ==> female
David ==> male
Cheryl ==> female

Number of end letters: 5
Accuracy = 64.63%
Alexander ==> male
Danielle ==> female
David ==> male
Cheryl ==> female
```

Figure 8: Gender identification output

We can see that the accuracy peaked at two letters and then started decreasing after that. Next, we'll look at another interesting problem - analyzing the sentiment of a text.

Building a sentiment analyzer

Sentiment analysis is the process of determining the sentiment of a piece of text. For example, it can be used to determine whether a movie review is positive or negative. This is one of the most popular applications of natural language processing. We can add more categories as well, depending on the problem at hand. This technique can be used to get a sense of how people feel about a product, brand, or topic. It is frequently used to analyze marketing campaigns, opinion polls, social media presence, product reviews on e-commerce sites, and so on. Let's see how to determine the sentiment of a movie review.

We will use a Naive Bayes classifier to build this sentiment analyzer. First, extract all the unique words from the text. The NLTK classifier needs this data to be arranged in the form of a dictionary so that it can ingest it. Once the text data is divided into training and testing datasets, the Naive Bayes classifier will be trained to classify the reviews into positive and negative. Afterward, the top most informative words to indicate positive and negative reviews can be calculated and displayed. This information is interesting because it shows what words are being used to denote various reactions.

Let's see how this can be achieved. First, create a new Python file and import the following packages:

```
from nltk.corpus import movie_reviews
from nltk.classify import NaiveBayesClassifier
from nltk.classify.util import accuracy as nltk_accuracy
```

Define a function to construct a dictionary object based on the input words and return it:

```
# Extract features from the input list of words
def extract_features(words):
    return dict([(word, True) for word in words])
```

Define the `main` function and load the labeled movie reviews:

```
if __name__=='__main__':
    # Load the reviews from the corpus
    fileids_pos = movie_reviews.fileids('pos')
    fileids_neg = movie_reviews.fileids('neg')
```

Extract the features from the movie reviews and label them accordingly:

```
    # Extract the features from the reviews
    features_pos = [(extract_features(movie_reviews.words(
            fileids=[f])), 'Positive') for f in fileids_pos]
    features_neg = [(extract_features(movie_reviews.words(
            fileids=[f])), 'Negative') for f in fileids_neg]
```

Define the split between training and testing. In this case, we will allocate 80% for training and 20% for testing:

```
# Define the train and test split (80% and 20%)
threshold = 0.8
num_pos = int(threshold * len(features_pos))
num_neg = int(threshold * len(features_neg))
```

Separate the feature vectors for training and testing:

```
# Create training and training datasets
features_train = features_pos[:num_pos] + features_neg[:num_neg]
features_test = features_pos[num_pos:] + features_neg[num_neg:]
```

Print the number of data points used for training and testing:

```
# Print the number of datapoints used
print('\nNumber of training datapoints:', len(features_train))
print('Number of test datapoints:', len(features_test))
```

Train a `NaiveBayesClassifier` using the training data and compute the accuracy using the inbuilt accuracy method available in NLTK:

```
# Train a Naive Bayes classifier
classifier = NaiveBayesClassifier.train(features_train)
print('\nAccuracy of the classifier:', nltk_accuracy(
        classifier, features_test))
```

Print the top `N` most informative words:

```
N = 15
print('\nTop ' + str(N) + ' most informative words:')
for i, item in enumerate(classifier.most_informative_features()):
    print(str(i+1) + '. ' + item[0])
    if i == N - 1:
        break
```

Define sample sentences to be used for testing:

```
# Test input movie reviews
input_reviews = [
    'The costumes in this movie were great',
    'I think the story was terrible and the characters were very
weak',
    'People say that the director of the movie is amazing',
    'This is such an idiotic movie. I will not recommend it to
anyone.'
]
```

Iterate through the sample data and predict the output:

```
    print("\nMovie review predictions:")
    for review in input_reviews:
        print("\nReview:", review)
```

Compute the probabilities for each class:

```
        # Compute the probabilities
        probabilities = classifier.prob_classify(extract_
features(review.split()))
```

Pick the maximum value among the probabilities:

```
        # Pick the maximum value
        predicted_sentiment = probabilities.max()
```

Print the predicted output class (positive or negative sentiment):

```
        # Print outputs
        print("Predicted sentiment:", predicted_sentiment)
        print("Probability:", round(probabilities.prob(predicted_
sentiment), 2))
```

The full code is given in the file `sentiment_analyzer.py`. If you run the code, you will get the following output:

```
Number of training datapoints: 1600
Number of test datapoints: 400

Accuracy of the classifier: 0.735

Top 15 most informative words:
1. outstanding
2. insulting
3. vulnerable
4. ludicrous
5. uninvolving
6. astounding
7. avoids
8. fascination
9. symbol
10. seagal
11. affecting
12. anna
13. darker
14. animators
15. idiotic
```

Figure 9: Sentiment analysis output

The preceding screenshot shows the top 15 most informative words. If you scroll down, you will see this:

```
Movie review predictions:

Review: The costumes in this movie were great
Predicted sentiment: Positive
Probability: 0.59

Review: I think the story was terrible and the characters were very weak
Predicted sentiment: Negative
Probability: 0.8

Review: People say that the director of the movie is amazing
Predicted sentiment: Positive
Probability: 0.6

Review: This is such an idiotic movie. I will not recommend it to anyone.
Predicted sentiment: Negative
Probability: 0.87
```

Figure 10: Movie review sentiment output

We can see and verify intuitively that the predictions are correct.

In this section, we constructed a sophisticated sentiment analyzer. We will continue our journey in the NLP space and learn the foundations of Latent Dirichlet Allocation.

Topic modeling using Latent Dirichlet Allocation

Topic modeling is the process of identifying patterns in text data that correspond to a topic. If the text contains multiple topics, then this technique can be used to identify and separate those themes within the input text. This technique can be used to uncover hidden thematic structure in a given set of documents.

Topic modeling helps us to organize documents in an optimal way, which can then be used for analysis. One thing to note about topic modeling algorithms is that they don't need labeled data. It is like unsupervised learning in that it will identify the patterns on its own. Given the enormous volumes of text data generated on the internet, topic modeling is important because it enables the summarization of vast amounts of data, which would otherwise not be possible.

Latent Dirichlet Allocation is a topic modeling technique, the underlying concept of which is that a given piece of text is a combination of multiple topics. Let's consider the following sentence: Data visualization is an important tool in financial analysis. This sentence has multiple topics, such as data, visualization, and finance. This combination helps to identify text in a large document. It is a statistical model that tries to capture concepts and create a model based on them. The model assumes that documents are generated from a random process based on these topics. A topic is a distribution over a fixed vocabulary of words. Let's see how to do topic modeling in Python.

The `gensim` library will be used in this section. This library has already been installed in the first section of this chapter. Make sure that you have it before you proceed. Create a new Python file and import the following packages:

```
from nltk.tokenize import RegexpTokenizer
from nltk.corpus import stopwords
from nltk.stem.snowball import SnowballStemmer
from gensim import models, corpora
```

Define a function to load the input data. The input file contains 10 line-separated sentences:

```
# Load input data
def load_data(input_file):
    data = []
    with open(input_file, 'r') as f:
        for line in f.readlines():
            data.append(line[:-1])

    return data
```

Define a function to process the input text. The first step is to tokenize it:

```
# Processor function for tokenizing, removing stop
# words, and stemming
def process(input_text):
    # Create a regular expression tokenizer
    tokenizer = RegexpTokenizer(r'\w+')
```

We then need to stem the tokenized text:

```
    # Create a Snowball stemmer
    stemmer = SnowballStemmer('english')
```

We need to remove the stop words from the input text because they don't add information. Let's get the list of stop words:

```
        # Get the list of stop words
        stop_words = stopwords.words('english')
```

Tokenize the input string:

```
    # Tokenize the input string
    tokens = tokenizer.tokenize(input_text.lower())
```

Remove the stop-words:

```
        # Remove the stop words
        tokens = [x for x in tokens if not x in stop_words]
```

Stem the tokenized words and return the list:

```
        # Perform stemming on the tokenized words
        tokens_stemmed = [stemmer.stem(x) for x in tokens]

        return tokens_stemmed
```

Define the `main` function and load the input data from the file `data.txt` provided for you:

```
    if __name__=='__main__':
        # Load input data
        data = load_data('data.txt')
```

Tokenize the text:

```
        # Create a list for sentence tokens
        tokens = [process(x) for x in data]
```

Create a dictionary based on the tokenized sentences:

```
        # Create a dictionary based on the sentence tokens
        dict_tokens = corpora.Dictionary(tokens)
```

Create a document-term matrix using the sentence tokens:

```
        # Create a document-term matrix
        doc_term_mat = [dict_tokens.doc2bow(token) for token in tokens]
```

We need to provide the number of topics as the input parameter. In this case, we know that the input text has two distinct topics. Let's specify that:

```
    # Define the number of topics for the LDA model
    num_topics = 2
```

Generate the `LatentDirichlet` model:

```
    # Generate the LDA model
    ldamodel = models.ldamodel.LdaModel(doc_term_mat,
            num_topics=num_topics, id2word=dict_tokens, passes=25)
```

Print the top five contributing words for each topic:

```
    num_words = 5
    print('\nTop ' + str(num_words) + ' contributing words to each
topic:')
    for item in ldamodel.print_topics(num_topics=num_topics, num_
words=num_words):
        print('\nTopic', item[0])

        # Print the contributing words along with
        # their relative contributions
        list_of_strings = item[1].split(' + ')
        for text in list_of_strings:
            weight = text.split('*')[0]
            word = text.split('*')[1]
            print(word, '==>', str(round(float(weight) * 100, 2)) +
'%')
```

The full code is given in the file `topic_modeler.py`. If you run the code, you will get the following output:

```
Top 5 contributing words to each topic:

Topic 0
mathemat ==> 2.7%
structur ==> 2.6%
set ==> 2.6%
formul ==> 2.6%
tradit ==> 1.6%

Topic 1
empir ==> 4.7%
expand ==> 3.3%
time ==> 2.0%
peopl ==> 2.0%
histor ==> 2.0%
```

Figure 11: Topic modeler output

We can see that it does a reasonably good job of separating the two topics - mathematics and history. If you look at the text, you can verify that each sentence is either about mathematics or history.

Summary

In this chapter, we learned about various underlying concepts in natural language processing. We discussed tokenization and how to separate input text into multiple tokens. We learned how to reduce words to their base forms using stemming and lemmatization. We implemented a text chunker to divide input text into chunks based on predefined conditions.

We discussed the *Bag of Words* model and built a document-term matrix for input text. We then learned how to categorize text using machine learning. We constructed a gender identifier using a heuristic. We also used machine learning to analyze the sentiments of movie reviews. Finally, we discussed topic modeling and implemented a system to identify topics in a given document.

In the next chapter, we will learn how to model sequential data using Hidden Markov Models and then use them to analyze stock market data.

16
Chatbots

In this chapter, we will learn about chatbots. We will understand what they are, and how they can be used. You will also learn how to create your own chatbot. We will cover the following topics:

- The future of chatbots
- Chatbots today
- Basic chatbot concepts
- Popular chatbot platforms
- DialogFlow:
    - Setting up DialogFlow
    - Integrating the chatbot into a website with a widget
    - Integrating the chatbot into a website using Python
    - Setting up a webhook in DialogFlow
    - Enabling webhooks for intents
    - Setting up training phrases for an intent
    - Setting up parameters and actions for an intent
    - Building fulfillment responses from a webhook
    - Checking responses from a webhook

We'll begin by talking about the future of chatbots and their many potential applications.

The future of chatbots

It is difficult to exactly predict how AI will upend our society in the next few years. Just like nuclear technology has been used to develop nuclear weapons and to power nuclear power plants, AI can also be used for noble causes or for nefarious purposes. It is not hard to imagine that militaries around the world have powerful weapons that take advantage of AI techniques. For example, using currently "off-the-shelf" technology, we could build a drone, give it the picture of the person that is an intended target, and let the drone hunt that person down until they are eliminated.

Even if the technology is used for more constructive use cases, it is hard to predict how the technological disruption will unfold in the next couple of years. There are various studies predicting, to some degree, that entire industries will no longer need as many workers as they have had in the past because of productivity increases powered by AI. Two "low-hanging fruit" examples are the trucking and transportation industry and the call center industry.

Voice interfaces in the last few years have been finally breaking through and pervading our lives more and more. Applications like Alexa, Siri, and Google Home have started to become embedded in our lives and our culture. In addition, messaging platforms like WeChat, Facebook Messenger, WhatsApp, and Slack create opportunities for businesses to interact with people and potentially monetize these interactions. These messaging platforms are getting so popular and pervasive that, in 2019, the four largest services have more active users than the four largest social networking platforms (4.1 billion versus 3.4 billion).

Call centers have already changed dramatically over the last few years. As technological advances continue with the use of chatbots, the cloud, and voice biometrics, companies can improve their customer service and handle more calls with less staff.

We are not there yet, but it is easy to visualize that, in the next 5 or 10 years, when you call your bank, only the most unusual edge cases will require human intervention and a huge percentage of the calls will be handled automatically.

This trend will only continue to accelerate. Currently, no one is going to confuse most chatbot conversation with a human conversation. But as they get better in the next few years, it will feel more natural and fluid. When we dial a call center, sometimes at least, one of the reasons for our call is to complain or vent in addition to getting a problem solved. As chatbots get better, they will be able to display what we perceive as sympathy and understanding. Additionally, they will have full access to all your previous calls and be able to develop a history and build a rapport by remembering snippets of previous conversations.

For example, it will not be difficult soon for chatbots to remember that you mentioned your kid's name and the next time that you call ask you how little Bobby is doing. Additionally, just like it is the case now when you communicate with your bank via different channels like the web, a phone app, or when speaking with someone at the branch, the chatbot will be able to access information entered through these other channels and use it to serve you better and faster. Again, we are not there yet, but a day can possibly come where we prefer to call customer service instead of using other channels like online access because it will be quicker and more efficient. As an example, I do find myself using Alexa more and more as she gets better, and I get more comfortable and familiar with her functionality and quirks. I am still working on trying to rattle her but have not yet achieved it.

Not just with Alexa but with other smart home assistants, many of us use them to:

- Listen to music
- Set alarms
- Create shopping lists
- Get weather forecasts
- Control devices around the house
- Order online commerce goods
- Book a plane ticket

But this experience could become more sophisticated. As they get better, they will surpass us in at least some aspects. For example, unless we program them in that way, chatbots will never get frustrated.

Regarding AI in general and chatbots in particular, the ethical implications of their continued progress is a constant topic. As chatbots get better and more human-like, regulators will probably force businesses to disclose when we are talking to a chatbot and not a human. This might not be a bad rule to have in place. However, we might get to the point where chatbots are so good that even though that disclosure is given at the beginning, we will soon forget that the other end is a computer and not a human that understands us and empathizes with us.

One powerful example of how good chatbots are getting at sounding natural is Google Duplex. You should be able to catch a demo of it here:

`https://www.youtube.com/watch?v=D5VN56jQMWM`

By the way, this technology is generally available, and you should be able to use it if you have an Android phone or an iPhone.

There is little doubt that chatbots will be prolific — in our homes, in our cars, in our clothes as wearables, in call centers, and on our phones. According to one estimate, the global market for chatbots is expected to grow from $4.2 billion in 2019 to $15.7 billion by 2024 with a combined annual growth rate of 30.2%. As it happens with other technologies, younger people that are growing up with this technology will never know what it was like to not have chatbots around to serve us and make our lives better.

This section discussed what chatbots might look like in the next few years. In the next section, we will come back to earth and make some suggestions about how to leverage existing chatbot technology to create great applications using the tools available today.

Chatbots today

In the previous section, we discussed what we believe will be possible in the coming years as the technology of AI evolves. As with any technology, we shouldn't wait until everything has been perfected. In this section and for the rest of the chapter, we'll focus on what is possible today and the best practices to make your own applications as useful and user friendly as possible.

In order to leverage the existing technology available today and given that current chatbots still need to be programmed specifically with domain data and specific intents, we should be careful to have a good design and a good plan in place to program our chatbot. Start with clearly defined goals for your chatbot and avoid trying to come up with a broad solution. Currently, chatbots that play in a well-defined and narrow domain space have a better chance of performing well and being useful than one that tries to be a "jack of all trades." A chatbot that is designed to give support during an online commerce experience cannot be used to diagnose car problems and will have to be reprogrammed in that domain. Focus the chatbot clearly on a specific goal and space and you will most likely create a better experience for your users by doing so.

To drive the point home, I will share a personal story. A few years ago, I visited a restaurant in Miami. As you know, English is the most common language in the US but less so in Miami. We looked at the menu, ordered our drinks, and then our appetizers. It was now time to order the main course. I decided to start some small talk with the waiter. I forget my specific question, but it was something along the lines of "How do you like living in Miami?" The panicked look on his face told me that he did not understand the question and no matter how many times, I tried to explain it, he wasn't going to. To put him at ease, I switched to Spanish and completed our little chat.

The takeaway here is that the waiter knew "restaurant English" and all the phrases and interactions required to complete restaurant transactions. But everything else was outside of his comfort zone. Similarly, when we develop our chatbot in the following sections, it will be able to communicate with our users as long as we stay in the intended domain. If the chatbot is developed to take restaurant reservations, it will not be able to help if the user's intent is to get a medical diagnosis.

Chatbots today are still somewhat narrow. As many things as we can do with Alexa, Siri, and Google Home, currently, they can only help us with specific tasks. They cannot yet handle certain human traits very well like empathy, sarcasm, and critical thinking. In their current state, chatbots will be able to help us with repetitive transactional tasks in a more human-centered way.

However, even though we should try to keep our chatbot as tight as possible on domain, that doesn't mean that we shouldn't try to inject a little "personality" into our bot. Alexa can be cheeky and humorous at times and you should strive for the same with your bots. This should result in higher engagement with your bot.

While chatting, people typically expect a certain level of mutual interest in the conversation and, consequently, that the conversation will take place in such a way that there will be answers that feed the subsequent questions, as well as answers that inform and promote the conversation. Using a little bit of slang will go a long way to making your bot more realistic and engaging.

Before we delve into the design of our own chatbot, let's cover some foundational concepts that will help us during development.

Chatbot concepts

Before we develop our code, let's set a baseline and visit some useful definitions related to chatbots.

Agent

An agent is a system that can handle all the conversations and route all the necessary actions. It is a natural-language understanding module that gets trained frequently to cater to use-specific requirements.

Intents

When two people communicate, they both have a reason as to why they started the communication. It might be as simple as catching up with a friend and finding out what they have been doing.

It could be that one of them is trying to sell something and so forth. These "intents" fall under three broad classifications:

- **The speaker is trying to entertain** - An example is when someone tells you a joke.
- **The speaker is trying to inform** - Someone asks what time is it, or, what is the temperature? And they receive the answer.
- **The speaker is trying to persuade** - The agenda is to try to sell something.

For most chatbots, their role is to fulfill commands and perform tasks. For this reason, the first task they need to perform is to ascertain the intent of the person that invoked them. Intents have elements such as context, training phase, actions and parameters, and responses.

Context

Context is used to give coherence and fluency to a discussion, preserving the key concepts that have already been used in the conversation.

Entities

This basically groups a set of words under a defined entity. For example, pen, pencil, paper, eraser, and notebook can be termed as stationaries. So, DialogFlow offers pre-built entities that are already trained, or we can build our custom entity and train them. This helps in reducing the redundancy of training phrases.

Integrations

Chatbot platforms like DialogFlow and Lex can integrate with most of the most popular conversation and messaging platforms like Google Assistant, Facebook Messenger, Kik, and Viber, among others.

Fulfillment

Fulfillment is a connecting service that allows you to take actions based on the end user's expressions and send dynamic responses back to the user. For example, if the user is looking for employee details, your service can fetch details from the database and respond to the user immediately with the results.

Utterances

Whenever we carry a conversation with someone, it is perfectly normal to use slightly different ways to ask the same question. For example, we might ask the question "How was your day today?," but there are a wide variety of ways to ask the same question. Examples include:

- Tell me about your day
- Did you have a good day?
- How was your day?
- How was work?

Humans are naturally adept at interpreting meaning from utterances and answering the question that the questioner meant to ask rather than what they actually asked. For example, a simple interpretation of the question "Did you have a good day?" would require the answer to be yes or no. But as humans, we are skilled enough to understand that the real meaning might be "Tell me about your day."

Many of the chatbot platforms out there are getting better at not requiring us to spell out every single utterance, but rather they are able to do some "fuzzy" matching and not require an entry for every single combination.

Wake words

Many chatbots like Alexa or Siri stay dormant until they are "woken" and become ready to receive commands. To wake them up, a "wake word" is needed. In the case of Alexa, the most common wake word used is "Alexa." In the case of Siri, the default wake word is "Hey Siri." And, in the case of the Starship Enterprise, the wake word is "Computer."

Launch words

Once a chatbot is woken up, many times we want the chatbot to perform an action for us, so we need to "launch" the action. Examples of some launch words are:

- Order
- Tell me
- Add
- Turn on

You can think of launch words as commands.

Slot values or entities

Slot values are words that will be converted into parameters. Let's look at a few examples:

- Order <u>milk</u>
- Tell me the capital of <u>Italy</u>
- Add <u>bread</u> to the shopping list
- Turn on the <u>oven</u>

The slot values have been underlined. A slot value can have a slot type. Just like a parameter can have parameter types (integer, string, and so on). Some slot types are built-in and custom slot types can also be created. Some examples of slot types are:

- Country names
- Email addresses
- Phone numbers
- Dates

Some chatbot platforms refer to slot types as entities.

Error Planning and Default Cases

A well-designed chatbot should always gracefully handle unforeseen cases. When a chatbot does not have a programmed answer for a specific interaction, it should be able to display default behavior that handles unforeseen conditions as gracefully as possible. For example, if a chatbot's function is to book domestic flights within the U.S. but a user solicits a charter flight to Vancouver, Canada, the chatbot should be able to gracefully tell the users that they only service the U.S. cities and ask them the destination again.

Webhooks

A webhook is an HTTP push API or web callback. It is also referred to as a reverse API, because it sends data from the application to the application consumers as soon as the event occurs. It obviates the need for the consumers to continuously poll the application.

Now that we've covered the foundational concepts we need to know to better work with chatbots, let's consider how we can create a useful, "well-architected" chatbot.

A well-architected chatbot

For a chatbot to be useful and efficient, it must possess certain qualities. We call a chatbot that possesses these qualities a "well-architected" chatbot. We list and define these qualities as follows:

Adaptability

An adaptable chatbot is one that can understand and adapt to all the utterances received. Even for utterances that are not explicitly programmed, there should be a graceful response to get the chatbot user back on track or alternatively use the opportunity to transfer the party to a live operator.

Personalization

As humans, we love to feel special. We love to hear our name and love for others to remember little things about us (our kids' names, our alma mater, and so on). A personalized chatbot remembers previous interactions and the information that they have collected about individual users.

Availability

A chatbot should be available to help the user. This goes beyond traditional platform availability. Of course, our chatbot should be always ready to assist and be accessed whenever it is needed. But this also applies to how quickly we can get the chatbot to help us to accomplish an intent. Think of the navigation trees in traditional **Interactive Voice Response** (**IVR**) systems, where we must press a lot of numbers before they divine the intent that we are trying to perform. This type of system has low availability.

Relatability

A chatbot that is relatable gives the user of the chatbot the perception that they are truly having a normal conversation.

We're almost ready to move on to developing our own chatbot. Before we do that, however, we should consider the major chatbot platforms that act as a foundation for our chatbot's development and distribution.

Chatbot platforms

Some of the most widely used chatbots are those made possible by platforms developed by major vendors such as Google, AWS, and Microsoft. You should carefully consider their service offerings when you are choosing the technology stack for your chatbot. All three of these big vendors provide reliable and scalable cloud computing services that will help you to implement and customize your chatbot according to your needs. As of now, the most famous platforms to easily create text- or voice-based bots are the following:

- DialogFlow (Google, formerly Api.ai)
- Azure Bot Service (Microsoft)
- Lex (AWS)
- Wit.ai (Facebook)
- Watson (IBM)

It is certainly possible to write powerful chatbots with the platforms listed here, as well as with other popular platforms. But we will now dive deeper into one platform in particular to gain a deeper understanding. Among the chatbot services, DialogFlow is a strong option for beginner users. We'll discuss DialogFlow in the following section, and we will use the platform for our chatbot's development in the remainder of the chapter.

Creating a chatbot using DialogFlow

Google has a long history of extensive research in machine learning and **Natural Language Processing** (**NLP**). And much of this research is reflected in their DialogFlow tool. DialogFlow integrates with Google Cloud Speech-to-Text API and other third-party services such as Google Assistant, Amazon Alexa, and Facebook Messenger.

It is possible to create chatbots that offer quite a bit of functionality without writing a line of code. Initially, we will review how the chatbot can be configured without code and by merely using the **Google Cloud Platform** (**GCP**) console. In the following sections of this chapter, we will demonstrate how the chatbot can be integrated with other services. The later sections in this chapter will require a basic understanding of the Python language.

Steps to get started

1. Sign up for free at `https://dialogflow.com` using a Google account.
2. For your chatbots to work properly, you will need to accept all the requested permissions by DialogFlow. This will allow you to manage data across the GCP services and let you integrate with the Google Assistant.
3. You can access the DialogFlow console at `https://console.dialogflow.com`.
4. Finally, create a new agent by selecting the primary language (other languages can be added later) and a Google Project identifier. The name of the project in the Google Cloud Console is needed to enable billing and other settings. Don't worry if you don't have an existing project: create a new one.

Now that you are signed up and ready to go, let's begin by getting DialogFlow set up.

DialogFlow setup

When you first sign into DialogFlow, you will be asked to allow certain permissions. It is recommended that you allow these permissions. Otherwise, the following exercises will not work correctly:

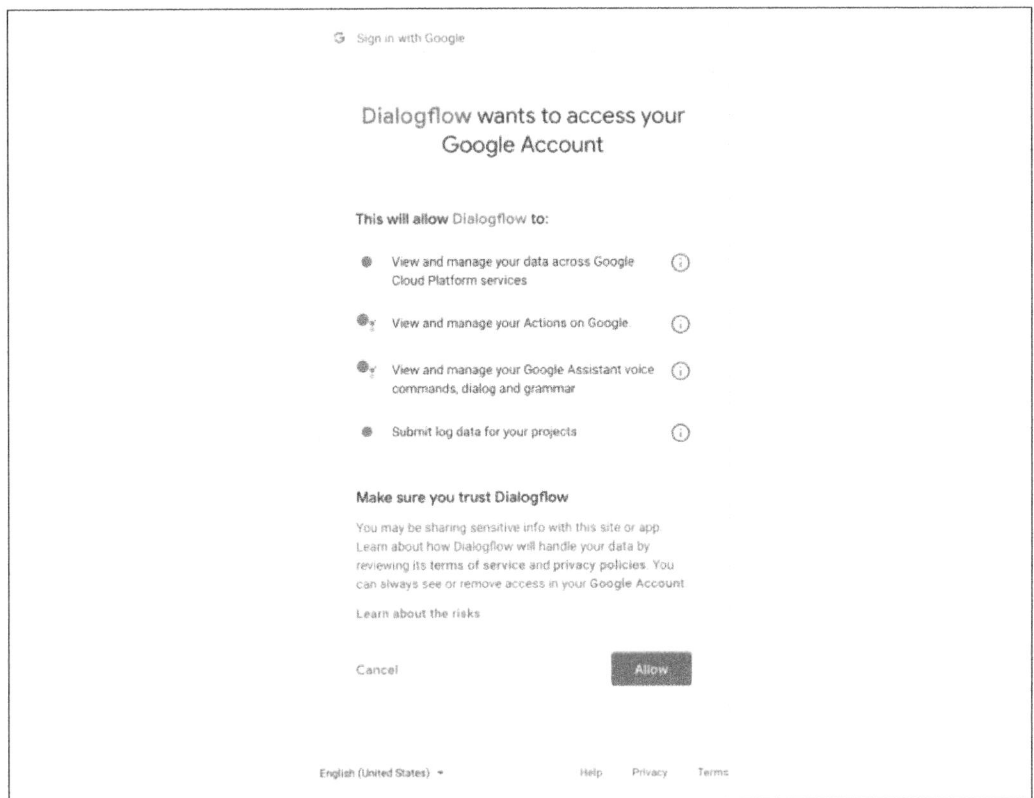

Figure 1: Google Cloud Console permissions to access the DialogFlow console

Development in DialogFlow leverages the two main concepts that we discussed previously – intent and context. An intent identifies the purpose of the utterance given by the user to the chatbot. Context gives coherence and fluency to the conversation.

After clicking on the **Intents** tab, you should see a screen like this:

Figure 2: DialogFlow chatbot intent creation

As we saw previously, another important concept in chatbot development is the slot type. In DialogFlow, we refer to slot types as entities. Entities enable the identification of common or parametrically recurring concepts in the conversation. Entities can be built-in or custom made. The use of entities makes chatbots more versatile and flexible. When clicking on the **Entities** tab, you should see this screen:

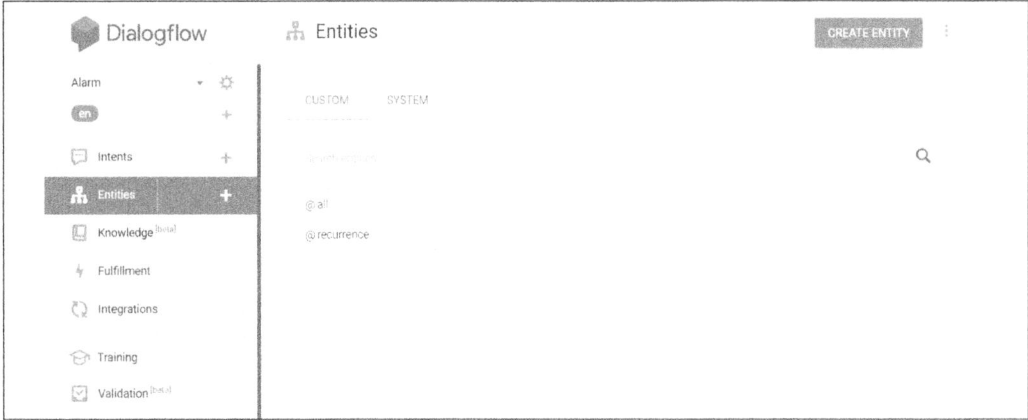

Figure 3: DialogFlow chatbot entity creation

Let's start with a basic example that uses only intents. First, we'll create the agent and then define some intents through the DialogFlow interface. It is possible to create these intents programmatically, but to keep the example simple we'll create the intents using the graphical interface. First, let's set up the fallback intent. This is the intent that will be invoked if no other intent is called:

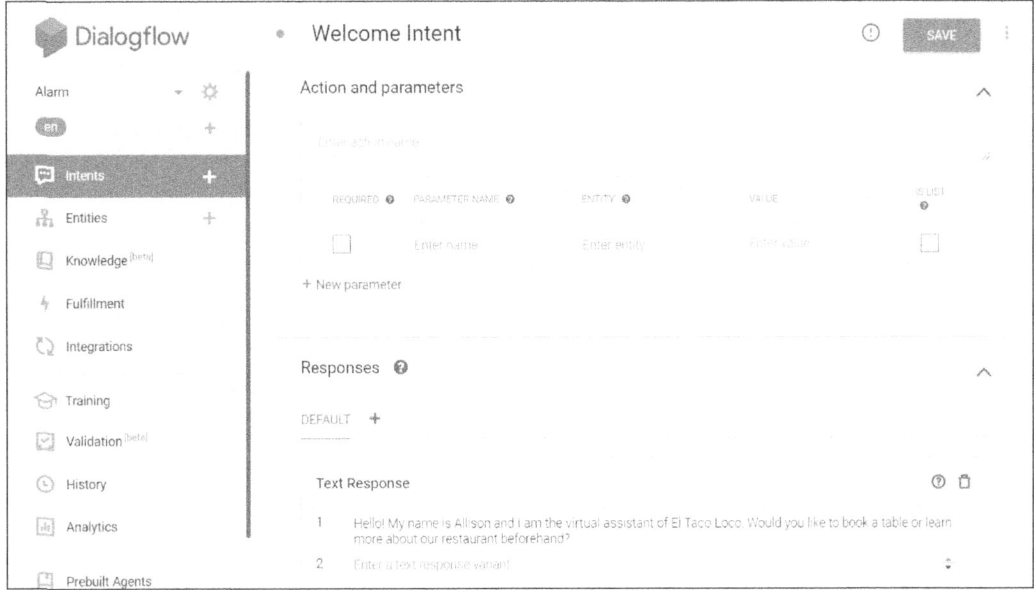

Figure 4: DialogFlow fallback intent creation

As you can see in *Figure 4*, just write in the **Try it now** form to get an answer. Initially, when no intents have been created yet, the chatbot will use the fallback intent. Having a fallback intent prevents the conversation from coming to a standstill.

As we browse the **Default Fallback Intent** we see the full list of **Responses**. As you can see, many responses have already been defined. When an intent is matched, the chatbot engine will randomly select an item as the answer.

Let's create our first intent. We can do this using the console. Make sure that you also fill in the **Training phrases** form. These are the sentences that we expect from the user that will trigger the intent. The more precise and comprehensive we are in constructing these sentences, the more success the chatbot will have in identifying the intent.

We can now proceed by inserting more intents to add more functionality to our chatbot. We can continuously test our chatbot using the helper on the right.

Hopefully, it is apparent that it is certainly possible to create powerful chatbots purely using intents. DialogFlow is doing most of the heavy lifting for us. To make the chatbot even more powerful, we can start adding context to the intents. And we can make our chatbot more flexible by adding parameters as we go from one intent to the other while maintaining the context of the conversation. In the next section of the tutorial, we'll see how we can integrate our chatbot into a website.

Integrating a chatbot into a website using a widget

There are two methods that can be used to integrate a DialogFlow chatbot into a website:

- Via a widget
- Using Python

We will start by visiting the first method, which is the easier way. This method integrates DialogFlow into a web page using an *iframe*. To use this method, select **Integrations** from the menu on the left and make sure that **Web Demo** is enabled. Copy the HTML code and paste it into a web page and, just like that, you will be able to use the chatbot on your site:

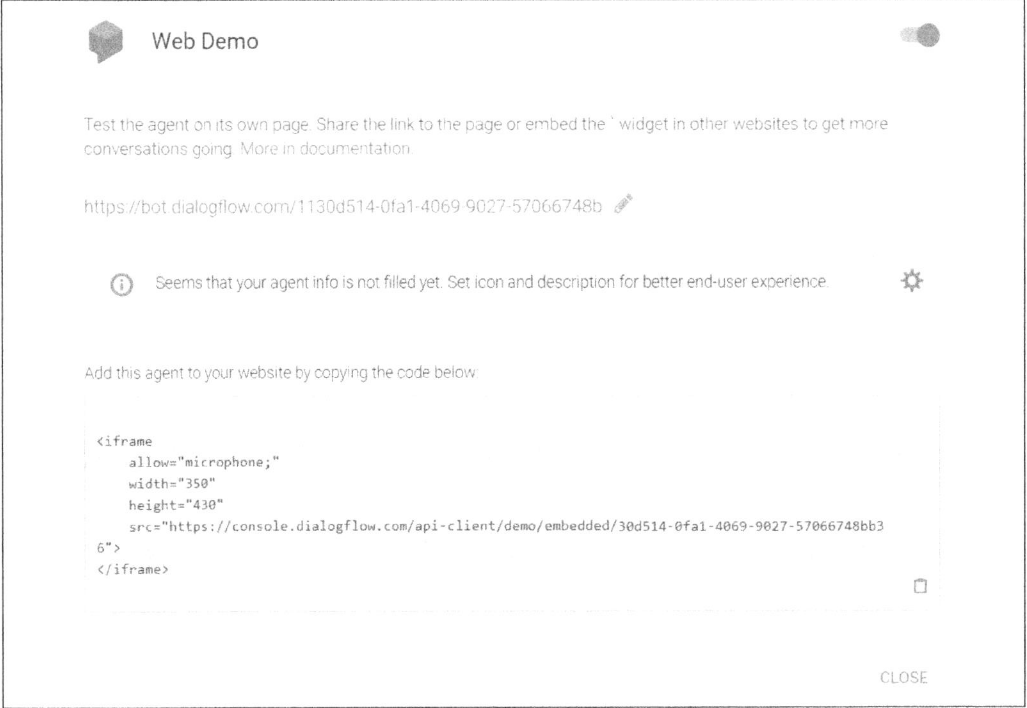

Figure 5: Integrating a chatbot into a website using the iframe

In the following section, we'll consider the second method - using Python. As we saw, the widget method to integrate our chatbot is extremely easy. However, we have little control over how the bot will be implemented. Integrating a chatbot into a site using Python gives the developer more control and flexibility in terms of how the chatbot can be deployed.

Integrating a chatbot into a website using Python

Another way to invoke a DialogFlow chatbot is by using Python. First, we need to install package requirements that are needed for the code to run:

```
$ pip3 install DialogFlow
$ pip3 install google-api-core
```

The code initializes a client session that takes the intent as input and finally returns a response, the so-called `fulfillment`, and the corresponding confidence as a decimal value. The sentence for which we want to get an answer is saved in the variable named `text_to_be_analyzed`. Edit the script by adding your sentence. Using Python, it is easy to create more custom logic. For example, you can catch an intent and then trigger a custom action:

```
# Install the following requirements:
# DialogFlow 0.5.1
# google-api-core 1.4.1

import DialogFlow
from google.api_core.exceptions import InvalidArgument

PROJECT_ID = 'google-project-id'
LANGUAGE_CODE = 'en-US'
GOOGLE_APPLICATION_CREDENTIALS = 'credentials.json'
SESSION_ID = 'current-user-id'

analyzed_text = "Hi! I'm Billy. I want tacos. Can you help me?"

session_client = DialogFlow.SessionsClient()
session = session_client.session_path(PROJECT_ID, SESSION_ID)

text_input = DialogFlow.types.TextInput(text=analyzed_text,
    language_code=LANGUAGE_CODE)
query_input = DialogFlow.types.QueryInput(text=text_input)
try:
    response = session_client.detect_intent(session=session,
    query_input=query_input)
except InvalidArgument:
    raise

print("Query text:", response.query_result.query_text)
print("Detected intent:",
```

```
        response.query_result.intent.display_name)
    print("Detected intent confidence:",
        response.query_result.intent_detection_confidence)
    print("Fulfillment text:",
        response.query_result.fulfillment_text)
```

As you can see, the function requires a `session_id`. This is a value that identifies the current session. For this reason, we suggest that you use the ID of the user to make it easily retrievable.

For the Python code to work, a new token is needed. In fact, version 2.0 of the DialogFlow API relies on an authentication system that is based on a private key associated with the GCP service account, instead of the access tokens. Using this procedure, it is possible to get a JSON format private key.

Fulfillment and webhooks

Now that we have established how a session can be created, let's use it for something useful. The purpose of having a session is to be able to make requests to the server and receive responses that can fulfill the request. In DialogFlow, requests are called webhooks and loosely correspond to responses. Fulfillment is a useful feature of DialogFlow: with fulfillment, we can communicate with the backend and generate dynamic responses. With fulfillment, we can develop a webhook that accepts a request from DialogFlow, processes the request, and responds with DialogFlow-compatible JSON.

In DialogFlow, a webhook is used to fetch data from the backend when certain webhook-enabled intents are invoked. The information from the intent is passed along to the webhook service and then a response is returned.

For this purpose, **ngrok** can be used. The ngrok software is a web tunneling tool that can be used to invoke webhooks. It enables the testing of APIs and webhooks using a local server. Another tool that will be used in this section of the tutorial is **Flask**. Flask is a lightweight web framework that can be used to create a webhook service that can invoke external applications. In our example, the external application that will be called is the DialogFlow agent. To use Flask, we first need to install it:

```
$ pip3 install Flask
```

To learn more about Flask, you can visit:

`https://pypi.org/project/Flask`

Creating webhook using Flask

First, we can create a basic Flask app:

```
# import flask dependencies
from flask import Flask

# initialize the flask app
app = Flask(__name__)

# default route
@app.route('/')
def index():
    return 'Hello World'

# create a route for webhook
@app.route('/webhook')
def webhook():
    return 'Hello World'

# run the app
if __name__ == '__main__':
   app.run()
```

Test the application using the following command:

```
$ python app.py or FLASK_APP=hello.py flask run
```

If you see the preceding output, this will confirm that the initial version of the application is working. So far, we are only using a local server, so it cannot be accessed by other external clients via the internet. To integrate it as a webhook for DialogFlow, we need to deploy it on a server that can be accessed via the internet. That's where the ngrok tool comes in. The tool can be downloaded here:

`https://ngrok.io`

To run ngrok, use the following command:

```
$ ngrok http <port_number>
```

For example:

```
$ ngrok http 5000
```

The output received should be something like this:

```
ngrok by @inconshreveable                                       (Ctrl+C to quit)

Session Status                online
Account
Version                       2.2.8
Region                        United States (us)
Web Interface                 http://127.0.0.1:4040
Forwarding                    http://886b69bc.ngrok.io -> localhost:5000
Forwarding                    https://886b69bc.ngrok.io -> localhost:5000

Connections                   ttl     opn     rt1     rt5     p50     p90
                              0       0       0.00    0.00    0.00    0.00
```

Figure 6: ngrok initialization output

In the next section, we'll look at how to set up a webhook in DialogFlow.

How to set up a webhook in DialogFlow

To set up the webhook in DialogFlow, on the left sidebar, select **Fulfillment** and enter the webhook URL generated by ngrok:

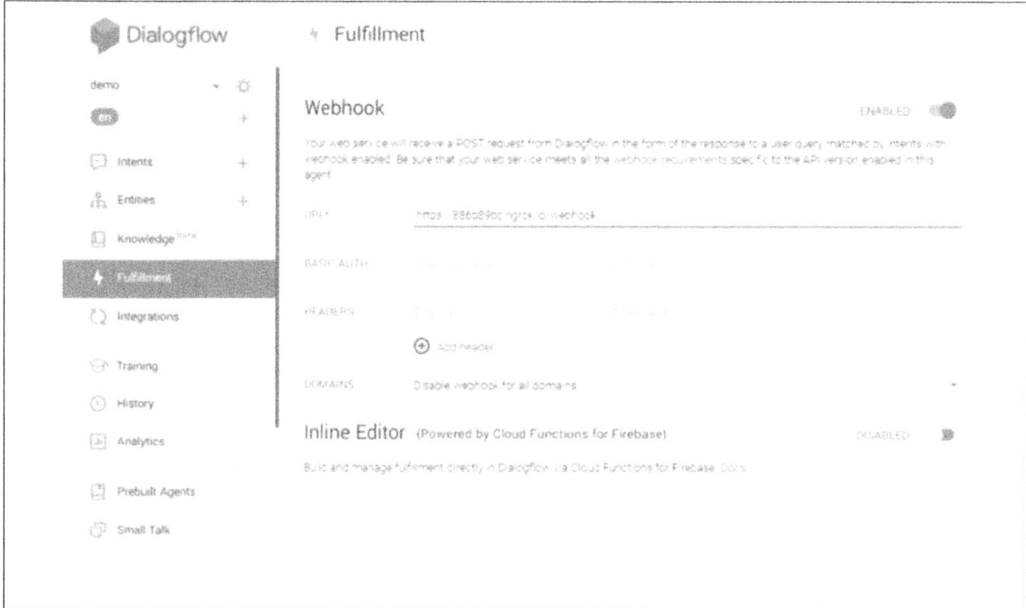

Figure 7: Dialogflow webhook setup

Make sure the suffix `/webhook` is added to the end of the URL. It should look like this:

```
https://886b89bc.ngrok.io/webhook
```

Not:

```
https:// 886b89bc.ngrok.io/
```

We will handle the request on a `/webhook` route and not an index route.

If the URL does not have the webhook suffix, you should get the following error:

`Webhook call failed. Error: 405 Method Not Allowed.`

Correct the URL to include the suffix and this should fix the error.

Next, the webhook needs to be enabled to support intents and to fetch server data. We'll look at how we can do this in the following section.

Enabling webhooks for intents

To enable webhooks for intents, open the intent that needs the webhook enabled, scroll down to the bottom of the page, and enable the option **Enable webhook call for this intent**:

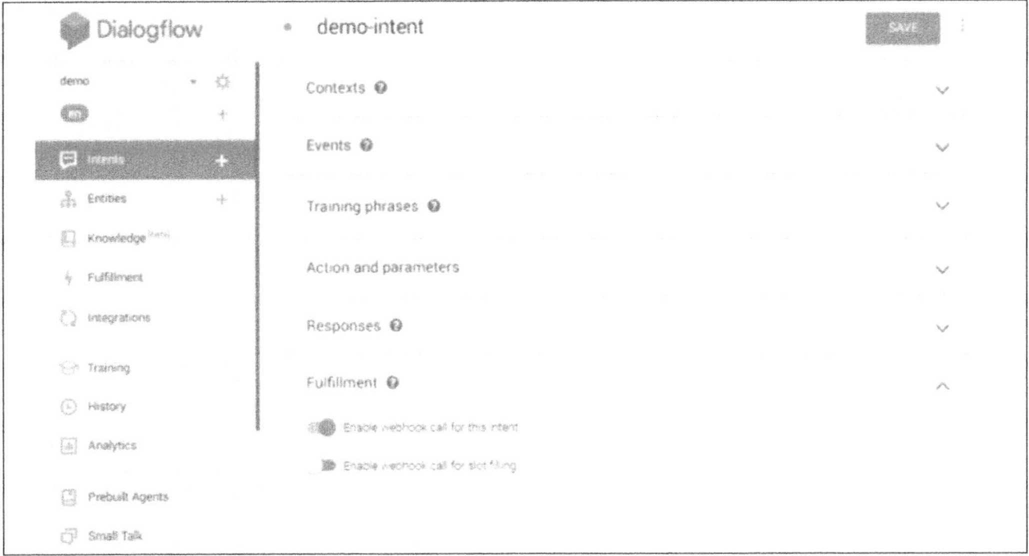

Figure 8: Dialogflow webhook enablement for intents

When the intent is triggered, it sends a request to the webhook and a response is sent back. We can now move on to setting up training phases.

Setting up training phrases for an intent

Training phrases are utterances that help the chatbot to determine which intent is being called. Here is an example of how that should be set up:

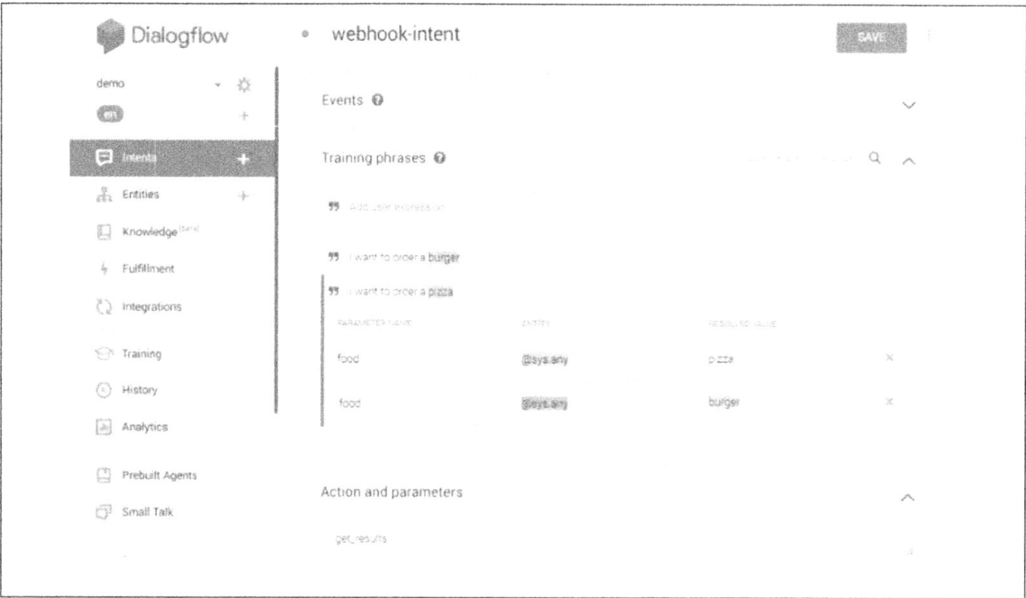

Figure 9: Dialogflow training phrase setup for intents

Next, we need to set up the parameters and actions.

Setting up parameters and actions for an intent

Actions and parameters need to be set up in the intent that can then be used in the webhook to process the request.

In the current example, `get_results` is set up as an **Action**. Whenever the intent calls the webhook using a `POST` request, `get_results` will be received as **Action**. If multiple intents exist that can invoke the webhook, the action will be used to make the distinction and, with this, generate different responses.

We can also pass **parameters** to our webhook. To do that, we can define the parameter name and its value. In this example, we are going to start very simply, but eventually we are going to allow the user to order food items from a restaurant. So for example, the user might say: "I want to order burgers and fries" and the chatbot will pass this utterance to the backend for validation, storage, and processing:

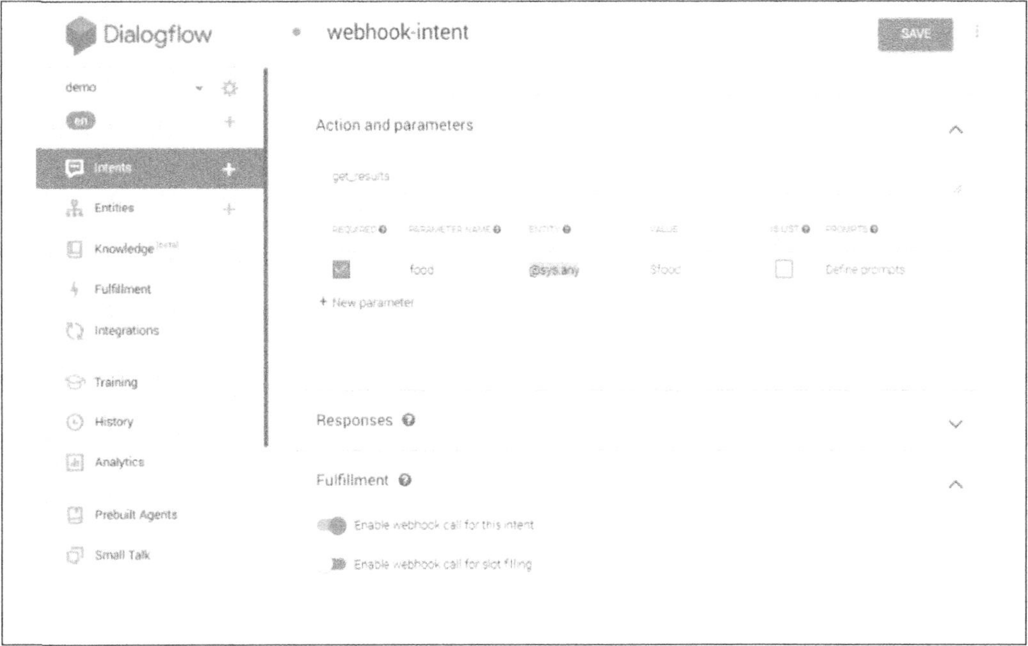

Figure 10: Dialogflow action and parameter setup

Actions and parameters are optional values. The webhook will still work even if the actions and parameters are not passed. To distinguish between intents that don't have actions, the intent name can be checked in the request JSON.

Building fulfillment responses from a webhook

Webhook responses should be constructed using a valid JSON response. This way, DialogFlow will be able to display messages properly in the frontend.

The responses can be constructed using Python. The following response types are available:

- Simple Response
- Basic Card
- Suggestions
- List Card
- Browse Carousel
- Carousel Response

The following code generates a simple JSON response with `fulfillment` text for DialogFlow:

```
# import flask dependencies
from flask import Flask, request, make_response, jsonify

# initialize the flask app
app = Flask(__name__)

# default route
@app.route('/)
def index():
    return 'Hello World'

# function for responses
def results():
    # build a request object
    req = request.get_json(force=True)

    # fetch action from json
    action = req.get('queryResult').get('action')

    # return a fulfillment response
    return {'fulfillmentText': 'This is a webhook response'}

# create a route for webhook
@app.route('/webhook', methods=['GET', 'POST'])
def webhook():
    # return response
    return make_response(jsonify(results()))

# run the app
if __name__ == '__main__':
   app.run()
You can see that we have fetched "action" from the request using
action = req.get('queryResult').get('action')
```

Initially, this is just a very simple example to demonstrate the request/response (webhook/fulfillment) mechanism. The user should see the following response for the intent:

`This is a webhook response.`

You can see that we have fetched `action` from the request using:

```
action = req.get('queryResult').get('action')
```

Actions were not used in this example, but they can be used for this purpose. We will now look at how to get a response from the server and how it can be handled depending on the response.

Checking responses from a webhook

Using the console on the right side of the window, the intent can be called, and the response can be checked. In the current example, the response will be as follows:

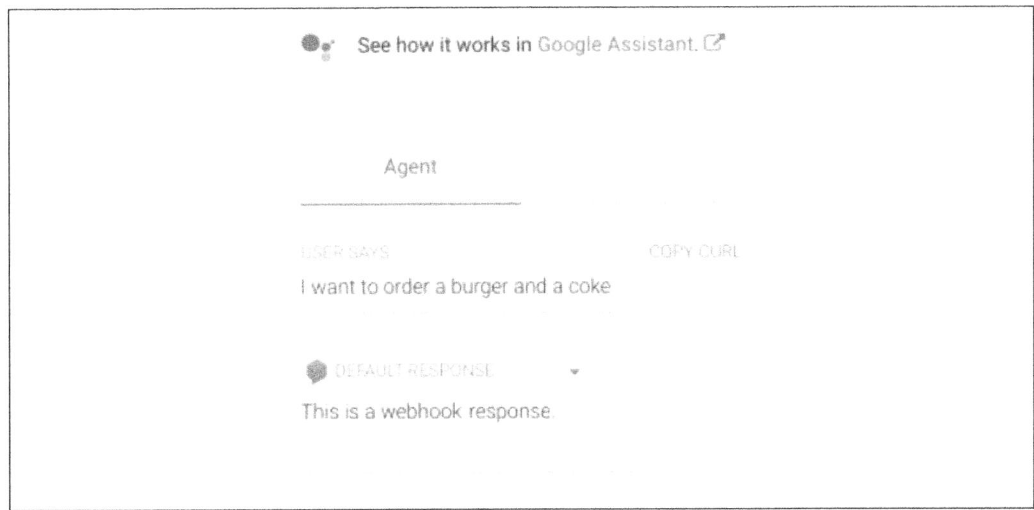

Figure 11: Dialogflow response validation

If we want to debug and troubleshoot the chatbot, we can click on **DIAGNOSTIC INFO**. There, we can view all the DialogFlow request details and the response sent back from the webhook. **DIAGNOSTIC INFO** can also be used for debugging if there is an error in the webhook.

The purpose of this chapter was to present a basic introduction to chatbots. Our chatbot at this point is not doing much other than demonstrating how to get a response from the server. We leave it to you to explore how to further enhance the chatbot. Some obvious enhancements include checking the requested food against an established menu to see if the item is available on the menu; checking the requested amount of food against the current inventory to see if the order can be fulfilled; storing the order in a backend database for accounting and tracking purposes; and connecting the chatbot to a robot or a backend system to actually fulfill the order.

Summary

In this chapter, we first learned about the potential future of chatbots and how they will affect our society as they get better. We then learned about the limitations of current chatbot technology and what the recommended best practices are given the current limitations. We learned about basic chatbot concepts and what the most popular chatbot platforms are.

Finally, we delved deeper into a chatbot platform developed by Google by the name of DialogFlow. We got familiar with this platform by performing a basic exercise and then learning how we can integrate with other backend services using webhooks. We went step by step to understand how to test the chatbot's functionality and make sure it was set up correctly.

In the next chapter, we will jump into another exciting topic and learn how to train sequential data and use it for time series analysis.

17 Sequential Data and Time Series Analysis

In this chapter, we are going to learn how to build sequence learning models. In order to do this, we will cover a number of topics to give us a good grasp of how to build and use these models. We will learn how to handle time series data in Pandas. We will gain an understanding of how to slice time series data and perform various operations on it and then we will discuss how to extract various statistics from time series data on a rolling basis. Following that, we will learn about Hidden Markov Models (HMM) and then implement a system to build those models. We will gain an understanding of how to use Conditional Random Fields to analyze sequences of alphabets, and finally we will discuss how to analyze stock market data using the techniques learned so far.

By the end of this chapter, you will have covered:

- Understanding sequential data
- Handling time series data with Pandas
- Slicing time series data
- Operating on time series data
- Extracting statistics from time series data
- Generating data using Hidden Markov Models
- Identifying alphabet sequences with Conditional Random Fields
- Stock market analysis

Let's begin by looking at and understanding sequential data.

Understanding sequential data

In the world of machine learning, we encounter many types of data, such as images, text, video, and sensor readings. Different types of data require different types of modeling techniques. Sequential data refers to data where the ordering is important. Sequential data can be found in many instances "out in the wild." Here are some examples:

Genomic Sequence Data - This perhaps is the best and most important example we have of sequential data. The sequence in which genes appear is what creates and maintains life at its most basic level. Genomics sequences contain the information that keep us alive.

Human Languages - Order is extremely important when communicating. If we started altering the sequence for the words in this book, it would not take long before the book would become completely incomprehensible!

Computer Languages - In most computer languages, the correct order of inputs is essential for anything to function properly. As an example, the sequence of symbols ">=" means "greater than or equal" in many computer languages but "=>" might mean assignment in some languages or produce a syntax error in others.

Time series data is a subclassification of sequential data. Some examples of time series data are as follows:

Stock market prices - The holy grail of time series data are stock prices. Many data scientists will at some point in their career try to use their data science skills to try to predict the stock market. And many of them will realize what a difficult endeavor it is and move on to other topics and problems. A few reasons why stock prediction is difficult are:

- At different times in the economic cycle, stocks react differently to economic conditions.
- There are many variables that affect stock prices, making it an incredibly complex system.
- Some of the most drastic movements in stocks happen outside of the market trading hours, making it hard to act on that information in real time.

Applications logs - By definition, applications logs have two components. The timestamp indicating when an action occurred, and the information or error being logged.

IoT activity - Activity in IoT devices happens in a temporal sequence manner and can therefore be used as time series data.

Time series data is time stamped values obtained from any data source such as sensors, microphones, stock markets, and so on. Time series data has a lot of important characteristics that need to be modeled in order to be effectively analyzed.

Measurements for certain parameters in time series data are taken at regular time intervals. These measurements are arranged and stored on a timeline, and the order of their appearance is critical. This order is used to extract patterns from the data.

In this chapter, we will see how to build models that describe time series data and sequential data in general. These models will be used to understand the behavior of the time series variable. We will then be able to use these models to predict and extrapolate values that the model has not previously seen.

Time series data analysis is used extensively in finance, sensor data analysis, speech recognition, economics, weather forecasting, manufacturing, and many more areas. In this chapter, we will extensively use a library called Pandas that handles the time series related operations.

Pandas is a powerful and popular Python package used for data manipulation and analysis. Specifically, it offers methods and operations for manipulating tables structures. It's a cute name that evokes furry bears but here's a piece of useless trivia. The name Pandas comes from the term *panel data*, which is an econometrics term for datasets that include observations over multiple time periods.

We will also use a couple of other useful packages like `hmmlearn` and `pystruct`. Make sure you install them before you proceed.

These packages can be installed by running the following commands:

```
$ pip3 install pandas
$ pip3 install hmmlearn
$ pip3 install pystruct
$ pip3 install cvxopt
$ pip3 install timeseries
```

If you get an error when installing `cvxopt`, you will find further instructions at `http://cvxopt.org/install`. Assuming you have successfully installed the packages, let's go ahead to the next section, where we'll look at how to handle time series data with Pandas.

Handling time series data with Pandas

Pandas is arguably the most important library in Python. Learning to use its methods well is paramount, and it will serve you well as you use Python for any of your other projects. In addition to time series analysis, many more functions can be performed with Pandas including:

- DataFrame manipulation with integrated indexing
- Methods to read data from a variety of different file formats and write data into in-memory data structures
- Data sorting
- Data filtering
- Missing value imputation
- Reshaping and pivoting datasets
- Label-based slicing, indexing, and creation of subsets
- Efficient column insertion and deletion
- Group by operations on datasets
- Merging and joining of datasets

In this section, we will use it to convert a sequence of numbers into time series data and visualize it. Pandas provides options to add timestamps, organize data, and then efficiently operate on it.

Create a new Python file and import the following packages:

```
import numpy as np
import matplotlib.pyplot as plt
import pandas as pd
```

Define a function to read the data from the input file. The parameter index indicates the column that contains the relevant data:

```
def read_data(input_file, index):
    # Read the data from the input file
    input_data = np.loadtxt(input_file, delimiter=',')
```

Define a `lambda` function to convert strings to Pandas date format:

```
    # Lambda function to convert strings to Pandas date format
    to_date = lambda x, y: str(int(x)) + '-' + str(int(y))
```

Use this `lambda` function to get the start date from the first line in the input file:

```
    # Extract the start date
    start = to_date(input_data[0, 0], input_data[0, 1])
```

The Pandas library needs the end date to be exclusive when we perform operations, so we need to increase the `date` field in the last line by one month:

```
    # Extract the end date
    if input_data[-1, 1] == 12:
        year = input_data[-1, 0] + 1
        month = 1
    else:
        year = input_data[-1, 0]
        month = input_data[-1, 1] + 1

    end = to_date(year, month)
```

Create a list of indices with dates using the start and end dates with a monthly frequency:

```
    # Create a date list with a monthly frequency
    date_indices = pd.date_range(start, end, freq='M')
```

Create a Pandas data series using the timestamps:

```
    # Add timestamps to the input data to create time series data
    output = pd.Series(input_data[:, index], index=date_indices)

    return output
```

Define the `main` function and specify the input file:

```
if __name__=='__main__':
    # Input filename
    input_file = 'data_2D.txt'
```

Specify the columns that contain the data:

```
    # Specify the columns that need to be converted
    # into time series data
    indices = [2, 3]
```

Iterate through the columns and read the data in each column:

```
# Iterate through the columns and plot the data
for index in indices:
    # Convert the column to timeseries format
    timeseries = read_data(input_file, index)
```

Plot the time series data:

```
    # Plot the data
    plt.figure()
    timeseries.plot()
    plt.title('Dimension ' + str(index - 1))

plt.show()
```

The full code is given in the file `timeseries.py`. If you run the code, you will see two screenshots.

The following screenshot indicates the data in the first dimension:

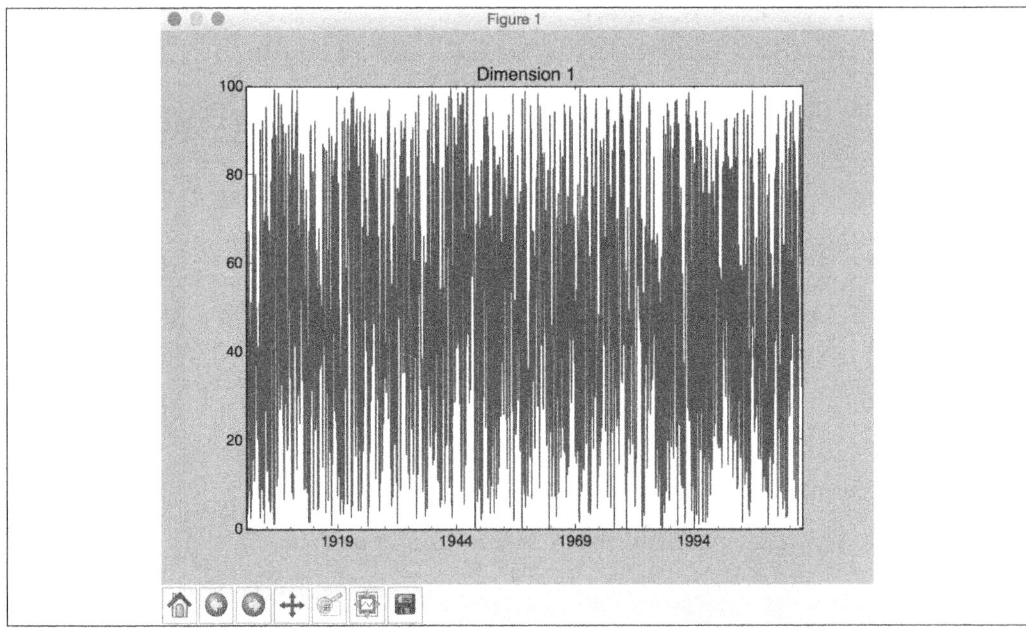

Figure 1: First dimension data plotted using daily data

The second screenshot indicates the data in the second dimension:

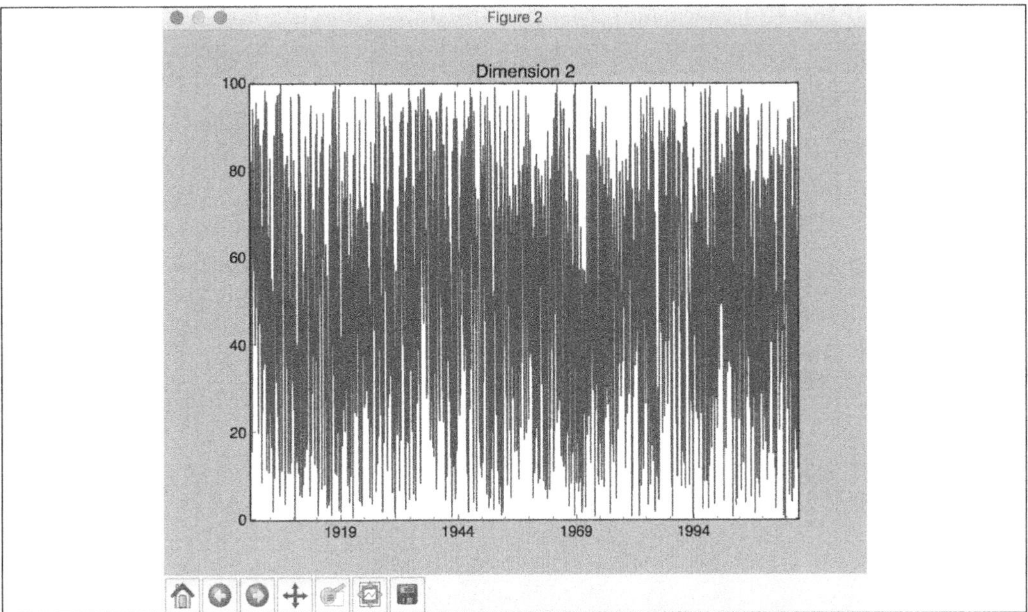

Figure 2: Second dimension data plotted using daily data

In this section, we set the foundation of how to use Pandas to load data from an external file, how to convert it into time series format, and then how to plot it and visualize it. In the next section, we will learn how to further manipulate the data.

Slicing time series data

Now that we loaded the time series data, let's see how we can slice it. The process of slicing refers to dividing the data into various sub-intervals and extracting relevant information. This is useful when we are working with time series datasets. Instead of using indices, we will use timestamps to slice our data.

Create a new Python file and import the following packages:

```
import numpy as np
import matplotlib.pyplot as plt
import pandas as pd

from timeseries import read_data
```

Load the third column (zero-indexed) from the input data file:

```
# Load input data
index = 2
data = read_data('data_2D.txt', index)
```

Define the start and end years, and then plot the data with year-level granularity:

```
# Plot data with year-level granularity
start = '2003'
end = '2011'
plt.figure()
data[start:end].plot()
plt.title('Input data from ' + start + ' to ' + end)
```

Define the start and end months, and then plot the data with month-level granularity:

```
# Plot data with month-level granularity
start = '1998-2'
end = '2006-7'
plt.figure()
data[start:end].plot()
plt.title('Input data from ' + start + ' to ' + end)


plt.show()
```

The full code is given in the file `slicer.py`. If you run the code, you will see two figures.

The first screenshot shows the data from *2003* to *2011*:

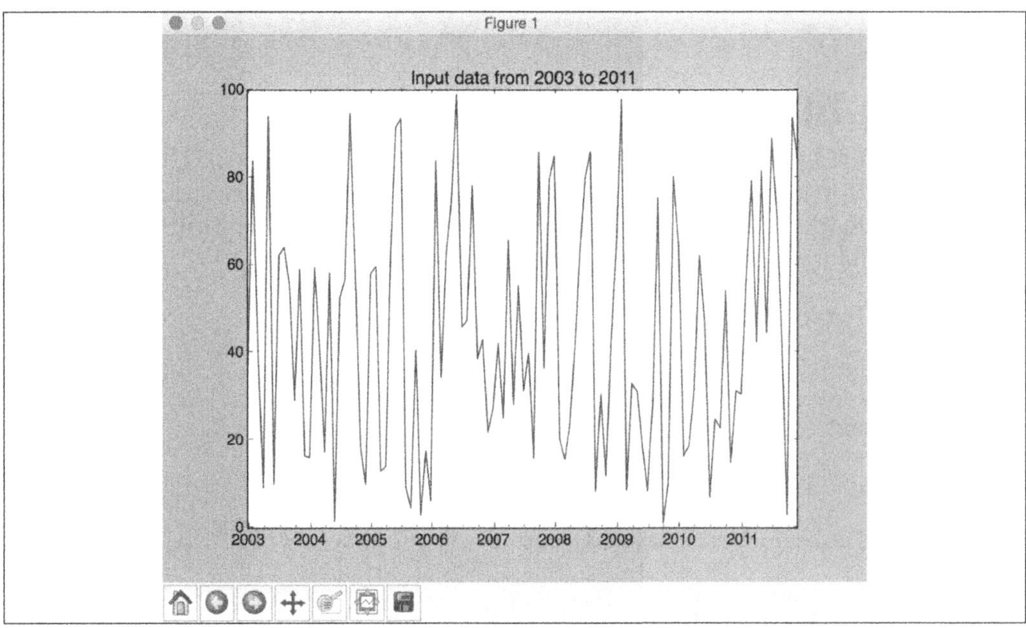

Figure 3: Data plotted using monthly ticks (2003 – 2011)

The second screenshot shows the data from *February 1998* to *July 2006*:

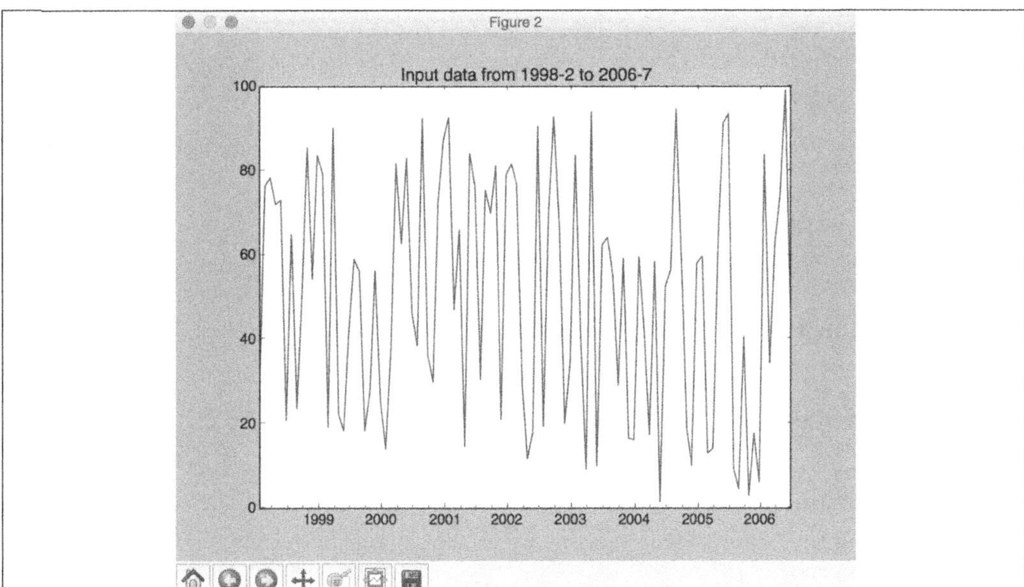

Figure 4: Data plotted using monthly ticks (1998 – 2006)

As we saw in the charts created in the previous section (*Figure 1* and *Figure 2*), they were hard to read. The data was "bunched up." By slicing the data using monthly ticks, it is much easier to visualize the up and downs in the data. In the next section, we will continue to learn about the different functionality available in the Pandas library such as filtering and summation and how this functionality can help to better analyze and visualize datasets.

Operating on time series data

The Pandas library can operate on time series data efficiently and perform various operations like filtering and addition. Conditions can be set, and Pandas will filter the dataset and return the right subset based on the condition. Time series data can be loaded and filtered as well. Let's look at another example to illustrate this.

Create a new Python file and import the following packages:

```
import numpy as np
import pandas as pd
import matplotlib.pyplot as plt


from timeseries import read_data
```

Define the input filename:

```
# Input filename
input_file = 'data_2D.txt'
```

Load the third and fourth columns into separate variables:

```
# Load data
x1 = read_data(input_file, 2)
x2 = read_data(input_file, 3)
```

Create a Pandas `DataFrame` object by naming the two dimensions:

```
# Create pandas dataframe for slicing
data = pd.DataFrame({'dim1': x1, 'dim2': x2})
```

Plot the data by specifying the start and end years:

```
# Plot data
start = '1968'
end = '1975'
data[start:end].plot()
plt.title('Data overlapped on top of each other')
```

Filter the data using conditions and then display it. In this case, we will take all the datapoints in `dim1` that are less than `45` and all the values in `dim2` that are greater than `30`:

```
# Filtering using conditions
# - 'dim1' is smaller than a certain threshold
# - 'dim2' is greater than a certain threshold
data[(data['dim1'] < 45) & (data['dim2'] > 30)].plot()
plt.title('dim1 < 45 and dim2 > 30')
```

We can also add two series in Pandas. Let's add `dim1` and `dim2` between the given start and end dates:

```
# Adding two dataframes
plt.figure()
diff = data[start:end]['dim1'] + data[start:end]['dim2']
diff.plot()
plt.title('Summation (dim1 + dim2)')

plt.show()
```

The full code is given in the file `operator.py`. If you run the code, you will see three screenshots. The first screenshot shows the data from *1968* to *1975*:

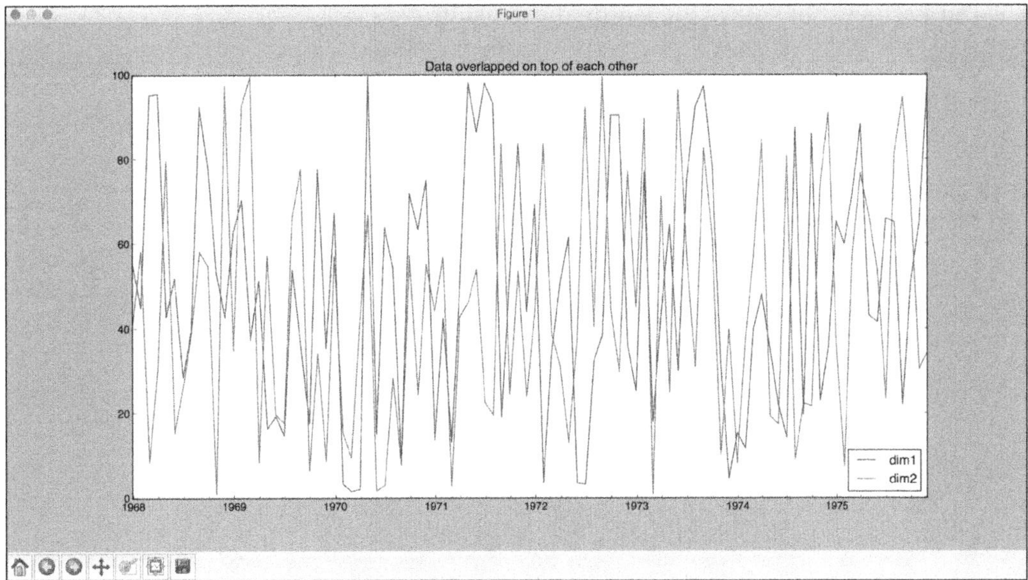

Figure 5: Overlapped data (1968 - 1975)

The second screenshot shows the filtered data:

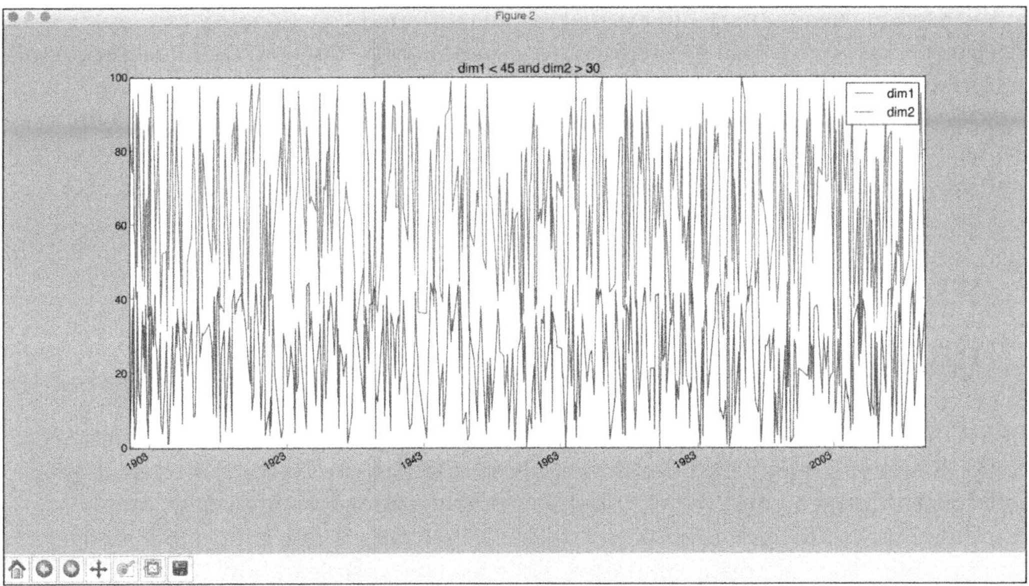

Figure 6: Data with dim < 45 and dim > 30 (1968 - 1975)

The third screenshot shows the summation result:

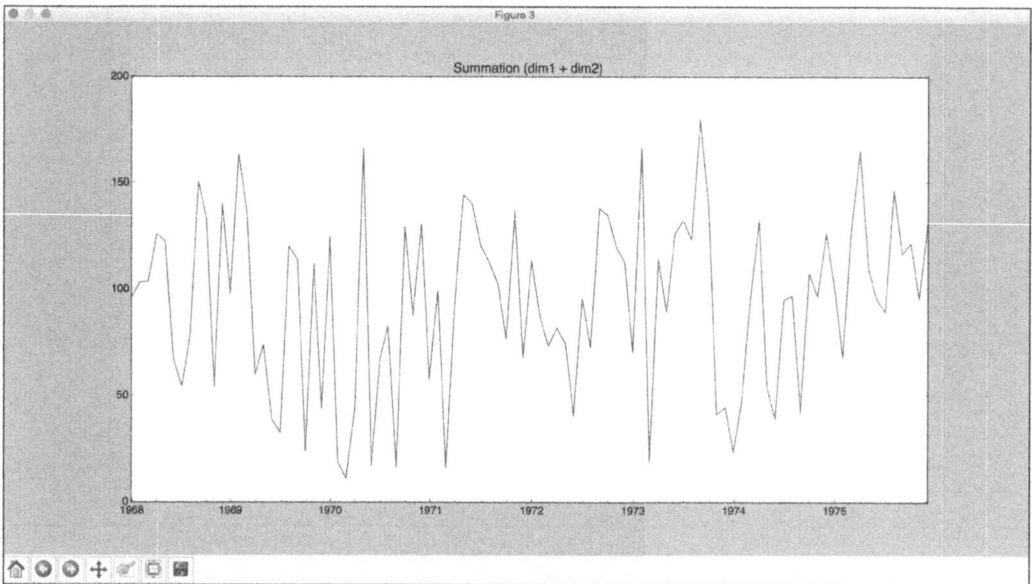

Figure 7: Summation of dim1 and dim2 (1968 - 1975)

In this section, we continued to learn about the different functionality available in the Pandas library including filtering and summation. In data science, it is important before selecting and training models to understand the datasets that are being analyzed. Pandas is a useful tool to accomplish this. In the next section, we will introduce two more useful libraries. These libraries are used to calculate various statistics about datasets.

Extracting statistics from time series data

In order to extract meaningful insights from time series data, we can generate statistics from it. Examples of these statistics are operations like mean, variance, correlation, maximum value, and so on. These statistics can be computed on a rolling basis using a window. We can use a predetermined window size and compute these statistics within that window. When we visualize the statistics over time, we might see interesting patterns. Let's see an example of how to extract these statistics from time series data.

Create a new Python file and import the following packages:

```
import numpy as np
import matplotlib.pyplot as plt
import pandas as pd

from timeseries import read_data
```

Define the input filename:

```
# Input filename
input_file = 'data_2D.txt'
```

Load the third and fourth columns into separate variables:

```
# Load input data in time series format
x1 = read_data(input_file, 2)
x2 = read_data(input_file, 3)
```

Create a Pandas `DataFrame` by naming the two dimensions:

```
# Create pandas dataframe for slicing
data = pd.DataFrame({'dim1': x1, 'dim2': x2})
```

Extract maximum and minimum values along each dimension:

```
# Extract max and min values
print('\nMaximum values for each dimension:')
print(data.max())
print('\nMinimum values for each dimension:')
print(data.min())
```

Extract the overall mean and the row-wise mean for the first `12` rows:

```
# Extract overall mean and row-wise mean values
print('\nOverall mean:')
print(data.mean())
print('\nRow-wise mean:')
print(data.mean(1)[:12])
```

Plot the rolling mean using a window size of `24`:

```
# Plot the rolling mean using a window size of 24
data.rolling(center=False, window=24).mean().plot()
plt.title('Rolling mean')
```

Print the correlation coefficients:

```
# Extract correlation coefficients
print('\nCorrelation coefficients:\n', data.corr())
```

Plot the rolling correlation using a window size of `60`:

```
# Plot rolling correlation using a window size of 60
plt.figure()
plt.title('Rolling correlation')
data['dim1'].rolling(window=60).corr(other=data['dim2']).plot()


plt.show()
```

The full code is given in the file `stats_extractor.py`. If you run the code, you will see two screenshots. The first screenshot shows the rolling mean:

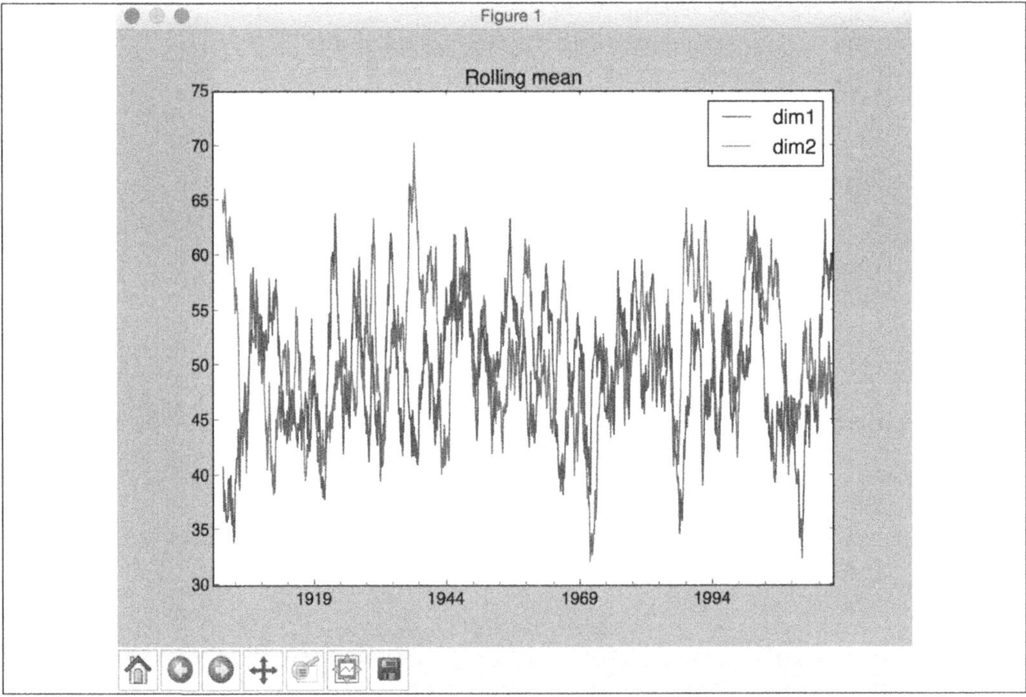

Figure 8: Rolling mean

The second screenshot shows the rolling correlation:

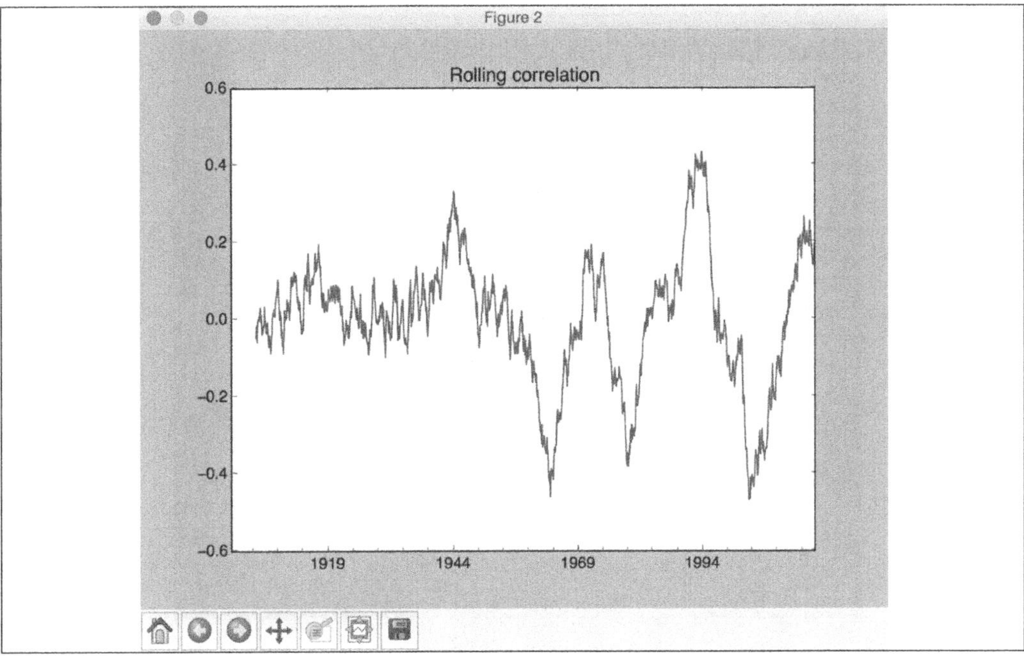

Figure 9: Rolling correlation

You should also see the following output:

```
Maximum values for each dimension:
dim1    99.98
dim2    99.97
dtype: float64

Minimum values for each dimension:
dim1    0.18
dim2    0.16
dtype: float64

Overall mean:
dim1    49.030541
dim2    50.983291
dtype: float64
```

Figure 10: Maximum and minimum dimension and overall mean

If you scroll down, you will see row-wise mean values and the correlation coefficients printed out:

```
Row-wise mean:
1900-01-31    85.595
1900-02-28    75.310
1900-03-31    27.700
1900-04-30    44.675
1900-05-31    31.295
1900-06-30    44.160
1900-07-31    67.415
1900-08-31    56.160
1900-09-30    51.495
1900-10-31    61.260
1900-11-30    30.925
1900-12-31    30.785
Freq: M, dtype: float64

Correlation coefficients:
          dim1     dim2
dim1  1.00000  0.00627
dim2  0.00627  1.00000
```

Figure 11: Row-wise mean and correlation coefficients

The correlation coefficients in the preceding figures indicate the level of correlation of each dimension with all the other dimensions. A correlation of `1.0` indicates perfect correlation, whereas a correlation of `0.0` indicates that the variables are not related to each other at all. `dim1` is perfectly correlated to `dim1` and `dim2` is perfectly correlated to `dim2`. This will always be the case in any confusion matrix. It is just saying that a variable is perfectly correlated to itself. Additionally, `dim1` has a low correlation to `dim2`. This means that `dim1` will have low power to predict the value of `dim2`. So far, we will not be becoming millionaires any time soon from our models and their ability to predict stock prices. In the next section, we will learn about a useful technique to analyze time series data called **Hidden Markov Models** (**HMMs**).

Generating data using Hidden Markov Models

A **Hidden Markov Model** (**HMM**) is a powerful analysis technique for analyzing sequential data. It assumes that the system being modeled is a Markov process with hidden states. This means that the underlying system can be one among a set of possible states.

It goes through a sequence of state transitions, thereby producing a sequence of outputs. We can only observe the outputs but not the states. Hence these states are hidden from us. Our goal is to model the data so that we can infer the state transitions of unknown data.

In order to understand HMMs, let's consider a version of the **traveling salesman problem** (**TSP**). In this example, a salesman must travel between the following three cities for his job – London, Barcelona, and New York. His goal is to minimize the traveling time so that he can be the most efficient. Considering his work commitments and schedule, we have a set of probabilities that dictate the chances of going from city *X* to city *Y*. In the following information given, *P(X -> Y)* indicates the probability of going from city *X* to city *Y*:

City	**Probability**
P(London -> London)	0.10
P(London -> Barcelona)	0.70
P(London -> NY)	0.20
P(Barcelona -> Barcelona)	0.15
P(Barcelona -> London)	0.75
P(Barcelona -> NY)	0.10
P(NY -> NY)	0.05
P(NY -> London)	0.60
P(NY -> Barcelona)	0.35

Let's represent this information with a transition matrix:

	London	**Barcelona**	**NY**
London	0.10	0.70	0.20
Barcelona	0.75	0.15	0.10
NY	0.60	0.35	0.05

Now that we have all the information, let's go ahead and set the problem statement. The salesman starts his journey on Tuesday from London, and plans something on Friday. But that will depend on where he is. What is the probability that he will be in Barcelona on Friday? This table will help us figure it out.

If we do not have a Markov Chain to model this problem, then we will not know what the travel schedule looks like. Our goal is to say with a good amount of certainty that he will be in each city on a given day.

If we denote the transition matrix by *T* and the current day by *X(i)*, then:

X(i+1) = X(i).T

In our case, Friday is 3 days away from Tuesday. This means we need to compute *X(i+3)*. The computations will look like this:

X(i+1) = X(i).T

X(i+2) = X(i+1).T

X(i+3) = X(i+2).T

So, in essence:

X(i+3) = X(i).T^3

We set *X(i)* to:

X(i) = [0.10 0.70 0.20]

The next step is to compute the cube of the matrix. There are many tools available online to perform matrix operations such as:

`http://matrix.reshish.com/multiplication.php`

If you do all the matrix calculations, then you will see that you will get the following probabilities for Thursday:

P(London) = 0.31

P(Barcelona) = 0.53

P(NY) = 0.16

We can see that there is a higher chance of him being in Barcelona than in any other city. This makes geographical sense as well because Barcelona is closer to London compared to New York. Let's see how to model HMMs in Python.

Create a new Python file and import the following packages:

```
import datetime

import numpy as np
import matplotlib.pyplot as plt
from hmmlearn.hmm import GaussianHMM

from timeseries import read_data
```

Load data from the input file:

```
# Load input data
data = np.loadtxt('data_1D.txt', delimiter=',')
```

Extract the third column for training:

```
# Extract the data column (third column) for training
X = np.column_stack([data[:, 2]])
```

Create a Gaussian HMM with `5` components and diagonal covariance:

```
# Create a Gaussian HMM
num_components = 5
hmm = GaussianHMM(n_components=num_components,
        covariance_type='diag', n_iter=1000)
```

Train the HMM:

```
# Train the HMM
print('\nTraining the Hidden Markov Model...')
hmm.fit(X)
```

Print the mean and variance values for each component of the HMM:

```
# Print HMM stats
print('\nMeans and variances:')
for i in range(hmm.n_components):
    print('\nHidden state', i+1)
    print('Mean =', round(hmm.means_[i][0], 2))
    print('Variance =', round(np.diag(hmm.covars_[i])[0], 2))
```

Generate `1200` samples using the trained HMM and plot them:

```
# Generate data using the HMM model
num_samples = 1200
generated_data, _ = hmm.sample(num_samples)
plt.plot(np.arange(num_samples), generated_data[:, 0], c='black')
plt.title('Generated data')

plt.show()
```

The full code is given in the file `hmm.py`. If you run the code, you will see the following screenshot, which shows the 1200 generated samples:

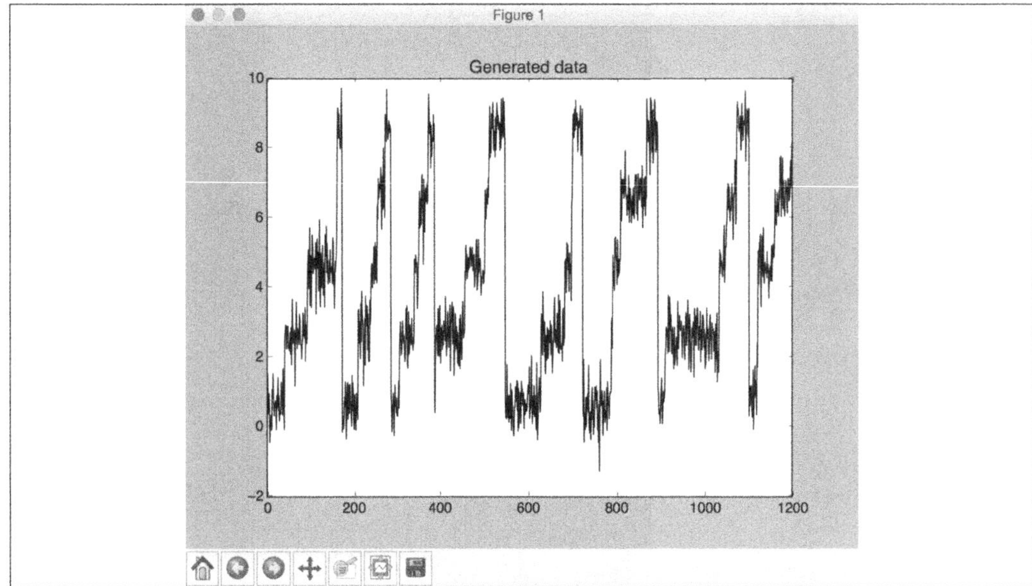

Figure 12: Generated data

You will also see the following output:

```
Training the Hidden Markov Model...

Means and variances:

Hidden state 1
Mean = 4.6
Variance = 0.25

Hidden state 2
Mean = 6.59
Variance = 0.25

Hidden state 3
Mean = 0.6
Variance = 0.25

Hidden state 4
Mean = 8.6
Variance = 0.26

Hidden state 5
Mean = 2.6
Variance = 0.26
```

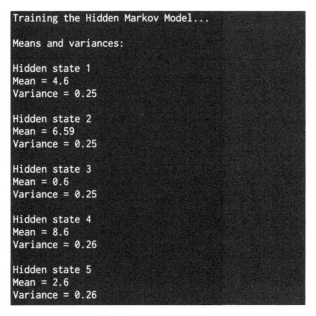

Figure 13: HMM training

The way we can interpret the chart is the different times it will take to traverse the sales routes, given the different itineraries. The second output indicates the mean and variances for these routes.

Now that we have learned about HMMs let's learn about another topic relevant to time series analysis. In the next section, we will learn about a probabilistic model commonly known as Conditional Random Fields and how they differ from HMMs.

Identifying alphabet sequences with Conditional Random Fields

Conditional Random Fields (**CRFs**) are probabilistic models that are frequently used to analyze structured data. We use them to label and segment sequential data in various forms. Following are some of the most common use cases where CRFs are applied:

- Handwriting recognition
- Character recognition
- Object detection
- Named entity recognition
- Gene prediction
- Image segmentation
- Part of speech tagging
- Noise reduction

One item of note regarding CRFs is that they are discriminative models. Contrast this with HMMs, which are generative models.

We can define a conditional probability distribution over a labeled sequence of measurements. We will use this to build a CRF model. In HMMs, we define a joint distribution over the observation sequence and the labels.

One of the main advantages of CRFs is that they are conditional by nature. This is not the case with HMMs. CRFs do not assume any independence between output observations. HMMs assume that the output at any given time is statistically independent of the previous data point. HMMs must make this assumption to ensure that the inference process works in a robust way. But this assumption is not always true. Real-world data is filled with temporal dependencies.

CRFs tend to outperform HMMs in a variety of applications such as natural language processing, speech recognition, biotechnology, and so on. In this section, we will discuss how to use CRFs to analyze and identify words.

This is a good use case that will highlight the ability to identify dependencies in the data. The order of letters for words in the English language is by no means random. For example, consider the word *random*. The probability that the next letter after the first letter is going to be a vowel is higher than the probability of it being a consonant. The probability that the second letter in a word is going to be the letter *x* is not zero. We can think of a couple words that meet this criterion - exempt, exact, exhibit, and so on. But what is the probability that the second letter in a word is an *x* given that the first letter is an *r*? We can't think of a word that fits that criterion. Even if they exist, there are not that many, so the probability is lower. CRFs take advantage of this fact.

Create a new Python file and import the following packages:

```
import os
import argparse
import string
import pickle

import numpy as np
import matplotlib.pyplot as plt
from pystruct.datasets import load_letters
from pystruct.models import ChainCRF
from pystruct.learners import FrankWolfeSSVM
```

Define a function to parse the input arguments. We can pass the `C` value as the input parameter. The `C` parameter controls how much we want to penalize misclassification. A higher value of `C` would mean that we are imposing a higher penalty for misclassification during training, but we might end up overfitting the model. On the other hand, if we choose a lower value for `C`, we are allowing the model to better generalize. But this also means that we are imposing a lower penalty for misclassification of training data points.

```
def build_arg_parser():
    parser = argparse.ArgumentParser(description='Trains a 
Conditional\
            Random Field classifier')
    parser.add_argument("--C", dest="c_val", required=False, 
type=float,
            default=1.0, help='C value to be used for training')
    return parser
```

Define a class to handle all the functionality of building the CRF model. We will use a chain CRF model with `FrankWolfeSSVM`:

```
# Class to model the CRF
class CRFModel(object):
    def __init__(self, c_val=1.0):
        self.clf = FrankWolfeSSVM(model=ChainCRF(),
                C=c_val, max_iter=50)
```

Define a function to load the training data:

```
    # Load the training data
    def load_data(self):
        alphabets = load_letters()
        X = np.array(alphabets['data'])
        y = np.array(alphabets['labels'])
        folds = alphabets['folds']

        return X, y, folds
```

Define a function to train the CRF model:

```
    # Train the CRF
    def train(self, X_train, y_train):
        self.clf.fit(X_train, y_train)
```

Define a function to evaluate the accuracy of the CRF model:

```
    # Evaluate the accuracy of the CRF
    def evaluate(self, X_test, y_test):
        return self.clf.score(X_test, y_test)
```

Define a function to run the trained CRF model on an unknown datapoint:

```
    # Run the CRF on unknown data
    def classify(self, input_data):
        return self.clf.predict(input_data)[0]
```

Define a function to extract a substring from the alphabets based on a list of indices:

```
# Convert indices to alphabets
def convert_to_letters(indices):
    # Create a numpy array of all alphabets
    alphabets = np.array(list(string.ascii_lowercase))
```

Extract the letters:

```
    # Extract the letters based on input indices
    output = np.take(alphabets, indices)
    output = ''.join(output)

    return output
```

Define the main function and parse the input arguments:

```
if __name__=='__main__':
    args = build_arg_parser().parse_args()
    c_val = args.c_val
```

Create the CRF model object:

```
    # Create the CRF model
    crf = CRFModel(c_val)
```

Load the input data and separate it into train and test sets:

```
    # Load the train and test data
    X, y, folds = crf.load_data()
    X_train, X_test = X[folds == 1], X[folds != 1]
    y_train, y_test = y[folds == 1], y[folds != 1]
```

Train the CRF model:

```
    # Train the CRF model
    print('\nTraining the CRF model...')
    crf.train(X_train, y_train)
```

Evaluate the accuracy of the CRF model and print it:

```
    # Evaluate the accuracy
    score = crf.evaluate(X_test, y_test)
    print('\nAccuracy score =', str(round(score*100, 2)) + '%')
```

Run it on some test data points and print the output:

```
    indices = range(3000, len(y_test), 200)
    for index in indices:
        print("\nOriginal  =", convert_to_letters(y_test[index]))
        predicted = crf.classify([X_test[index]])
        print("Predicted =", convert_to_letters(predicted))
```

The full code is given in the file `crf.py`. If you run the code, you should see the following output:

```
Training the CRF model...

Accuracy score = 77.93%

Original  = rojections
Predicted = rojectiong

Original  = uff
Predicted = ufr

Original  = kiing
Predicted = kiing

Original  = ecompress
Predicted = ecomertig

Original  = uzz
Predicted = vex

Original  = poiling
Predicted = aciting
```

Figure 14: CRF model training

If you scroll to the end, you should also see the following output:

```
Original  = abulously
Predicted = abuloualy

Original  = ormalization
Predicted = ormalisation

Original  = ake
Predicted = aka

Original  = afeteria
Predicted = ateteria

Original  = obble
Predicted = obble

Original  = hadow
Predicted = habow

Original  = ndustrialized
Predicted = ndusqrialyled

Original  = ympathetically
Predicted = ympnshetically
```

Figure 15: Original vs. predicted outputs

As we can see, it predicts most of the words correctly. Hopefully, we were able to illustrate the power of CRFs and how they differ from HMMs. In the next section, we will revisit HMMs and apply them in an example to analyze stock market data.

Stock market analysis

We will analyze stock market data in this section using HMMs. This is an example where the data is already organized and timestamped. We will use the dataset available in the `matplotlib` package. The dataset contains the stock values of various companies over the years. HMMs are generative models that can analyze such time series data and extract the underlying structure. We will use this model to analyze stock price variations and generate the outputs.

Please do not expect that the results generated by this model will be anywhere near production quality and that you will be able to use this model to perform live trading and make money doing so. It will provide a foundation that can be used to start thinking about how this can be accomplished. If you are so inclined, we encourage you to continue to enhance the model and stress it against different datasets and perhaps use it with current market data. We do not make any representations about how profitable or unprofitable the model might be.

Create a new Python file and import the following packages:

```
import datetime
import warnings

import numpy as np
import matplotlib.pyplot as plt
import yfinance as yf
from hmmlearn.hmm import GaussianHMM
```

Load historical stock market quotes from September 4, 1970 to May 17, 2016. You are free to choose any date range you wish:

```
# Load historical stock quotes from matplotlib package
start_date = datetime.date(1970, 9, 4)
end_date = datetime.date(2016, 5, 17)
intc = yf.Ticker('INTC').history(start=start_date, end=end_date)
```

Take the percentage difference of closing quotes each day:

```
# Take the percentage difference of closing stock prices
diff_percentages = 100.0 * np.diff(intc.Close) / intc.Close[:-1]
```

Stack the two data columns to create the training dataset:

```
# Stack the differences and volume values
# column-wise for training
training_data = np.column_stack([diff_percentages, intc.Volume[:-1]])
```

Create and train the Gaussian HMM with `7` components and diagonal covariance:

```
# Create and train Gaussian HMM
hmm = GaussianHMM(n_components=7, covariance_type='diag', n_iter=1000)
with warnings.catch_warnings():
    warnings.simplefilter('ignore')
    hmm.fit(training_data)
```

Use the trained HMM model to generate `300` samples. You can choose to generate any number of samples you want.

```
# Generate data using the HMM model
num_samples = 300
samples, _ = hmm.sample(num_samples)
```

Plot the generated values for difference percentages:

```
# Plot the difference percentages
plt.figure()
plt.title('Difference percentages')
plt.plot(np.arange(num_samples), samples[:, 0], c='black')
```

Plot the generated values for volume of shares traded:

```
# Plot the volume of shares traded
plt.figure()
plt.title('Volume of shares')
plt.plot(np.arange(num_samples), samples[:, 1], c='black')
plt.ylim(ymin=0)

plt.show()
```

The full code is given in the file `stock_market.py`. If you run the code, you will see the following two screenshots. The first screenshot shows the difference percentages generated by the HMM:

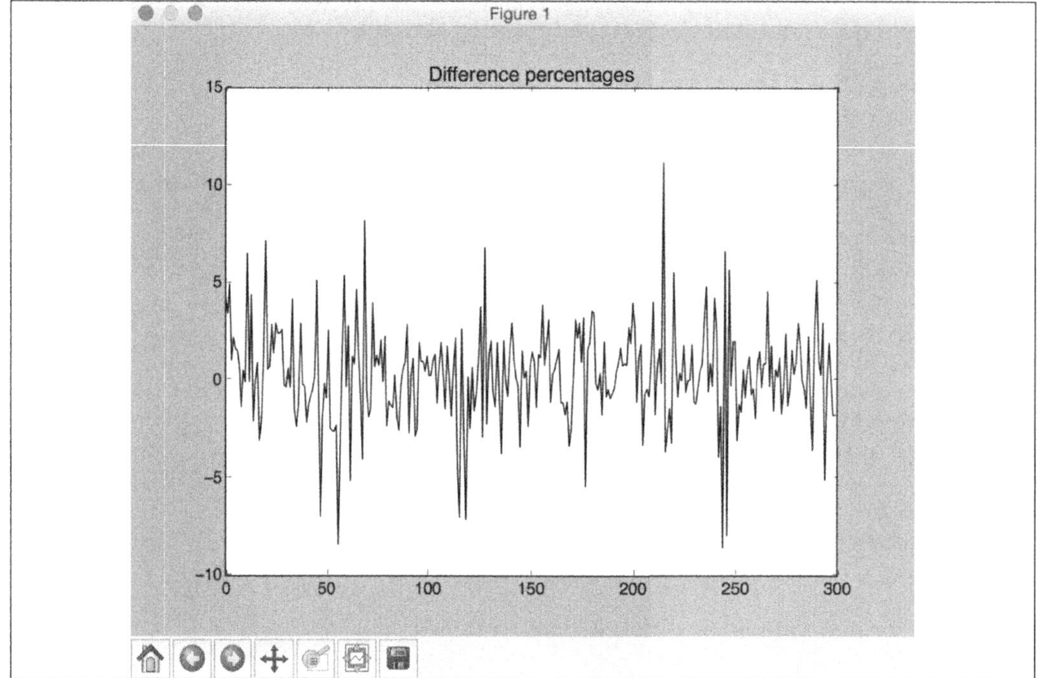

Figure 16: Difference percentages

The second screenshot shows the values generated by the HMM for volume of shares traded:

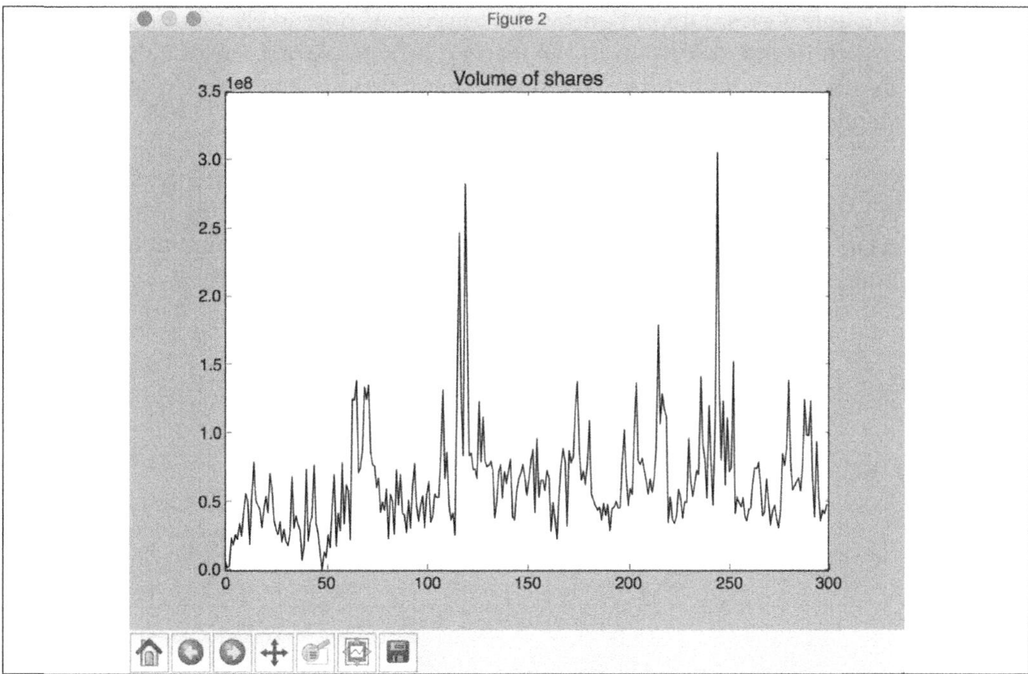

Figure 17: Volume of shares

We leave it to the reader to calculate the accuracy of the values predicted by the HMM model against the actual data points in the dataset. It will then take some work to use it to produce trading signals. As we mentioned at the beginning of the section, we do not recommend using this code to perform actual trades using real money.

Summary

In this chapter, we learned how to build sequence learning models. We understood how to handle time series data in Pandas. We discussed how to slice time series data and perform various operations on it. We learned how to extract various stats from time series data in a rolling manner. We understood Hidden Markov Models and then implemented a system to build that model.

We discussed how to use Conditional Random Fields to analyze sequences of alphabets. We learned how to analyze stock market data using various techniques. In the next chapter, we'll move on to learn about how AI can be implemented within the area of image recognition.

18
Image Recognition

In this chapter, we are going to learn about object detection and tracking. First, we will spend some time understanding why image recognition is important for machine learning. We will then learn about an image recognition package called OpenCV, which is a popular library for computer vision. We will also learn how to install OpenCV and discuss frame differencing to see how we can detect the moving parts in a video. We will learn how to track objects using color spaces, and how to use background subtraction to track objects. After that we will build an interactive object tracker using the CAMShift algorithm and learn how to build an optical flow-based tracker. We will discuss face detection and associated concepts such as Haar cascades and integral images. We will then use this technique to build an eye detector and tracker.

By the end of this chapter, you will know about:

- Installing OpenCV
- Frame differencing
- Tracking objects using color spaces
- Object tracking using background subtraction
- Building an interactive object tracker using the CAMShift algorithm
- Optical flow-based tracking
- Face detection and tracking
- Using Haar cascades for object detection
- Using integral images for feature extraction
- Eye detection and tracking

We'll begin by introducing OpenCV and we'll run through how to install it.

Importance of image recognition

As it has hopefully become clear from the topics in this book, artificial intelligence in general, and machine learning in particular, are some of the technologies that are driving the digital transformation happening in today's society. Being able to "see" is a critical component of the learning process in humans. Similarly, even though they use different method to "see," capturing images and recognizing what is contained in those images is of paramount importance to computers in order to create datasets to feed machine learning pipelines and obtain insight from that data.

An obvious example of this is self-driving technology. In this case computers, just like their human counterparts, need to be able to ingest gigabytes worth of data in any given second, analyze that data, and make life altering decisions in real time. I am very excited for the day when this technology becomes widely available; my estimation is that this will happen sooner rather than later. According to the World Health Organization there were 1.25 million road traffic deaths in 2013. A big percentage of this will likely be avoided when self-driving cars get deployed.

Self-driving technology is just one application of image recognition and the applications are almost limitless, only bounded by our imagination. Some of the other popular uses are:

Automated image classification - We can see first - hand examples of this in Google Photos and when uploading images to Facebook and seeing how Facebook gives us suggestions about who is in the picture.

Reverse image search - Google, among others, offers a feature where instead of using keywords as input and getting images as a result, you can use an image as the input and Google provides guesses as to what the image contains. You can try here:

`https://images.google.com/`

Optical character recognition - Converting images to text relies heavily on image recognition.

MRI and ultrasound interpretation - Some tools are outperforming humans in the recognition of cancers and other diseases.

Having considered some practical applications of image recognition, let's get into the package we'll be using in order to see it for ourselves.

OpenCV

We will be using a package called OpenCV in this chapter. **OpenCV** (**Open Source Computer Vision**) as the name implies is an open source cross-platform Python package that can be used to enable real-time computer vision. The tool has its origins in Intel Labs.

OpenCV can be used in conjunction with TensorFlow, PyTorch, and Caffe.

Installation

We will be using a package called OpenCV in this chapter. You can learn more about it here: `http://opencv.org`. Make sure to install it before you proceed. Here are the links to install OpenCV 3 with Python 3 on various operating systems:

- **Windows**: `https://solarianprogrammer.com/2016/09/17/install-opencv-3-with-python-3-on-windows`
- **Ubuntu**: `http://www.pyimagesearch.com/2015/07/20/install-opencv-3-0-and-python-3-4-on-ubuntu`
- **Mac**: `http://www.pyimagesearch.com/2015/06/29/install-opencv-3-0-and-python-3-4-on-osx`

Now that you have installed it, let's go to the next section where we'll discuss frame differencing.

Frame differencing

Frame differencing is one of the simplest techniques that can be used to identify the moving parts in a video. Intuitively, in most applications this is where the fun part exists. If we have a video of a runner, we probably want to analyze the runner as they run and not the background images. When we watch a movie, we focus mostly on the characters in the forefront while they talk and do things. We don't tend to focus on the boring picture frames in the background.

Occasionally, you get the one-off geek that finds a problem in a movie hidden in this background, as we saw a couple of times in recent episodes of *Game of Thrones* when people found a cup of Starbucks in the background, but this is the exception rather than the rule.

When we are looking at a live video stream, the differences between consecutive frames captured from the stream gives us a lot of information. Let's see how we can take the differences between consecutive frames and display the differences. The code in this section requires an attached camera, so make sure you have a camera on your machine.

Create a new Python file and import the following package:

```
import cv2
```

Define a function to compute the frame differences. Start by computing the difference between the current frame and the next frame:

```
# Compute the frame differences
def frame_diff(prev_frame, cur_frame, next_frame):
    # Difference between the current frame and the next frame
    diff_frames_1 = cv2.absdiff(next_frame, cur_frame)
```

Compute the difference between the current frame and the previous frame:

```
    # Difference between the current frame and the previous frame
    diff_frames_2 = cv2.absdiff(cur_frame, prev_frame)
```

Compute the bitwise AND between the two difference frames and return it:

```
    return cv2.bitwise_and(diff_frames_1, diff_frames_2)
```

Define a function to grab the current frame from the webcam. Start by reading it from the video capture object:

```
# Define a function to get the current frame from the webcam
def get_frame(cap, scaling_factor):
    # Read the current frame from the video capture object
    _, frame = cap.read()
```

Resize the frame based on the scaling factor and return it:

```
    # Resize the image
    frame = cv2.resize(frame, None, fx=scaling_factor,
            fy=scaling_factor, interpolation=cv2.INTER_AREA)
```

Convert the image to grayscale and return it:

```
    # Convert to grayscale
    gray = cv2.cvtColor(frame, cv2.COLOR_RGB2GRAY)

    return gray
```

Define the `main` function and initialize the video capture object:

```
if __name__=='__main__':
    # Define the video capture object
    cap = cv2.VideoCapture(0)
```

Define the scaling factor to resize the images:

```
    # Define the scaling factor for the images
    scaling_factor = 0.5
```

Grab the current frame, the next frame, and the frame after that:

```
    # Grab the current frame
    prev_frame = get_frame(cap, scaling_factor)

    # Grab the next frame
    cur_frame = get_frame(cap, scaling_factor)

    # Grab the frame after that
    next_frame = get_frame(cap, scaling_factor)
```

Iterate indefinitely until the user presses the *Esc* key. Start by computing the frame differences:

```
    # Keep reading the frames from the webcam
    # until the user hits the 'Esc' key
    while True:
        # Display the frame difference
        cv2.imshow('Object Movement', frame_diff(prev_frame,
                cur_frame, next_frame))
```

Update the `frame` variables:

```
        # Update the variables
        prev_frame = cur_frame
        cur_frame = next_frame
```

Grab the next frame from the webcam:

```
        # Grab the next frame
        next_frame = get_frame(cap, scaling_factor)
```

Check if the user pressed the *Esc* key. If so, exit the loop:

```
        # Check if the user hit the 'Esc' key
        key = cv2.waitKey(10)
        if key == 27:
            break
```

Once you exit the loop, make sure that all the windows are closed properly:

```
# Close all the windows
cv2.destroyAllWindows()
```

The full code is given in the file `frame_diff.py` provided to you. If you run the code, you will see an output window showing a live output. If you move around, you will see your silhouette as shown here:

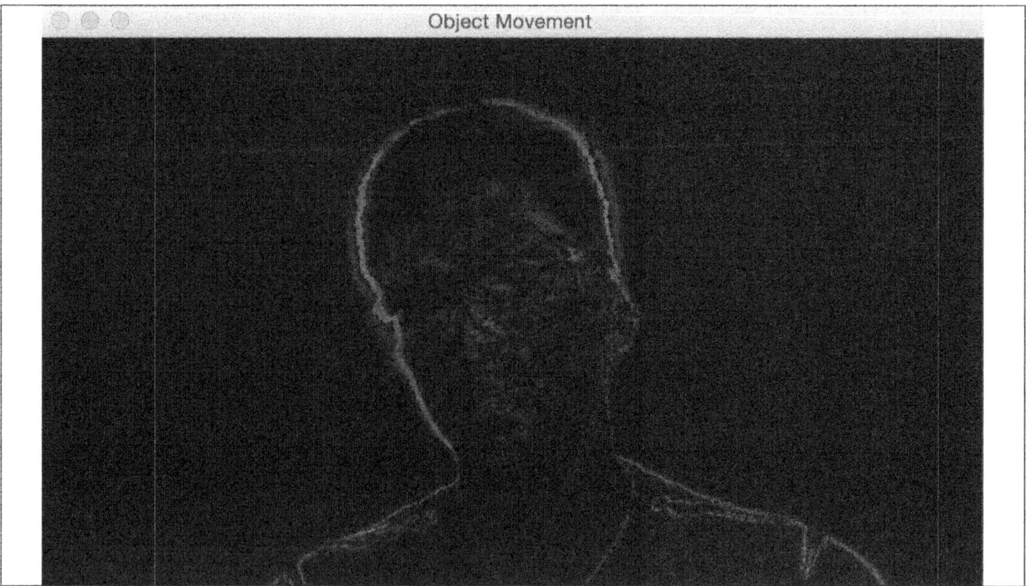

Figure 1: Silhouette images

The white lines in the preceding screenshot represent the silhouette. What did we achieve? Why is this important? Depending on the application, we might not need all the information that the original images provided. The original images had a lot more detail, a lot more contrast, and many more colors. Let's use the self-driving car example. We probably don't care that the car in front of us is red or green. We are much more concerned to know if the car is heading towards us and about to crash into us. By filtering all the extra non-relevant information, it allows other algorithms in the system to process the relevant information from images a lot more efficiently and therefore react to any impending danger more quickly.

Another instance where this filtering might be useful is if the space to load the video is limited or costly and we need to compress the images and make them more space efficient. We'll leave it up to the reader to come up with other scenarios where this might be useful but hopefully, we have given you enough to spark your imagination and creative juices.

The information obtained by frame differencing is useful, but we will not be able to build a robust tracker with it. It is sensitive to noise and it does not really track an object completely. To build a robust object tracker, we need to know what characteristics of the object can be used to track it accurately. This is where color spaces become relevant, which we will discuss in the next section.

Tracking objects using color spaces

An image can be represented using various color spaces. The RGB color space is probably the most popular color space, but it does not lend itself nicely to applications like object tracking. So, we will be using the HSV color space instead. It is an intuitive color space model that is closer to how humans perceive color. You can learn more about it here:

`https://en.wikipedia.org/wiki/HSL_and_HSV`

We can convert the captured frame from RGB to the HSV color space, and then use color thresholding to track any given object. We should note that we need to know the color distribution of the object so that we can select the appropriate ranges for thresholding.

Create a new Python file and import the following packages:

```
import cv2
import numpy as np
```

Define a function to grab the current frame from the webcam. Start by reading it from the video capture object:

```
# Define a function to get the current frame from the webcam
def get_frame(cap, scaling_factor):
    # Read the current frame from the video capture object
    _, frame = cap.read()
```

Resize the frame based on the scaling factor and return it:

```
    # Resize the image
    frame = cv2.resize(frame, None, fx=scaling_factor,
            fy=scaling_factor, interpolation=cv2.INTER_AREA)

    return frame
```

Define the `main` function. Start by initializing the video capture object:

```
if __name__=='__main__':
    # Define the video capture object
    cap = cv2.VideoCapture(0)
```

Define the scaling factor to be used to resize the captured frames:

```
# Define the scaling factor for the images
scaling_factor = 0.5
```

Iterate indefinitely until the user hits the *Esc* key. Grab the current frame to start:

```
# Keep reading the frames from the webcam
# until the user hits the 'Esc' key
while True:
    # Grab the current frame
    frame = get_frame(cap, scaling_factor)
```

Convert the image to the HSV color space using the inbuilt function available in OpenCV:

```
    # Convert the image to HSV colorspace
    hsv = cv2.cvtColor(frame, cv2.COLOR_BGR2HSV)
```

Define the approximate HSV color range for the color of human skin:

```
    # Define range of skin color in HSV
    lower = np.array([0, 70, 60])
    upper = np.array([50, 150, 255])
```

Threshold the HSV image to create the mask:

```
    # Threshold the HSV image to get only skin color
    mask = cv2.inRange(hsv, lower, upper)
```

Compute bitwise AND between the mask and the original image:

```
    # Bitwise-AND between the mask and original image
    img_bitwise_and = cv2.bitwise_and(frame, frame, mask=mask)
```

Run median blurring to smoothen the image:

```
    # Run median blurring
    img_median_blurred = cv2.medianBlur(img_bitwise_and, 5)
```

Display the input and output frames:

```
    # Display the input and output
    cv2.imshow('Input', frame)
    cv2.imshow('Output', img_median_blurred)
```

Check if the user pressed the *Esc* key. If so, then exit the loop:

```
    # Check if the user hit the 'Esc' key
    c = cv2.waitKey(5)
    if c == 27:
        break
```

Once you exit the loop, make sure that all the windows are properly closed:

```
# Close all the windows
cv2.destroyAllWindows()
```

The full code is given in the file `colorspaces.py` provided to you. If you run the code, you will get two screenshots. The window titled **Input** is the captured frame:

Figure 2: Captured frame

The second window titled **Output** shows the skin mask:

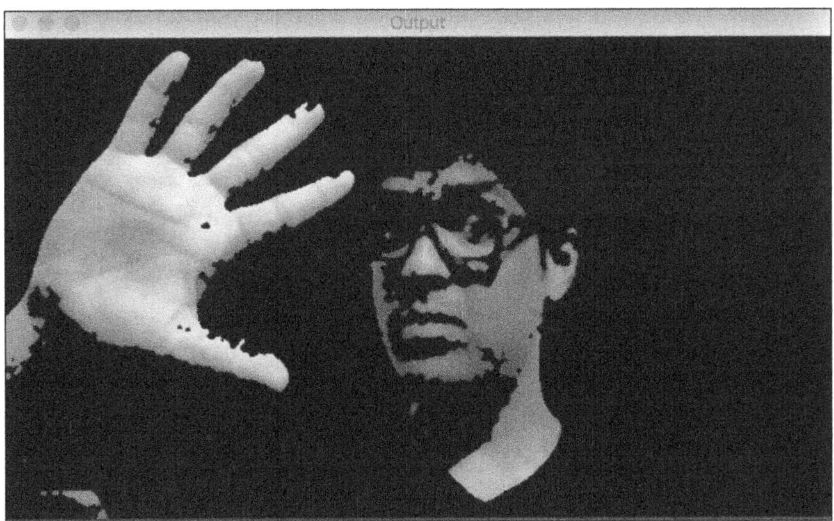

Figure 3: Output frame

As you can see in the output frame, we now only see one color in the image, and it corresponds to anything that is skin. Everything else is black. Similar to what we saw in the previous section, we filtered the image to contain only the information that we are interested in. In this case, the filtering was different, but the result is the fact that we now only have the information that is required to further process the image. Some applications that come to mind:

- Detecting abnormal skin conditions or discoloration.
- A security system that only turns on when it sees the color of human skin. This could be used in ports where humans might be hiding in containers.

Can you think of some other applications? In the next section, we will learn about another image transformation technique called background subtraction.

Object tracking using background subtraction

Background subtraction is a technique that models the background in a given video, and then uses that model to detect moving objects. This technique is used a lot in video compression as well as video surveillance. It performs well where we must detect moving objects within a static scene. The algorithm basically works by detecting the background, building a model for it, and then subtracting it from the current frame to obtain the foreground. This foreground corresponds to moving objects.

One of the main steps here is to build a model of the background. It is not the same as frame differencing because we are not differencing successive frames. We are modeling the background and updating it in real time, which makes it an adaptive algorithm that can adjust to a moving baseline. Therefore, it performs much better than frame differencing.

Create a new Python file and import the following packages:

```
import cv2
import numpy as np
```

Define a function to grab the current frame:

```
# Define a function to get the current frame from the webcam
def get_frame(cap, scaling_factor):
    # Read the current frame from the video capture object
    _, frame = cap.read()
```

Resize the frame and return it:

```
    # Resize the image
    frame = cv2.resize(frame, None, fx=scaling_factor,
            fy=scaling_factor, interpolation=cv2.INTER_AREA)

    return frame
```

Define the `main` function and initialize the video capture object:

```
if __name__=='__main__':
    # Define the video capture object
    cap = cv2.VideoCapture(0)
```

Define the background subtractor object:

```
    # Define the background subtractor object
    bg_subtractor = cv2.createBackgroundSubtractorMOG2()
```

Define the history and the learning rate. The following comment is self-explanatory as to what `history` is all about:

```
    # Define the number of previous frames to use to learn.
    # This factor controls the learning rate of the algorithm.
    # The learning rate refers to the rate at which your model
    # will learn about the background. Higher value for
    # 'history' indicates a slower learning rate. You can
    # play with this parameter to see how it affects the output.
    history = 100

    # Define the learning rate
    learning_rate = 1.0/history
```

Iterate indefinitely until the user presses the *Esc* key. Start by grabbing the current frame:

```
    # Keep reading the frames from the webcam
    # until the user hits the 'Esc' key
    while True:
        # Grab the current frame
        frame = get_frame(cap, 0.5)
```

Compute the `mask` using the background subtractor object defined earlier:

```
        # Compute the mask
        mask = bg_subtractor.apply(frame, learningRate=learning_rate)
```

Convert the `mask` from grayscale to RGB:

```
# Convert grayscale image to RGB color image
mask = cv2.cvtColor(mask, cv2.COLOR_GRAY2BGR)
```

Display the input and output images:

```
# Display the images
cv2.imshow('Input', frame)
cv2.imshow('Output', mask & frame)
```

Check if the user pressed the *Esc* key. If so, exit the loop:

```
# Check if the user hit the 'Esc' key
c = cv2.waitKey(10)
if c == 27:
    break
```

Once you exit the loop, make sure you release the video capture object and close all the windows properly:

```
# Release the video capture object
cap.release()

# Close all the windows
cv2.destroyAllWindows()
```

The full code is given in the file `background_subtraction.py` provided to you. If you run the code, you will see a window displaying the live output. If you move around, you will partially see yourself as shown here:

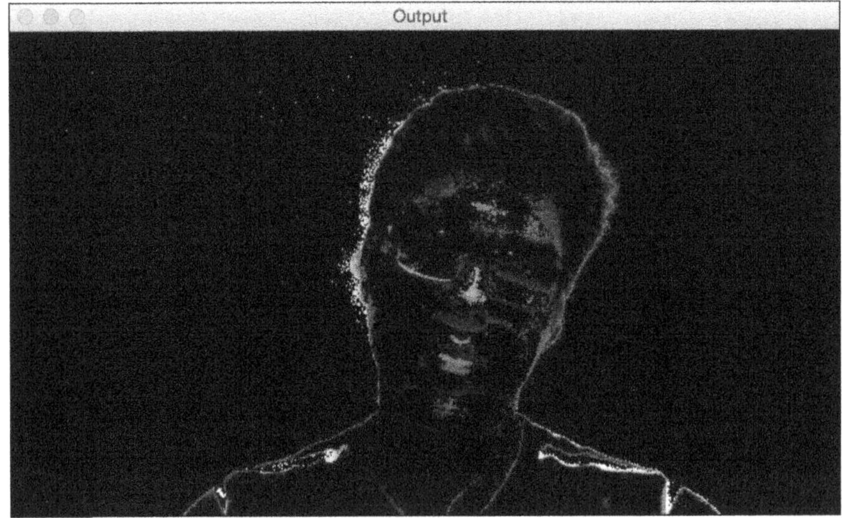

Figure 4: Background subtraction image

Once you stop moving around, it will start fading because you are now part of the background. The algorithm will consider you a part of the background and start updating the model accordingly:

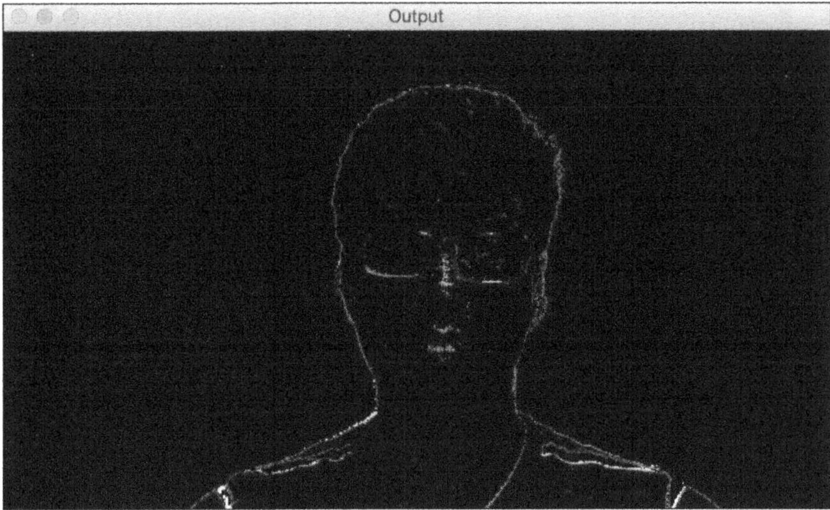

Figure 5: Background subtraction image

As you remain still, it will continue to fade as shown here:

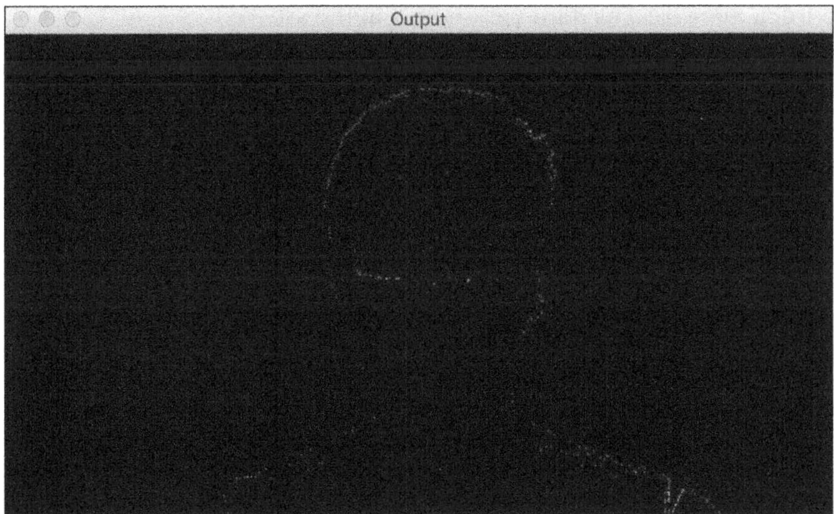

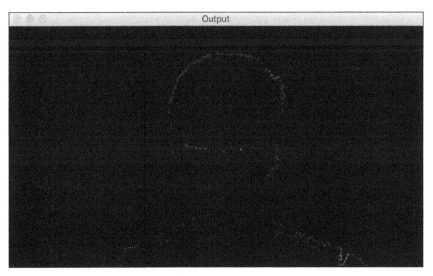

Figure 6: Background subtraction image

The process of fading indicates that the current scene is becoming part of the background model.

As you can already imagine, generating images only when there is movement will save a vast amount of storage. A simple example of when this would be useful would be with a security camera. Watching hours and hours of a camera focusing on an empty parking lot can be more boring than watching paint dry, but if the security system is only smart enough to record when there is movement in the frame, we will be able to discern the "interesting" portion of the video much quicker.

Color space-based tracking allows us to track colored objects, but we must define the color first. This seems restrictive! Let us see how we can select an object in a live video and then have a tracker that can track it. This is where the **CAMShift** algorithm, which stands for **Continuously Adaptive Mean Shift**, becomes relevant. This is basically an adaptive version of the Mean Shift algorithm. We'll discuss CAMShift in the next section.

Building an interactive object tracker using the CAMShift algorithm

In order to understand CAMShift, let's first see how Mean Shift works. Consider a region of interest in a given frame. We have selected this region because it contains the object of interest. We want to track this object, so we have drawn a rough boundary around it, which is what *region of interest* refers to. We want our object tracker to track this object as it moves around in the video.

To do this, we select a set of points based on the color histogram of that region and then compute the centroid. If the location of this centroid is at the geometric center of this region, then we know that the object hasn't moved. But if the location of the centroid is not at the geometric center of this region, then we know that the object has moved. This means that we need to move the enclosing boundary as well. The movement of the centroid is directly indicative of the direction of movement of the object. We need to move our bounding box so that the new centroid becomes the geometric center of this bounding box. We keep doing this for every frame and track the object in real time. Hence, this algorithm is called Mean Shift because the mean (that is, the centroid) keeps shifting and we track the object using this.

Let us see how this is related to CAMShift. One of the problems with Mean Shift is that the size of the object is not allowed to change over time. Once we draw a bounding box, it will stay constant regardless of how close or far away the object is from the camera. Therefore, we need to use CAMShift because it can adapt the size of the bounding box to the size of the object. If you want to explore it further, you can check out this link:

`http://docs.opencv.org/3.1.0/db/df8/tutorial_py_meanshift.html`

Let us see how to build a tracker.

Create a new Python file and import the following packages:

```
import cv2
import numpy as np
```

Define a class to handle all the functionality related to object tracking:

```
# Define a class to handle object tracking related functionality
class ObjectTracker(object):
    def __init__(self, scaling_factor=0.5):
        # Initialize the video capture object
        self.cap = cv2.VideoCapture(0)
```

Capture the current frame:

```
        # Capture the frame from the webcam
        _, self.frame = self.cap.read()
```

Set the scaling factor:

```
        # Scaling factor for the captured frame
        self.scaling_factor = scaling_factor
```

Resize the frame:

```
        # Resize the frame
        self.frame = cv2.resize(self.frame, None,
                fx=self.scaling_factor, fy=self.scaling_factor,
                interpolation=cv2.INTER_AREA)
```

Create a window to display the output:

```
        # Create a window to display the frame
        cv2.namedWindow('Object Tracker')
```

Set the mouse callback function to take input from the mouse:

```
        # Set the mouse callback function to track the mouse
        cv2.setMouseCallback('Object Tracker', self.mouse_event)
```

Initialize variables to track the rectangular selection:

```
        # Initialize variable related to rectangular region selection
        self.selection = None

        # Initialize variable related to starting position
        self.drag_start = None
```

```
        # Initialize variable related to the state of tracking
        self.tracking_state = 0
```

Define a function to track the mouse events:

```
    # Define a method to track the mouse events
    def mouse_event(self, event, x, y, flags, param):
        # Convert x and y coordinates into 16-bit numpy integers
        x, y = np.int16([x, y])
```

When the left button on the mouse is down, it indicates that the user has started drawing a rectangle:

```
        # Check if a mouse button down event has occurred
        if event == cv2.EVENT_LBUTTONDOWN:
            self.drag_start = (x, y)
            self.tracking_state = 0
```

If the user is currently dragging the mouse to set the size of the rectangular selection, track the width and height:

```
        # Check if the user has started selecting the region
        if self.drag_start:
            if flags & cv2.EVENT_FLAG_LBUTTON:
                # Extract the dimensions of the frame
                h, w = self.frame.shape[:2]
```

Set the starting *X* and *Y* coordinates of the rectangle:

```
                # Get the initial position
                xi, yi = self.drag_start
```

Get the maximum and minimum values of the coordinates to make it agnostic to the direction in which you drag the mouse to draw the rectangle:

```
                # Get the max and min values
                x0, y0 = np.maximum(0, np.minimum([xi, yi], [x, y]))
                x1, y1 = np.minimum([w, h], np.maximum([xi, yi], [x,
y]))
```

Reset the selection variable:

```
                # Reset the selection variable
                self.selection = None
```

Finalize the rectangular selection:

```
                # Finalize the rectangular selection
```

```
                if x1-x0 > 0 and y1-y0 > 0:
                    self.selection = (x0, y0, x1, y1)
```

If the selection is done, set the flag that indicates that we should start tracking the object within the rectangular region:

```
            else:
                # If the selection is done, start tracking
                self.drag_start = None
                if self.selection is not None:
                    self.tracking_state = 1
```

Define a method to track the object:

```
    # Method to start tracking the object
    def start_tracking(self):
        # Iterate until the user presses the Esc key
        while True:
            # Capture the frame from webcam
            _, self.frame = self.cap.read()
```

Resize the frame:

```
            # Resize the input frame
            self.frame = cv2.resize(self.frame, None,
                    fx=self.scaling_factor, fy=self.scaling_factor,
                    interpolation=cv2.INTER_AREA)
```

Create a copy of the frame. We will need it later:

```
            # Create a copy of the frame
            vis = self.frame.copy()
```

Convert the color space of the frame from RGB to HSV:

```
            # Convert the frame to HSV colorspace
            hsv = cv2.cvtColor(self.frame, cv2.COLOR_BGR2HSV)
```

Create the mask based on predefined thresholds:

```
            # Create the mask based on predefined thresholds
            mask = cv2.inRange(hsv, np.array((0., 60., 32.)),
            np.array((180., 255., 255.)))
```

Check if the user has selected the region:

```
            # Check if the user has selected the region
            if self.selection:
                # Extract the coordinates of the selected rectangle
```

```
        x0, y0, x1, y1 = self.selection

        # Extract the tracking window
        self.track_window = (x0, y0, x1-x0, y1-y0)
```

Extract the regions of interest from the HSV image as well as the mask. Compute the histogram of the region of interest based on these:

```
        # Extract the regions of interest
        hsv_roi = hsv[y0:y1, x0:x1]
        mask_roi = mask[y0:y1, x0:x1]

        # Compute the histogram of the region of
        # interest in the HSV image using the mask
        hist = cv2.calcHist( [hsv_roi], [0], mask_roi,
                [16], [0, 180] )
```

Normalize the histogram:

```
        # Normalize and reshape the histogram
        cv2.normalize(hist, hist, 0, 255, cv2.NORM_MINMAX)
        self.hist = hist.reshape(-1)
```

Extract the region of interest from the original frame:

```
        # Extract the region of interest from the frame
        vis_roi = vis[y0:y1, x0:x1]
```

Compute bitwise NOT of the region of interest. This is for display purposes only:

```
        # Compute the image negative (for display only)
        cv2.bitwise_not(vis_roi, vis_roi)
        vis[mask == 0] = 0
```

Check if the system is in the tracking mode:

```
    # Check if the system in the "tracking" mode
    if self.tracking_state == 1:
        # Reset the selection variable
        self.selection = None
```

Compute the histogram back projection:

```
        # Compute the histogram back projection
        hsv_backproj = cv2.calcBackProject([hsv], [0],
                self.hist, [0, 180], 1)
```

Compute bitwise AND between the histogram and the mask:

```
                    # Compute bitwise AND between histogram
                    # backprojection and the mask
                    hsv_backproj &= mask
```

Define termination criteria for the tracker:

```
                    # Define termination criteria for the tracker
                    term_crit = (cv2.TERM_CRITERIA_EPS | cv2.TERM_
CRITERIA_COUNT, 10, 1)
```

Apply the CAMShift algorithm to the back projected histogram:

```
                    # Apply CAMShift on 'hsv_backproj'
                    track_box, self.track_window = cv2.CamShift(hsv_
backproj, self.track_window, term_crit)
```

Draw an ellipse around the object and display it:

```
                    # Draw an ellipse around the object
                    cv2.ellipse(vis, track_box, (0, 255, 0), 2)

                # Show the output live video
                cv2.imshow('Object Tracker', vis)
```

If the user presses *Esc*, then exit the loop:

```
                # Stop if the user hits the 'Esc' key
                c = cv2.waitKey(5)
                if c == 27:
                    break
```

Once you exit the loop, make sure that all the windows are closed properly:

```
            # Close all the windows
            cv2.destroyAllWindows()
```

Define the `main` function and start tracking:

```
if __name__ == '__main__':
    # Start the tracker
    ObjectTracker().start_tracking()
```

The full code is given in the file `camshift.py` provided to you. If you run the code, you will see a window showing the live video from the webcam.

Take an object, hold it in your hand, and then draw a rectangle around it. Once you draw the rectangle, make sure to move the mouse pointer away from the final position. The image will look something like this:

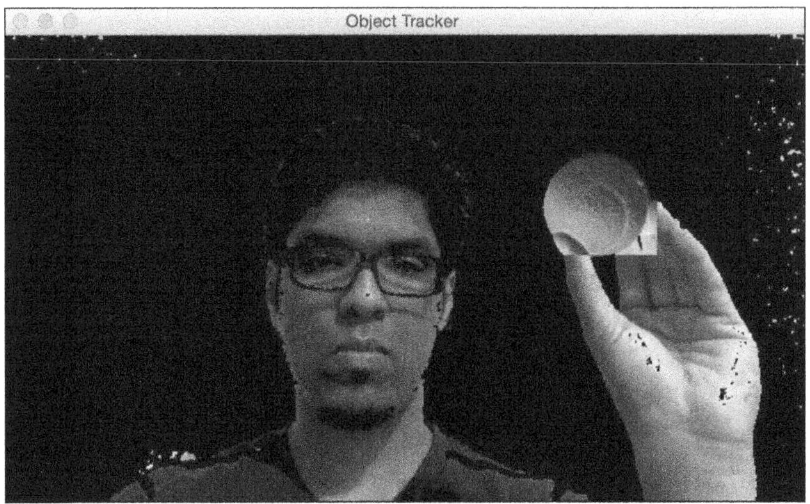

Figure 7: Object detection image

Once the selection is done, move the mouse pointer to a different position to lock the rectangle. This event will start the tracking process as seen in the following image:

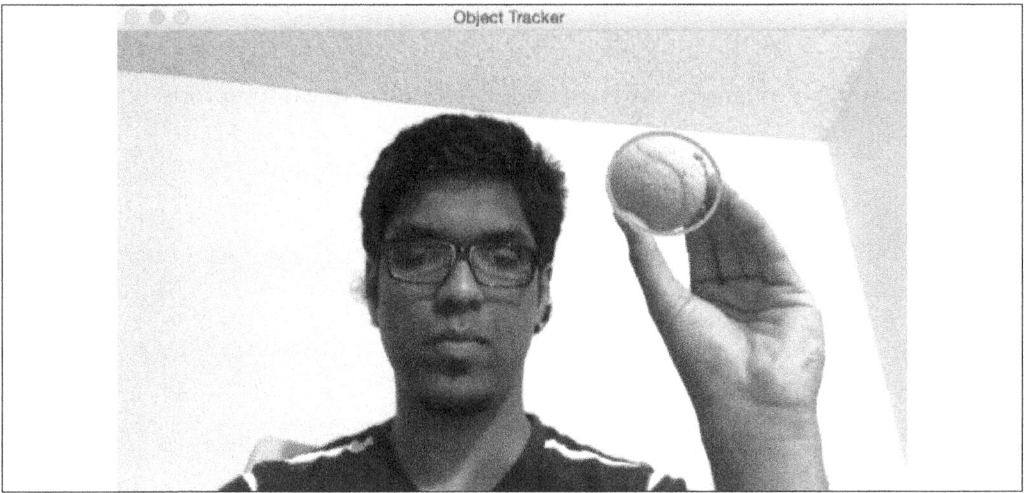

Figure 8: Object detection image 2

Let's move the object around to see if it's still being tracked

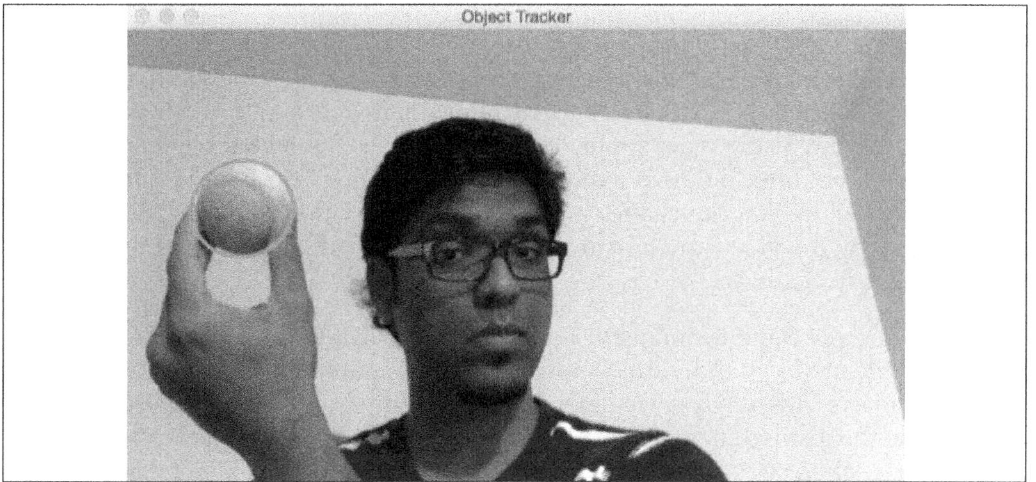

Figure 9: Object detection image 3

Looks like it's working well. You can move the object around to see how it's getting tracked in real time.

Hopefully, by now you are seeing the possibilities of the many applications of image recognition and have probably come up with your own ideas about how to apply what we have learned about so far. The technology that they use might be a little more sophisticated than what we are using in this chapter, but the concepts are not that different. Techniques like these are used by the NFL to *virtually* set the 10-yard marker on television and Major League Baseball paints the strike zone using similar techniques to the ones that we learned about in this section. The example that comes closest to what we saw here is what the Wimbledon tournament uses to ascertain where a tennis ball lands and determine if it's in or out. In the next section, we will learn about optical flow-based tracking. It is another useful technique for image recognition.

Optical flow-based tracking

In January 2020, it was announced that *The Irishman*, a movie directed by Martin Scorsese, was nominated for an Oscar. This movie details the life of truck driver, gangster, and teamster Frank Sheeran (played by Robert DeNiro). In the movie, we see Sheeran at different times in his life. From the time he was in his 20's to the time he was in his 80's. The whole time we saw DeNiro on the screen it was obvious that it was him and you could really tell that he was twenty years old or eighty years old.

In previous movies, this might have been achieved with makeup. For this movie, makeup was not used for this purpose. Instead they used special effects and they retouched DeNiro's face with *digital* makeup. Amazing, right?

For many years, making realistic faces with computers was extremely difficult, but Hollywood and its special effects artists have finally cracked the code. Obviously, they are using more sophisticated techniques than what we will cover in this chapter, but optical flow is a foundational technology to begin to achieve this functionality. Before you can change a person's face in a video, you must be able to track that face in the video any time it moves. This is one of the problems that optical flow can solve.

Optical flow is a popular technique used in computer vision. It uses image feature points to track an object. Individual feature points are tracked across successive frames in the live video. When we detect a set of feature points in a given frame, we compute the displacement vectors to keep track of it. We show the motion of these feature points between successive frames. These vectors are known as motion vectors. There are many ways to perform optical flow, but the **Lucas-Kanade** method is perhaps the most popular. Here is the original paper that describes this technique:

`http://cseweb.ucsd.edu/classes/sp02/cse252/lucaskanade81.pdf`

The first step is to extract the feature points from the current frame. For each feature point that is extracted, a 3×3 patch (of pixels) is created with the feature point at the center. We are assuming that all the points in each patch have a similar motion. The size of this window can be adjusted depending on the situation.

For each patch, we look for a match in its neighborhood in the previous frame. We pick the best match based on an error metric. The search area is bigger than 3×3 because we look for a bunch of different 3×3 patches to get the one that is closest to the current patch. Once we get that, the path from the center point of the current patch and the matched patch in the previous frame will become the motion vector. We similarly compute the motion vectors for all the other patches.

Create a new Python file and import the following packages:

```
import cv2
import numpy as np
```

Define a function to start tracking using optical flow. Start by initializing the video capture object and the scaling factor:

```
# Define a function to track the object
def start_tracking():
    # Initialize the video capture object
    cap = cv2.VideoCapture(0)
```

```
# Define the scaling factor for the frames
scaling_factor = 0.5
```

Define the number of frames to track and the number of frames to skip:

```
# Number of frames to track
num_frames_to_track = 5

# Skipping factor
num_frames_jump = 2
```

Initialize variables related to tracking paths and the frame index:

```
# Initialize variables
tracking_paths = []
frame_index = 0
```

Define the tracking parameters like the window size, maximum level, and the termination criteria:

```
# Define tracking parameters
tracking_params = dict(winSize = (11, 11), maxLevel = 2,
        criteria = (cv2.TERM_CRITERIA_EPS | cv2.TERM_CRITERIA_
COUNT,
            10, 0.03))
```

Iterate indefinitely until the user presses the *Esc* key. Start by capturing the current frame and resizing it:

```
# Iterate until the user hits the 'Esc' key
while True:
    # Capture the current frame
    _, frame = cap.read()

    # Resize the frame
    frame = cv2.resize(frame, None, fx=scaling_factor,
            fy=scaling_factor, interpolation=cv2.INTER_AREA)
```

Convert the frame from RGB to grayscale:

```
    # Convert to grayscale
    frame_gray = cv2.cvtColor(frame, cv2.COLOR_BGR2GRAY)
```

Create a copy of the frame:

```
    # Create a copy of the frame
    output_img = frame.copy()
```

Check if the length of tracking paths is greater than zero:

```
        if len(tracking_paths) > 0:
            # Get images
            prev_img, current_img = prev_gray, frame_gray
```

Organize the feature points:

```
            # Organize the feature points
            feature_points_0 = np.float32([tp[-1] for tp in \
                    tracking_paths]).reshape(-1, 1, 2)
```

Compute the optical flow based on the previous and current images by using the feature points and the tracking parameters:

```
            # Compute optical flow
            feature_points_1, _, _ = cv2.calcOpticalFlowPyrLK(
                    prev_img, current_img, feature_points_0,
                    None, **tracking_params)

            # Compute reverse optical flow
            feature_points_0_rev, _, _ = cv2.calcOpticalFlowPyrLK(
                    current_img, prev_img, feature_points_1,
                    None, **tracking_params)

            # Compute the difference between forward and
            # reverse optical flow
            diff_feature_points = abs(feature_points_0 - \
                    feature_points_0_rev).reshape(-1, 2).max(-1)
```

Extract the good feature points:

```
            # Extract the good points
            good_points = diff_feature_points < 1
```

Initialize the variable for the new tracking paths:

```
            # Initialize variable
            new_tracking_paths = []
```

Iterate through all the good feature points and draw circles around them:

```
            # Iterate through all the good feature points
            for tp, (x, y), good_points_flag in zip(tracking_paths,
                        feature_points_1.reshape(-1, 2), good_points):
                # If the flag is not true, then continue
                if not good_points_flag:
                    continue
```

Append the *X* and *Y* coordinates and don't exceed the number of frames we are supposed to track:

```
                # Append the X and Y coordinates and check if
                # its length greater than the threshold
                tp.append((x, y))
                if len(tp) > num_frames_to_track:
                    del tp[0]

                new_tracking_paths.append(tp)
```

Draw a circle around the point. Update the tracking paths and draw lines using the new tracking paths to show movement:

```
                # Draw a circle around the feature points
                cv2.circle(output_img, (x, y), 3, (0, 255, 0), -1)

            # Update the tracking paths
            tracking_paths = new_tracking_paths

            # Draw lines
            cv2.polylines(output_img, [np.int32(tp) for tp in \
                    tracking_paths], False, (0, 150, 0))
```

Go into this `if` condition after skipping the number of frames specified earlier:

```
        # Go into this 'if' condition after skipping the
        # right number of frames
        if not frame_index % num_frames_jump:
            # Create a mask and draw the circles
            mask = np.zeros_like(frame_gray)
            mask[:] = 255
            for x, y in [np.int32(tp[-1]) for tp in tracking_paths]:
                cv2.circle(mask, (x, y), 6, 0, -1)
```

Compute the good features to track using the inbuilt function along with parameters like mask, maximum corners, quality level, minimum distance, and the block size:

```
            # Compute good features to track
            feature_points = cv2.goodFeaturesToTrack(frame_gray,
                    mask = mask, maxCorners = 500, qualityLevel = 0.3,
                    minDistance = 7, blockSize = 7)
```

If the feature points exist, append them to the tracking paths:

```
            # Check if feature points exist. If so, append them
            # to the tracking paths
            if feature_points is not None:
                for x, y in np.float32(feature_points).reshape(-1, 2):
                    tracking_paths.append([(x, y)])
```

Update the variables related to frame index and the previous grayscale image:

```
            # Update variables
            frame_index += 1
            prev_gray = frame_gray
```

Display the output:

```
            # Display output
            cv2.imshow('Optical Flow', output_img)
```

Check if the user pressed the *Esc* key. If so, exit the loop:

```
            # Check if the user hit the 'Esc' key
            c = cv2.waitKey(1)
            if c == 27:
                break
```

Define the `main` function and start tracking. Once you stop the tracker, make sure that all the windows are closed properly:

```
if __name__ == '__main__':
    # Start the tracker
    start_tracking()

    # Close all the windows
    cv2.destroyAllWindows()
```

The full code is given in the file `optical_flow.py` provided to you. If you run the code, you will see a window showing the live video. You will see feature points as shown in the following screenshot:

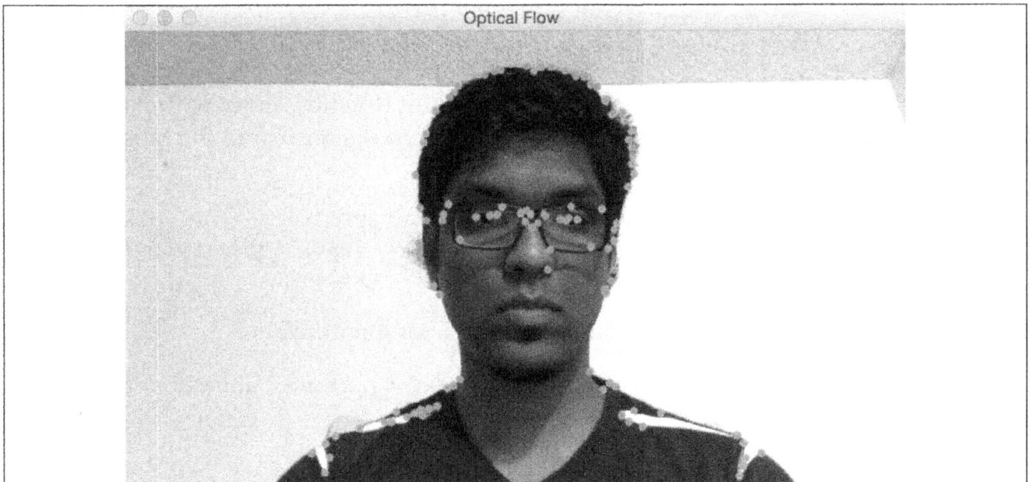

Figure 10: Object tracking image

If you move around, you will see lines showing the movement of those feature points:

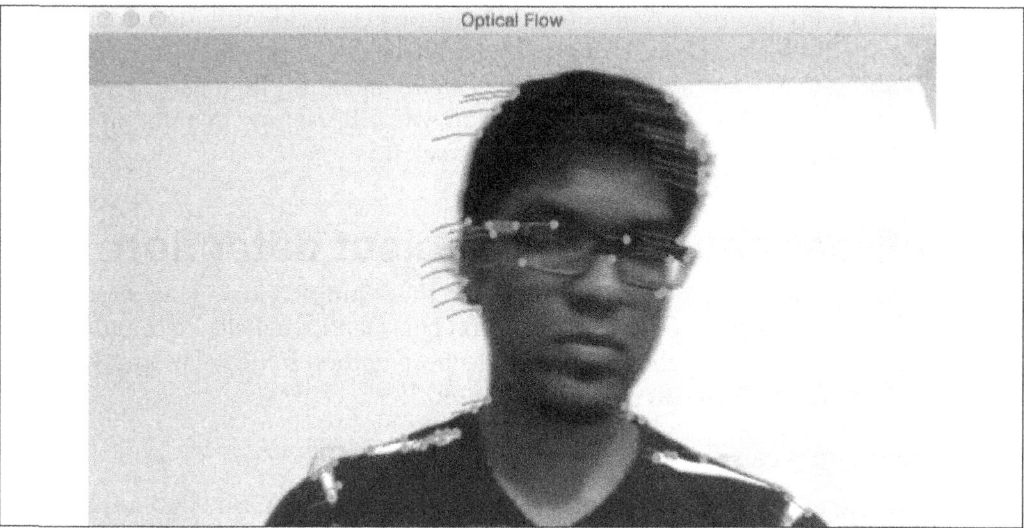

Figure 11: Object tracking image

If you then move in the opposite direction, the lines will also change their direction accordingly:

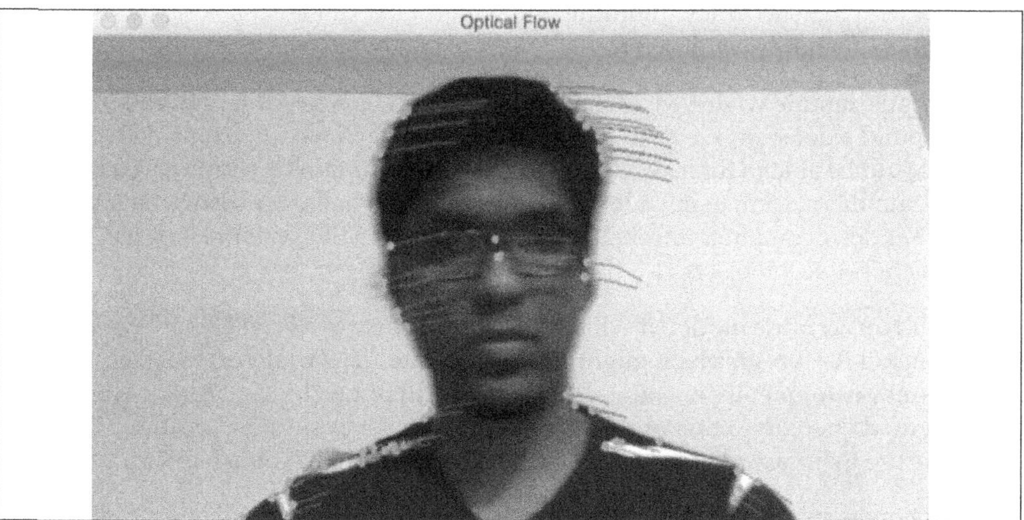

Figure 12: Object tracking image

Having seen those outputs, let's move on to the next section: *Face detection and tracking*.

Face detection and tracking

Face detection refers to detecting the location of a face in a given image. This is often confused with face recognition, which is the process of identifying who the person is. A typical biometric system utilizes both face detection and face recognition to perform the task. It uses face detection to locate the face and then uses face recognition to identify the person. In this section, we will see how to automatically detect the location of a face in a live video and track it.

Using Haar cascades for object detection

We will be using Haar cascades to detect faces in the example video. Haar cascades, in this case, refers to cascade classifiers based on Haar features. *Paul Viola* and *Michael Jones* first came up with this object detection method in their landmark research paper in 2001. You can check it out here:

`https://www.cs.cmu.edu/~efros/courses/LBMV07/Papers/viola-cvpr-01.pdf`

In their paper, they describe an effective machine learning technique that can be used to detect any object.

They use a boosted cascade of simple classifiers. This cascade is used to build an overall classifier that performs with high accuracy. The reason this is relevant is because it helps us circumvent the process of building a single-step classifier that performs with high accuracy. Building one such robust single-step classifier is a computationally intensive process.

Consider an example where we must detect an object like, say, a tennis ball. In order to build a detector, we need a system that can learn what a tennis ball looks like. It should be able to infer whether a given image contains a tennis ball. We need to train this system using a lot of images of tennis balls. We also need a lot of images that don't contain tennis balls as well. This helps the system learn how to differentiate between objects.

If we build an accurate model, it will be complex. Hence, we won't be able to run it in real time. If it's too simple, it might not be accurate. This trade-off between speed and accuracy is frequently encountered in the world of machine learning. The Viola-Jones method overcomes this problem by building a set of simple classifiers. These classifiers are then cascaded to form a unified classifier that's robust and accurate.

Let's see how to use this to perform face detection. In order to build a machine learning system to detect faces, we first need to build a feature extractor. The machine learning algorithms will use these features to understand what a face looks like. This is where Haar features become relevant.

They are just simple summations and differences of patches across the image. Haar features are easy to compute. In order to make it robust to scale, we do this at multiple image sizes. If you want to learn more about this in a tutorial format, you can check out this link:

`http://www.cs.ubc.ca/~lowe/425/slides/13-ViolaJones.pdf`

Once the features are extracted, we pass them through our boosted cascade of simple classifiers. We check various rectangular sub-regions in the image and keep discarding the ones that don't contain faces. This helps us arrive at the final answer quickly. In order to compute these features quickly, they used a concept known as integral images.

Using integral images for feature extraction

In order to compute Haar features, we must compute the summations and differences of many sub-regions in the image. We need to compute these summations and differences at multiple scales, which makes it a computationally intensive process. In order to build a real-time system, we use integral images. Consider the following figure:

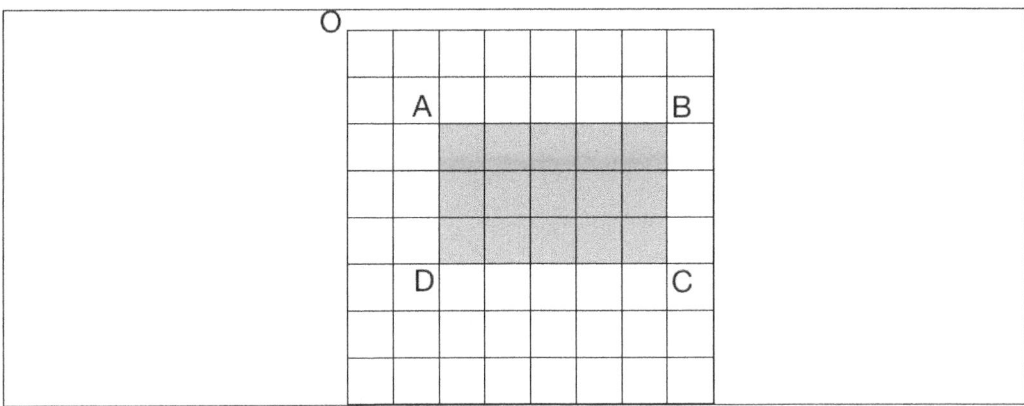

Figure 13: Area of ABCD

If we want to compute the sum of the rectangle **ABCD** in this image, we don't need to go through each pixel in that rectangular area. Let's say **OC** indicates the area of the rectangle formed by the top left corner **O** and the point **C** on the diagonally opposite corner of the rectangle. To calculate the area of the rectangle **ABCD**, we can use the following formula:

$$Area\ of\ the\ rectangle\ ABCD = OC - (OB + OD - OA)$$

What's so special about this formula? If you notice, we didn't have to iterate through anything or recalculate any rectangle areas. All the values on the right-hand side of the equation are already available because they were computed during earlier cycles. We directly used them to compute the area of this rectangle. What we effectively do is consider a larger rectangle, with **O** and **C** representing opposing diagonals, and then we "cut out" the white parts in order to just leave the blue area. Having considered that, let's see how to build a face detector.

Create a new Python file and import the following packages:

```
import cv2
import numpy as np
```

Load the Haar cascade file corresponding to face detection:

```
# Load the Haar cascade file
face_cascade = cv2.CascadeClassifier(
        'haar_cascade_files/haarcascade_frontalface_default.xml'

# Check if the cascade file has been loaded correctly
if face_cascade.empty():
        raise IOError('Unable to load the face cascade classifier xml
file')
```

Initialize the video capture object and define the scaling factor:

```
# Initialize the video capture object
cap = cv2.VideoCapture(0)

# Define the scaling factor
scaling_factor = 0.5
```

Iterate indefinitely until the user presses the *Esc* key. Capture the current frame:

```
# Iterate until the user hits the 'Esc' key
while True:
    # Capture the current frame
    _, frame = cap.read()
```

Resize the frame:

```
    # Resize the frame
    frame = cv2.resize(frame, None,
            fx=scaling_factor, fy=scaling_factor,
            interpolation=cv2.INTER_AREA)
```

Convert the image to grayscale:

```
    # Convert to grayscale
    gray = cv2.cvtColor(frame, cv2.COLOR_BGR2GRAY)
```

Run the face detector on the grayscale image:

```
# Run the face detector on the grayscale image
face_rects = face_cascade.detectMultiScale(gray, 1.3, 5)
```

Iterate through the detected faces and draw rectangles around them:

```
# Draw a rectangle around the face
for (x,y,w,h) in face_rects:
    cv2.rectangle(frame, (x,y), (x+w,y+h), (0,255,0), 3)
```

Display the output:

```
# Display the output
cv2.imshow('Face Detector', frame)
```

Check if the user pressed the *Esc* key. If so, exit the loop:

```
# Check if the user hit the 'Esc' key
c = cv2.waitKey(1)
if c == 27:
    break
```

Once you exit the loop, make sure to release the video capture object and close all the windows properly:

```
# Release the video capture object
cap.release()

# Close all the windows
cv2.destroyAllWindows()
```

The full code is given in the file `face_detector.py` provided to you. If you run the code, you will see something like this:

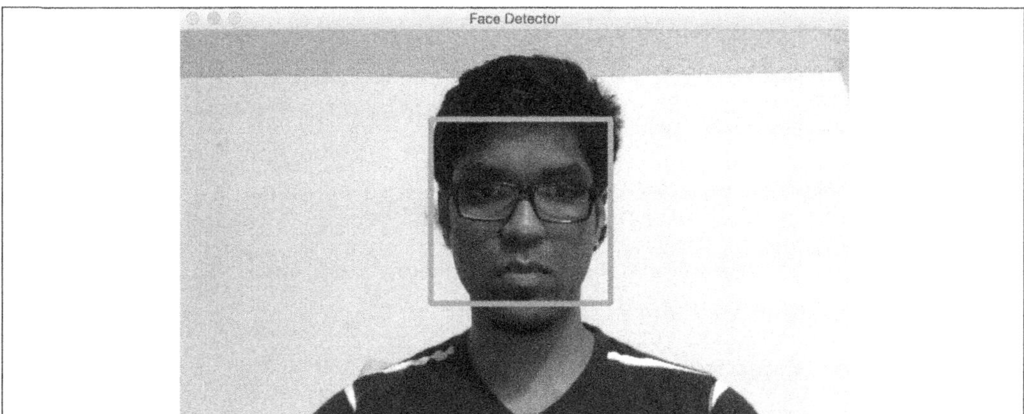

Figure 14: Face detection image

From face detection, we'll move onto a similar concept in the next section: *Eye detection and tracking*.

Eye detection and tracking

Eye detection works similarly to face detection. Instead of using a face cascade file, we will use an eye cascade file. Create a new Python file and import the following packages:

```
import cv2
import numpy as np
```

Load the Haar cascade files corresponding to face and eye detection:

```
# Load the Haar cascade files for face and eye
face_cascade = cv2.CascadeClassifier('haar_cascade_files/haarcascade_
frontalface_default.xml')
eye_cascade = cv2.CascadeClassifier('haar_cascade_files/haarcascade_
eye.xml')

# Check if the face cascade file has been loaded correctly
if face_cascade.empty():
    raise IOError('Unable to load the face cascade classifier xml
file')

# Check if the eye cascade file has been loaded correctly
if eye_cascade.empty():
    raise IOError('Unable to load the eye cascade classifier xml
file')
```

Initialize the video capture object and define the scaling factor:

```
# Initialize the video capture object
cap = cv2.VideoCapture(0)

# Define the scaling factor
ds_factor = 0.5
```

Iterate indefinitely until the user presses the *Esc* key:

```
# Iterate until the user hits the 'Esc' key
while True:
    # Capture the current frame
    _, frame = cap.read()
```

Resize the frame:

```
        # Resize the frame
        frame = cv2.resize(frame, None, fx=ds_factor, fy=ds_factor,
    interpolation=cv2.INTER_AREA)
```

Convert the frame from RGB to grayscale:

```
        # Convert to grayscale
        gray = cv2.cvtColor(frame, cv2.COLOR_BGR2GRAY)
```

Run the face detector:

```
        # Run the face detector on the grayscale image
        faces = face_cascade.detectMultiScale(gray, 1.3, 5)
```

For each face detected, run the eye detector within that region:

```
        # For each face that's detected, run the eye detector
        for (x,y,w,h) in faces:
            # Extract the grayscale face ROI
            roi_gray = gray[y:y+h, x:x+w]
```

Extract the region of interest and run the eye detector:

```
            # Extract the color face ROI
            roi_color = frame[y:y+h, x:x+w]

            # Run the eye detector on the grayscale ROI
            eyes = eye_cascade.detectMultiScale(roi_gray)
```

Draw circles around the eyes and display the output:

```
            # Draw circles around the eyes
            for (x_eye,y_eye,w_eye,h_eye) in eyes:
                center = (int(x_eye + 0.5*w_eye), int(y_eye + 0.5*h_eye))
                radius = int(0.3 * (w_eye + h_eye))
                color = (0, 255, 0)
                thickness = 3
                cv2.circle(roi_color, center, radius, color, thickness)

        # Display the output
        cv2.imshow('Eye Detector', frame)
```

If the user presses the *Esc* key, exit the loop:

```
        # Check if the user hit the 'Esc' key
        c = cv2.waitKey(1)
        if c == 27:
            break
```

Once you exit the loop, make sure to release the video capture object and close all the windows:

```
# Release the video capture object
cap.release()

# Close all the windows
cv2.destroyAllWindows()
```

The full code is given in the file `eye_detector.py` provided to you. If you run the code, you will see something like this:

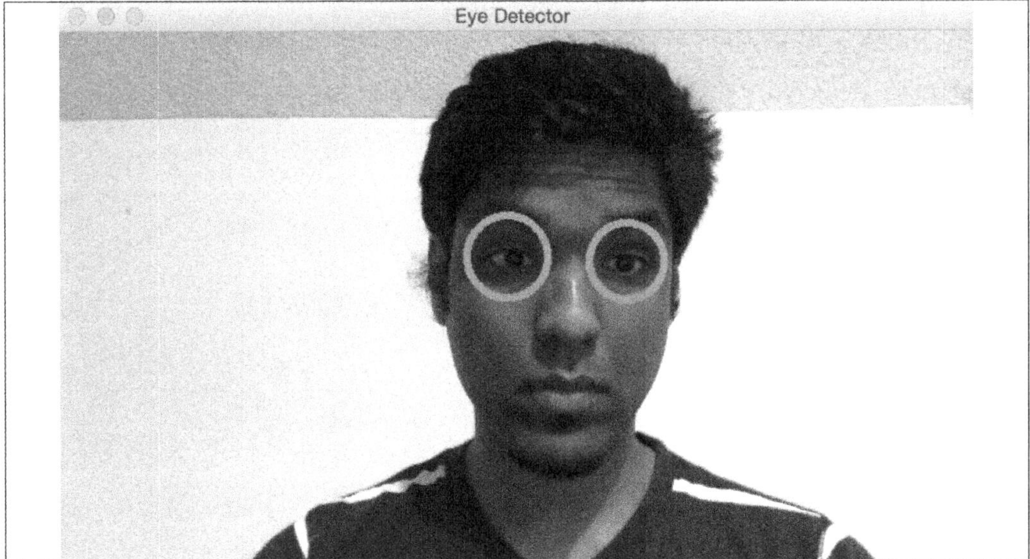

Figure 15: Eye detection image

Stealing an idea from the previous section, we could use the technique we learned in this section to add glasses to a character on screen in a movie (or a beard, or a mustache, and so on).

Another application that comes to mind is tracking the eyes of a truck driver and determining the rate at which they are blinking or maybe even if their eyes are closed to see if they are getting tired and asking them - perhaps forcing them - to pull over.

This chapter aimed to demonstrate how image recognition can be used in a wide array of applications. We look forward to hearing from you and learning how you apply the techniques that you learned in this chapter by combining them with your own ideas.

Summary

In this chapter, we learned about object detection and tracking. We understood how to install OpenCV with Python support on various operating systems. We learned about frame differencing and used it to detect the moving parts in a video. We discussed how to track human skin using color spaces. We talked about background subtraction and how it can be used to track objects in static scenes. We built an interactive object tracker using the CAMShift algorithm.

We learned how to build an optical flow-based tracker. We discussed face detection techniques and understood the concepts of Haar cascades and integral images. We used this technique to build an eye detector and tracker.

In the next chapter, we will discuss artificial neural networks and use those techniques to build an optical character recognition engine.

19
Neural Networks

In this chapter, we are going to learn about neural networks. We will start with an introduction to neural networks and the installation of the relevant library. We will then discuss perceptrons and how to build a classifier based on them. After that, we'll go deeper and learn about single-layer neural networks and multi-layer neural networks.

Later, we will see how to use neural networks to build a vector quantizer. We will analyze sequential data using recurrent neural networks, and finally we will use neural networks to build an optical character recognition engine. By the end of this chapter, we will have covered:

- An introduction to neural networks
- Building a Perceptron-based classifier
- Constructing a single-layer neural network
- Constructing a multilayer neural network
- Building a vector quantizer
- Analyzing sequential data using recurrent neural networks
- Visualizing characters in an **Optical Character Recognition** (OCR) database
- Building an **Optical Character Recognition** (OCR) engine

Let's begin with an introduction to neural networks.

Introduction to neural networks

One of the fundamental premises of AI is to build systems that can perform tasks that would normally require human intelligence. The human brain is amazing at learning new concepts. Why not use the model of the human brain to build a system? A neural network is a model designed to loosely simulate the learning process of the human brain.

Neural networks are designed such that they can identify the underlying patterns in data and learn from them. They can be used for various tasks such as classification, regression, and segmentation. One drawback of neural networks is that we need to convert any given data into a numerical format before feeding it into the neural network. For example, we deal with many different types of data including visual, textual, and time series. We need to figure out how to represent problems in a way that can be understood by neural networks. To understand this process, let's first consider how to build a neural network, and then how to train one.

Building a neural network

Some components of the human learning process are hierarchical. We have various parts in our brain's neural network and each stage corresponds to a different granularity. Some parts learn simple things and some parts learn more complex things. Let's consider the example of visually recognizing an object.

When we look at a box, the first part in our brain might identify simple things like corners and edges. The next part identifies the generic shape and the part after that identifies what kind of object it is. This process might differ for different brain functions, but you get the idea. Using this hierarchy, the human brain separates the tasks and identifies the given object.

To simulate the learning process of the human brain, a neural network is built using layers of neurons. These neurons are inspired by the biological neurons we discussed in the previous paragraph. Each layer in a neural network is a set of independent neurons. Each neuron in a layer is connected to neurons in the adjacent layer.

Training a neural network

If we are dealing with *N*-dimensional input data, then the input layer will consist of *N* neurons. If we have *M* distinct classes in our training data, then the output layer will consist of *M* neurons. The layers between the input and output layers are called hidden layers. A simple neural network will consist of a couple of layers and a deep neural network will consist of many layers.

So how can a neural network be used to classify data? The first step is to collect the appropriate training data and label it. Each neuron acts as a simple function and the neural network trains itself until the error goes below a certain a threshold.

The error is the difference between the predicted output and the actual output. Based on how big the error is, the neural network adjusts itself and retrains until it gets closer to the solution.

Enough about thinking of neural networks in the abstract. Time to get our hands dirty and learn by doing, just like we have been doing throughout this book. We will use a library called **NeuroLab** in this chapter. NeuroLab is a library that implements basic neural network algorithms. It has a variety of parameters that enables its configuration. Its interface is like the **Neural Network Toolbox** (**NNT**) package in **MATLAB**. The library is based on the NumPy package. You can find more about it at:

`https://pythonhosted.org/neurolab`

You can install it by running the following command on your Terminal:

```
$ pip3 install neurolab
```

Once you have installed it, you can proceed to the next section where we will build a Perceptron-based classifier.

Building a Perceptron-based classifier

Neurons, dendrites, and axons comprise the building blocks of the brain. Similarly, perceptrons are the most basic structure in a neural network.

The evolution of the neural networks has gone through many changes. Their development is grounded on the neurological work performed by Santiago Ramon y Cajal and Sir Charles Scott Sherrington. Ramon y Cajal was a pioneer in the exploration of the structure of nervous tissue and demonstrated that:

- Neurons can communicate with each other
- Neurons are physically separate from other neurons

Leveraging the research of Ramon y Cajal and Sherrington, Warren McCulloch and Walter Pitts in their 1943 paper, *A Logical Calculus of Ideas Immanent in Nervous Activity*, described an architecture borrowing from the structure of neurons having a binary threshold activation function analogous to first order logic sentences.

The following is a basic representation of McCulloch and Pitts neuron, otherwise called a Perceptron:

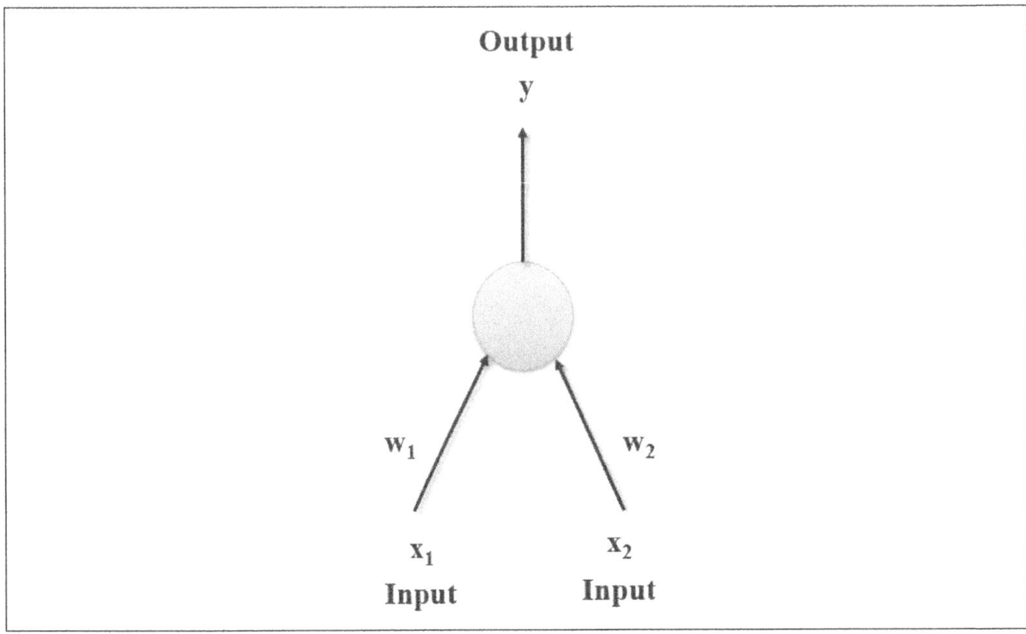

Figure 1: Basic Perceptron functionality

So, a Perceptron is a fundamental building block in many neural networks. It takes inputs, performs computation on them, and then produces an output. It uses a simple linear function to make the decision. Let's say we are dealing with an *N*-dimension input data point. A Perceptron computes the weighted summation of those *N* numbers and it then adds a constant to produce the output. The constant is called the bias of the neuron. It is worth noting that these simple Perceptrons can be used to design complex deep neural networks.

In this chapter, we will see how such a basic structure can be used to perform machine learning. In later chapters, we will see even more sophisticated examples, and some interesting applications of neural networks. Many neural networks, at their core, no matter how complicated they are, leverage the simple concept of the Perceptron. And that's why it's important to get a thorough understanding of this topic. Let's see how to build a Perceptron-based classifier using NeuroLab.

Create a new Python file and import the following packages:

```
import numpy as np
import matplotlib.pyplot as plt
import neurolab as nl
```

Load the input data from the text file `data_perceptron.txt` provided to you. Each line contains space - separated numbers, where the first two numbers are the features and the last number is the label:

```
# Load input data
text = np.loadtxt('data_perceptron.txt')
```

Separate the text into data points and labels:

```
# Separate datapoints and labels
data = text[:, :2]
labels = text[:, 2].reshape((text.shape[0], 1))
```

Plot the data points:

```
# Plot input data
plt.figure()
plt.scatter(data[:,0], data[:,1])
plt.xlabel('Dimension 1')
plt.ylabel('Dimension 2')
plt.title('Input data')
```

Define the maximum and minimum values that each dimension can take:

```
# Define minimum and maximum values for each dimension
dim1_min, dim1_max, dim2_min, dim2_max = 0, 1, 0, 1
```

Since the data is separated into two classes, we just need one bit to represent the output. So, the output layer will contain a single neuron.

```
# Number of neurons in the output layer
num_output = labels.shape[1]
```

We have a dataset where the data points are two-dimensional. Let's define a Perceptron with two input neurons, where we assign one neuron for each dimension.

```
# Define a perceptron with 2 input neurons (because we
# have 2 dimensions in the input data)
dim1 = [dim1_min, dim1_max]
dim2 = [dim2_min, dim2_max]
perceptron = nl.net.newp([dim1, dim2], num_output)
```

Train the perceptron with the training data:

```
# Train the perceptron using the data
error_progress = perceptron.train(data, labels, epochs=100, show=20,
lr=0.03)
```

Plot the training progress using the error metric:

```
# Plot the training progress
plt.figure()
plt.plot(error_progress)
plt.xlabel('Number of epochs')
plt.ylabel('Training error')
plt.title('Training error progress')
plt.grid()

plt.show()
```

The full code is given in the file `perceptron_classifier.py`. If you run the code, you will get two output screenshots. The first screenshot indicates the input data points:

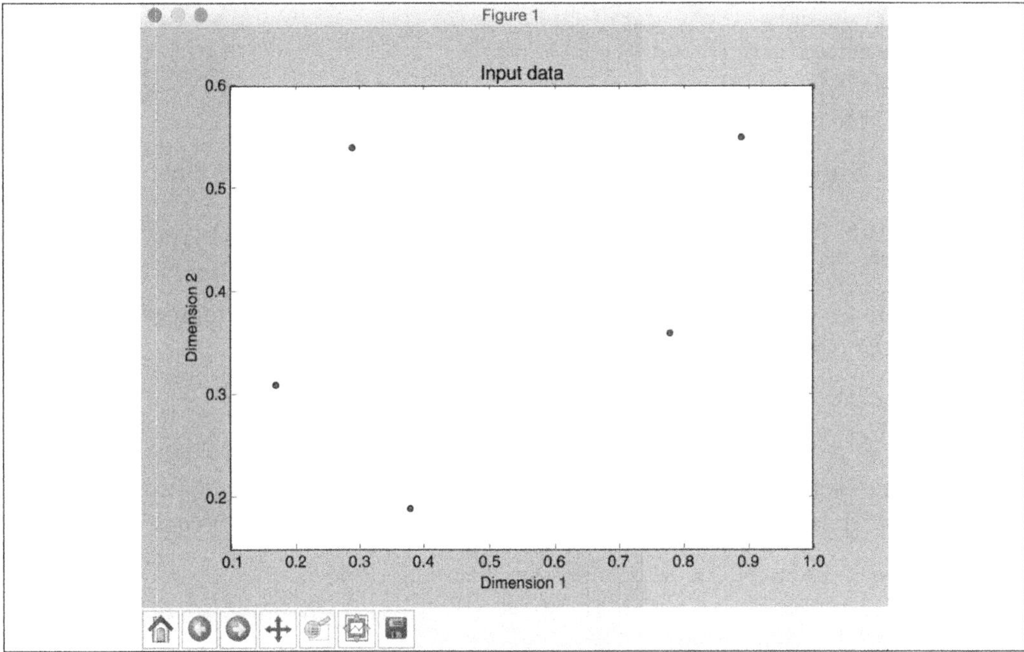

Figure 2: Plot of the training progress

The second screenshot represents the training progress using the error metric:

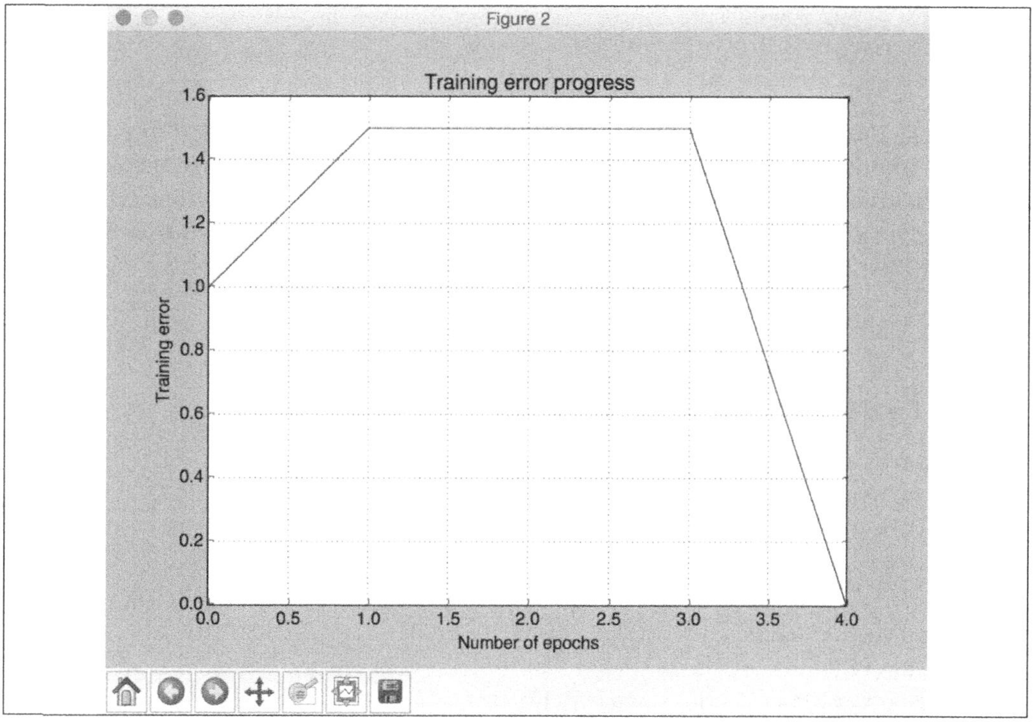

Figure 3: Plot of the training error

We can observe from the preceding screenshot that the error goes down to **0** at the end of the fourth epoch, which is exactly what we wanted to happen. If the error is **0**, it cannot be improved any further. In the next section, we'll enhance our model and create a single-layer neural network.

Constructing a single-layer neural network

Having a model that has a few perceptrons is a good start and it allowed us to get a fundamental understanding of this exciting concept, but to really solve problems, such a simple model will not be sufficient. The human brain has approximately 85 billion neurons. We won't be building a neural network that has that many nodes, but this number gives you an idea of what it takes to solve complicated problems. Before we build a model with billions of nodes, let's take the next step to building a network with a single-layer. This single-layer neural network consists of independent neurons acting on input data to produce an output. Let's get to it.

Create a new Python file and import the following packages:

```
import numpy as np
import matplotlib.pyplot as plt
import neurolab as nl
```

We will use the input data from the file `data_simple_nn.txt` provided to you. Each line in this file contains four numbers. The first two numbers form the datapoint and the last two numbers are the labels. Why do we need to assign two numbers for labels? Because we have four distinct classes in our dataset, so we need two bits to represent them. Let's go ahead and load the data:

```
# Load input data
text = np.loadtxt('data_simple_nn.txt')
```

Separate the data into data points and labels:

```
# Separate it into datapoints and labels
data = text[:, 0:2]
labels = text[:, 2:]
```

Plot the input data:

```
# Plot input data
plt.figure()
plt.scatter(data[:,0], data[:,1])
plt.xlabel('Dimension 1')
plt.ylabel('Dimension 2')
plt.title('Input data')
```

Extract the minimum and maximum values for each dimension (we don't need to hardcode it like we did in the previous section):

```
# Minimum and maximum values for each dimension
dim1_min, dim1_max = data[:,0].min(), data[:,0].max()
dim2_min, dim2_max = data[:,1].min(), data[:,1].max()
```

Define the number of neurons in the output layer:

```
# Define the number of neurons in the output layer
num_output = labels.shape[1]
```

Define a single-layer neural network using the above parameters:

```
# Define a single-layer neural network
dim1 = [dim1_min, dim1_max]
dim2 = [dim2_min, dim2_max]
nn = nl.net.newp([dim1, dim2], num_output)
```

Train the neural network using training data:

```
# Train the neural network
error_progress = nn.train(data, labels, epochs=100, show=20, lr=0.03)
```

Plot the training progress:

```
# Plot the training progress
plt.figure()
plt.plot(error_progress)
plt.xlabel('Number of epochs')
plt.ylabel('Training error')
plt.title('Training error progress')
plt.grid()

plt.show()
```

Define some sample test data points and run the network on those points:

```
# Run the classifier on test datapoints
print('\nTest results:')
data_test = [[0.4, 4.3], [4.4, 0.6], [4.7, 8.1]]
for item in data_test:
    print(item, '-->', nn.sim([item])[0])
```

The full code is given in the file `simple_neural_network.py`. If you run the code, you will get two screenshots. The first screenshot represents the input data points:

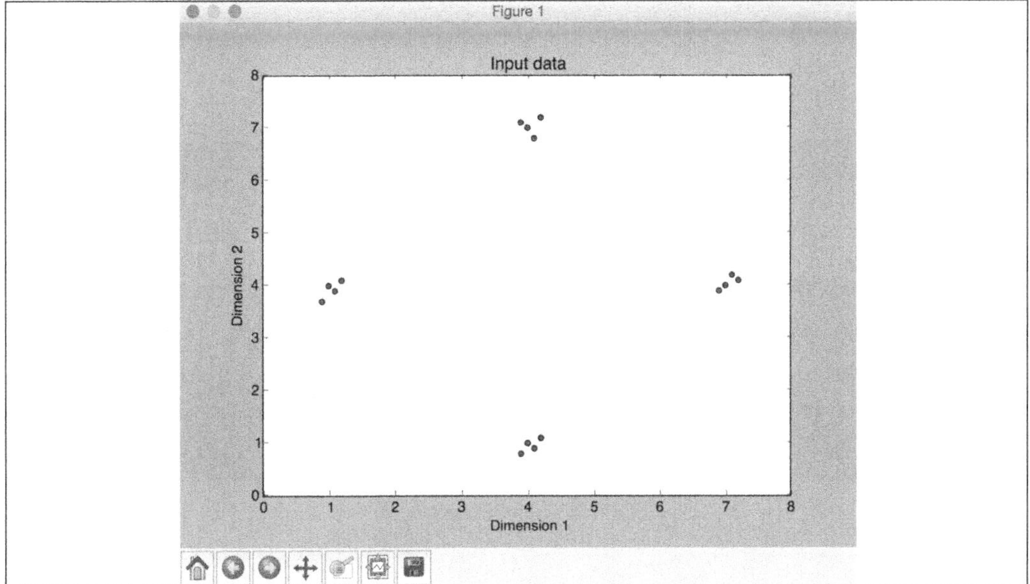

Figure 4: Plot of the data points

The second screenshot shows the training progress:

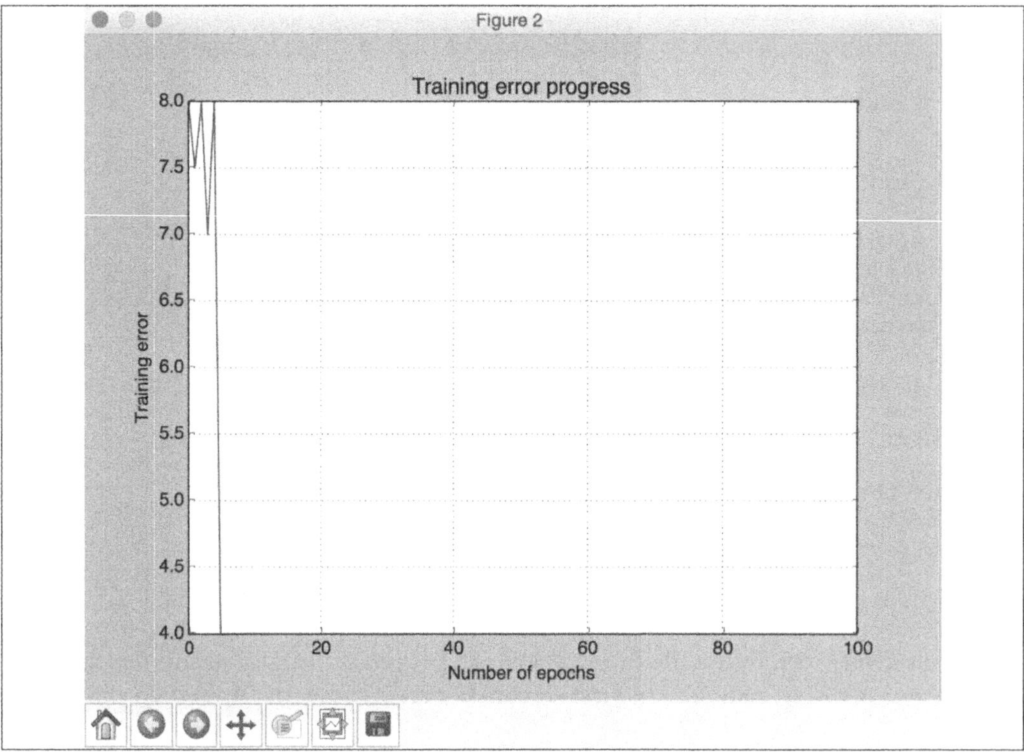

Figure 5: Plot of the training progress

Once you close the graphs, you should see the following output:

```
Epoch: 20; Error: 4.0;
Epoch: 40; Error: 4.0;
Epoch: 60; Error: 4.0;
Epoch: 80; Error: 4.0;
Epoch: 100; Error: 4.0;
The maximum number of train epochs is reached

Test results:
[0.4, 4.3] --> [ 0.  0.]
[4.4, 0.6] --> [ 1.  0.]
[4.7, 8.1] --> [ 1.  1.]
```

Figure 6: Training epochs

As we can see in *Figure 5*, the error quickly starts decreasing, signifying that our training is efficiently creating better and better predictions. In this case, the error did not go down to zero. But if we let the model run for a few more epochs, we expect that the error will continue to decrease. If you locate these test data points on a 2D graph, you can visually verify that the predicted outputs are correct.

Constructing a multi-layer neural network

So, we enhanced our model from a few nodes to a single-layer, but we are still far away from 85 billion nodes. We won't get to that in this section either, but let's take another step in the right direction. The human brain does not use a single-layer model. The output from some neurons becomes the input for other neurons and so on. A model that has this characteristic is known as a multi-layer neural network. This type of architecture yields higher accuracy, and it enables us to solve more complex and more varied problems. Let's see how we can use NeuroLab to build a multi-layer neural network.

Create a new Python file and import the following packages:

```
import numpy as np
import matplotlib.pyplot as plt
import neurolab as nl
```

In the previous two sections, we saw how to use a neural network as a classifier. In this section, we will see how to use a multi-layer neural network as a regressor. Generate some sample data points based on the equation *y = 3x^2 + 5* and then normalize the points:

```
# Generate some training data
min_val = -15
max_val = 15
num_points = 130
x = np.linspace(min_val, max_val, num_points)
y = 3 * np.square(x) + 5
y /= np.linalg.norm(y)
```

Reshape the preceding variables to create a training dataset:

```
# Create data and labels
data = x.reshape(num_points, 1)
labels = y.reshape(num_points, 1)
```

Plot the input data:

```
# Plot input data
plt.figure()
```

```
plt.scatter(data, labels)
plt.xlabel('Dimension 1')
plt.ylabel('Dimension 2')
plt.title('Input data')
```

Define a multi-layer neural network with two hidden layers. You are free to design a neural network any way you want. For this case, let's use `10` neurons in the first layer and `6` neurons in the second layer. Our task is to predict the value, so the output layer will contain a single neuron:

```
# Define a multilayer neural network with 2 hidden layers;
# First hidden layer consists of 10 neurons
# Second hidden layer consists of 6 neurons
# Output layer consists of 1 neuron
nn = nl.net.newff([[min_val, max_val]], [10, 6, 1])
```

Set the training algorithm to gradient descent:

```
# Set the training algorithm to gradient descent
nn.trainf = nl.train.train_gd
```

Train the neural network using the training data that was generated:

```
# Train the neural network
error_progress = nn.train(data, labels, epochs=2000, show=100,
goal=0.01)
```

Run the neural network on the training data points:

```
# Run the neural network on training datapoints
output = nn.sim(data)
y_pred = output.reshape(num_points)
```

Plot the training progress:

```
# Plot training error
plt.figure()
plt.plot(error_progress)
plt.xlabel('Number of epochs')
plt.ylabel('Error')
plt.title('Training error progress')
```

Plot the predicted output:

```
# Plot the output
x_dense = np.linspace(min_val, max_val, num_points * 2)
y_dense_pred = nn.sim(x_dense.reshape(x_dense.size,1)).reshape(x_
dense.size)

plt.figure()
plt.plot(x_dense, y_dense_pred, '-', x, y, '.', x, y_pred, 'p')
plt.title('Actual vs predicted')

plt.show()
```

The full code is given in the file `multilayer_neural_network.py`. If you run the code, you will get three screenshots. The first screenshot shows the input data:

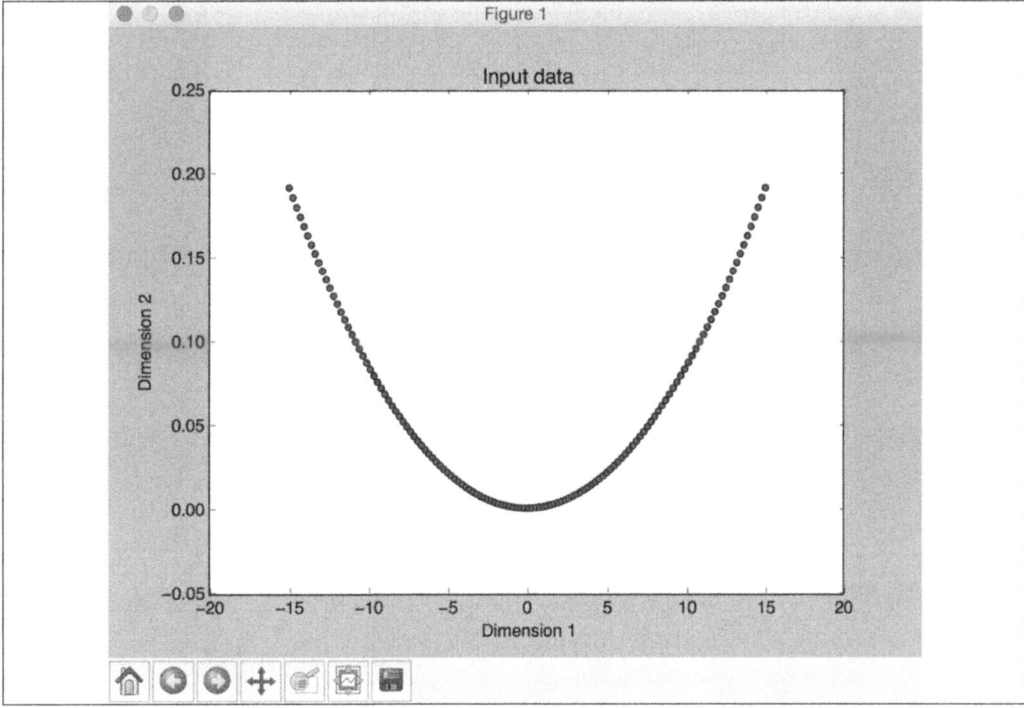

Figure 7: Plot of the input data

The second screenshot shows the training progress:

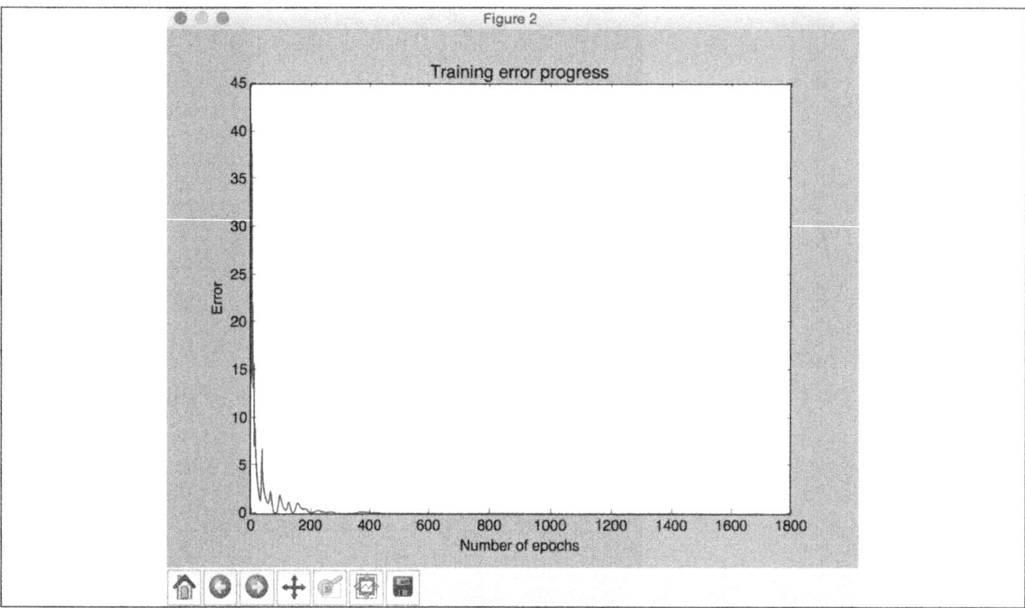

Figure 8: Plot of the training progress

The third screenshot shows the predicted output overlaid on top of the input data:

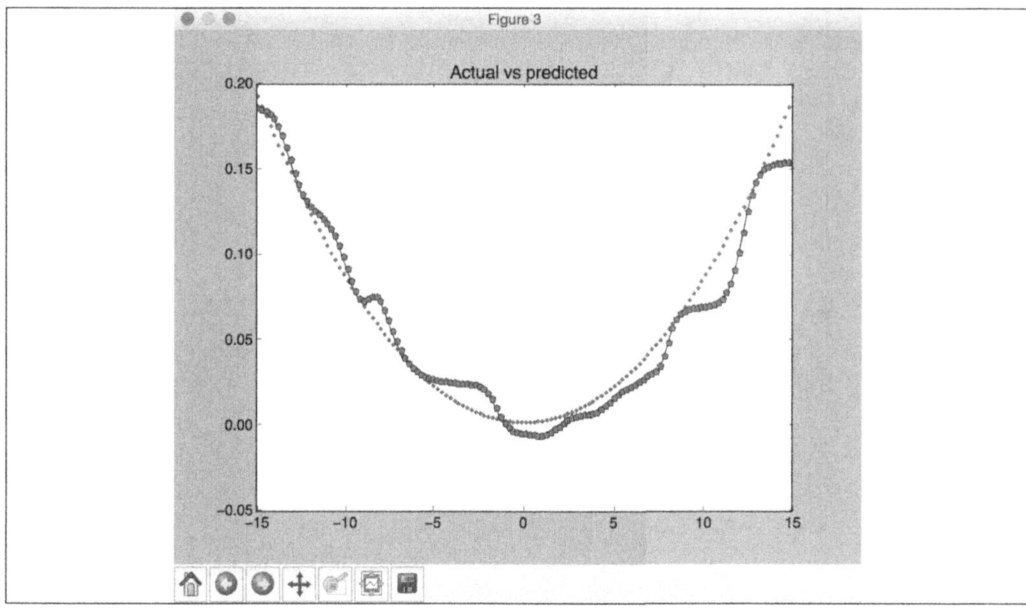

Figure 9: Plot of the output overlaid over the input data

The predicted output seems to follow somewhat closely the actual input. If you continue to train the network and reduce the error, you will see that the predicted output will match the input curve even more accurately.

You should also see the following printed out:

```
Epoch: 100; Error: 1.9247718251621995;
Epoch: 200; Error: 0.15723294798079526;
Epoch: 300; Error: 0.021680213116912858;
Epoch: 400; Error: 0.1381761995539017;
Epoch: 500; Error: 0.04392553381948737;
Epoch: 600; Error: 0.02975401597014979;
Epoch: 700; Error: 0.014228560930227126;
Epoch: 800; Error: 0.03460207842970052;
Epoch: 900; Error: 0.035934053149433196;
Epoch: 1000; Error: 0.025833284445815966;
Epoch: 1100; Error: 0.013672412879982398;
Epoch: 1200; Error: 0.01776586425692384;
Epoch: 1300; Error: 0.04310242610384976;
Epoch: 1400; Error: 0.03799681296096611;
Epoch: 1500; Error: 0.02467030041520845;
Epoch: 1600; Error: 0.010094873168855236;
Epoch: 1700; Error: 0.01210866043021068;
The goal of learning is reached
```

Figure 10: Training epochs

In the previous sections, we learned how to build basic neural networks and get a firm grasp and understanding of the fundamentals. In the next section, we will continue learning how to build neural networks. We will now learn how to build neural networks using vector quantizers.

Building a vector quantizer

Vector Quantization is a quantization technique where the input data is represented by a fixed number of representative points. It is the *N*-dimensional equivalent of rounding off a number. This technique is commonly used in multiple fields such as voice/image recognition, semantic analysis, and image/voice compression. The history of optimal vector quantization theory goes back to the 1950s in Bell Labs, where research was carried out to optimize signal transmission using discretization procedures. One advantage of vector quantizer neural networks is that they have high interpretability. Let's see how we can build a vector c.

Due to some issues with the current version of NeuroLab (v. 0.3.5), running the following code will throw an error. Fortunately, there is a fix for this, but it involves making a change in the NeuroLab package. Changing line **179** of the `net.py` file in the NeuroLab package (`layer_out.np['w'][n][st:i].fill(1.0)`) to `layer_out.np['w'][n][int(st):int(i)].fill(1.0))` should fix this issue. Readers are requested to use this workaround until the time that a fix is implemented in the official NeuroLab package.

Create a new Python file and import the following packages:

```
import numpy as np
import matplotlib.pyplot as plt
import neurolab as nl
```

Load the input data from the file `data_vector_quantization.txt`. Each line in this file contains six numbers. The first two numbers form the datapoint and the last four numbers form a one-hot encoded label. There are four classes overall.

```
# Load input data
text = np.loadtxt('data_vector_quantization.txt')
```

Separate the text into data and labels:

```
# Separate it into data and labels
data = text[:, 0:2]
labels = text[:, 2:]
```

Define a neural network with two layers where we have `10` neurons in the input layer and `4` neurons in the output layer:

```
# Define a neural network with 2 layers:
# 10 neurons in input layer and 4 neurons in output layer
num_input_neurons = 10
num_output_neurons = 4
weights = [1/num_output_neurons] * num_output_neurons
nn = nl.net.newlvq(nl.tool.minmax(data), num_input_neurons, weights)
```

Train the neural network using the training data:

```
# Train the neural network
_ = nn.train(data, labels, epochs=500, goal=-1)
```

In order to visualize the output clusters, let's create a grid of points:

```
# Create the input grid
xx, yy = np.meshgrid(np.arange(0, 10, 0.2), np.arange(0, 10, 0.2))
xx.shape = xx.size, 1
yy.shape = yy.size, 1
grid_xy = np.concatenate((xx, yy), axis=1)
```

Evaluate the grid of points using the neural network:

```
# Evaluate the input grid of points
grid_eval = nn.sim(grid_xy)
```

Extract the four classes:

```
# Define the 4 classes
class_1 = data[labels[:,0] == 1]
class_2 = data[labels[:,1] == 1]
class_3 = data[labels[:,2] == 1]
class_4 = data[labels[:,3] == 1]
```

Extract the grids corresponding to those four classes:

```
# Define X-Y grids for all the 4 classes
grid_1 = grid_xy[grid_eval[:,0] == 1]
grid_2 = grid_xy[grid_eval[:,1] == 1]
grid_3 = grid_xy[grid_eval[:,2] == 1]
grid_4 = grid_xy[grid_eval[:,3] == 1]
```

Plot the outputs:

```
# Plot the outputs
plt.plot(class_1[:,0], class_1[:,1], 'ko',
        class_2[:,0], class_2[:,1], 'ko',
        class_3[:,0], class_3[:,1], 'ko',
        class_4[:,0], class_4[:,1], 'ko')
plt.plot(grid_1[:,0], grid_1[:,1], 'm.',
        grid_2[:,0], grid_2[:,1], 'bx',
        grid_3[:,0], grid_3[:,1], 'c^',
        grid_4[:,0], grid_4[:,1], 'y+')
plt.axis([0, 10, 0, 10])
plt.xlabel('Dimension 1')
plt.ylabel('Dimension 2')
plt.title('Vector quantization')

plt.show()
```

The full code is given in the file `vector_quantizer.py`. If you run the code, you will get the following screenshot that shows the input data points and the boundaries between clusters:

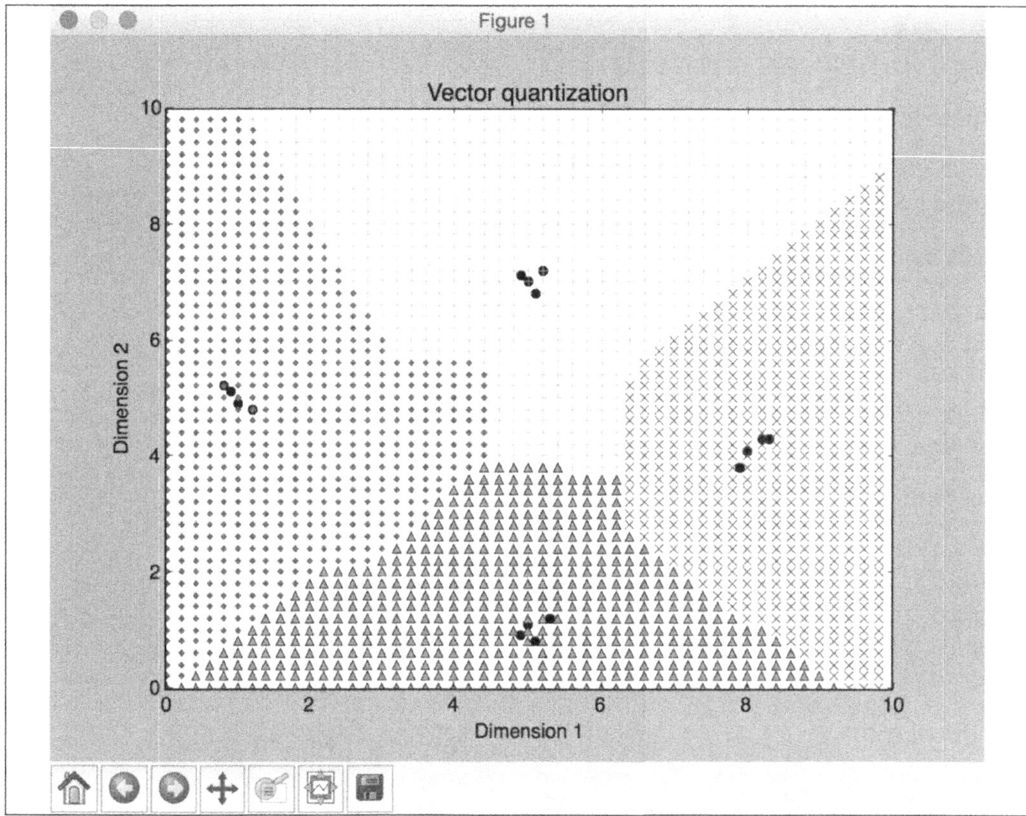

Figure 11: Plot of the input data points and boundaries between clusters

You should also see the following output:

```
Epoch: 100; Error: 0.0;
Epoch: 200; Error: 0.0;
Epoch: 300; Error: 0.0;
Epoch: 400; Error: 0.0;
Epoch: 500; Error: 0.0;
The maximum number of train epochs is reached
```

Figure 12: Training epochs

In the previous section, we learned how to build a neural network using vector quantizers. In the next section, we will continue learning about neural networks. Next, we will learn how to analyze sequential data using recurrent neural networks (RNNs).

Analyzing sequential data using recurrent neural networks

With all our neural network examples so far, we have been using static data. Neural networks can also be used effectively to build models that process sequential data. **Recurrent neural networks (RNNs)** are great at modeling sequential data. You can learn more about recurrent neural networks at:

`https://www.jeremyjordan.me/introduction-to-recurrent-neural-networks/`

When we are working with time series data, we normally cannot use generic learning models. We need to capture the temporal dependencies in the data so that a robust model can be built. Let's see how to build it.

Create a new Python file and import the following packages:

```
import numpy as np
import matplotlib.pyplot as plt
import neurolab as nl
```

Define a function to generate the waveforms. Start by defining four sine waves:

```
def get_data(num_points):
    # Create sine waveforms
    wave_1 = 0.5 * np.sin(np.arange(0, num_points))
    wave_2 = 3.6 * np.sin(np.arange(0, num_points))
    wave_3 = 1.1 * np.sin(np.arange(0, num_points))
    wave_4 = 4.7 * np.sin(np.arange(0, num_points))
```

Create varying amplitudes for the overall waveform:

```
    # Create varying amplitudes
    amp_1 = np.ones(num_points)
    amp_2 = 2.1 + np.zeros(num_points)
    amp_3 = 3.2 * np.ones(num_points)
    amp_4 = 0.8 + np.zeros(num_points)
```

Create the overall waveform:

```
    wave = np.array([wave_1, wave_2, wave_3, wave_4]).reshape(num_
points * 4, 1)
    amp = np.array([[amp_1, amp_2, amp_3, amp_4]]).reshape(num_points
* 4, 1)

    return wave, amp
```

Define a function to visualize the output of the neural network:

```
# Visualize the output
def visualize_output(nn, num_points_test):
    wave, amp = get_data(num_points_test)
    output = nn.sim(wave)
    plt.plot(amp.reshape(num_points_test * 4))
    plt.plot(output.reshape(num_points_test * 4))
```

Define the `main` function and create a waveform:

```
if __name__=='__main__':
    # Create some sample data
    num_points = 40
    wave, amp = get_data(num_points)
```

Create a recurrent neural network with two layers:

```
    # Create a recurrent neural network with 2 layers
    nn = nl.net.newelm([[-2, 2]], [10, 1], [nl.trans.TanSig(),
nl.trans.PureLin()])
```

Set the initializer functions for each layer:

```
    # Set the init functions for each layer
    nn.layers[0].initf = nl.init.InitRand([-0.1, 0.1], 'wb')
    nn.layers[1].initf = nl.init.InitRand([-0.1, 0.1], 'wb')
    nn.init()
```

Train the neural network:

```
    # Train the recurrent neural network
    error_progress = nn.train(wave, amp, epochs=1200, show=100,
goal=0.01)
```

Run the data through the network:

```
    # Run the training data through the network
    output = nn.sim(wave)
```

Plot the output:

```
    # Plot the results
    plt.subplot(211)
    plt.plot(error_progress)
    plt.xlabel('Number of epochs')
    plt.ylabel('Error (MSE)')

    plt.subplot(212)
```

```
plt.plot(amp.reshape(num_points * 4))
plt.plot(output.reshape(num_points * 4))
plt.legend(['Original', 'Predicted'])
```

Test the performance of the neural network on unknown test data:

```
# Testing the network performance on unknown data
plt.figure()

plt.subplot(211)
visualize_output(nn, 82)
plt.xlim([0, 300])

plt.subplot(212)
visualize_output(nn, 49)
plt.xlim([0, 300])

plt.show()
```

The full code is given in the file `recurrent_neural_network.py`. If you run the code, you will see two output figures. The upper half of the first screenshot shows the training progress and the lower half shows the predicted output overlaid on top of the input waveform:

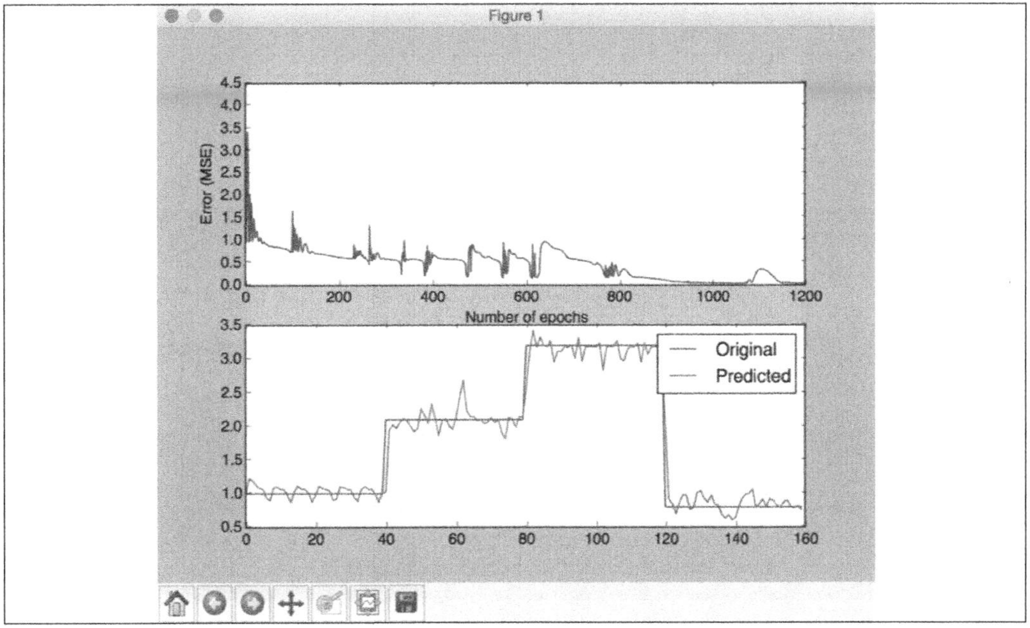

Figure 13: Plot of the output overlaid on top of the input waveform

The upper half of the following screenshot shows how the neural network simulates the waveform even though we increased the length of the waveform. The lower half of the screenshot shows the same for decreased length:

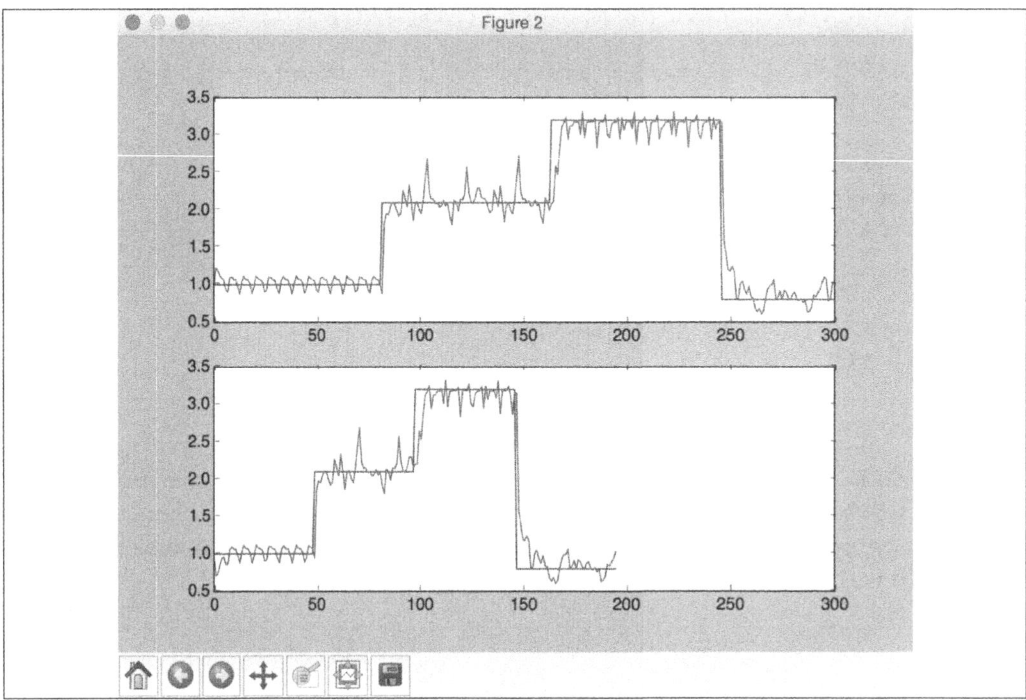

Figure 14: Plot of the simulation of the waveforms

You should also see the following output:

```
Epoch: 100; Error: 0.7378753203612153;
Epoch: 200; Error: 0.6276459886666788;
Epoch: 300; Error: 0.586316536629095;
Epoch: 400; Error: 0.7246461052491963;
Epoch: 500; Error: 0.7244266943409208;
Epoch: 600; Error: 0.5650581389122635;
Epoch: 700; Error: 0.5798180931911314;
Epoch: 800; Error: 0.19557566610789826;
Epoch: 900; Error: 0.10837074465396046;
Epoch: 1000; Error: 0.04330852391940663;
Epoch: 1100; Error: 0.3073835343028226;
Epoch: 1200; Error: 0.034685278416163604;
The maximum number of train epochs is reached
```

Figure 15: Training epochs

As you can see, the error continuously decreases until the maximum number of training epochs is reached. This concludes the section in which we showed how RNNs can be used to analyze time series data. In the next section, we will demonstrate a practical application of neural networks by looking at optical character recognition.

Visualizing characters in an optical character recognition database

Neural networks can also be used for optical character recognition. It is perhaps one of its most common use cases. Converting handwriting to computer characters has been a fundamental problem that many computer scientists have tried to solve and has yet remained elusive. We have made great advances but, for obvious reasons, 100% accuracy will remain out of reach. Why?

Think about this scenario. Have you ever written anything down and five minutes later, you are unable to read your own handwriting? Computers will always have this problem as well. There is an infinite number of ways to write down the number *6* and some of them will look more like a *0* or a *5* than a *6*. I might be wrong, but I think we will find a cure for cancer before we are able to find a reliable way for a computer to recognize a doctor's handwriting. We can already achieve high levels of accuracy and the *more beautiful* the handwriting, the easier it will be to read. The reason we keep on trying to solve this problem is because it's a worthwhile goal that has many applications. By way of a quick example, a doctor's time is highly valued. As the systems get better at recognizing their notes, they will be freed up to focus their energy on actually treating and helping patients and focus less on paperwork.

Optical Character Recognition (**OCR**) is the process of recognizing handwritten characters in images. Before building a model, let's familiarize ourselves with the dataset. We will be using the dataset available at:

`http://ai.stanford.edu/~btaskar/ocr`

You will be downloading a file called `letter.data`. For convenience, this file has been provided to you in the code bundle. Let's see how to load that data and visualize the characters.

Create a new Python file and import the following packages:

```
import os
import sys

import cv2
import numpy as np
```

Define the input file containing the OCR data:

```
# Define the input file
input_file = 'letter.data'
```

Define the visualization and other parameters required to load the data from that file:

```
# Define the visualization parameters
img_resize_factor = 12
start = 6
end = -1
height, width = 16, 8
```

Iterate through the lines of that file until the user presses the *Esc* key. Each line in that file is tab-separated. Read each line and scale it up to `255`:

```
# Iterate until the user presses the Esc key
with open(input_file, 'r') as f:
    for line in f.readlines():
        # Read the data
        data = np.array([255 * float(x) for x in line.split('\t')
[start:end]])
```

Reshape the 1D array into a 2D image:

```
        # Reshape the data into a 2D image
        img = np.reshape(data, (height, width))
```

Scale the image for visualization:

```
        # Scale the image
        img_scaled = cv2.resize(img, None, fx=img_resize_factor,
fy=img_resize_factor)
```

Display the image:

```
        # Display the image
        cv2.imshow('Image', img_scaled)
```

Check if the user has pressed the *Esc* key. If so, exit the loop:

```
        # Check if the user pressed the Esc key
        c = cv2.waitKey()
        if c == 27:
            break
```

The full code is given in the file `character_visualizer.py`. If you run the code, you will get an output screenshot displaying a character. You can keep pressing the space bar to see more characters. For example, an o might look like this:

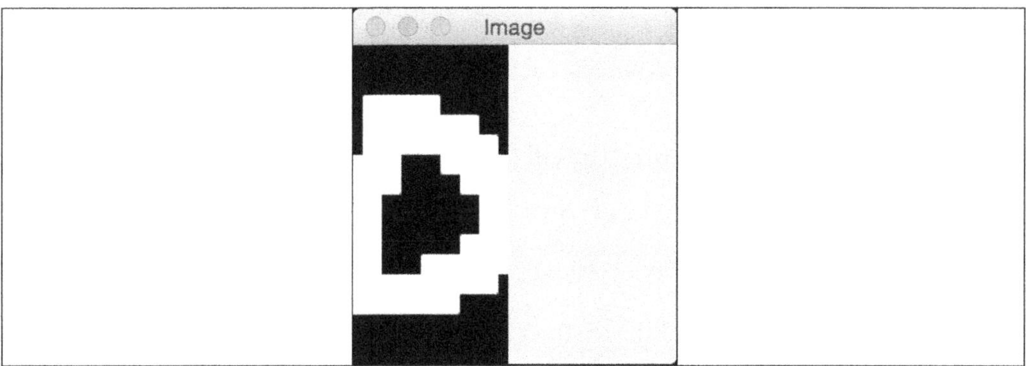

Figure 16: Plot of the letter O

And an `i` might look like this:

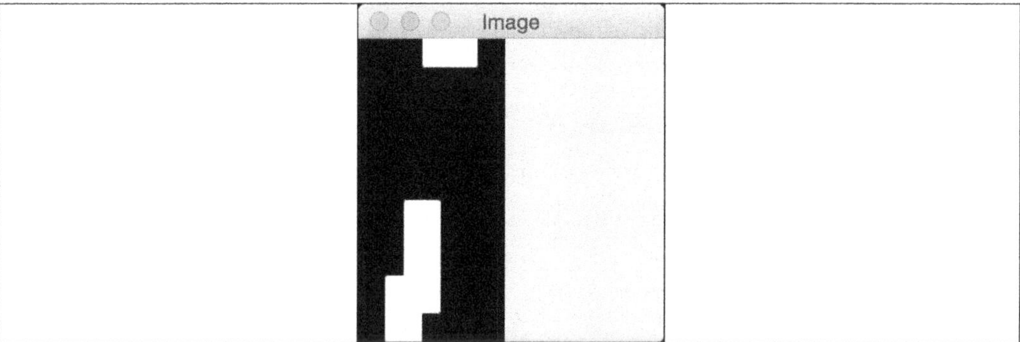

Figure 17: Plot of the letter I

So far, we have not *recognized* any characters. We have just come up with the way to visualize the dataset and verify that our model is making accurate predictions. We will build that in the next section.

Building an optical character recognition engine

Now that we have learned how to work with this data, let's build an optical character recognition system using neural networks.

Create a new Python file and import the following packages:

```
import numpy as np
import neurolab as nl
```

Define the input file:

```
# Define the input file
input_file = 'letter.data'
```

Define the number of data points that will be loaded:

```
# Define the number of datapoints to
# be loaded from the input file
num_datapoints = 50
```

Define the string containing all the distinct characters:

```
# String containing all the distinct characters
orig_labels = 'omandig'
```

Extract the number of distinct classes:

```
# Compute the number of distinct characters
num_orig_labels = len(orig_labels)
```

Define the train and test split. We will use 90% for training and 10% for testing:

```
# Define the training and testing parameters
num_train = int(0.9 * num_datapoints)
num_test = num_datapoints - num_train
```

Define the dataset extraction parameters:

```
# Define the dataset extraction parameters
start = 6
end = -1
```

Create the dataset:

```
# Creating the dataset
data = []
labels = []
with open(input_file, 'r') as f:
    for line in f.readlines():
        # Split the current line tabwise
        list_vals = line.split('\t')
```

If the label is not in our list of labels, we should skip it:

```
        # Check if the label is in our ground truth
        # labels. If not, we should skip it.
        if list_vals[1] not in orig_labels:
            continue
```

Extract the current label and append it to the main list:

```
        # Extract the current label and append it
        # to the main list
        label = np.zeros((num_orig_labels, 1))
        label[orig_labels.index(list_vals[1])] = 1
        labels.append(label)
```

Extract the character vector and append it to the main list:

```
        # Extract the character vector and append it to the main list
        cur_char = np.array([float(x) for x in list_vals[start:end]])
        data.append(cur_char)
```

Exit the loop once we have created the dataset:

```
        # Exit the loop once the required dataset has been created
        if len(data) >= num_datapoints:
            break
```

Convert the lists into NumPy arrays:

```
# Convert the data and labels to numpy arrays
data = np.asfarray(data)
labels = np.array(labels).reshape(num_datapoints, num_orig_labels)
```

Extract the number of dimensions:

```
# Extract the number of dimensions
num_dims = len(data[0])
```

Create a feedforward neural network and set the training algorithm to gradient descent:

```
# Create a feedforward neural network
nn = nl.net.newff([[0, 1] for _ in range(len(data[0]))],
        [128, 16, num_orig_labels])

# Set the training algorithm to gradient descent
nn.trainf = nl.train.train_gd
```

Train the neural network:

```
# Train the network
error_progress = nn.train(data[:num_train,:], labels[:num_train,:],
        epochs=10000, show=100, goal=0.01)
```

Predict the output for test data:

```
# Predict the output for test inputs
print('\nTesting on unknown data:')
predicted_test = nn.sim(data[num_train:, :])
for i in range(num_test):
    print('\nOriginal:', orig_labels[np.argmax(labels[i])])
    print('Predicted:', orig_labels[np.argmax(predicted_test[i])])
```

The full code is given in the file `ocr.py`. If you run the code, you should see the following output:

```
Epoch: 100; Error: 80.75182001223291;
Epoch: 200; Error: 49.823887961230206;
Epoch: 300; Error: 26.624261963923217;
Epoch: 400; Error: 31.131906412329677;
Epoch: 500; Error: 30.589610928772494;
Epoch: 600; Error: 23.129959531324324;
Epoch: 700; Error: 15.561849160600984;
Epoch: 800; Error: 9.52433563455828;
Epoch: 900; Error: 1.4032941634688987;
Epoch: 1000; Error: 1.1584148924740179;
Epoch: 1100; Error: 0.844934060039839;
Epoch: 1200; Error: 0.646187646028962;
Epoch: 1300; Error: 0.48881681329304894;
Epoch: 1400; Error: 0.4005475591737743;
Epoch: 1500; Error: 0.34145887283532067;
Epoch: 1600; Error: 0.29871068426249625;
Epoch: 1700; Error: 0.2657577763744411;
Epoch: 1800; Error: 0.23921810237252988;
Epoch: 1900; Error: 0.2172060084455509;
Epoch: 2000; Error: 0.19856823374761018;
Epoch: 2100; Error: 0.18253521958793384;
Epoch: 2200; Error: 0.16855895648078095;
```

Figure 18: Training epochs

It will keep going until 10,000 epochs. Once it's done, you should see the following output:

```
Epoch: 9500; Error: 0.032460181065798295;
Epoch: 9600; Error: 0.027044816600106478;
Epoch: 9700; Error: 0.022026328910164213;
Epoch: 9800; Error: 0.018353324233938713;
Epoch: 9900; Error: 0.01578969259136868;
Epoch: 10000; Error: 0.014064205770213847;
The maximum number of train epochs is reached

Testing on unknown data:

Original: o
Predicted: o

Original: m
Predicted: n

Original: m
Predicted: m

Original: a
Predicted: d

Original: n
Predicted: n
```

Figure 19: Training epochs

As we can see in the preceding screenshot, our model got three of them right. If you use a bigger dataset and train longer, then you should get higher accuracy. We leave it to you to see if they can get higher accuracy and better results by training the network longer and tweaking the configuration of the models.

Hopefully, this chapter got you excited about OCR in particular and neural networks in general. In subsequent chapters, we will review many other use cases for this technology that is at the forefront of the current machine learning revolution.

Summary

In this chapter, we learned about neural networks. We discussed how to build and train neural networks. We talked about perceptrons and built a classifier based on that. We learned about single-layer neural networks as well as multi-layer neural networks. We discussed how neural networks could be used to build a vector quantizer. We analyzed sequential data using recurrent neural networks. We then built an optical character recognition engine using neural networks. In the next chapter, we will learn about reinforcement learning and see how to build smart learning agents.

20
Deep Learning with Convolutional Neural Networks

In this chapter, we are going to learn about deep learning and **Convolutional Neural Networks (CNNs)**. CNNs have gained a lot of momentum over the last few years, especially in the field of image recognition. We will talk about the architecture of CNNs and the type of layers used inside. We are going to see how to use a package called TensorFlow. We will build a perceptron-based linear regressor. We are going to learn how to build an image classifier using a single-layer neural network.

We will then build an image classifier using a CNN. Image classifiers have many applications. It's a fancy name, but it's just the ability of computers to discern what an object is. For example, you might build a classifier that determines if something is a hotdog or not a hotdog. This is a lighthearted example, but image classifiers can also have life-or-death applications. Picture a drone that has image classification software embedded in it and it can distinguish between civilians and enemy combatants. No mistakes can be made in that sort of case.

This chapter covers the following topics:

- The basics of CNNs
- The architecture of CNNs
- The types of layers in a CNN
- Building a perceptron-based linear regressor
- Building an image classifier using a single-layer neural network
- Building an image classifier using a CNN

Let's begin by running through the basics.

The basics of Convolutional Neural Networks

CNNs in general, and **Generative Adversarial Networks (GANs)** in particular, have been in the news lately. A GAN is a class of CNN developed by Ian Goodfellow and his colleagues initially in 2014. In GANs, two neural networks compete against each other in a game (in a game theory sense). Given a dataset, a GAN learns to create new data examples similar to the training set. For example, it might be a little slow but there is a website that will generate faces of people that don't exist.

We'll let your imagination run wild but it would certainly be possible to create a film using some of these generated "humans" to star in the movie. There is other research to try to solve the converse. Given an image, can we determine if it's a GAN-generated image or a real person? You can play around with the website here:

`https://thispersondoesnotexist.com/`

To use it, just keep on refreshing the page and it will generate a new image every time. GANs were originally created as a generative model for unsupervised learning. GANs have also proven useful for semi-supervised learning, supervised learning, and reinforcement learning. Yann LeCun, one of the giants of AI, calls GANs, *the most interesting idea in the last 10 years in ML* [1]. Let's consider some other use cases and applications of GANs.

Generating more example data using GANs - Data is the ingredient in ML. In some cases, it is not possible to get enough data to feed to a model. Using GANs to generate more input data is a good way to generate additional quality data to feed into a model.

Security - ML has provided a boost to many industries. Regardless of the market sector, cyber security is always "top of mind" for the C-suite. GANs are used by some security vendors to handle cyberattacks. In simple terms, the GAN creates fake intrusions, and these intrusions are used to train models to identify these threats, enabling us to thwart genuine versions of these attacks.

Data manipulation - GANs can be used for "pseudo style transfers," that is, modifying some dimensions of the example without completely modifying it.

GANs can be used in voice applications. Given a speech, a GAN can be trained to reproduce famous voices.

In some famous examples, videos of Trump, Obama, or the Mona Lisa were modified using GANs and the developers made these figures say phrases they never said. They can be quite realistic. Or video or images can be changed to look like different people. Here is an example of the interposition of Nicolas Cage's face on top of an image of President Donald Trump created by MIT:

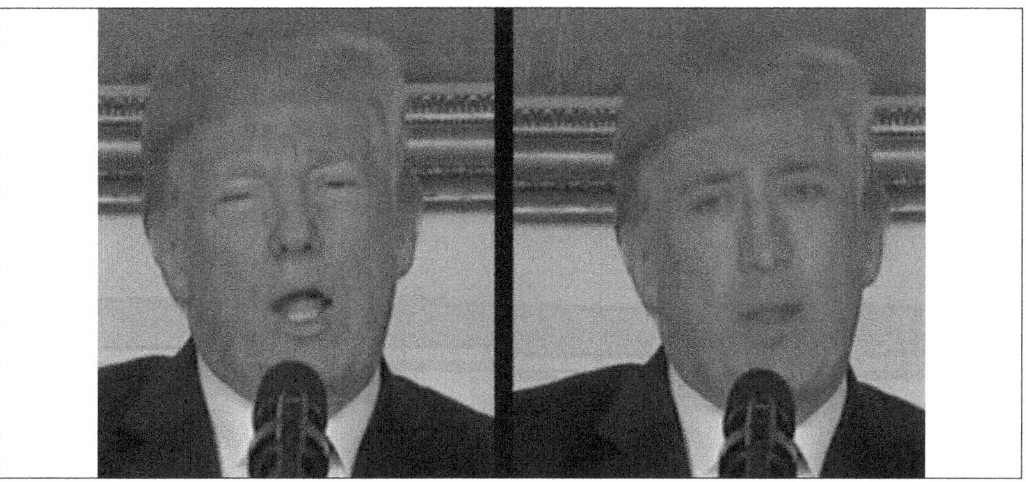

Figure 1: Nicolas Cage as President Donald Trump

These techniques can be ported to other domains such as natural language processing, speech processing, and so on. As an example, the GAN might tweak a sentence slightly, changing the meaning of the sentence.

Privacy - As part of their security strategy, many companies want to keep some of the data private and confidential. Obvious examples would come in the form of defense and military applications. GANs can be used while encrypting data; for example, to generate one-time throwaway keys.

In 2016, Google began research in order to better utilize GANs. The basic idea was to have one network creating a passkey and another network trying to crack it.

We saw how neural networks work throughout the previous two chapters. Neural networks consist of neurons that have weights and biases. These weights and biases are tuned during the training process to come up with a good learning model. Each neuron receives a set of inputs, processes it in some way, and then outputs a value.

If we build a neural network with many layers, it's called a deep neural network. The branch of AI dealing with these deep neural networks is referred to as deep learning.

One of the main disadvantages of ordinary neural networks is that they ignore the structure of input data. All data is converted to a single-dimensional array before feeding it into the network. This might work well with numeric data, but things get difficult when we deal with images.

Let's consider grayscale images. These images are 2D structures and we know that the spatial arrangement of pixels has a lot of hidden information. If we ignore this information, we will be losing a lot of underlying patterns. This is where CNNs come into the picture. CNNs take the 2D structure of the images into account when they process them.

CNNs are also made up of neurons consisting of weights and biases. These neurons accept input data, process it, and then output something. The goal of the network is to go from the raw image data in the input layer to the correct class in the output layer. The difference between ordinary neural networks and CNNs is in the type of layers we use and how we treat the input data. CNNs assume that the inputs are images, which allows them to extract properties specific to images. This makes CNNs way more efficient in dealing with images. Now that we've got the basics of CNNs covered, let's look at how they are built.

Architecture of CNNs

When we are working with ordinary neural networks, we need to convert the input data into a single vector. This vector acts as the input to the neural network, which then passes through the layers of the neural network. In these layers, each neuron is connected to all the neurons in the previous layer. It is also worth noting that the neurons within each layer are not connected to each other. They are only connected to the neurons in the adjacent layers. The last layer in the network is the output layer and it represents the final output.

If we use this structure for images, it will quickly become unmanageable. For example, let's consider an image dataset consisting of 256×256 RGB images. Since these are 3-channel images, there would be $256 * 256 * 3 = 196,608$ weights. Note that this is just for a single neuron! Each layer will have multiple neurons, so the number of weights tends to increase rapidly. This means that the model will now have an enormous number of parameters to tune during the training process. Therefore, it quickly becomes quite complex and time-consuming. Connecting each neuron to every neuron in the previous layer, called full connectivity, is clearly not going to work.

CNNs explicitly consider the structure of images when processing the data. The neurons in CNNs are arranged in 3 dimensions - width, height, and depth. Each neuron in the current layer is connected to a small patch of the output from the previous layer. It's like overlaying an *N*x*N* filter on the input image. This contrasts with a fully connected layer where each neuron is connected to all the neurons of the previous layer.

Since a single filter cannot capture all the nuances of the image, we do this *M* number of times to make sure we capture all the details. These *M* filters act as feature extractors. If you look at the outputs of these filters, we can see that they extract features like edges, corners, and so on. This is true for the initial layers in the CNN. As we progress through layers of the network, we will see that the latter layers extract higher-level features.

A CNN is a deep learning network. It is often used to recognize images. Understanding how it recognizes an image will help in gaining an understanding about how they work. Like any other neural network, it assigns weights and biases to elements in the image and is able to differentiate these elements from one another. The pre-processing used in a CNN is less compared to other classification models. When using primitive methods filters with enough training, CNNs can be trained to distinguish these filters and characteristics.

A CNN architecture, in its basic form, can be compared to the neurons and dendrites in the human brain, and it borrows its inspiration from the visual cortex. Individual neurons respond to stimuli in restricted regions of the visual field. This region is known as the Receptive Field. A grouping of these fields overlap with one another and thus cover the entire field of vision.

CNNs vs. perceptron neural networks

An image is a pixel-value matrix. Why couldn't we just flatten the input image? For example, a *7x7* image can be flattened into a *49x1* vector. We can then use this flattened image as input to a perceptron-based neural network.

When using basic binary (black and white) inputs, this method might show an average precision score while performing prediction of classes, but would have little to no accuracy when it comes to complex images having pixel dependencies throughout.

Let's analyze this for a second to get some understanding by thinking about how humans process an image. Think of an image that contains a diamond shape: ♦. Our brain can instantaneously process the image and realize that it's a diamond shape: ♦.

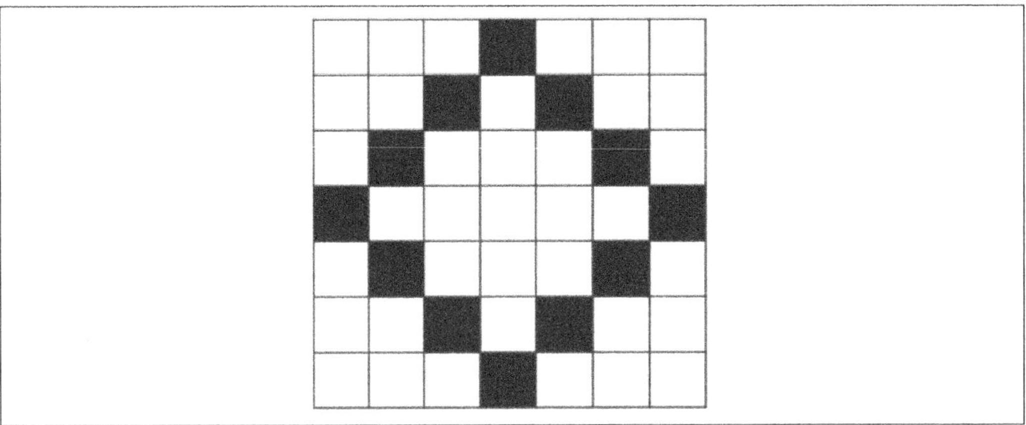

Figure 2: Diamond shape

What happens if we flatten it?

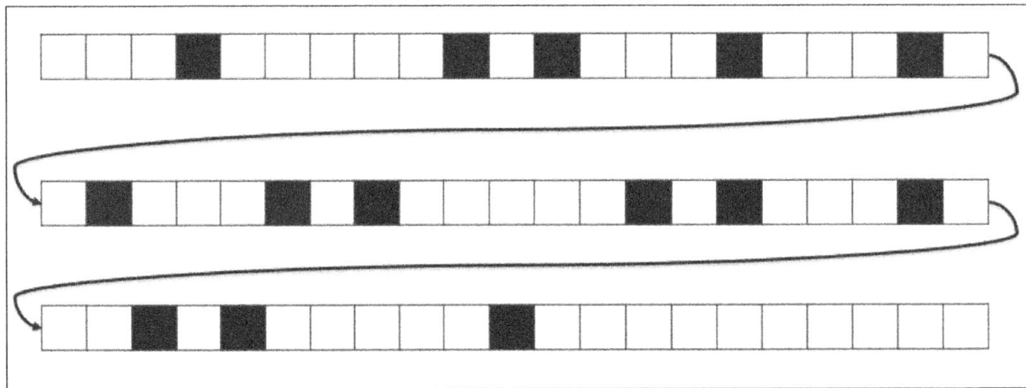

Figure 3: Diamond shape but flattened

It's not so easy to recognize, is it? Despite this, it is the same information. Something similar happens when using traditional neural networks rather than CNNs. The information that we had when the pixels were contiguous is now lost.

A CNN can capture spatial and temporal dependencies in an image through the application of relevant filters. The CNN architecture performs better upon a dataset because of the reduction in the number of parameters and the fact that weights are reused.

Now that we have a better understanding of CNN architecture and how images are processed, let's think about the layers that comprise a CNN.

Types of layers in a CNN

CNNs typically use the following types of layers:

Input layer - This layer takes the raw image data as it is.

Convolutional layer - This layer computes the convolutions between the neurons and the various patches in the input. If you need a quick refresher on image convolutions, you can check out this link:

`http://web.pdx.edu/~jduh/courses/Archive/geog481w07/Students/Ludwig_ImageConvolution.pdf`

The convolutional layer basically computes the dot product between the weights and a small patch in the output of the previous layer.

Rectified Linear Unit layer - This layer applies an activation function to the output of the previous layer. This function is usually something like *max(0, x)*. This layer is needed to add non-linearity to the network so that it can generalize well to any type of function.

Pooling layer - This layer samples the output of the previous layer resulting in a structure with smaller dimensions. Pooling helps us to keep only the prominent parts as we progress in the network. Max pooling is frequently used in the pooling layer, where we pick the maximum value in a given *KxK* window.

Fully Connected layer - This layer computes the output scores in the last layer. The resulting output is of the size *1x1xL*, where *L* is the number of classes in the training dataset.

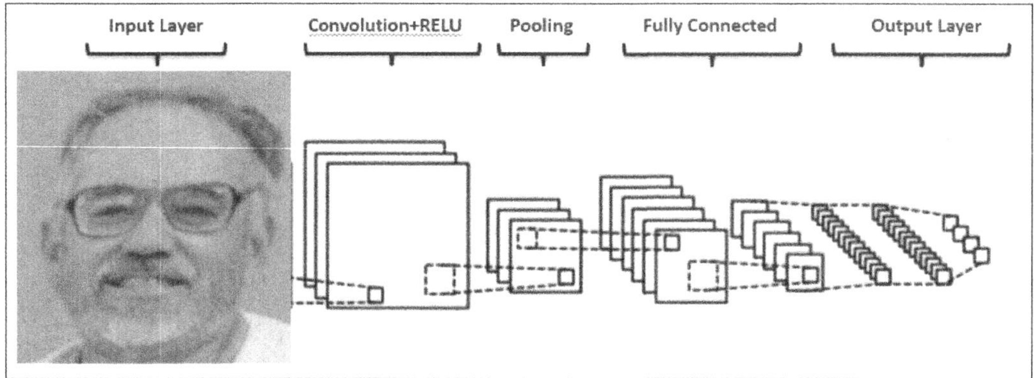

Figure 4: CNN layers

As we go from the input layer to the output layer in the network, the input image gets transformed from pixel values to the final class scores. Many different architectures for CNNs have been proposed and it's an active area of research. The accuracy and robustness of a model depends on many factors - the type of layers, depth of the network, the arrangement of various types of layers within the network, the functions chosen for each layer, training data, and so on.

Building a perceptron-based linear regressor

Before we build a CNN, let's set the stage with a more basic model and the see how we can improve using CNNs. In this section we will see how to build a linear regression model using perceptrons. We have already seen linear regression in previous chapters, but this section is about building a linear regression model using a neural network approach.

We will be using TensorFlow in this chapter. It is a popular deep learning package that's widely used to build various real-world systems. In this section, we will get familiar with how it works. Make sure to install it before you proceed. The installation instructions can be found here:

`https://www.tensorflow.org/get_started/os_setup`

Once you verify that it's installed, create a new Python file and import the following packages:

```
import numpy as np
import matplotlib.pyplot as plt
import tensorflow as tf
```

We will be generating some data points and see how to train a model using these data points.

Define the number of data points to be generated:

```
# Define the number of points to generate
num_points = 1200
```

Define the parameters that will be used to generate the data. We will be using the model of a line: $y = mx + c$:

```
# Generate the data based on equation y = mx + c
data = []
m = 0.2
c = 0.5
for i in range(num_points):
    # Generate 'x'
    x = np.random.normal(0.0, 0.8)
```

Generate some noise to add some variation in the data:

```
    # Generate some noise
    noise = np.random.normal(0.0, 0.04)
```

Compute the value of `y` using the equation:

```
    # Compute 'y'
    y = m*x + c + noise

    data.append([x, y])
```

Once you finish iterating, separate the data into input and output variables:

```
# Separate x and y
x_data = [d[0] for d in data]
y_data = [d[1] for d in data]
```

Plot the data:

```
# Plot the generated data
plt.plot(x_data, y_data, 'ro')
plt.title('Input data')
plt.show()
```

Generate weights and biases for the perceptron. For weights, we will use a uniform random number generator and set the biases to zero:

```
# Generate weights and biases
W = tf.Variable(tf.random_uniform([1], -1.0, 1.0))
b = tf.Variable(tf.zeros([1]))
```

Define the equation using TensorFlow variables:

```
# Define equation for 'y'
y = W * x_data + b
```

Define the loss function that can be used during the training process. The optimizer will try to minimize this value as much as possible.

```
# Define how to compute the loss
loss = tf.reduce_mean(tf.square(y - y_data))
```

Define the gradient descent optimizer and specify the loss function:

```
# Define the gradient descent optimizer
optimizer = tf.train.GradientDescentOptimizer(0.5)
train = optimizer.minimize(loss)
```

All the variables are in place, but they haven't been initialized yet. Let's do that:

```
# Initialize all the variables
init = tf.initialize_all_variables()
```

Start the TensorFlow session and run it using the initializer:

```
# Start the tensorflow session and run it
sess = tf.Session()
sess.run(init)
```

Start the training process:

```
# Start iterating
num_iterations = 10
for step in range(num_iterations):
    # Run the session
    sess.run(train)
```

Print the progress of the training process. The `loss` parameter will continue to decrease as we go through iterations:

```
    # Print the progress
    print('\nITERATION', step+1)
    print('W =', sess.run(W)[0])
```

```
print('b =', sess.run(b)[0])
print('loss =', sess.run(loss))
```

Plot the generated data and overlay the predicted model on top. In this case, the model is a line:

```
# Plot the input data
plt.plot(x_data, y_data, 'ro')

# Plot the predicted output line
plt.plot(x_data, sess.run(W) * x_data + sess.run(b))
```

Set the parameters for the plot:

```
# Set plotting parameters
plt.xlabel('Dimension 0')
plt.ylabel('Dimension 1')
plt.title('Iteration ' + str(step+1) + ' of ' + str(num_
iterations))
plt.show()
```

The full code is given in the file `linear_regression.py`. If you run the code, you should see following screenshot:

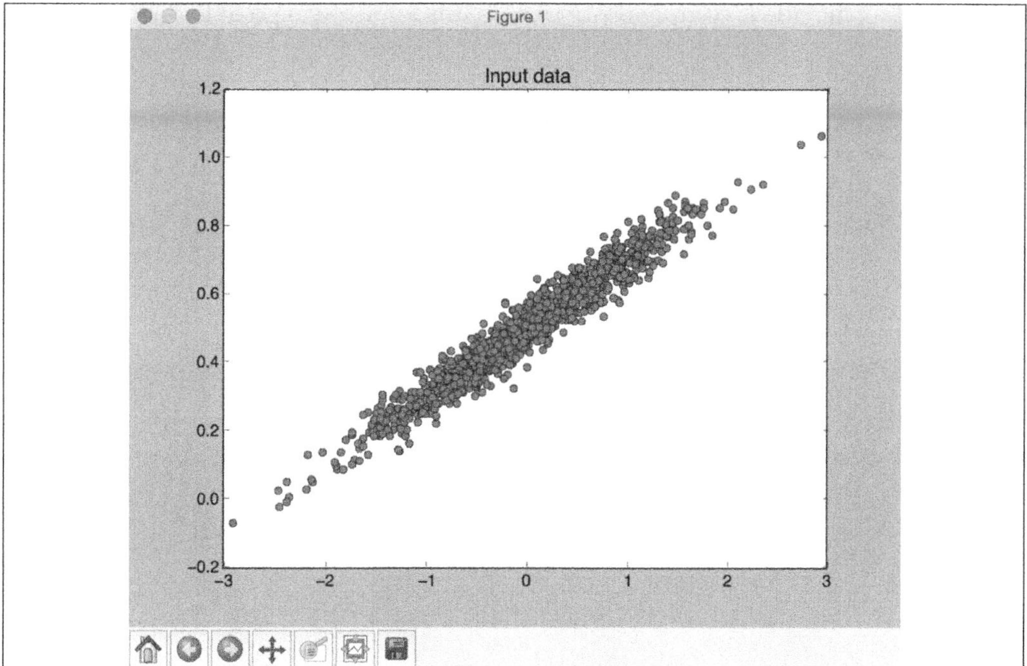

Figure 5: Plot of input data

If you close this window, you will see the training process. The first iteration looks like this:

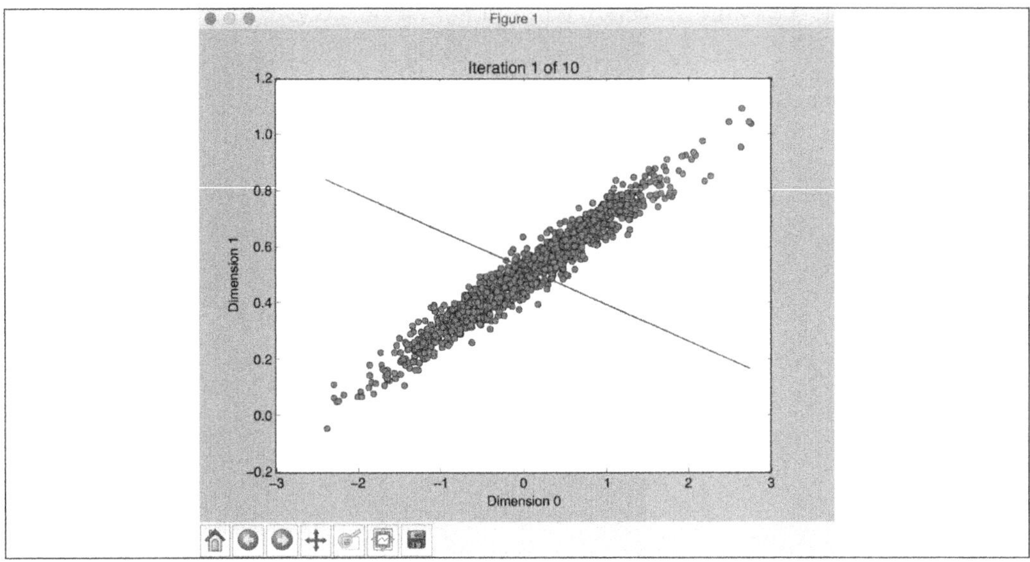

Figure 6: Plot of first iteration of the training process

As we can see, the line is completely off. Close this window to go to the next iteration:

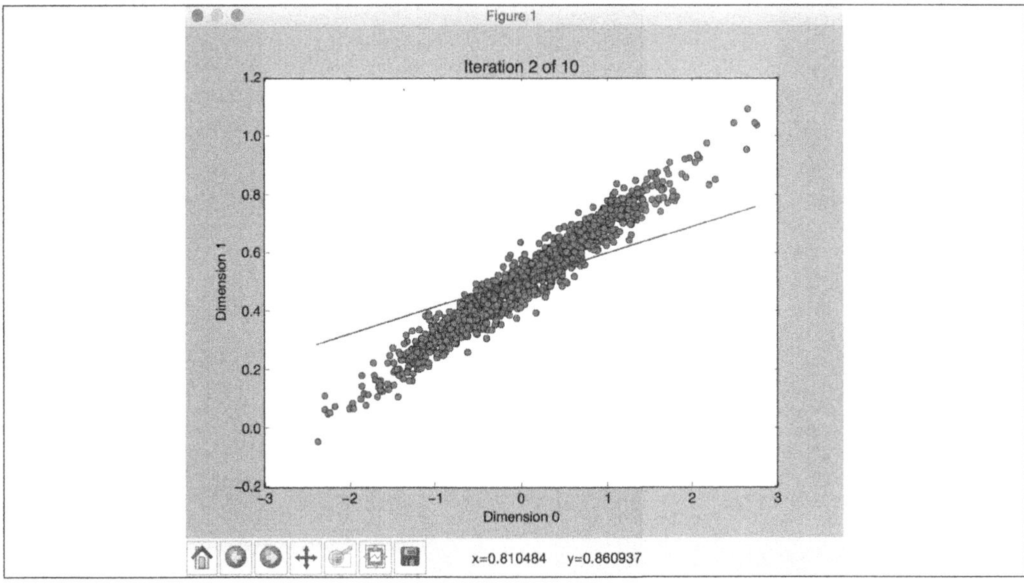

Figure 7: Plot of a subsequent iteration of the training process

The line seems better, but it's still off. Let's close this window and continue iterating:

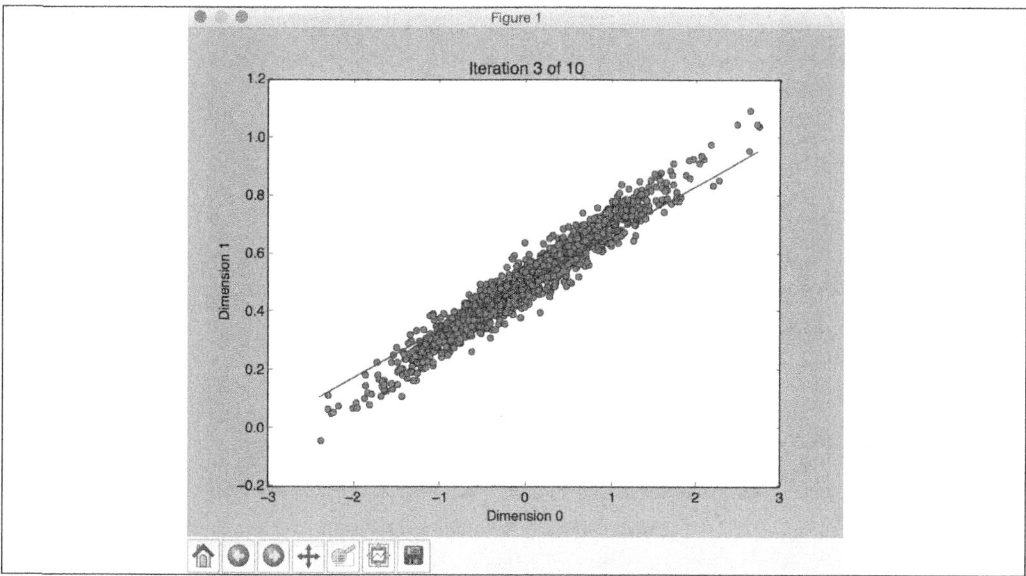

Figure 8: Plot of another subsequent iteration of the training process

It looks like the line is getting closer to the real model. If you continue iterating like this, the model gets better. The eighth iteration looks like this:

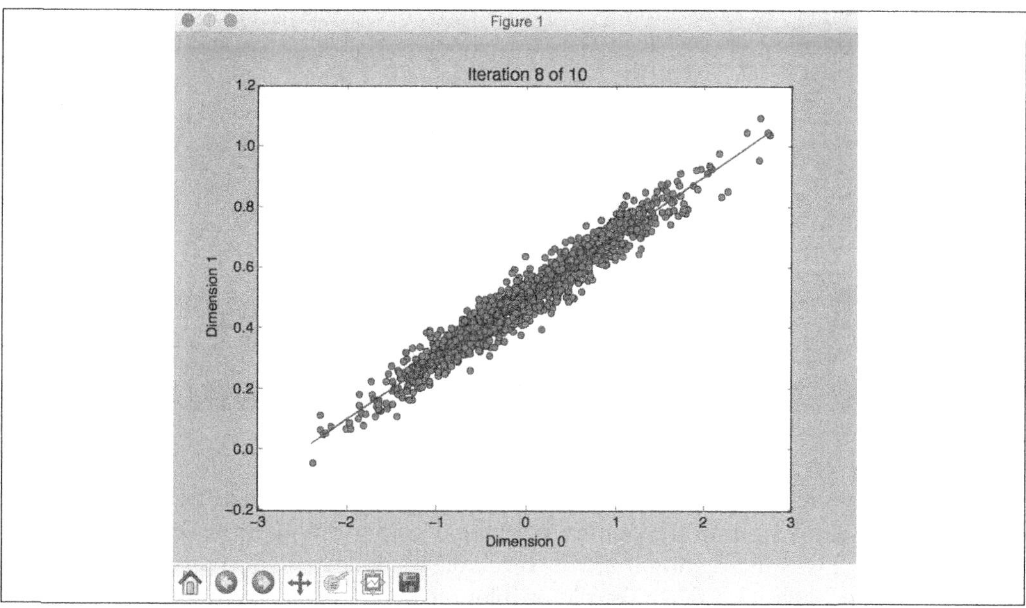

Figure 9: Plot of the eighth iteration of the training process

The line seems to fit the data well. Then, you should see this printed out:

```
ITERATION 1
W = -0.130961
b = 0.53005
loss = 0.0760343

ITERATION 2
W = 0.0917911
b = 0.508959
loss = 0.00960302

ITERATION 3
W = 0.164665
b = 0.502555
loss = 0.00250165

ITERATION 4
W = 0.188492
b = 0.500459
loss = 0.0017425
```

Figure 10: Initial output of the epochs

Once it finishes training, you will see the following:

```
ITERATION 7
W = 0.199662
b = 0.499477
loss = 0.00165175

ITERATION 8
W = 0.199934
b = 0.499453
loss = 0.00165165

ITERATION 9
W = 0.200023
b = 0.499445
loss = 0.00165164

ITERATION 10
W = 0.200052
b = 0.499443
loss = 0.00165164
```

Figure 11: Final output of the epochs

We can see how the values for `w` and `b` keep adjusting and we also see how the loss keeps on decreasing up until the point where the loss is so small that we can no longer see it decrease. It was interesting that we were able to achieve a good result quickly, but we gave our network a fairly simple problem to solve. Let's take it up a notch.

Building an image classifier using a single-layer neural network

Let's see how to create a single-layer neural network using TensorFlow and use it to build an image classifier. We will be using the MNIST image dataset to build our system. It is a dataset containing images of handwritten digits. Our goal is to build a classifier that can correctly identify the digit in each image.

Create a new Python file and import the following packages:

```
import tensorflow as tf
from tensorflow.examples.tutorials.mnist import input_data
```

Extract the MNIST image data. The `one_hot` flag specifies that we will be using one-hot encoding in our labels. It means that if we have *n* classes, then the label for a given data point will be an array of length *n*. Each element in this array corresponds to a given class. To specify a class, the value at the corresponding index will be set to *1* and everything else will be *0*:

```
# Get the MNIST data
mnist = input_data.read_data_sets("./mnist_data", one_hot=True)
```

The images in the database are *28x28*. We need to convert it to a single-dimensional array to create the input layer:

```
# The images are 28x28, so create the input layer
# with 784 neurons (28x28=784)
x = tf.placeholder(tf.float32, [None, 784])
```

Create a single-layer neural network with weights and biases. There are 10 distinct digits in the database. The number of neurons in the input layer is `784` and the number of neurons in the output layer is `10`:

```
# Create a layer with weights and biases.
# There are 10 distinct
# digits, so the output layer should have 10 classes
W = tf.Variable(tf.zeros([784, 10]))
b = tf.Variable(tf.zeros([10]))
```

Create the equation to be used for training:

```
# Create the equation for 'y' using y = W*x + b
y = tf.matmul(x, W) + b
```

Define the loss function and the gradient descent optimizer:

```
# Define the entropy loss and the gradient descent optimizer
y_loss = tf.placeholder(tf.float32, [None, 10])
loss = tf.reduce_mean(tf.nn.softmax_cross_entropy_with_
logits(logits=y, labels=y_loss))
optimizer = tf.train.GradientDescentOptimizer(0.5).minimize(loss)
```

Initialize all the variables:

```
# Initialize all the variables
init = tf.initialize_all_variables()
```

Create a TensorFlow session and run it:

```
# Create a session
session = tf.Session()
session.run(init)
```

Start the training process. We will train using batches where we run the optimizer on the current batch and then continue with the next batch for the next iteration. The first step in each iteration is to get the next batch of images to train on:

```
# Start training
num_iterations = 1200
batch_size = 90
for _ in range(num_iterations):
    # Get the next batch of images
    x_batch, y_batch = mnist.train.next_batch(batch_size)
```

Run the optimizer on this batch of images:

```
    # Train on this batch of images
    session.run(optimizer, feed_dict = {x: x_batch, y_loss: y_batch})
```

Once the training process is over, compute the accuracy using the test dataset:

```
# Compute the accuracy using test data
predicted = tf.equal(tf.argmax(y, 1), tf.argmax(y_loss, 1))
accuracy = tf.reduce_mean(tf.cast(predicted, tf.float32))
print('\nAccuracy =', session.run(accuracy, feed_dict = {
        x: mnist.test.images,
        y_loss: mnist.test.labels}))
```

The full code is given in the file `single_layer.py`. If you run the code, it will download the data to a folder called `mnist_data` in the current folder. This is the default option. If you want to change it, you can do so using the input argument. Once you run the code, you will get the following output:

```
Extracting ./mnist_data/train-images-idx3-ubyte.gz
Extracting ./mnist_data/train-labels-idx1-ubyte.gz
Extracting ./mnist_data/t10k-images-idx3-ubyte.gz
Extracting ./mnist_data/t10k-labels-idx1-ubyte.gz

Accuracy = 0.921
```

Figure 12: Output of the accuracy

As indicated by the output, the accuracy of the model is 92.1%. This is a quite low score. Let's see how we can improve using CNNs.

Building an image classifier using a Convolutional Neural Network

The image classifier in the previous section didn't perform that well. Getting 92.1% on the MNIST dataset is relatively easy. Let's see how we can use CNNs to achieve a much higher accuracy. We will build an image classifier using the same dataset, but with a CNN instead of a single-layer neural network.

Create a new Python file and import the following packages:

```
import argparse

import tensorflow as tf
from tensorflow.examples.tutorials.mnist import input_data
```

Define a function to create values for weights in each layer:

```
def get_weights(shape):
    data = tf.truncated_normal(shape, stddev=0.1)
    return tf.Variable(data)
```

Define a function to create values for biases in each layer:

```
def get_biases(shape):
    data = tf.constant(0.1, shape=shape)
    return tf.Variable(data)
```

Define a function to create a layer based on the input shape:

```
def create_layer(shape):
    # Get the weights and biases
    W = get_weights(shape)
    b = get_biases([shape[-1]])
```

```
        return W, b
```

Define a function to perform 2D convolution:

```
    def convolution_2d(x, W):
        return tf.nn.conv2d(x, W, strides=[1, 1, 1, 1],
                padding='SAME')
```

Define a function to perform a 2×2 max pooling operation:

```
    def max_pooling(x):
        return tf.nn.max_pool(x, ksize=[1, 2, 2, 1],
                strides=[1, 2, 2, 1], padding='SAME')
```

Extract the MNIST image data:

```
    # Get the MNIST data
    mnist = input_data.read_data_sets(args.input_dir, one_hot=True)
```

Create the input layer with `784` neurons:

```
    # The images are 28x28, so create the input layer
    # with 784 neurons (28x28=784)
    x = tf.placeholder(tf.float32, [None, 784])
```

We will be using convolutional neural networks that take advantage of the 2D structure of images. So, let's reshape `x` into a 4D tensor where the second and third dimensions specify the image dimensions:

```
    # Reshape 'x' into a 4D tensor
    x_image = tf.reshape(x, [-1, 28, 28, 1])
```

Create the first convolutional layer, which will extract `32` features for each 5×5 patch in the image:

```
    # Define the first convolutional layer
    W_conv1, b_conv1 = create_layer([5, 5, 1, 32])
```

Convolve the image with the weight tensor computed in the previous step, and then add the bias tensor to it. We then need to apply the **Rectified Linear Unit** (**ReLU**) function to the output:

```
    # Convolve the image with weight tensor, add the
    # bias, and then apply the ReLU function
    h_conv1 = tf.nn.relu(convolution_2d(x_image, W_conv1) + b_conv1)
```

Apply the 2×2 max pooling operator to the output of the previous step:

```
    # Apply the max pooling operator
    h_pool1 = max_pooling(h_conv1)
```

Create the second convolutional layer to compute `64` features for each 5×5 patch:

```
# Define the second convolutional layer
W_conv2, b_conv2 = create_layer([5, 5, 32, 64])
```

Convolve the output of the previous layer with the weight tensor computed in the previous step, and then add the bias tensor to it. We then need to apply the ReLU function to the output:

```
# Convolve the output of previous layer with the
# weight tensor, add the bias, and then apply
# the ReLU function
h_conv2 = tf.nn.relu(convolution_2d(h_pool1, W_conv2) + b_conv2)
```

Apply the 2×2 max pooling operator to the output of the previous step:

```
# Apply the max pooling operator
h_pool2 = max_pooling(h_conv2)
```

The image size is now reduced to 7×7. Create a fully connected layer with `1024` neurons:

```
# Define the fully connected layer
W_fc1, b_fc1 = create_layer([7 * 7 * 64, 1024])
```

Reshape the output of the previous layer:

```
# Reshape the output of the previous layer
h_pool2_flat = tf.reshape(h_pool2, [-1, 7*7*64])
```

Multiply the output of the previous layer with the weight tensor of the fully connected layer, and then add the bias tensor to it. We then apply the ReLU function to the output:

```
# Multiply the output of previous layer by the
# weight tensor, add the bias, and then apply
# the ReLU function
h_fc1 = tf.nn.relu(tf.matmul(h_pool2_flat, W_fc1) + b_fc1)
```

In order to reduce overfitting, we need to create a dropout layer. Let's create a TensorFlow placeholder for the probability values, which specify the probability of a neuron's output being kept during dropout:

```
# Define the dropout layer using a probability placeholder
# for all the neurons
keep_prob = tf.placeholder(tf.float32)
h_fc1_drop = tf.nn.dropout(h_fc1, keep_prob)
```

Define the readout layer with `10` output neurons corresponding to the 10 classes in our dataset. Compute the output:

```
# Define the readout layer (output layer)
W_fc2, b_fc2 = create_layer([1024, 10])
y_conv = tf.matmul(h_fc1_drop, W_fc2) + b_fc2
```

Define the `loss` function and `optimizer` function:

```
# Define the entropy loss and the optimizer
y_loss = tf.placeholder(tf.float32, [None, 10])
loss = tf.reduce_mean(tf.nn.softmax_cross_entropy_with_logits(y_conv,
y_loss))
optimizer = tf.train.AdamOptimizer(1e-4).minimize(loss)
```

Define how the accuracy should be computed:

```
# Define the accuracy computation
predicted = tf.equal(tf.argmax(y_conv, 1), tf.argmax(y_loss, 1))
accuracy = tf.reduce_mean(tf.cast(predicted, tf.float32))
```

Create and run a session after initializing the variables:

```
# Create and run a session
sess = tf.InteractiveSession()
init = tf.initialize_all_variables()
sess.run(init)
```

Start the training process:

```
# Start training
num_iterations = 21000
batch_size = 75
print('\nTraining the model.')
for i in range(num_iterations):
    # Get the next batch of images
    batch = mnist.train.next_batch(batch_size)
```

Print the accuracy progress every `50` iterations:

```
    # Print progress
    if i % 50 == 0:
        cur_accuracy = accuracy.eval(feed_dict = {
                x: batch[0], y_loss: batch[1], keep_prob: 1.0})
        print('Iteration', i, ', Accuracy =', cur_accuracy)
```

Run the optimizer on the current batch:

```
    # Train on the current batch
    optimizer.run(feed_dict = {x: batch[0], y_loss: batch[1], keep_
prob: 0.5})
```

Once the training process is over, compute the accuracy using the test dataset:

```
# Compute accuracy using test data
print('Test accuracy =', accuracy.eval(feed_dict = {
        x: mnist.test.images, y_loss: mnist.test.labels,
        keep_prob: 1.0}))
```

The full code is given in the file `cnn.py`. If you run the code, you will get the following output:

```
Extracting ./mnist_data/train-images-idx3-ubyte.gz
Extracting ./mnist_data/train-labels-idx1-ubyte.gz
Extracting ./mnist_data/t10k-images-idx3-ubyte.gz
Extracting ./mnist_data/t10k-labels-idx1-ubyte.gz

Training the model....
Iteration 0 , Accuracy = 0.0533333
Iteration 50 , Accuracy = 0.813333
Iteration 100 , Accuracy = 0.8
Iteration 150 , Accuracy = 0.906667
Iteration 200 , Accuracy = 0.84
Iteration 250 , Accuracy = 0.92
Iteration 300 , Accuracy = 0.933333
Iteration 350 , Accuracy = 0.866667
Iteration 400 , Accuracy = 0.973333
Iteration 450 , Accuracy = 0.933333
Iteration 500 , Accuracy = 0.906667
Iteration 550 , Accuracy = 0.853333
Iteration 600 , Accuracy = 0.973333
Iteration 650 , Accuracy = 0.973333
Iteration 700 , Accuracy = 0.96
Iteration 750 , Accuracy = 0.933333
```

Figure 13: Output of the accuracy

As you continue iterating, the accuracy keeps increasing as shown in the following screenshot:

```
Iteration 2900 , Accuracy = 0.973333
Iteration 2950 , Accuracy = 1.0
Iteration 3000 , Accuracy = 0.973333
Iteration 3050 , Accuracy = 1.0
Iteration 3100 , Accuracy = 0.986667
Iteration 3150 , Accuracy = 1.0
Iteration 3200 , Accuracy = 1.0
Iteration 3250 , Accuracy = 1.0
Iteration 3300 , Accuracy = 1.0
Iteration 3350 , Accuracy = 1.0
Iteration 3400 , Accuracy = 0.986667
Iteration 3450 , Accuracy = 0.946667
Iteration 3500 , Accuracy = 0.973333
Iteration 3550 , Accuracy = 0.973333
Iteration 3600 , Accuracy = 1.0
Iteration 3650 , Accuracy = 0.986667
Iteration 3700 , Accuracy = 1.0
Iteration 3750 , Accuracy = 1.0
Iteration 3800 , Accuracy = 0.986667
Iteration 3850 , Accuracy = 0.986667
Iteration 3900 , Accuracy = 1.0
```

Figure 14: Output of the accuracy

Now that we have the output, we can see that the accuracy of a convolutional neural network is much higher than a simple neural network. This is actually quite an improvement from the accuracy achieved in the last section, where we did not use CNNs. CNNs to the rescue!

Summary

In this chapter, we learned about deep learning and CNNs. We discussed what CNNs are and why we need them. We talked about the architecture of CNNs. We learned about the various type of layers used within a CNN. We discussed how to use TensorFlow. We used it to build a perceptron-based linear regressor. We learned how to build an image classifier using a single-layer neural network. We then built an image classifier using a CNN.

In the next chapter we will learn about CNNs' other popular brother - **Recurrent Neural Networks (RNNs)**. Like CNNs, RNNs have taken flight and are extremely popular right now. They have achieved impressive results against previous models; in some cases, in some cases, even surpassing human performance.

Reference

1. Yann LeCun's response to a question on Quora: `https://www.quora.com/What-are-some-recent-and-potentially-upcoming-breakthroughs-in-deep-learning`

21
Recurrent Neural Networks and Other Deep Learning Models

In this chapter, we are going to learn about deep learning and **Recurrent Neural Networks** (**RNNs**). Like CNNs covered in previous chapters, RNNs have also gained a lot of momentum over the last few years. In the case of RNNs, they are heavily used in the area of speech recognition. Many of today's chatbots have built their foundation on RNN technologies. There has been some success predicting financial markets using RNNs. As an example, we might have a text with a sequence of words, and we have an objective to predict the next word in the sequence.

We will discuss the architecture of RNNs and their components. We will continue using TensorFlow, which we started learning about in the previous chapter. We will use TensorFlow to quickly build RNNs. We will also learn how to build an RNN classifier using a single layer neural network. We will then build an image classifier using a CNN.

By the end of this chapter, you will know:

- The basics of RNNs
- The architecture of RNNs
- The types of layers in an RNN
- The details of a language modeling use case
- How to build an initial RNN classifier using basic algorithms
- How to enhance an RNN using more advanced techniques

Let's start off by going through the basics of RNNs.

The basics of Recurrent Neural Networks

RNNs are another type of popular model that is currently gaining a lot of traction. As we discussed in *Chapter 1, Introduction to Artificial Intelligence*, the study of neural networks in general and RNNs in particular is the domain of the *connectionist* tribe (as described in Pedro Domingos' AI classification). RNNs are frequently used to tackle **Natural Language Processing** (**NLP**) and **Natural Language Understanding** (**NLU**) problems.

The math behind RNNs can be overwhelming at times. Before we get into the nitty gritty of RNNs, keep this thought in mind: a race car driver does not need to fully understand the mechanics of their car to make it go fast and win races. Similarly, we don't necessarily need to fully understand how RNNs work under the hood to make them do useful and sometimes impressive work for us. Francois Chollet, the creator of the Keras library, describes **Long Short-Term Memory** (**LSTM**) networks - which are a form of RNNs - like this:

> *"You don't need to understand everything about the specific architecture of an LSTM cell; as a human, it shouldn't be your job to understand it. Just keep in mind what the LSTM cell is meant to do: allow past information to be reinjected at a later time."*

Now let's get into some of the basics of neural networks. As suggested by their name, *neural* networks take inspiration from the architecture of the brain's neurons. Neurons in a neural network quite roughly mimic the architecture and the functionality of a human neuron. There is much we don't understand about the architecture of the brain in general and neurons in particular. But at a basic level, a neuron takes inputs and, if a threshold is reached, it fires an output. In mathematical terms, an *artificial* neuron is a container for a mathematical function, and its only task is to deliver an output by applying the given inputs to the function.

Now that we have learned about what makes neural networks *tick* and what makes them fire, let's learn about some of the common functions that are used to trigger them. These functions are commonly referred to as *activation functions* because they activate when thresholds are met. You can use any kind of function as your activation function, but the following are some common functions that are used as activation functions:

- Step function
- Sigmoid function
- Tanh function
- ReLU function

Each of these will be described in more detail in the following sections.

Step function

A step function is a simple function. As simple as it gets. If the output is above a certain threshold, the function fires. Otherwise it doesn't. Graphically:

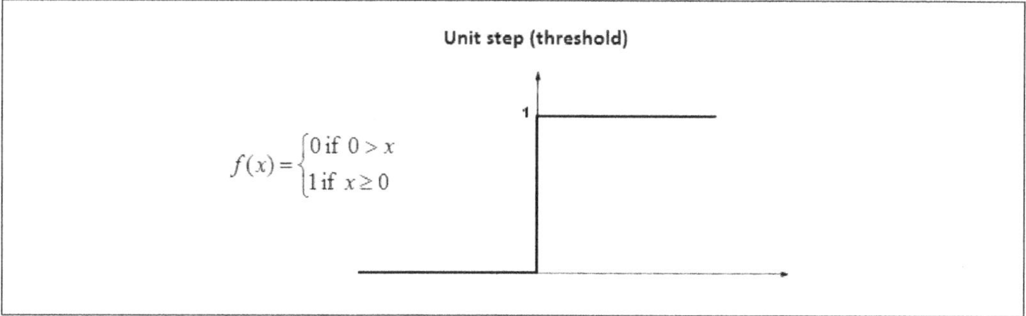

Figure 1: Unit step function

The output is *1* if the value of x is greater than or equal to zero and *0* if the value of x is less than zero. As can be seen, a step function is non-differentiable at zero. A neural network typically uses backpropagation along with gradient descent to calculate weights of different layers. Since the step function is non-differentiable at zero, it therefore is not able to progress down the gradient descent and fails while trying to update its weights.

To overcome this issue, we can use a sigmoid function instead.

Sigmoid function

A sigmoid function (also known as a logistic function) is defined as follows:

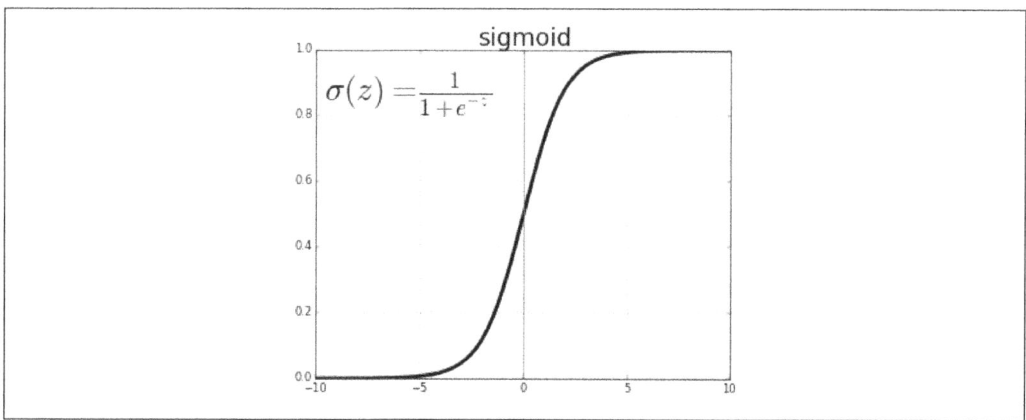

Figure 2: Sigmoid function

The value of the function tends to *0* when *z* (the independent variable) tends to negative infinity and tends to *1* when *z* tends to infinity.

The sigmoid function suffers from a disadvantage. It is prone to the problem of vanishing gradients. As can be seen from the graphic, sigmoid function values are in a small range between 0 and 1. The sigmoid function has steep gradients. Thus, in many instances, a large change in the input produces a small change in the output. This problem is known as a *vanishing gradient*. The problem exponentially increases with an increase in the number of layers in a network, so it is hard to scale neural networks that use this function.

One of the reasons the sigmoid function is used is because its output always falls between 0 and 1. Therefore, it is useful with models where the prediction output needs to be a probability. A probability always falls in the range of 0 and 1. So, in these cases sigmoid is an appropriate function to use.

We will now look at the *tanh* function, which overcomes some of the problems with the sigmoid function.

Tanh function

The *tanh(z)* function is a rescaled version of the sigmoid function. Its output ranges from *-1* to *-1* instead of *0* to *1*.

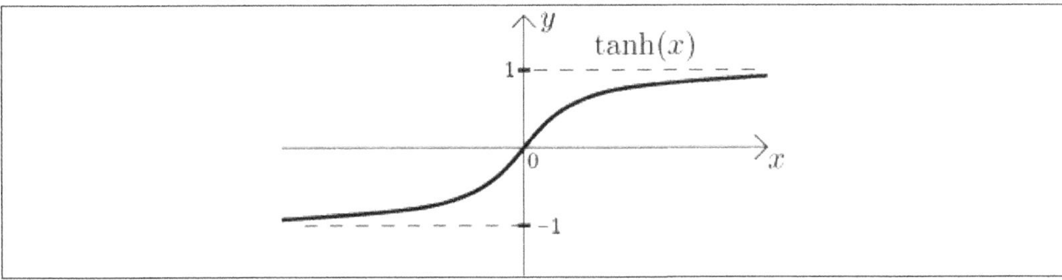

Figure 3: Tanh function

The main reason why we would use the *tanh* function instead of the sigmoid function is because since values are centered around 0, the derivatives are higher. A higher gradient helps to produce a better learning rate and therefore allows the models to be trained quicker. However, the vanishing gradients problem is still present when using the *tanh* function.

We will now learn about another function: the ReLU function.

ReLU function

The **Rectified Linear Unit (ReLU)** function is likely the most popular activation function in CNN and RNN models. The function returns 0 when given a negative input. When given any positive value, it returns that value back. So, it can be written as:

$$f(x)=max\ (0,\ x)$$

Graphically it looks like this:

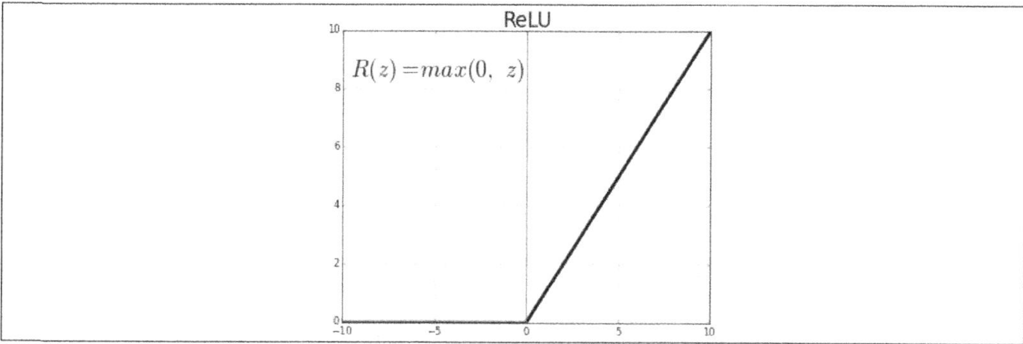

Figure 4: ReLU function

Within the ReLU variations, the Leaky ReLU implementation is one of the most popular. It returns the same value as the regular ReLU for positive numbers. But instead of returning *0* for negative values, it has a constant slope (less than *1*).

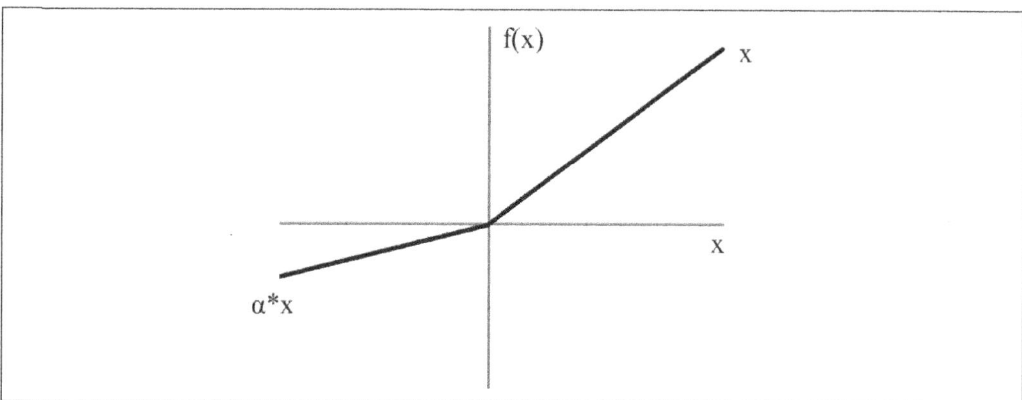

Figure 5: Leaky ReLU function

That slope is a parameter set by the user of the function when setting up the model. The slope is identified by *a*. For example, for *a=0.3*, the activation function would be:

$$f(x) = max\ (0.3*x,\ x)$$

A Leaky ReLU has the theoretical advantage that, by being influenced by *x* at all values, it may make better use of the information given by all the inputs.

Given the characteristics and advantages of ReLU, it is often the activation function of choice for deep learning practitioners and researchers alike.

Now that we've covered some basic features of RNNs and have discussed some of their key functions, let's dive into their actual architecture.

Architecture of RNNs

The main concept behind an RNN is to take advantage of previous information in a sequence. In a traditional neural network, it is assumed that all inputs and outputs are independent of one another. In some domains and use cases, this assumption is not correct, and we can take advantage of this interconnectedness.

I will use a personal example. I believe that in many cases, I can predict what my wife will say next based on a couple initial sentences. I tend to believe that I have a high accuracy rate with my predictive ability. That said, if you ask my wife, she may tell you a quite different story! A similar concept is being used by Google's email service, Gmail. If you are a user of the service, you will have noticed that, from 2019, it started making suggestions when it thinks it can complete a sentence. If it guesses right, all you do is hit the tab key and the sentence is completed. If it doesn't, you can continue typing and it might give a different suggestion based on the new input. I am not privy to the internals of the implementation of this service, but one can assume that they are using RNN technology, since RNNs are very adept at this kind of problem.

The reason RNNs are called recurrent is because these algorithms perform the same task for every element of a sequence, and the output depends on the previous computations. You can also think of RNNs as having a "memory" that stores information about what has happened and has been calculated up to this point. Theoretically, there is no limit to the length of sequence RNNs are capable of drawing information from. Practically, they are usually implemented in such a way that they only look back a few steps. Here is a figure that is commonly used to represent an RNN:

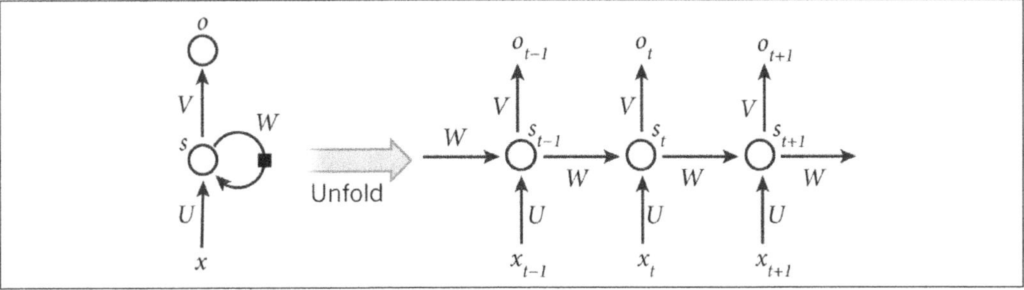

Figure 6: A recurrent neural network and the unfolding in time of the computation involved in its forward computation

Source: LeCun, Bengio, and G. Hinton, 2015, Deep learning, Nature

The preceding diagram represents an RNN being unrolled or unfolded as a full network. The term *unrolling* is used to mean that the network is laid out step by step for the whole sequence. As example, if the previous three words are being used to predict the next word, the network is to be *unrolled* into a 3-layer network, one layer for each word. The formulas that govern the computation happening in an RNN are as follows:

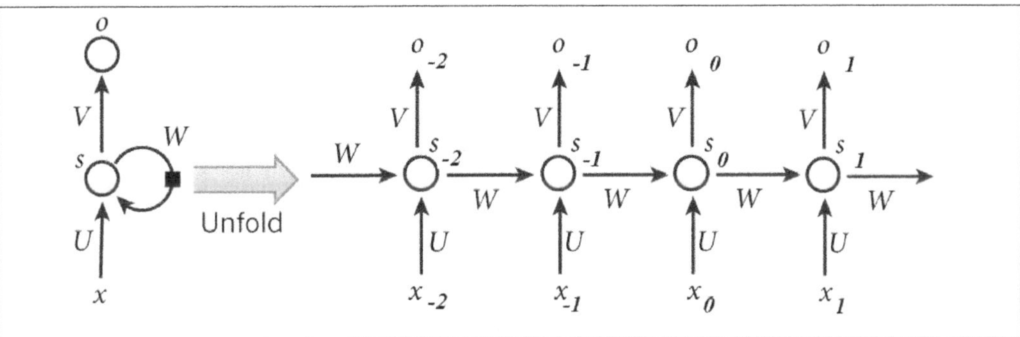

Figure 7: A 3-layer recurrent neural network

Source: LeCun, Bengio, and G. Hinton, 2015, Deep learning, Nature

x_t is the input at time step *t*. In this case, x_1 could be a one-hot attribute that corresponds to the 2nd word in a sentence.

s_t is the hidden state at time step *t*. You can think of it as the *memory* of the network. s_t is calculated using the previous hidden state and the input at the current step:

$$s_t = f(U_{x_t} + W_{s_{t-1}})$$

The function *f* that is most commonly used is a nonlinearity function like *tanh* or *ReLU*. *s-1*, which is required to calculate the 1st hidden state, is typically initialized to zero.

o_t is the output at step *t*. For example, if we wanted to predict the next word in a sentence it would be a vector of probabilities across our vocabulary:

$$o_t = softmax(V_{s_t})$$

There are a few things to note here. You can think of the hidden state s_t as the memory of the network. s_t captures information about what happened in all the previous time steps. The output at step o_t is calculated solely based on the memory at time *t*. As was mentioned previously, it's more complicated in practice because s_t can only capture information about a finite number of previous steps.

Unlike a traditional deep neural network, which uses different parameters at each layer, an RNN shares the same parameters (*U*, *V*, and *W*, shown previously) across all steps. This is because the same task is being performed for each step, but with different inputs. This greatly reduces the total number of parameters that need to be tracked.

The previous diagram has outputs for each time step, but depending on the task, this may not be needed. As an example, when performing sentiment analysis, it is common to be interested in the sentiment of the whole sentence rather than each individual word. Similarly, we may not need inputs at each time step. The main feature of an RNN is its hidden state, which captures some information about a sequence.

It is now time to delve deeper into a specific example. We will learn how we can use RNNs to predict the next word in a sentence. Let's make some predictions.

A language modeling use case

Our goal is to build a language model using an RNN. Here's what that means. Let's say we have a sentence of *m* words. A language model allows us to predict the probability of observing the sentence (in a given dataset) as:

$$P(w_1, \dots, w_m) = \prod_{i=1}^{m} P(w_i | w_1, \dots, w_{i-1})$$

In words, the probability of a sentence is the product of probabilities of each word given the words that came before it. So, the probability of the sentence "Please let me know if you have any questions" would be the probability of "questions" given "Please let me know if you have any..." multiplied by the probability of "any" given "Please let me know if you have..." and so on.

How is that useful? Why is it important to assign a probability to the observation of a given sentence?

First, a model like this can be used as a scoring mechanism. A language model can be used to pick the most probable next word. Intuitively, the most probable next word is likely to be grammatically correct.

Language Modeling has an important application. Because it can predict the probability of a word given the preceding words, it can be used for **Natural Text Generation** (**NTG**). Given an existing word sequence, a word is suggested from the list of words with the highest probabilities, and the process is repeated until a full sentence is generated.

Note that, in the preceding equation, the probability of each word is conditioned on all previous words. In more real-world situations, models may have a hard time representing long-term dependencies due to computational or memory constraints. For this reason, most models are typically limited to looking only at a small number of the previous words.

Enough theory. We are now ready to start writing some code and to learn how we can train an RNN to generate text.

Training an RNN

As we discussed at the beginning of the chapter, the applications of RNNs are wide and varied across a plethora of industries. In our case, we will only perform a quick example in order to more firmly understand the basic mechanics of RNNs.

The input data that we will be trying to model with our RNN is the mathematical *cosine* function.

So first let's define our input data and store it into a NumPy array.

```
import numpy as np
import math
import matplotlib.pyplot as plt

input_data = np.array([math.cos(x) for x in np.arange(200)])

plt.plot(input_data[:50])
plt.show
```

The preceding statement will plot the data so we can visualize what our input data looks like. You should get an output like this:

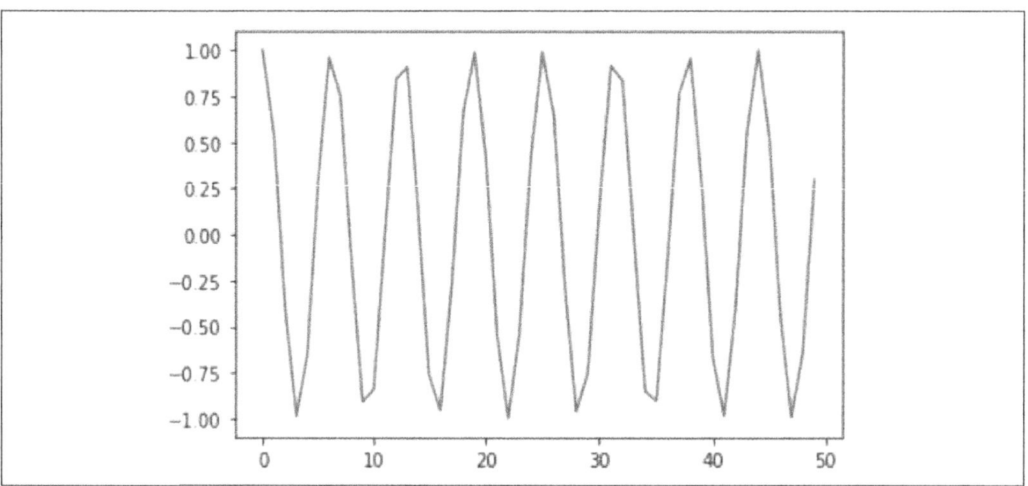

Figure 8: Visualization of input data

Let's now split the input data into two sets so we can use one portion for training and another portion for validation. Perhaps not the optimal split from a training standpoint, but to keep things simple, let's split the data right down the middle.

```
X = []
Y = []

size = 50
number_of_records = len(input_data) - size

for i in range(number_of_records - 50):
  X.append(input_data[i:i+size])
  Y.append(input_data[i+size])

X = np.array(X)
X = np.expand_dims(X, axis=2)

Y = np.array(Y)
Y = np.expand_dims(Y, axis=1)
```

And let's print the shape of the resulting training array:

```
X.shape, Y.shape
```

You should see output like this:

```
((100, 50, 1), (100, 1))
```

And let's create the validation set:

```
X_valid = []
Y_valid = []

for i in range(number_of_records - 50, number_of_records):
    X_valid.append(input_data[i:i+size])
    Y_valid.append(input_data[i+size])

X_valid = np.array(X_valid)
X_valid = np.expand_dims(X_valid, axis=2)

Y_valid = np.array(Y_valid)
Y_valid = np.expand_dims(Y_valid, axis=1)
```

Next let's define the parameters that will be used by the RNN. For example, we are defining the hidden layer to contain `100` units:

```
learning_rate = 0.0001
number_of_epochs = 5
sequence_length = 50
hidden_layer_size = 100
output_layer_size = 1

back_prop_truncate = 5
min_clip_value = -10
max_clip_value = 10
```

And let's define the weights for the connections between the various layers:

```
W1 = np.random.uniform(0, 1, (hidden_layer_size, sequence_length))
W2 = np.random.uniform(0, 1, (hidden_layer_size, hidden_layer_size))
W3 = np.random.uniform(0, 1, (output_layer_size, hidden_layer_size))
```

In the preceding code:

- `W1` is the weight matrix for weights between the input and hidden layers
- `W2` is the weight matrix for weights between the hidden and output layers
- `W3` is the weight matrix for shared weights in the RNN layer (hidden layer)

The activation function that we will use for our RNN is a sigmoid function. Refer to the previous chapter for a thorough discussion about activation functions in general and the sigmoid function in particular.

```
def sigmoid(x):
    return 1 / (1 + np.exp(-x))
```

We now have everything lined up and we can begin to train our model. We will iterate for `25` epochs. You will clearly see in the results the point at which the model and the actual data begin to converge. Make sure to stop the training when convergence is achieved. Otherwise, we will overfit the data and our model will produce good numbers with the training data, but it will not be performant with data it has not yet seen.

Run the program a couple times. Once you see the data starting to converge, you can adjust the value of the "number of epochs."

Here is the outline of the steps that will be performed during training:

1. Check the loss on the training data
    - Perform a forward pass
    - Calculate the error
2. Check the loss on the validation data
    - Perform a forward pass
    - Calculate the error
3. Start the training
    - Perform a forward pass
    - Backpropagate the error
    - Update the weights

```
for epoch in range(number_of_epochs):
  # check loss on train
  loss = 0.0

  # do a forward pass to get prediction
  for i in range(Y.shape[0]):
    x, y = X[i], Y[i]
    prev_act = np.zeros((hidden_layer_size, 1))
    for t in range(sequence_length):
      new_input = np.zeros(x.shape)
      new_input[t] = x[t]
      mul_w1 = np.dot(W1, new_input)
```

```
      mul_w2 = np.dot(W2, prev_act)
      add = mul_w2 + mul_w1
      act = sigmoid(add)
      mul_w3 = np.dot(W3, act)
      prev_act = act

  # calculate error
    loss_per_record = (y - mul_w3)**2 / 2
    loss += loss_per_record
  loss = loss / float(y.shape[0])

  # check loss on validation
  val_loss = 0.0
  for i in range(Y_valid.shape[0]):
    x, y = X_valid[i], Y_valid[i]
    prev_act = np.zeros((hidden_layer_size, 1))
    for t in range(sequence_length):
      new_input = np.zeros(x.shape)
      new_input[t] = x[t]
      mul_w1 = np.dot(W1, new_input)
      mul_w2 = np.dot(W2, prev_act)
      add = mul_w2 + mul_w1
      act = sigmoid(add)
      mul_w3 = np.dot(W3, act)
      prev_act = act

    loss_per_record = (y - mul_w3)**2 / 2
    val_loss += loss_per_record
  val_loss = val_loss / float(y.shape[0])

  print('Epoch: ', epoch + 1, ', Loss: ', loss, ', Val Loss: ', val_
loss)

  # train model
  for i in range(Y.shape[0]):
    x, y = X[i], Y[i]

    layers = []
    prev_act = np.zeros((hidden_layer_size, 1))
    dW1 = np.zeros(W1.shape)
    dW3 = np.zeros(W3.shape)
    dW2 = np.zeros(W2.shape)

    dW1_t = np.zeros(W1.shape)
```

```
    dW3_t = np.zeros(W3.shape)
    dW2_t = np.zeros(W2.shape)

    dW1_i = np.zeros(W1.shape)
    dW2_i = np.zeros(W2.shape)

    # forward pass
    for t in range(sequence_length):
      new_input = np.zeros(x.shape)
      new_input[t] = x[t]
      mul_w1 = np.dot(W1, new_input)
      mul_w2 = np.dot(W2, prev_act)
      add = mul_w2 + mul_w1
      act = sigmoid(add)
      mul_w3 = np.dot(W3, act)
      layers.append({'act':act, 'prev_act':prev_act})
      prev_act = act

    # derivative of pred
    dmul_w3 = (mul_w3 - y)

    # backward pass
    for t in range(sequence_length):
      dW3_t = np.dot(dmul_w3, np.transpose(layers[t]['act']))
      dsv = np.dot(np.transpose(W3), dmul_w3)

      ds = dsv
      dadd = add * (1 - add) * ds

      dmul_w2 = dadd * np.ones_like(mul_w2)

      dprev_act = np.dot(np.transpose(W2), dmul_w2)


      for i in range(t-1, max(-1, t-back_prop_truncate-1), -1):
        ds = dsv + dprev_act
        dadd = add * (1 - add) * ds

        dmul_w2 = dadd * np.ones_like(mul_w2)
        dmul_w1 = dadd * np.ones_like(mul_w1)

        dW2_i = np.dot(W2, layers[t]['prev_act'])
        dprev_act = np.dot(np.transpose(W2), dmul_w2)
```

```
            new_input = np.zeros(x.shape)
            new_input[t] = x[t]
            dW1_i = np.dot(W1, new_input)
            dx = np.dot(np.transpose(W1), dmul_w1)

            dW1_t += dW1_i
            dW2_t += dW2_i

          dW3 += dW3_t
          dW1 += dW1_t
          dW2 += dW2_t

          if dW1.max() > max_clip_value:
            dW1[dW1 > max_clip_value] = max_clip_value
          if dW3.max() > max_clip_value:
            dW3[dW3 > max_clip_value] = max_clip_value
          if dW2.max() > max_clip_value:
            dW2[dW2 > max_clip_value] = max_clip_value


          if dW1.min() < min_clip_value:
            dW1[dW1 < min_clip_value] = min_clip_value
          if dW3.min() < min_clip_value:
            dW3[dW3 < min_clip_value] = min_clip_value
          if dW2.min() < min_clip_value:
            dW2[dW2 < min_clip_value] = min_clip_value

        # update
        W1 -= learning_rate * dW1
        W3 -= learning_rate * dW3
        W2 -= learning_rate * dW2
```

The output should look something like this:

```
Epoch:  1 , Loss:  [[121041.93042362]] , Val Loss:  [[60516.00234376]]
Epoch:  2 , Loss:  [[76845.00778255]] , Val Loss:  [[38418.55786001]]
Epoch:  3 , Loss:  [[42648.08514127]] , Val Loss:  [[21321.11337615]]
Epoch:  4 , Loss:  [[18451.16022513]] , Val Loss:  [[9223.66775589]]
Epoch:  5 , Loss:  [[4238.41635421]] , Val Loss:  [[2118.31929096]]
```

Figure 9: RNN training output with 5 epochs

As you can see, the loss and the validation loss keep on decreasing with every epoch. We could probably run the model for a few more epochs and make sure that the results have converged.

Here is an example of a run with 10 epochs:

```
Epoch:  1 , Loss:  [[95567.55451649]] , Val Loss:  [[47779.37198851]]
Epoch:  2 , Loss:  [[56854.28788942]] , Val Loss:  [[28423.75551176]]
Epoch:  3 , Loss:  [[28141.02126203]] , Val Loss:  [[14068.13903485]]
Epoch:  4 , Loss:  [[9427.75131975]] , Val Loss:  [[4712.5209022]]
Epoch:  5 , Loss:  [[701.30645776]] , Val Loss:  [[350.32328326]]
Epoch:  6 , Loss:  [[24.4862044]] , Val Loss:  [[12.26924361]]
Epoch:  7 , Loss:  [[27.61131066]] , Val Loss:  [[13.83388386]]
Epoch:  8 , Loss:  [[28.77439377]] , Val Loss:  [[14.45462133]]
Epoch:  9 , Loss:  [[31.02608915]] , Val Loss:  [[15.53625882]]
Epoch:  10 , Loss:  [[25.79425679]] , Val Loss:  [[12.95839331]]
```

Figure 10: RNN training output with 10 epochs

As you can see, after epoch 6, the results have now converged. Finding out the optimal number of epochs is a *trial and error* process. From these results, 6 appears to be approximately the right number of epochs.

We are almost at the end of the road for this example. Let's plot the initial input dataset against the predicted values and see how we make out. Here is the relevant code:

```
preds = []
for i in range(Y_valid.shape[0]):
  x, y = X_valid[i], Y_valid[i]
  prev_act = np.zeros((hidden_layer_size, 1))
  # For each time step...
  for t in range(sequence_length):
    mul_w1 = np.dot(W1, x)
    mul_w2 = np.dot(W2, prev_act)
    add = mul_w2 + mul_w1
    act = sigmoid(add)
    mul_w3 = np.dot(W3, act)
    prev_act = act

  preds.append(mul_w3)

preds = np.array(preds)

plt.plot(preds[:, 0, 0], 'g')
plt.plot(Y_valid[:, 0], 'r')
plt.show()
```

And here are the results:

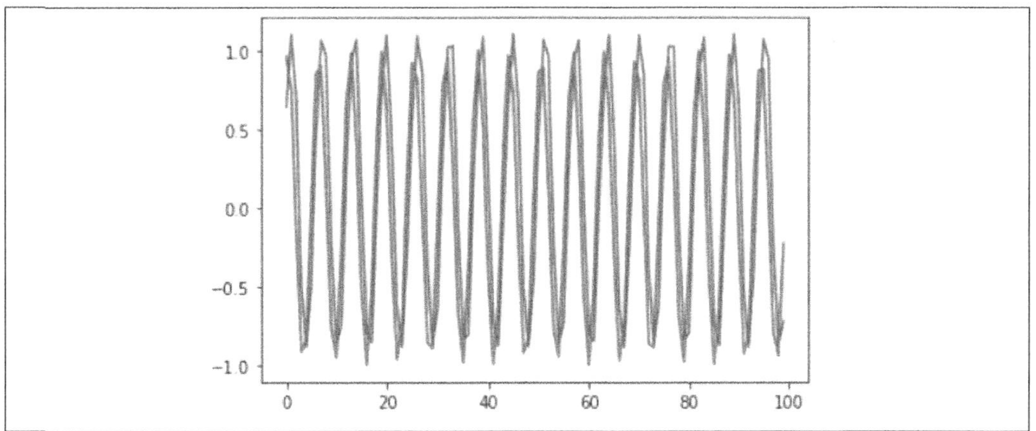

Figure 11: RNN training predicted vs. actual plot

As we can see, the predicted values versus the initial values are fairly aligned so that's a nice result. RNNs are stochastic in nature, so the next time we run the example the alignment might be better or worse. You will likely see a different alignment.

Finally, let's calculate the **Root Mean Square Error** (**RMSE**) score:

```
from sklearn.metrics import mean_squared_error
math.sqrt(mean_squared_error(Y_valid[:, 0], preds[:, 0, 0]))
```

RMSE is the square root of a variance. It can be interpreted as the standard deviation of the unexplained variance. It has the useful property of having in the same units as the response variable. Lower values of RMSE indicate a better fit.

In this case, we get a low score, which indicates that our model is producing decent predictions:

```
0.5691944360057564
```

This was a simple example of an RNN in action. And, as you saw, it was no simple two-line program! This highlights the fact that RNNs are not trivial to implement, and applying them to complex tasks is a real undertaking.

Additionally, RNNs are computationally expensive, and therefore generating accurate predictions can take a lot time; this is all but a certainty if we don't have access to suitable hardware.

Nonetheless, many breakthroughs have been made with RNNs, and the data science community continues to find new applications for them continuously. Not only that, but their performance and their accuracy are ever improving. We leave it to you to increase the performance and capabilities of the neural network we have designed up to this point, and to come up with your own examples on how the network can then be applied to other domains. Happy coding.

Summary

In this chapter, we continued to learn about deep learning and learned the basics of RNNs. We then discussed what the basic concepts of the architecture of an RNN are and why these concepts are important. After learning the basics, we looked at some of the potential uses of RNNs and landed on using it to implement a language model. Initially we implemented the language model using basic techniques and we started adding more and more complexity to the model to understand higher-level concepts.

We hope you are as excited as we are to go to the next chapter where we will learn how to create intelligent agents using reinforcement learning.

22

Creating Intelligent Agents with Reinforcement Learning

In this chapter, we are going to learn about **reinforcement learning** (**RL**). We will discuss the premise of RL. We will talk about the differences between RL and supervised learning. We will go through some real-world examples of RL and see how it manifests itself in various forms. We will learn about the building blocks of RL and the various concepts involved. We will then create an environment in Python to see how it works in practice. We will then use these concepts to build a learning agent.

In this chapter, we will cover the following topics:

- Understanding what it means to learn
- Reinforcement learning versus supervised learning
- Real-world examples of RL
- Building blocks of RL
- Creating an environment
- Building a learning agent

Before we move into RL itself, let's first think about what it actually means to learn; after all, it will help us to understand it before we go about trying to implement it!

Understanding what it means to learn

The concept of learning is fundamental to Artificial Intelligence. We want machines to understand the process of learning so that they can do it on their own. Humans learn by observing and interacting with their surroundings. When you go to a new place, you quickly scan and see what's happening around you.

Nobody is teaching you what to do here. You are observing and interacting with the environment around you. By building this connection with the environment, we tend to gather a lot of information about what's causing different things. We learn about cause and effect, what actions lead to what results, and what we need to do in order to achieve something.

We use this learning process everywhere in our lives. We gather all this knowledge about our surroundings and, in turn, learn how we respond to that. Let's consider the example of an orator. Whenever good orators are giving speeches in public, they are aware of how the crowd is reacting to what they are saying. If the crowd is not responding to it, then the orator changes the speech in real-time to ensure that the crowd is engaged. As we can see, the orator is trying to influence the environment through his/her behavior. We can say that the orator *learned* from interaction with the crowd in order to act and achieve a certain goal. This learning process - observing the environment, acting, assessing the consequences of that action, adapting, and acting again - is one of the most fundamental ideas in Artificial Intelligence on which many topics are based. Let's talk about RL by keeping this in mind.

RL refers to the process of learning what to do and mapping situations to certain actions in order to maximize the reward. In most paradigms of machine learning, a learning agent is told what actions to take in order to achieve certain results. In the case of reinforcement leaning, the learning agent is not told what actions to take. Instead, it must discover what actions yield the highest reward by trying them out. These actions tend to affect the immediate reward as well as the next situation. This means that all the subsequent rewards will be affected too.

A good way to think about RL is by understanding that we are defining a learning problem and not a learning method. So, we can say that any method that can solve our problem can be considered as an RL method. RL is characterized by two distinguishing features - trial and error learning, and delayed reward. An RL agent uses these two features to learn from the consequences of its actions.

Reinforcement learning versus supervised learning

A lot of current research is focused on supervised learning. RL might seem a bit like supervised learning, but it is not. The process of supervised learning refers to learning from labeled samples. While this is a useful technique, it is not enough to start learning from interactions. When we want to design a machine to navigate unknown terrains, this kind of learning is not going to help us. We don't have training samples available beforehand.

We need an agent that can learn from its own experience by interacting with the unknown terrain. This is where RL really shines.

Let's consider the exploration stage when the agent is interacting with the new environment in order to learn. How much can it explore? At this point, the agent doesn't know how big the environment is, and in many cases, it won't be able to explore all the possibilities. So, what should the agent do? Should it learn from its limited experience or wait until it explores further before acting? This is one of the main challenges of RL. In order to get a higher reward, an agent must favor the actions that have been tried and tested. But in order to discover such actions, it should keep trying newer actions that have not been selected before. Researchers have studied this trade-off between exploration and exploitation extensively over the years and it's still an active topic.

Real-world examples of reinforcement learning

Let's see where RL occurs in the real world. This will help us understand how it works and what possible applications can be built using this concept:

Game playing - Let's consider a board game like Go or Chess. In order to determine the best move, the players need to think about various factors. The number of possibilities is so large that it is not possible to perform a brute-force search. If we were to build a machine to play such a game using traditional techniques, we would need to specify many rules to cover all these possibilities. RL completely bypasses this problem. We do not need to manually specify any logic rules. The learning agent simply learns by example and playing games against itself.

For a more thorough discussion on this topic refer to the *Gaming* section in *Chapter 2, Fundamental Use Cases for Artificial Intelligence*.

Robotics - Let's consider a robot whose job is to explore a new building. It should make sure it has enough power left to come back to the base station. This robot must decide if it should make decisions by considering the trade-off between the amount of information collected and the ability to get back to the base station safely.

For more on this topic jump to the *Shipping and warehouse management* section in *Chapter 2, Fundamental Use Cases for Artificial Intelligence*.

Industrial controllers - Consider the case of scheduling elevators. A good scheduler will spend the least amount of power and service the highest number of people. For problems like these, RL agents can learn how to do this in a simulated environment. They can then take that knowledge to come up with optimal scheduling.

Babies - Machines don't have a monopoly on utilizing RL; newborns undergo much the same process as they struggle to walk in the first few months. They learn by trying it repeatedly until they learn how to balance. It's interesting to see the different locomotion methods that babies find until they figure out that walking (or running!) is the most efficient.

If you observe these examples closely, you will see there are some common traits. All of them involve interacting with the environment. The learning agent (be they machine, baby, or otherwise) aims to achieve a certain goal even though there's uncertainty about the environment. The actions of an agent will change the future state of that environment. This impacts the opportunities available at later times as the agent continues to interact with the environment.

Having discussed what RL is and having covered some real-life examples, let's now get into its workings. We'll start off by talking about the building blocks of the RL system.

Building blocks of reinforcement learning

Apart from the interaction between the agent and the environment, there are other factors at play within the RL system:

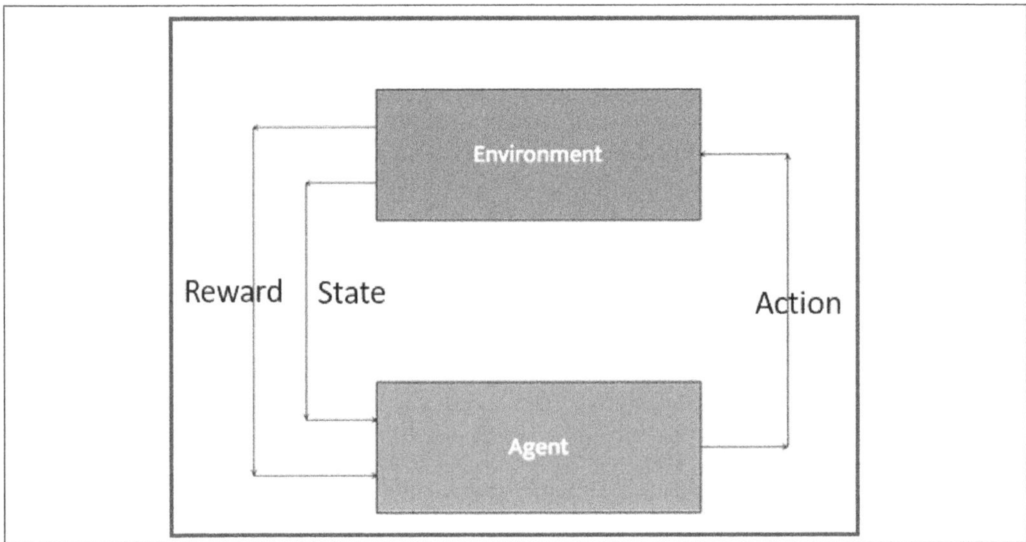

Figure 1: Components of reinforcement learning

Typically, RL agents perform the following steps:

1. There is a set of states related to the agent and the environment. At a given point of time, the agent observes an input state to sense the environment.
2. There are policies that govern what action needs to be taken. These policies act as decision-making functions. The action is determined based on the input state using these policies.
3. The agent takes the action based on the previous step.
4. The environment reacts in response to that action. The agent receives reinforcement, also known as reward, from the environment.
5. The agent calculates and records the information about this reward. It's important to note that this reward is received for this state/action pair so that it can be used to take more rewarding actions in the future given a certain state.

RL systems can do multiple things simultaneously – learn by performing a trial-and-error search, learn the model of the environment it is in, and then use that model to plan the next steps. In the next section, we will get our hands dirty and start playing with reinforcement learning systems written in Python using a popular framework.

Creating an environment

We will be using a package called **OpenAI Gym** to build RL agents. You can learn more about it here: `https://gym.openai.com`. It can be installed using `pip` by running the following command:

```
$ pip3 install gym
```

You can find various tips and tricks related to its installation here:

`https://github.com/openai/gym#installation`

Now that you have installed it, let's go ahead and write some code.

Create a new Python file and import the following packages:

```
import argparse

import gym
```

Define a function to parse the input arguments. The input arguments will be used to specify the type of environment to be run:

```
def build_arg_parser():
    parser = argparse.ArgumentParser(description='Run an environment')
```

```
    parser.add_argument('--input-env', dest='input_env',
required=True,
            choices=['cartpole', 'mountaincar', 'pendulum', 'taxi',
'lake'],
            help='Specify the name of the environment')
    return parser
```

Define the `main` function and parse the input arguments:

```
if __name__=='__main__':
    args = build_arg_parser().parse_args()
    input_env = args.input_env
```

Create a mapping from the input argument string to the names of the environments as specified in the OpenAI Gym package:

```
    name_map = {'cartpole': 'CartPole-v0',
                'mountaincar': 'MountainCar-v0',
                'pendulum': 'Pendulum-v0',
                'taxi': 'Taxi-v1',
                'lake': 'FrozenLake-v0'}
```

Create the environment based on the input argument and reset it:

```
    # Create the environment and reset it
    env = gym.make(name_map[input_env])
    env.reset()
```

Iterate `1000` times and take a random action during each step:

```
    # Iterate 1000 times
    for _ in range(1000):
        # Render the environment
        env.render()

        # take a random action
        env.step(env.action_space.sample())
```

The full code is given in the file `run_environment.py`. If you want to know how to run the code, run it with the `help` argument as shown in the following figure:

```
$ python3 run_environment.py --help
usage: run_environment.py [-h] --input-env
                          {cartpole,mountaincar,pendulum,taxi,lake}

Run an environment

optional arguments:
  -h, --help            show this help message and exit
  --input-env {cartpole,mountaincar,pendulum,taxi,lake}
                        Specify the name of the environment
```

Figure 2: Command to run the Python program

Let's run it with the cartpole environment. Run the following command:

```
$ python3 run_environment.py --input-env cartpole
```

If you run it, you will see a window showing a **cartpole** moving to your right. The following screenshot shows the initial position:

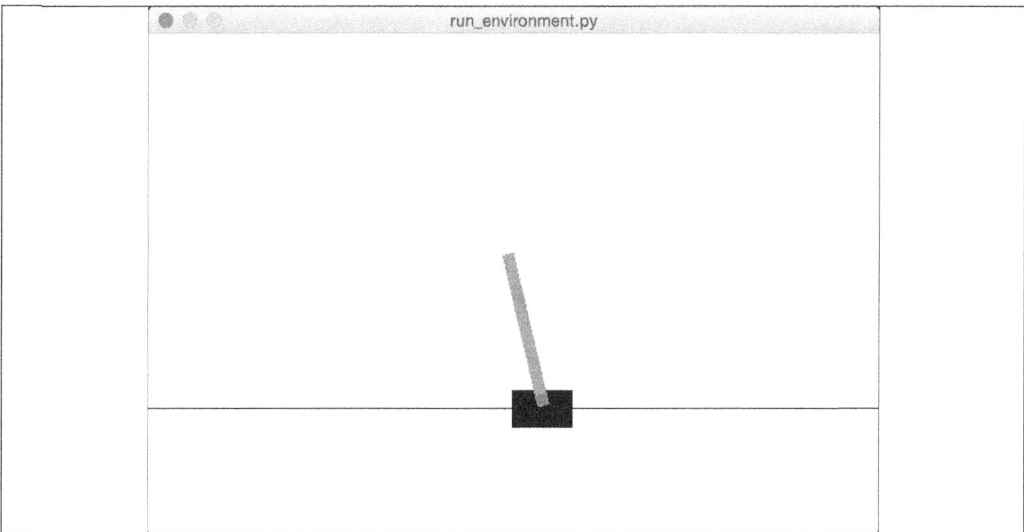

Figure 3: Cartpole example output

In the next second or so, you will see it moving as shown in the following screenshot:

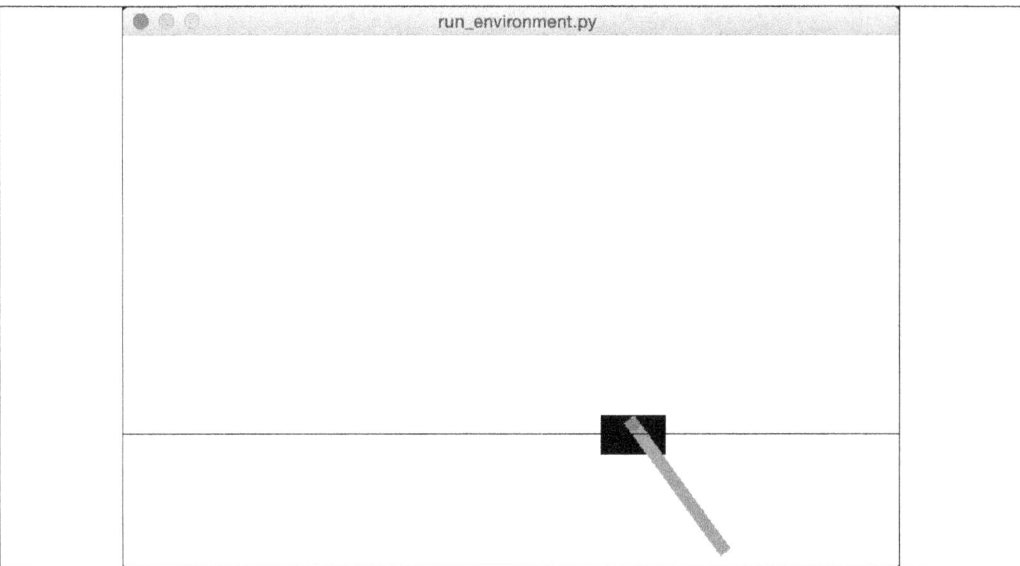

Figure 4: Cartpole example output 2

Towards the end, you will see it going out of the window as shown in the following screenshot:

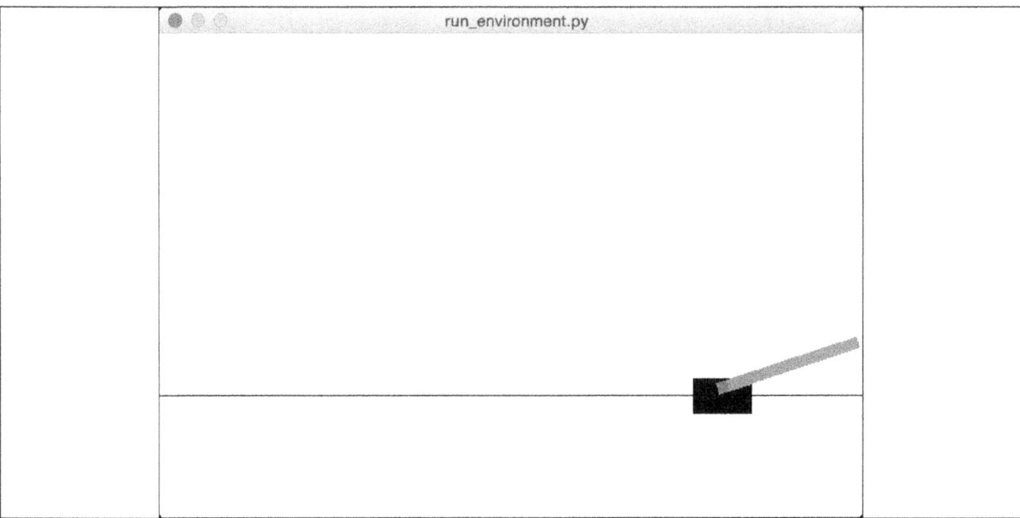

Figure 5: Cartpole example output 3

Let's run it with the `mountaincar` argument. Run the following command:

```
$ python3 run_environment.py --input-env mountaincar
```

If you run the code, you will see the following figure initially:

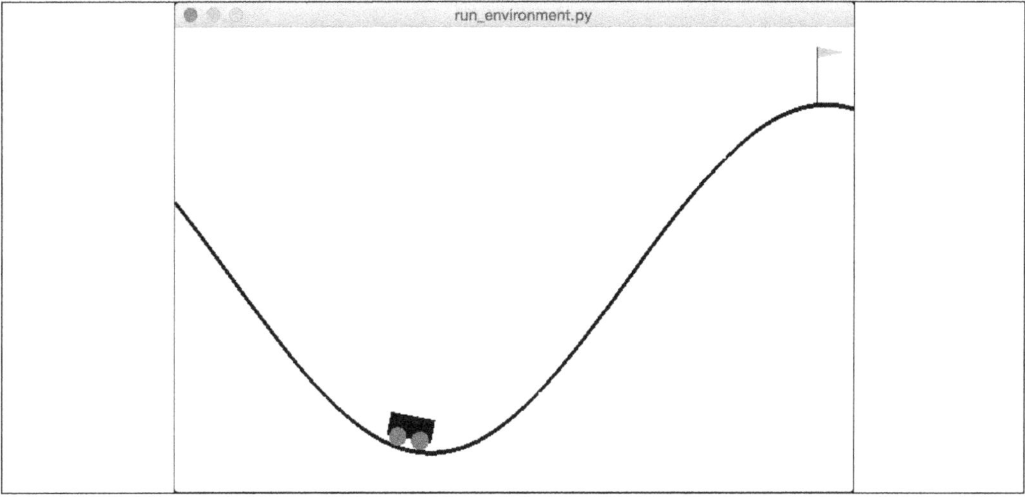

Figure 6: Mountain car example output

If you let it run for a few seconds, you will see that the car oscillates more in order to reach the flag:

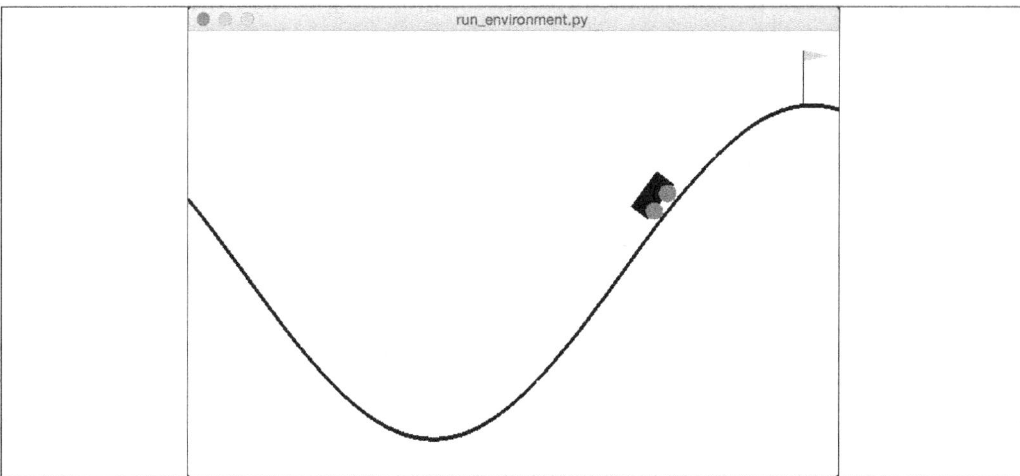

Figure 7: Mountain car example output 2

It will keep taking longer strides as shown in the following figure:

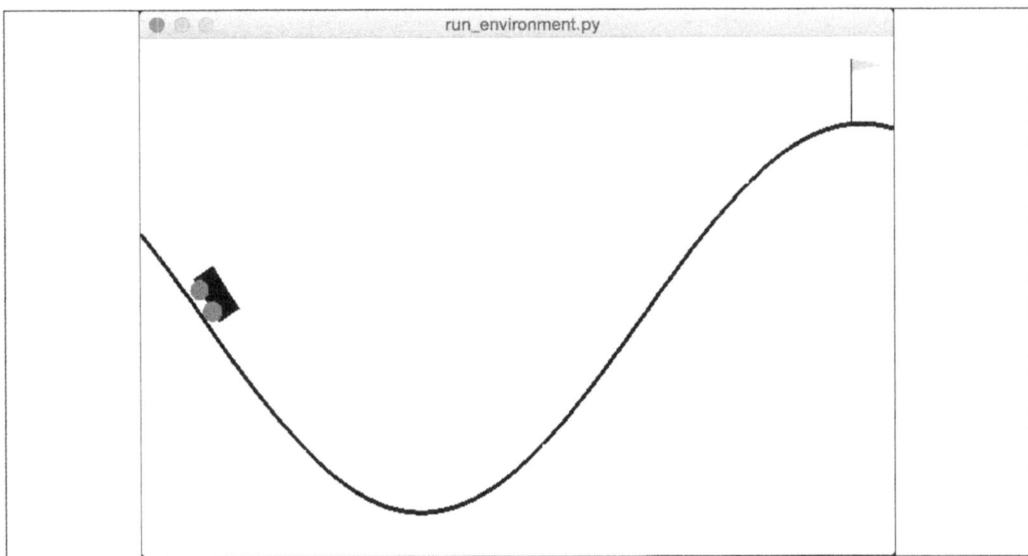

Figure 8: Mountain car example output 3

In the first example in this section, nothing too exciting happened. It was just a cartpole moving around. The example did allow us to get a basic understanding of the RL framework we are using. The second example was a little more exciting. It actually had a goal (to touch the flag). Achieving a goal is usually how reinforcement problems are framed. In the next example, we'll continue making things more interesting and we will set our sights on a slightly more complicated goal.

Building a learning agent

In this section, we will build upon the work from our first cartpole example. Initially, the cartpole was just moving around. We are now going to try to balance the pole on top of the cart and try to make sure the pole stays upright. Ready to learn some more? Let's get to it.

First, create a new Python file and import the following packages:

```
import argparse
import gym
```

Define a function to parse the input arguments:

```
def build_arg_parser():
    parser = argparse.ArgumentParser(description='Run an environment')
```

```
    parser.add_argument('--input-env', dest='input_env',
required=True,
            choices=['cartpole', 'mountaincar', 'pendulum'],
            help='Specify the name of the environment')
    return parser
```

Parse the input arguments:

```
if __name__=='__main__':
    args = build_arg_parser().parse_args()
    input_env = args.input_env
```

Build a mapping from the input arguments to the names of the environments in the OpenAI Gym package:

```
    name_map = {'cartpole': 'CartPole-v0',
                'mountaincar': 'MountainCar-v0',
                'pendulum': 'Pendulum-v0'}
```

Create the environment based on the input argument:

```
    # Create the environment
    env = gym.make(name_map[input_env])
```

Start iterating by resetting the environment:

```
    # Start iterating
    for _ in range(20):
        # Reset the environment
        observation = env.reset()
```

For each reset, iterate `100` times. Start by rendering the environment:

```
        # Iterate 100 times
        for i in range(100):
            # Render the environment
            env.render()
```

Print the current observation and take an action based on the available action space:

```
            # Print the current observation
            print(observation)

            # Take action
            action = env.action_space.sample()
```

Extract the consequences of taking the current action:

```
            # Extract the observation, reward, status and
```

```
            # other info based on the action taken
            observation, reward, done, info = env.step(action)
```

Check if we have achieved our goal:

```
            # Check if it's done
            if done:
                print('Episode finished after {} timesteps'.
format(i+1))
                break
```

The full code is given in the file `balancer.py`. If you want to know how to run the code, run it with the `help` argument as shown in the following screenshot:

```
$ python3 balancer.py --help
usage: balancer.py [-h] --input-env {cartpole,mountaincar,pendulum}

Run an environment

optional arguments:
  -h, --help            show this help message and exit
  --input-env {cartpole,mountaincar,pendulum}
                        Specify the name of the environment
```

Figure 9: Command to run the Python balancer example

Let's run the code with the `cartpole` environment. Run the following command:

`$ python3 balancer.py --input-env cartpole`

If you run the code, you will see that the cartpole balances itself:

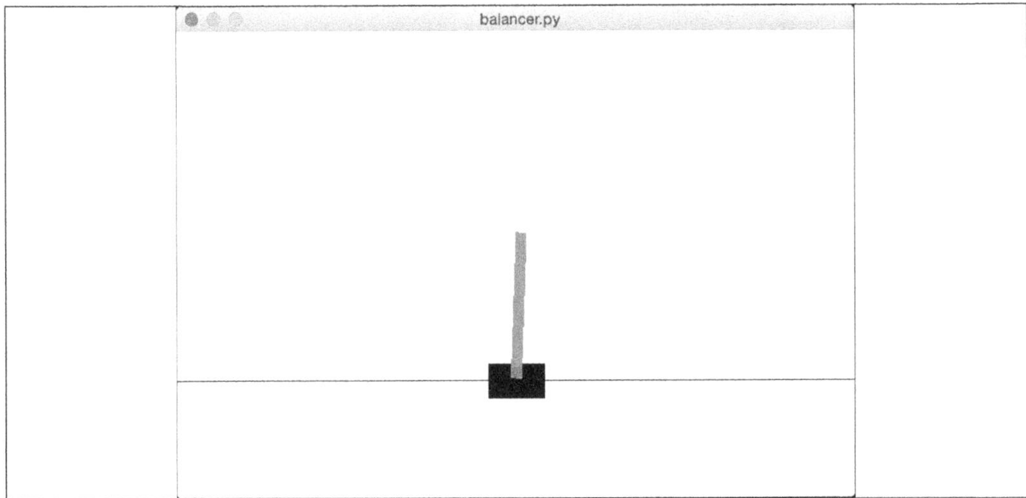

Figure 10: Cartpole example output 4

If you let it run for a few seconds, you will see that the cartpole is still standing as shown in the following screenshot:

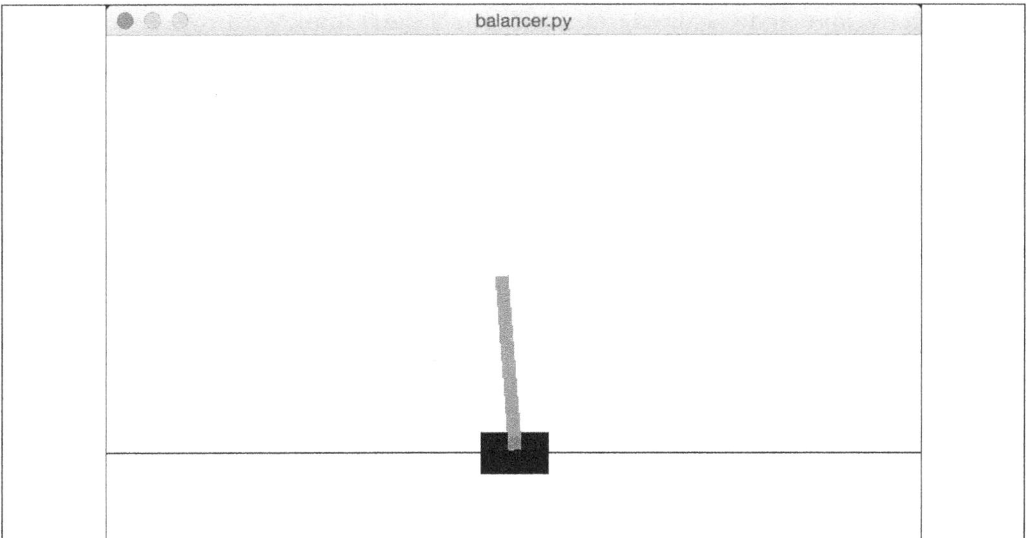

Figure 11: Cartpole example output 5

You should see a lot of information printed out. If you look at one of the episodes, it will look something like this:

```
[ 0.01704777  0.03379922 -0.01628054  0.02868271]
[ 0.01772375 -0.16108552 -0.01570689  0.31618481]
[ 0.01450204  0.03425659 -0.00938319  0.01859014]
[ 0.01518717 -0.16072954 -0.00901139  0.30829785]
[ 0.01197258 -0.35572194 -0.00284543  0.59812526]
[ 0.00485814 -0.16056029  0.00911707  0.30454742]
[ 0.00164694 -0.35581098  0.01520802  0.60009165]
[-0.00546928 -0.16090505  0.02720986  0.31223756]
[-0.00868738 -0.35640386  0.03345461  0.61337594]
[-0.01581546 -0.55197696  0.04572213  0.91640525]
[-0.026855   -0.3575021   0.06405023  0.63843544]
[-0.03400504 -0.16332896  0.07681894  0.36659087]
[-0.03727162 -0.3594537   0.08415076  0.68247294]
[-0.04446069 -0.5556372   0.09780022  1.00041801]
[-0.05557344 -0.75192055  0.11780858  1.32214352]
[-0.07061185 -0.55846765  0.14425145  1.06853119]
[-0.0817812  -0.36551752  0.16562207  0.82437502]
[-0.08909155 -0.56247052  0.18210957  1.16423244]
[-0.10034096 -0.75943464  0.20539422  1.50803784]
Episode finished after 19 timesteps
```

Figure 12: Episode output

Different episodes take a different number of steps to finish. If you scroll through the information printed out, you will be able to see that. Hopefully, when you run this example, you will see that the cartpole does indeed balance at least most of the time. With the knowledge gained in this chapter, I don't think we are ready to beat AlphaZero playing the game of Go. But we got the fundamentals on how systems like these are built.

Summary

In this chapter, we learned about RL systems. We discussed the premise of RL and how we can set it up. We talked about the differences between RL and supervised learning. We went through some real-world examples of RL and saw how various systems use it in different forms.

We discussed the building blocks of RL and concepts such as agent, environment, policy, reward, and so on. We then created an environment in Python to see it all in action. Finally, we used these concepts to build an RL agent.

In the next chapter, we will go into a rather different topic and learn how big data technologies can help us make our machine learning systems more robust and efficient.

23
Artificial Intelligence and Big Data

In this chapter, we are going to learn what big data is and how big data technologies can be used in the context of artificial intelligence. We will discuss how big data can help accelerate machine learning pipelines. We will also discuss when it is a good idea to use big data techniques and when they are overkill, using some examples to further our understanding. We will learn about the building blocks of a machine learning pipeline that uses big data and the various challenges involved, and we will create an environment in Python to see how it works in practice. By the end of this chapter, we will have covered:

- Big data basics
- The three V's of big data
- Big data as it applies to artificial intelligence and machine learning
- A machine learning pipeline using big data
- Apache Hadoop
- Apache Spark
- Apache Impala
- NoSQL databases

Let's begin with the basics of big data.

Big data basics

There is an activity that you regularly perform today that you rarely did ten years ago, and certainly never did twenty years ago. Yet, if you were told you could never do this again, you would feel completely hamstrung. You probably already did it a few times today, or at least this week. What am I talking about? Want to take a guess? I am talking about performing a Google search.

Google hasn't been around that long, yet we are so dependent on it now. It has disrupted and upended a big swath of industries including magazine publishing, phone directories, newspapers, and so on. Nowadays, whenever we have a knowledge itch, we use Google to scratch it. This is especially the case due to our permanent link to the internet via cell phones. Google has almost become an extension of us.

Yet, have you stopped to think about the mechanics behind all of this incredible knowledge-finding? We literally have billions of documents at our fingertips that can be accessed in a few milliseconds and, as if by magic, the most relevant documents generally show up in the first few results, usually giving us the answer we are looking for. I sometimes get the feeling that Google is reading my mind and knows what I want before I start typing the keywords.

One of the fundamental technologies that Google uses to give these answers is what is commonly referred to as big data. But what is big data? The name itself doesn't give us much. *Data* could be anything that is stored on a computer and *big* is a relative term. Before we define what *big data* is, let me give you one of my favorite observations that I have seen regarding the topic:

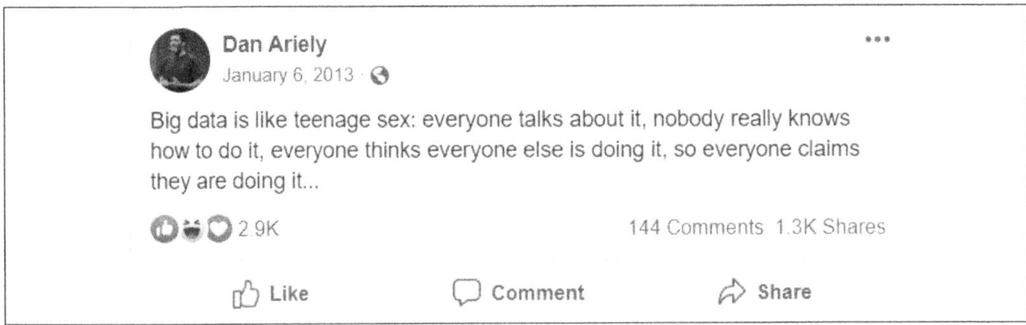

Figure 1: Big data analogy

This quote drives the point home that big data means different things to different people. This is starting to change, but traditional databases have had a ceiling as far as how much information we can store and how big they can scale. If you are using new technologies like Hadoop, Spark, NoSQL databases, and graph databases, you are using big data. Nothing is infinite, but these technologies can scale out (instead of scaling up) and can therefore scale much more efficiently and on a bigger scale. Nothing can scale infinitely, but there is a fundamental difference between legacy technologies like traditional databases and new technologies like Hadoop and Spark. With the advent of vendors and tools like Snowflake it is starting to also become possible to handle petabyte size databases using plain-old SQL.

As a business grows and its resources needs go up, if they are using a traditional architecture, they would *scale up* by upgrading to a bigger, more powerful machine. Predictably, this method of growth will hit a limit. Hardware makers manufacture machines that are only so big.

Conversely, if a business is using new technologies and they reach a bottleneck, they can break the bottleneck by *scaling out* and adding a new machine to the mix rather replacing the hardware. Since we are adding firepower, this new addition does not have to be bigger. It typically is identical to the old machines. This method of growth is a lot more scalable. We can potentially have hundreds and thousands of machines working together to solve a problem.

This collaboration by a set of computing resources is normally referred to as a *cluster*. A cluster is a collection of uniform *nodes* that collaborate in a common goal such as storing and analyzing vast amounts of structured or unstructured data. These clusters normally run open source distributed processing software on low-cost commodity hardware.

Such clusters run Hadoop's open source distributed processing software on low-cost commodity computers. Clusters are often referred to as *shared nothing* systems because the only resource that is shared between the nodes is the network that connects them.

A cluster architecture can greatly boost processing speed for data analysis. The architecture is also highly scalable: when the cluster's processing power is overwhelmed by a certain workload, additional nodes can easily be added to increase throughput. Moreover, a cluster architecture is inherently fault-tolerant.

Each data component is redundantly copied on multiple nodes, which ensures that data cannot be lost because of a single node failure. Data loss is not impossible, but it is extremely unlikely.

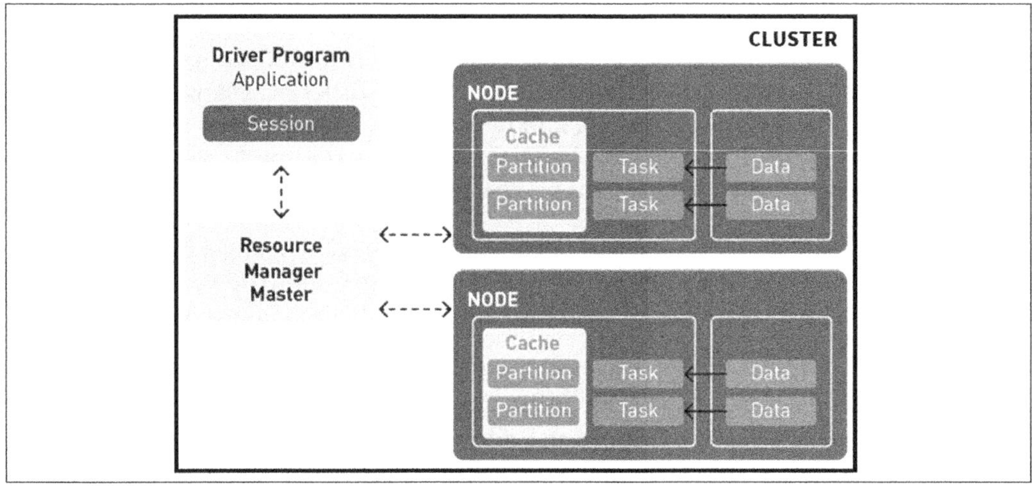

Figure 2: Clusters and Nodes

In order to better understand big data, let's continue working with one of the best examples of leveraging big data technologies. Let's continue analyzing Google Search. For obvious reasons, much of the actual inner workings of Google Search are proprietary. We are speculating but most likely the exact details of how Google works is only known to a few employees inside Google.

It's possible that no one person fully knows or understands every detail of Google Search. The rest of us make educated guesses based on morsels of information released by Google every now and again.

It is still informative (and fun) to speculate how it might work. Google's interface makes it look easy and it doesn't seem like it is doing much other than taking request with a set of words and returning a response based on that request. I still remember the first time I ever saw the Google Search page and being thoroughly confused and not being certain if the page was done loading. This was in the days of dial-up modems and Yahoo was a bigger player than Google. If you have visited the Yahoo home page lately and have seen how busy it still is, you would understand my predicament. But there is a lot that is happening behind the scenes with a simple Google Search request. Going one level deeper, these are the steps being taken:

1. Receive the query
2. Parsing of the query
3. Establish and standardize word order

4. Look up information in the Google index. As it performs this lookup, the results are personalized by considering:
    - Personal preferences
    - Previous search history
    - Personal information Google know about you (which is A LOT)
5. Ranking of results (most of the work to rank the results has been done before the query is sent)
6. Send back the response

Here is a sample query, how many results it found, and the time it took to return the results:

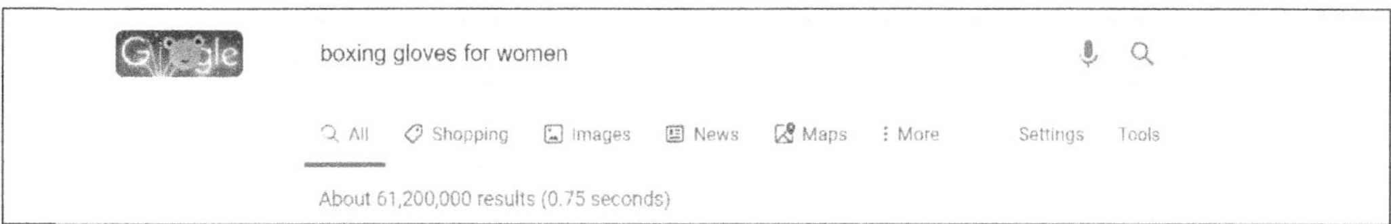

Figure 3: Google Search, with the number of results shown

One important consideration is that Google does not search the internet when you submit a query. By the time a query is made a lot of work has been done for you in order to respond quickly. In the following sections, we'll discuss some of this activity that goes on in the background.

Crawling

For Google to provide results, it needs to know what's available. There is no magical central repository that has all web pages and web sites, so Google constantly searches for new sites and pages and adds them to its list of known pages. This discovery process is known as crawling.

Some pages are in Google's list of sites because Google has previously crawled them. Some pages are discovered when Google follows a link from a known page to a new page. Still other pages are discovered when a website is submitted by a site owner or agent to make Google aware of the site and its sitemap.

Indexing

Once a page is discovered and added to Google's list of sites, Google tries to understand its contents. This process is called indexing. Google analyzes a site's content and catalogs the images and video from the site.

The results are then stored in the Google index. As you can imagine, this index truly meets the definition of big data.

By creating this index, Google searches its index of the internet instead of searching the internet. This might seem like a small detail but it's a huge reason why Google Search is so fast.

Think of it this way. When you go to the library, you can look for a book in one of two ways. You can go to the card catalog (assuming it's an old school library) or you can walk around the aisles until you find the book you are looking for. Which method do you think will be faster?

Compare the information that is contained in a typical library with the data that is contained in the Google universe and we quickly realize how important it is to go against the index instead of the raw data.

Google works similarly to a library card catalog, except its "catalog," or index, contains pointers to a huge amount of web pages and is vastly greater than the index in your local library's catalog. According to Google's own documentation, they admit that its index is at least 100 Petabytes, and is likely many multiples of that. More information can be found here:

`https://www.google.com/search/howsearchworks/crawling-indexing/`

In case you are the curious sort, there is a cool website that will give you a real-time estimate of how many web pages have been indexed. Give it a try:

`http://www.worldwidewebsize.com/`

Ranking

When you are looking for the answer to a question using a search engine, Google uses many factors to give the most relevant answer. One of the most important is the concept of *PageRank*. We'll leave the reader to find out more about that concept. Google uses other criteria to determine relevancy including:

- User language settings
- Previous search history
- Geographical location
- Type, Make, and Model of the device (desktop or phone)

For example, searching for *pharmacy* would provide a different result for a user in Bangalore than the result a user in London would get.

As we see in the previous section there is a lot of work that Google does a priori to make searches fast. But this is not all that Google does to provide its magic. How else does Google speed up search?

Worldwide datacenters

Like the Coca-Cola formula, Google likes to keep some of its *secret sauce* ingredients secret, so Google does not release details about how many data centers they have and where they are located. One thing is for certain, they have a lot of them and they're all over the world.

Regardless, when you submit a query to Google, a smart network router shepherds your search query to the datacenter(s) that is located closest to you and that is available to perform your search.

More information can be found here:

`https://netvantagemarketing.com/blog/how-does-google-return-results-so-damn-fast/`

Distributed lookups

So, Google has many datacenters, and each one of these datacenters house hundreds if not thousands of commodity servers. These computers are connected and work together in a synchronized manner to execute user requests. When a search query arrives at the datacenter, a master server receives the request and it in turn breaks the job down into smaller batches and assigns lookup jobs to several slave nodes. Each of these slave nodes is assigned a partition of the Google web index and assigned the task to return the most relevant results for a given query. These results are returned to the master server which in turn further filters, organizes, and sorts the consolidated results before sending it back to the requester.

When a query is submitted to Google, it is leveraging the capabilities of some of this army of servers. These servers can handle simultaneous lookups.

Custom software

The vast majority, if not all the critical software that powers these servers, was custom-built by Google engineers for the exclusive use of Google including:

- Custom spiders to crawl web sites
- Proprietary internal databases

- Custom programming languages
- A proprietary filesystem called **Google File System** (**GFS**) or Colossus

Hopefully you feel like you have a better understanding of what is big data. Let's add a little confusion now, and let's see why size is not the only thing that matters when it comes to big data.

The three V's of big data

It wasn't that long ago that it was customary to purge any log produced by an application after 90 days or so. Companies lately have come to the realization that they were throwing away gold nuggets of information. Additionally, storage has become cheap enough that it's a no brainer to keep these logs. Also, the cloud, the internet, and general advances in technology create even more data now. The number of devices storing and transmitting data, from smartphones to IoT gadgets, industrial sensors, and surveillance cameras have proliferated exponentially around the world, contributing to an explosion in the volume of data.

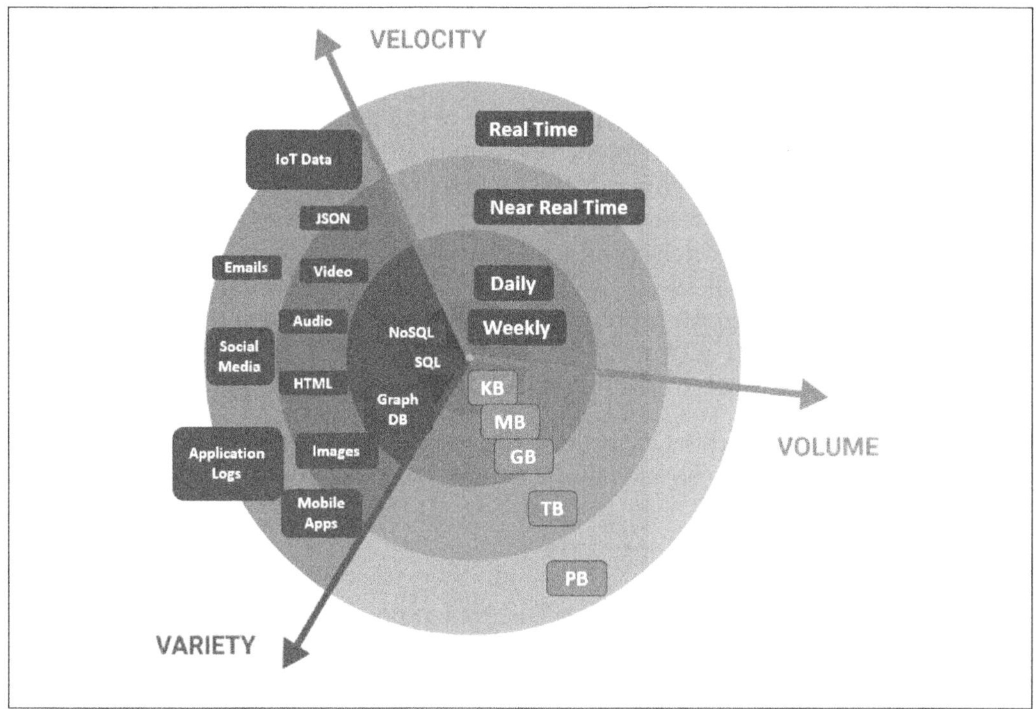

Figure 4: The three V's of big data

According to IBM, 2.5 exabytes of data were generated every day in 2012. That's a big number by any measure. Also, about 75% of data is unstructured, coming from sources such as text, voice, and video.

The fact that so much of the new data being created is not structured brings up another good point regarding big data. The volume of data is not the only characteristic of big data that makes it difficult to process. There are at least two other items to consider when processing data that increase the processing complexity. They are typically referred to as velocity and variety. Let's look closer at what is commonly referred to as the three V's.

Volume

Volume is the characteristic most commonly associated with big data for obvious reasons. Let's visit a few more examples of this and what big data means in this context.

Among other services, Facebook stores images. Big deal, right? But let's review some statistics regarding Facebook:

- Facebook has more users than China has people
- About 500,000 people create a new profile every day
- Facebook is storing roughly 250 billion images

That's big data and that's volume. These numbers will keep on getting bigger for Facebook and for the world around us in general. Consider that the number of cellphones in the world now exceeds the number of people in the world and each of them is continuously collecting data and sending it to the Googles, Apples, and Facebooks of the world. The big data challenge will just keep on getting bigger. Pile on the IoT and smart home devices that are now becoming popular and maybe we will start getting overwhelmed now.

Velocity

Velocity is the measure of how fast the data is coming in. Dealing with terabytes and petabytes of data is one challenge. Another perhaps bigger challenge is dealing with the fact that this data is probably not static and continues to grow. Not only do we have to receive it as it's getting generated, but it also probably needs to be processed, transformed, analyzed, and used for training, in some cases.

If all we had to worry about was the volume of the data, we could potentially use legacy technologies to process the data and eventually get the job done. The velocity at which the data comes in creates the need to process the data in an expeditious and efficient way and, most importantly, use it at a fast rate to derive insights from it.

Staying with the Facebook example. 250 billion images are certainly a big number and the rest of the statistics certainly qualify as big numbers. But this is not a static number.

Consider that back in 2012 every minute:

- 510,000 comments were posted
- 293,000 statuses were updated
- 136,000 photos were uploaded

It is hard to fathom the enormity of this volume. Daily, this translates to about:

- 735 million comments per day
- 421 million status updates per day
- 195 million image uploads per day

Facebook is being tighter lipped nowadays about their metrics so more recent statistics are hard to come by. Many more interesting statistics about Facebook traffic and other popular sites can be found here:
`http://thesocialskinny.com/100-social-media-statistics-for-2012/`

When it comes to data, Facebook must ingest it, process it, index it, store it, and later, be able to retrieve it. These numbers will vary slightly depending on what source you believe and how recent the data is. Facebook has recently been on the news for political reasons. Forget about all the polemics around it. Can you imagine the technological problem they have on their hands to identify if an image is offensive, controversial, political, true or not, and so on - based on the volume and velocity that we are describing above?

As you can imagine these numbers just keep getting bigger. Like in Physics, you don't just have velocity, you might also have acceleration.

Variety

In the good old days, most data was stored in neat columns and rows. As we collect more and more data, this is no longer the case. We are collecting and storing photographs, sensor data, IoT device information, tweets, encrypted packets, voice, video, and so on. Each of these are very different from each other. This data isn't the neat rows and columns and database joins of days of yore. Much of it is unstructured. That means that it cannot be easily stored in a database and indexed.

To better our understanding, let's start with a simple example. Assume you are the plaintiff attorney for an upcoming important case. As part of discovery, the defense team recently sent you a bunch of online and physical files (in a legal context, *discovery* is a process where the plaintiff and the defense exchange the evidence they will be presenting during the trial so that they can each present rebuttals). These files include voicemails, phone recordings, emails, videotaped depositions, physical files, emails (with attachments), and computer files.

The defense is legally required to produce all documents relevant to the case, but they are not required to organize it for you. It is not uncommon for them to send you extra information to add to the confusion. The defense would love nothing more than for you to miss some critical information that might be the crux to cracking your case wide open and getting a positive outcome for your client. The courts are most definitely going to put a deadline and milestones on when you will need to present your case. Even though you are not dealing with Facebook-level numbers as far as volume and velocity, in this case, the variety of your data is more complex than most Facebook data. And that's what makes your job difficult.

We won't go into full detail about how to tackle this project, but let's highlight some tasks that will have to be addressed, which machine learning and big data will help you address:

1. Scan and perform OCR on the physical files.
2. Transcribe the voice mails, phone call recordings, and videotaped depositions. Index them. We are trying to standardize the data format into machine-readable computer files than can be scanned and searched uniformly.
3. Detach the attachments from the emails.
4. Index and make all the information searchable (there are open source and proprietary tools that can help with this process like Solr, Sinequa, Elastic Search, and Amazon Kendra).

In this section, we have identified some of the ways to sift through all this insanity using big data tools and glean insights to solve problems, discern patterns, and identify opportunities using machine learning. In the following sections, we will learn about the actual tools that are available to accomplish this.

Big data and machine learning

Big data technologies are leveraged successfully by technology companies around the world. Today's enterprises understand the power of big data, and they realize that it can be even more powerful when used in conjunction with machine learning.

Machine learning systems coupled with big data technology help businesses in a multitude of ways including managing, analyzing, and using the captured data far more strategically than ever before.

As companies capture and generate ever increasing volumes of data, this presents both a challenge and a great opportunity. Fortunately, these two technologies complement each other symbiotically. Businesses are constantly coming up with new models that increase the computational requirements of the resulting workloads. New advances in big data enable and facilitate the processing of these new use cases. Data scientists are seeing that current architectures can handle this increased workload. They are therefore coming up with new ways to analyze this data, and are deriving ever-deeper insights from the current data that is available.

Well-crafted algorithms thrive with large datasets, meaning the more the data, the more effective the learning. With the emergence of big data together coupled with advancements in computing power, machine learning continues to evolve at an accelerating pace. With the steadily increasing proliferation of big data analysis in the field of machine learning, machines and devices continue to get smarter and keep on taking on tasks previously reserved for humans.

These companies are creating data pipelines that then feed machine learning models to constantly improve operations. Take as an example Amazon. Like Google, Amazon can be tight-lipped about some of its statistics. Fortunately, some information is available. In 2017, Amazon shipped 5 billion items worldwide. That's 13 million items per day or at least 150 items per second. If we were to use traditional data technologies to process this amount of data and apply machine learning models to this data, we would receive more transactions before we are able to make useful inferences. By using big data techniques, Amazon can process these transactions and use machine learning to gain useful insights from its operations.

A specific example is Amazon's sophisticated fraud detection algorithms. It is extremely important that cases of fraudulent behavior are caught. Ideally, they want to catch it before it happens. Given the volume of its transactions, many of these checks need to happen simultaneously. Interestingly, in some instances, Amazon does not try to minimize the amount of fraud but rather they choose to maximize client satisfaction and service usability. For example, much of the fraud that occurs in the AWS service occurs when people use prepaid cards. One simple solution to minimize fraud would be to disallow the use of prepaid cards but Amazon still accepts this type of payment, and instead they push their data scientists to come up with solutions to minimize fraud even if users choose to use this payment form.

While on the topic of fraud it is also interesting to note that Amazon announced in the 2019 edition of their re:Invent conference a new service called **Fraud Detector**. It uses some of the same techniques that Amazon uses to catch fraud and allows users of the service to prevent fraud in their own operations and transactions. More information about the service can be found here:

`https://aws.amazon.com/fraud-detector/`

In the previous sections, we learned how big data technologies are powerful by themselves. The main point of this section is to understand that machine learning is one of the workloads that a big data cluster can successfully take on and process in a massively parallel manner. Many big data stacks like the Hadoop stack have built-in machine learning components (like Mahout), but we are not constrained to using only these components to train machine learning models. These stacks can be combined with other best of breed ML libraries like Scikit-Learn, Theano, Torch, Caffe, and TensorFlow. Now that we have discussed how big data can help us to create machine learning models, let's learn more about some of the most popular big data tools available today.

Apache Hadoop

Hadoop is a popular open source framework under the umbrella of the Apache Software Foundation that facilitates the networking of multiple computer machines to process, transform, and analyze massively large datasets. We'll talk about this more in the next section. With the advent of the new Hadoop component called **Apache Spark**, there are other ways to process this data but initially, many workloads were handled by using the *MapReduce* programming paradigm.

The Hadoop framework is utilized by many Fortune 500 companies, including Facebook, Netflix, and others.

Hadoop can integrate with a variety of other technology solutions and third-party software including machine learning tools.

Hadoop is arguably the best open source tool for building scalable big data solutions. It can work with massive distributed datasets and can be easily integrated with other technologies and frameworks. Let's learn about some of the core concepts in the Hadoop ecosystem.

MapReduce

The Hadoop core relies heavily on MapReduce. MapReduce is a programming design pattern used for processing, transforming, and generating big datasets using parallel, distributed cluster computing. The MapReduce model accomplishes the processing of large-scale datasets by orchestrating distributed resources, running multiple jobs in parallel, and synchronizing communications and data transfers between the nodes. It gracefully handles when individual nodes go down by replicating the data across the nodes.

MapReduce only really makes sense in the context of a multi-node cluster architecture model. The idea behind MapReduce is that many problems can be broken down into two steps. Mapping and reducing.

A MapReduce implementation is comprised of a map component, which performs mapping, filtering, and/or sorting (for example mapping images of different household items into queues, one queue for each type of item), and a reduce component, which completes a summary operation (continuing the example, counting the number of images in each queue, giving us frequencies for the household items).

Apache Hive

There are many components that comprise the Hadoop ecosystem and there are complete books that cover the topic. For example, we recommend *Mastering Hadoop 3* by Manish Kumar and Chanchal Singh. Many of these components are beyond the scope of this book, but one important component of Hadoop that we should cover before we close the topic is Apache Hive.

Apache Hive is a data warehouse software component built on top of Apache Hadoop that supports data querying and analysis. Apache Hive supports a SQL-like interface to fetch data stored in the various databases and file systems supported by Hadoop. Without Hive, complex Java code needs to be implemented to provide the necessary MapReduce logic. Apache Hive provides an abstraction to support SQL-like queries (HiveQL) into the underlying Java without having to implement complex low-level Java code.

Since most data warehousing applications support SQL-based query languages, Hive facilitates and enables portability of SQL-based applications into Hadoop. Hive was initially developed by Facebook, but it is now integrated into the Hadoop ecosystem and used by a large swath of Fortune 500 companies.

Apache Spark

Apache Spark is another popular open source framework that falls under the umbrella of the Apache Software Foundation. For many use cases, Spark can be used instead of Hadoop to solve the same problems.

Hadoop was developed first, and for that reason it has plenty of mindshare as well as implementations. But in many instances, Spark can be a superior alternative. The main reason for this is the fact that Hadoop handles most of its processing by reading and writing files to HDFS on disk, whereas Spark processes data in RAM using a concept known as an RDD, or Resilient Distributed Dataset.

Resilient distributed datasets

Resilient Distributed Datasets (**RDD**) are a foundational component of Spark. RDDs have the following characteristics:

- Immutability
- Distributed
- Always reside in memory, not in disk storage

Datasets in RDD are split into logical partitions, which are redundantly stored across various nodes in the cluster. These objects may be user-defined classes. Initially RDD could only be created using the Scala language but Java and Python are also supported now.

More formally, an RDD is an immutable, partitioned record set. RDDs are generated through a sequence of deterministic operations. RDDs are a resilient set of in-memory objects that can be operated on parallelly and at scale.

RDDs can be created using one of two methods:

1. By parallelizing an existing set in the driver program
2. By making a reference to a dataset from external disk storage, like for example a shared file system, S3, HBase, HDFS, or any other external data source that supports a Hadoop compatible input format

Spark makes use of the concept of RDD to achieve faster and more efficient MapReduce operations. With the second version of Spark a simpler data structure is also now supported that simplifies the processing of datasets. These are DataFrames.

DataFrames

A new abstraction in Spark is DataFrames. DataFrames were first supported with the introduction of Spark 2.0 as an alternative interface to RDDs. These two interfaces are somewhat similar. DataFrames organize data into named columns. It is conceptually equivalent to a table in a relational database or DataFrames in the Python's pandas package or R. This makes DataFrames easier to use than RDDs. RDDs don't support a similar set of column-level header references.

DataFrames can be generated from a variety of data sources including:

- Structured data files in Hive (for example, Parquet, ORC, JSON)
- Hive tables
- External databases (via JDBC)
- Existing RDDs

The DataFrame API is available in Scala, Java, Python, and R.

SparkSQL

SparkSQL is to Spark what Hive is to Hadoop. It allows users of the Spark framework to query DataFrames much like SQL tables in traditional relational databases.

SparkSQL adds a level of abstraction to allow the querying of data stored in RDDs, DataFrames, and external sources creating a uniform interface to all these data sources. Providing this uniform interface makes it easy for developers to create complex SQL queries that go against a heterogeneous variety of sources such as HDFS files, S3, traditional databases, and so on.

More specifically, SparkSQL enables users to:

- Run SQL queries over imported data and existing RDDs
- Import data from Apache Parquet files, ORC files, and Hive tables
- Output RDDs and DataFrames to Hive tables or Apache Parquet files

SparkSQL has columnar storage, a cost-based optimizer, and code generation to speed up queries. It can support thousands of nodes using the Spark engine.

SparkSQL can run Hive queries without modification. It rewrites the Hive front-end and meta store, allowing full compatibility with existing Hive data.

Apache Impala

In some ways like Apache Spark, Apache Impala is an open source **massively parallel processing** (**MPP**) SQL engine for data that is stored in a cluster that is running on Apache Hadoop. It runs on top of Apache Hadoop.

Impala provides a scalable parallel SQL database engine to Hadoop, that allows developers to create and run low-latency SQL queries to data stored in Apache HBase, Amazon S3, and HDFS without having to move or transform data prior to reading it.

Impala integrates easily with Hadoop and supports the same file and data formats, metadata, and security and resource management frameworks used by MapReduce, Apache Hive, and Apache Pig as well as other tools in the Hadoop stack.

Impala is used by analysts and data scientists. The folks perform analytics on data stored in Hadoop via SQL, BI tools as well as machine learning libraries, packages, and tools. The result is large-scale data processing (via MapReduce).

Queries can be launched on the same system using the same data and metadata without having to migrate datasets into a specialized system and without having to convert to proprietary file formats to perform even simple analysis.

Features supported include:

- HDFS and Apache HBase are supported formats
- Reads Hadoop file formats such as:
    - Text (CSV, JSON, XML)
    - Parquet
    - SequenceFile
    - Avro
    - LZO
    - RCFile
- Supports Hadoop security (such as Kerberos authentication)
- Fine-grained, role-based authorization with Apache Sentry
- Uses metadata, ODBC drivers, and SQL syntax from Apache Hive

More information about Impala and its history can be found in the Impala documentation:

`https://impala.apache.org/`

As well as here:

`https://en.wikipedia.org/wiki/Apache_Impala`

Let's now analyze another important technology that can greatly enhance the processing of large datasets. We will now try to understand what NoSQL databases are.

NoSQL Databases

Before we delve deeper into specific types of NoSQL databases, let's first understand what a NoSQL database is. It's not a great name, but it is hard to come up with anything better. As the name implies a NoSQL database is any database that is not a SQL database. It comprises a variety of database technologies that had to be built in response to market demands for products that were able to handle bigger workloads and larger and more diverse datasets.

Data is the new oil and it exists in a wide variety of places. Log files, audio, video, click streams, IoT data, and emails are some examples of the data that needs to be processed and analyzed. Traditional SQL databases require a structured schema before the data can be used. Additionally, they were not built to take advantage of commodity storage and processing power easily available today.

Types of NoSQL databases

Document databases - Document databases are used to store semi-structured data. They use a key that is paired with a complex data structure known as a document. Documents can contain many types of data structures such as primitive values (like integers, Booleans, and strings), different key-value pairs, or key-array pairs, or even nested documents.

Graph databases - Graph databases use graph structures for semantic queries with nodes, edges, and attributes to represent and store data. The emphasis on graph databases are the relationships in the data. Some sample uses cases for graph databases:

- The information contained in Facebook and the relationships between friends in the network.
- Transactions, customers, and accounts for a bank. That is, *Customer A* using *Account X* sent money to *Customer B* that has *Account Y*.

- Ancestry information for a family. Examples of relationships in the case are spouses, siblings, parents, children, uncles, and so on.

Examples of graph databases are:

- Neo4J
- Giraph
- Tiger Graph
- Amazon Neptune
- Azure Cosmos

Key-values databases - Key-value databases are the simplest type of NoSQL databases. Every single item in the database is stored using an *attribute* name (or *key*), together with its value. Some examples of key-value stores are:

- Riak
- RocksDB
- Apache Ignite
- Berkeley DB
- ArangoDB
- Redis

Wide-column databases - Wide-column databases are optimized for queries over large datasets, and store columns of data together, instead of rows. Examples of these type of databases are Cassandra and HBase.

Let's now push further into more detail on some of the most popular implementations of NoSQL databases.

Apache Cassandra

Apache Cassandra is an open source, distributed, NoSQL database. It can handle vast amounts of data. It leverages a horizontal architecture that can use many commodity servers for its processing. It provides high availability because it has an architecture with no single points of failure. Cassandra relies on clusters that can span across multiple datacenters and regions. It uses asynchronous masterless replication while providing low latency operations for its users.

Avinash Lakshman (one of the authors of Amazon's DynamoDB) and Prashant Malik initially developed Cassandra at Facebook. Facebook released Cassandra as an open-source project and in 2010 it became a top-level Apache project.

MongoDB

MongoDB is a document-oriented horizontally scalable database. It stores data using the JSON data format. It's often used to store website data, and it is also popular for content management and caching applications. It supports a replication and high availability configuration to greatly minimize data loss.

Depending on the type of queries it can be a highly performant system. It was written in C++. It fully supports indices, it has a rich query language and can be configured to provide high availability across data centers.

Redis

Redis is another open source NoSQL database. It is a key-value store. It supports hashes, sets, strings, sorted sets, and lists in a key. For this reason, Redis is also called as a data structure server. Redis supports running atomic operations like incrementing values present in a hash, set intersection computation, string appending, difference, and union. Redis leverages in-memory datasets to achieve high performance. Redis supports most of the most popular programming languages such as Python, Java, Scala, C++, and so on.

Neo4j

Neo4j is a graph database management system developed by Neo4j, Inc. It was initially released in February 2010. It supports ACID-compliant transactions within a native graph storage and processing. Neo4j is perhaps the most popular graph database.

Neo4j has an open source version and a paid version. The open source version of Neo4j is available in a GPL3-licensed open source "community edition," whereas with the closed-source commercial license you can have online backup and high availability extensions. Neo also licenses Neo4j with these extensions under closed-source commercial terms.

Neo4j is implemented in Java and supports the most popular languages using the Cypher Query Language through a transactional HTTP endpoint, or through the binary "bolt" protocol.

There are dozens of other popular database implementations. We barely grazed the surface of that universe. It is our sincere hope that you feel better prepared to tackle your next data science project with the concepts we covered in the book.

Summary

In this chapter, initially we laid a foundation of the core and basic concepts around big data. We then learned about many different technologies related to big data. We learned about the "grand daddy" of them all when it comes to big data technologies - Hadoop. We also learned about perhaps the currently most popular big data tool in the market today, which is Spark.

Finally, we learned about another technology that is commonly used in big data implementations, and that is NoSQL databases. NoSQL database engines power many of the biggest workloads in Fortune 500 companies as well as serving millions of pages in the most common websites that exist today.

For all the amazing and exciting applications that exist for machine learning today, it is our firm belief that we are only scratching the surface of what is possible. It is our sincere hope that you feel you have a better grasp of the concepts involved in doing machine learning, but more importantly, it is our wish that your curiosity has been piqued and this book sparks in you a life-long interest of this beautiful topic.

We are excited to see what you do with the knowledge contained not only in this chapter, but in this book. Hopefully, you found the book engaging, entertaining, and useful. And we hope that you had as much fun reading it as we had writing. We wish you continued success in all your endeavors.

Other Books You May Enjoy

If you enjoyed this book, you may be interested in these other books by Packt:

Python Machine Learning - Third Edition

Sebastian Raschka, Vahid Mirjalili

ISBN: 978-1-78995-575-0

- Master the frameworks, models, and techniques that enable machines to 'learn' from data
- Use scikit-learn for machine learning and TensorFlow for deep learning
- Apply machine learning to image classification, sentiment analysis, intelligent web applications, and more
- Build and train neural networks, GANs, and other models
- Discover best practices for evaluating and tuning models
- Predict continuous target outcomes using regression analysis
- Dig deeper into textual and social media data using sentiment analysis

AI Crash Course

Hadelin de Ponteves

ISBN: 978-1-83864-535-9

- Master the key skills of deep learning, reinforcement learning, and deep reinforcement learning
- Understand Q-learning and deep Q-learning
- Learn from friendly, plain English explanations and practical activities
- Build fun projects, including a virtual-self-driving car
- Use AI to solve real-world business problems and win classic video games
- Build an intelligent, virtual robot warehouse worker

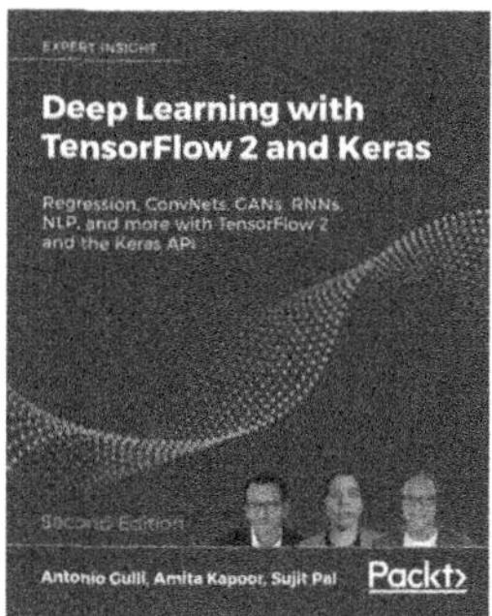

Deep Learning with TensorFlow 2 and Keras - Second Edition

Antonio Gulli, Amita Kapoor, Sujit Pal

ISBN: 978-1-83882-341-2

- Build machine learning and deep learning systems with TensorFlow 2 and the Keras API
- Use Regression analysis, the most popular approach to machine learning
- Understand ConvNets (convolutional neural networks) and how they are essential for deep learning systems such as image classifiers
- Use GANs (generative adversarial networks) to create new data that fits with existing patterns
- Discover RNNs (recurrent neural networks) that can process sequences of input intelligently, using one part of a sequence to correctly interpret another
- Apply deep learning to natural human language and interpret natural language texts to produce an appropriate response
- Train your models on the cloud and put TF to work in real environments
- Explore how Google tools can automate simple ML workflows without the need for complex modeling

Leave a review - let other readers know what you think

Please share your thoughts on this book with others by leaving a review on the site that you bought it from. If you purchased the book from Amazon, please leave us an honest review on this book's Amazon page. This is vital so that other potential readers can see and use your unbiased opinion to make purchasing decisions, we can understand what our customers think about our products, and our authors can see your feedback on the title that they have worked with Packt to create. It will only take a few minutes of your time, but is valuable to other potential customers, our authors, and Packt. Thank you!

Index

Symbols

A

B

C

D

E

F

G

H

I

J

K

L

M

Q

R

S

Made in the USA
Monee, IL
04 September 2021